# CRAFTING INTERPRETERS

## ROBERT NYSTROM

 genever benning

ISBN 978-0-9905829-3-9

*To Ginny, I miss your stupid face.*

# Table of Contents

# Design Notes

# Acknowledgements

When the first copy of "Game Programming Patterns" sold, I guess I had the right to call myself an author. But it took time to feel comfortable with that label. Thank you to everyone who bought copies of my first book, and to the publishers and translators who brought it to other languages. You gave me the confidence to believe I could tackle a project of this scope. Well, that, and massively underestimating what I was getting myself into, but that's on me.

A fear particular to technical writing is *getting stuff wrong*. Tests and static analysis only get you so far. Once the code and prose is in ink on paper, there's no fixing it. I am deeply grateful to the many people who filed issues and pull requests on the open source repo for the book. Special thanks go to cm1776, who filed 145 tactfully worded issues pointing out hundreds of code errors, typos, and unclear sentences. The book is more accurate and readable because of you all.

I'm grateful to my copy editor Kari Somerton who braved a heap of computer science jargon and an unfamilar workflow in order to fix my many grammar errors and stylistic inconsistencies.

When the pandemic turned everyone's life upside down, a number of people reached out to tell me that my book provided a helpful distraction. This book that I spent six years writing forms a chapter in my own life's story and I'm grateful to the readers who contacted me and made that chapter more meaningful.

Finally, the deepest thanks go to my wife Megan and my daughters Lily and Gretchen. You patiently endured the time I had to sink into the book, and my stress while writing it. There's no one I'd rather be stuck at home with.

# Welcome

This may be the beginning of a grand adventure. Programming languages encompass a huge space to explore and play in. Plenty of room for your own creations to share with others or just enjoy yourself. Brilliant computer scientists and software engineers have spent entire careers traversing this land without ever reaching the end. If this book is your first entry into the country, welcome.

The pages of this book give you a guided tour through some of the world of languages. But before we strap on our hiking boots and venture out, we should familiarize ourselves with the territory. The chapters in this part introduce you to the basic concepts used by programming languages and how those concepts are organized.

We will also get acquainted with Lox, the language we'll spend the rest of the book implementing (twice).

# Introduction

1

> *"Fairy tales are more than true: not because they tell us that dragons exist, but because they tell us that dragons can be beaten."*
>
> — G.K. Chesterton by way of Neil Gaiman, *Coraline*

I'm really excited we're going on this journey together. This is a book on implementing interpreters for programming languages. It's also a book on how to design a language worth implementing. It's the book I wish I'd had when I first started getting into languages, and it's the book I've been writing in my head for nearly a decade.

In these pages, we will walk step-by-step through two complete interpreters for a full-featured language. I assume this is your first foray into languages, so I'll cover each concept and line of code you need to build a complete, usable, fast language implementation.

In order to cram two full implementations inside one book without it turning into a doorstop, this text is lighter on theory than others. As we build each piece of the system, I will introduce the history and concepts behind it. I'll try to get you familiar with the lingo so that if you ever find yourself at a cocktail party full of PL (programming language) researchers, you'll fit in.

To my friends and family, sorry I've been so absentminded!

Strangely enough, a situation I have found myself in multiple times. You wouldn't believe how much some of them can drink.

Static type systems in particular require rigorous formal reasoning. Hacking on a type system has the same feel as proving a theorem in mathematics.

It turns out this is no coincidence. In the early half of last century, Haskell Curry and William Alvin Howard showed that they are two sides of the same coin: the Curry-Howard isomorphism.

But we're mostly going to spend our brain juice getting the language up and running. This is not to say theory isn't important. Being able to reason precisely and formally about syntax and semantics is a vital skill when working on a language. But, personally, I learn best by doing. It's hard for me to wade through paragraphs full of abstract concepts and really absorb them. But if I've coded something, run it, and debugged it, then I *get* it.

That's my goal for you. I want you to come away with a solid intuition of how a real language lives and breathes. My hope is that when you read other, more theoretical books later, the concepts there will firmly stick in your mind, adhered to this tangible substrate.

## 1.1  Why Learn This Stuff?

Every introduction to every compiler book seems to have this section. I don't know what it is about programming languages that causes such existential doubt. I don't think ornithology books worry about justifying their existence. They assume the reader loves birds and start teaching.

But programming languages are a little different. I suppose it is true that the odds of any of us creating a broadly successful, general-purpose programming language are slim. The designers of the world's widely used languages could fit in a Volkswagen bus, even without putting the pop-top camper up. If joining that elite group was the *only* reason to learn languages, it would be hard to justify. Fortunately, it isn't.

### 1.1.1  Little languages are everywhere

For every successful general-purpose language, there are a thousand successful niche ones. We used to call them "little languages", but inflation in the jargon economy led to the name "domain-specific languages". These are pidgins tailor-built to a specific task. Think application scripting languages, template engines, markup formats, and configuration files.

A random selection of some little languages you might run into.

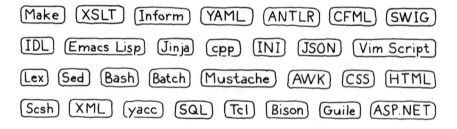

Almost every large software project needs a handful of these. When you can, it's good to reuse an existing one instead of rolling your own. Once you factor in documentation, debuggers, editor support, syntax highlighting, and all of the other trappings, doing it yourself becomes a tall order.

But there's still a good chance you'll find yourself needing to whip up a parser or other tool when there isn't an existing library that fits your needs. Even when you are reusing some existing implementation, you'll inevitably end up needing to debug and maintain it and poke around in its guts.

### 1.1.2 Languages are great exercise

Long distance runners sometimes train with weights strapped to their ankles or at high altitudes where the atmosphere is thin. When they later unburden themselves, the new relative ease of light limbs and oxygen-rich air enables them to run farther and faster.

Implementing a language is a real test of programming skill. The code is complex and performance critical. You must master recursion, dynamic arrays, trees, graphs, and hash tables. You probably use hash tables at least in your day-to-day programming, but do you *really* understand them? Well, after we've crafted our own from scratch, I guarantee you will.

While I intend to show you that an interpreter isn't as daunting as you might believe, implementing one well is still a challenge. Rise to it, and you'll come away a stronger programmer, and smarter about how you use data structures and algorithms in your day job.

### 1.1.3 One more reason

This last reason is hard for me to admit, because it's so close to my heart. Ever since I learned to program as a kid, I felt there was something magical about languages. When I first tapped out BASIC programs one key at a time I couldn't conceive how BASIC *itself* was made.

Later, the mixture of awe and terror on my college friends' faces when talking about their compilers class was enough to convince me language hackers were a different breed of human—some sort of wizards granted privileged access to arcane arts.

It's a charming image, but it has a darker side. *I* didn't feel like a wizard, so I was left thinking I lacked some inborn quality necessary to join the cabal. Though I've been fascinated by languages ever since I doodled made-up keywords in my school notebook, it took me decades to muster the courage to try to really learn them. That "magical" quality, that sense of exclusivity, excluded *me*.

When I did finally start cobbling together my own little interpreters, I quickly learned that, of course, there is no magic at all. It's just code, and the people who hack on languages are just people.

There *are* a few techniques you don't often encounter outside of languages, and some parts are a little difficult. But not more difficult than other obstacles you've overcome. My hope is that if you've felt intimidated by languages and this book helps you overcome that fear, maybe I'll leave you just a tiny bit braver than you were before.

And, who knows, maybe you *will* make the next great language. Someone has to.

Its practitioners don't hesitate to play up this image. Two of the seminal texts on programming languages feature a dragon and a wizard on their covers.

→ craftinginterpreters.com/dragon
→ craftinginterpreters.com/wizard

## 1.2   How the Book Is Organized

This book is broken into three parts. You're reading the first one now. It's a couple of chapters to get you oriented, teach you some of the lingo that language hackers use, and introduce you to Lox, the language we'll be implementing.

Each of the other two parts builds one complete Lox interpreter. Within those parts, each chapter is structured the same way. The chapter takes a single language feature, teaches you the concepts behind it, and walks you through an implementation.

It took a good bit of trial and error on my part, but I managed to carve up the two interpreters into chapter-sized chunks that build on the previous chapters but require nothing from later ones. From the very first chapter, you'll have a working program you can run and play with. With each passing chapter, it grows increasingly full-featured until you eventually have a complete language.

Aside from copious, scintillating English prose, chapters have a few other delightful facets:

### 1.2.1  The code

We're about *crafting* interpreters, so this book contains real code. Every single line of code needed is included, and each snippet tells you where to insert it in your ever-growing implementation.

Many other language books and language implementations use tools like Lex and Yacc, so-called **compiler-compilers**, that automatically generate some of the source files for an implementation from some higher-level description. There are pros and cons to tools like those, and strong opinions—some might say religious convictions—on both sides.

We will abstain from using them here. I want to ensure there are no dark corners where magic and confusion can hide, so we'll write everything by hand. As you'll see, it's not as bad as it sounds, and it means you really will understand each line of code and how both interpreters work.

Yacc is a tool that takes in a grammar file and produces a source file for a compiler, so it's sort of like a "compiler" that outputs a compiler, which is where we get the term "compiler-compiler".

Yacc wasn't the first of its ilk, which is why it's named "Yacc"—*Yet Another Compiler-Compiler*. A later similar tool is Bison, named as a pun on the pronunciation of Yacc like "yak".

A book has different constraints from the "real world" and so the coding style here might not always reflect the best way to write maintainable production software. If I seem a little cavalier about, say, omitting `private` or declaring a global variable, understand I do so to keep the code easier on your eyes. The pages here aren't as wide as your IDE and every character counts.

Also, the code doesn't have many comments. That's because each handful of lines is surrounded by several paragraphs of honest-to-God prose explaining it. When you write a book to accompany your program, you are welcome to omit comments too. Otherwise, you should probably use `//` a little more than I do.

If you find all of these little self-references and puns charming and fun, you'll fit right in here. If not, well, maybe the language nerd sense of humor is an acquired taste.

While the book contains every line of code and teaches what each means, it does not describe the machinery needed to compile and run the interpreter. I assume you can slap together a makefile or a project in your IDE of choice in order to get the code to run. Those kinds of instructions get out of date quickly, and I want this book to age like XO brandy, not backyard hooch.

### 1.2.2  Snippets

Since the book contains literally every line of code needed for the implementations, the snippets are quite precise. Also, because I try to keep the program in a runnable state even when major features are missing, sometimes we add temporary code that gets replaced in later snippets.

A snippet with all the bells and whistles looks like this:

**lox/Scanner.java**
*in* scanToken()
*replace 1 line*

```
      default:
        Lox.error(line, "Unexpected character.");
        break;
```

In the center, you have the new code to add. It may have a few faded out lines above or below to show where it goes in the existing surrounding code. There is also a little blurb telling you in which file and where to place the snippet. If that blurb says "replace _ lines", there is some existing code between the faded lines that you need to remove and replace with the new snippet.

### 1.2.3  Asides

Asides contain biographical sketches, historical background, references to related topics, and suggestions of other areas to explore. There's nothing that you *need* to know in them to understand later parts of the book, so you can skip them if you want. I won't judge you, but I might be a little sad.

Well, some asides do, at least. Most of them are just dumb jokes and amateurish drawings.

### 1.2.4  Challenges

Each chapter ends with a few exercises. Unlike textbook problem sets, which tend to review material you already covered, these are to help you learn *more* than what's in the chapter. They force you to step off the guided path and explore on your own. They will make you research other languages, figure out how to implement features, or otherwise get you out of your comfort zone.

Vanquish the challenges and you'll come away with a broader understanding and possibly a few bumps and scrapes. Or skip them if you want to stay inside the comfy confines of the tour bus. It's your book.

A word of warning: the challenges often ask you to make changes to the interpreter you're building. You'll want to implement those in a copy of your code. The later chapters assume your interpreter is in a pristine ("unchallenged"?) state.

### 1.2.5  Design notes

Most "programming language" books are strictly programming language *implementation* books. They rarely discuss how one might happen to *design* the language being implemented. Implementation is fun because it is so precisely defined. We programmers seem to have an affinity for things that are black and white, ones and zeroes.

Personally, I think the world needs only so many implementations of FORTRAN 77. At some point, you find yourself designing a *new* language. Once you start playing *that* game, then the softer, human side of the equation becomes paramount. Things like which features are easy to learn, how to balance innovation and familiarity, what syntax is more readable and to whom.

All of that stuff profoundly affects the success of your new language. I want your language to succeed, so in some chapters I end with a "design note", a little essay on some corner of the human aspect of programming languages. I'm no expert on this—I don't know if anyone really is—so take these with a large pinch of salt. That should make them tastier food for thought, which is my main aim.

I know a lot of language hackers whose careers are based on this. You slide a language spec under their door, wait a few months, and code and benchmark results come out.

Hopefully your new language doesn't hardcode assumptions about the width of a punched card into its grammar.

## 1.3  The First Interpreter

We'll write our first interpreter, jlox, in Java. The focus is on *concepts*. We'll write the simplest, cleanest code we can to correctly implement the semantics of the language. This will get us comfortable with the basic techniques and also hone

The book uses Java and C, but readers have ported the code to many other languages. If the languages I picked aren't your bag, take a look at those:
→ craftinginterpreters.com/ports

our understanding of exactly how the language is supposed to behave.

Java is a great language for this. It's high level enough that we don't get overwhelmed by fiddly implementation details, but it's still pretty explicit. Unlike in scripting languages, there tends to be less complex machinery hiding under the hood, and you've got static types to see what data structures you're working with.

I also chose Java specifically because it is an object-oriented language. That paradigm swept the programming world in the '90s and is now the dominant way of thinking for millions of programmers. Odds are good you're already used to organizing code into classes and methods, so we'll keep you in that comfort zone.

While academic language folks sometimes look down on object-oriented languages, the reality is that they are widely used even for language work. GCC and LLVM are written in C++, as are most JavaScript virtual machines. Object-oriented languages are ubiquitous, and the tools and compilers *for* a language are often written *in* the same language.

And, finally, Java is hugely popular. That means there's a good chance you already know it, so there's less for you to learn to get going in the book. If you aren't that familiar with Java, don't freak out. I try to stick to a fairly minimal subset of it. I use the diamond operator from Java 7 to make things a little more terse, but that's about it as far as "advanced" features go. If you know another object-oriented language, like C# or C++, you can muddle through.

By the end of part II, we'll have a simple, readable implementation. It's not very fast, but it's correct. However, we are only able to accomplish that by building on the Java virtual machine's own runtime facilities. We want to learn how Java *itself* implements those things.

A compiler reads files in one language, translates them, and outputs files in another language. You can implement a compiler in any language, including the same language it compiles, a process called **self-hosting**.

You can't compile your compiler using itself yet, but if you have another compiler for your language written in some other language, you use *that* one to compile your compiler once. Now you can use the compiled version of your own compiler to compile future versions of itself, and you can discard the original one compiled from the other compiler. This is called **bootstrapping**, from the image of pulling yourself up by your own bootstraps.

I pronounce the name like "sea-locks", but you can say it "clocks" or even "cloch", where you pronounce the "x" like the Greeks do if it makes you happy.

Did you think this was just an interpreter book? It's a compiler book as well. Two for the price of one!

## 1.4  The Second Interpreter

So in the next part, we start all over again, but this time in C. C is the perfect language for understanding how an implementation *really* works, all the way down to the bytes in memory and the code flowing through the CPU.

A big reason that we're using C is so I can show you things C is particularly good at, but that *does* mean you'll need to be pretty comfortable with it. You don't have to be the reincarnation of Dennis Ritchie, but you shouldn't be spooked by pointers either.

If you aren't there yet, pick up an introductory book on C and chew through it, then come back here when you're done. In return, you'll come away from this book an even stronger C programmer. That's useful given how many language implementations are written in C: Lua, CPython, and Ruby's MRI, to name a few.

In our C interpreter, clox, we are forced to implement for ourselves all the things Java gave us for free. We'll write our own dynamic array and hash table. We'll decide how objects are represented in memory, and build a garbage collector to reclaim them.

Our Java implementation was focused on being correct. Now that we have that down, we'll turn to also being *fast*. Our C interpreter will contain a compiler that translates Lox to an efficient bytecode representation (don't worry, I'll get into what that means soon), which it then executes. This is the same technique used by implementations of Lua, Python, Ruby, PHP, and many other successful languages.

We'll even try our hand at benchmarking and optimization. By the end, we'll have a robust, accurate, fast interpreter for our language, able to keep up with other professional caliber implementations out there. Not bad for one book and a few thousand lines of code.

## CHALLENGES

1. There are at least six domain-specific languages used in the little system I cobbled together to write and publish this book. What are they?

2. Get a "Hello, world!" program written and running in Java. Set up whatever makefiles or IDE projects you need to get it working. If you have a debugger, get comfortable with it and step through your program as it runs.

3. Do the same thing for C. To get some practice with pointers, define a doubly linked list of heap-allocated strings. Write functions to insert, find, and delete items from it. Test them.

The repository for the book is here:
→ craftinginterpreters.com/repo

## DESIGN NOTE: WHAT'S IN A NAME?

One of the hardest challenges in writing this book was coming up with a name for the language it implements. I went through *pages* of candidates before I found one that worked. As you'll discover on the first day you start building your own language, naming is deviously hard. A good name satisfies a few criteria:

1. **It isn't in use.** You can run into all sorts of trouble, legal and social, if you inadvertently step on someone else's name.

2. **It's easy to pronounce.** If things go well, hordes of people will be saying and writing your language's name. Anything longer than a couple of syllables or a handful of letters will annoy them to no end.

3. **It's distinct enough to search for.** People will Google your language's name to learn about it, so you want a word that's rare enough that most results point to your docs. Though, with the amount of AI search engines are packing today, that's less of an issue. Still, you won't be doing your users any favors if you name your language "for".

4. **It doesn't have negative connotations across a number of cultures.** This is hard to be on guard for, but it's worth considering. The designer of Nimrod ended up renaming his language to "Nim" because too many people remember that Bugs Bunny used "Nimrod" as an insult. (Bugs was using it ironically.)

If your potential name makes it through that gauntlet, keep it. Don't get hung up on trying to find an appellation that captures the quintessence of your language. If the names of the world's other successful languages teach us anything, it's that the name doesn't matter much. All you need is a reasonably unique token.

# A Map of the Territory

2

*"You must have a map, no matter how rough. Otherwise you wander all over the place. In* The Lord of the Rings *I never made anyone go farther than he could on a given day."*

— J. R. R. Tolkien

We don't want to wander all over the place, so before we set off, let's scan the territory charted by previous language implementers. It will help us understand where we are going and the alternate routes others have taken.

First, let me establish a shorthand. Much of this book is about a language's *implementation*, which is distinct from the *language itself* in some sort of Platonic ideal form. Things like "stack", "bytecode", and "recursive descent", are nuts and bolts one particular implementation might use. From the user's perspective, as long as the resulting contraption faithfully follows the language's specification, it's all implementation detail.

We're going to spend a lot of time on those details, so if I have to write "language *implementation*" every single time I mention them, I'll wear my fingers off. Instead, I'll use "language" to refer to either a language or an implementation of it, or both, unless the distinction matters.

## 2.1  The Parts of a Language

Engineers have been building programming languages since the Dark Ages of computing. As soon as we could talk to computers, we discovered doing so was too hard, and we enlisted their help. I find it fascinating that even though today's machines are literally a million times faster and have orders of magnitude more storage, the way we build programming languages is virtually unchanged.

Though the area explored by language designers is vast, the trails they've carved through it are few. Not every language takes the exact same path—some take a shortcut or two—but otherwise they are reassuringly similar, from Rear Admiral Grace Hopper's first COBOL compiler all the way to some hot, new, transpile-to-JavaScript language whose "documentation" consists entirely of a single, poorly edited README in a Git repository somewhere.

I visualize the network of paths an implementation may choose as climbing a mountain. You start off at the bottom with the program as raw source text, literally just a string of characters. Each phase analyzes the program and transforms it to some higher-level representation where the semantics—what the author wants the computer to do—become more apparent.

Eventually we reach the peak. We have a bird's-eye view of the user's program and can see what their code *means*. We begin our descent down the other side of the mountain. We transform this highest-level representation down to successively lower-level forms to get closer and closer to something we know how to make the CPU actually execute.

There are certainly dead ends, sad little cul-de-sacs of CS papers with zero citations and now-forgotten optimizations that only made sense when memory was measured in individual bytes.

Let's trace through each of those trails and points of interest. Our journey begins on the left with the bare text of the user's source code:

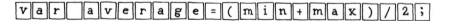

### 2.1.1 Scanning

The first step is **scanning**, also known as **lexing**, or (if you're trying to impress someone) **lexical analysis**. They all mean pretty much the same thing. I like "lexing" because it sounds like something an evil supervillain would do, but I'll use "scanning" because it seems to be marginally more commonplace.

A **scanner** (or **lexer**) takes in the linear stream of characters and chunks them together into a series of something more akin to "words". In programming languages, each of these words is called a **token**. Some tokens are single characters, like ( and ,. Others may be several characters long, like numbers (123), string literals ("hi!"), and identifiers (min).

*"Lexical" comes from the Greek root "lex", meaning "word".*

Some characters in a source file don't actually mean anything. Whitespace is often insignificant, and comments, by definition, are ignored by the language. The scanner usually discards these, leaving a clean sequence of meaningful tokens.

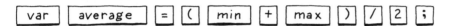

### 2.1.2 Parsing

The next step is **parsing**. This is where our syntax gets a **grammar**—the ability to compose larger expressions and statements out of smaller parts. Did you ever diagram sentences in English class? If so, you've done what a parser does, except that English has thousands and thousands of "keywords" and an overflowing cornucopia of ambiguity. Programming languages are much simpler.

A **parser** takes the flat sequence of tokens and builds a tree structure that mirrors the nested nature of the grammar. These trees have a couple of different names—**parse tree** or **abstract syntax tree**—depending on how close to the bare syntactic structure of the source language they are. In practice, language hackers usually call them **syntax trees**, **ASTs**, or often just **trees**.

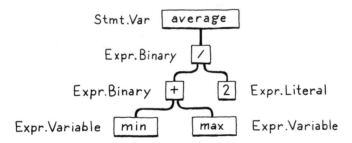

Parsing has a long, rich history in computer science that is closely tied to the artificial intelligence community. Many of the techniques used today to parse programming languages were originally conceived to parse *human* languages by AI researchers who were trying to get computers to talk to us.

It turns out human languages were too messy for the rigid grammars those parsers could handle, but they were a perfect fit for the simpler artificial grammars of programming languages. Alas, we flawed humans still manage to use those simple grammars incorrectly, so the parser's job also includes letting us know when we do by reporting **syntax errors**.

### 2.1.3  Static analysis

The first two stages are pretty similar across all implementations. Now, the individual characteristics of each language start coming into play. At this point, we know the syntactic structure of the code—things like which expressions are nested in which—but we don't know much more than that.

In an expression like a  +  b, we know we are adding a and b, but we don't know what those names refer to. Are they local variables? Global? Where are they defined?

The first bit of analysis that most languages do is called **binding** or **resolution**. For each **identifier**, we find out where that name is defined and wire the two together. This is where **scope** comes into play—the region of source code where a certain name can be used to refer to a certain declaration.

The language we'll build in this book is dynamically typed, so it will do its type checking later, at runtime.

If the language is statically typed, this is when we type check. Once we know where a and b are declared, we can also figure out their types. Then if those types don't support being added to each other, we report a **type error**.

Take a deep breath. We have attained the summit of the mountain and a sweeping view of the user's program. All this semantic insight that is visible to us from analysis needs to be stored somewhere. There are a few places we can squirrel it away:

- Often, it gets stored right back as **attributes** on the syntax tree itself—extra fields in the nodes that aren't initialized during parsing but get filled in later.

- Other times, we may store data in a lookup table off to the side. Typically, the keys to this table are identifiers—names of variables and declarations. In that case, we call it a **symbol table** and the values it associates with each key tell us what that identifier refers to.

- The most powerful bookkeeping tool is to transform the tree into an entirely new data structure that more directly expresses the semantics of the code. That's the next section.

Everything up to this point is considered the **front end** of the implementation. You might guess everything after this is the **back end**, but no. Back in the days of yore when "front end" and "back end" were coined, compilers were much simpler. Later researchers invented new phases to stuff between the two halves. Rather than discard the old terms, William Wulf and company lumped those new phases into the charming but spatially paradoxical name **middle end**.

### 2.1.4  Intermediate representations

You can think of the compiler as a pipeline where each stage's job is to organize the data representing the user's code in a way that makes the next stage simpler to implement. The front end of the pipeline is specific to the source language the program is written in. The back end is concerned with the final architecture where the program will run.

There are a few established styles of IRs out there. Hit your search engine of choice and look for "control flow graph", "static single-assignment", "continuation-passing style", and "three-address code".

In the middle, the code may be stored in some **intermediate representation** (**IR**) that isn't tightly tied to either the source or destination forms (hence "intermediate"). Instead, the IR acts as an interface between these two languages.

This lets you support multiple source languages and target platforms with less effort. Say you want to implement Pascal, C, and Fortran compilers, and you want to target x86, ARM, and, I dunno, SPARC. Normally, that means you're signing up to write *nine* full compilers: Pascal→x86, C→ARM, and every other combination.

A shared intermediate representation reduces that dramatically. You write *one* front end for each source language that produces the IR. Then *one* back end for each target architecture. Now you can mix and match those to get every combination.

There's another big reason we might want to transform the code into a form that makes the semantics more apparent...

If you've ever wondered how GCC supports so many crazy languages and architectures, like Modula-3 on Motorola 68k, now you know. Language front ends target one of a handful of IRs, mainly GIMPLE and RTL. Target back ends like the one for 68k then take those IRs and produce native code.

## 2.1.5 Optimization

Once we understand what the user's program means, we are free to swap it out with a different program that has the *same semantics* but implements them more efficiently—we can **optimize** it.

A simple example is **constant folding**: if some expression always evaluates to the exact same value, we can do the evaluation at compile time and replace the code for the expression with its result. If the user typed in this:

```
pennyArea = 3.14159 * (0.75 / 2) * (0.75 / 2);
```

we could do all of that arithmetic in the compiler and change the code to:

```
pennyArea = 0.4417860938;
```

Optimization is a huge part of the programming language business. Many language hackers spend their entire careers here, squeezing every drop of performance they can out of their compilers to get their benchmarks a fraction of a percent faster. It can become a sort of obsession.

We're mostly going to hop over that rathole in this book. Many successful languages have surprisingly few compile-time optimizations. For example, Lua and CPython generate relatively unoptimized code, and focus most of their performance effort on the runtime.

If you can't resist poking your foot into that hole, some keywords to get you started are "constant propagation", "common subexpression elimination", "loop invariant code motion", "global value numbering", "strength reduction", "scalar replacement of aggregates", "dead code elimination", and "loop unrolling".

## 2.1.6 Code generation

We have applied all of the optimizations we can think of to the user's program. The last step is converting it to a form the machine can actually run. In other words, **generating code** (or **code gen**), where "code" here usually refers to the kind of primitive assembly-like instructions a CPU runs and not the kind of "source code" a human might want to read.

Finally, we are in the **back end**, descending the other side of the mountain. From here on out, our representation of the code becomes more and more primitive, like evolution run in reverse, as we get closer to something our simple-minded machine can understand.

We have a decision to make. Do we generate instructions for a real CPU or a virtual one? If we generate real machine code, we get an executable that the OS can load directly onto the chip. Native code is lightning fast, but generating it is a lot of work. Today's architectures have piles of instructions, complex pipelines,

For example, the AAD ("ASCII Adjust AX Before Division") instruction lets you perform division, which sounds useful. Except that instruction takes, as operands, two binary-coded decimal digits packed into a single 16-bit register. When was the last time *you* needed BCD on a 16-bit machine?

and enough historical baggage to fill a 747's luggage bay.

Speaking the chip's language also means your compiler is tied to a specific architecture. If your compiler targets x86 machine code, it's not going to run on an ARM device. All the way back in the '60s, during the Cambrian explosion of computer architectures, that lack of portability was a real obstacle.

To get around that, hackers like Martin Richards and Niklaus Wirth, of BCPL and Pascal fame, respectively, made their compilers produce *virtual* machine code. Instead of instructions for some real chip, they produced code for a hypothetical, idealized machine. Wirth called this **p-code** for *portable*, but today, we generally call it **bytecode** because each instruction is often a single byte long.

These synthetic instructions are designed to map a little more closely to the language's semantics, and not be so tied to the peculiarities of any one computer architecture and its accumulated historical cruft. You can think of it like a dense, binary encoding of the language's low-level operations.

### 2.1.7  Virtual machine

If your compiler produces bytecode, your work isn't over once that's done. Since there is no chip that speaks that bytecode, it's your job to translate. Again, you have two options. You can write a little mini-compiler for each target architecture that converts the bytecode to native code for that machine. You still have to do work for each chip you support, but this last stage is pretty simple and you get to reuse the rest of the compiler pipeline across all of the machines you support. You're basically using your bytecode as an intermediate representation.

The basic principle here is that the farther down the pipeline you push the architecture-specific work, the more of the earlier phases you can share across architectures.

There is a tension, though. Many optimizations, like register allocation and instruction selection, work best when they know the strengths and capabilities of a specific chip. Figuring out which parts of your compiler can be shared and which should be target-specific is an art.

Or you can write a **virtual machine** (**VM**), a program that emulates a hypothetical chip supporting your virtual architecture at runtime. Running bytecode in a VM is slower than translating it to native code ahead of time because every instruction must be simulated at runtime each time it executes. In return, you get simplicity and portability. Implement your VM in, say, C, and you can run your language on any platform that has a C compiler. This is how the second interpreter we build in this book works.

The term "virtual machine" also refers to a different kind of abstraction. A **system virtual machine** emulates an entire hardware platform and operating system in software. This is how you can play Windows games on your Linux machine, and how cloud providers give customers the user experience of controlling their own "server" without needing to physically allocate separate computers for each user.

The kind of VMs we'll talk about in this book are **language virtual machines** or **process virtual machines** if you want to be unambiguous.

### 2.1.8  Runtime

We have finally hammered the user's program into a form that we can execute. The last step is running it. If we compiled it to machine code, we simply tell the operating system to load the executable and off it goes. If we compiled it to bytecode, we need to start up the VM and load the program into that.

In both cases, for all but the basest of low-level languages, we usually need some services that our language provides while the program is running. For example, if the language automatically manages memory, we need a garbage collector going in order to reclaim unused bits. If our language supports "instance of" tests so you can see what kind of object you have, then we need some representation to keep track of the type of each object during execution.

All of this stuff is going at runtime, so it's called, appropriately, the **runtime**. In a fully compiled language, the code implementing the runtime gets inserted directly into the resulting executable. In, say, Go, each compiled application has its own copy of Go's runtime directly embedded in it. If the language is run inside an interpreter or VM, then the runtime lives there. This is how most implementations of languages like Java, Python, and JavaScript work.

## 2.2 Shortcuts and Alternate Routes

That's the long path covering every possible phase you might implement. Many languages do walk the entire route, but there are a few shortcuts and alternate paths.

### 2.2.1 Single-pass compilers

Some simple compilers interleave parsing, analysis, and code generation so that they produce output code directly in the parser, without ever allocating any syntax trees or other IRs. These **single-pass compilers** restrict the design of the language. You have no intermediate data structures to store global information about the program, and you don't revisit any previously parsed part of the code. That means as soon as you see some expression, you need to know enough to correctly compile it.

Pascal and C were designed around this limitation. At the time, memory was so precious that a compiler might not even be able to hold an entire *source file* in memory, much less the whole program. This is why Pascal's grammar requires type declarations to appear first in a block. It's why in C you can't call a function above the code that defines it unless you have an explicit forward declaration that tells the compiler what it needs to know to generate code for a call to the later function.

> **Syntax-directed translation** is a structured technique for building these all-at-once compilers. You associate an *action* with each piece of the grammar, usually one that generates output code. Then, whenever the parser matches that chunk of syntax, it executes the action, building up the target code one rule at a time.

### 2.2.2 Tree-walk interpreters

Some programming languages begin executing code right after parsing it to an AST (with maybe a bit of static analysis applied). To run the program, the interpreter traverses the syntax tree one branch and leaf at a time, evaluating each node as it goes.

This implementation style is common for student projects and little languages, but is not widely used for general-purpose languages since it tends to be slow. Some people use "interpreter" to mean only these kinds of implementations, but others define that word more generally, so I'll use the inarguably explicit **tree-walk interpreter** to refer to these. Our first interpreter rolls this way.

> A notable exception is early versions of Ruby, which were tree walkers. At 1.9, the canonical implementation of Ruby switched from the original MRI (Matz's Ruby Interpreter) to Koichi Sasada's YARV (Yet Another Ruby VM). YARV is a bytecode virtual machine.

### 2.2.3 Transpilers

Writing a complete back end for a language can be a lot of work. If you have some existing generic IR to target, you could bolt your front end onto that. Otherwise, it seems like you're stuck. But what if you treated some other *source language* as if it were an intermediate representation?

You write a front end for your language. Then, in the back end, instead of doing all the work to *lower* the semantics to some primitive target language, you produce a string of valid source code for some other language that's about as high level as yours. Then, you use the existing compilation tools for *that* language as your escape route off the mountain and down to something you can execute.

They used to call this a **source-to-source compiler** or a **transcompiler**. After the rise of languages that compile to JavaScript in order to run in the browser, they've affected the hipster sobriquet **transpiler**.

> The first transcompiler, XLT86, translated 8080 assembly into 8086 assembly. That might seem straightforward, but keep in mind the 8080 was an 8-bit chip and the 8086 a 16-bit chip that could use each register as a pair of 8-bit ones. XLT86 did data flow analysis to track register usage in the source program and then efficiently map it to the register set of the 8086.

XLT86 was written by Gary Kildall, a tragic hero of computer science if there ever was one. One of the first people to recognize the promise of microcomputers, he created PL/M and CP/M, the first high-level language and OS for them.

He was a sea captain, business owner, licensed pilot, and motorcyclist. A TV host with the Kris Kristofferson-esque look sported by dashing bearded dudes in the '80s. He took on Bill Gates and, like many, lost, before meeting his end in a biker bar under mysterious circumstances. He died too young, but sure as hell lived before he did.

JS used to be the *only* way to execute code in a browser. Thanks to WebAssembly, compilers now have a second, lower-level language they can target that runs on the web.

While the first transcompiler translated one assembly language to another, today, most transpilers work on higher-level languages. After the viral spread of UNIX to machines various and sundry, there began a long tradition of compilers that produced C as their output language. C compilers were available everywhere UNIX was and produced efficient code, so targeting C was a good way to get your language running on a lot of architectures.

Web browsers are the "machines" of today, and their "machine code" is JavaScript, so these days it seems almost every language out there has a compiler that targets JS since that's the main way to get your code running in a browser.

The front end—scanner and parser—of a transpiler looks like other compilers. Then, if the source language is only a simple syntactic skin over the target language, it may skip analysis entirely and go straight to outputting the analogous syntax in the destination language.

If the two languages are more semantically different, you'll see more of the typical phases of a full compiler including analysis and possibly even optimization. Then, when it comes to code generation, instead of outputting some binary language like machine code, you produce a string of grammatically correct source (well, destination) code in the target language.

Either way, you then run that resulting code through the output language's existing compilation pipeline, and you're good to go.

### 2.2.4  Just-in-time compilation

This last one is less a shortcut and more a dangerous alpine scramble best reserved for experts. The fastest way to execute code is by compiling it to machine code, but you might not know what architecture your end user's machine supports. What to do?

You can do the same thing that the HotSpot Java Virtual Machine (JVM), Microsoft's Common Language Runtime (CLR), and most JavaScript interpreters do. On the end user's machine, when the program is loaded—either from source in the case of JS, or platform-independent bytecode for the JVM and CLR—you compile it to native code for the architecture their computer supports. Naturally enough, this is called **just-in-time compilation**. Most hackers just say "JIT", pronounced like it rhymes with "fit".

This is, of course, exactly where the HotSpot JVM gets its name.

The most sophisticated JITs insert profiling hooks into the generated code to see which regions are most performance critical and what kind of data is flowing through them. Then, over time, they will automatically recompile those hotspots with more advanced optimizations.

## 2.3  Compilers and Interpreters

Now that I've stuffed your head with a dictionary's worth of programming language jargon, we can finally address a question that's plagued coders since time immemorial: What's the difference between a compiler and an interpreter?

It turns out this is like asking the difference between a fruit and a vegetable. That seems like a binary either-or choice, but actually "fruit" is a *botanical* term and "vegetable" is *culinary*. One does not strictly imply the negation of the other.

There are fruits that aren't vegetables (apples) and vegetables that aren't fruits (carrots), but also edible plants that are both fruits *and* vegetables, like tomatoes.

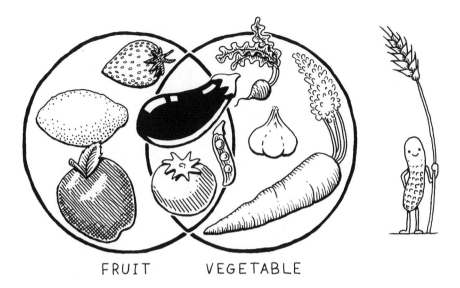

Peanuts (which are not even nuts) and cereals like wheat are actually fruit, but I got this drawing wrong. What can I say, I'm a software engineer, not a botanist. I should probably erase the little peanut guy, but he's so cute that I can't bear to.

Now *pine nuts*, on the other hand, are plant-based foods that are neither fruits nor vegetables. At least as far as I can tell.

FRUIT        VEGETABLE

So, back to languages:

- **Compiling** is an *implementation technique* that involves translating a source language to some other—usually lower-level—form. When you generate bytecode or machine code, you are compiling. When you transpile to another high-level language, you are compiling too.

- When we say a language implementation "is a **compiler**", we mean it translates source code to some other form but doesn't execute it. The user has to take the resulting output and run it themselves.

- Conversely, when we say an implementation "is an **interpreter**", we mean it takes in source code and executes it immediately. It runs programs "from source".

Like apples and oranges, some implementations are clearly compilers and *not* interpreters. GCC and Clang take your C code and compile it to machine code. An end user runs that executable directly and may never even know which tool was used to compile it. So those are *compilers* for C.

In older versions of Matz's canonical implementation of Ruby, the user ran Ruby from source. The implementation parsed it and executed it directly by traversing the syntax tree. No other translation occurred, either internally or in any user-visible form. So this was definitely an *interpreter* for Ruby.

But what of CPython? When you run your Python program using it, the code is parsed and converted to an internal bytecode format, which is then executed inside the VM. From the user's perspective, this is clearly an interpreter—they run their program from source. But if you look under CPython's scaly skin, you'll see that there is definitely some compiling going on.

The answer is that it is both. CPython *is* an interpreter, and it *has* a compiler. In practice, most scripting languages work this way, as you can see:

The Go tool is even more of a horticultural curiosity. If you run `go build`, it compiles your Go source code to machine code and stops. If you type `go run`, it does that, then immediately executes the generated executable.

So `go` *is* a compiler (you can use it as a tool to compile code without running it), *is* an interpreter (you can invoke it to immediately run a program from source), and also *has* a compiler (when you use it as an interpreter, it is still compiling internally).

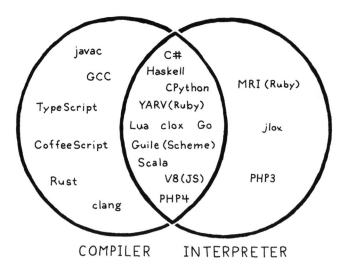

That overlapping region in the center is where our second interpreter lives too, since it internally compiles to bytecode. So while this book is nominally about interpreters, we'll cover some compilation too.

## 2.4  Our Journey

That's a lot to take in all at once. Don't worry. This isn't the chapter where you're expected to *understand* all of these pieces and parts. I just want you to know that they are out there and roughly how they fit together.

This map should serve you well as you explore the territory beyond the guided path we take in this book. I want to leave you yearning to strike out on your own and wander all over that mountain.

Henceforth, I promise to tone down the whole mountain metaphor thing.

But, for now, it's time for our own journey to begin. Tighten your bootlaces, cinch up your pack, and come along. From here on out, all you need to focus on is the path in front of you.

---

**CHALLENGES**

1. Pick an open source implementation of a language you like. Download the source code and poke around in it. Try to find the code that implements the scanner and parser. Are they handwritten, or generated using tools like Lex and Yacc? (`.l` or `.y` files usually imply the latter.)

2. Just-in-time compilation tends to be the fastest way to implement dynamically typed languages, but not all of them use it. What reasons are there to *not* JIT?

3. Most Lisp implementations that compile to C also contain an interpreter that lets them execute Lisp code on the fly as well. Why?

# The Lox Language

3

*"What nicer thing can you do for somebody than make them breakfast?"*

— Anthony Bourdain

We'll spend the rest of this book illuminating every dark and sundry corner of the Lox language, but it seems cruel to have you immediately start grinding out code for the interpreter without at least a glimpse of what we're going to end up with.

At the same time, I don't want to drag you through reams of language lawyering and specification-ese before you get to touch your text editor. So this will be a gentle, friendly introduction to Lox. It will leave out a lot of details and edge cases. We've got plenty of time for those later.

A tutorial isn't very fun if you can't try the code out yourself. Alas, you don't have a Lox interpreter yet, since you haven't built one!

Fear not. You can use mine:

→ craftinginterpreters.com/repo

## 3.1  Hello, Lox

Here's your very first taste of Lox:

Your first taste of Lox, the language, that is. I don't know if you've ever had the cured, cold-smoked salmon before. If not, give it a try too.

```
// Your first Lox program!
print "Hello, world!";
```

As that `//` line comment and the trailing semicolon imply, Lox's syntax is a member of the C family. (There are no parentheses around the string because `print` is a built-in statement, and not a library function.)

Now, I won't claim that C has a *great* syntax. If we wanted something elegant, we'd probably mimic Pascal or Smalltalk. If we wanted to go full Scandinavian-furniture-minimalism, we'd do a Scheme. Those all have their virtues.

I'm surely biased, but I think Lox's syntax is pretty clean. C's most egregious grammar problems are around types. Dennis Ritchie had this idea called "declaration reflects use", where variable declarations mirror the operations you would have to perform on the variable to get to a value of the base type. Clever idea, but I don't think it worked out great in practice.

Lox doesn't have static types, so we avoid that.

What C-like syntax has instead is something you'll often find more valuable in a language: *familiarity*. I know you are already comfortable with that style because the two languages we'll be using to *implement* Lox—Java and C—also inherit it. Using a similar syntax for Lox gives you one less thing to learn.

## 3.2  A High-Level Language

While this book ended up bigger than I was hoping, it's still not big enough to fit a huge language like Java in it. In order to fit two complete implementations of Lox in these pages, Lox itself has to be pretty compact.

Now that JavaScript has taken over the world and is used to build ginormous applications, it's hard to think of it as a "little scripting language". But Brendan Eich hacked the first JS interpreter into Netscape Navigator in *ten days* to make buttons animate on web pages. JavaScript has grown up since then, but it was once a cute little language.

Because Eich slapped JS together with roughly the same raw materials and time as an episode of MacGyver, it has some weird semantic corners where the duct tape and paper clips show through. Things like variable hoisting, dynamically bound `this`, holes in arrays, and implicit conversions.

I had the luxury of taking my time on Lox, so it should be a little cleaner.

When I think of languages that are small but useful, what comes to mind are high-level "scripting" languages like JavaScript, Scheme, and Lua. Of those three, Lox looks most like JavaScript, mainly because most C-syntax languages do. As we'll learn later, Lox's approach to scoping hews closely to Scheme. The C flavor of Lox we'll build in Part III is heavily indebted to Lua's clean, efficient implementation.

Lox shares two other aspects with those three languages:

### 3.2.1  Dynamic typing

Lox is dynamically typed. Variables can store values of any type, and a single variable can even store values of different types at different times. If you try to perform an operation on values of the wrong type—say, dividing a number by a string—then the error is detected and reported at runtime.

There are plenty of reasons to like static types, but they don't outweigh the pragmatic reasons to pick dynamic types for Lox. A static type system is a ton of work to learn and implement. Skipping it gives you a simpler language and a shorter book. We'll get our interpreter up and executing bits of code sooner if we defer our type checking to runtime.

### 3.2.2  Automatic memory management

After all, the two languages we'll be using to *implement* Lox are both statically typed.

High-level languages exist to eliminate error-prone, low-level drudgery, and what could be more tedious than manually managing the allocation and freeing of storage? No one rises and greets the morning sun with, "I can't wait to figure out the correct place to call `free()` for every byte of memory I allocate today!"

There are two main techniques for managing memory: **reference counting** and **tracing garbage collection** (usually just called **garbage collection** or **GC**). Ref counters are much simpler to implement—I think that's why Perl, PHP, and Python all started out using them. But, over time, the limitations of ref counting become too troublesome. All of those languages eventually ended up adding a full tracing GC, or at least enough of one to clean up object cycles.

Tracing garbage collection has a fearsome reputation. It is a little harrowing working at the level of raw memory. Debugging a GC can sometimes leave you seeing hex dumps in your dreams. But, remember, this book is about dispelling magic and slaying those monsters, so we *are* going to write our own garbage collector. I think you'll find the algorithm is quite simple and a lot of fun to implement.

In practice, ref counting and tracing are more ends of a continuum than opposing sides. Most ref counting systems end up doing some tracing to handle cycles, and the write barriers of a generational collector look a bit like retain calls if you squint.

For lots more on this, look up a paper called "A Unified Theory of Garbage Collection".

## 3.3 Data Types

In Lox's little universe, the atoms that make up all matter are the built-in data types. There are only a few:

- **Booleans.** You can't code without logic and you can't logic without Boolean values. "True" and "false", the yin and yang of software. Unlike some ancient languages that repurpose an existing type to represent truth and falsehood, Lox has a dedicated Boolean type. We may be roughing it on this expedition, but we aren't *savages*.

  There are two Boolean values, obviously, and a literal for each one.

Boolean variables are the only data type in Lox named after a person, George Boole, which is why "Boolean" is capitalized. He died in 1864, nearly a century before digital computers turned his algebra into electricity. I wonder what he'd think to see his name all over billions of lines of Java code.

```
true;  // Not false.
false; // Not *not* false.
```

- **Numbers.** Lox has only one kind of number: double-precision floating point. Since floating-point numbers can also represent a wide range of integers, that covers a lot of territory, while keeping things simple.

  Full-featured languages have lots of syntax for numbers—hexadecimal, scientific notation, octal, all sorts of fun stuff. We'll settle for basic integer and decimal literals.

```
1234;  // An integer.
12.34; // A decimal number.
```

- **Strings.** We've already seen one string literal in the first example. Like most languages, they are enclosed in double quotes.

```
"I am a string";
"";      // The empty string.
"123";   // This is a string, not a number.
```

As we'll see when we get to implementing them, there is quite a lot of complexity hiding in that innocuous sequence of characters.

Even that word "character" is a trickster. Is it ASCII? Unicode? A code point or a "grapheme cluster"? Fixed-length or variable-length encoding?

- **Nil.** There's one last built-in value who's never invited to the party but always seems to show up. It represents "no value". It's called "null" in many other languages. In Lox we spell it `nil`. (When we get to implementing it, that will help distinguish when we're talking about Lox's `nil` versus Java or C's `null`.)

There are good arguments for not having a null value in a language since null pointer errors are the scourge of our industry. If we were doing a statically typed language, it would be worth trying to ban it. In a dynamically typed one, though, eliminating it is often more annoying than having it.

## 3.4 Expressions

If built-in data types and their literals are atoms, then **expressions** must be the molecules. Most of these will be familiar.

### 3.4.1 Arithmetic

Lox features the basic arithmetic operators you know and love from C and other languages:

```
add + me;
subtract - me;
multiply * me;
divide / me;
```

There are some operators that have more than two operands and the operators are interleaved between them. The only one in wide usage is the "conditional" or "ternary" operator of C and friends:

```
cond ? thenArm : elseArm;
```

Some call these **mixfix** operators. A few languages let you define your own operators and control how they are positioned—their "fixity".

The subexpressions on either side of the operator are **operands**. Because there are *two* of them, these are called **binary** operators. (It has nothing to do with the ones-and-zeroes use of "binary".) Because the operator is fixed *in* the middle of the operands, these are also called **infix** operators (as opposed to **prefix** operators where the operator comes before the operands, and **postfix** where it comes after).

One arithmetic operator is actually *both* an infix and a prefix one. The – operator can also be used to negate a number.

```
-negateMe;
```

All of these operators work on numbers, and it's an error to pass any other types to them. The exception is the + operator—you can also pass it two strings to concatenate them.

### 3.4.2 Comparison and equality

Moving along, we have a few more operators that always return a Boolean result. We can compare numbers (and only numbers), using Ye Olde Comparison Operators.

```
less < than;
lessThan <= orEqual;
greater > than;
greaterThan >= orEqual;
```

We can test two values of any kind for equality or inequality.

```
1 == 2;         // false.
"cat" != "dog"; // true.
```

Even different types.

```
314 == "pi"; // false.
```

Values of different types are *never* equivalent.

```
123 == "123"; // false.
```

I'm generally against implicit conversions.

### 3.4.3 Logical operators

The not operator, a prefix !, returns `false` if its operand is true, and vice versa.

```
!true;  // false.
!false; // true.
```

The other two logical operators really are control flow constructs in the guise of expressions. An and expression determines if two values are *both* true. It returns the left operand if it's false, or the right operand otherwise.

```
true and false; // false.
true and true;  // true.
```

And an or expression determines if *either* of two values (or both) are true. It returns the left operand if it is true and the right operand otherwise.

```
false or false; // false.
true or false;  // true.
```

> I used and and or for these instead of && and || because Lox doesn't use & and | for bitwise operators. It felt weird to introduce the double-character forms without the single-character ones.
>
> I also kind of like using words for these since they are really control flow structures and not simple operators.

The reason and and or are like control flow structures is that they **short-circuit**. Not only does and return the left operand if it is false, it doesn't even *evaluate* the right one in that case. Conversely (contrapositively?), if the left operand of an or is true, the right is skipped.

### 3.4.4 Precedence and grouping

All of these operators have the same precedence and associativity that you'd expect coming from C. (When we get to parsing, we'll get *way* more precise about that.) In cases where the precedence isn't what you want, you can use ( ) to group stuff.

```
var average = (min + max) / 2;
```

Since they aren't very technically interesting, I've cut the remainder of the typical operator menagerie out of our little language. No bitwise, shift, modulo, or conditional operators. I'm not grading you, but you will get bonus points in my heart if you augment your own implementation of Lox with them.

Those are the expression forms (except for a couple related to specific features that we'll get to later), so let's move up a level.

## 3.5  Statements

Now we're at statements. Where an expression's main job is to produce a *value*, a statement's job is to produce an *effect*. Since, by definition, statements don't evaluate to a value, to be useful they have to otherwise change the world in some way—usually modifying some state, reading input, or producing output.

You've seen a couple of kinds of statements already. The first one was:

```
print "Hello, world!";
```

Baking `print` into the language instead of just making it a core library function is a hack. But it's a *useful* hack for us: it means our in-progress interpreter can start producing output before we've implemented all of the machinery required to define functions, look them up by name, and call them.

A `print` statement evaluates a single expression and displays the result to the user. You've also seen some statements like:

```
"some expression";
```

An expression followed by a semicolon (;) promotes the expression to statement-hood. This is called (imaginatively enough), an **expression statement**.

If you want to pack a series of statements where a single one is expected, you can wrap them up in a **block**.

```
{
  print "One statement.";
  print "Two statements.";
}
```

Blocks also affect scoping, which leads us to the next section...

## 3.6  Variables

This is one of those cases where not having `nil` and forcing every variable to be initialized to some value would be more annoying than dealing with `nil` itself.

You declare variables using `var` statements. If you omit the initializer, the variable's value defaults to `nil`.

```
var imAVariable = "here is my value";
var iAmNil;
```

Once declared, you can, naturally, access and assign a variable using its name.

Can you tell that I tend to work on this book in the morning before I've had anything to eat?

```
var breakfast = "bagels";
print breakfast; // "bagels".
breakfast = "beignets";
print breakfast; // "beignets".
```

I won't get into the rules for variable scope here, because we're going to spend a surprising amount of time in later chapters mapping every square inch of the rules. In most cases, it works like you would expect coming from C or Java.

## 3.7 Control Flow

It's hard to write useful programs if you can't skip some code or execute some more than once. That means control flow. In addition to the logical operators we already covered, Lox lifts three statements straight from C.

An `if` statement executes one of two statements based on some condition.

```
if (condition) {
  print "yes";
} else {
  print "no";
}
```

A `while` loop executes the body repeatedly as long as the condition expression evaluates to true.

```
var a = 1;
while (a < 10) {
  print a;
  a = a + 1;
}
```

Finally, we have `for` loops.

```
for (var a = 1; a < 10; a = a + 1) {
  print a;
}
```

This loop does the same thing as the previous `while` loop. Most modern languages also have some sort of `for-in` or `foreach` loop for explicitly iterating over various sequence types. In a real language, that's nicer than the crude C-style `for` loop we got here. Lox keeps it basic.

## 3.8 Functions

A function call expression looks the same as it does in C.

```
makeBreakfast(bacon, eggs, toast);
```

You can also call a function without passing anything to it.

```
makeBreakfast();
```

Unlike in, say, Ruby, the parentheses are mandatory in this case. If you leave

We already have **and** and **or** for branching, and we *could* use recursion to repeat code, so that's theoretically sufficient. It would be pretty awkward to program that way in an imperative-styled language, though.

Scheme, on the other hand, has no built-in looping constructs. It *does* rely on recursion for repetition. Smalltalk has no built-in branching constructs, and relies on dynamic dispatch for selectively executing code.

I left **do** **while** loops out of Lox because they aren't that common and wouldn't teach you anything that you won't already learn from **while**. Go ahead and add it to your implementation if it makes you happy. It's your party.

This is a concession I made because of how the implementation is split across chapters. A **for-in** loop needs some sort of dynamic dispatch in the iterator protocol to handle different kinds of sequences, but we don't get that until after we're done with control flow. We could circle back and add **for-in** loops later, but I didn't think doing so would teach you anything super interesting.

them off, the name doesn't *call* the function, it just refers to it.

A language isn't very fun if you can't define your own functions. In Lox, you do that with `fun`.

```
fun printSum(a, b) {
  print a + b;
}
```

Now's a good time to clarify some terminology. Some people throw around "parameter" and "argument" like they are interchangeable and, to many, they are. We're going to spend a lot of time splitting the finest of downy hairs around semantics, so let's sharpen our words. From here on out:

- An **argument** is an actual value you pass to a function when you call it. So a function *call* has an *argument* list. Sometimes you hear **actual parameter** used for these.

- A **parameter** is a variable that holds the value of the argument inside the body of the function. Thus, a function *declaration* has a *parameter* list. Others call these **formal parameters** or simply **formals**.

The body of a function is always a block. Inside it, you can return a value using a `return` statement.

```
fun returnSum(a, b) {
  return a + b;
}
```

If execution reaches the end of the block without hitting a `return`, it implicitly returns `nil`.

### 3.8.1 Closures

Functions are *first class* in Lox, which just means they are real values that you can get a reference to, store in variables, pass around, etc. This works:

```
fun addPair(a, b) {
  return a + b;
}

fun identity(a) {
  return a;
}

print identity(addPair)(1, 2); // Prints "3".
```

Since function declarations are statements, you can declare local functions inside another function.

```
fun outerFunction() {
  fun localFunction() {
    print "I'm local!";
  }

  localFunction();
}
```

If you combine local functions, first-class functions, and block scope, you run into this interesting situation:

```
fun returnFunction() {
  var outside = "outside";

  fun inner() {
    print outside;
  }

  return inner;
}

var fn = returnFunction();
fn();
```

Here, `inner()` accesses a local variable declared outside of its body in the surrounding function. Is this kosher? Now that lots of languages have borrowed this feature from Lisp, you probably know the answer is yes.

For that to work, `inner()` has to "hold on" to references to any surrounding variables that it uses so that they stay around even after the outer function has returned. We call functions that do this **closures**. These days, the term is often used for *any* first-class function, though it's sort of a misnomer if the function doesn't happen to close over any variables.

As you can imagine, implementing these adds some complexity because we can no longer assume variable scope works strictly like a stack where local variables evaporate the moment the function returns. We're going to have a fun time learning how to make these work correctly and efficiently.

Peter J. Landin coined the term "closure". Yes, he invented damn near half the terms in programming languages. Most of them came out of one incredible paper, "The Next 700 Programming Languages".

In order to implement these kind of functions, you need to create a data structure that bundles together the function's code and the surrounding variables it needs. He called this a "closure" because it *closes over* and holds on to the variables it needs.

## 3.9 Classes

Since Lox has dynamic typing, lexical (roughly, "block") scope, and closures, it's about halfway to being a functional language. But as you'll see, it's *also* about halfway to being an object-oriented language. Both paradigms have a lot going for them, so I thought it was worth covering some of each.

Since classes have come under fire for not living up to their hype, let me first explain why I put them into Lox and this book. There are really two questions:

### 3.9.1 Why might any language want to be object oriented?

Now that object-oriented languages like Java have sold out and only play arena shows, it's not cool to like them anymore. Why would anyone make a *new* language with objects? Isn't that like releasing music on 8-track?

It is true that the "all inheritance all the time" binge of the '90s produced some monstrous class hierarchies, but **object-oriented programming** (**OOP**) is still pretty rad. Billions of lines of successful code have been written in OOP languages, shipping millions of apps to happy users. Likely a majority of working programmers today are using an object-oriented language. They can't all be *that* wrong.

In particular, for a dynamically typed language, objects are pretty handy. We need *some* way of defining compound data types to bundle blobs of stuff together.

If we can also hang methods off of those, then we avoid the need to prefix all of our functions with the name of the data type they operate on to avoid colliding with similar functions for different types. In, say, Racket, you end up having to name your functions like `hash-copy` (to copy a hash table) and `vector-copy` (to copy a vector) so that they don't step on each other. Methods are scoped to the object, so that problem goes away.

### 3.9.2  Why is Lox object oriented?

I could claim objects are groovy but still out of scope for the book. Most programming language books, especially ones that try to implement a whole language, leave objects out. To me, that means the topic isn't well covered. With such a widespread paradigm, that omission makes me sad.

Given how many of us spend all day *using* OOP languages, it seems like the world could use a little documentation on how to *make* one. As you'll see, it turns out to be pretty interesting. Not as hard as you might fear, but not as simple as you might presume, either.

### 3.9.3  Classes or prototypes

When it comes to objects, there are actually two approaches to them, classes and prototypes. Classes came first, and are more common thanks to C++, Java, C#, and friends. Prototypes were a virtually forgotten offshoot until JavaScript accidentally took over the world.

In class-based languages, there are two core concepts: instances and classes. Instances store the state for each object and have a reference to the instance's class. Classes contain the methods and inheritance chain. To call a method on an instance, there is always a level of indirection. You look up the instance's class and then you find the method *there*:

In a statically typed language like C++, method lookup typically happens at compile time based on the *static* type of the instance, giving you **static dispatch**. In contrast, **dynamic dispatch** looks up the class of the actual instance object at runtime. This is how virtual methods in statically typed languages and all methods in a dynamically typed language like Lox work.

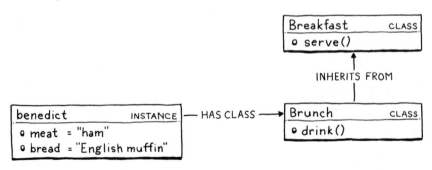

Prototype-based languages merge these two concepts. There are only objects—no classes—and each individual object may contain state and methods. Objects can directly inherit from each other (or "delegate to" in prototypal lingo):

In practice the line between class-based and prototype-based languages blurs. JavaScript's "constructor function" notion pushes you pretty hard towards defining class-like objects. Meanwhile, class-based Ruby is perfectly happy to let you attach methods to individual instances.

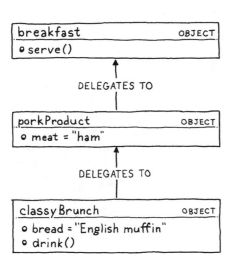

This means that in some ways prototypal languages are more fundamental than classes. They are really neat to implement because they're *so* simple. Also, they can express lots of unusual patterns that classes steer you away from.

But I've looked at a *lot* of code written in prototypal languages—including some of my own devising. Do you know what people generally do with all of the power and flexibility of prototypes?...They use them to reinvent classes.

I don't know *why* that is, but people naturally seem to prefer a class-based (Classic? Classy?) style. Prototypes *are* simpler in the language, but they seem to accomplish that only by pushing the complexity onto the user. So, for Lox, we'll save our users the trouble and bake classes right in.

Larry Wall, Perl's inventor/prophet calls this the "waterbed theory". Some complexity is essential and cannot be eliminated. If you push it down in one place, it swells up in another.

Prototypal languages don't so much *eliminate* the complexity of classes as they do make the *user* take that complexity by building their own class-like metaprogramming libraries.

### 3.9.4  Classes in Lox

Enough rationale, let's see what we actually have. Classes encompass a constellation of features in most languages. For Lox, I've selected what I think are the brightest stars. You declare a class and its methods like so:

```
class Breakfast {
  cook() {
    print "Eggs a-fryin'!";
  }

  serve(who) {
    print "Enjoy your breakfast, " + who + ".";
  }
}
```

They are still just as fun, though.

The body of a class contains its methods. They look like function declarations but without the fun keyword. When the class declaration is executed, Lox creates a class object and stores that in a variable named after the class. Just like functions, classes are first class in Lox.

```
// Store it in variables.
var someVariable = Breakfast;

// Pass it to functions.
someFunction(Breakfast);
```

Next, we need a way to create instances. We could add some sort of new keyword, but to keep things simple, in Lox the class itself is a factory function for instances. Call a class like a function, and it produces a new instance of itself.

```
var breakfast = Breakfast();
print breakfast; // "Breakfast instance".
```

### 3.9.5  Instantiation and initialization

Classes that only have behavior aren't super useful. The idea behind object-oriented programming is encapsulating behavior *and state* together. To do that, you need fields. Lox, like other dynamically typed languages, lets you freely add properties onto objects.

```
breakfast.meat = "sausage";
breakfast.bread = "sourdough";
```

Assigning to a field creates it if it doesn't already exist.

If you want to access a field or method on the current object from within a method, you use good old this.

```
class Breakfast {
  serve(who) {
    print "Enjoy your " + this.meat + " and " +
        this.bread + ", " + who + ".";
  }

  // ...
}
```

Part of encapsulating data within an object is ensuring the object is in a valid state when it's created. To do that, you can define an initializer. If your class has a method named init(), it is called automatically when the object is constructed. Any parameters passed to the class are forwarded to its initializer.

```
class Breakfast {
  init(meat, bread) {
    this.meat = meat;
    this.bread = bread;
  }

  // ...
}


var baconAndToast = Breakfast("bacon", "toast");
baconAndToast.serve("Dear Reader");
// "Enjoy your bacon and toast, Dear Reader."
```

## 3.9.6 Inheritance

Every object-oriented language lets you not only define methods, but reuse them across multiple classes or objects. For that, Lox supports single inheritance. When you declare a class, you can specify a class that it inherits from using a less-than (<) operator.

```
class Brunch < Breakfast {
  drink() {
    print "How about a Bloody Mary?";
  }
}
```

Here, Brunch is the **derived class** or **subclass**, and Breakfast is the **base class** or **superclass**.

Every method defined in the superclass is also available to its subclasses.

```
var benedict = Brunch("ham", "English muffin");
benedict.serve("Noble Reader");
```

Even the `init()` method gets inherited. In practice, the subclass usually wants to define its own `init()` method too. But the original one also needs to be called so that the superclass can maintain its state. We need some way to call a method on our own *instance* without hitting our own *methods*.

As in Java, you use `super` for that.

```
class Brunch < Breakfast {
  init(meat, bread, drink) {
    super.init(meat, bread);
    this.drink = drink;
  }
}
```

Why the < operator? I didn't feel like introducing a new keyword like `extends`. Lox doesn't use `:` for anything else so I didn't want to reserve that either. Instead, I took a page from Ruby and used <.

If you know any type theory, you'll notice it's not a *totally* arbitrary choice. Every instance of a subclass is an instance of its superclass too, but there may be instances of the superclass that are not instances of the subclass. That means, in the universe of objects, the set of subclass objects is smaller than the superclass's set, though type nerds usually use <: for that relation.

Lox is different from C++, Java, and C#, which do not inherit constructors, but similar to Smalltalk and Ruby, which do.

That's about it for object orientation. I tried to keep the feature set minimal. The structure of the book did force one compromise. Lox is not a *pure* object-oriented language. In a true OOP language every object is an instance of a class, even primitive values like numbers and Booleans.

Because we don't implement classes until well after we start working with the built-in types, that would have been hard. So values of primitive types aren't real objects in the sense of being instances of classes. They don't have methods or properties. If I were trying to make Lox a real language for real users, I would fix that.

## 3.10  The Standard Library

We're almost done. That's the whole language, so all that's left is the "core" or "standard" library—the set of functionality that is implemented directly in the interpreter and that all user-defined behavior is built on top of.

This is the saddest part of Lox. Its standard library goes beyond minimalism and veers close to outright nihilism. For the sample code in the book, we only need to demonstrate that code is running and doing what it's supposed to do. For that, we already have the built-in `print` statement.

Later, when we start optimizing, we'll write some benchmarks and see how long it takes to execute code. That means we need to track time, so we'll define one built-in function, `clock()`, that returns the number of seconds since the program started.

And…that's it. I know, right? It's embarrassing.

If you wanted to turn Lox into an actual useful language, the very first thing you should do is flesh this out. String manipulation, trigonometric functions, file I/O, networking, heck, even *reading input from the user* would help. But we don't need any of that for this book, and adding it wouldn't teach you anything interesting, so I've left it out.

Don't worry, we'll have plenty of exciting stuff in the language itself to keep us busy.

### CHALLENGES

1. Write some sample Lox programs and run them (you can use the implementations of Lox in my repository). Try to come up with edge case behavior I didn't specify here. Does it do what you expect? Why or why not?

2. This informal introduction leaves a *lot* unspecified. List several open questions you have about the language's syntax and semantics. What do you think the answers should be?

3. Lox is a pretty tiny language. What features do you think it is missing that would make it annoying to use for real programs? (Aside from the standard library, of course.)

## DESIGN NOTE: EXPRESSIONS AND STATEMENTS

Lox has both expressions and statements. Some languages omit the latter. Instead, they treat declarations and control flow constructs as expressions too. These "everything is an expression" languages tend to have functional pedigrees and include most Lisps, SML, Haskell, Ruby, and CoffeeScript.

To do that, for each "statement-like" construct in the language, you need to decide what value it evaluates to. Some of those are easy:

- An `if` expression evaluates to the result of whichever branch is chosen. Likewise, a `switch` or other multi-way branch evaluates to whichever case is picked.

- A variable declaration evaluates to the value of the variable.

- A block evaluates to the result of the last expression in the sequence.

Some get a little stranger. What should a loop evaluate to? A `while` loop in CoffeeScript evaluates to an array containing each element that the body evaluated to. That can be handy, or a waste of memory if you don't need the array.

You also have to decide how these statement-like expressions compose with other expressions—you have to fit them into the grammar's precedence table. For example, Ruby allows:

```
puts 1 + if true then 2 else 3 end + 4
```

Is this what you'd expect? Is it what your *users* expect? How does this affect how you design the syntax for your "statements"? Note that Ruby has an explicit **end** to tell when the `if` expression is complete. Without it, the + 4 would likely be parsed as part of the **else** clause.

Turning every statement into an expression forces you to answer a few hairy questions like that. In return, you eliminate some redundancy. C has both blocks for sequencing statements, and the comma operator for sequencing expressions. It has both the `if` statement and the `?:` conditional operator. If everything was an expression in C, you could unify each of those.

Languages that do away with statements usually also feature **implicit returns**—a function automatically returns whatever value its body evaluates to without need for some explicit **return** syntax. For small functions and methods, this is really handy. In fact, many languages that do have statements have added syntax like => to be able to define functions whose body is the result of evaluating a single expression.

But making *all* functions work that way can be a little strange. If you aren't careful, your function will leak a return value even if you only intend it to produce a side effect. In practice, though, users of these languages don't find it to be a problem.

For Lox, I gave it statements for prosaic reasons. I picked a C-like syntax for familiarity's sake, and trying to take the existing C statement syntax and interpret it like expressions gets weird pretty fast.

# A Tree-Walk Interpreter

PART II

With this part, we begin jlox, the first of our two interpreters. Programming languages are a huge topic with piles of concepts and terminology to cram into your brain all at once. Programming language theory requires a level of mental rigor that you probably haven't had to summon since your last calculus final. (Fortunately there isn't too much theory in this book.)

Implementing an interpreter uses a few architectural tricks and design patterns uncommon in other kinds of applications, so we'll be getting used to the engineering side of things too. Given all of that, we'll keep the code we have to write as simple and plain as possible.

In less than two thousand lines of clean Java code, we'll build a complete interpreter for Lox that implements every single feature of the language, exactly as we've specified. The first few chapters work front-to-back through the phases of the interpreter—scanning, parsing, and evaluating code. After that, we add language features one at a time, growing a simple calculator into a full-fledged scripting language.

# Scanning

4

*"Take big bites. Anything worth doing is worth overdoing."*

— Robert A. Heinlein, *Time Enough for Love*

The first step in any compiler or interpreter is scanning. The scanner takes in raw source code as a series of characters and groups it into a series of chunks we call **tokens**. These are the meaningful "words" and "punctuation" that make up the language's grammar.

Scanning is a good starting point for us too because the code isn't very hard— pretty much a `switch` statement with delusions of grandeur. It will help us warm up before we tackle some of the more interesting material later. By the end of this chapter, we'll have a full-featured, fast scanner that can take any string of Lox source code and produce the tokens that we'll feed into the parser in the next chapter.

This task has been variously called "scanning" and "lexing" (short for "lexical analysis") over the years. Way back when computers were as big as Winnebagos but had less memory than your watch, some people used "scanner" only to refer to the piece of code that dealt with reading raw source code characters from disk and buffering them in memory. Then "lexing" was the subsequent phase that did useful stuff with the characters.

These days, reading a source file into memory is trivial, so it's rarely a distinct phase in the compiler. Because of that, the two terms are basically interchangeable.

## 4.1 The Interpreter Framework

Since this is our first real chapter, before we get to actually scanning some code we need to sketch out the basic shape of our interpreter, jlox. Everything starts with a class in Java.

lox/Lox.java
*create new file*

```java
package com.craftinginterpreters.lox;

import java.io.BufferedReader;
import java.io.IOException;
import java.io.InputStreamReader;
import java.nio.charset.Charset;
import java.nio.file.Files;
import java.nio.file.Paths;
import java.util.List;

public class Lox {
  public static void main(String[] args) throws IOException {
    if (args.length > 1) {
      System.out.println("Usage: jlox [script]");
      System.exit(64);
    } else if (args.length == 1) {
      runFile(args[0]);
    } else {
      runPrompt();
    }
  }
}
```

For exit codes, I'm using the conventions defined in the UNIX "sysexits.h" header. It's the closest thing to a standard I could find.

Stick that in a text file, and go get your IDE or Makefile or whatever set up. I'll be right here when you're ready. Good? OK!

Lox is a scripting language, which means it executes directly from source. Our interpreter supports two ways of running code. If you start jlox from the command line and give it a path to a file, it reads the file and executes it.

lox/Lox.java
*add after* main()

```java
private static void runFile(String path) throws IOException {
  byte[] bytes = Files.readAllBytes(Paths.get(path));
  run(new String(bytes, Charset.defaultCharset()));
}
```

If you want a more intimate conversation with your interpreter, you can also run it interactively. Fire up jlox without any arguments, and it drops you into a prompt where you can enter and execute code one line at a time.

lox/Lox.java
*add after* runFile()

```java
private static void runPrompt() throws IOException {
  InputStreamReader input = new InputStreamReader(System.in);
  BufferedReader reader = new BufferedReader(input);

  for (;;) {
    System.out.print("> ");
    String line = reader.readLine();
    if (line == null) break;
    run(line);
  }
}
```

An interactive prompt is also called a "REPL" (pronounced like "rebel" but with a "p"). The name comes from Lisp where implementing one is as simple as wrapping a loop around a few built-in functions:

```
(print (eval (read)))
```

Working outwards from the most nested call, you **R**ead a line of input, **E**valuate it, **P**rint the result, then **L**oop and do it all over again.

The readLine() function, as the name so helpfully implies, reads a line of input from the user on the command line and returns the result. To kill an interactive command-line app, you usually type Control-D. Doing so signals an "end-of-file" condition to the program. When that happens `readLine()` returns `null`, so we check for that to exit the loop.

Both the prompt and the file runner are thin wrappers around this core function:

```
private static void run(String source) {
  Scanner scanner = new Scanner(source);
  List<Token> tokens = scanner.scanTokens();

  // For now, just print the tokens.
  for (Token token : tokens) {
    System.out.println(token);
  }
}
```

*lox/Lox.java*
*add after* `runPrompt()`

It's not super useful yet since we haven't written the interpreter, but baby steps, you know? Right now, it prints out the tokens our forthcoming scanner will emit so that we can see if we're making progress.

## 4.1.1 Error handling

While we're setting things up, another key piece of infrastructure is *error handling*. Textbooks sometimes gloss over this because it's more a practical matter than a formal computer science-y problem. But if you care about making a language that's actually *usable*, then handling errors gracefully is vital.

The tools our language provides for dealing with errors make up a large portion of its user interface. When the user's code is working, they aren't thinking about our language at all—their headspace is all about *their program*. It's usually only when things go wrong that they notice our implementation.

When that happens, it's up to us to give the user all the information they need to understand what went wrong and guide them gently back to where they are trying to go. Doing that well means thinking about error handling all through the implementation of our interpreter, starting now.

Having said all that, for *this* interpreter, what we'll build is pretty bare bones. I'd love to talk about interactive debuggers, static analyzers, and other fun stuff, but there's only so much ink in the pen.

```
static void error(int line, String message) {
  report(line, "", message);
}

private static void report(int line, String where,
                           String message) {
  System.err.println(
      "[line " + line + "] Error" + where + ": " + message);
  hadError = true;
}
```

*lox/Lox.java*
*add after* `run()`

This `error()` function and its `report()` helper tells the user some syntax error occurred on a given line. That is really the bare minimum to be able to claim you even *have* error reporting.

Imagine if you accidentally left a dangling comma in some function call and the interpreter printed out:

```
Error: Unexpected "," somewhere in your code. Good luck finding it!
```

That's not very helpful. We need to at least point them to the right line. Even better would be the beginning and end column so they know *where* in the line. Even better than *that* is to *show* the user the offending line, like:

```
Error: Unexpected "," in argument list.

  15 | function(first, second,);
                             ^-- Here.
```

I'd love to implement something like that in this book but the honest truth is that it's a lot of grungy string manipulation code. Very useful for users, but not super fun to read in a book and not very technically interesting. So we'll stick with just a line number. In your own interpreters, please do as I say and not as I do.

The primary reason we're sticking this error reporting function in the main Lox class is because of that `hadError` field. It's defined here:

*lox/Lox.java*
*in class* Lox

```
public class Lox {
  static boolean hadError = false;
```

We'll use this to ensure we don't try to execute code that has a known error. Also, it lets us exit with a non-zero exit code like a good command line citizen should.

*lox/Lox.java*
*in* runFile()

```
    run(new String(bytes, Charset.defaultCharset()));

    // Indicate an error in the exit code.
    if (hadError) System.exit(65);
  }
```

We need to reset this flag in the interactive loop. If the user makes a mistake, it shouldn't kill their entire session.

*lox/Lox.java*
*in* runPrompt()

```
      run(line);
      hadError = false;
    }
```

The other reason I pulled the error reporting out here instead of stuffing it into the scanner and other phases where the error might occur is to remind you that it's good engineering practice to separate the code that *generates* the errors from the code that *reports* them.

Various phases of the front end will detect errors, but it's not really their job to know how to present that to a user. In a full-featured language implementation, you will likely have multiple ways errors get displayed: on stderr, in an IDE's error window, logged to a file, etc. You don't want that code smeared all over your scanner and parser.

Ideally, we would have an actual abstraction, some kind of "ErrorReporter" interface that gets passed to the scanner and parser so that we can swap out different reporting strategies. For our simple interpreter here, I didn't do that, but I

I had exactly that when I first implemented jlox. I ended up tearing it out because it felt over-engineered for the minimal interpreter in this book.

did at least move the code for error reporting into a different class.

With some rudimentary error handling in place, our application shell is ready. Once we have a Scanner class with a scanTokens() method, we can start running it. Before we get to that, let's get more precise about what tokens are.

## 4.2 Lexemes and Tokens

Here's a line of Lox code:

```
var language = "lox";
```

Here, var is the keyword for declaring a variable. That three-character sequence "v-a-r" means something. But if we yank three letters out of the middle of language, like "g-u-a", those don't mean anything on their own.

That's what lexical analysis is about. Our job is to scan through the list of characters and group them together into the smallest sequences that still represent something. Each of these blobs of characters is called a **lexeme**. In that example line of code, the lexemes are:

The lexemes are only the raw substrings of the source code. However, in the process of grouping character sequences into lexemes, we also stumble upon some other useful information. When we take the lexeme and bundle it together with that other data, the result is a token. It includes useful stuff like:

### 4.2.1 Token type

Keywords are part of the shape of the language's grammar, so the parser often has code like, "If the next token is while then do…" That means the parser wants to know not just that it has a lexeme for some identifier, but that it has a *reserved* word, and *which* keyword it is.

The parser could categorize tokens from the raw lexeme by comparing the strings, but that's slow and kind of ugly. Instead, at the point that we recognize a lexeme, we also remember which *kind* of lexeme it represents. We have a different type for each keyword, operator, bit of punctuation, and literal type.

After all, string comparison ends up looking at individual characters, and isn't that the scanner's job?

```
package com.craftinginterpreters.lox;

enum TokenType {
  // Single-character tokens.
  LEFT_PAREN, RIGHT_PAREN, LEFT_BRACE, RIGHT_BRACE,
  COMMA, DOT, MINUS, PLUS, SEMICOLON, SLASH, STAR,

  // One or two character tokens.
  BANG, BANG_EQUAL, EQUAL, EQUAL_EQUAL,
  GREATER, GREATER_EQUAL, LESS, LESS_EQUAL,
```

lox/TokenType.java
*create new file*

*continued on next page…*

...from previous page

```
  // Literals.
  IDENTIFIER, STRING, NUMBER,

  // Keywords.
  AND, CLASS, ELSE, FALSE, FUN, FOR, IF, NIL, OR,
  PRINT, RETURN, SUPER, THIS, TRUE, VAR, WHILE,

  EOF
}
```

## 4.2.2 Literal value

There are lexemes for literal values—numbers and strings and the like. Since the scanner has to walk each character in the literal to correctly identify it, it can also convert that textual representation of a value to the living runtime object that will be used by the interpreter later.

## 4.2.3 Location information

Back when I was preaching the gospel about error handling, we saw that we need to tell users *where* errors occurred. Tracking that starts here. In our simple interpreter, we note only which line the token appears on, but more sophisticated implementations include the column and length too.

We take all of this data and wrap it in a class.

lox/Token.java
create new file

```java
package com.craftinginterpreters.lox;

class Token {
  final TokenType type;
  final String lexeme;
  final Object literal;
  final int line;

  Token(TokenType type, String lexeme, Object literal, int line) {
    this.type = type;
    this.lexeme = lexeme;
    this.literal = literal;
    this.line = line;
  }

  public String toString() {
    return type + " " + lexeme + " " + literal;
  }
}
```

Some token implementations store the location as two numbers: the offset from the beginning of the source file to the beginning of the lexeme, and the length of the lexeme. The scanner needs to know these anyway, so there's no overhead to calculate them.

An offset can be converted to line and column positions later by looking back at the source file and counting the preceding newlines. That sounds slow, and it is. However, you need to do it *only when you need to actually display a line and column to the user*. Most tokens never appear in an error message. For those, the less time you spend calculating position information ahead of time, the better.

Now we have an object with enough structure to be useful for all of the later phases of the interpreter.

## 4.3 Regular Languages and Expressions

Now that we know what we're trying to produce, let's, well, produce it. The core of the scanner is a loop. Starting at the first character of the source code, the scanner figures out what lexeme the character belongs to, and consumes it and any following characters that are part of that lexeme. When the scanner reaches the end of that lexeme, it emits a token.

Then it loops back and does it again, starting from the very next character in the source code. It keeps doing that, eating characters and occasionally, uh, excreting tokens, until it reaches the end of the input.

Lexical analygator.

The part of the loop where we look at a handful of characters to figure out which kind of lexeme it "matches" may sound familiar. If you know regular expressions, you might consider defining a regex for each kind of lexeme and using those to match characters. For example, Lox has the same rules as C for identifiers (variable names and the like). This regex matches one:

```
[a-zA-Z_][a-zA-Z_0-9]*
```

If you did think of regular expressions, your intuition is a deep one. The rules that determine how a particular language groups characters into lexemes are called its **lexical grammar**. In Lox, as in most programming languages, the rules of that grammar are simple enough for the language to be classified a **regular language**. That's the same "regular" as in regular expressions.

You very precisely *can* recognize all of the different lexemes for Lox using regexes if you want to, and there's a pile of interesting theory underlying why that is and what it means. Tools like Lex or Flex are designed expressly to let you do this—throw a handful of regexes at them, and they give you a complete scanner back.

Since our goal is to understand how a scanner does what it does, we won't be delegating that task. We're about handcrafted goods.

It pains me to gloss over the theory so much, especially when it's as interesting as I think the Chomsky hierarchy and finite-state machines are. But the honest truth is other books cover this better than I could. *Compilers: Principles, Techniques, and Tools* (universally known as "the dragon book") is the canonical reference.

Lex was created by Mike Lesk and Eric Schmidt. Yes, the same Eric Schmidt who was executive chairman of Google. I'm not saying programming languages are a surefire path to wealth and fame, but we *can* count at least one mega billionaire among us.

## 4.4 The Scanner Class

Without further ado, let's make ourselves a scanner.

lox/Scanner.java
*create new file*

```java
package com.craftinginterpreters.lox;

import java.util.ArrayList;
import java.util.HashMap;
import java.util.List;
import java.util.Map;

import static com.craftinginterpreters.lox.TokenType.*;

class Scanner {
  private final String source;
  private final List<Token> tokens = new ArrayList<>();

  Scanner(String source) {
    this.source = source;
  }
}
```

I know static imports are considered bad style by some, but they save me from having to sprinkle **TokenType.** all over the scanner and parser. Forgive me, but every character counts in a book.

We store the raw source code as a simple string, and we have a list ready to fill with tokens we're going to generate. The aforementioned loop that does that looks like this:

lox/Scanner.java
*add after* Scanner()

```java
List<Token> scanTokens() {
  while (!isAtEnd()) {
    // We are at the beginning of the next lexeme.
    start = current;
    scanToken();
  }

  tokens.add(new Token(EOF, "", null, line));
  return tokens;
}
```

The scanner works its way through the source code, adding tokens until it runs out of characters. Then it appends one final "end of file" token. That isn't strictly needed, but it makes our parser a little cleaner.

This loop depends on a couple of fields to keep track of where the scanner is in the source code.

lox/Scanner.java
*in class* Scanner

```java
  private final List<Token> tokens = new ArrayList<>();
  private int start = 0;
  private int current = 0;
  private int line = 1;

  Scanner(String source) {
```

The **start** and **current** fields are offsets that index into the string. The **start** field points to the first character in the lexeme being scanned, and **current** points at the character currently being considered. The **line** field tracks what source line **current** is on so we can produce tokens that know their location.

Then we have one little helper function that tells us if we've consumed all the characters.

```java
private boolean isAtEnd() {
  return current >= source.length();
}
```

lox/Scanner.java
*add after* scanTokens()

## 4.5  Recognizing Lexemes

In each turn of the loop, we scan a single token. This is the real heart of the scanner. We'll start simple. Imagine if every lexeme were only a single character long. All you would need to do is consume the next character and pick a token type for it. Several lexemes *are* only a single character in Lox, so let's start with those.

```java
private void scanToken() {
  char c = advance();
  switch (c) {
    case '(': addToken(LEFT_PAREN); break;
    case ')': addToken(RIGHT_PAREN); break;
    case '{': addToken(LEFT_BRACE); break;
    case '}': addToken(RIGHT_BRACE); break;
    case ',': addToken(COMMA); break;
    case '.': addToken(DOT); break;
    case '-': addToken(MINUS); break;
    case '+': addToken(PLUS); break;
    case ';': addToken(SEMICOLON); break;
    case '*': addToken(STAR); break;
  }
}
```

lox/Scanner.java
*add after* scanTokens()

Wondering why / isn't in here? Don't worry, we'll get to it.

Again, we need a couple of helper methods.

```java
private char advance() {
  return source.charAt(current++);
}

private void addToken(TokenType type) {
  addToken(type, null);
}

private void addToken(TokenType type, Object literal) {
  String text = source.substring(start, current);
  tokens.add(new Token(type, text, literal, line));
}
```

lox/Scanner.java
*add after* isAtEnd()

The `advance()` method consumes the next character in the source file and returns it. Where `advance()` is for input, `addToken()` is for output. It grabs the text of the current lexeme and creates a new token for it. We'll use the other overload to handle tokens with literal values soon.

### 4.5.1 Lexical errors

Before we get too far in, let's take a moment to think about errors at the lexical level. What happens if a user throws a source file containing some characters Lox doesn't use, like @#^, at our interpreter? Right now, those characters get silently discarded. They aren't used by the Lox language, but that doesn't mean the interpreter can pretend they aren't there. Instead, we report an error.

*lox/Scanner.java*
*in* scanToken()

```
    case '*': addToken(STAR); break;

    default:
      Lox.error(line, "Unexpected character.");
      break;
  }
```

Note that the erroneous character is still *consumed* by the earlier call to advance(). That's important so that we don't get stuck in an infinite loop.

The code reports each invalid character separately, so this shotguns the user with a blast of errors if they accidentally paste a big blob of weird text. Coalescing a run of invalid characters into a single error would give a nicer user experience.

Note also that we *keep scanning*. There may be other errors later in the program. It gives our users a better experience if we detect as many of those as possible in one go. Otherwise, they see one tiny error and fix it, only to have the next error appear, and so on. Syntax error Whac-A-Mole is no fun.

(Don't worry. Since hadError gets set, we'll never try to *execute* any of the code, even though we keep going and scan the rest of it.)

### 4.5.2 Operators

We have single-character lexemes working, but that doesn't cover all of Lox's operators. What about !? It's a single character, right? Sometimes, yes, but if the very next character is an equals sign, then we should instead create a != lexeme. Note that the ! and = are *not* two independent operators. You can't write !      = in Lox and have it behave like an inequality operator. That's why we need to scan != as a single lexeme. Likewise, <, >, and = can all be followed by = to create the other equality and comparison operators.

For all of these, we need to look at the second character.

*lox/Scanner.java*
*in* scanToken()

```
    case '*': addToken(STAR); break;
    case '!':
      addToken(match('=') ? BANG_EQUAL : BANG);
      break;
    case '=':
      addToken(match('=') ? EQUAL_EQUAL : EQUAL);
      break;
    case '<':
      addToken(match('=') ? LESS_EQUAL : LESS);
      break;
    case '>':
      addToken(match('=') ? GREATER_EQUAL : GREATER);
      break;

    default:
```

Those cases use this new method:

```
private boolean match(char expected) {
  if (isAtEnd()) return false;
  if (source.charAt(current) != expected) return false;

  current++;
  return true;
}
```

lox/Scanner.java
*add after* scanToken()

It's like a conditional advance(). We only consume the current character if it's what we're looking for.

Using match(), we recognize these lexemes in two stages. When we reach, for example, !, we jump to its switch case. That means we know the lexeme *starts* with !. Then we look at the next character to determine if we're on a != or merely a !.

## 4.6 Longer Lexemes

We're still missing one operator: / for division. That character needs a little special handling because comments begin with a slash too.

```
    break;
  case '/':
    if (match('/')) {
      // A comment goes until the end of the line.
      while (peek() != '\n' && !isAtEnd()) advance();
    } else {
      addToken(SLASH);
    }
    break;

  default:
```

lox/Scanner.java
*in* scanToken()

This is similar to the other two-character operators, except that when we find a second /, we don't end the token yet. Instead, we keep consuming characters until we reach the end of the line.

This is our general strategy for handling longer lexemes. After we detect the beginning of one, we shunt over to some lexeme-specific code that keeps eating characters until it sees the end.

We've got another helper:

```
private char peek() {
  if (isAtEnd()) return '\0';
  return source.charAt(current);
}
```

lox/Scanner.java
*add after* match()

It's sort of like advance(), but doesn't consume the character. This is called **lookahead**. Since it only looks at the current unconsumed character, we have *one character of lookahead*. The smaller this number is, generally, the faster the

Technically, match() is doing lookahead too. advance() and peek() are the fundamental operators and match() combines them.

scanner runs. The rules of the lexical grammar dictate how much lookahead we need. Fortunately, most languages in wide use peek only one or two characters ahead.

Comments are lexemes, but they aren't meaningful, and the parser doesn't want to deal with them. So when we reach the end of the comment, we *don't* call addToken(). When we loop back around to start the next lexeme, start gets reset and the comment's lexeme disappears in a puff of smoke.

While we're at it, now's a good time to skip over those other meaningless characters: newlines and whitespace.

lox/Scanner.java
*in* scanToken()

```
        break;

    case ' ':
    case '\r':
    case '\t':
      // Ignore whitespace.
      break;

    case '\n':
      line++;
      break;

    default:
      Lox.error(line, "Unexpected character.");
```

When encountering whitespace, we simply go back to the beginning of the scan loop. That starts a new lexeme *after* the whitespace character. For newlines, we do the same thing, but we also increment the line counter. (This is why we used peek() to find the newline ending a comment instead of match(). We want that newline to get us here so we can update line.)

Our scanner is getting smarter. It can handle fairly free-form code like:

```
// this is a comment
(( )){} // grouping stuff
!*+-/=<> <= == // operators
```

### 4.6.1  String literals

Now that we're comfortable with longer lexemes, we're ready to tackle literals. We'll do strings first, since they always begin with a specific character, ".

lox/Scanner.java
*in* scanToken()

```
        break;

    case '"': string(); break;

    default:
```

That calls:

```
private void string() {
  while (peek() != '"' && !isAtEnd()) {
    if (peek() == '\n') line++;
    advance();
  }

  if (isAtEnd()) {
    Lox.error(line, "Unterminated string.");
    return;
  }

  advance(); // The closing ".

  // Trim the surrounding quotes.
  String value = source.substring(start + 1, current - 1);
  addToken(STRING, value);
}
```

lox/Scanner.java
*add after* scanToken()

Like with comments, we consume characters until we hit the " that ends the string. We also gracefully handle running out of input before the string is closed and report an error for that.

For no particular reason, Lox supports multi-line strings. There are pros and cons to that, but prohibiting them was a little more complex than allowing them, so I left them in. That does mean we also need to update line when we hit a newline inside a string.

Finally, the last interesting bit is that when we create the token, we also produce the actual string *value* that will be used later by the interpreter. Here, that conversion only requires a substring() to strip off the surrounding quotes. If Lox supported escape sequences like \n, we'd unescape those here.

## 4.6.2 Number literals

All numbers in Lox are floating point at runtime, but both integer and decimal literals are supported. A number literal is a series of digits optionally followed by a . and one or more trailing digits.

```
1234
12.34
```

We don't allow a leading or trailing decimal point, so these are both invalid:

```
.1234
1234.
```

We could easily support the former, but I left it out to keep things simple. The latter gets weird if we ever want to allow methods on numbers like 123.sqrt(). To recognize the beginning of a number lexeme, we look for any digit. It's kind of tedious to add cases for every decimal digit, so we'll stuff it in the default case instead.

Since we look only for a digit to start a number, that means −123 is not a number *literal*. Instead, −123, is an *expression* that applies − to the number literal 123. In practice, the result is the same, though it has one interesting edge case if we were to add method calls on numbers. Consider:

```
print -123.abs();
```

This prints −123 because negation has lower precedence than method calls. We could fix that by making − part of the number literal. But then consider:

```
var n = 123;
print -n.abs();
```

This still produces −123, so now the language seems inconsistent. No matter what you do, some case ends up weird.

lox/Scanner.java
*in* scanToken()
*replace 1 line*

```
default:
  if (isDigit(c)) {
    number();
  } else {
    Lox.error(line, "Unexpected character.");
  }
  break;
```

This relies on this little utility:

lox/Scanner.java
*add after* peek()

```
private boolean isDigit(char c) {
  return c >= '0' && c <= '9';
}
```

Once we know we are in a number, we branch to a separate method to consume the rest of the literal, like we do with strings.

lox/Scanner.java
*add after* scanToken()

```
private void number() {
  while (isDigit(peek())) advance();

  // Look for a fractional part.
  if (peek() == '.' && isDigit(peekNext())) {
    // Consume the "."
    advance();

    while (isDigit(peek())) advance();
  }

  addToken(NUMBER,
      Double.parseDouble(source.substring(start, current)));
}
```

The Java standard library provides `Character.isDigit()`, which seems like a good fit. Alas, that method allows things like Devanagari digits, full-width numbers, and other funny stuff we don't want.

We consume as many digits as we find for the integer part of the literal. Then we look for a fractional part, which is a decimal point (.) followed by at least one digit. If we do have a fractional part, again, we consume as many digits as we can find.

Looking past the decimal point requires a second character of lookahead since we don't want to consume the . until we're sure there is a digit *after* it. So we add:

lox/Scanner.java
*add after* peek()

```
private char peekNext() {
  if (current + 1 >= source.length()) return '\0';
  return source.charAt(current + 1);
}
```

I could have made `peek()` take a parameter for the number of characters ahead to look instead of defining two functions, but that would allow *arbitrarily far* lookahead. Providing these two functions makes it clearer to a reader of the code that our scanner looks ahead at most two characters.

Finally, we convert the lexeme to its numeric value. Our interpreter uses Java's `Double` type to represent numbers, so we produce a value of that type. We're using Java's own parsing method to convert the lexeme to a real Java double. We could implement that ourselves, but, honestly, unless you're trying to cram for an upcoming programming interview, it's not worth your time.

The remaining literals are Booleans and `nil`, but we handle those as keywords, which gets us to…

# 4.7 Reserved Words and Identifiers

Our scanner is almost done. The only remaining pieces of the lexical grammar to implement are identifiers and their close cousins, the reserved words. You might think we could match keywords like or in the same way we handle multiple-character operators like <=.

```
case 'o':
  if (match('r')) {
    addToken(OR);
  }
  break;
```

Consider what would happen if a user named a variable orchid. The scanner would see the first two letters, or, and immediately emit an or keyword token. This gets us to an important principle called **maximal munch**. When two lexical grammar rules can both match a chunk of code that the scanner is looking at, *whichever one matches the most characters wins.*

That rule states that if we can match orchid as an identifier and or as a keyword, then the former wins. This is also why we tacitly assumed, previously, that <= should be scanned as a single <= token and not < followed by =.

Maximal munch means we can't easily detect a reserved word until we've reached the end of what might instead be an identifier. After all, a reserved word *is* an identifier, it's just one that has been claimed by the language for its own use. That's where the term **reserved word** comes from.

So we begin by assuming any lexeme starting with a letter or underscore is an identifier.

Consider this nasty bit of C code:

```
---a;
```

Is it valid? That depends on how the scanner splits the lexemes. What if the scanner sees it like this:

```
- --a;
```

Then it could be parsed. But that would require the scanner to know about the grammatical structure of the surrounding code, which entangles things more than we want. Instead, the maximal munch rule says that it is *always* scanned like:

```
-- -a;
```

It scans it that way even though doing so leads to a syntax error later in the parser.

```
    default:
      if (isDigit(c)) {
        number();
      } else if (isAlpha(c)) {
        identifier();
      } else {
        Lox.error(line, "Unexpected character.");
      }
```

lox/Scanner.java
*in* scanToken()

The rest of the code lives over here:

```
private void identifier() {
  while (isAlphaNumeric(peek())) advance();

  addToken(IDENTIFIER);
}
```

lox/Scanner.java
*add after* scanToken()

We define that in terms of this helper:

```
private boolean isAlpha(char c) {
  return (c >= 'a' && c <= 'z') ||
         (c >= 'A' && c <= 'Z') ||
          c == '_';
}
```

lox/Scanner.java
*add after* peekNext()

And this one:

lox/Scanner.java
*add after* isAlpha()

```java
private boolean isAlphaNumeric(char c) {
  return isAlpha(c) || isDigit(c);
}
```

That gets identifiers working. To handle keywords, we see if the identifier's lexeme is one of the reserved words. If so, we use a token type specific to that keyword. We define the set of reserved words in a map.

lox/Scanner.java
*in class* Scanner

```java
private static final Map<String, TokenType> keywords;

static {
  keywords = new HashMap<>();
  keywords.put("and",    AND);
  keywords.put("class",  CLASS);
  keywords.put("else",   ELSE);
  keywords.put("false",  FALSE);
  keywords.put("for",    FOR);
  keywords.put("fun",    FUN);
  keywords.put("if",     IF);
  keywords.put("nil",    NIL);
  keywords.put("or",     OR);
  keywords.put("print",  PRINT);
  keywords.put("return", RETURN);
  keywords.put("super",  SUPER);
  keywords.put("this",   THIS);
  keywords.put("true",   TRUE);
  keywords.put("var",    VAR);
  keywords.put("while",  WHILE);
}
```

Then, after we scan an identifier, we check to see if it matches anything in the map.

lox/Scanner.java
*in* identifier()
*replace 1 line*

```java
    while (isAlphaNumeric(peek())) advance();

    String text = source.substring(start, current);
    TokenType type = keywords.get(text);
    if (type == null) type = IDENTIFIER;
    addToken(type);
  }
```

If so, we use that keyword's token type. Otherwise, it's a regular user-defined identifier.

And with that, we now have a complete scanner for the entire Lox lexical grammar. Fire up the REPL and type in some valid and invalid code. Does it produce the tokens you expect? Try to come up with some interesting edge cases and see if it handles them as it should.

## CHALLENGES

1. The lexical grammars of Python and Haskell are not *regular*. What does that mean, and why aren't they?

2. Aside from separating tokens—distinguishing `print foo` from `printfoo`—spaces aren't used for much in most languages. However, in a couple of dark corners, a space *does* affect how code is parsed in CoffeeScript, Ruby, and the C preprocessor. Where and what effect does it have in each of those languages?

3. Our scanner here, like most, discards comments and whitespace since those aren't needed by the parser. Why might you want to write a scanner that does *not* discard those? What would it be useful for?

4. Add support to Lox's scanner for C-style `/* ... */` block comments. Make sure to handle newlines in them. Consider allowing them to nest. Is adding support for nesting more work than you expected? Why?

## DESIGN NOTE: IMPLICIT SEMICOLONS

Programmers today are spoiled for choice in languages and have gotten picky about syntax. They want their language to look clean and modern. One bit of syntactic lichen that almost every new language scrapes off (and some ancient ones like BASIC never had) is ; as an explicit statement terminator.

Instead, they treat a newline as a statement terminator where it makes sense to do so. The "where it makes sense" part is the challenging bit. While *most* statements are on their own line, sometimes you need to spread a single statement across a couple of lines. Those intermingled newlines should not be treated as terminators.

Most of the obvious cases where the newline should be ignored are easy to detect, but there are a handful of nasty ones:

- A return value on the next line:

```
if (condition) return
"value"
```

  Is "value" the value being returned, or do we have a `return` statement with no value followed by an expression statement containing a string literal?

- A parenthesized expression on the next line:

```
func
(parenthesized)
```

  Is this a call to `func(parenthesized)`, or two expression statements, one for `func` and one for a parenthesized expression?

- A - on the next line:

```
first
-second
```

  Is this `first - second`—an infix subtraction—or two expression statements, one for `first` and one to negate `second`?

In all of these, either treating the newline as a separator or not would both produce valid code, but possibly not the code the user wants. Across languages, there is an unsettling variety of rules used to decide which newlines are separators. Here are a couple:

- Lua completely ignores newlines, but carefully controls its grammar such that no separator between statements is needed at all in most cases. This is perfectly legit:

```
a = 1 b = 2
```

  Lua avoids the `return` problem by requiring a `return` statement to be the very last statement in a block. If there is a value after `return` before the keyword **end**, it *must* be for the `return`. For the other two cases, they allow an explicit ; and expect users to use that. In practice, that almost never happens because there's no point in a parenthesized or unary negation expression statement.

- Go handles newlines in the scanner. If a newline appears following one of a handful of token types that are known to potentially end a statement, the newline is treated like a semicolon. Otherwise it is ignored. The Go team provides a canonical code formatter, gofmt, and the ecosystem is fervent about its use, which ensures that idiomatic styled code works well with this simple rule.

- Python treats all newlines as significant unless an explicit backslash is used at the end of a line to continue it to the next line. However, newlines anywhere inside a pair of brackets ((), [], or {}) are ignored. Idiomatic style strongly prefers the latter.

  This rule works well for Python because it is a highly statement-oriented language. In particular, Python's grammar ensures a statement never appears inside an expression. C does the same, but many other languages which have a "lambda" or function literal syntax do not.

  An example in JavaScript:

```
console.log(function() {
  statement();
});
```

  Here, the `console.log()` *expression* contains a function literal which in turn contains the *statement* `statement();`.

  Python would need a different set of rules for implicitly joining lines if you could get back *into* a statement where newlines should become meaningful while still nested inside brackets.

  And now you know why Python's `lambda` allows only a single expression body.

- JavaScript's "automatic semicolon insertion" rule is the real odd one. Where other languages assume most newlines *are* meaningful and only a few should be ignored in multi-line statements, JS assumes the opposite. It treats all of your newlines as meaningless whitespace *unless* it encounters a parse error. If it does, it goes back and tries turning the previous newline into a semicolon to get something grammatically valid.

  This design note would turn into a design diatribe if I went into complete detail about how that even *works*, much less all the various ways that JavaScript's "solution" is a bad idea. It's a mess. JavaScript is the only language I know where many style guides demand explicit semicolons after every statement even though the language theoretically lets you elide them.

If you're designing a new language, you almost surely *should* avoid an explicit statement terminator. Programmers are creatures of fashion like other humans, and semicolons are as passé as ALL CAPS KEYWORDS. Just make sure you pick a set of rules that make sense for your language's particular grammar and idioms. And don't do what JavaScript did.

# Representing Code

5

*"To dwellers in a wood, almost every species of tree has its voice as well as its feature."*

— Thomas Hardy, *Under the Greenwood Tree*

In the last chapter, we took the raw source code as a string and transformed it into a slightly higher-level representation: a series of tokens. The parser we'll write in the next chapter takes those tokens and transforms them yet again, into an even richer, more complex representation.

Before we can produce that representation, we need to define it. That's the subject of this chapter. Along the way, we'll cover some theory around formal grammars, feel the difference between functional and object-oriented programming, go over a couple of design patterns, and do some metaprogramming.

Before we do all that, let's focus on the main goal—a representation for code. It should be simple for the parser to produce and easy for the interpreter to consume. If you haven't written a parser or interpreter yet, those requirements aren't exactly illuminating. Maybe your intuition can help. What is your brain doing when you play the part of a *human* interpreter? How do you mentally evaluate an arithmetic expression like this:

```
1 + 2 * 3 - 4
```

Because you understand the order of operations—the old "Please Excuse My

I was so worried about this being one of the most boring chapters in the book that I kept stuffing more fun ideas into it until I ran out of room.

Dear Aunt Sally" stuff—you know that the multiplication is evaluated before the addition or subtraction. One way to visualize that precedence is using a tree. Leaf nodes are numbers, and interior nodes are operators with branches for each of their operands.

In order to evaluate an arithmetic node, you need to know the numeric values of its subtrees, so you have to evaluate those first. That means working your way from the leaves up to the root—a *post-order* traversal:

A. Starting with the full tree, evaluate the bottom-most operation, 2 ∗ 3.

B. Now we can evaluate the +.

C. Next, the −.

D. The final answer.

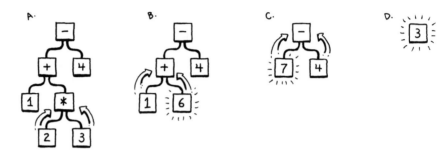

That's not to say a tree is the *only* possible representation of our code. In Part III, we'll generate bytecode, another representation that isn't as human friendly but is closer to the machine.

If I gave you an arithmetic expression, you could draw one of these trees pretty easily. Given a tree, you can evaluate it without breaking a sweat. So it intuitively seems like a workable representation of our code is a tree that matches the grammatical structure—the operator nesting—of the language.

We need to get more precise about what that grammar is then. Like lexical grammars in the last chapter, there is a long ton of theory around syntactic grammars. We're going into that theory a little more than we did when scanning because it turns out to be a useful tool throughout much of the interpreter. We start by moving one level up the Chomsky hierarchy...

## 5.1  Context-Free Grammars

In the last chapter, the formalism we used for defining the lexical grammar—the rules for how characters get grouped into tokens—was called a *regular language*. That was fine for our scanner, which emits a flat sequence of tokens. But regular languages aren't powerful enough to handle expressions which can nest arbitrarily deeply.

We need a bigger hammer, and that hammer is a **context-free grammar** (**CFG**). It's the next heaviest tool in the toolbox of **formal grammars**. A formal grammar takes a set of atomic pieces it calls its "alphabet". Then it defines a (usually infinite) set of "strings" that are "in" the grammar. Each string is a sequence of "letters" in the alphabet.

I'm using all those quotes because the terms get a little confusing as you move from lexical to syntactic grammars. In our scanner's grammar, the alphabet consists of individual characters and the strings are the valid lexemes—roughly "words". In the syntactic grammar we're talking about now, we're at a different level of granularity. Now each "letter" in the alphabet is an entire token and a "string" is a sequence of *tokens*—an entire expression.

Oof. Maybe a table will help:

| Terminology | | Lexical grammar | Syntactic grammar |
|---|---|---|---|
| The "alphabet" is... | → | Characters | Tokens |
| A "string" is... | → | Lexeme or token | Expression |
| It's implemented by the... | → | Scanner | Parser |

A formal grammar's job is to specify which strings are valid and which aren't. If we were defining a grammar for English sentences, "eggs are tasty for breakfast" would be in the grammar, but "tasty breakfast for are eggs" would probably not.

### 5.1.1  Rules for grammars

How do we write down a grammar that contains an infinite number of valid strings? We obviously can't list them all out. Instead, we create a finite set of rules. You can think of them as a game that you can "play" in one of two directions.

If you start with the rules, you can use them to *generate* strings that are in the grammar. Strings created this way are called **derivations** because each is *derived* from the rules of the grammar. In each step of the game, you pick a rule and follow what it tells you to do. Most of the lingo around formal grammars comes from playing them in this direction. Rules are called **productions** because they *produce* strings in the grammar.

Each production in a context-free grammar has a **head**—its name—and a **body**, which describes what it generates. In its pure form, the body is simply a list of symbols. Symbols come in two delectable flavors:

> Restricting heads to a single symbol is a defining feature of context-free grammars. More powerful formalisms like **unrestricted grammars** allow a sequence of symbols in the head as well as in the body.

- A **terminal** is a letter from the grammar's alphabet. You can think of it like a literal value. In the syntactic grammar we're defining, the terminals are individual lexemes—tokens coming from the scanner like if or 1234.

  These are called "terminals", in the sense of an "end point" because they don't lead to any further "moves" in the game. You simply produce that one symbol.

- A **nonterminal** is a named reference to another rule in the grammar. It means "play that rule and insert whatever it produces here". In this way, the grammar composes.

There is one last refinement: you may have multiple rules with the same name. When you reach a nonterminal with that name, you are allowed to pick any of the rules for it, whichever floats your boat.

To make this concrete, we need a way to write down these production rules. People have been trying to crystallize grammar all the way back to Pāṇini's *Ashtadhyayi*, which codified Sanskrit grammar a mere couple thousand years ago. Not much progress happened until John Backus and company needed a notation for specifying ALGOL 58 and came up with **Backus-Naur form (BNF)**. Since then, nearly everyone uses some flavor of BNF, tweaked to their own tastes.

> Yes, we need to define a syntax to use for the rules that define our syntax. Should we specify that *metasyntax* too? What notation do we use for *it*? It's languages all the way down!

I tried to come up with something clean. Each rule is a name, followed by an arrow (→), followed by a sequence of symbols, and finally ending with a semico-

Yes, I really am going to be using breakfast examples throughout this entire book. Sorry.

lon (`;`). Terminals are quoted strings, and nonterminals are lowercase words.

Using that, here's a grammar for breakfast menus:

```
breakfast  → protein "with" breakfast "on the side" ;
breakfast  → protein ;
breakfast  → bread ;

protein    → crispiness "crispy" "bacon" ;
protein    → "sausage" ;
protein    → cooked "eggs" ;

crispiness → "really" ;
crispiness → "really" crispiness ;

cooked     → "scrambled" ;
cooked     → "poached" ;
cooked     → "fried" ;

bread      → "toast" ;
bread      → "biscuits" ;
bread      → "English muffin" ;
```

We can use this grammar to generate random breakfasts. Let's play a round and see how it works. By age-old convention, the game starts with the first rule in the grammar, here `breakfast`. There are three productions for that, and we randomly pick the first one. Our resulting string looks like:

```
protein "with" breakfast "on the side"
```

We need to expand that first nonterminal, `protein`, so we pick a production for that. Let's pick:

```
protein → cooked "eggs" ;
```

Next, we need a production for `cooked`, and so we pick `"poached"`. That's a terminal, so we add that. Now our string looks like:

```
"poached" "eggs" "with" breakfast "on the side"
```

The next non-terminal is `breakfast` again. The first `breakfast` production we chose recursively refers back to the `breakfast` rule. Recursion in the grammar is a good sign that the language being defined is context-free instead of regular. In particular, recursion where the recursive nonterminal has productions on both sides implies that the language is not regular.

We could keep picking the first production for `breakfast` over and over again yielding all manner of breakfasts like "bacon with sausage with scrambled eggs with bacon…" We won't though. This time we'll pick `bread`. There are three rules for that, each of which contains only a terminal. We'll pick "English muffin".

With that, every nonterminal in the string has been expanded until it finally contains only terminals and we're left with:

Imagine that we've recursively expanded the `breakfast` rule here several times, like "bacon with bacon with bacon with…" In order to complete the string correctly, we need to add an *equal* number of "on the side" bits to the end. Tracking the number of required trailing parts is beyond the capabilities of a regular grammar. Regular grammars can express *repetition*, but they can't *keep count* of how many repetitions there are, which is necessary to ensure that the string has the same number of `with` and `on the side` parts.

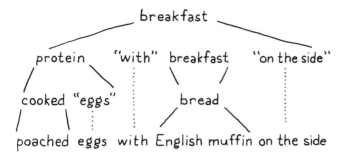

Throw in some ham and Hollandaise, and you've got eggs Benedict.

Any time we hit a rule that had multiple productions, we just picked one arbitrarily. It is this flexibility that allows a short number of grammar rules to encode a combinatorially larger set of strings. The fact that a rule can refer to itself—directly or indirectly—kicks it up even more, letting us pack an infinite number of strings into a finite grammar.

## 5.1.2 Enhancing our notation

Stuffing an infinite set of strings in a handful of rules is pretty fantastic, but let's take it further. Our notation works, but it's tedious. So, like any good language designer, we'll sprinkle a little syntactic sugar on top—some extra convenience notation. In addition to terminals and nonterminals, we'll allow a few other kinds of expressions in the body of a rule:

- Instead of repeating the rule name each time we want to add another production for it, we'll allow a series of productions separated by a pipe (|).

```
bread → "toast" | "biscuits" | "English muffin" ;
```

- Further, we'll allow parentheses for grouping and then allow | within that to select one from a series of options within the middle of a production.

```
protein → ( "scrambled" | "poached" | "fried" ) "eggs" ;
```

- Using recursion to support repeated sequences of symbols has a certain appealing purity, but it's kind of a chore to make a separate named sub-rule each time we want to loop. So, we also use a postfix * to allow the previous symbol or group to be repeated zero or more times.

```
crispiness → "really" "really"* ;
```

This is how the Scheme programming language works. It has no built-in looping functionality at all. Instead, *all* repetition is expressed in terms of recursion.

- A postfix + is similar, but requires the preceding production to appear at least once.

```
crispiness → "really"+ ;
```

- A postfix ? is for an optional production. The thing before it can appear zero or one time, but not more.

```
breakfast → protein ( "with" breakfast "on the side" )? ;
```

With all of those syntactic niceties, our breakfast grammar condenses down to:

```
breakfast → protein ( "with" breakfast "on the side" )?
          | bread ;

protein   → "really"+ "crispy" "bacon"
          | "sausage"
          | ( "scrambled" | "poached" | "fried" ) "eggs" ;

bread     → "toast" | "biscuits" | "English muffin" ;
```

Not too bad, I hope. If you're used to grep or using regular expressions in your text editor, most of the punctuation should be familiar. The main difference is that symbols here represent entire tokens, not single characters.

We'll use this notation throughout the rest of the book to precisely describe Lox's grammar. As you work on programming languages, you'll find that context-free grammars (using this or EBNF or some other notation) help you crystallize your informal syntax design ideas. They are also a handy medium for communicating with other language hackers about syntax.

The rules and productions we define for Lox are also our guide to the tree data structure we're going to implement to represent code in memory. Before we can do that, we need an actual grammar for Lox, or at least enough of one for us to get started.

### 5.1.3  A Grammar for Lox expressions

In the previous chapter, we did Lox's entire lexical grammar in one fell swoop. Every keyword and bit of punctuation is there. The syntactic grammar is larger, and it would be a real bore to grind through the entire thing before we actually get our interpreter up and running.

Instead, we'll crank through a subset of the language in the next couple of chapters. Once we have that mini-language represented, parsed, and interpreted, then later chapters will progressively add new features to it, including the new syntax. For now, we are going to worry about only a handful of expressions:

- **Literals.** Numbers, strings, Booleans, and `nil`.

- **Unary expressions.** A prefix `!` to perform a logical not, and `-` to negate a number.

- **Binary expressions.** The infix arithmetic (`+`, `-`, `*`, `/`) and logic operators (`==`, `!=`, `<`, `<=`, `>`, `>=`) we know and love.

- **Parentheses.** A pair of `(` and `)` wrapped around an expression.

That gives us enough syntax for expressions like:

```
1 - (2 * 3) < 4 == false
```

Using our handy dandy new notation, here's a grammar for those:

```
expression      → literal | unary | binary | grouping ;
literal         → NUMBER | STRING | "true" | "false" | "nil" ;
grouping        → "(" expression ")" ;
unary           → ( "-" | "!" ) expression ;
binary          → expression operator expression ;
operator        → "==" | "!=" | "<" | "<=" | ">" | ">="
                | "+"  | "-"  | "*" | "/" ;
```

There's one bit of extra metasyntax here. In addition to quoted strings for terminals that match exact lexemes, we CAPITALIZE terminals that are a single lexeme whose text representation may vary. NUMBER is any number literal, and STRING is any string literal. Later, we'll do the same for IDENTIFIER.

This grammar is actually ambiguous, which we'll see when we get to parsing it. But it's good enough for now.

*If you're so inclined, try using this grammar to generate a few expressions like we did with the breakfast grammar before. Do the resulting expressions look right to you? Can you make it generate anything wrong like 1 + / 3?*

## 5.2  Implementing Syntax Trees

Finally, we get to write some code. That little expression grammar is our skeleton. Since the grammar is recursive—note how grouping, unary, and binary all refer back to expression—our data structure will form a tree. Since this structure represents the syntax of our language, it's called a **syntax tree**.

Our scanner used a single Token class to represent all kinds of lexemes. To distinguish the different kinds—think the number 123 versus the string "123"—we included a simple TokenType enum. Syntax trees are not so homogeneous. Unary expressions have a single operand, binary expressions have two, and literals have none.

We *could* mush that all together into a single Expression class with an arbitrary list of children. Some compilers do. But I like getting the most out of Java's type system. So we'll define a base class for expressions. Then, for each kind of expression—each production under expression—we create a subclass that has fields for the nonterminals specific to that rule. This way, we get a compile error if we, say, try to access the second operand of a unary expression.

Something like this:

*In particular, we're defining an **abstract syntax tree** (**AST**). In a **parse tree**, every single grammar production becomes a node in the tree. An AST elides productions that aren't needed by later phases.*

*Tokens aren't entirely homogeneous either. Tokens for literals store the value, but other kinds of lexemes don't need that state. I have seen scanners that use different classes for literals and other kinds of lexemes, but I figured I'd keep things simpler.*

```java
package com.craftinginterpreters.lox;

abstract class Expr {
  static class Binary extends Expr {
    Binary(Expr left, Token operator, Expr right) {
      this.left = left;
      this.operator = operator;
      this.right = right;
    }

    final Expr left;
    final Token operator;
    final Expr right;
  }
  // Other expressions...
}
```

*I avoid abbreviations in my code because they trip up a reader who doesn't know what they stand for. But in compilers I've looked at, "Expr" and "Stmt" are so ubiquitous that I may as well start getting you used to them now.*

Expr is the base class that all expression classes inherit from. As you can see from `Binary`, the subclasses are nested inside of it. There's no technical need for this, but it lets us cram all of the classes into a single Java file.

## 5.2.1  Disoriented objects

You'll note that, much like the Token class, there aren't any methods here. It's a dumb structure. Nicely typed, but merely a bag of data. This feels strange in an object-oriented language like Java. Shouldn't the class *do stuff*?

The problem is that these tree classes aren't owned by any single domain. Should they have methods for parsing since that's where the trees are created? Or interpreting since that's where they are consumed? Trees span the border between those territories, which means they are really owned by *neither*.

In fact, these types exist to enable the parser and interpreter to *communicate*. That lends itself to types that are simply data with no associated behavior. This style is very natural in functional languages like Lisp and ML where *all* data is separate from behavior, but it feels odd in Java.

Functional programming aficionados right now are jumping up to exclaim "See! Object-oriented languages are a bad fit for an interpreter!" I won't go that far. You'll recall that the scanner itself was admirably suited to object-orientation. It had all of the mutable state to keep track of where it was in the source code, a well-defined set of public methods, and a handful of private helpers.

My feeling is that each phase or part of the interpreter works fine in an object-oriented style. It is the data structures that flow between them that are stripped of behavior.

## 5.2.2  Metaprogramming the trees

Java can express behavior-less classes, but I wouldn't say that it's particularly great at it. Eleven lines of code to stuff three fields in an object is pretty tedious, and when we're all done, we're going to have 21 of these classes.

I don't want to waste your time or my ink writing all that down. Really, what is the essence of each subclass? A name, and a list of typed fields. That's it. We're smart language hackers, right? Let's automate.

Instead of tediously handwriting each class definition, field declaration, constructor, and initializer, we'll hack together a script that does it for us. It has a description of each tree type—its name and fields—and it prints out the Java code needed to define a class with that name and state.

This script is a tiny Java command-line app that generates a file named "Expr.java":

Picture me doing an awkward robot dance when you read that. "AU-TO-MATE."

I got the idea of scripting the syntax tree classes from Jim Hugunin, creator of Jython and IronPython.

An actual scripting language would be a better fit for this than Java, but I'm trying not to throw too many languages at you.

**tool/GenerateAst.java**
*create new file*

```java
package com.craftinginterpreters.tool;

import java.io.IOException;
import java.io.PrintWriter;
import java.util.Arrays;
import java.util.List;
```

*continued on next page...*

```java
public class GenerateAst {
  public static void main(String[] args) throws IOException {
    if (args.length != 1) {
      System.err.println("Usage: generate_ast <output directory>");
      System.exit(64);
    }
    String outputDir = args[0];
  }
}
```

...from previous page

Note that this file is in a different package, .tool instead of .lox. This script isn't part of the interpreter itself. It's a tool *we*, the people hacking on the interpreter, run ourselves to generate the syntax tree classes. When it's done, we treat "Expr.java" like any other file in the implementation. We are merely automating how that file gets authored.

To generate the classes, it needs to have some description of each type and its fields.

```java
    String outputDir = args[0];
    defineAst(outputDir, "Expr", Arrays.asList(
      "Binary   : Expr left, Token operator, Expr right",
      "Grouping : Expr expression",
      "Literal  : Object value",
      "Unary    : Token operator, Expr right"
    ));
  }
```

**tool/GenerateAst.java**
*in* main()

For brevity's sake, I jammed the descriptions of the expression types into strings. Each is the name of the class followed by : and the list of fields, separated by commas. Each field has a type and a name.

The first thing defineAst() needs to do is output the base Expr class.

```java
  private static void defineAst(
      String outputDir, String baseName, List<String> types)
      throws IOException {
    String path = outputDir + "/" + baseName + ".java";
    PrintWriter writer = new PrintWriter(path, "UTF-8");

    writer.println("package com.craftinginterpreters.lox;");
    writer.println();
    writer.println("import java.util.List;");
    writer.println();
    writer.println("abstract class " + baseName + " {");

    writer.println("}");
    writer.close();
  }
```

**tool/GenerateAst.java**
*add after* main()

When we call this, baseName is "Expr", which is both the name of the class and the name of the file it outputs. We pass this as an argument instead of hardcoding the name because we'll add a separate family of classes later for statements.

Inside the base class, we define each subclass.

**tool/GenerateAst.java**
*in* defineAst()

```java
writer.println("abstract class " + baseName + " {");

  // The AST classes.
  for (String type : types) {
    String className = type.split(":")[0].trim();
    String fields = type.split(":")[1].trim();
    defineType(writer, baseName, className, fields);
  }
writer.println("}");
```

This isn't the world's most elegant string manipulation code, but that's fine. It only runs on the exact set of class definitions we give it. Robustness ain't a priority.

That code, in turn, calls:

**tool/GenerateAst.java**
*add after* defineAst()

```java
private static void defineType(
    PrintWriter writer, String baseName,
    String className, String fieldList) {
  writer.println("  static class " + className + " extends " +
      baseName + " {");

  // Constructor.
  writer.println("    " + className + "(" + fieldList + ") {");

  // Store parameters in fields.
  String[] fields = fieldList.split(", ");
  for (String field : fields) {
    String name = field.split(" ")[1];
    writer.println("      this." + name + " = " + name + ";");
  }

  writer.println("    }");

  // Fields.
  writer.println();
  for (String field : fields) {
    writer.println("    final " + field + ";");
  }

  writer.println("  }");
}
```

There we go. All of that glorious Java boilerplate is done. It declares each field in the class body. It defines a constructor for the class with parameters for each field and initializes them in the body.

Appendix II contains the code generated by this script once we've finished implementing jlox and defined all of its syntax tree nodes.

Compile and run this Java program now and it blasts out a new ".java" file containing a few dozen lines of code. That file's about to get even longer.

# 5.3  Working with Trees

Put on your imagination hat for a moment. Even though we aren't there yet, consider what the interpreter will do with the syntax trees. Each kind of expression in Lox behaves differently at runtime. That means the interpreter needs to select a different chunk of code to handle each expression type. With tokens, we can simply switch on the TokenType. But we don't have a "type" enum for the syntax trees, just a separate Java class for each one.

We could write a long chain of type tests:

```java
if (expr instanceof Expr.Binary) {
  // ...
} else if (expr instanceof Expr.Grouping) {
  // ...
} else // ...
```

But all of those sequential type tests are slow. Expression types whose names are alphabetically later would take longer to execute because they'd fall through more if cases before finding the right type. That's not my idea of an elegant solution.

We have a family of classes and we need to associate a chunk of behavior with each one. The natural solution in an object-oriented language like Java is to put those behaviors into methods on the classes themselves. We could add an abstract interpret() method on Expr which each subclass would then implement to interpret itself.

This exact thing is literally called the "Interpreter pattern" in *Design Patterns: Elements of Reusable Object-Oriented Software*, by Erich Gamma, et al.

This works alright for tiny projects, but it scales poorly. Like I noted before, these tree classes span a few domains. At the very least, both the parser and interpreter will mess with them. As you'll see later, we need to do name resolution on them. If our language was statically typed, we'd have a type checking pass.

If we added instance methods to the expression classes for every one of those operations, that would smush a bunch of different domains together. That violates separation of concerns and leads to hard-to-maintain code.

## 5.3.1  The expression problem

This problem is more fundamental than it may seem at first. We have a handful of types, and a handful of high-level operations like "interpret". For each pair of type and operation, we need a specific implementation. Picture a table:

|          | interpret() | resolve() | analyze() |
|----------|-------------|-----------|-----------|
| Binary   | ...         | ...       | ...       |
| Grouping | ...         | ...       | ...       |
| Literal  | ...         | ...       | ...       |
| Unary    | ...         | ...       | ...       |

Rows are types, and columns are operations. Each cell represents the unique piece of code to implement that operation on that type.

An object-oriented language like Java assumes that all of the code in one row naturally hangs together. It figures all the things you do with a type are likely related to each other, and the language makes it easy to define them together as methods inside the same class.

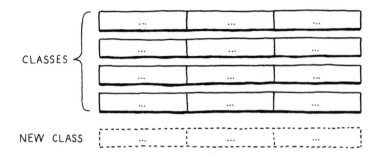

This makes it easy to extend the table by adding new rows. Simply define a new class. No existing code has to be touched. But imagine if you want to add a new *operation*—a new column. In Java, that means cracking open each of those existing classes and adding a method to it.

Functional paradigm languages in the ML family flip that around. There, you don't have classes with methods. Types and functions are totally distinct. To implement an operation for a number of different types, you define a single function. In the body of that function, you use *pattern matching*—sort of a type-based switch on steroids—to implement the operation for each type all in one place.

This makes it trivial to add new operations—simply define another function that pattern matches on all of the types.

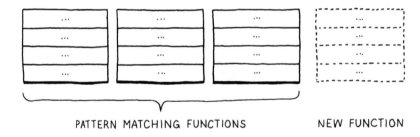

But, conversely, adding a new type is hard. You have to go back and add a new case to all of the pattern matches in all of the existing functions.

Each style has a certain "grain" to it. That's what the paradigm name literally says—an object-oriented language wants you to *orient* your code along the rows of types. A functional language instead encourages you to lump each column's worth of code together into a *function*.

A bunch of smart language nerds noticed that neither style made it easy to add *both* rows and columns to the table. They called this difficulty the "expression problem" because—like we are now—they first ran into it when they were trying to figure out the best way to model expression syntax tree nodes in a compiler.

People have thrown all sorts of language features, design patterns, and programming tricks to try to knock that problem down but no perfect language has finished it off yet. In the meantime, the best we can do is try to pick a language whose orientation matches the natural architectural seams in the program we're writing.

ML, short for "metalanguage" was created by Robin Milner and friends and forms one of the main branches in the great programming language family tree. Its children include SML, Caml, OCaml, Haskell, and F#. Even Scala, Rust, and Swift bear a strong resemblance.

Much like Lisp, it is one of those languages that is so full of good ideas that language designers today are still rediscovering them over forty years later.

Languages with *multimethods*, like Common Lisp's CLOS, Dylan, and Julia do support adding both new types and operations easily. What they typically sacrifice is either static type checking, or separate compilation.

Object-orientation works fine for many parts of our interpreter, but these tree classes rub against the grain of Java. Fortunately, there's a design pattern we can bring to bear on it.

## 5.3.2  The Visitor pattern

The **Visitor pattern** is the most widely misunderstood pattern in all of *Design Patterns*, which is really saying something when you look at the software architecture excesses of the past couple of decades.

The trouble starts with terminology. The pattern isn't about "visiting", and the "accept" method in it doesn't conjure up any helpful imagery either. Many think the pattern has to do with traversing trees, which isn't the case at all. We *are* going to use it on a set of classes that are tree-like, but that's a coincidence. As you'll see, the pattern works as well on a single object.

The Visitor pattern is really about approximating the functional style within an OOP language. It lets us add new columns to that table easily. We can define all of the behavior for a new operation on a set of types in one place, without having to touch the types themselves. It does this the same way we solve almost every problem in computer science: by adding a layer of indirection.

Before we apply it to our auto-generated Expr classes, let's walk through a simpler example. Say we have two kinds of pastries: beignets and crullers.

```
abstract class Pastry {
}

class Beignet extends Pastry {
}

class Cruller extends Pastry {
}
```

We want to be able to define new pastry operations—cooking them, eating them, decorating them, etc.—without having to add a new method to each class every time. Here's how we do it. First, we define a separate interface.

```
interface PastryVisitor {
  void visitBeignet(Beignet beignet);
  void visitCruller(Cruller cruller);
}
```

Each operation that can be performed on pastries is a new class that implements that interface. It has a concrete method for each type of pastry. That keeps the code for the operation on both types all nestled snugly together in one class.

Given some pastry, how do we route it to the correct method on the visitor based on its type? Polymorphism to the rescue! We add this method to Pastry:

```
abstract class Pastry {
  abstract void accept(PastryVisitor visitor);
}
```

Each subclass implements it.

A beignet (pronounced "ben-yay", with equal emphasis on both syllables) is a deep-fried pastry in the same family as doughnuts. When the French colonized North America in the 1700s, they brought beignets with them. Today, in the US, they are most strongly associated with the cuisine of New Orleans.

My preferred way to consume them is fresh out of the fryer at Café du Monde, piled high in powdered sugar, and washed down with a cup of café au lait while I watch tourists staggering around trying to shake off their hangover from the previous night's revelry.

In *Design Patterns*, both of these methods are confusingly named `visit()`, and they rely on overloading to distinguish them. This leads some readers to think that the correct visit method is chosen *at runtime* based on its parameter type. That isn't the case. Unlike over*riding*, over*loading* is statically dispatched at compile time.

Using distinct names for each method makes the dispatch more obvious, and also shows you how to apply this pattern in languages that don't support overloading.

```
class Beignet extends Pastry {
  @Override
  void accept(PastryVisitor visitor) {
    visitor.visitBeignet(this);
  }
}
```

And:

```
class Cruller extends Pastry {
  @Override
  void accept(PastryVisitor visitor) {
    visitor.visitCruller(this);
  }
}
```

To perform an operation on a pastry, we call its `accept()` method and pass in the visitor for the operation we want to execute. The pastry—the specific subclass's overriding implementation of `accept()`—turns around and calls the appropriate visit method on the visitor and passes *itself* to it.

That's the heart of the trick right there. It lets us use polymorphic dispatch on the *pastry* classes to select the appropriate method on the *visitor* class. In the table, each pastry class is a row, but if you look at all of the methods for a single visitor, they form a *column*.

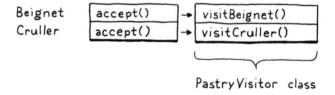

We added one `accept()` method to each class, and we can use it for as many visitors as we want without ever having to touch the pastry classes again. It's a clever pattern.

### 5.3.3 Visitors for expressions

Another common refinement is an additional "context" parameter that is passed to the visit methods and then sent back through as a parameter to `accept()`. That lets operations take an additional parameter. The visitors we'll define in the book don't need that, so I omitted it.

OK, let's weave it into our expression classes. We'll also refine the pattern a little. In the pastry example, the visit and `accept()` methods don't return anything. In practice, visitors often want to define operations that produce values. But what return type should `accept()` have? We can't assume every visitor class wants to produce the same type, so we'll use generics to let each implementation fill in a return type.

First, we define the visitor interface. Again, we nest it inside the base class so that we can keep everything in one file.

```
  writer.println("abstract class " + baseName + " {");

  defineVisitor(writer, baseName, types);

  // The AST classes.
```
tool/GenerateAst.java
in defineAst()

That function generates the visitor interface.

```
private static void defineVisitor(
    PrintWriter writer, String baseName, List<String> types) {
  writer.println("  interface Visitor<R> {");

  for (String type : types) {
    String typeName = type.split(":")[0].trim();
    writer.println("    R visit" + typeName + baseName + "(" +
        typeName + " " + baseName.toLowerCase() + ");");
  }

  writer.println("  }");
}
```
tool/GenerateAst.java
add after defineAst()

Here, we iterate through all of the subclasses and declare a visit method for each one. When we define new expression types later, this will automatically include them.

Inside the base class, we define the abstract `accept()` method.

```
    defineType(writer, baseName, className, fields);
  }

  // The base accept() method.
  writer.println();
  writer.println("  abstract <R> R accept(Visitor<R> visitor);");

  writer.println("}");
```
tool/GenerateAst.java
in defineAst()

Finally, each subclass implements that and calls the right visit method for its own type.

```
    writer.println("    }");

    // Visitor pattern.
    writer.println();
    writer.println("    @Override");
    writer.println("    <R> R accept(Visitor<R> visitor) {");
    writer.println("      return visitor.visit" +
        className + baseName + "(this);");
    writer.println("    }");

    // Fields.
```
tool/GenerateAst.java
in defineType()

There we go. Now we can define operations on expressions without having to muck with the classes or our generator script. Compile and run this generator script to output an updated "Expr.java" file. It contains a generated Visitor interface and a set of expression node classes that support the Visitor pattern using it.

Before we end this rambling chapter, let's implement that Visitor interface and see the pattern in action.

## 5.4  A (Not Very) Pretty Printer

When we debug our parser and interpreter, it's often useful to look at a parsed syntax tree and make sure it has the structure we expect. We could inspect it in the debugger, but that can be a chore.

Instead, we'd like some code that, given a syntax tree, produces an unambiguous string representation of it. Converting a tree to a string is sort of the opposite of a parser, and is often called "pretty printing" when the goal is to produce a string of text that is valid syntax in the source language.

That's not our goal here. We want the string to very explicitly show the nesting structure of the tree. A printer that returned 1 + 2 * 3 isn't super helpful if what we're trying to debug is whether operator precedence is handled correctly. We want to know if the + or * is at the top of the tree.

To that end, the string representation we produce isn't going to be Lox syntax. Instead, it will look a lot like, well, Lisp. Each expression is explicitly parenthesized, and all of its subexpressions and tokens are contained in that.

Given a syntax tree like:

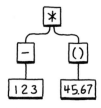

It produces:

```
(* (- 123) (group 45.67))
```

Not exactly "pretty", but it does show the nesting and grouping explicitly. To implement this, we define a new class.

lox/AstPrinter.java
*create new file*

```
package com.craftinginterpreters.lox;

class AstPrinter implements Expr.Visitor<String> {
  String print(Expr expr) {
    return expr.accept(this);
  }
}
```

As you can see, it implements the visitor interface. That means we need visit methods for each of the expression types we have so far.

```
    return expr.accept(this);
  }

  @Override
  public String visitBinaryExpr(Expr.Binary expr) {
    return parenthesize(expr.operator.lexeme,
                        expr.left, expr.right);
  }

  @Override
  public String visitGroupingExpr(Expr.Grouping expr) {
    return parenthesize("group", expr.expression);
  }

  @Override
  public String visitLiteralExpr(Expr.Literal expr) {
    if (expr.value == null) return "nil";
    return expr.value.toString();
  }

  @Override
  public String visitUnaryExpr(Expr.Unary expr) {
    return parenthesize(expr.operator.lexeme, expr.right);
  }
}
```

lox/AstPrinter.java
*add after* print()

Literal expressions are easy—they convert the value to a string with a little check to handle Java's `null` standing in for Lox's `nil`. The other expressions have subexpressions, so they use this `parenthesize()` helper method:

```
  private String parenthesize(String name, Expr... exprs) {
    StringBuilder builder = new StringBuilder();

    builder.append("(").append(name);
    for (Expr expr : exprs) {
      builder.append(" ");
      builder.append(expr.accept(this));
    }
    builder.append(")");

    return builder.toString();
  }
```

lox/AstPrinter.java
*add after* visitUnaryExpr()

It takes a name and a list of subexpressions and wraps them all up in parentheses, yielding a string like:

```
(+ 1 2)
```

Note that it calls `accept()` on each subexpression and passes in itself. This is the recursive step that lets us print an entire tree.

This recursion is also why people think the Visitor pattern itself has to do with trees.

We don't have a parser yet, so it's hard to see this in action. For now, we'll hack together a little `main()` method that manually instantiates a tree and prints it.

**lox/AstPrinter.java**
*add after* `parenthesize()`

```java
public static void main(String[] args) {
    Expr expression = new Expr.Binary(
        new Expr.Unary(
            new Token(TokenType.MINUS, "-", null, 1),
            new Expr.Literal(123)),
        new Token(TokenType.STAR, "*", null, 1),
        new Expr.Grouping(
            new Expr.Literal(45.67)));

    System.out.println(new AstPrinter().print(expression));
}
```

If we did everything right, it prints:

```
(* (- 123) (group 45.67))
```

You can go ahead and delete this method. We won't need it. Also, as we add new syntax tree types, I won't bother showing the necessary visit methods for them in AstPrinter. If you want to (and you want the Java compiler to not yell at you), go ahead and add them yourself. It will come in handy in the next chapter when we start parsing Lox code into syntax trees. Or, if you don't care to maintain AstPrinter, feel free to delete it. We won't need it again.

## CHALLENGES

1. Earlier, I said that the |, *, and + forms we added to our grammar metasyntax were just syntactic sugar. Take this grammar:

```
expr → expr ( "(" ( expr ("," expr)* )? ")" | "." IDENTIFIER )+
     | IDENTIFIER
     | NUMBER
```

   Produce a grammar that matches the same language but does not use any of that notational sugar.
   *Bonus:* What kind of expression does this bit of grammar encode?

2. The Visitor pattern lets you emulate the functional style in an object-oriented language. Devise a complementary pattern for a functional language. It should let you bundle all of the operations on one type together and let you define new types easily.

   (SML or Haskell would be ideal for this exercise, but Scheme or another Lisp works as well.)

3. In reverse Polish notation (RPN), the operands to an arithmetic operator are both placed before the operator, so `1 + 2` becomes `1 2 +`. Evaluation proceeds from left to right. Numbers are pushed onto an implicit stack. An arithmetic operator pops the top two numbers, performs the operation, and pushes the result. Thus, this:

```
(1 + 2) * (4 - 3)
```

   in RPN becomes:

```
1 2 + 4 3 - *
```

   Define a visitor class for our syntax tree classes that takes an expression, converts it to RPN, and returns the resulting string.

# Parsing Expressions

6

*"Grammar, which knows how to control even kings."*

— Molière

This chapter marks the first major milestone of the book. Many of us have cobbled together a mishmash of regular expressions and substring operations to extract some sense out of a pile of text. The code was probably riddled with bugs and a beast to maintain. Writing a *real* parser—one with decent error handling, a coherent internal structure, and the ability to robustly chew through a sophisticated syntax—is considered a rare, impressive skill. In this chapter, you will attain it.

It's easier than you think, partially because we front-loaded a lot of the hard work in the last chapter. You already know your way around a formal grammar. You're familiar with syntax trees, and we have some Java classes to represent them. The only remaining piece is parsing—transmogrifying a sequence of tokens into one of those syntax trees.

Some CS textbooks make a big deal out of parsers. In the '60s, computer scientists—understandably tired of programming in assembly language—started designing more sophisticated, human-friendly languages like Fortran and ALGOL. Alas, they weren't very *machine*-friendly for the primitive computers of the time.

These pioneers designed languages that they honestly weren't even sure how to write compilers for, and then did groundbreaking work inventing parsing and

"Parse" comes to English from the Old French "pars" for "part of speech". It means to take a text and map each word to the grammar of the language. We use it here in the same sense, except that our language is a little more modern than Old French.

Like many rites of passage, you'll probably find it looks a little smaller, a little less daunting when it's behind you than when it loomed ahead.

Imagine how harrowing assembly programming on those old machines must have been that they considered *Fortran* to be an improvement.

compiling techniques that could handle these new, big languages on those old, tiny machines.

Classic compiler books read like fawning hagiographies of these heroes and their tools. The cover of *Compilers: Principles, Techniques, and Tools* literally has a dragon labeled "complexity of compiler design" being slain by a knight bearing a sword and shield branded "LALR parser generator" and "syntax-directed translation". They laid it on thick.

A little self-congratulation is well-deserved, but the truth is you don't need to know most of that stuff to bang out a high quality parser for a modern machine. As always, I encourage you to broaden your education and take it in later, but this book omits the trophy case.

## 6.1  Ambiguity and the Parsing Game

In the last chapter, I said you can "play" a context-free grammar like a game in order to *generate* strings. Parsers play that game in reverse. Given a string—a series of tokens—we map those tokens to terminals in the grammar to figure out which rules could have generated that string.

The "could have" part is interesting. It's entirely possible to create a grammar that is *ambiguous*, where different choices of productions can lead to the same string. When you're using the grammar to *generate* strings, that doesn't matter much. Once you have the string, who cares how you got to it?

When parsing, ambiguity means the parser may misunderstand the user's code. As we parse, we aren't just determining if the string is valid Lox code, we're also tracking which rules match which parts of it so that we know what part of the language each token belongs to. Here's the Lox expression grammar we put together in the last chapter:

```
expression      → literal
                | unary
                | binary
                | grouping ;

literal         → NUMBER | STRING | "true" | "false" | "nil" ;
grouping        → "(" expression ")" ;
unary           → ( "-" | "!" ) expression ;
binary          → expression operator expression ;
operator        → "==" | "!=" | "<" | "<=" | ">" | ">="
                | "+" | "-" | "*" | "/" ;
```

This is a valid string in that grammar:

But there are two ways we could have generated it. One way is:

1. Starting at `expression`, pick `binary`.

2. For the left-hand `expression`, pick `NUMBER`, and use 6.

3. For the operator, pick `"/"`.

4. For the right-hand `expression`, pick `binary` again.

5. In that nested `binary` expression, pick 3 - 1.

Another is:

1. Starting at `expression`, pick `binary`.

2. For the left-hand `expression`, pick `binary` again.

3. In that nested `binary` expression, pick 6 / 3.

4. Back at the outer `binary`, for the operator, pick `"-"`.

5. For the right-hand `expression`, pick `NUMBER`, and use 1.

Those produce the same *strings*, but not the same *syntax trees*:

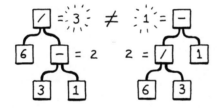

In other words, the grammar allows seeing the expression as (6 / 3) - 1 or 6 / (3 - 1). The `binary` rule lets operands nest any which way you want. That in turn affects the result of evaluating the parsed tree. The way mathematicians have addressed this ambiguity since blackboards were first invented is by defining rules for precedence and associativity.

- **Precedence** determines which operator is evaluated first in an expression containing a mixture of different operators. Precedence rules tell us that we evaluate the / before the – in the above example. Operators with higher precedence are evaluated before operators with lower precedence. Equivalently, higher precedence operators are said to "bind tighter".

- **Associativity** determines which operator is evaluated first in a series of the *same* operator. When an operator is **left-associative** (think "left-to-right"), operators on the left evaluate before those on the right. Since – is left-associative, this expression:

5 - 3 - 1

While not common these days, some languages specify that certain pairs of operators have *no* relative precedence. That makes it a syntax error to mix those operators in an expression without using explicit grouping.

Likewise, some operators are **non-associative**. That means it's an error to use that operator more than once in a sequence. For example, Perl's range operator isn't associative, so a `..` b is OK, but a `..` b `..` c is an error.

is equivalent to:

```
(5 - 3) - 1
```

Assignment, on the other hand, is **right-associative**. This:

```
a = b = c
```

is equivalent to:

```
a = (b = c)
```

Without well-defined precedence and associativity, an expression that uses multiple operators is ambiguous—it can be parsed into different syntax trees, which could in turn evaluate to different results. We'll fix that in Lox by applying the same precedence rules as C, going from lowest to highest.

| Name | Operators | Associates |
|------|-----------|------------|
| Equality | == != | Left |
| Comparison | > >= < <= | Left |
| Term | - + | Left |
| Factor | / * | Left |
| Unary | ! - | Right |

Right now, the grammar stuffs all expression types into a single `expression` rule. That same rule is used as the non-terminal for operands, which lets the grammar accept any kind of expression as a subexpression, regardless of whether the precedence rules allow it.

We fix that by stratifying the grammar. We define a separate rule for each precedence level.

Instead of baking precedence right into the grammar rules, some parser generators let you keep the same ambiguous-but-simple grammar and then add in a little explicit operator precedence metadata on the side in order to disambiguate.

```
expression    → ...
equality      → ...
comparison    → ...
term          → ...
factor        → ...
unary         → ...
primary       → ...
```

Each rule here only matches expressions at its precedence level or higher. For example, unary matches a unary expression like `!negated` or a primary expression like `1234`. And `term` can match `1 + 2` but also `3 * 4 / 5`. The final `primary` rule covers the highest-precedence forms—literals and parenthesized expressions.

We just need to fill in the productions for each of those rules. We'll do the easy ones first. The top `expression` rule matches any expression at any precedence level. Since `equality` has the lowest precedence, if we match that, then it covers everything.

```
expression      → equality
```

Over at the other end of the precedence table, a primary expression contains all the literals and grouping expressions.

```
primary         → NUMBER | STRING | "true" | "false" | "nil"
                | "(" expression ")" ;
```

A unary expression starts with a unary operator followed by the operand. Since unary operators can nest— `!!true` is a valid if weird expression—the operand can itself be a unary operator. A recursive rule handles that nicely.

```
unary           → ( "!" | "-" ) unary ;
```

But this rule has a problem. It never terminates.

Remember, each rule needs to match expressions at that precedence level *or higher*, so we also need to let this match a primary expression.

```
unary           → ( "!" | "-" ) unary
                | primary ;
```

That works.

The remaining rules are all binary operators. We'll start with the rule for multiplication and division. Here's a first try:

```
factor          → factor ( "/" | "*" ) unary
                | unary ;
```

The rule recurses to match the left operand. That enables the rule to match a series of multiplication and division expressions like `1 * 2 / 3`. Putting the recursive production on the left side and `unary` on the right makes the rule left-associative and unambiguous.

All of this is correct, but the fact that the first symbol in the body of the rule is the same as the head of the rule means this production is **left-recursive**. Some parsing techniques, including the one we're going to use, have trouble with left recursion. (Recursion elsewhere, like we have in `unary` and the indirect recursion for grouping in `primary` are not a problem.)

There are many grammars you can define that match the same language. The choice for how to model a particular language is partially a matter of taste and partially a pragmatic one. This rule is correct, but not optimal for how we intend to parse it. Instead of a left recursive rule, we'll use a different one.

```
factor          → unary ( ( "/" | "*" ) unary )* ;
```

We define a factor expression as a flat *sequence* of multiplications and divisions. This matches the same syntax as the previous rule, but better mirrors the code we'll write to parse Lox. We use the same structure for all of the other binary operator precedence levels, giving us this complete expression grammar:

We could eliminate `expression` and simply use `equality` in the other rules that contain expressions, but using `expression` makes those other rules read a little better.

Also, in later chapters when we expand the grammar to include assignment and logical operators, we'll only need to change the production for `expression` instead of touching every rule that contains an expression.

In principle, it doesn't matter whether you treat multiplication as left- or right-associative—you get the same result either way. Alas, in the real world with limited precision, roundoff and overflow mean that associativity can affect the result of a sequence of multiplications. Consider:

```
print 0.1 * (0.2 * 0.3);
print (0.1 * 0.2) * 0.3;
```

In languages like Lox that use IEEE 754 double-precision floating-point numbers, the first evaluates to `0.006`, while the second yields `0.006000000000000001`. Sometimes that tiny difference matters.

```
expression    → equality ;
equality      → comparison ( ( "!=" | "==" ) comparison )* ;
comparison    → term ( ( ">" | ">=" | "<" | "<=" ) term )* ;
term          → factor ( ( "-" | "+" ) factor )* ;
factor        → unary ( ( "/" | "*" ) unary )* ;
unary         → ( "!" | "-" ) unary
              | primary ;
primary       → NUMBER | STRING | "true" | "false" | "nil"
              | "(" expression ")" ;
```

This grammar is more complex than the one we had before, but in return we have eliminated the previous one's ambiguity. It's just what we need to make a parser.

## 6.2  Recursive Descent Parsing

There is a whole pack of parsing techniques whose names are mostly combinations of "L" and "R"—LL(k), LR(1), LALR—along with more exotic beasts like parser combinators, Earley parsers, the shunting yard algorithm, and packrat parsing. For our first interpreter, one technique is more than sufficient: **recursive descent**.

Recursive descent is the simplest way to build a parser, and doesn't require using complex parser generator tools like Yacc, Bison or ANTLR. All you need is straightforward handwritten code. Don't be fooled by its simplicity, though. Recursive descent parsers are fast, robust, and can support sophisticated error handling. In fact, GCC, V8 (the JavaScript VM in Chrome), Roslyn (the C# compiler written in C#) and many other heavyweight production language implementations use recursive descent. It rocks.

It's called "recursive *descent*" because it walks *down* the grammar. Confusingly, we also use direction metaphorically when talking about "high" and "low" precedence, but the orientation is reversed. In a top-down parser, you reach the lowest-precedence expressions first because they may in turn contain subexpressions of higher precedence.

Recursive descent is considered a **top-down parser** because it starts from the top or outermost grammar rule (here expression) and works its way down into the nested subexpressions before finally reaching the leaves of the syntax tree. This is in contrast with bottom-up parsers like LR that start with primary expressions and compose them into larger and larger chunks of syntax.

A recursive descent parser is a literal translation of the grammar's rules straight into imperative code. Each rule becomes a function. The body of the rule translates to code roughly like:

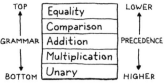

CS people really need to get together and straighten out their metaphors. Don't even get me started on which direction a stack grows or why trees have their roots on top.

| Grammar notation | Code representation |
| --- | --- |
| Terminal | Code to match and consume a token |
| Nonterminal | Call to that rule's function |
| \| | if or switch statement |
| * or + | while or for loop |
| ? | if statement |

The descent is described as "recursive" because when a grammar rule refers to itself—directly or indirectly—that translates to a recursive function call.

## 6.2.1  The parser class

Each grammar rule becomes a method inside this new class:

```
package com.craftinginterpreters.lox;

import java.util.List;
import static com.craftinginterpreters.lox.TokenType.*;

class Parser {
  private final List<Token> tokens;
  private int current = 0;

  Parser(List<Token> tokens) {
    this.tokens = tokens;
  }
}
```

lox/Parser.java
*create new file*

Like the scanner, the parser consumes a flat input sequence, only now we're reading tokens instead of characters. We store the list of tokens and use `current` to point to the next token eagerly waiting to be parsed.

We're going to run straight through the expression grammar now and translate each rule to Java code. The first rule, `expression`, simply expands to the `equality` rule, so that's straightforward.

```
private Expr expression() {
  return equality();
}
```

lox/Parser.java
*add after* Parser()

Each method for parsing a grammar rule produces a syntax tree for that rule and returns it to the caller. When the body of the rule contains a nonterminal—a reference to another rule—we call that other rule's method.

The rule for equality is a little more complex.

This is why left recursion is problematic for recursive descent. The function for a left-recursive rule immediately calls itself, which calls itself again, and so on, until the parser hits a stack overflow and dies.

```
equality        → comparison ( ( "!=" | "==" ) comparison )* ;
```

In Java, that becomes:

```
private Expr equality() {
  Expr expr = comparison();
  while (match(BANG_EQUAL, EQUAL_EQUAL)) {
    Token operator = previous();
    Expr right = comparison();
    expr = new Expr.Binary(expr, operator, right);
  }

  return expr;
}
```

lox/Parser.java
*add after* expression()

Let's step through it. The first `comparison` nonterminal in the body translates to the first call to `comparison()` in the method. We take that result and store it in a local variable.

Then, the ( `...` )\* loop in the rule maps to a `while` loop. We need to know when to exit that loop. We can see that inside the rule, we must first find either a `!=` or `==` token. So, if we *don't* see one of those, we must be done with the sequence of equality operators. We express that check using a handy `match()` method.

lox/Parser.java<br>*add after* equality()

```java
private boolean match(TokenType... types) {
  for (TokenType type : types) {
    if (check(type)) {
      advance();
      return true;
    }
  }
  return false;
}
```

This checks to see if the current token has any of the given types. If so, it consumes the token and returns `true`. Otherwise, it returns `false` and leaves the current token alone. The `match()` method is defined in terms of two more fundamental operations.

The `check()` method returns `true` if the current token is of the given type. Unlike `match()`, it never consumes the token, it only looks at it.

lox/Parser.java<br>*add after* match()

```java
private boolean check(TokenType type) {
  if (isAtEnd()) return false;
  return peek().type == type;
}
```

The `advance()` method consumes the current token and returns it, similar to how our scanner's corresponding method crawled through characters.

lox/Parser.java<br>*add after* check()

```java
private Token advance() {
  if (!isAtEnd()) current++;
  return previous();
}
```

These methods bottom out on the last handful of primitive operations.

lox/Parser.java<br>*add after* advance()

```java
private boolean isAtEnd() {
  return peek().type == EOF;
}

private Token peek() {
  return tokens.get(current);
}

private Token previous() {
  return tokens.get(current - 1);
}
```

isAtEnd() checks if we've run out of tokens to parse. peek() returns the current token we have yet to consume, and previous() returns the most recently consumed token. The latter makes it easier to use match() and then access the just-matched token.

That's most of the parsing infrastructure we need. Where were we? Right, so if we are inside the while loop in equality(), then we know we have found a != or == operator and must be parsing an equality expression.

We grab the matched operator token so we can track which kind of equality expression we have. Then we call comparison() again to parse the right-hand operand. We combine the operator and its two operands into a new Expr.Binary syntax tree node, and then loop around. For each iteration, we store the resulting expression back in the same expr local variable. As we zip through a sequence of equality expressions, that creates a left-associative nested tree of binary operator nodes.

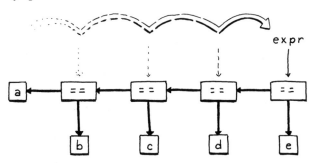

Parsing a == b == c == d == e. For each iteration, we create a new binary expression using the previous one as the left operand.

The parser falls out of the loop once it hits a token that's not an equality operator. Finally, it returns the expression. Note that if the parser never encounters an equality operator, then it never enters the loop. In that case, the equality() method effectively calls and returns comparison(). In that way, this method matches an equality operator *or anything of higher precedence*.

Moving on to the next rule…

```
comparison      → term ( ( ">" | ">=" | "<" | "<=" ) term )* ;
```

Translated to Java:

```java
private Expr comparison() {
  Expr expr = term();

  while (match(GREATER, GREATER_EQUAL, LESS, LESS_EQUAL)) {
    Token operator = previous();
    Expr right = term();
    expr = new Expr.Binary(expr, operator, right);
  }

  return expr;
}
```

lox/Parser.java
*add after* equality()

The grammar rule is virtually identical to equality and so is the corresponding code. The only differences are the token types for the operators we match, and the method we call for the operands—now term() instead of comparison(). The remaining two binary operator rules follow the same pattern.

If you wanted to do some clever Java 8, you could create a helper method for parsing a left-associative series of binary operators given a list of token types, and an operand method handle to simplify this redundant code.

In order of precedence, first addition and subtraction:

lox/Parser.java
*add after* `comparison()`

```java
private Expr term() {
  Expr expr = factor();

  while (match(MINUS, PLUS)) {
    Token operator = previous();
    Expr right = factor();
    expr = new Expr.Binary(expr, operator, right);
  }

  return expr;
}
```

And finally, multiplication and division:

lox/Parser.java
*add after* `term()`

```java
private Expr factor() {
  Expr expr = unary();

  while (match(SLASH, STAR)) {
    Token operator = previous();
    Expr right = unary();
    expr = new Expr.Binary(expr, operator, right);
  }

  return expr;
}
```

That's all of the binary operators, parsed with the correct precedence and associativity. We're crawling up the precedence hierarchy and now we've reached the unary operators.

```
unary          → ( "!" | "-" ) unary
               | primary ;
```

The code for this is a little different.

lox/Parser.java
*add after* `factor()`

```java
private Expr unary() {
  if (match(BANG, MINUS)) {
    Token operator = previous();
    Expr right = unary();
    return new Expr.Unary(operator, right);
  }

  return primary();
}
```

The fact that the parser looks ahead at upcoming tokens to decide how to parse puts recursive descent into the category of **predictive parsers**.

Again, we look at the current token to see how to parse. If it's a ! or −, we must have a unary expression. In that case, we grab the token and then recursively call `unary()` again to parse the operand. Wrap that all up in a unary expression syntax tree and we're done.

Otherwise, we must have reached the highest level of precedence, primary expressions.

```
primary        → NUMBER | STRING | "true" | "false" | "nil"
               | "(" expression ")" ;
```

Most of the cases for the rule are single terminals, so parsing is straightforward.

```
private Expr primary() {
  if (match(FALSE)) return new Expr.Literal(false);
  if (match(TRUE)) return new Expr.Literal(true);
  if (match(NIL)) return new Expr.Literal(null);

  if (match(NUMBER, STRING)) {
    return new Expr.Literal(previous().literal);
  }

  if (match(LEFT_PAREN)) {
    Expr expr = expression();
    consume(RIGHT_PAREN, "Expect ')' after expression.");
    return new Expr.Grouping(expr);
  }
}
```

lox/Parser.java
*add after* unary()

The interesting branch is the one for handling parentheses. After we match an opening ( and parse the expression inside it, we *must* find a ) token. If we don't, that's an error.

# 6.3  Syntax Errors

A parser really has two jobs:

1. Given a valid sequence of tokens, produce a corresponding syntax tree.

2. Given an *invalid* sequence of tokens, detect any errors and tell the user about their mistakes.

Don't underestimate how important the second job is! In modern IDEs and editors, the parser is constantly reparsing code—often while the user is still editing it—in order to syntax highlight and support things like auto-complete. That means it will encounter code in incomplete, half-wrong states *all the time*.

When the user doesn't realize the syntax is wrong, it is up to the parser to help guide them back onto the right path. The way it reports errors is a large part of your language's user interface. Good syntax error handling is hard. By definition, the code isn't in a well-defined state, so there's no infallible way to know what the user *meant* to write. The parser can't read your mind.

There are a couple of hard requirements for when the parser runs into a syntax error. A parser must:

Not yet at least. With the way things are going in machine learning these days, who knows what the future will bring?

Philosophically speaking, if an error isn't detected and the interpreter runs the code, is it *really* an error?

- **Detect and report the error.** If it doesn't detect the error and passes the resulting malformed syntax tree on to the interpreter, all manner of horrors may be summoned.

- **Avoid crashing or hanging.** Syntax errors are a fact of life, and language tools have to be robust in the face of them. Segfaulting or getting stuck in an infinite loop isn't allowed. While the source may not be valid *code*, it's still a valid *input to the parser* because users use the parser to learn what syntax is allowed.

Those are the table stakes if you want to get in the parser game at all, but you really want to raise the ante beyond that. A decent parser should:

- **Be fast.** Computers are thousands of times faster than they were when parser technology was first invented. The days of needing to optimize your parser so that it could get through an entire source file during a coffee break are over. But programmer expectations have risen as quickly, if not faster. They expect their editors to reparse files in milliseconds after every keystroke.

- **Report as many distinct errors as there are.** Aborting after the first error is easy to implement, but it's annoying for users if every time they fix what they think is the one error in a file, a new one appears. They want to see them all.

- **Minimize *cascaded* errors.** Once a single error is found, the parser no longer really knows what's going on. It tries to get itself back on track and keep going, but if it gets confused, it may report a slew of ghost errors that don't indicate other real problems in the code. When the first error is fixed, those phantoms disappear, because they reflect only the parser's own confusion. Cascaded errors are annoying because they can scare the user into thinking their code is in a worse state than it is.

You know you want to push it.

The last two points are in tension. We want to report as many separate errors as we can, but we don't want to report ones that are merely side effects of an earlier one.

The way a parser responds to an error and keeps going to look for later errors is called **error recovery**. This was a hot research topic in the '60s. Back then, you'd hand a stack of punch cards to the secretary and come back the next day to see if the compiler succeeded. With an iteration loop that slow, you *really* wanted to find every single error in your code in one pass.

Today, when parsers complete before you've even finished typing, it's less of an issue. Simple, fast error recovery is fine.

### 6.3.1  Panic mode error recovery

Of all the recovery techniques devised in yesteryear, the one that best stood the test of time is called—somewhat alarmingly—**panic mode**. As soon as the parser detects an error, it enters panic mode. It knows at least one token doesn't make sense given its current state in the middle of some stack of grammar productions.

Before it can get back to parsing, it needs to get its state and the sequence of forthcoming tokens aligned such that the next token does match the rule being parsed. This process is called **synchronization**.

To do that, we select some rule in the grammar that will mark the synchronization point. The parser fixes its parsing state by jumping out of any nested productions until it gets back to that rule. Then it synchronizes the token stream by discarding tokens until it reaches one that can appear at that point in the rule.

Any additional real syntax errors hiding in those discarded tokens aren't reported, but it also means that any mistaken cascaded errors that are side effects of the initial error aren't *falsely* reported either, which is a decent trade-off.

The traditional place in the grammar to synchronize is between statements. We don't have those yet, so we won't actually synchronize in this chapter, but we'll get the machinery in place for later.

## 6.3.2  Entering panic mode

Back before we went on this side trip around error recovery, we were writing the code to parse a parenthesized expression. After parsing the expression, the parser looks for the closing ) by calling consume(). Here, finally, is that method:

```
private Token consume(TokenType type, String message) {
  if (check(type)) return advance();

  throw error(peek(), message);
}
```

lox/Parser.java
*add after* match()

It's similar to match() in that it checks to see if the next token is of the expected type. If so, it consumes the token and everything is groovy. If some other token is there, then we've hit an error. We report it by calling this:

```
private ParseError error(Token token, String message) {
  Lox.error(token, message);
  return new ParseError();
}
```

lox/Parser.java
*add after* previous()

First, that shows the error to the user by calling:

```
static void error(Token token, String message) {
  if (token.type == TokenType.EOF) {
    report(token.line, " at end", message);
  } else {
    report(token.line, " at '" + token.lexeme + "'", message);
  }
}
```

lox/Lox.java
*add after* report()

This reports an error at a given token. It shows the token's location and the token itself. This will come in handy later since we use tokens throughout the interpreter to track locations in code.

After we report the error, the user knows about their mistake, but what does the *parser* do next? Back in error(), we create and return a ParseError, an instance of this new class:

lox/Parser.java
*nest inside class* Parser

```
class Parser {
  private static class ParseError extends RuntimeException {}

  private final List<Token> tokens;
```

Another way to handle common syntax errors is with **error productions**. You augment the grammar with a rule that *successfully* matches the *erroneous* syntax. The parser safely parses it but then reports it as an error instead of producing a syntax tree.

For example, some languages have a unary + operator, like +123, but Lox does not. Instead of getting confused when the parser stumbles onto a + at the beginning of an expression, we could extend the unary rule to allow it.

```
unary  →  ("!"|"-"|"+")
          unary
        | primary ;
```

This lets the parser consume + without going into panic mode or leaving the parser in a weird state.

Error productions work well because you, the parser author, know *how* the code is wrong and what the user was likely trying to do. That means you can give a more helpful message to get the user back on track, like, "Unary '+' expressions are not supported." Mature parsers tend to accumulate error productions like barnacles since they help users fix common mistakes.

I say "probably" because we could hit a semicolon separating clauses in a for loop. Our synchronization isn't perfect, but that's OK. We've already reported the first error precisely, so everything after that is kind of "best effort".

This is a simple sentinel class we use to unwind the parser. The `error()` method *returns* the error instead of *throwing* it because we want to let the calling method inside the parser decide whether to unwind or not. Some parse errors occur in places where the parser isn't likely to get into a weird state and we don't need to synchronize. In those places, we simply report the error and keep on truckin'.

For example, Lox limits the number of arguments you can pass to a function. If you pass too many, the parser needs to report that error, but it can and should simply keep on parsing the extra arguments instead of freaking out and going into panic mode.

In our case, though, the syntax error is nasty enough that we want to panic and synchronize. Discarding tokens is pretty easy, but how do we synchronize the parser's own state?

### 6.3.3 Synchronizing a recursive descent parser

With recursive descent, the parser's state—which rules it is in the middle of recognizing—is not stored explicitly in fields. Instead, we use Java's own call stack to track what the parser is doing. Each rule in the middle of being parsed is a call frame on the stack. In order to reset that state, we need to clear out those call frames.

The natural way to do that in Java is exceptions. When we want to synchronize, we *throw* that ParseError object. Higher up in the method for the grammar rule we are synchronizing to, we'll catch it. Since we synchronize on statement boundaries, we'll catch the exception there. After the exception is caught, the parser is in the right state. All that's left is to synchronize the tokens.

We want to discard tokens until we're right at the beginning of the next statement. That boundary is pretty easy to spot—it's one of the main reasons we picked it. *After* a semicolon, we're probably finished with a statement. Most statements start with a keyword—for, if, return, var, etc. When the *next* token is any of those, we're probably about to start a statement.

This method encapsulates that logic:

lox/Parser.java
*add after* error()

```
private void synchronize() {
  advance();
  while (!isAtEnd()) {
    if (previous().type == SEMICOLON) return;

    switch (peek().type) {
      case CLASS: case FOR: case FUN: case IF: case PRINT:
      case RETURN: case VAR: case WHILE:
        return;
    }

    advance();
  }
}
```

It discards tokens until it thinks it has found a statement boundary. After catching a ParseError, we'll call this and then we are hopefully back in sync. When it works well, we have discarded tokens that would have likely caused cascaded errors anyway, and now we can parse the rest of the file starting at the next statement.

Alas, we don't get to see this method in action, since we don't have statements yet. We'll get to that in a couple of chapters. For now, if an error occurs, we'll panic and unwind all the way to the top and stop parsing. Since we can parse only a single expression anyway, that's no big loss.

## 6.4 Wiring up the Parser

We are mostly done parsing expressions now. There is one other place where we need to add a little error handling. As the parser descends through the parsing methods for each grammar rule, it eventually hits `primary()`. If none of the cases in there match, it means we are sitting on a token that can't start an expression. We need to handle that error too.

```
  if (match(LEFT_PAREN)) {
    Expr expr = expression();
    consume(RIGHT_PAREN, "Expect ')' after expression.");
    return new Expr.Grouping(expr);
  }

  throw error(peek(), "Expect expression.");
}
```

*lox/Parser.java*
*in* `primary()`

With that, all that remains in the parser is to define an initial method to kick it off. That method is called, naturally enough, `parse()`.

```
Expr parse() {
  try {
    return expression();
  } catch (ParseError error) {
    return null;
  }
}
```

*lox/Parser.java*
*add after* `Parser()`

We'll revisit this method later when we add statements to the language. For now, it parses a single expression and returns it. We also have some temporary code to exit out of panic mode. Syntax error recovery is the parser's job, so we don't want the ParseError exception to escape into the rest of the interpreter.

When a syntax error does occur, this method returns `null`. That's OK. The parser promises not to crash or hang on invalid syntax, but it doesn't promise to return a *usable syntax tree* if an error is found. As soon as the parser reports an error, `hadError` gets set, and subsequent phases are skipped.

Finally, we can hook up our brand new parser to the main Lox class and try it out. We still don't have an interpreter, so for now, we'll parse to a syntax tree and then use the AstPrinter class from the last chapter to display it.

Delete the old code to print the scanned tokens and replace it with this:

lox/Lox.java
*in* run()
*replace 5 lines*

```
List<Token> tokens = scanner.scanTokens();
Parser parser = new Parser(tokens);
Expr expression = parser.parse();

// Stop if there was a syntax error.
if (hadError) return;

System.out.println(new AstPrinter().print(expression));
}
```

It is possible to define a more complex grammar than Lox's that's difficult to parse using recursive descent. Predictive parsing gets tricky when you may need to look ahead a large number of tokens to figure out what you're sitting on.

In practice, most languages are designed to avoid that. Even in cases where they aren't, you can usually hack around it without too much pain. If you can parse C++ using recursive descent—which many C++ compilers do—you can parse anything.

Congratulations, you have crossed the threshold! That really is all there is to handwriting a parser. We'll extend the grammar in later chapters with assignment, statements, and other stuff, but none of that is any more complex than the binary operators we tackled here.

Fire up the interpreter and type in some expressions. See how it handles precedence and associativity correctly? Not bad for less than 200 lines of code.

## CHALLENGES

1. In C, a block is a statement form that allows you to pack a series of statements where a single one is expected. The comma operator is an analogous syntax for expressions. A comma-separated series of expressions can be given where a single expression is expected (except inside a function call's argument list). At runtime, the comma operator evaluates the left operand and discards the result. Then it evaluates and returns the right operand.

   Add support for comma expressions. Give them the same precedence and associativity as in C. Write the grammar, and then implement the necessary parsing code.

2. Likewise, add support for the C-style conditional or "ternary" operator ? : . What precedence level is allowed between the ? and : ? Is the whole operator left-associative or right-associative?

3. Add error productions to handle each binary operator appearing without a left-hand operand. In other words, detect a binary operator appearing at the beginning of an expression. Report that as an error, but also parse and discard a right-hand operand with the appropriate precedence.

## DESIGN NOTE: LOGIC VERSUS HISTORY

Let's say we decide to add bitwise & and | operators to Lox. Where should we put them in the precedence hierarchy? C—and most languages that follow in C's foot-steps—place them below ==. This is widely considered a mistake because it means common operations like testing a flag require parentheses.

```
if (flags & FLAG_MASK == SOME_FLAG) { ... } // Wrong.
if ((flags & FLAG_MASK) == SOME_FLAG) { ... } // Right.
```

Should we fix this for Lox and put bitwise operators higher up the precedence table than C does? There are two strategies we can take.

You almost never want to use the result of an == expression as the operand to a bitwise operator. By making bitwise bind tighter, users don't need to parenthesize as often. So if we do that, and users assume the precedence is chosen logically to minimize parentheses, they're likely to infer it correctly.

This kind of internal consistency makes the language easier to learn because there are fewer edge cases and exceptions users have to stumble into and then correct. That's good, because before users can use our language, they have to load all of that syntax and semantics into their heads. A simpler, more rational language *makes sense*.

But, for many users there is an even faster shortcut to getting our language's ideas into their wetware—*use concepts they already know*. Many newcomers to our language will be coming from some other language or languages. If our language uses some of the same syntax or semantics as those, there is much less for the user to learn (and *unlearn*).

This is particularly helpful with syntax. You may not remember it well today, but way back when you learned your very first programming language, code probably looked alien and unapproachable. Only through painstaking effort did you learn to read and accept it. If you design a novel syntax for your new language, you force users to start that process all over again.

Taking advantage of what users already know is one of the most powerful tools you can use to ease adoption of your language. It's almost impossible to overestimate how valuable this is. But it faces you with a nasty problem: What happens when the thing the users all know *kind of sucks*? C's bitwise operator precedence is a mistake that doesn't make sense. But it's a *familiar* mistake that millions have already gotten used to and learned to live with.

Do you stay true to your language's own internal logic and ignore history? Do you start from a blank slate and first principles? Or do you weave your language into the rich tapestry of programming history and give your users a leg up by starting from something they already know?

There is no perfect answer here, only trade-offs. You and I are obviously biased towards liking novel languages, so our natural inclination is to burn the history books and start our own story.

In practice, it's often better to make the most of what users already know. Getting them to come to your language requires a big leap. The smaller you can make that chasm, the more people will be willing to cross it. But you can't *always* stick to history, or your language won't have anything new and compelling to give people a *reason* to jump over.

# Evaluating Expressions

7

*"You are my creator, but I am your master; Obey!"*

— Mary Shelley, *Frankenstein*

If you want to properly set the mood for this chapter, try to conjure up a thunderstorm, one of those swirling tempests that likes to yank open shutters at the climax of the story. Maybe toss in a few bolts of lightning. In this chapter, our interpreter will take breath, open its eyes, and execute some code.

A decrepit Victorian mansion is optional, but adds to the ambiance.

There are all manner of ways that language implementations make a computer do what the user's source code commands. They can compile it to machine code, translate it to another high-level language, or reduce it to some bytecode format for a virtual machine to run. For our first interpreter, though, we are going to take the simplest, shortest path and execute the syntax tree itself.

Right now, our parser only supports expressions. So, to "execute" code, we will evaluate an expression and produce a value. For each kind of expression syntax we can parse—literal, operator, etc.—we need a corresponding chunk of code that knows how to evaluate that tree and produce a result. That raises two questions:

1. What kinds of values do we produce?

2. How do we organize those chunks of code?

Taking them on one at a time...

## 7.1  Representing Values

In Lox, values are created by literals, computed by expressions, and stored in variables. The user sees these as *Lox* objects, but they are implemented in the underlying language our interpreter is written in. That means bridging the lands of Lox's dynamic typing and Java's static types. A variable in Lox can store a value of any (Lox) type, and can even store values of different types at different points in time. What Java type might we use to represent that?

Given a Java variable with that static type, we must also be able to determine which kind of value it holds at runtime. When the interpreter executes a + operator, it needs to tell if it is adding two numbers or concatenating two strings. Is there a Java type that can hold numbers, strings, Booleans, and more? Is there one that can tell us what its runtime type is? There is! Good old java.lang.Object.

In places in the interpreter where we need to store a Lox value, we can use Object as the type. Java has boxed versions of its primitive types that all subclass Object, so we can use those for Lox's built-in types:

| Lox type | Java representation |
| --- | --- |
| Any Lox value | Object |
| nil | null |
| Boolean | Boolean |
| number | Double |
| string | String |

Given a value of static type Object, we can determine if the runtime value is a number or a string or whatever using Java's built-in `instanceof` operator. In other words, the JVM's own object representation conveniently gives us every-

Here, I'm using "value" and "object" pretty much interchangeably.

Later in the C interpreter we'll make a slight distinction between them, but that's mostly to have unique terms for two different corners of the implementation—in-place versus heap-allocated data. From the user's perspective, the terms are synonymous.

thing we need to implement Lox's built-in types. We'll have to do a little more work later when we add Lox's notions of functions, classes, and instances, but Object and the boxed primitive classes are sufficient for the types we need right now.

Another thing we need to do with values is manage their memory, and Java does that too. A handy object representation and a really nice garbage collector are the main reasons we're writing our first interpreter in Java.

## 7.2  Evaluating Expressions

Next, we need blobs of code to implement the evaluation logic for each kind of expression we can parse. We could stuff that code into the syntax tree classes in something like an `interpret()` method. In effect, we could tell each syntax tree node, "Interpret thyself". This is the Gang of Four's Interpreter design pattern. It's a neat pattern, but like I mentioned earlier, it gets messy if we jam all sorts of logic into the tree classes.

Instead, we're going to reuse our groovy Visitor pattern. In the previous chapter, we created an AstPrinter class. It took in a syntax tree and recursively traversed it, building up a string which it ultimately returned. That's almost exactly what a real interpreter does, except instead of concatenating strings, it computes values.

We start with a new class.

```
package com.craftinginterpreters.lox;

class Interpreter implements Expr.Visitor<Object> {
}
```

lox/Interpreter.java
*create new file*

The class declares that it's a visitor. The return type of the visit methods will be Object, the root class that we use to refer to a Lox value in our Java code. To satisfy the Visitor interface, we need to define visit methods for each of the four expression tree classes our parser produces. We'll start with the simplest...

### 7.2.1  Evaluating literals

The leaves of an expression tree—the atomic bits of syntax that all other expressions are composed of—are literals. Literals are almost values already, but the distinction is important. A literal is a *bit of syntax* that produces a value. A literal always appears somewhere in the user's source code. Lots of values are produced by computation and don't exist anywhere in the code itself. Those aren't literals. A literal comes from the parser's domain. Values are an interpreter concept, part of the runtime's world.

In the next chapter, when we implement variables, we'll add identifier expressions, which are also leaf nodes.

So, much like we converted a literal *token* into a literal *syntax tree node* in the parser, now we convert the literal tree node into a runtime value. That turns out to be trivial.

```
  @Override
  public Object visitLiteralExpr(Expr.Literal expr) {
    return expr.value;
  }
```

lox/Interpreter.java
*in class* Interpreter

We eagerly produced the runtime value way back during scanning and stuffed it in the token. The parser took that value and stuck it in the literal tree node, so to evaluate a literal, we simply pull it back out.

### 7.2.2  Evaluating parentheses

The next simplest node to evaluate is grouping—the node you get as a result of using explicit parentheses in an expression.

lox/Interpreter.java
*in class* Interpreter

```
@Override
public Object visitGroupingExpr(Expr.Grouping expr) {
    return evaluate(expr.expression);
}
```

Some parsers don't define tree nodes for parentheses. Instead, when parsing a parenthesized expression, they simply return the node for the inner expression. We do create a node for parentheses in Lox because we'll need it later to correctly handle the left-hand sides of assignment expressions.

A grouping node has a reference to an inner node for the expression contained inside the parentheses. To evaluate the grouping expression itself, we recursively evaluate that subexpression and return it.

We rely on this helper method which simply sends the expression back into the interpreter's visitor implementation:

lox/Interpreter.java
*in class* Interpreter

```
private Object evaluate(Expr expr) {
    return expr.accept(this);
}
```

### 7.2.3  Evaluating unary expressions

Like grouping, unary expressions have a single subexpression that we must evaluate first. The difference is that the unary expression itself does a little work afterwards.

lox/Interpreter.java
*add after* visitLiteralExpr()

```
@Override
public Object visitUnaryExpr(Expr.Unary expr) {
    Object right = evaluate(expr.right);

    switch (expr.operator.type) {
      case MINUS:
        return -(double)right;
    }

    // Unreachable.
    return null;
}
```

First, we evaluate the operand expression. Then we apply the unary operator itself to the result of that. There are two different unary expressions, identified by the type of the operator token.

Shown here is -, which negates the result of the subexpression. The subexpression must be a number. Since we don't *statically* know that in Java, we cast it before performing the operation. This type cast happens at runtime when the - is evaluated. That's the core of what makes a language dynamically typed right there.

You're probably wondering what happens if the cast fails. Fear not, we'll get into that soon.

You can start to see how evaluation recursively traverses the tree. We can't evaluate the unary operator itself until after we evaluate its operand subexpression. That means our interpreter is doing a **post-order traversal**—each node evaluates its children before doing its own work.

The other unary operator is logical not.

```
switch (expr.operator.type) {
  case BANG:
    return !isTruthy(right);
  case MINUS:
```

lox/Interpreter.java
*in* visitUnaryExpr()

The implementation is simple, but what is this "truthy" thing about? We need to make a little side trip to one of the great questions of Western philosophy: *What is truth?*

## 7.2.4  Truthiness and falsiness

OK, maybe we're not going to really get into the universal question, but at least inside the world of Lox, we need to decide what happens when you use something other than true or false in a logic operation like ! or any other place where a Boolean is expected.

We *could* just say it's an error because we don't roll with implicit conversions, but most dynamically typed languages aren't that ascetic. Instead, they take the universe of values of all types and partition them into two sets, one of which they define to be "true", or "truthful", or (my favorite) "truthy", and the rest which are "false" or "falsey". This partitioning is somewhat arbitrary and gets weird in a few languages.

Lox follows Ruby's simple rule: false and nil are falsey, and everything else is truthy. We implement that like so:

In JavaScript, strings are truthy, but empty strings are not. Arrays are truthy but empty arrays are…also truthy. The number 0 is falsey, but the *string* "0" is truthy.

In Python, empty strings are falsey like in JS, but other empty sequences are falsey too.

In PHP, both the number 0 and the string "0" are falsey. Most other non-empty strings are truthy.

Get all that?

```
private boolean isTruthy(Object object) {
  if (object == null) return false;
  if (object instanceof Boolean) return (boolean)object;
  return true;
}
```

lox/Interpreter.java
*add after* visitUnaryExpr()

## 7.2.5  Evaluating binary operators

On to the last expression tree class, binary operators. There's a handful of them, and we'll start with the arithmetic ones.

```
@Override
public Object visitBinaryExpr(Expr.Binary expr) {
  Object left = evaluate(expr.left);
  Object right = evaluate(expr.right);

  switch (expr.operator.type) {
    case MINUS:
      return (double)left - (double)right;
    case SLASH:
```

lox/Interpreter.java
*add after* evaluate()

*continued on next page…*

...from previous page

Did you notice we pinned down a subtle corner of the language semantics here? In a binary expression, we evaluate the operands in left-to-right order. If those operands have side effects, that choice is user visible, so this isn't simply an implementation detail.

If we want our two interpreters to be consistent (hint: we do), we'll need to make sure clox does the same thing.

```
        return (double)left / (double)right;
      case STAR:
        return (double)left * (double)right;
    }

    // Unreachable.
    return null;
  }
```

I think you can figure out what's going on here. The main difference from the unary negation operator is that we have two operands to evaluate.

I left out one arithmetic operator because it's a little special.

*lox/Interpreter.java*
*in* visitBinaryExpr()

```
    switch (expr.operator.type) {
      case MINUS:
        return (double)left - (double)right;
      case PLUS:
        if (left instanceof Double && right instanceof Double) {
          return (double)left + (double)right;
        }

        if (left instanceof String && right instanceof String) {
          return (String)left + (String)right;
        }

        break;
      case SLASH:
```

We could have defined an operator specifically for string concatenation. That's what Perl (.), Lua (..), Smalltalk (,), Haskell (++), and others do.

I thought it would make Lox a little more approachable to use the same syntax as Java, JavaScript, Python, and others. This means that the + operator is **overloaded** to support both adding numbers and concatenating strings. Even in languages that don't use + for strings, they still often overload it for adding both integers and floating-point numbers.

The + operator can also be used to concatenate two strings. To handle that, we don't just assume the operands are a certain type and *cast* them, we dynamically *check* the type and choose the appropriate operation. This is why we need our object representation to support instanceof.

Next up are the comparison operators.

*lox/Interpreter.java*
*in* visitBinaryExpr()

```
    switch (expr.operator.type) {
      case GREATER:
        return (double)left > (double)right;
      case GREATER_EQUAL:
        return (double)left >= (double)right;
      case LESS:
        return (double)left < (double)right;
      case LESS_EQUAL:
        return (double)left <= (double)right;
      case MINUS:
```

They are basically the same as arithmetic. The only difference is that where the arithmetic operators produce a value whose type is the same as the operands (numbers or strings), the comparison operators always produce a Boolean.

The last pair of operators are equality.

*lox/Interpreter.java*
*in* visitBinaryExpr()

```
      case BANG_EQUAL: return !isEqual(left, right);
      case EQUAL_EQUAL: return isEqual(left, right);
```

Unlike the comparison operators which require numbers, the equality operators support operands of any type, even mixed ones. You can't ask Lox if 3 is *less* than "three", but you can ask if it's *equal* to it.

Spoiler alert: it's not.

Like truthiness, the equality logic is hoisted out into a separate method.

```
private boolean isEqual(Object a, Object b) {
  if (a == null && b == null) return true;
  if (a == null) return false;

  return a.equals(b);
}
```

**lox/Interpreter.java**
*add after* isTruthy()

This is one of those corners where the details of how we represent Lox objects in terms of Java matter. We need to correctly implement *Lox's* notion of equality, which may be different from Java's.

What do you expect this to evaluate to:

```
(0 / 0) == (0 / 0)
```

Fortunately, the two are pretty similar. Lox doesn't do implicit conversions in equality and Java does not either. We do have to handle nil/null specially so that we don't throw a NullPointerException if we try to call equals() on null. Otherwise, we're fine. Java's equals() method on Boolean, Double, and String have the behavior we want for Lox.

And that's it! That's all the code we need to correctly interpret a valid Lox expression. But what about an *invalid* one? In particular, what happens when a subexpression evaluates to an object of the wrong type for the operation being performed?

According to IEEE 754, which specifies the behavior of double-precision numbers, dividing a zero by zero gives you the special **NaN** ("not a number") value. Strangely enough, NaN is *not* equal to itself.

In Java, the == operator on primitive doubles preserves that behavior, but the equals() method on the Double class does not. Lox uses the latter, so doesn't follow IEEE. These kinds of subtle incompatibilities occupy a dismaying fraction of language implementers' lives.

## 7.3  Runtime Errors

I was cavalier about jamming casts in whenever a subexpression produces an Object and the operator requires it to be a number or a string. Those casts can fail. Even though the user's code is erroneous, if we want to make a usable language, we are responsible for handling that error gracefully.

It's time for us to talk about **runtime errors**. I spilled a lot of ink in the previous chapters talking about error handling, but those were all *syntax* or *static* errors. Those are detected and reported before *any* code is executed. Runtime errors are failures that the language semantics demand we detect and report while the program is running (hence the name).

Right now, if an operand is the wrong type for the operation being performed, the Java cast will fail and the JVM will throw a ClassCastException. That unwinds the whole stack and exits the application, vomiting a Java stack trace onto the user. That's probably not what we want. The fact that Lox is implemented in Java should be a detail hidden from the user. Instead, we want them to understand that a *Lox* runtime error occurred, and give them an error message relevant to our language and their program.

The Java behavior does have one thing going for it, though. It correctly stops executing any code when the error occurs. Let's say the user enters some expression like:

We could simply not detect or report a type error at all. This is what C does if you cast a pointer to some type that doesn't match the data that is actually being pointed to. C gains flexibility and speed by allowing that, but is also famously dangerous. Once you misinterpret bits in memory, all bets are off.

Few modern languages accept unsafe operations like that. Instead, most are **memory safe** and ensure—through a combination of static and runtime checks—that a program can never incorrectly interpret the value stored in a piece of memory.

```
2 * (3 / -"muffin")
```

I don't know, man, *can* you negate a muffin?

You can't negate a muffin, so we need to report a runtime error at that inner –expression. That in turn means we can't evaluate the / expression since it has no meaningful right operand. Likewise for the ⋆. So when a runtime error occurs deep in some expression, we need to escape all the way out.

We could print a runtime error and then abort the process and exit the application entirely. That has a certain melodramatic flair. Sort of the programming language interpreter equivalent of a mic drop.

Tempting as that is, we should probably do something a little less cataclysmic. While a runtime error needs to stop evaluating the *expression*, it shouldn't kill the *interpreter*. If a user is running the REPL and has a typo in a line of code, they should still be able to keep the session going and enter more code after that.

### 7.3.1  Detecting runtime errors

Our tree-walk interpreter evaluates nested expressions using recursive method calls, and we need to unwind out of all of those. Throwing an exception in Java is a fine way to accomplish that. However, instead of using Java's own cast failure, we'll define a Lox-specific one so that we can handle it how we want.

Before we do the cast, we check the object's type ourselves. So, for unary –, we add:

*lox/Interpreter.java*
*in* visitUnaryExpr()

```
        case MINUS:
            checkNumberOperand(expr.operator, right);
            return -(double)right;
```

The code to check the operand is:

*lox/Interpreter.java*
*add after* visitUnaryExpr()

```
  private void checkNumberOperand(Token operator, Object operand) {
    if (operand instanceof Double) return;
    throw new RuntimeError(operator, "Operand must be a number.");
  }
```

When the check fails, it throws one of these:

*lox/RuntimeError.java*
*create new file*

```
package com.craftinginterpreters.lox;

class RuntimeError extends RuntimeException {
  final Token token;

  RuntimeError(Token token, String message) {
    super(message);
    this.token = token;
  }
}
```

I admit the name "RuntimeError" is confusing since Java defines a RuntimeException class. An annoying thing about building interpreters is your names often collide with ones already taken by the implementation language. Just wait until we support Lox classes.

Unlike the Java cast exception, our class tracks the token that identifies where in the user's code the runtime error came from. As with static errors, this helps the user know where to fix their code.

We need similar checking for the binary operators. Since I promised you every single line of code needed to implement the interpreters, I'll run through them all.

Greater than:

```
case GREATER:
  checkNumberOperands(expr.operator, left, right);
  return (double)left > (double)right;
```
lox/Interpreter.java
*in* visitBinaryExpr()

Greater than or equal to:

```
case GREATER_EQUAL:
  checkNumberOperands(expr.operator, left, right);
  return (double)left >= (double)right;
```
lox/Interpreter.java
*in* visitBinaryExpr()

Less than:

```
case LESS:
  checkNumberOperands(expr.operator, left, right);
  return (double)left < (double)right;
```
lox/Interpreter.java
*in* visitBinaryExpr()

Less than or equal to:

```
case LESS_EQUAL:
  checkNumberOperands(expr.operator, left, right);
  return (double)left <= (double)right;
```
lox/Interpreter.java
*in* visitBinaryExpr()

Subtraction:

```
case MINUS:
  checkNumberOperands(expr.operator, left, right);
  return (double)left - (double)right;
```
lox/Interpreter.java
*in* visitBinaryExpr()

Division:

```
case SLASH:
  checkNumberOperands(expr.operator, left, right);
  return (double)left / (double)right;
```
lox/Interpreter.java
*in* visitBinaryExpr()

Multiplication:

```
case STAR:
  checkNumberOperands(expr.operator, left, right);
  return (double)left * (double)right;
```
lox/Interpreter.java
*in* visitBinaryExpr()

All of those rely on this validator, which is virtually the same as the unary one:

```
private void checkNumberOperands(Token operator,
                                 Object left, Object right) {
  if (left instanceof Double && right instanceof Double) return;

  throw new RuntimeError(operator, "Operands must be numbers.");
}
```
lox/Interpreter.java
*add after* checkNumberOperand()

The last remaining operator, again the odd one out, is addition. Since + is overloaded for numbers and strings, it already has code to check the types. All we need to do is fail if neither of the two success cases match.

lox/Interpreter.java
*in* visitBinaryExpr()
*replace 1 line*

```
        return (String)left + (String)right;
    }

    throw new RuntimeError(expr.operator,
        "Operands must be two numbers or two strings.");
  case SLASH:
```

*Another subtle semantic choice: We evaluate* both *operands before checking the type of* either. *Imagine we have a function* **say**() *that prints its argument then returns it. Using that, we write:*

```
say("left") - say("right");
```

*Our interpreter prints "left" and "right" before reporting the runtime error. We could have instead specified that the left operand is checked before even evaluating the right.*

That gets us detecting runtime errors deep in the innards of the evaluator. The errors are getting thrown. The next step is to write the code that catches them. For that, we need to wire up the Interpreter class into the main Lox class that drives it.

## 7.4 Hooking Up the Interpreter

The visit methods are sort of the guts of the Interpreter class, where the real work happens. We need to wrap a skin around them to interface with the rest of the program. The Interpreter's public API is simply one method.

lox/Interpreter.java
*in class* Interpreter

```
void interpret(Expr expression) {
  try {
    Object value = evaluate(expression);
    System.out.println(stringify(value));
  } catch (RuntimeError error) {
    Lox.runtimeError(error);
  }
}
```

This takes in a syntax tree for an expression and evaluates it. If that succeeds, evaluate() returns an object for the result value. interpret() converts that to a string and shows it to the user. To convert a Lox value to a string, we rely on:

lox/Interpreter.java
*add after* isEqual()

```
private String stringify(Object object) {
  if (object == null) return "nil";

  if (object instanceof Double) {
    String text = object.toString();
    if (text.endsWith(".0")) {
      text = text.substring(0, text.length() - 2);
    }
    return text;
  }

  return object.toString();
}
```

This is another of those pieces of code like isTruthy() that crosses the membrane between the user's view of Lox objects and their internal representation in Java.

It's pretty straightforward. Since Lox was designed to be familiar to someone coming from Java, things like Booleans look the same in both languages. The two edge cases are nil, which we represent using Java's null, and numbers.

Lox uses double-precision numbers even for integer values. In that case, they should print without a decimal point. Since Java has both floating point and integer types, it wants you to know which one you're using. It tells you by adding an explicit .0 to integer-valued doubles. We don't care about that, so we hack it off the end.

### 7.4.1  Reporting runtime errors

If a runtime error is thrown while evaluating the expression, interpret() catches it. This lets us report the error to the user and then gracefully continue. All of our existing error reporting code lives in the Lox class, so we put this method there too:

```
static void runtimeError(RuntimeError error) {
  System.err.println(error.getMessage() +
      "\n[line " + error.token.line + "]");
  hadRuntimeError = true;
}
```

*lox/Lox.java*
*add after* error()

We use the token associated with the RuntimeError to tell the user what line of code was executing when the error occurred. Even better would be to give the user an entire call stack to show how they *got* to be executing that code. But we don't have function calls yet, so I guess we don't have to worry about it.

After showing the error, runtimeError() sets this field:

```
static boolean hadError = false;
static boolean hadRuntimeError = false;

public static void main(String[] args) throws IOException {
```

*lox/Lox.java*
*in class* Lox

That field plays a small but important role.

```
    run(new String(bytes, Charset.defaultCharset()));

    // Indicate an error in the exit code.
    if (hadError) System.exit(65);
    if (hadRuntimeError) System.exit(70);
  }
```

*lox/Lox.java*
*in* runFile()

If the user is running a Lox script from a file and a runtime error occurs, we set an exit code when the process quits to let the calling process know. Not everyone cares about shell etiquette, but we do.

### 7.4.2  Running the interpreter

Now that we have an interpreter, the Lox class can start using it.

Yet again, we take care of this edge case with numbers to ensure that jlox and clox work the same. Handling weird corners of the language like this will drive you crazy but is an important part of the job.

Users rely on these details—either deliberately or inadvertently—and if the implementations aren't consistent, their program will break when they run it on different interpreters.

If the user is running the REPL, we don't care about tracking runtime errors. After they are reported, we simply loop around and let them input new code and keep going.

**lox/Lox.java**
*in class* Lox

```java
public class Lox {
  private static final Interpreter interpreter = new Interpreter();
  static boolean hadError = false;
```

We make the field static so that successive calls to `run()` inside a REPL session reuse the same interpreter. That doesn't make a difference now, but it will later when the interpreter stores global variables. Those variables should persist throughout the REPL session.

Finally, we remove the line of temporary code from the last chapter for printing the syntax tree and replace it with this:

**lox/Lox.java**
*in* run()
*replace 1 line*

```java
    // Stop if there was a syntax error.
    if (hadError) return;

    interpreter.interpret(expression);
  }
```

We have an entire language pipeline now: scanning, parsing, and execution. Congratulations, you now have your very own arithmetic calculator.

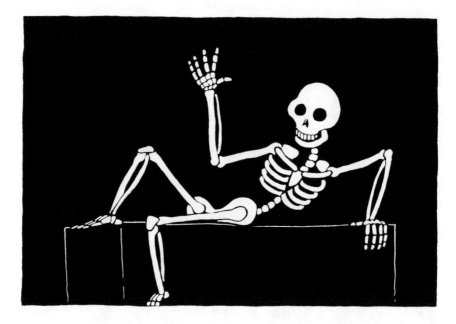

As you can see, the interpreter is pretty bare bones. But the Interpreter class and the Visitor pattern we've set up today form the skeleton that later chapters will stuff full of interesting guts—variables, functions, etc. Right now, the interpreter doesn't do very much, but it's alive!

## CHALLENGES

1. Allowing comparisons on types other than numbers could be useful. The operators might have a reasonable interpretation for strings. Even comparisons among mixed types, like 3 < "pancake" could be handy to enable things like ordered collections of heterogeneous types. Or it could simply lead to bugs and confusion.

   Would you extend Lox to support comparing other types? If so, which pairs of types do you allow and how do you define their ordering? Justify your choices and compare them to other languages.

2. Many languages define + such that if *either* operand is a string, the other is converted to a string and the results are then concatenated. For example, "scone" + 4 would yield scone4. Extend the code in `visitBinaryExpr()` to support that.

3. What happens right now if you divide a number by zero? What do you think should happen? Justify your choice. How do other languages you know handle division by zero, and why do they make the choices they do?

   Change the implementation in `visitBinaryExpr()` to detect and report a runtime error for this case.

## DESIGN NOTE: STATIC AND DYNAMIC TYPING

Some languages, like Java, are statically typed which means type errors are detected and reported at compile time before any code is run. Others, like Lox, are dynamically typed and defer checking for type errors until runtime right before an operation is attempted. We tend to consider this a black-and-white choice, but there is actually a continuum between them.

It turns out even most statically typed languages do *some* type checks at runtime. The type system checks most type rules statically, but inserts runtime checks in the generated code for other operations.

For example, in Java, the *static* type system assumes a cast expression will always safely succeed. After you cast some value, you can statically treat it as the destination type and not get any compile errors. But downcasts can fail, obviously. The only reason the static checker can presume that casts always succeed without violating the language's soundness guarantees, is because the cast is checked *at runtime* and throws an exception on failure.

A more subtle example is covariant arrays in Java and C#. The static subtyping rules for arrays allow operations that are not sound. Consider:

```
Object[] stuff = new Integer[1];
stuff[0] = "not an int!";
```

This code compiles without any errors. The first line upcasts the Integer array and stores it in a variable of type Object array. The second line stores a string in one of its cells. The Object array type statically allows that—strings *are* Objects—but the actual Integer array that **stuff** refers to at runtime should never have a string in it! To avoid that catastrophe, when you store a value in an array, the JVM does a *runtime* check to make sure it's an allowed type. If not, it throws an ArrayStoreException.

Java could have avoided the need to check this at runtime by disallowing the cast on the first line. It could make arrays *invariant* such that an array of Integers is *not* an array of Objects. That's statically sound, but it prohibits common and safe patterns of code that only read from arrays. Covariance is safe if you never *write* to the array. Those patterns were particularly important for usability in Java 1.0 before it supported generics. James Gosling and the other Java designers traded off a little static safety and performance—those array store checks take time—in return for some flexibility.

There are few modern statically typed languages that don't make that trade-off *somewhere*. Even Haskell will let you run code with non-exhaustive matches. If you find yourself designing a statically typed language, keep in mind that you can sometimes give users more flexibility without sacrificing *too* many of the benefits of static safety by deferring some type checks until runtime.

On the other hand, a key reason users choose statically typed languages is because of the confidence the language gives them that certain kinds of errors can *never* occur when their program is run. Defer too many type checks until runtime, and you erode that confidence.

# Statements and State

8

*"All my life, my heart has yearned for a thing I cannot name."*

— André Breton, *Mad Love*

The interpreter we have so far feels less like programming a real language and more like punching buttons on a calculator. "Programming" to me means building up a system out of smaller pieces. We can't do that yet because we have no way to bind a name to some data or function. We can't compose software without a way to refer to the pieces.

To support bindings, our interpreter needs internal state. When you define a variable at the beginning of the program and use it at the end, the interpreter has to hold on to the value of that variable in the meantime. So in this chapter, we will give our interpreter a brain that can not just process, but *remember*.

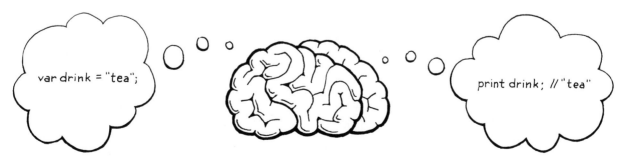

You could make a language that treats variable declarations as expressions that both create a binding and produce a value. The only language I know that does that is Tcl. Scheme seems like a contender, but note that after a `let` expression is evaluated, the variable it bound is forgotten. The `define` syntax is not an expression.

State and statements go hand in hand. Since statements, by definition, don't evaluate to a value, they need to do something else to be useful. That something is called a **side effect**. It could mean producing user-visible output or modifying some state in the interpreter that can be detected later. The latter makes them a great fit for defining variables or other named entities.

In this chapter, we'll do all of that. We'll define statements that produce output (`print`) and create state (`var`). We'll add expressions to access and assign to variables. Finally, we'll add blocks and local scope. That's a lot to stuff into one chapter, but we'll chew through it all one bite at a time.

## 8.1  Statements

We start by extending Lox's grammar with statements. They aren't very different from expressions. We start with the two simplest kinds:

1. An **expression statement** lets you place an expression where a statement is expected. They exist to evaluate expressions that have side effects. You may not notice them, but you use them all the time in C, Java, and other languages. Any time you see a function or method call followed by a `;`, you're looking at an expression statement.

Pascal is an outlier. It distinguishes between *procedures* and *functions*. Functions return values, but procedures cannot. There is a statement form for calling a procedure, but functions can only be called where an expression is expected. There are no expression statements in Pascal.

2. A `print` **statement** evaluates an expression and displays the result to the user. I admit it's weird to bake printing right into the language instead of making it a library function. Doing so is a concession to the fact that we're building this interpreter one chapter at a time and want to be able to play with it before it's all done. To make print a library function, we'd have to wait until we had all of the machinery for defining and calling functions before we could witness any side effects.

I will note with only a modicum of defensiveness that BASIC and Python have dedicated `print` statements and they are real languages. Granted, Python did remove their `print` statement in 3.0…

New syntax means new grammar rules. In this chapter, we finally gain the ability to parse an entire Lox script. Since Lox is imperative and dynamically typed, the "top level" of a script is simply a list of statements. The new rules are:

```
program        → statement* EOF ;

statement      → exprStmt
               | printStmt ;

exprStmt       → expression ";" ;
printStmt      → "print" expression ";" ;
```

The first rule is now `program`, which is the starting point for the grammar and represents a complete Lox script or REPL entry. A program is a list of statements followed by the special "end of file" token. The mandatory end token ensures the parser consumes the entire input and doesn't silently ignore erroneous unconsumed tokens at the end of a script.

Right now, `statement` only has two cases for the two kinds of statements we've described. We'll fill in more later in this chapter and in the following ones. The next step is turning this grammar into something we can store in memory — syntax trees.

## 8.1.1  Statement syntax trees

There is no place in the grammar where both an expression and a statement are allowed. The operands of, say, + are always expressions, never statements. The body of a `while` loop is always a statement.

Since the two syntaxes are disjoint, we don't need a single base class that they all inherit from. Splitting expressions and statements into separate class hierarchies enables the Java compiler to help us find dumb mistakes like passing a statement to a Java method that expects an expression.

That means a new base class for statements. As our elders did before us, we will use the cryptic name "Stmt". With great foresight, I have designed our little AST metaprogramming script in anticipation of this. That's why we passed in "Expr" as a parameter to `defineAst()`. Now we add another call to define Stmt and its subclasses.

Not really foresight: I wrote all the code for the book before I sliced it into chapters.

```
    "Unary    : Token operator, Expr right"
  ));

  defineAst(outputDir, "Stmt", Arrays.asList(
    "Expression : Expr expression",
    "Print      : Expr expression"
  ));
}
```

tool/GenerateAst.java
*in* main()

Run the AST generator script and behold the resulting "Stmt.java" file with the syntax tree classes we need for expression and `print` statements. Don't forget to add the file to your IDE project or makefile or whatever.

## 8.1.2  Parsing statements

The parser's `parse()` method that parses and returns a single expression was a temporary hack to get the last chapter up and running. Now that our grammar has the correct starting rule, `program`, we can turn `parse()` into the real deal.

```
List<Stmt> parse() {
  List<Stmt> statements = new ArrayList<>();
  while (!isAtEnd()) {
    statements.add(statement());
  }

  return statements;
}
```

lox/Parser.java
*method* parse()
*replace 7 lines*

What about the code we had in here for catching **ParseError** exceptions? We'll put better parse error handling in place soon when we add support for additional statement types.

This parses a series of statements, as many as it can find until it hits the end of the input. This is a pretty direct translation of the `program` rule into recursive descent style. We must also chant a minor prayer to the Java verbosity gods since we are using ArrayList now.

lox/Parser.java

```
package com.craftinginterpreters.lox;

import java.util.ArrayList;
import java.util.List;
```

A program is a list of statements, and we parse one of those statements using this method:

lox/Parser.java<br>add after expression()

```
private Stmt statement() {
  if (match(PRINT)) return printStatement();

  return expressionStatement();
}
```

A little bare bones, but we'll fill it in with more statement types later. We determine which specific statement rule is matched by looking at the current token. A print token means it's obviously a print statement.

If the next token doesn't look like any known kind of statement, we assume it must be an expression statement. That's the typical final fallthrough case when parsing a statement, since it's hard to proactively recognize an expression from its first token.

Each statement kind gets its own method. First print:

lox/Parser.java<br>add after statement()

```
private Stmt printStatement() {
  Expr value = expression();
  consume(SEMICOLON, "Expect ';' after value.");
  return new Stmt.Print(value);
}
```

Since we already matched and consumed the print token itself, we don't need to do that here. We parse the subsequent expression, consume the terminating semicolon, and emit the syntax tree.

If we didn't match a print statement, we must have one of these:

lox/Parser.java<br>add after printStatement()

```
private Stmt expressionStatement() {
  Expr expr = expression();
  consume(SEMICOLON, "Expect ';' after expression.");
  return new Stmt.Expression(expr);
}
```

Similar to the previous method, we parse an expression followed by a semicolon. We wrap that Expr in a Stmt of the right type and return it.

### 8.1.3  Executing statements

We're running through the previous couple of chapters in microcosm, working our way through the front end. Our parser can now produce statement syntax trees, so the next and final step is to interpret them. As in expressions, we use the Visitor pattern, but we have a new visitor interface, Stmt.Visitor, to implement since statements have their own base class.

We add that to the list of interfaces Interpreter implements.

```
class Interpreter implements Expr.Visitor<Object>,
                             Stmt.Visitor<Void> {
  void interpret(Expr expression) {
```

lox/Interpreter.java
*replace 1 line*

Java doesn't let you use lowercase "void"
as a generic type argument for obscure
reasons having to do with type erasure
and the stack. Instead, there is a separate
"Void" type specifically for this use. Sort
of a "boxed void", like "Integer" is for "int".

Unlike expressions, statements produce no values, so the return type of the visit methods is Void, not Object. We have two statement types, and we need a visit method for each. The easiest is expression statements.

lox/Interpreter.java
*add after* evaluate()

```
  @Override
  public Void visitExpressionStmt(Stmt.Expression stmt) {
    evaluate(stmt.expression);
    return null;
  }
```

We evaluate the inner expression using our existing `evaluate()` method and discard the value. Then we return `null`. Java requires that to satisfy the special capitalized Void return type. Weird, but what can you do?

The `print` statement's visit method isn't much different.

Appropriately enough, we discard the
value returned by evaluate() by
placing that call inside a *Java* expression
statement.

lox/Interpreter.java
*add after* visitExpressionStmt()

```
  @Override
  public Void visitPrintStmt(Stmt.Print stmt) {
    Object value = evaluate(stmt.expression);
    System.out.println(stringify(value));
    return null;
  }
```

Before discarding the expression's value, we convert it to a string using the `stringify()` method we introduced in the last chapter and then dump it to stdout.

Our interpreter is able to visit statements now, but we have some work to do to feed them to it. First, modify the old `interpret()` method in the Interpreter class to accept a list of statements—in other words, a program.

lox/Interpreter.java
*method* interpret()
*replace 8 lines*

```
  void interpret(List<Stmt> statements) {
    try {
      for (Stmt statement : statements) {
        execute(statement);
      }
    } catch (RuntimeError error) {
      Lox.runtimeError(error);
    }
  }
```

This replaces the old code which took a single expression. The new code relies on this tiny helper method:

lox/Interpreter.java
*add after* evaluate()

```
  private void execute(Stmt stmt) {
    stmt.accept(this);
  }
```

That's the statement analogue to the `evaluate()` method we have for expressions. Since we're working with lists now, we need to let Java know.

lox/Interpreter.java

```
package com.craftinginterpreters.lox;

import java.util.List;

class Interpreter implements Expr.Visitor<Object>,
```

The main Lox class is still trying to parse a single expression and pass it to the interpreter. We fix the parsing line like so:

lox/Lox.java
*in* run()
*replace 1 line*

```
    Parser parser = new Parser(tokens);
    List<Stmt> statements = parser.parse();

    // Stop if there was a syntax error.
```

And then replace the call to the interpreter with this:

lox/Lox.java
*in* run()
*replace 1 line*

```
    if (hadError) return;

    interpreter.interpret(statements);
  }
```

Basically just plumbing the new syntax through. OK, fire up the interpreter and give it a try. At this point, it's worth sketching out a little Lox program in a text file to run as a script. Something like:

```
print "one";
print true;
print 2 + 1;
```

It almost looks like a real program! Note that the REPL, too, now requires you to enter a statement instead of a simple expression. Don't forget your semicolons.

## 8.2  Global Variables

Now that we have statements, we can start working on state. Before we get into all of the complexity of lexical scoping, we'll start off with the easiest kind of variables—globals. We need two new constructs.

Global state gets a bad rap. Sure, lots of global state—especially *mutable* state—makes it hard to maintain large programs. It's good software engineering to minimize how much you use.

But when you're slapping together a simple programming language or, heck, even learning your first language, the flat simplicity of global variables helps. My first language was BASIC and, though I outgrew it eventually, it was nice that I didn't have to wrap my head around scoping rules before I could make a computer do fun stuff.

1. A **variable declaration** statement brings a new variable into the world.

   ```
   var beverage = "espresso";
   ```

   This creates a new binding that associates a name (here "beverage") with a value (here, the string "espresso").

2. Once that's done, a **variable expression** accesses that binding. When the identifier "beverage" is used as an expression, it looks up the value bound to that name and returns it.

   ```
   print beverage; // "espresso".
   ```

Later, we'll add assignment and block scope, but that's enough to get moving.

## 8.2.1 Variable syntax

As before, we'll work through the implementation from front to back, starting with the syntax. Variable declarations are statements, but they are different from other statements, and we're going to split the statement grammar in two to handle them. That's because the grammar restricts where some kinds of statements are allowed.

The clauses in control flow statements—think the then and else branches of an if statement or the body of a while—are each a single statement. But that statement is not allowed to be one that declares a name. This is OK:

```
if (monday) print "Ugh, already?";
```

But this is not:

```
if (monday) var beverage = "espresso";
```

We *could* allow the latter, but it's confusing. What is the scope of that beverage variable? Does it persist after the if statement? If so, what is its value on days other than Monday? Does the variable exist at all on those days?

Code like this is weird, so C, Java, and friends all disallow it. It's as if there are two levels of "precedence" for statements. Some places where a statement is allowed—like inside a block or at the top level—allow any kind of statement, including declarations. Others allow only the "higher" precedence statements that don't declare names.

To accommodate the distinction, we add another rule for kinds of statements that declare names.

> In this analogy, block statements work sort of like parentheses do for expressions. A block is itself in the "higher" precedence level and can be used anywhere, like in the clauses of an if statement. But the statements it *contains* can be lower precedence. You're allowed to declare variables and other names inside the block. The curlies let you escape back into the full statement grammar from a place where only some statements are allowed.

```
program        → declaration* EOF ;

declaration    → varDecl
               | statement ;

statement      → exprStmt
               | printStmt ;
```

Declaration statements go under the new declaration rule. Right now, it's only variables, but later it will include functions and classes. Any place where a declaration is allowed also allows non-declaring statements, so the declaration rule falls through to statement. Obviously, you can declare stuff at the top level of a script, so program routes to the new rule.

The rule for declaring a variable looks like:

```
varDecl        → "var" IDENTIFIER ( "=" expression )? ";" ;
```

Like most statements, it starts with a leading keyword. In this case, var. Then an identifier token for the name of the variable being declared, followed by an optional initializer expression. Finally, we put a bow on it with the semicolon.

To access a variable, we define a new kind of primary expression.

```
primary        → "true" | "false" | "nil"
               | NUMBER | STRING
               | "(" expression ")"
               | IDENTIFIER ;
```

That IDENTIFIER clause matches a single identifier token, which is understood to be the name of the variable being accessed.

These new grammar rules get their corresponding syntax trees. Over in the AST generator, we add a new statement node for a variable declaration.

**tool/GenerateAst.java**
*in main()*
*add "," to previous line*

```
      "Expression : Expr expression",
      "Var        : Token name, Expr initializer"
    ));
```

It stores the name token so we know what it's declaring, along with the initializer expression. (If there isn't an initializer, that field is null.)

Then we add an expression node for accessing a variable.

**tool/GenerateAst.java**
*in main()*
*add "," to previous line*

```
      "Literal  : Object value",
      "Variable : Token name"
    ));
```

It's simply a wrapper around the token for the variable name. That's it. As always, don't forget to run the AST generator script so that you get updated "Expr.java" and "Stmt.java" files.

### 8.2.2  Parsing variables

Before we parse variable statements, we need to shift around some code to make room for the new declaration rule in the grammar. The top level of a program is now a list of declarations, so the entrypoint method to the parser changes.

**lox/Parser.java**
*in parse()*
*replace 1 line*

```
List<Stmt> parse() {
  List<Stmt> statements = new ArrayList<>();
  while (!isAtEnd()) {
    statements.add(declaration());
  }
  return statements;
}
```

That calls this new method:

**lox/Parser.java**
*add after expression()*

```
  private Stmt declaration() {
    try {
      if (match(VAR)) return varDeclaration();
      return statement();
    } catch (ParseError error) {
      synchronize();
      return null;
    }
  }
```

Hey, do you remember way back in that earlier chapter when we put the infra-structure in place to do error recovery? We are finally ready to hook that up.

This declaration() method is the method we call repeatedly when parsing a series of statements in a block or a script, so it's the right place to synchro-nize when the parser goes into panic mode. The whole body of this method is wrapped in a try block to catch the exception thrown when the parser begins error recovery. This gets it back to trying to parse the beginning of the next statement or declaration.

The real parsing happens inside the try block. First, it looks to see if we're at a variable declaration by looking for the leading var keyword. If not, it falls through to the existing statement() method that parses print and expres-sion statements.

Remember how statement() tries to parse an expression statement if no other statement matches? And expression() reports a syntax error if it can't parse an expression at the current token? That chain of calls ensures we report an error if a valid declaration or statement isn't parsed.

When the parser matches a var token, it branches to:

```
private Stmt varDeclaration() {
  Token name = consume(IDENTIFIER, "Expect variable name.");

  Expr initializer = null;
  if (match(EQUAL)) {
    initializer = expression();
  }

  consume(SEMICOLON, "Expect ';' after variable declaration.");
  return new Stmt.Var(name, initializer);
}
```

lox/Parser.java
*add after* printStatement()

As always, the recursive descent code follows the grammar rule. The parser has already matched the var token, so next it requires and consumes an identifier token for the variable name.

Then, if it sees an = token, it knows there is an initializer expression and pars-es it. Otherwise, it leaves the initializer null. Finally, it consumes the required semicolon at the end of the statement. All this gets wrapped in a Stmt.Var syntax tree node and we're groovy.

Parsing a variable expression is even easier. In primary(), we look for an identifier token.

```
    return new Expr.Literal(previous().literal);
  }

  if (match(IDENTIFIER)) {
    return new Expr.Variable(previous());
  }

  if (match(LEFT_PAREN)) {
```

lox/Parser.java
*in* primary()

That gives us a working front end for declaring and using variables. All that's left is to feed it into the interpreter. Before we get to that, we need to talk about where variables live in memory.

## 8.3 Environments

The bindings that associate variables to values need to be stored somewhere. Ever since the Lisp folks invented parentheses, this data structure has been called an **environment**.

I like to imagine the environment literally, as a sylvan wonderland where variables and values frolic.

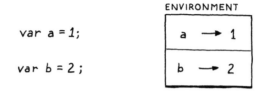

ENVIRONMENT

```
var a = 1;          a  ⟶  1

var b = 2;          b  ⟶  2
```

Java calls them **maps** or **hashmaps**. Other languages call them **hash tables**, **dictionaries** (Python and C#), **hashes** (Ruby and Perl), **tables** (Lua), or **associative arrays** (PHP). Way back when, they were known as **scatter tables**.

You can think of it like a map where the keys are variable names and the values are the variable's, uh, values. In fact, that's how we'll implement it in Java. We could stuff that map and the code to manage it right into Interpreter, but since it forms a nicely delineated concept, we'll pull it out into its own class.

Start a new file and add:

lox/Environment.java
*create new file*

```java
package com.craftinginterpreters.lox;

import java.util.HashMap;
import java.util.Map;

class Environment {
  private final Map<String, Object> values = new HashMap<>();
}
```

There's a Java Map in there to store the bindings. It uses bare strings for the keys, not tokens. A token represents a unit of code at a specific place in the source text, but when it comes to looking up variables, all identifier tokens with the same name should refer to the same variable (ignoring scope for now). Using the raw string ensures all of those tokens refer to the same map key.

There are two operations we need to support. First, a variable definition binds a new name to a value.

lox/Environment.java
*in class* Environment

```java
  void define(String name, Object value) {
    values.put(name, value);
  }
```

Not exactly brain surgery, but we have made one interesting semantic choice. When we add the key to the map, we don't check to see if it's already present. That means that this program works:

```
var a = "before";
print a; // "before".
var a = "after";
print a; // "after".
```

A variable statement doesn't just define a *new* variable, it can also be used to *re*define an existing variable. We could choose to make this an error instead. The user may not intend to redefine an existing variable. (If they did mean to, they probably would have used assignment, not `var`.) Making redefinition an error would help them find that bug.

However, doing so interacts poorly with the REPL. In the middle of a REPL session, it's nice to not have to mentally track which variables you've already defined. We could allow redefinition in the REPL but not in scripts, but then users would have to learn two sets of rules, and code copied and pasted from one form to the other might not work.

So, to keep the two modes consistent, we'll allow it—at least for global variables. Once a variable exists, we need a way to look it up.

My rule about variables and scoping is, "When in doubt, do what Scheme does". The Scheme folks have probably spent more time thinking about variable scope than we ever will—one of the main goals of Scheme was to introduce lexical scoping to the world—so it's hard to go wrong if you follow in their footsteps.

Scheme allows redefining variables at the top level.

```
class Environment {
  private final Map<String, Object> values = new HashMap<>();

  Object get(Token name) {
    if (values.containsKey(name.lexeme)) {
      return values.get(name.lexeme);
    }

    throw new RuntimeError(name,
        "Undefined variable '" + name.lexeme + "'.");
  }
}
```

**lox/Environment.java**
*in class* Environment

This is a little more semantically interesting. If the variable is found, it simply returns the value bound to it. But what if it's not? Again, we have a choice:

- Make it a syntax error.

- Make it a runtime error.

- Allow it and return some default value like `nil`.

Lox is pretty lax, but the last option is a little *too* permissive to me. Making it a syntax error—a compile-time error—seems like a smart choice. Using an undefined variable is a bug, and the sooner you detect the mistake, the better.

The problem is that *using* a variable isn't the same as *referring* to it. You can refer to a variable in a chunk of code without immediately evaluating it if that chunk of code is wrapped inside a function. If we make it a static error to *mention* a variable before it's been declared, it becomes much harder to define recursive functions.

We could accommodate single recursion—a function that calls itself—by declaring the function's own name before we examine its body. But that doesn't help with mutually recursive procedures that call each other. Consider:

```
fun isOdd(n) {
  if (n == 0) return false;
  return isEven(n - 1);
}

fun isEven(n) {
  if (n == 0) return true;
  return isOdd(n - 1);
}
```

Granted, this is probably not the most efficient way to tell if a number is even or odd (not to mention the bad things that happen if you pass a non-integer or negative number to them). Bear with me.

Some statically typed languages like Java and C# solve this by specifying that the top level of a program isn't a sequence of imperative statements. Instead, a program is a set of declarations which all come into being simultaneously. The implementation declares *all* of the names before looking at the bodies of *any* of the functions.

Older languages like C and Pascal don't work like this. Instead, they force you to add explicit *forward declarations* to declare a name before it's fully defined. That was a concession to the limited computing power at the time. They wanted to be able to compile a source file in one single pass through the text, so those compilers couldn't gather up all of the declarations first before processing function bodies.

The `isEven()` function isn't defined by the time we are looking at the body of `isOdd()` where it's called. If we swap the order of the two functions, then `isOdd()` isn't defined when we're looking at `isEven()`'s body.

Since making it a *static* error makes recursive declarations too difficult, we'll defer the error to runtime. It's OK to refer to a variable before it's defined as long as you don't *evaluate* the reference. That lets the program for even and odd numbers work, but you'd get a runtime error in:

```
print a;
var a = "too late!";
```

As with type errors in the expression evaluation code, we report a runtime error by throwing an exception. The exception contains the variable's token so we can tell the user where in their code they messed up.

### 8.3.1 Interpreting global variables

The Interpreter class gets an instance of the new Environment class.

*lox/Interpreter.java*
*in class* Interpreter

```
class Interpreter implements Expr.Visitor<Object>,
                             Stmt.Visitor<Void> {
  private Environment environment = new Environment();

  void interpret(List<Stmt> statements) {
```

We store it as a field directly in Interpreter so that the variables stay in memory as long as the interpreter is still running.

We have two new syntax trees, so that's two new visit methods. The first is for declaration statements.

*lox/Interpreter.java*
*add after* visitPrintStmt()

```
@Override
public Void visitVarStmt(Stmt.Var stmt) {
  Object value = null;
  if (stmt.initializer != null) {
    value = evaluate(stmt.initializer);
  }

  environment.define(stmt.name.lexeme, value);
  return null;
}
```

If the variable has an initializer, we evaluate it. If not, we have another choice to make. We could have made this a syntax error in the parser by *requiring* an initializer. Most languages don't, though, so it feels a little harsh to do so in Lox.

We could make it a runtime error. We'd let you define an uninitialized variable, but if you accessed it before assigning to it, a runtime error would occur. It's not a bad idea, but most dynamically typed languages don't do that. Instead, we'll keep it simple and say that Lox sets a variable to nil if it isn't explicitly initialized.

```
var a;
print a; // "nil".
```

Thus, if there isn't an initializer, we set the value to `null`, which is the Java representation of Lox's `nil` value. Then we tell the environment to bind the variable to that value.

Next, we evaluate a variable expression.

```
@Override
public Object visitVariableExpr(Expr.Variable expr) {
  return environment.get(expr.name);
}
```

lox/Interpreter.java
*add after* visitUnaryExpr()

This simply forwards to the environment which does the heavy lifting to make sure the variable is defined. With that, we've got rudimentary variables working. Try this out:

```
var a = 1;
var b = 2;
print a + b;
```

We can't reuse *code* yet, but we can start to build up programs that reuse *data*.

# 8.4 Assignment

It's possible to create a language that has variables but does not let you reassign—or **mutate**—them. Haskell is one example. SML supports only mutable references and arrays—variables cannot be reassigned. Rust steers you away from mutation by requiring a `mut` modifier to enable assignment.

Mutating a variable is a side effect and, as the name suggests, some language folks think side effects are dirty or inelegant. Code should be pure math that produces values—crystalline, unchanging ones—like an act of divine creation. Not some grubby automaton that beats blobs of data into shape, one imperative grunt at a time.

Lox is not so austere. Lox is an imperative language, and mutation comes with the territory. Adding support for assignment doesn't require much work. Global variables already support redefinition, so most of the machinery is there now. Mainly, we're missing an explicit assignment notation.

I find it delightful that the same group of people who pride themselves on dispassionate logic are also the ones who can't resist emotionally loaded terms for their work: "pure", "side effect", "lazy", "persistent", "first-class", "higher-order".

## 8.4.1 Assignment syntax

That little = syntax is more complex than it might seem. Like most C-derived languages, assignment is an expression and not a statement. As in C, it is the lowest precedence expression form. That means the rule slots between `expression` and `equality` (the next lowest precedence expression).

In some other languages, like Pascal, Python, and Go, assignment is a statement.

```
expression    → assignment ;
assignment    → IDENTIFIER "=" assignment
              | equality ;
```

This says an `assignment` is either an identifier followed by an = and an expression for the value, or an `equality` (and thus any other) expression. Later, `assignment` will get more complex when we add property setters on objects, like:

```
instance.field = "value";
```

The easy part is adding the new syntax tree node.

tool/GenerateAst.java
*in* main()

```
defineAst(outputDir, "Expr", Arrays.asList(
  "Assign   : Token name, Expr value",
  "Binary   : Expr left, Token operator, Expr right",
```

It has a token for the variable being assigned to, and an expression for the new value. After you run the AstGenerator to get the new Expr.Assign class, swap out the body of the parser's existing `expression()` method to match the updated rule.

lox/Parser.java
*in* expression()
*replace 1 line*

```
private Expr expression() {
  return assignment();
}
```

Here is where it gets tricky. A single token lookahead recursive descent parser can't see far enough to tell that it's parsing an assignment until *after* it has gone through the left-hand side and stumbled onto the =. You might wonder why it even needs to. After all, we don't know we're parsing a + expression until after we've finished parsing the left operand.

The difference is that the left-hand side of an assignment isn't an expression that evaluates to a value. It's a sort of pseudo-expression that evaluates to a "thing" you can assign to. Consider:

```
var a = "before";
a = "value";
```

On the second line, we don't *evaluate* a (which would return the string "before"). We figure out what variable a refers to so we know where to store the right-hand side expression's value. The classic terms for these two constructs are **l-value** and **r-value**. All of the expressions that we've seen so far that produce values are r-values. An l-value "evaluates" to a storage location that you can assign into.

We want the syntax tree to reflect that an l-value isn't evaluated like a normal expression. That's why the Expr.Assign node has a *Token* for the left-hand side, not an Expr. The problem is that the parser doesn't know it's parsing an l-value until it hits the =. In a complex l-value, that may occur many tokens later.

```
makeList().head.next = node;
```

We have only a single token of lookahead, so what do we do? We use a little trick, and it looks like this:

In fact, the names come from assignment expressions: *l*-values appear on the *left* side of the = in an assignment, and *r*-values on the *right*.

Since the receiver of a field assignment can be any expression, and expressions can be as long as you want to make them, it may take an *unbounded* number of tokens of lookahead to find the =.

```
  private Expr assignment() {
    Expr expr = equality();

    if (match(EQUAL)) {
      Token equals = previous();
      Expr value = assignment();

      if (expr instanceof Expr.Variable) {
        Token name = ((Expr.Variable)expr).name;
        return new Expr.Assign(name, value);
      }

      error(equals, "Invalid assignment target.");
    }

    return expr;
  }
```

lox/Parser.java
*add after* expressionStatement()

We *report* an error if the left-hand side isn't a valid assignment target, but we don't *throw* it because the parser isn't in a confused state where we need to go into panic mode and synchronize.

Most of the code for parsing an assignment expression looks similar to that of the other binary operators like +. We parse the left-hand side, which can be any expression of higher precedence. If we find an =, we parse the right-hand side and then wrap it all up in an assignment expression tree node.

One slight difference from binary operators is that we don't loop to build up a sequence of the same operator. Since assignment is right-associative, we instead recursively call `assignment()` to parse the right-hand side.

The trick is that right before we create the assignment expression node, we look at the left-hand side expression and figure out what kind of assignment target it is. We convert the r-value expression node into an l-value representation.

This conversion works because it turns out that every valid assignment target happens to also be valid syntax as a normal expression. Consider a complex field assignment like:

```
newPoint(x + 2, 0).y = 3;
```

The left-hand side of that assignment could also work as a valid expression.

```
newPoint(x + 2, 0).y;
```

The first example sets the field, the second gets it.

This means we can parse the left-hand side *as if it were* an expression and then after the fact produce a syntax tree that turns it into an assignment target. If the left-hand side expression isn't a valid assignment target, we fail with a syntax error. That ensures we report an error on code like this:

```
a + b = c;
```

Right now, the only valid target is a simple variable expression, but we'll add fields later. The end result of this trick is an assignment expression tree node that knows what it is assigning to and has an expression subtree for the value being assigned. All with only a single token of lookahead and no backtracking.

You can still use this trick even if there are assignment targets that are not valid expressions. Define a **cover grammar**, a looser grammar that accepts all of the valid expression *and* assignment target syntaxes. When you hit an =, report an error if the left-hand side isn't within the valid assignment target grammar. Conversely, if you *don't* hit an =, report an error if the left-hand side isn't a valid *expression*.

Way back in the parsing chapter, I said we represent parenthesized expressions in the syntax tree because we'll need them later. This is why. We need to be able to distinguish these cases:

```
a = 3;   // OK.
(a) = 3; // Error.
```

### 8.4.2  Assignment semantics

We have a new syntax tree node, so our interpreter gets a new visit method.

*lox/Interpreter.java*
*add after* visitVarStmt()

```java
@Override
public Object visitAssignExpr(Expr.Assign expr) {
  Object value = evaluate(expr.value);
  environment.assign(expr.name, value);
  return value;
}
```

For obvious reasons, it's similar to variable declaration. It evaluates the right-hand side to get the value, then stores it in the named variable. Instead of using **define()** on Environment, it calls this new method:

*lox/Environment.java*
*add after* get()

```java
void assign(Token name, Object value) {
  if (values.containsKey(name.lexeme)) {
    values.put(name.lexeme, value);
    return;
  }

  throw new RuntimeError(name,
      "Undefined variable '" + name.lexeme + "'.");
}
```

Unlike Python and Ruby, Lox doesn't do implicit variable declaration.

The key difference between assignment and definition is that assignment is not allowed to create a *new* variable. In terms of our implementation, that means it's a runtime error if the key doesn't already exist in the environment's variable map.

The last thing the **visit()** method does is return the assigned value. That's because assignment is an expression that can be nested inside other expressions, like so:

```
var a = 1;
print a = 2; // "2".
```

Maybe a little better than that. Unlike some old BASICs, Lox can handle variable names longer than two characters.

Our interpreter can now create, read, and modify variables. It's about as sophisticated as early BASICs. Global variables are simple, but writing a large program when any two chunks of code can accidentally step on each other's state is no fun. We want *local* variables, which means it's time for *scope*.

## 8.5  Scope

A **scope** defines a region where a name maps to a certain entity. Multiple scopes enable the same name to refer to different things in different contexts. In my house, "Bob" usually refers to me. But maybe in your town you know a different Bob. Same name, but different dudes based on where you say it.

**Lexical scope** (or the less commonly heard **static scope**) is a specific style of scoping where the text of the program itself shows where a scope begins and ends. In Lox, as in most modern languages, variables are lexically scoped. When you see an expression that uses some variable, you can figure out which variable declaration it refers to just by statically reading the code.

For example:

```
{
  var a = "first";
  print a; // "first".
}


{
  var a = "second";
  print a; // "second".
}
```

Here, we have two blocks with a variable a declared in each of them. You and I can tell just from looking at the code that the use of a in the first print statement refers to the first a, and the second one refers to the second.

This is in contrast to **dynamic scope** where you don't know what a name refers to until you execute the code. Lox doesn't have dynamically scoped *variables*, but methods and fields on objects are dynamically scoped.

```
class Saxophone {
  play() {
    print "Careless Whisper";
  }
}

class GolfClub {
  play() {
    print "Fore!";
  }
}

fun playIt(thing) {
  thing.play();
}
```

When playIt() calls thing.play(), we don't know if we're about to hear "Careless Whisper" or "Fore!" It depends on whether you pass a Saxophone or a GolfClub to the function, and we don't know that until runtime.

Scope and environments are close cousins. The former is the theoretical concept, and the latter is the machinery that implements it. As our interpreter works its way through code, syntax tree nodes that affect scope will change the environment. In a C-ish syntax like Lox's, scope is controlled by curly-braced blocks. (That's why we call it **block scope**.)

"Lexical" comes from the Greek "lexikos" which means "related to words". When we use it in programming languages, it usually means a thing you can figure out from source code itself without having to execute anything.

Lexical scope came onto the scene with ALGOL. Earlier languages were often dynamically scoped. Computer scientists back then believed dynamic scope was faster to execute. Today, thanks to early Scheme hackers, we know that isn't true. If anything, it's the opposite.

Dynamic scope for variables lives on in some corners. Emacs Lisp defaults to dynamic scope for variables. The binding macro in Clojure provides it. The widely disliked with statement in JavaScript turns properties on an object into dynamically scoped variables.

```
{
  var a = "in block";
}
print a; // Error! No more "a".
```

The beginning of a block introduces a new local scope, and that scope ends when execution passes the closing }. Any variables declared inside the block disappear.

### 8.5.1  Nesting and shadowing

A first cut at implementing block scope might work like this:

1. As we visit each statement inside the block, keep track of any variables declared.

2. After the last statement is executed, tell the environment to delete all of those variables.

That would work for the previous example. But remember, one motivation for local scope is encapsulation—a block of code in one corner of the program shouldn't interfere with some other block. Check this out:

```
// How loud?
var volume = 11;

// Silence.
volume = 0;

// Calculate size of 3x4x5 cuboid.
{
  var volume = 3 * 4 * 5;
  print volume;
}
```

Look at the block where we calculate the volume of the cuboid using a local declaration of volume. After the block exits, the interpreter will delete the *global* volume variable. That ain't right. When we exit the block, we should remove any variables declared inside the block, but if there is a variable with the same name declared outside of the block, *that's a different variable*. It shouldn't get touched.

When a local variable has the same name as a variable in an enclosing scope, it **shadows** the outer one. Code inside the block can't see it any more—it is hidden in the "shadow" cast by the inner one—but it's still there.

When we enter a new block scope, we need to preserve variables defined in outer scopes so they are still around when we exit the inner block. We do that by defining a fresh environment for each block containing only the variables defined in that scope. When we exit the block, we discard its environment and restore the previous one.

We also need to handle enclosing variables that are *not* shadowed.

```
var global = "outside";
{
  var local = "inside";
  print global + local;
}
```

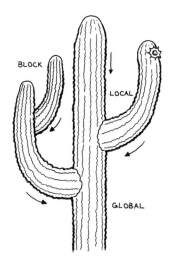

Here, `global` lives in the outer global environment and `local` is defined inside the block's environment. In that `print` statement, both of those variables are in scope. In order to find them, the interpreter must search not only the current innermost environment, but also any enclosing ones.

We implement this by chaining the environments together. Each environment has a reference to the environment of the immediately enclosing scope. When we look up a variable, we walk that chain from innermost out until we find the variable. Starting at the inner scope is how we make local variables shadow outer ones.

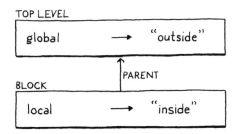

While the interpreter is running, the environments form a linear list of objects, but consider the full set of environments created during the entire execution. An outer scope may have multiple blocks nested within it, and each will point to the outer one, giving a tree-like structure, though only one path through the tree exists at a time.

The boring name for this is a **parent-pointer tree**, but I much prefer the evocative **cactus stack**.

Before we add block syntax to the grammar, we'll beef up our Environment class with support for this nesting. First, we give each environment a reference to its enclosing one.

```
class Environment {
  final Environment enclosing;
  private final Map<String, Object> values = new HashMap<>();
```

lox/Environment.java
*in class* Environment

This field needs to be initialized, so we add a couple of constructors.

```
  Environment() {
    enclosing = null;
  }

  Environment(Environment enclosing) {
    this.enclosing = enclosing;
  }
```

lox/Environment.java
*in class* Environment

The no-argument constructor is for the global scope's environment, which ends the chain. The other constructor creates a new local scope nested inside the given outer one.

We don't have to touch the `define()` method—a new variable is always declared in the current innermost scope. But variable lookup and assignment work with existing variables and they need to walk the chain to find them. First, lookup:

lox/Environment.java
*in* get()

```
        return values.get(name.lexeme);
    }

    if (enclosing != null) return enclosing.get(name);

    throw new RuntimeError(name,
        "Undefined variable '" + name.lexeme + "'.");
```

If the variable isn't found in this environment, we simply try the enclosing one. That in turn does the same thing recursively, so this will ultimately walk the entire chain. If we reach an environment with no enclosing one and still don't find the variable, then we give up and report an error as before.

Assignment works the same way.

It's likely faster to iteratively walk the chain, but I think the recursive solution is prettier. We'll do something *much* faster in clox.

lox/Environment.java
*in* assign()

```
        values.put(name.lexeme, value);
        return;
    }

    if (enclosing != null) {
      enclosing.assign(name, value);
      return;
    }

    throw new RuntimeError(name,
```

Again, if the variable isn't in this environment, it checks the outer one, recursively.

## 8.5.2 Block syntax and semantics

Now that Environments nest, we're ready to add blocks to the language. Behold the grammar:

```
statement       → exprStmt
                | printStmt
                | block ;

block           → "{" declaration* "}" ;
```

A block is a (possibly empty) series of statements or declarations surrounded by curly braces. A block is itself a statement and can appear anywhere a statement is allowed. The syntax tree node looks like this:

tool/GenerateAst.java
*in* main()

```
defineAst(outputDir, "Stmt", Arrays.asList(
  "Block      : List<Stmt> statements",
  "Expression : Expr expression",
```

As always, don't forget to run "GenerateAst.java".

It contains the list of statements that are inside the block. Parsing is straightforward. Like other statements, we detect the beginning of a block by its leading token—in this case the {. In the statement() method, we add:

```
   if (match(PRINT)) return printStatement();
   if (match(LEFT_BRACE)) return new Stmt.Block(block());

   return expressionStatement();
```

lox/Parser.java
*in* statement()

All the real work happens here:

```
private List<Stmt> block() {
  List<Stmt> statements = new ArrayList<>();

  while (!check(RIGHT_BRACE) && !isAtEnd()) {
    statements.add(declaration());
  }

  consume(RIGHT_BRACE, "Expect '}' after block.");
  return statements;
}
```

lox/Parser.java
*add after* expressionStatement()

We create an empty list and then parse statements and add them to the list until we reach the end of the block, marked by the closing }. Note that the loop also has an explicit check for `isAtEnd()`. We have to be careful to avoid infinite loops, even when parsing invalid code. If the user forgets a closing }, the parser needs to not get stuck.

That's it for syntax. For semantics, we add another visit method to Interpreter.

Having block() return the raw list of statements and leaving it to statement() to wrap the list in a Stmt.Block looks a little odd. I did it that way because we'll reuse block() later for parsing function bodies and we don't want that body wrapped in a Stmt.Block.

```
@Override
public Void visitBlockStmt(Stmt.Block stmt) {
  executeBlock(stmt.statements, new Environment(environment));
  return null;
}
```

lox/Interpreter.java
*add after* execute()

To execute a block, we create a new environment for the block's scope and pass it off to this other method:

```
void executeBlock(List<Stmt> statements,
                  Environment environment) {
  Environment previous = this.environment;
  try {
    this.environment = environment;

    for (Stmt statement : statements) {
      execute(statement);
    }
  } finally {
    this.environment = previous;
  }
}
```

lox/Interpreter.java
*add after* execute()

Manually changing and restoring a mutable environment field feels inelegant. Another classic approach is to explicitly pass the environment as a parameter to each visit method. To "change" the environment, you pass a different one as you recurse down the tree. You don't have to restore the old one, since the new one lives on the Java stack and is implicitly discarded when the interpreter returns from the block's visit method.

I considered that for jlox, but it's kind of tedious and verbose adding an environment parameter to every single visit method. To keep the book a little simpler, I went with the mutable field.

This new method executes a list of statements in the context of a given environment. Up until now, the `environment` field in Interpreter always pointed to the same environment—the global one. Now, that field represents the *current* environment. That's the environment that corresponds to the innermost scope containing the code to be executed.

To execute code within a given scope, this method updates the interpreter's `environment` field, visits all of the statements, and then restores the previous value. As is always good practice in Java, it restores the previous environment using a finally clause. That way it gets restored even if an exception is thrown.

Surprisingly, that's all we need to do in order to fully support local variables, nesting, and shadowing. Go ahead and try this out:

```
var a = "global a";
var b = "global b";
var c = "global c";
{
  var a = "outer a";
  var b = "outer b";
  {
    var a = "inner a";
    print a;
    print b;
    print c;
  }
  print a;
  print b;
  print c;
}
print a;
print b;
print c;
```

Our little interpreter can remember things now. We are inching closer to something resembling a full-featured programming language.

## CHALLENGES

1. The REPL no longer supports entering a single expression and automatically printing its result value. That's a drag. Add support to the REPL to let users type in both statements and expressions. If they enter a statement, execute it. If they enter an expression, evaluate it and display the result value.

2. Maybe you want Lox to be a little more explicit about variable initialization. Instead of implicitly initializing variables to `nil`, make it a runtime error to access a variable that has not been initialized or assigned to, as in:

```
// No initializers.
var a;
var b;

a = "assigned";
print a; // OK, was assigned first.

print b; // Error!
```

3. What does the following program do?

```
var a = 1;
{
  var a = a + 2;
  print a;
}
```

What did you *expect* it to do? Is it what you think it should do? What does analogous code in other languages you are familiar with do? What do you think users will expect this to do?

## DESIGN NOTE: IMPLICIT VARIABLE DECLARATION

Lox has distinct syntax for declaring a new variable and assigning to an existing one. Some languages collapse those to only assignment syntax. Assigning to a non-existent variable automatically brings it into being. This is called **implicit variable declaration** and exists in Python, Ruby, and CoffeeScript, among others. JavaScript has an explicit syntax to declare variables, but can also create new variables on assignment. Visual Basic has an option to enable or disable implicit variables.

When the same syntax can assign or create a variable, each language must decide what happens when it isn't clear about which behavior the user intends. In particular, each language must choose how implicit declaration interacts with shadowing, and which scope an implicitly declared variable goes into.

- In Python, assignment always creates a variable in the current function's scope, even if there is a variable with the same name declared outside of the function.

- Ruby avoids some ambiguity by having different naming rules for local and global variables. However, blocks in Ruby (which are more like closures than like "blocks" in C) have their own scope, so it still has the problem. Assignment in Ruby assigns to an existing variable outside of the current block if there is one with the same name. Otherwise, it creates a new variable in the current block's scope.

- CoffeeScript, which takes after Ruby in many ways, is similar. It explicitly disallows shadowing by saying that assignment always assigns to a variable in an outer scope if there is one, all the way up to the outermost global scope. Otherwise, it creates the variable in the current function scope.

- In JavaScript, assignment modifies an existing variable in any enclosing scope, if found. If not, it implicitly creates a new variable in the *global* scope.

The main advantage to implicit declaration is simplicity. There's less syntax and no "declaration" concept to learn. Users can just start assigning stuff and the language figures it out.

Older, statically typed languages like C benefit from explicit declaration because they give the user a place to tell the compiler what type each variable has and how much storage to allocate for it. In a dynamically typed, garbage-collected language, that isn't really necessary, so you can get away with making declarations implicit. It feels a little more "scripty", more "you know what I mean".

But is that a good idea? Implicit declaration has some problems.

- A user may intend to assign to an existing variable, but may have misspelled it. The interpreter doesn't know that, so it goes ahead and silently creates some new variable and the variable the user wanted to assign to still has its old value. This is particularly heinous in JavaScript where a typo will create a *global* variable, which may in turn interfere with other code.

- JS, Ruby, and CoffeeScript use the presence of an existing variable with the same name—even in an outer scope—to determine whether or not an assignment creates a new variable or assigns to an existing one. That means adding a new variable in a surrounding scope can change the meaning of existing code. What was once a local variable may silently turn into an assignment to that new outer variable.

- In Python, you may *want* to assign to some variable outside of the current function instead of creating a new variable in the current one, but you can't.

Over time, the languages I know with implicit variable declaration ended up adding more features and complexity to deal with these problems.

- Implicit declaration of global variables in JavaScript is universally considered a mistake today. "Strict mode" disables it and makes it a compile error.

- Python added a `global` statement to let you explicitly assign to a global variable from within a function. Later, as functional programming and nested functions became more popular, they added a similar `nonlocal` statement to assign to variables in enclosing functions.

- Ruby extended its block syntax to allow declaring certain variables to be explicitly local to the block even if the same name exists in an outer scope.

Given those, I think the simplicity argument is mostly lost. There is an argument that implicit declaration is the right *default* but I personally find that less compelling.

My opinion is that implicit declaration made sense in years past when most scripting languages were heavily imperative and code was pretty flat. As programmers have gotten more comfortable with deep nesting, functional programming, and closures, it's become much more common to want access to variables in outer scopes. That makes it more likely that users will run into the tricky cases where it's not clear whether they intend their assignment to create a new variable or reuse a surrounding one.

So I prefer explicitly declaring variables, which is why Lox requires it.

# Control Flow

*"Logic, like whiskey, loses its beneficial effect when taken in too large quantities."*

— Edward John Moreton Drax Plunkett, Lord Dunsany

Compared to last chapter's grueling marathon, today is a lighthearted frolic through a daisy meadow. But while the work is easy, the reward is surprisingly large.

Right now, our interpreter is little more than a calculator. A Lox program can only do a fixed amount of work before completing. To make it run twice as long you have to make the source code twice as lengthy. We're about to fix that. In this chapter, our interpreter takes a big step towards the programming language major leagues: *Turing-completeness*.

# 9.1 Turing Machines (Briefly)

In the early part of last century, mathematicians stumbled into a series of confusing paradoxes that led them to doubt the stability of the foundation they had built their work upon. To address that crisis, they went back to square one. Starting from a handful of axioms, logic, and set theory, they hoped to rebuild mathematics on top of an impervious foundation.

The most famous is **Russell's paradox**. Initially, set theory allowed you to define any sort of set. If you could describe it in English, it was valid. Naturally, given mathematicians' predilection for self-reference, sets can contain other sets. So Russell, rascal that he was, came up with: *R is the set of all sets that do not contain themselves.*

Does R contain itself? If it doesn't, then according to the second half of the definition it should. But if it does, then it no longer meets the definition. Cue mind exploding.

They wanted to rigorously answer questions like, "Can all true statements be proven?", "Can we compute all functions that we can define?", or even the more general question, "What do we mean when we claim a function is 'computable'?"

They presumed the answer to the first two questions would be "yes". All that remained was to prove it. It turns out that the answer to both is "no", and astonishingly, the two questions are deeply intertwined. This is a fascinating corner of mathematics that touches fundamental questions about what brains are able to do and how the universe works. I can't do it justice here.

They proved the answer to the first question is "no" by showing that the function that returns the truth value of a given statement is *not* a computable one.

What I do want to note is that in the process of proving that the answer to the first two questions is "no", Alan Turing and Alonzo Church devised a precise answer to the last question—a definition of what kinds of functions are computable. They each crafted a tiny system with a minimum set of machinery that is still powerful enough to compute any of a (very) large class of functions.

Turing called his inventions "a-machines" for "automatic". He wasn't so self-aggrandizing as to put his *own* name on them. Later mathematicians did that for him. That's how you get famous while still retaining some modesty.

These are now considered the "computable functions". Turing's system is called a **Turing machine**. Church's is the **lambda calculus**. Both are still widely used as the basis for models of computation and, in fact, many modern functional programming languages use the lambda calculus at their core.

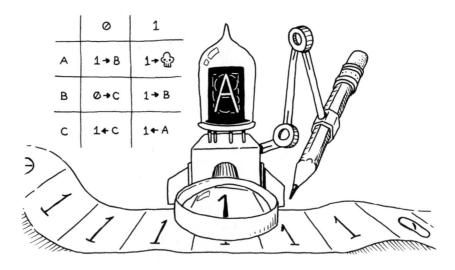

Turing machines have better name recognition—there's no Hollywood film about Alonzo Church yet—but the two formalisms are equivalent in power. In fact, any programming language with some minimal level of expressiveness is powerful enough to compute *any* computable function.

You can prove that by writing a simulator for a Turing machine in your language. Since Turing proved his machine can compute any computable function, by extension, that means your language can too. All you need to do is translate the function into a Turing machine, and then run that on your simulator.

If your language is expressive enough to do that, it's considered **Turing-complete**. Turing machines are pretty dang simple, so it doesn't take much power to do this. You basically need arithmetic, a little control flow, and the ability to allocate and use (theoretically) arbitrary amounts of memory. We've got the first. By the end of this chapter, we'll have the second.

We *almost* have the third too. You can create and concatenate strings of arbitrary size, so you can *store* unbounded memory. But we don't have any way to access parts of a string.

## 9.2 Conditional Execution

Enough history, let's jazz up our language. We can divide control flow roughly into two kinds:

- **Conditional** or **branching control flow** is used to *not* execute some piece of code. Imperatively, you can think of it as jumping *ahead* over a region of code.

- **Looping control flow** executes a chunk of code more than once. It jumps *back* so that you can do something again. Since you don't usually want *infinite* loops, it typically has some conditional logic to know when to stop looping as well.

Branching is simpler, so we'll start there. C-derived languages have two main conditional execution features, the if statement and the perspicaciously named "conditional" operator (?:). An if statement lets you conditionally execute statements and the conditional operator lets you conditionally execute expressions.

The conditional operator is also called the "ternary" operator because it's the only operator in C that takes three operands.

For simplicity's sake, Lox doesn't have a conditional operator, so let's get our if statement on. Our statement grammar gets a new production.

```
statement        → exprStmt
                 | ifStmt
                 | printStmt
                 | block ;

ifStmt           → "if" "(" expression ")" statement
                 ( "else" statement )? ;
```

The semicolons in the rules aren't quoted, which means they are part of the grammar metasyntax, not Lox's syntax. A block does not have a ; at the end and an if statement doesn't either, unless the then or else statement happens to be one that ends in a semicolon.

An if statement has an expression for the condition, then a statement to execute if the condition is truthy. Optionally, it may also have an else keyword and a statement to execute if the condition is falsey. The syntax tree node has fields for each of those three pieces.

```
    "Expression : Expr expression",
    "If         : Expr condition, Stmt thenBranch," +
                " Stmt elseBranch",
    "Print      : Expr expression",
```

**tool/GenerateAst.java**
*in* main()

Like other statements, the parser recognizes an if statement by the leading if keyword.

```
private Stmt statement() {
  if (match(IF)) return ifStatement();
  if (match(PRINT)) return printStatement();
```

**lox/Parser.java**
*in* statement()

When it finds one, it calls this new method to parse the rest:

lox/Parser.java
*add after* statement()

```java
private Stmt ifStatement() {
  consume(LEFT_PAREN, "Expect '(' after 'if'.");
  Expr condition = expression();
  consume(RIGHT_PAREN, "Expect ')' after if condition.");

  Stmt thenBranch = statement();
  Stmt elseBranch = null;
  if (match(ELSE)) {
    elseBranch = statement();
  }

  return new Stmt.If(condition, thenBranch, elseBranch);
}
```

The parentheses around the condition are only half useful. You need some kind of delimiter *between* the condition and the then statement, otherwise the parser can't tell when it has reached the end of the condition expression. But the *opening* parenthesis after if doesn't do anything useful. Dennis Ritchie put it there so he could use ) as the ending delimiter without having unbalanced parentheses.

Other languages like Lua and some BASICs use a keyword like **then** as the ending delimiter and don't have anything before the condition. Go and Swift instead require the statement to be a braced block. That lets them use the { at the beginning of the statement to tell when the condition is done.

As usual, the parsing code hews closely to the grammar. It detects an else clause by looking for the preceding else keyword. If there isn't one, the elseBranch field in the syntax tree is null.

That seemingly innocuous optional else has, in fact, opened up an ambiguity in our grammar. Consider:

```
if (first) if (second) whenTrue(); else whenFalse();
```

Here's the riddle: Which if statement does that else clause belong to? This isn't just a theoretical question about how we notate our grammar. It actually affects how the code executes:

- If we attach the else to the first if statement, then whenFalse() is called if first is falsey, regardless of what value second has.

- If we attach it to the second if statement, then whenFalse() is only called if first is truthy and second is falsey.

Since else clauses are optional, and there is no explicit delimiter marking the end of the if statement, the grammar is ambiguous when you nest ifs in this way. This classic pitfall of syntax is called the **dangling else** problem.

Here, formatting highlights the two ways the else could be parsed. But note that since whitespace characters are ignored by the parser, this is only a guide to the human reader.

```
if(first)                          if(first)
    if (second)                        if (second)
        whenTrue();                        whenTrue();
else                               else
    whenFalse();                       whenFalse();
```

It is possible to define a context-free grammar that avoids the ambiguity directly, but it requires splitting most of the statement rules into pairs, one that allows an if with an else and one that doesn't. It's annoying.

Instead, most languages and parsers avoid the problem in an ad hoc way. No matter what hack they use to get themselves out of the trouble, they always choose the same interpretation—the else is bound to the nearest if that precedes it.

Our parser conveniently does that already. Since ifStatement() eagerly looks for an else before returning, the innermost call to a nested series will claim the else clause for itself before returning to the outer if statements.

Syntax in hand, we are ready to interpret.

```
@Override
public Void visitIfStmt(Stmt.If stmt) {
  if (isTruthy(evaluate(stmt.condition))) {
    execute(stmt.thenBranch);
  } else if (stmt.elseBranch != null) {
    execute(stmt.elseBranch);
  }
  return null;
}
```

lox/Interpreter.java
*add after* visitExpressionStmt()

The interpreter implementation is a thin wrapper around the self-same Java code. It evaluates the condition. If truthy, it executes the then branch. Otherwise, if there is an else branch, it executes that.

If you compare this code to how the interpreter handles other syntax we've implemented, the part that makes control flow special is that Java if statement. Most other syntax trees always evaluate their subtrees. Here, we may not evaluate the then or else statement. If either of those has a side effect, the choice not to evaluate it becomes user visible.

## 9.3 Logical Operators

Since we don't have the conditional operator, you might think we're done with branching, but no. Even without the ternary operator, there are two other operators that are technically control flow constructs—the logical operators and and or.

These aren't like other binary operators because they **short-circuit**. If, after evaluating the left operand, we know what the result of the logical expression must be, we don't evaluate the right operand. For example:

```
false and sideEffect();
```

For an and expression to evaluate to something truthy, both operands must be truthy. We can see as soon as we evaluate the left false operand that that isn't going to be the case, so there's no need to evaluate sideEffect() and it gets skipped.

This is why we didn't implement the logical operators with the other binary operators. Now we're ready. The two new operators are low in the precedence table. Similar to || and && in C, they each have their own precedence with or lower than and. We slot them right between assignment and equality.

I've always wondered why they don't have the same precedence, like the various comparison or equality operators do.

```
expression     → assignment ;
assignment     → IDENTIFIER "=" assignment
               | logic_or ;
logic_or       → logic_and ( "or" logic_and )* ;
logic_and      → equality ( "and" equality )* ;
```

The *syntax* doesn't care that they
short-circuit. That's a semantic concern.

Instead of falling back to `equality`, `assignment` now cascades to `logic_or`. The two new rules, `logic_or` and `logic_and`, are similar to other binary operators. Then `logic_and` calls out to `equality` for its operands, and we chain back to the rest of the expression rules.

We could reuse the existing Expr.Binary class for these two new expressions since they have the same fields. But then `visitBinaryExpr()` would have to check to see if the operator is one of the logical operators and use a different code path to handle the short circuiting. I think it's cleaner to define a new class for these operators so that they get their own visit method.

tool/GenerateAst.java
*in* main()

```
"Literal  : Object value",
"Logical  : Expr left, Token operator, Expr right",
"Unary    : Token operator, Expr right",
```

To weave the new expressions into the parser, we first change the parsing code for assignment to call `or()`.

lox/Parser.java
*in* assignment()
*replace 1 line*

```
private Expr assignment() {
  Expr expr = or();

  if (match(EQUAL)) {
```

The code to parse a series of `or` expressions mirrors other binary operators.

lox/Parser.java
*add after* assignment()

```
private Expr or() {
  Expr expr = and();

  while (match(OR)) {
    Token operator = previous();
    Expr right = and();
    expr = new Expr.Logical(expr, operator, right);
  }

  return expr;
}
```

Its operands are the next higher level of precedence, the new `and` expression.

lox/Parser.java
*add after* or()

```
private Expr and() {
  Expr expr = equality();

  while (match(AND)) {
    Token operator = previous();
    Expr right = equality();
    expr = new Expr.Logical(expr, operator, right);
  }

  return expr;
}
```

That calls `equality()` for its operands, and with that, the expression parser is all tied back together again. We're ready to interpret.

```
@Override
public Object visitLogicalExpr(Expr.Logical expr) {
  Object left = evaluate(expr.left);

  if (expr.operator.type == TokenType.OR) {
    if (isTruthy(left)) return left;
  } else {
    if (!isTruthy(left)) return left;
  }

  return evaluate(expr.right);
}
```

lox/Interpreter.java
add after visitLiteralExpr()

If you compare this to the earlier chapter's visitBinaryExpr() method, you can see the difference. Here, we evaluate the left operand first. We look at its value to see if we can short-circuit. If not, and only then, do we evaluate the right operand.

The other interesting piece here is deciding what actual value to return. Since Lox is dynamically typed, we allow operands of any type and use truthiness to determine what each operand represents. We apply similar reasoning to the result. Instead of promising to literally return true or false, a logic operator merely guarantees it will return a value with appropriate truthiness.

Fortunately, we have values with proper truthiness right at hand—the results of the operands themselves. So we use those. For example:

```
print "hi" or 2; // "hi".
print nil or "yes"; // "yes".
```

On the first line, "hi" is truthy, so the or short-circuits and returns that. On the second line, nil is falsey, so it evaluates and returns the second operand, "yes".

That covers all of the branching primitives in Lox. We're ready to jump ahead to loops. You see what I did there? *Jump. Ahead.* Get it? See, it's like a reference to…oh, forget it.

## 9.4  While Loops

Lox features two looping control flow statements, while and for. The while loop is the simpler one, so we'll start there. Its grammar is the same as in C.

```
statement       → exprStmt
                | ifStmt
                | printStmt
                | whileStmt
                | block ;

whileStmt       → "while" "(" expression ")" statement ;
```

We add another clause to the statement rule that points to the new rule for while. It takes a while keyword, followed by a parenthesized condition expression, then a statement for the body. That new grammar rule gets a syntax tree node.

```
    "Print       : Expr expression",
    "While       : Expr condition, Stmt body"
));;
```

The node stores the condition and body. Here you can see why it's nice to have separate base classes for expressions and statements. The field declarations make it clear that the condition is an expression and the body is a statement.

Over in the parser, we follow the same process we used for if statements. First, we add another case in **statement()** to detect and match the leading keyword.

```
    if (match(PRINT)) return printStatement();
    if (match(WHILE)) return whileStatement();
    if (match(LEFT_BRACE)) return new Stmt.Block(block());
```

That delegates the real work to this method:

```
  private Stmt whileStatement() {
    consume(LEFT_PAREN, "Expect '(' after 'while'.");
    Expr condition = expression();
    consume(RIGHT_PAREN, "Expect ')' after condition.");
    Stmt body = statement();

    return new Stmt.While(condition, body);
  }
```

The grammar is dead simple and this is a straight translation of it to Java. Speaking of translating straight to Java, here's how we execute the new syntax:

```
  @Override
  public Void visitWhileStmt(Stmt.While stmt) {
    while (isTruthy(evaluate(stmt.condition))) {
      execute(stmt.body);
    }
    return null;
  }
```

Like the visit method for if, this visitor uses the corresponding Java feature. This method isn't complex, but it makes Lox much more powerful. We can finally write a program whose running time isn't strictly bound by the length of the source code.

## 9.5  For Loops

We're down to the last control flow construct, Ye Olde C-style for loop. I probably don't need to remind you, but it looks like this:

```
for (var i = 0; i < 10; i = i + 1) print i;
```

In grammarese, that's:

```
statement      → exprStmt
               | forStmt
               | ifStmt
               | printStmt
               | whileStmt
               | block ;

forStmt        → "for" "(" ( varDecl | exprStmt | ";" )
                 expression? ";"
                 expression? ")" statement ;
```

Inside the parentheses, you have three clauses separated by semicolons:

1. The first clause is the *initializer*. It is executed exactly once, before anything else. It's usually an expression, but for convenience, we also allow a variable declaration. In that case, the variable is scoped to the rest of the `for` loop— the other two clauses and the body.

2. Next is the *condition*. As in a `while` loop, this expression controls when to exit the loop. It's evaluated once at the beginning of each iteration, including the first. If the result is truthy, it executes the loop body. Otherwise, it bails.

3. The last clause is the *increment*. It's an arbitrary expression that does some work at the end of each loop iteration. The result of the expression is discarded, so it must have a side effect to be useful. In practice, it usually increments a variable.

Any of these clauses can be omitted. Following the closing parenthesis is a statement for the body, which is typically a block.

### 9.5.1 Desugaring

That's a lot of machinery, but note that none of it does anything you couldn't do with the statements we already have. If `for` loops didn't support initializer clauses, you could just put the initializer expression before the `for` statement. Without an increment clause, you could simply put the increment expression at the end of the body yourself.

In other words, Lox doesn't *need* `for` loops, they just make some common code patterns more pleasant to write. These kinds of features are called **syntactic sugar**. For example, the previous `for` loop could be rewritten like so:

```
{
  var i = 0;
  while (i < 10) {
    print i;
    i = i + 1;
  }
}
```

Most modern languages have a higher-level looping statement for iterating over arbitrary user-defined sequences. C# has `foreach`, Java has "enhanced for", even C++ has range-based `for` statements now. Those offer cleaner syntax than C's `for` statement by implicitly calling into an iteration protocol that the object being looped over supports.

I love those. For Lox, though, we're limited by building up the interpreter a chapter at a time. We don't have objects and methods yet, so we have no way of defining an iteration protocol that the `for` loop could use. So we'll stick with the old school C `for` loop. Think of it as "vintage". The fixie of control flow statements.

This delightful turn of phrase was coined by Peter J. Landin in 1964 to describe how some of the nice expression forms supported by languages like ALGOL were a sweetener sprinkled over the more fundamental—but presumably less palatable—lambda calculus underneath.

This script has the exact same semantics as the previous one, though it's not as easy on the eyes. Syntactic sugar features like Lox's `for` loop make a language more pleasant and productive to work in. But, especially in sophisticated language implementations, every language feature that requires back-end support and optimization is expensive.

Oh, how I wish the accepted term for this was "caramelization". Why introduce a metaphor if you aren't going to stick with it?

We can have our cake and eat it too by **desugaring**. That funny word describes a process where the front end takes code using syntax sugar and translates it to a more primitive form that the back end already knows how to execute.

We're going to desugar `for` loops to the `while` loops and other statements the interpreter already handles. In our simple interpreter, desugaring really doesn't save us much work, but it does give me an excuse to introduce you to the technique. So, unlike the previous statements, we *won't* add a new syntax tree node. Instead, we go straight to parsing. First, add an import we'll need soon.

**lox/Parser.java**

```
import java.util.ArrayList;
import java.util.Arrays;
import java.util.List;
```

Like every statement, we start parsing a `for` loop by matching its keyword.

**lox/Parser.java**
*in* `statement()`

```
private Stmt statement() {
  if (match(FOR)) return forStatement();
  if (match(IF)) return ifStatement();
```

Here is where it gets interesting. The desugaring is going to happen here, so we'll build this method a piece at a time, starting with the opening parenthesis before the clauses.

**lox/Parser.java**
*add after* `statement()`

```
private Stmt forStatement() {
  consume(LEFT_PAREN, "Expect '(' after 'for'.");

  // More here...
}
```

The first clause following that is the initializer.

**lox/Parser.java**
*in* `forStatement()`
*replace 1 line*

```
  consume(LEFT_PAREN, "Expect '(' after 'for'.");

  Stmt initializer;
  if (match(SEMICOLON)) {
    initializer = null;
  } else if (match(VAR)) {
    initializer = varDeclaration();
  } else {
    initializer = expressionStatement();
  }
}
```

In a previous chapter, I said we can split expression and statement syntax trees into two separate class hierarchies because there's no single place in the grammar that allows both an expression and a statement. That wasn't *entirely* true, I guess.

If the token following the ( is a semicolon then the initializer has been omitted. Otherwise, we check for a `var` keyword to see if it's a variable declaration. If neither of those matched, it must be an expression. We parse that and wrap it in an expression statement so that the initializer is always of type Stmt.

Next up is the condition.

```
    initializer = expressionStatement();
  }

  Expr condition = null;
  if (!check(SEMICOLON)) {
    condition = expression();
  }
  consume(SEMICOLON, "Expect ';' after loop condition.");
}
```

lox/Parser.java
in forStatement()

Again, we look for a semicolon to see if the clause has been omitted. The last clause is the increment.

```
  consume(SEMICOLON, "Expect ';' after loop condition.");

  Expr increment = null;
  if (!check(RIGHT_PAREN)) {
    increment = expression();
  }
  consume(RIGHT_PAREN, "Expect ')' after for clauses.");
}
```

lox/Parser.java
in forStatement()

It's similar to the condition clause except this one is terminated by the closing parenthesis. All that remains is the body.

Is it just me or does that sound morbid? "All that remained…was the *body*".

```
  consume(RIGHT_PAREN, "Expect ')' after for clauses.");
  Stmt body = statement();

  return body;
}
```

lox/Parser.java
in forStatement()

We've parsed all of the various pieces of the for loop and the resulting AST nodes are sitting in a handful of Java local variables. This is where the desugaring comes in. We take those and use them to synthesize syntax tree nodes that express the semantics of the for loop, like the hand-desugared example I showed you earlier.

The code is a little simpler if we work backward, so we start with the increment clause.

```
  Stmt body = statement();

  if (increment != null) {
    body = new Stmt.Block(
        Arrays.asList(
            body,
            new Stmt.Expression(increment)));
  }

  return body;
```

lox/Parser.java
in forStatement()

The increment, if there is one, executes after the body in each iteration of the loop. We do that by replacing the body with a little block that contains the original body followed by an expression statement that evaluates the increment.

lox/Parser.java
*in* forStatement()

```
    }

    if (condition == null) condition = new Expr.Literal(true);
    body = new Stmt.While(condition, body);

    return body;
```

Next, we take the condition and the body and build the loop using a primitive while loop. If the condition is omitted, we jam in true to make an infinite loop.

lox/Parser.java
*in* forStatement()

```
    body = new Stmt.While(condition, body);

    if (initializer != null) {
      body = new Stmt.Block(Arrays.asList(initializer, body));
    }

    return body;
```

Finally, if there is an initializer, it runs once before the entire loop. We do that by, again, replacing the whole statement with a block that runs the initializer and then executes the loop.

That's it. Our interpreter now supports C-style for loops and we didn't have to touch the Interpreter class at all. Since we desugared to nodes the interpreter already knows how to visit, there is no more work to do.

Finally, Lox is powerful enough to entertain us, at least for a few minutes. Here's a tiny program to print the first 21 elements in the Fibonacci sequence:

```
var a = 0;
var temp;

for (var b = 1; a < 10000; b = temp + b) {
  print a;
  temp = a;
  a = b;
}
```

## CHALLENGES

1. A few chapters from now, when Lox supports first-class functions and dynamic dispatch, we technically won't *need* branching statements built into the language. Show how conditional execution can be implemented in terms of those. Name a language that uses this technique for its control flow.

2. Likewise, looping can be implemented using those same tools, provided our interpreter supports an important optimization. What is it, and why is it necessary? Name a language that uses this technique for iteration.

3. Unlike Lox, most other C-style languages also support `break` and `continue` statements inside loops. Add support for `break` statements.

   The syntax is a `break` keyword followed by a semicolon. It should be a syntax error to have a `break` statement appear outside of any enclosing loop. At runtime, a `break` statement causes execution to jump to the end of the nearest enclosing loop and proceeds from there. Note that the `break` may be nested inside other blocks and `if` statements that also need to be exited.

## DESIGN NOTE: SPOONFULS OF SYNTACTIC SUGAR

When you design your own language, you choose how much syntactic sugar to pour into the grammar. Do you make an unsweetened health food where each semantic operation maps to a single syntactic unit, or some decadent dessert where every bit of behavior can be expressed ten different ways? Successful languages inhabit all points along this continuum.

On the extreme acrid end are those with ruthlessly minimal syntax like Lisp, Forth, and Smalltalk. Lispers famously claim their language "has no syntax", while Smalltalkers proudly show that you can fit the entire grammar on an index card. This tribe has the philosophy that the *language* doesn't need syntactic sugar. Instead, the minimal syntax and semantics it provides are powerful enough to let library code be as expressive as if it were part of the language itself.

Near these are languages like C, Lua, and Go. They aim for simplicity and clarity over minimalism. Some, like Go, deliberately eschew both syntactic sugar and the kind of syntactic extensibility of the previous category. They want the syntax to get out of the way of the semantics, so they focus on keeping both the grammar and libraries simple. Code should be obvious more than beautiful.

Somewhere in the middle you have languages like Java, C#, and Python. Eventually you reach Ruby, C++, Perl, and D—languages which have stuffed so much syntax into their grammar, they are running out of punctuation characters on the keyboard.

To some degree, location on the spectrum correlates with age. It's relatively easy to add bits of syntactic sugar in later releases. New syntax is a crowd pleaser, and it's less likely to break existing programs than mucking with the semantics. Once added, you can never take it away, so languages tend to sweeten with time. One of the main benefits of creating a new language from scratch is it gives you an opportunity to scrape off those accumulated layers of frosting and start over.

Syntactic sugar has a bad rap among the PL intelligentsia. There's a real fetish for minimalism in that crowd. There is some justification for that. Poorly designed, unneeded syntax raises the cognitive load without adding enough expressiveness to carry its weight. Since there is always pressure to cram new features into the language, it takes discipline and a focus on simplicity to avoid bloat. Once you add some syntax, you're stuck with it, so it's smart to be parsimonious.

At the same time, most successful languages do have fairly complex grammars, at least by the time they are widely used. Programmers spend a ton of time in their language of choice, and a few niceties here and there really can improve the comfort and efficiency of their work.

Striking the right balance—choosing the right level of sweetness for your language—relies on your own sense of taste.

# Functions

# 10

*"And that is also the way the human mind works—by the compounding of old ideas into new structures that become new ideas that can themselves be used in compounds, and round and round endlessly, growing ever more remote from the basic earthbound imagery that is each language's soil."*

— Douglas R. Hofstadter, *I Am a Strange Loop*

This chapter marks the culmination of a lot of hard work. The previous chapters add useful functionality in their own right, but each also supplies a piece of a puzzle. We'll take those pieces—expressions, statements, variables, control flow, and lexical scope—add a couple more, and assemble them all into support for real user-defined functions and function calls.

## 10.1 Function Calls

You're certainly familiar with C-style function call syntax, but the grammar is more subtle than you may realize. Calls are typically to named functions like:

```
average(1, 2);
```

The name *is* part of the call syntax in Pascal. You can call only named functions or functions stored directly in variables.

But the name of the function being called isn't actually part of the call syntax. The thing being called—the **callee**—can be any expression that evaluates to a function. (Well, it does have to be a pretty *high precedence* expression, but parentheses take care of that.) For example:

```
getCallback()();
```

There are two call expressions here. The first pair of parentheses has `getCallback` as its callee. But the second call has the entire `getCallback()` expression as its callee. It is the parentheses following an expression that indicate a function call. You can think of a call as sort of like a postfix operator that starts with (.

This "operator" has higher precedence than any other operator, even the unary ones. So we slot it into the grammar by having the `unary` rule bubble up to a new `call` rule.

The rule uses ⋆ to allow matching a series of calls like `fn(1)(2)(3)`. Code like that isn't common in C-style languages, but it is in the family of languages derived from ML. There, the normal way of defining a function that takes multiple arguments is as a series of nested functions. Each function takes one argument and returns a new function. That function consumes the next argument, returns yet another function, and so on. Eventually, once all of the arguments are consumed, the last function completes the operation.

This style, called **currying**, after Haskell Curry (the same guy whose first name graces that *other* well-known functional language), is baked directly into the language syntax so it's not as weird looking as it would be here.

```
unary          → ( "!" | "-" ) unary | call ;
call           → primary ( "(" arguments? ")" )* ;
```

This rule matches a primary expression followed by zero or more function calls. If there are no parentheses, this parses a bare primary expression. Otherwise, each call is recognized by a pair of parentheses with an optional list of arguments inside. The argument list grammar is:

```
arguments      → expression ( "," expression )* ;
```

This rule requires at least one argument expression, followed by zero or more other expressions, each preceded by a comma. To handle zero-argument calls, the `call` rule itself considers the entire `arguments` production to be optional.

I admit, this seems more grammatically awkward than you'd expect for the incredibly common "zero or more comma-separated things" pattern. There are some sophisticated metasyntaxes that handle this better, but in our BNF and in many language specs I've seen, it is this cumbersome.

Over in our syntax tree generator, we add a new node.

**tool/GenerateAst.java**
*in* main()

```
"Binary   : Expr left, Token operator, Expr right",
"Call     : Expr callee, Token paren, List<Expr> arguments",
"Grouping : Expr expression",
```

It stores the callee expression and a list of expressions for the arguments. It also stores the token for the closing parenthesis. We'll use that token's location when we report a runtime error caused by a function call.

Crack open the parser. Where `unary()` used to jump straight to `primary()`, change it to call, well, `call()`.

**lox/Parser.java**
*in* unary()
*replace 1 line*

```
    return new Expr.Unary(operator, right);
  }

  return call();
}
```

Its definition is:

```
private Expr call() {
  Expr expr = primary();

  while (true) {
    if (match(LEFT_PAREN)) {
      expr = finishCall(expr);
    } else {
      break;
    }
  }

  return expr;
}
```

lox/Parser.java
*add after* unary()

This code would be simpler as
`while (match(LEFT_PAREN))`
instead of the silly `while (true)`
and `break`. Don't worry, it will make
sense when we expand the parser later to
handle properties on objects.

The code here doesn't quite line up with the grammar rules. I moved a few things around to make the code cleaner—one of the luxuries we have with a handwritten parser. But it's roughly similar to how we parse infix operators. First, we parse a primary expression, the "left operand" to the call. Then, each time we see a (, we call finishCall() to parse the call expression using the previously parsed expression as the callee. The returned expression becomes the new expr and we loop to see if the result is itself called.

The code to parse the argument list is in this helper:

```
private Expr finishCall(Expr callee) {
  List<Expr> arguments = new ArrayList<>();
  if (!check(RIGHT_PAREN)) {
    do {
      arguments.add(expression());
    } while (match(COMMA));
  }

  Token paren = consume(RIGHT_PAREN,
                        "Expect ')' after arguments.");

  return new Expr.Call(callee, paren, arguments);
}
```

lox/Parser.java
*add after* unary()

This is more or less the arguments grammar rule translated to code, except that we also handle the zero-argument case. We check for that case first by seeing if the next token is ). If it is, we don't try to parse any arguments.

Otherwise, we parse an expression, then look for a comma indicating that there is another argument after that. We keep doing that as long as we find commas after each expression. When we don't find a comma, then the argument list must be done and we consume the expected closing parenthesis. Finally, we wrap the callee and those arguments up into a call AST node.

## 10.1.1  Maximum argument counts

Right now, the loop where we parse arguments has no bound. If you want to call a function and pass a million arguments to it, the parser would have no problem with it. Do we want to limit that?

Other languages have various approaches. The C standard says a conforming implementation has to support *at least* 127 arguments to a function, but doesn't say there's any upper limit. The Java specification says a method can accept *no more than* 255 arguments.

Our Java interpreter for Lox doesn't really need a limit, but having a maximum number of arguments will simplify our bytecode interpreter in Part III. We want our two interpreters to be compatible with each other, even in weird corner cases like this, so we'll add the same limit to jlox.

The limit is 254 arguments if the method is an instance method. That's because `this`—the receiver of the method—works like an argument that is implicitly passed to the method, so it claims one of the slots.

**lox/Parser.java**
*in* `finishCall()`

```
do {
    if (arguments.size() >= 255) {
        error(peek(), "Can't have more than 255 arguments.");
    }
    arguments.add(expression());
```

Note that the code here *reports* an error if it encounters too many arguments, but it doesn't *throw* the error. Throwing is how we kick into panic mode which is what we want if the parser is in a confused state and doesn't know where it is in the grammar anymore. But here, the parser is still in a perfectly valid state—it just found too many arguments. So it reports the error and keeps on keepin' on.

### 10.1.2 Interpreting function calls

We don't have any functions we can call, so it seems weird to start implementing calls first, but we'll worry about that when we get there. First, our interpreter needs a new import.

**lox/Interpreter.java**

```
import java.util.ArrayList;
import java.util.List;
```

As always, interpretation starts with a new visit method for our new call expression node.

**lox/Interpreter.java**
*add after* `visitBinaryExpr()`

This is another one of those subtle semantic choices. Since argument expressions may have side effects, the order they are evaluated could be user visible. Even so, some languages like Scheme and C don't specify an order. This gives compilers freedom to reorder them for efficiency, but means users may be unpleasantly surprised if arguments aren't evaluated in the order they expect.

```
@Override
public Object visitCallExpr(Expr.Call expr) {
    Object callee = evaluate(expr.callee);

    List<Object> arguments = new ArrayList<>();
    for (Expr argument : expr.arguments) {
        arguments.add(evaluate(argument));
    }

    LoxCallable function = (LoxCallable)callee;
    return function.call(this, arguments);
}
```

First, we evaluate the expression for the callee. Typically, this expression is just an identifier that looks up the function by its name, but it could be anything.

Then we evaluate each of the argument expressions in order and store the resulting values in a list.

Once we've got the callee and the arguments ready, all that remains is to perform the call. We do that by casting the callee to a LoxCallable and then invoking a `call()` method on it. The Java representation of any Lox object that can be called like a function will implement this interface. That includes user-defined functions, naturally, but also class objects since classes are "called" to construct new instances. We'll also use it for one more purpose shortly.

There isn't too much to this new interface.

I stuck "Lox" before the name to distinguish it from the Java standard library's own Callable interface. Alas, all the good simple names are already taken.

```java
package com.craftinginterpreters.lox;

import java.util.List;

interface LoxCallable {
  Object call(Interpreter interpreter, List<Object> arguments);
}
```

lox/LoxCallable.java
*create new file*

We pass in the interpreter in case the class implementing `call()` needs it. We also give it the list of evaluated argument values. The implementer's job is then to return the value that the call expression produces.

### 10.1.3  Call type errors

Before we get to implementing LoxCallable, we need to make the visit method a little more robust. It currently ignores a couple of failure modes that we can't pretend won't occur. First, what happens if the callee isn't actually something you can call? What if you try to do this:

```
"totally not a function"();
```

Strings aren't callable in Lox. The runtime representation of a Lox string is a Java string, so when we cast that to LoxCallable, the JVM will throw a ClassCastException. We don't want our interpreter to vomit out some nasty Java stack trace and die. Instead, we need to check the type ourselves first.

```java
    }

    if (!(callee instanceof LoxCallable)) {
      throw new RuntimeError(expr.paren,
          "Can only call functions and classes.");
    }

    LoxCallable function = (LoxCallable)callee;
```

lox/Interpreter.java
*in* visitCallExpr()

We still throw an exception, but now we're throwing our own exception type, one that the interpreter knows to catch and report gracefully.

### 10.1.4 Checking arity

The other problem relates to the function's **arity**. Arity is the fancy term for the number of arguments a function or operation expects. Unary operators have arity one, binary operators two, etc. With functions, the arity is determined by the number of parameters it declares.

```
fun add(a, b, c) {
  print a + b + c;
}
```

This function defines three parameters, a, b, and c, so its arity is three and it expects three arguments. So what if you try to call it like this:

```
add(1, 2, 3, 4); // Too many.
add(1, 2);       // Too few.
```

Different languages take different approaches to this problem. Of course, most statically typed languages check this at compile time and refuse to compile the code if the argument count doesn't match the function's arity. JavaScript discards any extra arguments you pass. If you don't pass enough, it fills in the missing parameters with the magic sort-of-like-null-but-not-really value undefined. Python is stricter. It raises a runtime error if the argument list is too short or too long.

I think the latter is a better approach. Passing the wrong number of arguments is almost always a bug, and it's a mistake I do make in practice. Given that, the sooner the implementation draws my attention to it, the better. So for Lox, we'll take Python's approach. Before invoking the callable, we check to see if the argument list's length matches the callable's arity.

**lox/Interpreter.java**
*in* visitCallExpr ()

```java
LoxCallable function = (LoxCallable)callee;
if (arguments.size() != function.arity()) {
  throw new RuntimeError(expr.paren, "Expected " +
      function.arity() + " arguments but got " +
      arguments.size() + ".");
}

return function.call(this, arguments);
```

That requires a new method on the LoxCallable interface to ask it its arity.

**lox/LoxCallable.java**
*in interface* LoxCallable

```java
interface LoxCallable {
  int arity();
  Object call(Interpreter interpreter, List<Object> arguments);
```

We *could* push the arity checking into the concrete implementation of call(). But, since we'll have multiple classes implementing LoxCallable, that would end up with redundant validation spread across a few classes. Hoisting it up into the visit method lets us do it in one place.

## 10.2  Native Functions

We can theoretically call functions, but we have no functions to call yet. Before we get to user-defined functions, now is a good time to introduce a vital but often overlooked facet of language implementations—**native functions**. These are functions that the interpreter exposes to user code but that are implemented in the host language (in our case Java), not the language being implemented (Lox).

Sometimes these are called **primitives**, **external functions**, or **foreign functions**. Since these functions can be called while the user's program is running, they form part of the implementation's runtime. A lot of programming language books gloss over these because they aren't conceptually interesting. They're mostly grunt work.

But when it comes to making your language actually good at doing useful stuff, the native functions your implementation provides are key. They provide access to the fundamental services that all programs are defined in terms of. If you don't provide native functions to access the file system, a user's going to have a hell of a time writing a program that reads and displays a file.

Many languages also allow users to provide their own native functions. The mechanism for doing so is called a **foreign function interface** (FFI), **native extension**, **native interface**, or something along those lines. These are nice because they free the language implementer from providing access to every single capability the underlying platform supports. We won't define an FFI for jlox, but we will add one native function to give you an idea of what it looks like.

### 10.2.1  Telling time

When we get to Part III and start working on a much more efficient implementation of Lox, we're going to care deeply about performance. Performance work requires measurement, and that in turn means **benchmarks**. These are programs that measure the time it takes to exercise some corner of the interpreter.

We could measure the time it takes to start up the interpreter, run the benchmark, and exit, but that adds a lot of overhead—JVM startup time, OS shenanigans, etc. That stuff does matter, of course, but if you're just trying to validate an optimization to some piece of the interpreter, you don't want that overhead obscuring your results.

A nicer solution is to have the benchmark script itself measure the time elapsed between two points in the code. To do that, a Lox program needs to be able to tell time. There's no way to do that now—you can't implement a useful clock "from scratch" without access to the underlying clock on the computer.

So we'll add clock(), a native function that returns the number of seconds that have passed since some fixed point in time. The difference between two successive invocations tells you how much time elapsed between the two calls. This function is defined in the global scope, so let's ensure the interpreter has access to that.

Curiously, two names for these functions—"native" and "foreign"—are antonyms. Maybe it depends on the perspective of the person choosing the term. If you think of yourself as "living" within the runtime's implementation (in our case, Java) then functions written in that are "native". But if you have the mindset of a *user* of your language, then the runtime is implemented in some other "foreign" language.

Or it may be that "native" refers to the machine code language of the underlying hardware. In Java, "native" methods are ones implemented in C or C++ and compiled to native machine code.

A classic native function almost every language provides is one to print text to stdout. In Lox, I made print a built-in statement so that we could get stuff on screen in the chapters before this one.

Once we have functions, we could simplify the language by tearing out the old print syntax and replacing it with a native function. But that would mean that examples early in the book wouldn't run on the interpreter from later chapters and vice versa. So, for the book, I'll leave it alone.

If you're building an interpreter for your *own* language, though, you may want to consider it.

**lox/Interpreter.java**
*in class* Interpreter
*replace 1 line*

```
class Interpreter implements Expr.Visitor<Object>,
                             Stmt.Visitor<Void> {
  final Environment globals = new Environment();
  private Environment environment = globals;

  void interpret(List<Stmt> statements) {
```

The `environment` field in the interpreter changes as we enter and exit local scopes. It tracks the *current* environment. This new `globals` field holds a fixed reference to the outermost global environment.

When we instantiate an Interpreter, we stuff the native function in that global scope.

```java
private Environment environment = globals;

Interpreter() {
  globals.define("clock", new LoxCallable() {
    @Override
    public int arity() { return 0; }

    @Override
    public Object call(Interpreter interpreter,
                       List<Object> arguments) {
      return (double)System.currentTimeMillis() / 1000.0;
    }

    @Override
    public String toString() { return "<native fn>"; }
  });
}

void interpret(List<Stmt> statements) {
```

In Lox, functions and variables occupy the same namespace. In Common Lisp, the two live in their own worlds. A function and variable with the same name don't collide. If you call the name, it looks up the function. If you refer to it, it looks up the variable. This does require jumping through some hoops when you do want to refer to a function as a first-class value.

Richard P. Gabriel and Kent Pitman coined the terms "Lisp-1" to refer to languages like Scheme that put functions and variables in the same namespace, and "Lisp-2" for languages like Common Lisp that partition them. Despite being totally opaque, those names have since stuck. Lox is a Lisp-1.

This defines a variable named "clock". Its value is a Java anonymous class that implements LoxCallable. The `clock()` function takes no arguments, so its arity is zero. The implementation of `call()` calls the corresponding Java function and converts the result to a double value in seconds.

If we wanted to add other native functions—reading input from the user, working with files, etc.—we could add them each as their own anonymous class that implements LoxCallable. But for the book, this one is really all we need.

Let's get ourselves out of the function-defining business and let our users take over...

## 10.3  Function Declarations

A named function declaration isn't really a single primitive operation. It's syntactic sugar for two distinct steps: (1) creating a new function object, and (2) binding a new variable to it. If Lox had syntax for anonymous functions, we wouldn't need function declaration statements. You could just do:

```
var add = fun (a, b) {
  print a + b;
};
```

However, since named functions are the common case, I went ahead and gave Lox nice syntax for them.

We finally get to add a new production to the `declaration` rule we introduced back when we added variables. Function declarations, like variables, bind a new name. That means they are allowed only in places where a declaration is permitted.

```
declaration    → funDecl | varDecl | statement ;
```

The updated `declaration` rule references this new rule:

```
funDecl        → "fun" function ;
function       → IDENTIFIER "(" parameters? ")" block ;
```

The main `funDecl` rule uses a separate helper rule `function`. A function *declaration statement* is the `fun` keyword followed by the actual function-y stuff. When we get to classes, we'll reuse that `function` rule for declaring methods. Those look similar to function declarations, but aren't preceded by `fun`.

The function itself is a name followed by the parenthesized parameter list and the body. The body is always a braced block, using the same grammar rule that block statements use. The parameter list uses this rule:

```
parameters     → IDENTIFIER ( "," IDENTIFIER )* ;
```

It's like the earlier `arguments` rule, except that each parameter is an identifier, not an expression. That's a lot of new syntax for the parser to chew through, but the resulting AST node isn't too bad.

```
      "Expression : Expr expression",
      "Function   : Token name, List<Token> params," +
                   " List<Stmt> body",
      "If         : Expr condition, Stmt thenBranch," +
```

A function node has a name, a list of parameters (their names), and then the body. We store the body as the list of statements contained inside the curly braces.

Over in the parser, we weave in the new declaration.

```
    try {
      if (match(FUN)) return function("function");
      if (match(VAR)) return varDeclaration();
```

Like other statements, a function is recognized by the leading keyword. When we encounter `fun`, we call `function`. That corresponds to the `function` grammar rule since we already matched and consumed the `fun` keyword. We'll build the method up a piece at a time, starting with this:

```
    private Stmt.Function function(String kind) {
      Token name = consume(IDENTIFIER, "Expect " + kind + " name.");
    }
```

Right now, it only consumes the identifier token for the function's name. You might be wondering about that funny little `kind` parameter. Just like we reuse the grammar rule, we'll reuse the `function()` method later to parse methods inside classes. When we do that, we'll pass in "method" for `kind` so that the error messages are specific to the kind of declaration being parsed.

Next, we parse the parameter list and the parentheses wrapped around it.

```
      Token name = consume(IDENTIFIER, "Expect " + kind + " name.");
      consume(LEFT_PAREN, "Expect '(' after " + kind + " name.");
      List<Token> parameters = new ArrayList<>();
      if (!check(RIGHT_PAREN)) {
        do {
          if (parameters.size() >= 255) {
            error(peek(), "Can't have more than 255 parameters.");
          }
```

Methods are too classy to have fun.

tool/GenerateAst.java
*in* main()

lox/Parser.java
*in* declaration()

lox/Parser.java
*add after* expressionStatement()

lox/Parser.java
*in* function()

*continued on next page...*

```
        parameters.add(
            consume(IDENTIFIER, "Expect parameter name."));
    } while (match(COMMA));
  }
  consume(RIGHT_PAREN, "Expect ')' after parameters.");
}
```

This is like the code for handling arguments in a call, except not split out into a helper method. The outer `if` statement handles the zero parameter case, and the inner `while` loop parses parameters as long as we find commas to separate them. The result is the list of tokens for each parameter's name.

Just like we do with arguments to function calls, we validate at parse time that you don't exceed the maximum number of parameters a function is allowed to have.

Finally, we parse the body and wrap it all up in a function node.

**lox/Parser.java**
*in* `function()`

```
  consume(RIGHT_PAREN, "Expect ')' after parameters.");
  consume(LEFT_BRACE, "Expect '{' before " + kind + " body.");
  List<Stmt> body = block();
  return new Stmt.Function(name, parameters, body);
}
```

Note that we consume the { at the beginning of the body here before calling `block()`. That's because `block()` assumes the brace token has already been matched. Consuming it here lets us report a more precise error message if the { isn't found since we know it's in the context of a function declaration.

## 10.4 Function Objects

We've got some syntax parsed so usually we're ready to interpret, but first we need to think about how to represent a Lox function in Java. We need to keep track of the parameters so that we can bind them to argument values when the function is called. And, of course, we need to keep the code for the body of the function so that we can execute it.

That's basically what the Stmt.Function class is. Could we just use that? Almost, but not quite. We also need a class that implements LoxCallable so that we can call it. We don't want the runtime phase of the interpreter to bleed into the front end's syntax classes so we don't want Stmt.Function itself to implement that. Instead, we wrap it in a new class.

**lox/LoxFunction.java**
*create new file*

```
package com.craftinginterpreters.lox;

import java.util.List;

class LoxFunction implements LoxCallable {
  private final Stmt.Function declaration;
  LoxFunction(Stmt.Function declaration) {
    this.declaration = declaration;
  }
}
```

We implement the `call()` of LoxCallable like so:

```java
@Override
public Object call(Interpreter interpreter,
                   List<Object> arguments) {
  Environment environment = new Environment(interpreter.globals);
  for (int i = 0; i < declaration.params.size(); i++) {
    environment.define(declaration.params.get(i).lexeme,
        arguments.get(i));
  }

  interpreter.executeBlock(declaration.body, environment);
  return null;
}
```

lox/LoxFunction.java
add after LoxFunction()

This handful of lines of code is one of the most fundamental, powerful pieces of our interpreter. As we saw in the chapter on statements and state, managing name environments is a core part of a language implementation. Functions are deeply tied to that.

Parameters are core to functions, especially the fact that a function *encapsulates* its parameters—no other code outside of the function can see them. This means each function gets its own environment where it stores those variables.

Further, this environment must be created dynamically. Each function *call* gets its own environment. Otherwise, recursion would break. If there are multiple calls to the same function in play at the same time, each needs its *own* environment, even though they are all calls to the same function.

For example, here's a convoluted way to count to three:

We'll dig even deeper into environments in the next chapter.

```lox
fun count(n) {
  if (n > 1) count(n - 1);
  print n;
}

count(3);
```

Imagine we pause the interpreter right at the point where it's about to print 1 in the innermost nested call. The outer calls to print 2 and 3 haven't printed their values yet, so there must be environments somewhere in memory that still store the fact that n is bound to 3 in one context, 2 in another, and 1 in the innermost, like:

That's why we create a new environment at each *call*, not at the function *declaration*. The `call()` method we saw earlier does that. At the beginning of the call, it creates a new environment. Then it walks the parameter and argument lists in lockstep. For each pair, it creates a new variable with the parameter's name and binds it to the argument's value.

So, for a program like this:

```
fun add(a, b, c) {
  print a + b + c;
}

add(1, 2, 3);
```

At the point of the call to add(), the interpreter creates something like this:

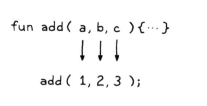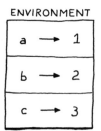

Then call() tells the interpreter to execute the body of the function in this new function-local environment. Up until now, the current environment was the environment where the function was being called. Now, we teleport from there inside the new parameter space we've created for the function.

This is all that's required to pass data into the function. By using different environments when we execute the body, calls to the same function with the same code can produce different results.

Once the body of the function has finished executing, executeBlock() discards that function-local environment and restores the previous one that was active back at the callsite. Finally, call() returns null, which returns nil to the caller. (We'll add return values later.)

Mechanically, the code is pretty simple. Walk a couple of lists. Bind some new variables. Call a method. But this is where the crystalline *code* of the function declaration becomes a living, breathing *invocation*. This is one of my favorite snippets in this entire book. Feel free to take a moment to meditate on it if you're so inclined.

Done? OK. Note when we bind the parameters, we assume the parameter and argument lists have the same length. This is safe because visitCallExpr() checks the arity before calling call(). It relies on the function reporting its arity to do that.

lox/LoxFunction.java
*add after* LoxFunction()

```java
@Override
public int arity() {
  return declaration.params.size();
}
```

That's most of our object representation. While we're in here, we may as well implement toString().

lox/LoxFunction.java
*add after* LoxFunction()

```java
@Override
public String toString() {
  return "<fn " + declaration.name.lexeme + ">";
}
```

This gives nicer output if a user decides to print a function value.

```
fun add(a, b) {
  print a + b;
}

print add; // "<fn add>".
```

### 10.4.1 Interpreting function declarations

We'll come back and refine LoxFunction soon, but that's enough to get started. Now we can visit a function declaration.

```
  @Override
  public Void visitFunctionStmt(Stmt.Function stmt) {
    LoxFunction function = new LoxFunction(stmt);
    environment.define(stmt.name.lexeme, function);
    return null;
  }
```

lox/Interpreter.java
*add after* visitExpressionStmt()

This is similar to how we interpret other literal expressions. We take a function *syntax node*—a compile-time representation of the function—and convert it to its runtime representation. Here, that's a LoxFunction that wraps the syntax node.

Function declarations are different from other literal nodes in that the declaration *also* binds the resulting object to a new variable. So, after creating the LoxFunction, we create a new binding in the current environment and store a reference to it there.

With that, we can define and call our own functions all within Lox. Give it a try:

```
fun sayHi(first, last) {
  print "Hi, " + first + " " + last + "!";
}

sayHi("Dear", "Reader");
```

I don't know about you, but that looks like an honest-to-God programming language to me.

## 10.5 Return Statements

We can get data into functions by passing parameters, but we've got no way to get results back *out*. If Lox were an expression-oriented language like Ruby or Scheme, the body would be an expression whose value is implicitly the function's result. But in Lox, the body of a function is a list of statements which don't produce values, so we need dedicated syntax for emitting a result. In other words, return statements.

The Hotel California of data.

I'm sure you can guess the grammar already.

```
statement       → exprStmt
                | forStmt
                | ifStmt
                | printStmt
                | returnStmt
                | whileStmt
                | block ;

returnStmt      → "return" expression? ";" ;
```

We've got one more—the final, in fact—production under the venerable `statement` rule. A `return` statement is the `return` keyword followed by an optional expression and terminated with a semicolon.

The return value is optional to support exiting early from a function that doesn't return a useful value. In statically typed languages, "void" functions don't return a value and non-void ones do. Since Lox is dynamically typed, there are no true void functions. The compiler has no way of preventing you from taking the result value of a call to a function that doesn't contain a `return` statement.

```
fun procedure() {
  print "don't return anything";
}

var result = procedure();
print result; // ?
```

This means every Lox function must return *something*, even if it contains no `return` statements at all. We use `nil` for this, which is why LoxFunction's implementation of `call()` returns `null` at the end. In that same vein, if you omit the value in a `return` statement, we simply treat it as equivalent to:

```
return nil;
```

Over in our AST generator, we add a new node.

**tool/GenerateAst.java**
*in* main()

```
      "Print      : Expr expression",
      "Return     : Token keyword, Expr value",
      "Var        : Token name, Expr initializer",
```

It keeps the `return` keyword token so we can use its location for error reporting, and the value being returned, if any. We parse it like other statements, first by recognizing the initial keyword.

**lox/Parser.java**
*in* statement()

```
    if (match(PRINT)) return printStatement();
    if (match(RETURN)) return returnStatement();
    if (match(WHILE)) return whileStatement();
```

That branches out to a new method.

```
private Stmt returnStatement() {
  Token keyword = previous();
  Expr value = null;
  if (!check(SEMICOLON)) {
    value = expression();
  }

  consume(SEMICOLON, "Expect ';' after return value.");
  return new Stmt.Return(keyword, value);
}
```

lox/Parser.java
*add after* printStatement()

After snagging the previously consumed `return` keyword, we look for a value expression. Since many different tokens can potentially start an expression, it's hard to tell if a return value is *present*. Instead, we check if it's *absent*. Since a semicolon can't begin an expression, if the next token is that, we know there must not be a value.

## 10.5.1  Returning from calls

Interpreting a `return` statement is tricky. You can return from anywhere within the body of a function, even deeply nested inside other statements. When the return is executed, the interpreter needs to jump all the way out of whatever context it's currently in and cause the function call to complete, like some kind of jacked up control flow construct.

For example, say we're running this program and we're about to execute the `return` statement:

```
fun count(n) {
  while (n < 100) {
    if (n == 3) return n; // <--
    print n;
    n = n + 1;
  }
}

count(1);
```

The Java call stack currently looks roughly like this:

```
Interpreter.visitReturnStmt()
Interpreter.visitIfStmt()
Interpreter.executeBlock()
Interpreter.visitBlockStmt()
Interpreter.visitWhileStmt()
Interpreter.executeBlock()
LoxFunction.call()
Interpreter.visitCallExpr()
```

We need to get from the top of the stack all the way back to `call()`. I don't know about you, but to me that sounds like exceptions. When we execute a `return` statement, we'll use an exception to unwind the interpreter past the visit methods of all of the containing statements back to the code that began executing the body.

The visit method for our new AST node looks like this:

lox/Interpreter.java
add after visitPrintStmt()

```java
@Override
public Void visitReturnStmt(Stmt.Return stmt) {
  Object value = null;
  if (stmt.value != null) value = evaluate(stmt.value);

  throw new Return(value);
}
```

If we have a return value, we evaluate it, otherwise, we use nil. Then we take that value and wrap it in a custom exception class and throw it.

lox/Return.java
create new file

```java
package com.craftinginterpreters.lox;

class Return extends RuntimeException {
  final Object value;

  Return(Object value) {
    super(null, null, false, false);
    this.value = value;
  }
}
```

This class wraps the return value with the accoutrements Java requires for a runtime exception class. The weird super constructor call with those null and false arguments disables some JVM machinery that we don't need. Since we're using our exception class for control flow and not actual error handling, we don't need overhead like stack traces.

We want this to unwind all the way to where the function call began, the call() method in LoxFunction.

lox/LoxFunction.java
in call()
replace 1 line

```java
          arguments.get(i));
  }

  try {
    interpreter.executeBlock(declaration.body, environment);
  } catch (Return returnValue) {
    return returnValue.value;
  }
  return null;
```

For the record, I'm not generally a fan of using exceptions for control flow. But inside a heavily recursive tree-walk interpreter, it's the way to go. Since our own syntax tree evaluation is so heavily tied to the Java call stack, we're pressed to do some heavyweight call stack manipulation occasionally, and exceptions are a handy tool for that.

We wrap the call to executeBlock() in a try-catch block. When it catches a return exception, it pulls out the value and makes that the return value from call(). If it never catches one of these exceptions, it means the function reached the end of its body without hitting a return statement. In that case, it implicitly returns nil.

Let's try it out. We finally have enough power to support this classic example—a recursive function to calculate Fibonacci numbers:

```
fun fib(n) {
  if (n <= 1) return n;
  return fib(n - 2) + fib(n - 1);
}

for (var i = 0; i < 20; i = i + 1) {
  print fib(i);
}
```

You might notice this is pretty slow. Obviously, recursion isn't the most efficient way to calculate Fibonacci numbers, but as a microbenchmark, it does a good job of stress testing how fast our interpreter implements function calls.

As you can see, the answer is "not very fast". That's OK. Our C interpreter will be faster.

This tiny program exercises almost every language feature we have spent the past several chapters implementing—expressions, arithmetic, branching, looping, variables, functions, function calls, parameter binding, and returns.

## 10.6  Local Functions and Closures

Our functions are pretty full featured, but there is one hole to patch. In fact, it's a big enough gap that we'll spend most of the next chapter sealing it up, but we can get started here.

LoxFunction's implementation of `call()` creates a new environment where it binds the function's parameters. When I showed you that code, I glossed over one important point: What is the *parent* of that environment?

Right now, it is always `globals`, the top-level global environment. That way, if an identifier isn't defined inside the function body itself, the interpreter can look outside the function in the global scope to find it. In the Fibonacci example, that's how the interpreter is able to look up the recursive call to `fib` inside the function's own body—`fib` is a global variable.

But recall that in Lox, function declarations are allowed *anywhere* a name can be bound. That includes the top level of a Lox script, but also the inside of blocks or other functions. Lox supports **local functions** that are defined inside another function, or nested inside a block.

Consider this classic example:

```
fun makeCounter() {
  var i = 0;
  fun count() {
    i = i + 1;
    print i;
  }

  return count;
}

var counter = makeCounter();
counter(); // "1".
counter(); // "2".
```

Here, `count()` uses `i`, which is declared outside of itself in the containing function `makeCounter()`. `makeCounter()` returns a reference to the `count()` function and then its own body finishes executing completely.

Meanwhile, the top-level code invokes the returned `count()` function. That executes the body of count(), which assigns to and reads i, even though the function where i was defined has already exited.

If you've never encountered a language with nested functions before, this might seem crazy, but users do expect it to work. Alas, if you run it now, you get an undefined variable error in the call to counter() when the body of count() tries to look up i. That's because the environment chain in effect looks like this:

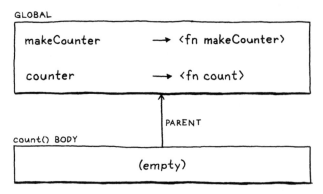

When we call count() (through the reference to it stored in counter), we create a new empty environment for the function body. The parent of that is the global environment. We lost the environment for makeCounter() where i is bound.

Let's go back in time a bit. Here's what the environment chain looked like right when we declared count() inside the body of makeCounter():

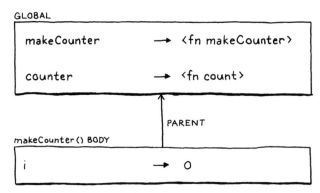

So at the point where the function is declared, we can see i. But when we return from makeCounter() and exit its body, the interpreter discards that environment. Since the interpreter doesn't keep the environment surrounding count() around, it's up to the function object itself to hang on to it.

This data structure is called a **closure** because it "closes over" and holds on to the surrounding variables where the function is declared. Closures have been around since the early Lisp days, and language hackers have come up with all manner of ways to implement them. For jlox, we'll do the simplest thing that works. In LoxFunction, we add a field to store an environment.

"Closure" is yet another term coined by Peter J. Landin. I assume before he came along that computer scientists communicated with each other using only primitive grunts and pawing hand gestures.

**lox/LoxFunction.java**
*in class* LoxFunction

```
private final Stmt.Function declaration;
private final Environment closure;

LoxFunction(Stmt.Function declaration) {
```

We initialize that in the constructor.

```
LoxFunction(Stmt.Function declaration, Environment closure) {
  this.closure = closure;
  this.declaration = declaration;
```

*lox/LoxFunction.java*
*constructor LoxFunction()*
*replace 1 line*

When we create a LoxFunction, we capture the current environment.

```
public Void visitFunctionStmt(Stmt.Function stmt) {
  LoxFunction function = new LoxFunction(stmt, environment);
  environment.define(stmt.name.lexeme, function);
```

*lox/Interpreter.java*
*in visitFunctionStmt()*
*replace 1 line*

This is the environment that is active when the function is *declared* not when it's *called*, which is what we want. It represents the lexical scope surrounding the function declaration. Finally, when we call the function, we use that environment as the call's parent instead of going straight to globals.

```
                    List<Object> arguments) {
  Environment environment = new Environment(closure);
  for (int i = 0; i < declaration.params.size(); i++) {
```

*lox/LoxFunction.java*
*in call()*
*replace 1 line*

This creates an environment chain that goes from the function's body out through the environments where the function is declared, all the way out to the global scope. The runtime environment chain matches the textual nesting of the source code like we want. The end result when we call that function looks like this:

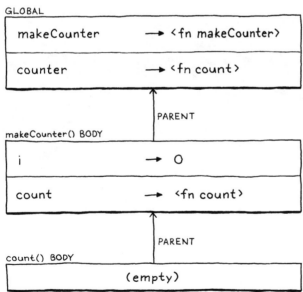

Now, as you can see, the interpreter can still find i when it needs to because it's in the middle of the environment chain. Try running that makeCounter() example now. It works!

Functions let us abstract over, reuse, and compose code. Lox is much more powerful than the rudimentary arithmetic calculator it used to be. Alas, in our rush to cram closures in, we let a bit of dynamic scoping leak into the interpreter. In the next chapter, we will explore deeper into lexical scope and close that hole.

## CHALLENGES

1. Our interpreter carefully checks that the number of arguments passed to a function matches the number of parameters it expects. Since this check is done at runtime on every call, it has a performance cost. Smalltalk implementations don't have that problem. Why not?

2. Lox's function declaration syntax performs two independent operations. It creates a function and also binds it to a name. This improves usability for the common case where you do want to associate a name with the function. But in functional-styled code, you often want to create a function to immediately pass it to some other function or return it. In that case, it doesn't need a name.

    Languages that encourage a functional style usually support **anonymous functions** or **lambdas**—an expression syntax that creates a function without binding it to a name. Add anonymous function syntax to Lox so that this works:

    ```
    fun thrice(fn) {
      for (var i = 1; i <= 3; i = i + 1) {
        fn(i);
      }
    }

    thrice(fun (a) {
      print a;
    });
    // "1".
    // "2".
    // "3".
    ```

    How do you handle the tricky case of an anonymous function expression occurring in an expression statement:

    ```
    fun () {};
    ```

3. Is this program valid?

    ```
    fun scope(a) {
      var a = "local";
    }
    ```

    In other words, are a function's parameters in the *same* scope as its local variables, or in an outer scope? What does Lox do? What about other languages you are familiar with? What do you think a language *should* do?

# Resolving and Binding

11

*"Once in a while you find yourself in an odd situation. You get into it by degrees and in the most natural way but, when you are right in the midst of it, you are suddenly astonished and ask yourself how in the world it all came about."*

— Thor Heyerdahl, *Kon-Tiki*

Oh, no! Our language implementation is taking on water! Way back when we added variables and blocks, we had scoping nice and tight. But when we later added closures, a hole opened in our formerly waterproof interpreter. Most real programs are unlikely to slip through this hole, but as language implementers, we take a sacred vow to care about correctness even in the deepest, dampest corners of the semantics.

We will spend this entire chapter exploring that leak, and then carefully patching it up. In the process, we will gain a more rigorous understanding of lexical scoping as used by Lox and other languages in the C tradition. We'll also get a chance to learn about *semantic analysis*—a powerful technique for extracting meaning from the user's source code without having to run it.

## 11.1  Static Scope

A quick refresher: Lox, like most modern languages, uses *lexical* scoping. This means that you can figure out which declaration a variable name refers to just by reading the text of the program. For example:

```
var a = "outer";
{
  var a = "inner";
  print a;
}
```

This is still nowhere near as precise as a real language specification. Those docs must be so explicit that even a Martian or an outright malicious programmer would be forced to implement the correct semantics provided they followed the letter of the spec.

That exactitude is important when a language may be implemented by competing companies who want their product to be incompatible with the others to lock customers onto their platform. For this book, we can thankfully ignore those kinds of shady shenanigans.

Here, we know that the a being printed is the variable declared on the previous line, and not the global one. Running the program doesn't—*can't*—affect this. The scope rules are part of the *static* semantics of the language, which is why they're also called *static scope*. I haven't spelled out those scope rules, but now is the time for precision:

**A variable usage refers to the preceding declaration with the same name in the innermost scope that encloses the expression where the variable is used.**

There's a lot to unpack in that:

- I say "variable usage" instead of "variable expression" to cover both variable expressions and assignments. Likewise with "expression where the variable is used".

In JavaScript, variables declared using `var` are implicitly "hoisted" to the beginning of the block. Any use of that name in the block will refer to that variable, even if the use appears before the declaration. When you write this in JavaScript:

```
{
  console.log(a);
  var a = "value";
}
```

It behaves like:

```
{
  var a; // Hoist.
  console.log(a);
  a = "value";
}
```

That means that in some cases you can read a variable before its initializer has run—an annoying source of bugs. The alternate `let` syntax for declaring variables was added later to address this problem.

- "Preceding" means appearing before *in the program text*.

```
var a = "outer";
{
  print a;
  var a = "inner";
}
```

Here, the a being printed is the outer one since it appears before the print statement that uses it. In most cases, in straight line code, the declaration preceding in *text* will also precede the usage in *time*. But that's not always true. As we'll see, functions may defer a chunk of code such that its *dynamic temporal* execution no longer mirrors the *static textual* ordering.

- "Innermost" is there because of our good friend shadowing. There may be more than one variable with the given name in enclosing scopes, as in:

```
var a = "outer";
{
  var a = "inner";
  print a;
}
```

Our rule disambiguates this case by saying the innermost scope wins.

Since this rule makes no mention of any runtime behavior, it implies that a variable expression always refers to the same declaration through the entire execution of the program. Our interpreter so far *mostly* implements the rule correctly. But when we added closures, an error snuck in.

```
var a = "global";
{
  fun showA() {
    print a;
  }

  showA();
  var a = "block";
  showA();
}
```

Before you type this in and run it, decide what you think it *should* print.

OK... got it? If you're familiar with closures in other languages, you'll expect it to print "global" twice. The first call to showA() should definitely print "global" since we haven't even reached the declaration of the inner a yet. And by our rule that a variable expression always resolves to the same variable, that implies the second call to showA() should print the same thing.

Alas, it prints:

```
global
block
```

Let me stress that this program never reassigns any variable and contains only a single print statement. Yet, somehow, that print statement for a never-assigned variable prints two different values at different points in time. We definitely broke something somewhere.

> I know, it's a totally pathological, contrived program. It's just *weird*. No reasonable person would ever write code like this. Alas, more of your life than you'd expect will be spent dealing with bizarro snippets of code like this if you stay in the programming language game for long.

### 11.1.1 Scopes and mutable environments

In our interpreter, environments are the dynamic manifestation of static scopes. The two mostly stay in sync with each other—we create a new environment when we enter a new scope, and discard it when we leave the scope. There is one other operation we perform on environments: binding a variable in one. This is where our bug lies.

Let's walk through that problematic example and see what the environments look like at each step. First, we declare a in the global scope.

That gives us a single environment with a single variable in it. Then we enter the block and execute the declaration of showA().

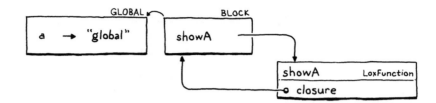

We get a new environment for the block. In that, we declare one name, showA, which is bound to the LoxFunction object we create to represent the function. That object has a closure field that captures the environment where the function was declared, so it has a reference back to the environment for the block.

Now we call showA().

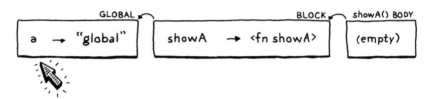

The interpreter dynamically creates a new environment for the function body of showA(). It's empty since that function doesn't declare any variables. The parent of that environment is the function's closure—the outer block environment.

Inside the body of showA(), we print the value of a. The interpreter looks up this value by walking the chain of environments. It gets all the way to the global environment before finding it there and printing "global". Great.

Next, we declare the second a, this time inside the block.

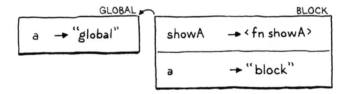

It's in the same block—the same scope—as showA(), so it goes into the same environment, which is also the same environment showA()'s closure refers to. This is where it gets interesting. We call showA() again.

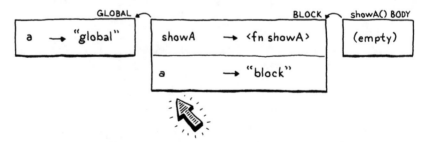

We create a new empty environment for the body of showA() again, wire it up to that closure, and run the body. When the interpreter walks the chain of environments to find a, it now discovers the *new* a in the block environment. Boo.

I chose to implement environments in a way that I hoped would agree with your informal intuition around scopes. We tend to consider all of the code within a block as being within the same scope, so our interpreter uses a single environment to represent that. Each environment is a mutable hash table. When a new local variable is declared, it gets added to the existing environment for that scope.

That intuition, like many in life, isn't quite right. A block is not necessarily all the same scope. Consider:

```
{
  var a;
  // 1.
  var b;
  // 2.
}
```

At the first marked line, only a is in scope. At the second line, both a and b are. If you define a "scope" to be a set of declarations, then those are clearly not the same scope—they don't contain the same declarations. It's like each var statement splits the block into two separate scopes, the scope before the variable is declared and the one after, which includes the new variable.

But in our implementation, environments do act like the entire block is one scope, just a scope that changes over time. Closures do not like that. When a function is declared, it captures a reference to the current environment. The function *should* capture a frozen snapshot of the environment *as it existed at the moment the function was declared*. But instead, in the Java code, it has a reference to the actual mutable environment object. When a variable is later declared in the scope that environment corresponds to, the closure sees the new variable, even though the declaration does *not* precede the function.

Some languages make this split explicit. In Scheme and ML, when you declare a local variable using `let`, you also delineate the subsequent code where the new variable is in scope. There is no implicit "rest of the block".

## 11.1.2  Persistent environments

There is a style of programming that uses what are called **persistent data structures**. Unlike the squishy data structures you're familiar with in imperative programming, a persistent data structure can never be directly modified. Instead, any "modification" to an existing structure produces a brand new object that contains all of the original data and the new modification. The original is left unchanged.

If we were to apply that technique to Environment, then every time you declared a variable it would return a *new* environment that contained all of the previously declared variables along with the one new name. Declaring a variable would do the implicit "split" where you have an environment before the variable is declared and one after:

This sounds like it might waste tons of memory and time copying the structure for each operation. In practice, persistent data structures share most of their data between the different "copies".

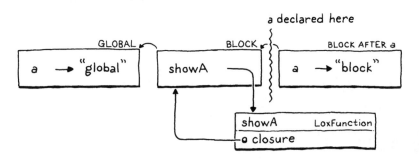

A closure retains a reference to the Environment instance in play when the function was declared. Since any later declarations in that block would produce new Environment objects, the closure wouldn't see the new variables and our bug would be fixed.

This is a legit way to solve the problem, and it's the classic way to implement environments in Scheme interpreters. We could do that for Lox, but it would mean going back and changing a pile of existing code.

I won't drag you through that. We'll keep the way we represent environments the same. Instead of making the data more statically structured, we'll bake the static resolution into the access *operation* itself.

## 11.2  Semantic Analysis

Our interpreter **resolves** a variable—tracks down which declaration it refers to—each and every time the variable expression is evaluated. If that variable is swaddled inside a loop that runs a thousand times, that variable gets re-resolved a thousand times.

We know static scope means that a variable usage always resolves to the same declaration, which can be determined just by looking at the text. Given that, why are we doing it dynamically every time? Doing so doesn't just open the hole that leads to our annoying bug, it's also needlessly slow.

A better solution is to resolve each variable use *once*. Write a chunk of code that inspects the user's program, finds every variable mentioned, and figures out which declaration each refers to. This process is an example of a **semantic analysis**. Where a parser tells only if a program is grammatically correct (a *syntactic* analysis), semantic analysis goes farther and starts to figure out what pieces of the program actually mean. In this case, our analysis will resolve variable bindings. We'll know not just that an expression *is* a variable, but *which* variable it is.

There are a lot of ways we could store the binding between a variable and its declaration. When we get to the C interpreter for Lox, we'll have a *much* more efficient way of storing and accessing local variables. But for jlox, I want to minimize the collateral damage we inflict on our existing codebase. I'd hate to throw out a bunch of mostly fine code.

Instead, we'll store the resolution in a way that makes the most out of our existing Environment class. Recall how the accesses of a are interpreted in the problematic example.

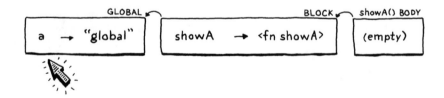

In the first (correct) evaluation, we look at three environments in the chain before finding the global declaration of a. Then, when the inner a is later declared in a block scope, it shadows the global one.

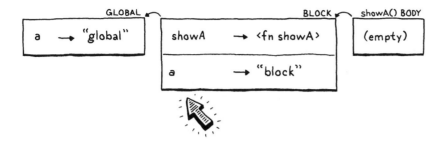

The next lookup walks the chain, finds a in the *second* environment and stops there. Each environment corresponds to a single lexical scope where variables are declared. If we could ensure a variable lookup always walked the *same* number of links in the environment chain, that would ensure that it found the same variable in the same scope every time.

To "resolve" a variable usage, we only need to calculate how many "hops" away the declared variable will be in the environment chain. The interesting question is *when* to do this calculation—or, put differently, where in our interpreter's implementation do we stuff the code for it?

Since we're calculating a static property based on the structure of the source code, the obvious answer is in the parser. That is the traditional home, and is where we'll put it later in clox. It would work here too, but I want an excuse to show you another technique. We'll write our resolver as a separate pass.

### 11.2.1 A variable resolution pass

After the parser produces the syntax tree, but before the interpreter starts executing it, we'll do a single walk over the tree to resolve all of the variables it contains. Additional passes between parsing and execution are common. If Lox had static types, we could slide a type checker in there. Optimizations are often implemented in separate passes like this too. Basically, any work that doesn't rely on state that's only available at runtime can be done in this way.

Our variable resolution pass works like a sort of mini-interpreter. It walks the tree, visiting each node, but a static analysis is different from a dynamic execution:

- **There are no side effects.** When the static analysis visits a print statement, it doesn't actually print anything. Calls to native functions or other operations that reach out to the outside world are stubbed out and have no effect.

- **There is no control flow.** Loops are visited only once. Both branches are visited in if statements. Logic operators are not short-circuited.

## 11.3  A Resolver Class

Like everything in Java, our variable resolution pass is embodied in a class.

```
package com.craftinginterpreters.lox;

import java.util.HashMap;
```

Variable resolution touches each node once, so its performance is $O(n)$ where $n$ is the number of syntax tree nodes. More sophisticated analyses may have greater complexity, but most are carefully designed to be linear or not far from it. It's an embarrassing faux pas if your compiler gets exponentially slower as the user's program grows.

**lox/Resolver.java**
*create new file*

*continued on next page...*

...from previous page

```
import java.util.List;
import java.util.Map;
import java.util.Stack;

class Resolver implements Expr.Visitor<Void>, Stmt.Visitor<Void> {
  private final Interpreter interpreter;

  Resolver(Interpreter interpreter) {
    this.interpreter = interpreter;
  }
}
```

Since the resolver needs to visit every node in the syntax tree, it implements the visitor abstraction we already have in place. Only a few kinds of nodes are interesting when it comes to resolving variables:

- A block statement introduces a new scope for the statements it contains.

- A function declaration introduces a new scope for its body and binds its parameters in that scope.

- A variable declaration adds a new variable to the current scope.

- Variable and assignment expressions need to have their variables resolved.

The rest of the nodes don't do anything special, but we still need to implement visit methods for them that traverse into their subtrees. Even though a + expression doesn't *itself* have any variables to resolve, either of its operands might.

## 11.3.1 Resolving blocks

We start with blocks since they create the local scopes where all the magic happens.

lox/Resolver.java
add after Resolver()

```
@Override
public Void visitBlockStmt(Stmt.Block stmt) {
  beginScope();
  resolve(stmt.statements);
  endScope();
  return null;
}
```

This begins a new scope, traverses into the statements inside the block, and then discards the scope. The fun stuff lives in those helper methods. We start with the simple one.

lox/Resolver.java
add after Resolver()

```
void resolve(List<Stmt> statements) {
  for (Stmt statement : statements) {
    resolve(statement);
  }
}
```

This walks a list of statements and resolves each one. It in turn calls:

```
private void resolve(Stmt stmt) {
  stmt.accept(this);
}
```
lox/Resolver.java
*add after* visitBlockStmt()

While we're at it, let's add another overload that we'll need later for resolving an expression.

```
private void resolve(Expr expr) {
  expr.accept(this);
}
```
lox/Resolver.java
*add after* resolve(Stmt stmt)

These methods are similar to the evaluate() and execute() methods in Interpreter—they turn around and apply the Visitor pattern to the given syntax tree node.

The real interesting behavior is around scopes. A new block scope is created like so:

```
private void beginScope() {
  scopes.push(new HashMap<String, Boolean>());
}
```
lox/Resolver.java
*add after* resolve()

Lexical scopes nest in both the interpreter and the resolver. They behave like a stack. The interpreter implements that stack using a linked list—the chain of Environment objects. In the resolver, we use an actual Java Stack.

```
  private final Interpreter interpreter;
  private final Stack<Map<String, Boolean>> scopes = new Stack<>();

  Resolver(Interpreter interpreter) {
```
lox/Resolver.java
*in class* Resolver

This field keeps track of the stack of scopes currently, uh, in scope. Each element in the stack is a Map representing a single block scope. Keys, as in Environment, are variable names. The values are Booleans, for a reason I'll explain soon.

The scope stack is only used for local block scopes. Variables declared at the top level in the global scope are not tracked by the resolver since they are more dynamic in Lox. When resolving a variable, if we can't find it in the stack of local scopes, we assume it must be global.

Since scopes are stored in an explicit stack, exiting one is straightforward.

```
private void endScope() {
  scopes.pop();
}
```
lox/Resolver.java
*add after* beginScope()

Now we can push and pop a stack of empty scopes. Let's put some things in them.

## 11.3.2  Resolving variable declarations

Resolving a variable declaration adds a new entry to the current innermost scope's map. That seems simple, but there's a little dance we need to do.

lox/Resolver.java
*add after* visitBlockStmt()

```java
@Override
public Void visitVarStmt(Stmt.Var stmt) {
  declare(stmt.name);
  if (stmt.initializer != null) {
    resolve(stmt.initializer);
  }
  define(stmt.name);
  return null;
}
```

We split binding into two steps, declaring then defining, in order to handle funny edge cases like this:

```
var a = "outer";
{
  var a = a;
}
```

What happens when the initializer for a local variable refers to a variable with the same name as the variable being declared? We have a few options:

1. **Run the initializer, then put the new variable in scope.** Here, the new local a would be initialized with "outer", the value of the *global* one. In other words, the previous declaration would desugar to:

   ```
   var temp = a; // Run the initializer.
   var a;        // Declare the variable.
   a = temp;     // Initialize it.
   ```

2. **Put the new variable in scope, then run the initializer.** This means you could observe a variable before it's initialized, so we would need to figure out what value it would have then. Probably nil. That means the new local a would be re-initialized to its own implicitly initialized value, nil. Now the desugaring would look like:

   ```
   var a; // Define the variable.
   a = a; // Run the initializer.
   ```

3. **Make it an error to reference a variable in its initializer.** Have the interpreter fail either at compile time or runtime if an initializer mentions the variable being initialized.

Do either of those first two options look like something a user actually *wants*? Shadowing is rare and often an error, so initializing a shadowing variable based on the value of the shadowed one seems unlikely to be deliberate.

The second option is even less useful. The new variable will *always* have the value nil. There is never any point in mentioning it by name. You could use an explicit nil instead.

Since the first two options are likely to mask user errors, we'll take the third. Further, we'll make it a compile error instead of a runtime one. That way, the user is alerted to the problem before any code is run.

In order to do that, as we visit expressions, we need to know if we're inside

the initializer for some variable. We do that by splitting binding into two steps.
The first is **declaring** it.

```
private void declare(Token name) {
  if (scopes.isEmpty()) return;

  Map<String, Boolean> scope = scopes.peek();
  scope.put(name.lexeme, false);
}
```

lox/Resolver.java
*add after* endScope()

Declaration adds the variable to the innermost scope so that it shadows any outer one and so that we know the variable exists. We mark it as "not ready yet" by
binding its name to `false` in the scope map. The value associated with a key in
the scope map represents whether or not we have finished resolving that variable's initializer.

After declaring the variable, we resolve its initializer expression in that same
scope where the new variable now exists but is unavailable. Once the initializer
expression is done, the variable is ready for prime time. We do that by **defining**
it.

```
private void define(Token name) {
  if (scopes.isEmpty()) return;
  scopes.peek().put(name.lexeme, true);
}
```

lox/Resolver.java
*add after* declare()

We set the variable's value in the scope map to `true` to mark it as fully initialized
and available for use. It's alive!

### 11.3.3  Resolving variable expressions

Variable declarations—and function declarations, which we'll get to—write to
the scope maps. Those maps are read when we resolve variable expressions.

```
@Override
public Void visitVariableExpr(Expr.Variable expr) {
  if (!scopes.isEmpty() &&
      scopes.peek().get(expr.name.lexeme) == Boolean.FALSE) {
    Lox.error(expr.name,
        "Can't read local variable in its own initializer.");
  }

  resolveLocal(expr, expr.name);
  return null;
}
```

lox/Resolver.java
*add after* visitVarStmt()

First, we check to see if the variable is being accessed inside its own initializer.
This is where the values in the scope map come into play. If the variable exists in
the current scope but its value is `false`, that means we have declared it but not
yet defined it. We report that error.

After that check, we actually resolve the variable itself using this helper:

lox/Resolver.java
*add after* define()

```java
private void resolveLocal(Expr expr, Token name) {
  for (int i = scopes.size() - 1; i >= 0; i--) {
    if (scopes.get(i).containsKey(name.lexeme)) {
      interpreter.resolve(expr, scopes.size() - 1 - i);
      return;
    }
  }
}
```

This looks, for good reason, a lot like the code in Environment for evaluating a variable. We start at the innermost scope and work outwards, looking in each map for a matching name. If we find the variable, we resolve it, passing in the number of scopes between the current innermost scope and the scope where the variable was found. So, if the variable was found in the current scope, we pass in 0. If it's in the immediately enclosing scope, 1. You get the idea.

If we walk through all of the block scopes and never find the variable, we leave it unresolved and assume it's global. We'll get to the implementation of that resolve() method a little later. For now, let's keep on cranking through the other syntax nodes.

### 11.3.4  Resolving assignment expressions

The other expression that references a variable is assignment. Resolving one looks like this:

lox/Resolver.java
*add after* visitVarStmt()

```java
@Override
public Void visitAssignExpr(Expr.Assign expr) {
  resolve(expr.value);
  resolveLocal(expr, expr.name);
  return null;
}
```

First, we resolve the expression for the assigned value in case it also contains references to other variables. Then we use our existing resolveLocal() method to resolve the variable that's being assigned to.

### 11.3.5  Resolving function declarations

Finally, functions. Functions both bind names and introduce a scope. The name of the function itself is bound in the surrounding scope where the function is declared. When we step into the function's body, we also bind its parameters into that inner function scope.

lox/Resolver.java
*add after* visitBlockStmt()

```java
@Override
public Void visitFunctionStmt(Stmt.Function stmt) {
  declare(stmt.name);
  define(stmt.name);
  resolveFunction(stmt);
  return null;
}
```

Similar to `visitVariableStmt()`, we declare and define the name of the function in the current scope. Unlike variables, though, we define the name eagerly, before resolving the function's body. This lets a function recursively refer to itself inside its own body.

Then we resolve the function's body using this:

```
private void resolveFunction(Stmt.Function function) {
  beginScope();
  for (Token param : function.params) {
    declare(param);
    define(param);
  }
  resolve(function.body);
  endScope();
}
```

lox/Resolver.java
*add after* resolve()

It's a separate method since we will also use it for resolving Lox methods when we add classes later. It creates a new scope for the body and then binds variables for each of the function's parameters.

Once that's ready, it resolves the function body in that scope. This is different from how the interpreter handles function declarations. At *runtime*, declaring a function doesn't do anything with the function's body. The body doesn't get touched until later when the function is called. In a *static* analysis, we immediately traverse into the body right then and there.

## 11.3.6  Resolving the other syntax tree nodes

That covers the interesting corners of the grammars. We handle every place where a variable is declared, read, or written, and every place where a scope is created or destroyed. Even though they aren't affected by variable resolution, we also need visit methods for all of the other syntax tree nodes in order to recurse into their subtrees. Sorry this bit is boring, but bear with me. We'll go kind of "top down" and start with statements.

I did say the book would have every single line of code for these interpreters. I didn't say they'd all be exciting.

An expression statement contains a single expression to traverse.

```
@Override
public Void visitExpressionStmt(Stmt.Expression stmt) {
  resolve(stmt.expression);
  return null;
}
```

lox/Resolver.java
*add after* visitBlockStmt()

An if statement has an expression for its condition and one or two statements for the branches.

```
@Override
public Void visitIfStmt(Stmt.If stmt) {
  resolve(stmt.condition);
  resolve(stmt.thenBranch);
  if (stmt.elseBranch != null) resolve(stmt.elseBranch);
  return null;
}
```

lox/Resolver.java
*add after* visitFunctionStmt()

Here, we see how resolution is different from interpretation. When we resolve an `if` statement, there is no control flow. We resolve the condition and *both* branches. Where a dynamic execution steps only into the branch that *is* run, a static analysis is conservative—it analyzes any branch that *could* be run. Since either one could be reached at runtime, we resolve both.

Like expression statements, a `print` statement contains a single subexpression.

lox/Resolver.java<br>add after `visitIfStmt()`

```java
@Override
public Void visitPrintStmt(Stmt.Print stmt) {
  resolve(stmt.expression);
  return null;
}
```

Same deal for return.

lox/Resolver.java<br>add after `visitPrintStmt()`

```java
@Override
public Void visitReturnStmt(Stmt.Return stmt) {
  if (stmt.value != null) {
    resolve(stmt.value);
  }

  return null;
}
```

As in `if` statements, with a `while` statement, we resolve its condition and resolve the body exactly once.

lox/Resolver.java<br>add after `visitVarStmt()`

```java
@Override
public Void visitWhileStmt(Stmt.While stmt) {
  resolve(stmt.condition);
  resolve(stmt.body);
  return null;
}
```

That covers all the statements. On to expressions...

Our old friend the binary expression. We traverse into and resolve both operands.

lox/Resolver.java<br>add after `visitAssignExpr()`

```java
@Override
public Void visitBinaryExpr(Expr.Binary expr) {
  resolve(expr.left);
  resolve(expr.right);
  return null;
}
```

Calls are similar—we walk the argument list and resolve them all. The thing being called is also an expression (usually a variable expression), so that gets resolved too.

```
@Override
public Void visitCallExpr(Expr.Call expr) {
  resolve(expr.callee);

  for (Expr argument : expr.arguments) {
    resolve(argument);
  }

  return null;
}
```

lox/Resolver.java
add after visitBinaryExpr()

Parentheses are easy.

```
@Override
public Void visitGroupingExpr(Expr.Grouping expr) {
  resolve(expr.expression);
  return null;
}
```

lox/Resolver.java
add after visitCallExpr()

Literals are easiest of all.

```
@Override
public Void visitLiteralExpr(Expr.Literal expr) {
  return null;
}
```

lox/Resolver.java
add after visitGroupingExpr()

A literal expression doesn't mention any variables and doesn't contain any sub-expressions so there is no work to do.

Since a static analysis does no control flow or short-circuiting, logical expressions are exactly the same as other binary operators.

```
@Override
public Void visitLogicalExpr(Expr.Logical expr) {
  resolve(expr.left);
  resolve(expr.right);
  return null;
}
```

lox/Resolver.java
add after visitLiteralExpr()

And, finally, the last node. We resolve its one operand.

```
@Override
public Void visitUnaryExpr(Expr.Unary expr) {
  resolve(expr.right);
  return null;
}
```

lox/Resolver.java
add after visitLogicalExpr()

With all of these visit methods, the Java compiler should be satisfied that Resolver fully implements Stmt.Visitor and Expr.Visitor. Now is a good time to take a break, have a snack, maybe a little nap.

## 11.4  Interpreting Resolved Variables

Let's see what our resolver is good for. Each time it visits a variable, it tells the interpreter how many scopes there are between the current scope and the scope where the variable is defined. At runtime, this corresponds exactly to the number of *environments* between the current one and the enclosing one where the interpreter can find the variable's value. The resolver hands that number to the interpreter by calling this:

lox/Interpreter.java
*add after* execute()

```
void resolve(Expr expr, int depth) {
  locals.put(expr, depth);
}
```

We want to store the resolution information somewhere so we can use it when the variable or assignment expression is later executed, but where? One obvious place is right in the syntax tree node itself. That's a fine approach, and that's where many compilers store the results of analyses like this.

We could do that, but it would require mucking around with our syntax tree generator. Instead, we'll take another common approach and store it off to the side in a map that associates each syntax tree node with its resolved data.

I *think* I've heard this map called a "side table" since it's a tabular data structure that stores data separately from the objects it relates to. But whenever I try to Google for that term, I get pages about furniture.

Interactive tools like IDEs often incrementally reparse and re-resolve parts of the user's program. It may be hard to find all of the bits of state that need recalculating when they're hiding in the foliage of the syntax tree. A benefit of storing this data outside of the nodes is that it makes it easy to *discard* it—simply clear the map.

lox/Interpreter.java
*in class* Interpreter

```
private Environment environment = globals;
private final Map<Expr, Integer> locals = new HashMap<>();

Interpreter() {
```

You might think we'd need some sort of nested tree structure to avoid getting confused when there are multiple expressions that reference the same variable, but each expression node is its own Java object with its own unique identity. A single monolithic map doesn't have any trouble keeping them separated.

As usual, using a collection requires us to import a couple of names.

lox/Interpreter.java

```
import java.util.ArrayList;
import java.util.HashMap;
import java.util.List;
```

And:

lox/Interpreter.java

```
import java.util.List;
import java.util.Map;

class Interpreter implements Expr.Visitor<Object>,
```

### 11.4.1  Accessing a resolved variable

Our interpreter now has access to each variable's resolved location. Finally, we get to make use of that. We replace the visit method for variable expressions with this:

```java
public Object visitVariableExpr(Expr.Variable expr) {
    return lookUpVariable(expr.name, expr);
}
```

*lox/Interpreter.java*
*in* visitVariableExpr()
*replace 1 line*

That delegates to:

```java
private Object lookUpVariable(Token name, Expr expr) {
    Integer distance = locals.get(expr);
    if (distance != null) {
        return environment.getAt(distance, name.lexeme);
    } else {
        return globals.get(name);
    }
}
```

*lox/Interpreter.java*
*add after* visitVariableExpr()

There are a couple of things going on here. First, we look up the resolved distance in the map. Remember that we resolved only *local* variables. Globals are treated specially and don't end up in the map (hence the name locals). So, if we don't find a distance in the map, it must be global. In that case, we look it up, dynamically, directly in the global environment. That throws a runtime error if the variable isn't defined.

If we *do* get a distance, we have a local variable, and we get to take advantage of the results of our static analysis. Instead of calling get(), we call this new method on Environment:

```java
Object getAt(int distance, String name) {
    return ancestor(distance).values.get(name);
}
```

*lox/Environment.java*
*add after* define()

The old get() method dynamically walks the chain of enclosing environments, scouring each one to see if the variable might be hiding in there somewhere. But now we know exactly which environment in the chain will have the variable. We reach it using this helper method:

```java
Environment ancestor(int distance) {
    Environment environment = this;
    for (int i = 0; i < distance; i++) {
        environment = environment.enclosing;
    }

    return environment;
}
```

*lox/Environment.java*
*add after* define()

The way the interpreter assumes the variable is in that map feels like flying blind. The interpreter code trusts that the resolver did its job and resolved the variable correctly. This implies a deep coupling between these two classes. Each line of resolver code that touches a scope must have its exact match in the interpreter for modifying an environment. This kind of coupling is a frequent source of subtle bugs—which I found out myself when writing the book—so pay close attention when touching code like this.

This walks a fixed number of hops up the parent chain and returns the environment there. Once we have that, getAt() simply returns the value of the variable in that environment's map. It doesn't even have to check to see if the variable is there—we know it will be because the resolver already found it before.

### 11.4.2  Assigning to a resolved variable

We can also use a variable by assigning to it. The changes to visiting an assignment expression are similar.

lox/Interpreter.java
in visitAssignExpr()
replace 1 line

```java
public Object visitAssignExpr(Expr.Assign expr) {
  Object value = evaluate(expr.value);

  Integer distance = locals.get(expr);
  if (distance != null) {
    environment.assignAt(distance, expr.name, value);
  } else {
    globals.assign(expr.name, value);
  }

  return value;
```

Again, we look up the variable's scope distance. If not found, we assume it's global and handle it the same way as before. Otherwise, we call this new method:

lox/Environment.java
add after getAt()

```java
void assignAt(int distance, Token name, Object value) {
  ancestor(distance).values.put(name.lexeme, value);
}
```

As getAt() is to get(), assignAt() is to assign(). It walks a fixed number of environments, and then stuffs the new value in that map.

Those are the only changes to Interpreter. This is why I chose a representation for our resolved data that was minimally invasive. All of the rest of the nodes continue working as they did before. Even the code for modifying environments is unchanged.

### 11.4.3  Running the resolver

We do need to actually *run* the resolver, though. We insert the new pass after the parser does its magic.

lox/Lox.java
in run()

```java
// Stop if there was a syntax error.
if (hadError) return;

Resolver resolver = new Resolver(interpreter);
resolver.resolve(statements);

interpreter.interpret(statements);
```

We don't run the resolver if there are any parse errors. If the code has a syntax error, it's never going to run, so there's little value in resolving it. If the syntax is clean, we tell the resolver to do its thing. The resolver has a reference to the interpreter and pokes the resolution data directly into it as it walks over variables. When the interpreter runs next, it has everything it needs.

At least, that's true if the resolver *succeeds*. But what about errors during resolution?

# 11.5 Resolution Errors

Since we are doing a semantic analysis pass, we have an opportunity to make Lox's semantics more precise, and to help users catch bugs early before running their code. Take a look at this bad boy:

```
fun bad() {
  var a = "first";
  var a = "second";
}
```

We do allow declaring multiple variables with the same name in the *global* scope, but doing so in a local scope is probably a mistake. If they knew the variable already existed, they would have assigned to it instead of using var. And if they *didn't* know it existed, they probably didn't intend to overwrite the previous one.

We can detect this mistake statically while resolving.

```
    Map<String, Boolean> scope = scopes.peek();
    if (scope.containsKey(name.lexeme)) {
      Lox.error(name,
          "Already a variable with this name in this scope.");
    }

    scope.put(name.lexeme, false);
```

*lox/Resolver.java*
*in* declare()

When we declare a variable in a local scope, we already know the names of every variable previously declared in that same scope. If we see a collision, we report an error.

## 11.5.1 Invalid return errors

Here's another nasty little script:

```
return "at top level";
```

This executes a return statement, but it's not even inside a function at all. It's top-level code. I don't know what the user *thinks* is going to happen, but I don't think we want Lox to allow this.

We can extend the resolver to detect this statically. Much like we track scopes as we walk the tree, we can track whether or not the code we are currently visiting is inside a function declaration.

```
  private final Stack<Map<String, Boolean>> scopes = new Stack<>();
  private FunctionType currentFunction = FunctionType.NONE;

  Resolver(Interpreter interpreter) {
```

*lox/Resolver.java*
*in class* Resolver

Instead of a bare Boolean, we use this funny enum:

lox/Resolver.java
*add after* Resolver ()

```
private enum FunctionType {
  NONE,
  FUNCTION
}
```

It seems kind of dumb now, but we'll add a couple more cases to it later and then it will make more sense. When we resolve a function declaration, we pass that in.

lox/Resolver.java
*in* visitFunctionStmt()
*replace 1 line*

```
    define(stmt.name);

    resolveFunction(stmt, FunctionType.FUNCTION);
    return null;
```

Over in `resolveFunction()`, we take that parameter and store it in the field before resolving the body.

lox/Resolver.java
*method* resolveFunction()
*replace 1 line*

```
private void resolveFunction(
    Stmt.Function function, FunctionType type) {
  FunctionType enclosingFunction = currentFunction;
  currentFunction = type;

  beginScope();
```

We stash the previous value of the field in a local variable first. Remember, Lox has local functions, so you can nest function declarations arbitrarily deeply. We need to track not just that we're in a function, but *how many* we're in.

We could use an explicit stack of FunctionType values for that, but instead we'll piggyback on the JVM. We store the previous value in a local on the Java stack. When we're done resolving the function body, we restore the field to that value.

lox/Resolver.java
*in* resolveFunction()

```
    endScope();
    currentFunction = enclosingFunction;
  }
```

Now that we can always tell whether or not we're inside a function declaration, we check that when resolving a `return` statement.

lox/Resolver.java
*in* visitReturnStmt()

```
public Void visitReturnStmt(Stmt.Return stmt) {
  if (currentFunction == FunctionType.NONE) {
    Lox.error(stmt.keyword, "Can't return from top-level code.");
  }

  if (stmt.value != null) {
```

Neat, right?

There's one more piece. Back in the main Lox class that stitches everything together, we are careful to not run the interpreter if any parse errors are encountered. That check runs *before* the resolver so that we don't try to resolve syntactically invalid code.

But we also need to skip the interpreter if there are resolution errors, so we add *another* check.

```
resolver.resolve(statements);

// Stop if there was a resolution error.
if (hadError) return;

interpreter.interpret(statements);
```

lox/Lox.java
*in* run()

You could imagine doing lots of other analysis in here. For example, if we added `break` statements to Lox, we would probably want to ensure they are only used inside loops.

We could go farther and report warnings for code that isn't necessarily *wrong* but probably isn't useful. For example, many IDEs will warn if you have unreachable code after a `return` statement, or a local variable whose value is never read. All of that would be pretty easy to add to our static visiting pass, or as separate passes.

But, for now, we'll stick with that limited amount of analysis. The important part is that we fixed that one weird annoying edge case bug, though it might be surprising that it took this much work to do it.

The choice of how many different analyses to lump into a single pass is difficult. Many small isolated passes, each with their own responsibility, are simpler to implement and maintain. However, there is a real runtime cost to traversing the syntax tree itself, so bundling multiple analyses into a single pass is usually faster.

## CHALLENGES

1. Why is it safe to eagerly define the variable bound to a function's name when other variables must wait until after they are initialized before they can be used?

2. How do other languages you know handle local variables that refer to the same name in their initializer, like:

```
var a = "outer";
{
  var a = a;
}
```

Is it a runtime error? Compile error? Allowed? Do they treat global variables differently? Do you agree with their choices? Justify your answer.

3. Extend the resolver to report an error if a local variable is never used.

4. Our resolver calculates *which* environment the variable is found in, but it's still looked up by name in that map. A more efficient environment representation would store local variables in an array and look them up by index.

   Extend the resolver to associate a unique index for each local variable declared in a scope. When resolving a variable access, look up both the scope the variable is in and its index and store that. In the interpreter, use that to quickly access a variable by its index instead of using a map.

# Classes

12

*"One has no right to love or hate anything if one has not acquired a thorough knowledge of its nature. Great love springs from great knowledge of the beloved object, and if you know it but little you will be able to love it only a little or not at all."*

— Leonardo da Vinci

We're eleven chapters in, and the interpreter sitting on your machine is nearly a complete scripting language. It could use a couple of built-in data structures like lists and maps, and it certainly needs a core library for file I/O, user input, etc. But the language itself is sufficient. We've got a little procedural language in the same vein as BASIC, Tcl, Scheme (minus macros), and early versions of Python and Lua.

If this were the '80s, we'd stop here. But today, many popular languages support "object-oriented programming". Adding that to Lox will give users a familiar set of tools for writing larger programs. Even if you personally don't like OOP, this chapter and the next will help you understand how others design and build object systems.

If you *really* hate classes, though, you can skip these two chapters. They are fairly isolated from the rest of the book. Personally, I find it's good to learn more about the things I dislike. Things look simple at a distance, but as I get closer, details emerge and I gain a more nuanced perspective.

## 12.1 OOP and Classes

There are three broad paths to object-oriented programming: classes, prototypes, and multimethods. Classes came first and are the most popular style. With the rise of JavaScript (and to a lesser extent Lua), prototypes are more widely known than they used to be. I'll talk more about those later. For Lox, we're taking the, ahem, classic approach.

Since you've written about a thousand lines of Java code with me already, I'm assuming you don't need a detailed introduction to object orientation. The main goal is to bundle data with the code that acts on it. Users do that by declaring a *class* that:

1. Exposes a *constructor* to create and initialize new *instances* of the class

2. Provides a way to store and access *fields* on instances

3. Defines a set of *methods* shared by all instances of the class that operate on each instances' state.

That's about as minimal as it gets. Most object-oriented languages, all the way back to Simula, also do inheritance to reuse behavior across classes. We'll add that in the next chapter. Even kicking that out, we still have a lot to get through. This is a big chapter and everything doesn't quite come together until we have all of the above pieces, so gather your stamina.

Multimethods are the approach you're least likely to be familiar with. I'd love to talk more about them—I designed a hobby language around them once and they are *super rad*—but there are only so many pages I can fit in. If you'd like to learn more, take a look at CLOS (the object system in Common Lisp), Dylan, Julia, or Raku.

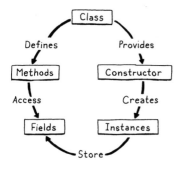

It's like the circle of life, *sans* Sir Elton John.

## 12.2 Class Declarations

Like we do, we're gonna start with syntax. A `class` statement introduces a new name, so it lives in the `declaration` grammar rule.

```
declaration     → classDecl
                | funDecl
                | varDecl
                | statement ;

classDecl       → "class" IDENTIFIER "{" function* "}" ;
```

The new `classDecl` rule relies on the `function` rule we defined earlier. To refresh your memory:

```
function        → IDENTIFIER "(" parameters? ")" block ;
parameters      → IDENTIFIER ( "," IDENTIFIER )* ;
```

In plain English, a class declaration is the `class` keyword, followed by the class's name, then a curly-braced body. Inside that body is a list of method declarations. Unlike function declarations, methods don't have a leading `fun` keyword. Each method is a name, parameter list, and body.

Here's an example:

```
class Breakfast {
  cook() {
    print "Eggs a-fryin'!";
  }

  serve(who) {
    print "Enjoy your breakfast, " + who + ".";
  }
}
```

Like most dynamically typed languages, fields are not explicitly listed in the class declaration. Instances are loose bags of data and you can freely add fields to them as you see fit using normal imperative code.

Over in our AST generator, the `classDecl` grammar rule gets its own statement node.

```
      "Block      : List<Stmt> statements",
      "Class      : Token name, List<Stmt.Function> methods",
      "Expression : Expr expression",
```

tool/GenerateAst.java<br>in main()

It stores the class's name and the methods inside its body. Methods are represented by the existing Stmt.Function class that we use for function declaration AST nodes. That gives us all the bits of state that we need for a method: name, parameter list, and body.

A class can appear anywhere a named declaration is allowed, triggered by the leading `class` keyword.

```
    try {
      if (match(CLASS)) return classDeclaration();
      if (match(FUN)) return function("function");
```

lox/Parser.java<br>in declaration()

That calls out to:

```
  private Stmt classDeclaration() {
    Token name = consume(IDENTIFIER, "Expect class name.");
    consume(LEFT_BRACE, "Expect '{' before class body.");

    List<Stmt.Function> methods = new ArrayList<>();
    while (!check(RIGHT_BRACE) && !isAtEnd()) {
      methods.add(function("method"));
    }

    consume(RIGHT_BRACE, "Expect '}' after class body.");

    return new Stmt.Class(name, methods);
  }
```

lox/Parser.java<br>add after declaration()

There's more meat to this than most of the other parsing methods, but it roughly follows the grammar. We've already consumed the `class` keyword, so we look for the expected class name next, followed by the opening curly brace. Once inside the body, we keep parsing method declarations until we hit the closing brace. Each method declaration is parsed by a call to `function()`, which we defined back in the chapter where functions were introduced.

Like we do in any open-ended loop in the parser, we also check for hitting the end of the file. That won't happen in correct code since a class should have a closing brace at the end, but it ensures the parser doesn't get stuck in an infinite loop if the user has a syntax error and forgets to correctly end the class body.

We wrap the name and list of methods into a Stmt.Class node and we're done. Previously, we would jump straight into the interpreter, but now we need to plumb the node through the resolver first.

*lox/Resolver.java*
*add after* `visitBlockStmt()`

```java
@Override
public Void visitClassStmt(Stmt.Class stmt) {
  declare(stmt.name);
  define(stmt.name);
  return null;
}
```

We aren't going to worry about resolving the methods themselves yet, so for now all we need to do is declare the class using its name. It's not common to declare a class as a local variable, but Lox permits it, so we need to handle it correctly.

Now we interpret the class declaration.

*lox/Interpreter.java*
*add after* `visitBlockStmt()`

```java
@Override
public Void visitClassStmt(Stmt.Class stmt) {
  environment.define(stmt.name.lexeme, null);
  LoxClass klass = new LoxClass(stmt.name.lexeme);
  environment.assign(stmt.name, klass);
  return null;
}
```

This looks similar to how we execute function declarations. We declare the class's name in the current environment. Then we turn the class *syntax node* into a LoxClass, the *runtime* representation of a class. We circle back and store the class object in the variable we previously declared. That two-stage variable binding process allows references to the class inside its own methods.

We will refine it throughout the chapter, but the first draft of LoxClass looks like this:

*lox/LoxClass.java*
*create new file*

```java
package com.craftinginterpreters.lox;

import java.util.List;
import java.util.Map;

class LoxClass {
  final String name;

  LoxClass(String name) {
    this.name = name;
  }
```

*continued on next page...*

```
  @Override
  public String toString() {
    return name;
  }
}
```

*…from previous page*

Literally a wrapper around a name. We don't even store the methods yet. Not super useful, but it does have a toString() method so we can write a trivial script and test that class objects are actually being parsed and executed.

```
class DevonshireCream {
  serveOn() {
    return "Scones";
  }
}

print DevonshireCream; // Prints "DevonshireCream".
```

## 12.3  Creating Instances

We have classes, but they don't do anything yet. Lox doesn't have "static" methods that you can call right on the class itself, so without actual instances, classes are useless. Thus instances are the next step.

While some syntax and semantics are fairly standard across OOP languages, the way you create new instances isn't. Ruby, following Smalltalk, creates instances by calling a method on the class object itself, a recursively graceful approach. Some, like C++ and Java, have a **new** keyword dedicated to birthing a new object. Python has you "call" the class itself like a function. (JavaScript, ever weird, sort of does both.)

I took a minimal approach with Lox. We already have class objects, and we already have function calls, so we'll use call expressions on class objects to create new instances. It's as if a class is a factory function that generates instances of itself. This feels elegant to me, and also spares us the need to introduce syntax like **new**. Therefore, we can skip past the front end straight into the runtime.

Right now, if you try this:

```
class Bagel {}
Bagel();
```

You get a runtime error. visitCallExpr() checks to see if the called object implements LoxCallable and reports an error since LoxClass doesn't. Not *yet*, that is.

In Smalltalk, even *classes* are created by calling methods on an existing object, usually the desired superclass. It's sort of a turtles-all-the-way-down thing. It ultimately bottoms out on a few magical classes like Object and Metaclass that the runtime conjures into being *ex nihilo*.

```
import java.util.Map;

class LoxClass implements LoxCallable {
  final String name;
```

**lox/LoxClass.java**
*replace 1 line*

Implementing that interface requires two methods.

lox/LoxClass.java
add after toString()

```java
@Override
public Object call(Interpreter interpreter,
                   List<Object> arguments) {
  LoxInstance instance = new LoxInstance(this);
  return instance;
}

@Override
public int arity() {
  return 0;
}
```

The interesting one is `call()`. When you "call" a class, it instantiates a new LoxInstance for the called class and returns it. The `arity()` method is how the interpreter validates that you passed the right number of arguments to a callable. For now, we'll say you can't pass any. When we get to user-defined constructors, we'll revisit this.

That leads us to LoxInstance, the runtime representation of an instance of a Lox class. Again, our first implementation starts small.

lox/LoxInstance.java
create new file

```java
package com.craftinginterpreters.lox;

import java.util.HashMap;
import java.util.Map;

class LoxInstance {
  private LoxClass klass;

  LoxInstance(LoxClass klass) {
    this.klass = klass;
  }

  @Override
  public String toString() {
    return klass.name + " instance";
  }
}
```

Like LoxClass, it's pretty bare bones, but we're only getting started. If you want to give it a try, here's a script to run:

```
class Bagel {}
var bagel = Bagel();

print bagel; // Prints "Bagel instance".
```

This program doesn't do much, but it's starting to do *something*.

# 12.4 Properties on Instances

We have instances, so we should make them useful. We're at a fork in the road. We could add behavior first—methods—or we could start with state—properties. We're going to take the latter because, as we'll see, the two get entangled in an interesting way and it will be easier to make sense of them if we get properties working first.

Lox follows JavaScript and Python in how it handles state. Every instance is an open collection of named values. Methods on the instance's class can access and modify properties, but so can outside code. Properties are accessed using a . syntax.

```
someObject.someProperty
```

An expression followed by . and an identifier reads the property with that name from the object the expression evaluates to. That dot has the same precedence as the parentheses in a function call expression, so we slot it into the grammar by replacing the existing call rule with:

```
call            → primary ( "(" arguments? ")" | "." IDENTIFIER )* ;
```

After a primary expression, we allow a series of any mixture of parenthesized calls and dotted property accesses. "Property access" is a mouthful, so from here on out, we'll call these "get expressions".

Allowing code outside of the class to directly modify an object's fields goes against the object-oriented credo that a class *encapsulates* state. Some languages take a more principled stance. In Smalltalk, fields are accessed using simple identifiers—essentially, variables that are only in scope inside a class's methods. Ruby uses @ followed by a name to access a field in an object. That syntax is only meaningful inside a method and always accesses state on the current object.

Lox, for better or worse, isn't quite so pious about its OOP faith.

## 12.4.1 Get expressions

The syntax tree node is:

```
"Call     : Expr callee, Token paren, List<Expr> arguments",
"Get      : Expr object, Token name",
"Grouping : Expr expression",
```

tool/GenerateAst.java
*in* main()

Following the grammar, the new parsing code goes in our existing call() method.

```
while (true) {
  if (match(LEFT_PAREN)) {
    expr = finishCall(expr);
  } else if (match(DOT)) {
    Token name = consume(IDENTIFIER,
        "Expect property name after '.'.");
    expr = new Expr.Get(expr, name);
  } else {
    break;
  }
}
```

lox/Parser.java
*in* call()

The outer while loop there corresponds to the * in the grammar rule. We zip along the tokens building up a chain of calls and gets as we find parentheses and dots, like so:

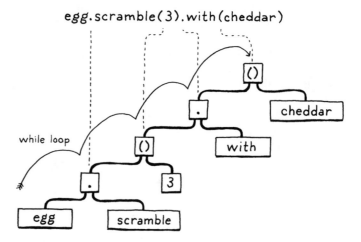

Instances of the new Expr.Get node feed into the resolver.

lox/Resolver.java
add after visitCallExpr()

```java
@Override
public Void visitGetExpr(Expr.Get expr) {
  resolve(expr.object);
  return null;
}
```

You can literally see that property dispatch in Lox is dynamic since we don't process the property name during the static resolution pass.

OK, not much to that. Since properties are looked up dynamically, they don't get resolved. During resolution, we recurse only into the expression to the left of the dot. The actual property access happens in the interpreter.

lox/Interpreter.java
add after visitCallExpr()

```java
@Override
public Object visitGetExpr(Expr.Get expr) {
  Object object = evaluate(expr.object);
  if (object instanceof LoxInstance) {
    return ((LoxInstance) object).get(expr.name);
  }

  throw new RuntimeError(expr.name,
      "Only instances have properties.");
}
```

First, we evaluate the expression whose property is being accessed. In Lox, only instances of classes have properties. If the object is some other type like a number, invoking a getter on it is a runtime error.

If the object is a LoxInstance, then we ask it to look up the property. It must be time to give LoxInstance some actual state. A map will do fine.

lox/LoxInstance.java
in class LoxInstance

```java
  private LoxClass klass;
  private final Map<String, Object> fields = new HashMap<>();

  LoxInstance(LoxClass klass) {
```

Each key in the map is a property name and the corresponding value is the property's value. To look up a property on an instance:

```
Object get(Token name) {
  if (fields.containsKey(name.lexeme)) {
    return fields.get(name.lexeme);
  }

  throw new RuntimeError(name,
      "Undefined property '" + name.lexeme + "'.");
}
```

An interesting edge case we need to handle is what happens if the instance doesn't *have* a property with the given name. We could silently return some dummy value like nil, but my experience with languages like JavaScript is that this behavior masks bugs more often than it does anything useful. Instead, we'll make it a runtime error.

So the first thing we do is see if the instance actually has a field with the given name. Only then do we return it. Otherwise, we raise an error.

Note how I switched from talking about "properties" to "fields". There is a subtle difference between the two. Fields are named bits of state stored directly in an instance. Properties are the named, uh, *things*, that a get expression may return. Every field is a property, but as we'll see, not every property is a field.

In theory, we can now read properties on objects. But since there's no way to actually stuff any state into an instance, there are no fields to access. Before we can test out reading, we must support writing.

### 12.4.2 Set expressions

Setters use the same syntax as getters, except they appear on the left side of an assignment.

```
someObject.someProperty = value;
```

In grammar land, we extend the rule for assignment to allow dotted identifiers on the left-hand side.

```
assignment      → ( call "." )? IDENTIFIER "=" assignment
                | logic_or ;
```

Unlike getters, setters don't chain. However, the reference to call allows any high-precedence expression before the last dot, including any number of *getters*, as in:

lox/LoxInstance.java
*add after* LoxInstance()

Doing a hash table lookup for every field access is fast enough for many language implementations, but not ideal. High performance VMs for languages like JavaScript use sophisticated optimizations like "hidden classes" to avoid that overhead.

Paradoxically, many of the optimizations invented to make dynamic languages fast rest on the observation that—even in those languages—most code is fairly static in terms of the types of objects it works with and their fields.

Ooh, foreshadowing. Spooky!

Note here that only the *last* part, the `.meat` is the *setter*. The `.omelette` and `.filling` parts are both *get* expressions.

Just as we have two separate AST nodes for variable access and variable assignment, we need a second setter node to complement our getter node.

tool/GenerateAst.java
*in* main()

```
"Logical  : Expr left, Token operator, Expr right",
"Set      : Expr object, Token name, Expr value",
"Unary    : Token operator, Expr right",
```

In case you don't remember, the way we handle assignment in the parser is a little funny. We can't easily tell that a series of tokens is the left-hand side of an assignment until we reach the =. Now that our assignment grammar rule has `call` on the left side, which can expand to arbitrarily large expressions, that final = may be many tokens away from the point where we need to know we're parsing an assignment.

Instead, the trick we do is parse the left-hand side as a normal expression. Then, when we stumble onto the equal sign after it, we take the expression we already parsed and transform it into the correct syntax tree node for the assignment.

We add another clause to that transformation to handle turning an Expr.Get expression on the left into the corresponding Expr.Set.

lox/Parser.java
*in* assignment()

```
      return new Expr.Assign(name, value);
    } else if (expr instanceof Expr.Get) {
      Expr.Get get = (Expr.Get)expr;
      return new Expr.Set(get.object, get.name, value);
    }
```

That's parsing our syntax. We push that node through into the resolver.

lox/Resolver.java
*add after* visitLogicalExpr()

```
@Override
public Void visitSetExpr(Expr.Set expr) {
  resolve(expr.value);
  resolve(expr.object);
  return null;
}
```

Again, like Expr.Get, the property itself is dynamically evaluated, so there's nothing to resolve there. All we need to do is recurse into the two subexpressions of Expr.Set, the object whose property is being set, and the value it's being set to.

That leads us to the interpreter.

lox/Interpreter.java
*add after* visitLogicalExpr()

```
@Override
public Object visitSetExpr(Expr.Set expr) {
  Object object = evaluate(expr.object);

  if (!(object instanceof LoxInstance)) {
    throw new RuntimeError(expr.name,
                           "Only instances have fields.");
  }
```

*continued on next page…*

```
    Object value = evaluate(expr.value);
    ((LoxInstance)object).set(expr.name, value);
    return value;
  }
```

...from previous page

We evaluate the object whose property is being set and check to see if it's a
LoxInstance. If not, that's a runtime error. Otherwise, we evaluate the value being set and store it on the instance. That relies on a new method in LoxInstance.

```
  void set(Token name, Object value) {
    fields.put(name.lexeme, value);
  }
```

lox/LoxInstance.java
add after get()

No real magic here. We stuff the values straight into the Java map where fields
live. Since Lox allows freely creating new fields on instances, there's no need to
see if the key is already present.

We hit another semantic edge case in
`visitSetExpr()`. There are three
distinct operations:

1. Evaluate the object.

2. Raise a runtime error if it's not an
   instance of a class.

3. Evaluate the value.

The order that those are performed in
could be user visible, which means we
need to carefully specify it and ensure our
implementations do these in the same
order.

## 12.5  Methods on Classes

You can create instances of classes and stuff data into them, but the class itself
doesn't really *do* anything. Instances are just maps and all instances are more or
less the same. To make them feel like instances *of classes*, we need behavior—
methods.

Our helpful parser already parses method declarations, so we're good there.
We also don't need to add any new parser support for method *calls*. We already
have . (getters) and () (function calls). A "method call" simply chains those
together.

That raises an interesting question. What happens when those two expressions
are pulled apart? Assuming that `method` in this example is a method on the class
of `object` and not a field on the instance, what should the following piece of
code do?

```
var m = object.method;
m(argument);
```

This program "looks up" the method and stores the result—whatever that is—in
a variable and then calls that object later. Is this allowed? Can you treat a method
like it's a function on the instance?

What about the other direction?

```
class Box {}

fun notMethod(argument) {
  print "called function with " + argument;
}

var box = Box();
box.function = notMethod;
box.function("argument");
```

This program creates an instance and then stores a function in a field on it. Then it calls that function using the same syntax as a method call. Does that work?

Different languages have different answers to these questions. One could write a treatise on it. For Lox, we'll say the answer to both of these is yes, it does work. We have a couple of reasons to justify that. For the second example—calling a function stored in a field—we want to support that because first-class functions are useful and storing them in fields is a perfectly normal thing to do.

The first example is more obscure. One motivation is that users generally expect to be able to hoist a subexpression out into a local variable without changing the meaning of the program. You can take this:

```
breakfast(omelette.filledWith(cheese), sausage);
```

And turn it into this:

```
var eggs = omelette.filledWith(cheese);
breakfast(eggs, sausage);
```

And it does the same thing. Likewise, since the . and the () in a method call *are* two separate expressions, it seems you should be able to hoist the *lookup* part into a variable and then call it later. We need to think carefully about what the *thing* you get when you look up a method is, and how it behaves, even in weird cases like:

A motivating use for this is callbacks. Often, you want to pass a callback whose body simply invokes a method on some object. Being able to look up the method and pass it directly saves you the chore of manually declaring a function to wrap it. Compare this:

```
fun callback(a, b, c) {
  obj.method(a, b, c);
}

takeCallback(callback);
```

With this:

```
takeCallback(obj.method);
```

```
class Person {
  sayName() {
    print this.name;
  }
}

var jane = Person();
jane.name = "Jane";

var method = jane.sayName;
method(); // ?
```

If you grab a handle to a method on some instance and call it later, does it "remember" the instance it was pulled off from? Does this inside the method still refer to that original object?

Here's a more pathological example to bend your brain:

```
class Person {
  sayName() {
    print this.name;
  }
}

var jane = Person();
jane.name = "Jane";

var bill = Person();
bill.name = "Bill";

bill.sayName = jane.sayName;
bill.sayName(); // ?
```

Does that last line print "Bill" because that's the instance that we *called* the method through, or "Jane" because it's the instance where we first grabbed the method?

Equivalent code in Lua and JavaScript would print "Bill". Those languages don't really have a notion of "methods". Everything is sort of functions-in-fields, so it's not clear that jane "owns" sayName any more than bill does.

Lox, though, has real class syntax so we do know which callable things are methods and which are functions. Thus, like Python, C#, and others, we will have methods "bind" this to the original instance when the method is first grabbed. Python calls these **bound methods**.

I know, imaginative name, right?

In practice, that's usually what you want. If you take a reference to a method on some object so you can use it as a callback later, you want to remember the instance it belonged to, even if that callback happens to be stored in a field on some other object.

OK, that's a lot of semantics to load into your head. Forget about the edge cases for a bit. We'll get back to those. For now, let's get basic method calls working. We're already parsing the method declarations inside the class body, so the next step is to resolve them.

```
    define(stmt.name);

    for (Stmt.Function method : stmt.methods) {
      FunctionType declaration = FunctionType.METHOD;
      resolveFunction(method, declaration);
    }

    return null;
```

lox/Resolver.java
*in* visitClassStmt()

Storing the function type in a local variable is pointless right now, but we'll expand this code before too long and it will make more sense.

We iterate through the methods in the class body and pass each one to the resolveFunction() method we wrote for handling function declarations already. The only difference is that we pass in a new FunctionType enum value.

```
    NONE,
    METHOD
  }
```

lox/Resolver.java
*in enum* FunctionType
*add "," to previous line*

That's going to be important when we resolve `this` expressions. For now, don't worry about it. The interesting stuff is in the interpreter.

```
    environment.define(stmt.name.lexeme, null);

    Map<String, LoxFunction> methods = new HashMap<>();
    for (Stmt.Function method : stmt.methods) {
      LoxFunction function = new LoxFunction(method, environment);
      methods.put(method.name.lexeme, function);
    }

    LoxClass klass = new LoxClass(stmt.name.lexeme, methods);
    environment.assign(stmt.name, klass);
```

When we interpret a class declaration statement, we turn the syntactic representation of the class—its AST node—into its runtime representation. Now, we need to do that for the methods contained in the class as well. Each method declaration blossoms into a LoxFunction object.

We take all of those and wrap them up into a map, keyed by the method names. That gets stored in LoxClass.

lox/LoxClass.java
in class LoxClass
replace 4 lines

```
  final String name;
  private final Map<String, LoxFunction> methods;

  LoxClass(String name, Map<String, LoxFunction> methods) {
    this.name = name;
    this.methods = methods;
  }

  @Override
  public String toString() {
```

Where an instance stores state, the class stores behavior. LoxInstance has its map of fields, and LoxClass gets a map of methods. Even though methods are owned by the class, they are still accessed through instances of that class.

```
  Object get(Token name) {
    if (fields.containsKey(name.lexeme)) {
      return fields.get(name.lexeme);
    }

    LoxFunction method = klass.findMethod(name.lexeme);
    if (method != null) return method;

    throw new RuntimeError(name, // [hidden]
        "Undefined property '" + name.lexeme + "'.");
```

Looking for a field first implies that fields shadow methods, a subtle but important semantic point.

When looking up a property on an instance, if we don't find a matching field, we look for a method with that name on the instance's class. If found, we return that. This is where the distinction between "field" and "property" becomes meaningful. When accessing a property, you might get a field—a bit of state stored on the instance—or you could hit a method defined on the instance's class.

The method is looked up using this:

```
LoxFunction findMethod(String name) {
  if (methods.containsKey(name)) {
    return methods.get(name);
  }

  return null;
}
```

lox/LoxClass.java
*add after* LoxClass()

You can probably guess this method is going to get more interesting later. For now, a simple map lookup on the class's method table is enough to get us started. Give it a try:

```
class Bacon {
  eat() {
    print "Crunch crunch crunch!";
  }
}

Bacon().eat(); // Prints "Crunch crunch crunch!".
```

Apologies if you prefer chewy bacon over crunchy. Feel free to adjust the script to your taste.

## 12.6 This

We can define both behavior and state on objects, but they aren't tied together yet. Inside a method, we have no way to access the fields of the "current" object—the instance that the method was called on—nor can we call other methods on that same object.

To get at that instance, it needs a name. Smalltalk, Ruby, and Swift use "self". Simula, C++, Java, and others use "this". Python uses "self" by convention, but you can technically call it whatever you like.

For Lox, since we generally hew to Java-ish style, we'll go with "this". Inside a method body, a `this` expression evaluates to the instance that the method was called on. Or, more specifically, since methods are accessed and then invoked as two steps, it will refer to the object that the method was *accessed* from.

That makes our job harder. Peep at:

"I" would have been a great choice, but using "i" for loop variables predates OOP and goes all the way back to Fortran. We are victims of the incidental choices of our forebears.

```
class Egotist {
  speak() {
    print this;
  }
}

var method = Egotist().speak;
method();
```

On the second-to-last line, we grab a reference to the `speak()` method off an instance of the class. That returns a function, and that function needs to remember the instance it was pulled off of so that *later*, on the last line, it can still find it when the function is called.

We need to take `this` at the point that the method is accessed and attach it to the function somehow so that it stays around as long as we need it to. Hmm…a way to store some extra data that hangs around a function, eh? That sounds an awful lot like a *closure*, doesn't it?

If we defined `this` as a sort of hidden variable in an environment that surrounds the function returned when looking up a method, then uses of `this` in the body would be able to find it later. LoxFunction already has the ability to hold on to a surrounding environment, so we have the machinery we need.

Let's walk through an example to see how it works:

```
class Cake {
  taste() {
    var adjective = "delicious";
    print "The " + this.flavor + " cake is " + adjective + "!";
  }
}

var cake = Cake();
cake.flavor = "German chocolate";
cake.taste(); // Prints "The German chocolate cake is delicious!".
```

When we first evaluate the class definition, we create a LoxFunction for `taste()`. Its closure is the environment surrounding the class, in this case the global one. So the LoxFunction we store in the class's method map looks like so:

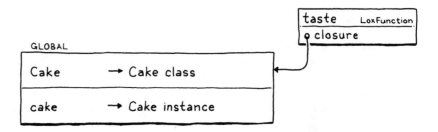

When we evaluate the `cake.taste` get expression, we create a new environment that binds `this` to the object the method is accessed from (here, `cake`). Then we make a *new* LoxFunction with the same code as the original one but using that new environment as its closure.

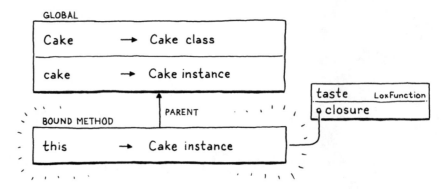

This is the LoxFunction that gets returned when evaluating the get expression for the method name. When that function is later called by a ( ) expression, we create an environment for the method body as usual.

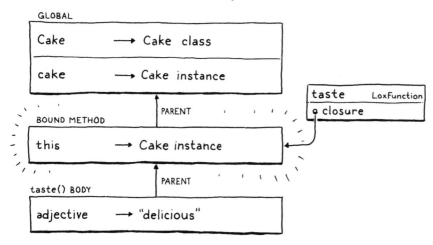

The parent of the body environment is the environment we created earlier to bind this to the current object. Thus any use of this inside the body successfully resolves to that instance.

Reusing our environment code for implementing this also takes care of interesting cases where methods and functions interact, like:

```
class Thing {
  getCallback() {
    fun localFunction() {
      print this;
    }

    return localFunction;
  }
}

var callback = Thing().getCallback();
callback();
```

In, say, JavaScript, it's common to return a callback from inside a method. That callback may want to hang on to and retain access to the original object—the this value—that the method was associated with. Our existing support for closures and environment chains should do all this correctly.

Let's code it up. The first step is adding new syntax for this.

```
      "Set      : Expr object, Token name, Expr value",
      "This     : Token keyword",
      "Unary    : Token operator, Expr right",
```

**tool/GenerateAst.java**
*in* main()

Parsing is simple since it's a single token which our lexer already recognizes as a reserved word.

lox/Parser.java
*in* primary()

```
      return new Expr.Literal(previous().literal);
    }

    if (match(THIS)) return new Expr.This(previous());

    if (match(IDENTIFIER)) {
```

You can start to see how **this** works like a variable when we get to the resolver.

lox/Resolver.java
*add after* visitSetExpr()

```
@Override
public Void visitThisExpr(Expr.This expr) {
    resolveLocal(expr, expr.keyword);
    return null;
}
```

We resolve it exactly like any other local variable using "this" as the name for the "variable". Of course, that's not going to work right now, because "this" *isn't* declared in any scope. Let's fix that over in visitClassStmt().

lox/Resolver.java
*in* visitClassStmt()

```
    define(stmt.name);

    beginScope();
    scopes.peek().put("this", true);

    for (Stmt.Function method : stmt.methods) {
```

Before we step in and start resolving the method bodies, we push a new scope and define "this" in it as if it were a variable. Then, when we're done, we discard that surrounding scope.

lox/Resolver.java
*in* visitClassStmt()

```
    }

    endScope();

    return null;
```

Now, whenever a **this** expression is encountered (at least inside a method) it will resolve to a "local variable" defined in an implicit scope just outside of the block for the method body.

The resolver has a new *scope* for **this**, so the interpreter needs to create a corresponding *environment* for it. Remember, we always have to keep the resolver's scope chains and the interpreter's linked environments in sync with each other. At runtime, we create the environment after we find the method on the instance. We replace the previous line of code that simply returned the method's LoxFunction with this:

lox/LoxInstance.java
*in* get()
*replace 1 line*

```
    LoxFunction method = klass.findMethod(name.lexeme);
    if (method != null) return method.bind(this);

    throw new RuntimeError(name, // [hidden]
        "Undefined property '" + name.lexeme + "'.");
```

Note the new call to `bind()`. That looks like so:

```
LoxFunction bind(LoxInstance instance) {
  Environment environment = new Environment(closure);
  environment.define("this", instance);
  return new LoxFunction(declaration, environment);
}
```

lox/LoxFunction.java
add after LoxFunction()

There isn't much to it. We create a new environment nestled inside the method's original closure. Sort of a closure-within-a-closure. When the method is called, that will become the parent of the method body's environment.

We declare "this" as a variable in that environment and bind it to the given instance, the instance that the method is being accessed from. *Et voilà*, the returned LoxFunction now carries around its own little persistent world where "this" is bound to the object.

The remaining task is interpreting those `this` expressions. Similar to the resolver, it is the same as interpreting a variable expression.

```
@Override
public Object visitThisExpr(Expr.This expr) {
  return lookUpVariable(expr.keyword, expr);
}
```

lox/Interpreter.java
add after visitSetExpr()

Go ahead and give it a try using that cake example from earlier. With less than twenty lines of code, our interpreter handles `this` inside methods even in all of the weird ways it can interact with nested classes, functions inside methods, handles to methods, etc.

## 12.6.1  Invalid uses of this

Wait a minute. What happens if you try to use `this` *outside* of a method? What about:

```
print this;
```

Or:

```
fun notAMethod() {
  print this;
}
```

There is no instance for `this` to point to if you're not in a method. We could give it some default value like `nil` or make it a runtime error, but the user has clearly made a mistake. The sooner they find and fix that mistake, the happier they'll be.

Our resolution pass is a fine place to detect this error statically. It already detects `return` statements outside of functions. We'll do something similar for `this`. In the vein of our existing FunctionType enum, we define a new ClassType one.

lox/Resolver.java
*add after enum* FunctionType

```
  }

  private enum ClassType {
    NONE,
    CLASS
  }

  private ClassType currentClass = ClassType.NONE;

  void resolve(List<Stmt> statements) {
```

Yes, it could be a Boolean. When we get to inheritance, it will get a third value, hence the enum right now. We also add a corresponding field, `currentClass`. Its value tells us if we are currently inside a class declaration while traversing the syntax tree. It starts out NONE which means we aren't in one.

When we begin to resolve a class declaration, we change that.

lox/Resolver.java
*in* visitClassStmt()

```
  public Void visitClassStmt(Stmt.Class stmt) {
    ClassType enclosingClass = currentClass;
    currentClass = ClassType.CLASS;

    declare(stmt.name);
```

As with `currentFunction`, we store the previous value of the field in a local variable. This lets us piggyback onto the JVM to keep a stack of `currentClass` values. That way we don't lose track of the previous value if one class nests inside another.

Once the methods have been resolved, we "pop" that stack by restoring the old value.

lox/Resolver.java
*in* visitClassStmt()

```
    endScope();

    currentClass = enclosingClass;
    return null;
```

When we resolve a `this` expression, the `currentClass` field gives us the bit of data we need to report an error if the expression doesn't occur nestled inside a method body.

lox/Resolver.java
*in* visitThisExpr()

```
  public Void visitThisExpr(Expr.This expr) {
    if (currentClass == ClassType.NONE) {
      Lox.error(expr.keyword,
          "Can't use 'this' outside of a class.");
      return null;
    }

    resolveLocal(expr, expr.keyword);
```

That should help users use `this` correctly, and it saves us from having to handle misuse at runtime in the interpreter.

## 12.7  Constructors and Initializers

We can do almost everything with classes now, and as we near the end of the chapter we find ourselves strangely focused on a beginning. Methods and fields let us encapsulate state and behavior together so that an object always *stays* in a valid configuration. But how do we ensure a brand new object *starts* in a good state?

For that, we need constructors. I find them one of the trickiest parts of a language to design, and if you peer closely at most other languages, you'll see cracks around object construction where the seams of the design don't quite fit together perfectly. Maybe there's something intrinsically messy about the moment of birth.

"Constructing" an object is actually a pair of operations:

1. The runtime *allocates* the memory required for a fresh instance. In most languages, this operation is at a fundamental level beneath what user code is able to access.

2. Then, a user-provided chunk of code *initializes* the unformed object.

The latter is what we tend to think of when we hear "constructor", but the language itself has usually done some groundwork for us before we get to that point. In fact, our Lox interpreter already has that covered when it creates a new LoxInstance object.

We'll do the remaining part—user-defined initialization—now. Languages have a variety of notations for the chunk of code that sets up a new object for a class. C++, Java, and C# use a method whose name matches the class name. Ruby and Python call it `init()`. The latter is nice and short, so we'll do that.

In LoxClass's implementation of LoxCallable, we add a few more lines.

```
                    List<Object> arguments) {
    LoxInstance instance = new LoxInstance(this);
    LoxFunction initializer = findMethod("init");
    if (initializer != null) {
      initializer.bind(instance).call(interpreter, arguments);
    }

    return instance;
```

*lox/LoxClass.java*
*in* call()

When a class is called, after the LoxInstance is created, we look for an "init" method. If we find one, we immediately bind and invoke it just like a normal method call. The argument list is forwarded along.

That argument list means we also need to tweak how a class declares its arity.

```
  public int arity() {
    LoxFunction initializer = findMethod("init");
    if (initializer == null) return 0;
    return initializer.arity();
  }
```

*lox/LoxClass.java*
*in* arity()
*replace 1 line*

If there is an initializer, that method's arity determines how many arguments you must pass when you call the class itself. We don't *require* a class to define an

A few examples: In Java, even though final fields must be initialized, it is still possible to read one *before* it has been. Exceptions—a huge, complex feature—were added to C++ mainly as a way to emit errors from constructors.

C++'s "placement new" is a rare example where the innards of allocation are laid bare for the programmer to prod.

initializer, though, as a convenience. If you don't have an initializer, the arity is still zero.

That's basically it. Since we bind the `init()` method before we call it, it has access to `this` inside its body. That, along with the arguments passed to the class, are all you need to be able to set up the new instance however you desire.

## 12.7.1 Invoking init() directly

As usual, exploring this new semantic territory rustles up a few weird creatures. Consider:

```
class Foo {
  init() {
    print this;
  }
}
```

```
var foo = Foo();
print foo.init();
```

Can you "re-initialize" an object by directly calling its `init()` method? If you do, what does it return? A reasonable answer would be `nil` since that's what it appears the body returns.

However—and I generally dislike compromising to satisfy the implementation—it will make clox's implementation of constructors much easier if we say that `init()` methods always return `this`, even when directly called. In order to keep jlox compatible with that, we add a little special case code in LoxFunction.

Maybe "dislike" is too strong a claim. It's reasonable to have the constraints and resources of your implementation affect the design of the language. There are only so many hours in the day, and if a cut corner here or there lets you get more features to users in less time, it may very well be a net win for their happiness and productivity. The trick is figuring out *which* corners to cut that won't cause your users and future self to curse your shortsightedness.

**lox/LoxFunction.java**
*in* `call()`

```
    return returnValue.value;
  }

  if (isInitializer) return closure.getAt(0, "this");
  return null;
```

If the function is an initializer, we override the actual return value and forcibly return `this`. That relies on a new `isInitializer` field.

**lox/LoxFunction.java**
*in class* LoxFunction
*replace 1 line*

```
  private final Environment closure;

  private final boolean isInitializer;

  LoxFunction(Stmt.Function declaration, Environment closure,
              boolean isInitializer) {
    this.isInitializer = isInitializer;
    this.closure = closure;
    this.declaration = declaration;
```

We can't simply see if the name of the LoxFunction is "init" because the user could have defined a *function* with that name. In that case, there *is* no `this` to return. To avoid *that* weird edge case, we'll directly store whether the LoxFunction represents an initializer method. That means we need to go back and fix the few places where we create LoxFunctions.

```
  public Void visitFunctionStmt(Stmt.Function stmt) {
    LoxFunction function = new LoxFunction(stmt, environment,
                                   false);
    environment.define(stmt.name.lexeme, function);
```

lox/Interpreter.java
*in* visitFunctionStmt()
*replace 1 line*

For actual function declarations, isInitializer is always false. For methods, we check the name.

```
    for (Stmt.Function method : stmt.methods) {
      LoxFunction function = new LoxFunction(method, environment,
          method.name.lexeme.equals("init"));
      methods.put(method.name.lexeme, function);
```

lox/Interpreter.java
*in* visitClassStmt()
*replace 1 line*

And then in bind() where we create the closure that binds this to a method, we pass along the original method's value.

```
    environment.define("this", instance);
    return new LoxFunction(declaration, environment,
                           isInitializer);
  }
```

lox/LoxFunction.java
*in* bind()
*replace 1 line*

## 12.7.2  Returning from init()

We aren't out of the woods yet. We've been assuming that a user-written initializer doesn't explicitly return a value because most constructors don't. What should happen if a user tries:

```
class Foo {
  init() {
    return "something else";
  }
}
```

It's definitely not going to do what they want, so we may as well make it a static error. Back in the resolver, we add another case to FunctionType.

```
  FUNCTION,
  INITIALIZER,
  METHOD
```

lox/Resolver.java
*in enum* FunctionType

We use the visited method's name to determine if we're resolving an initializer or not.

```
    FunctionType declaration = FunctionType.METHOD;
    if (method.name.lexeme.equals("init")) {
      declaration = FunctionType.INITIALIZER;
    }

    resolveFunction(method, declaration);
```

lox/Resolver.java
*in* visitClassStmt()

When we later traverse into a `return` statement, we check that field and make it an error to return a value from inside an `init()` method.

```
    if (stmt.value != null) {
      if (currentFunction == FunctionType.INITIALIZER) {
        Lox.error(stmt.keyword,
            "Can't return a value from an initializer.");
      }

      resolve(stmt.value);
```

We're *still* not done. We statically disallow returning a *value* from an initializer, but you can still use an empty early `return`.

```
class Foo {
  init() {
    return;
  }
}
```

That is actually kind of useful sometimes, so we don't want to disallow it entirely. Instead, it should return `this` instead of `nil`. That's an easy fix over in LoxFunction.

```
    } catch (Return returnValue) {
      if (isInitializer) return closure.getAt(0, "this");

      return returnValue.value;
```

If we're in an initializer and execute a `return` statement, instead of returning the value (which will always be `nil`), we again return `this`.

Phew! That was a whole list of tasks but our reward is that our little interpreter has grown an entire programming paradigm. Classes, methods, fields, `this`, and constructors. Our baby language is looking awfully grown-up.

## CHALLENGES

1. We have methods on instances, but there is no way to define "static" methods that can be called directly on the class object itself. Add support for them. Use a **class** keyword preceding the method to indicate a static method that hangs off the class object.

```
class Math {
  class square(n) {
    return n * n;
  }
}

print Math.square(3); // Prints "9".
```

   You can solve this however you like, but the "metaclasses" used by Smalltalk and Ruby are a particularly elegant approach. *Hint: Make LoxClass extend LoxInstance and go from there.*

2. Most modern languages support "getters" and "setters"—members on a class that look like field reads and writes but that actually execute user-defined code. Extend Lox to support getter methods. These are declared without a parameter list. The body of the getter is executed when a property with that name is accessed.

```
class Circle {
  init(radius) {
    this.radius = radius;
  }

  area {
    return 3.141592653 * this.radius * this.radius;
  }
}

var circle = Circle(4);
print circle.area; // Prints roughly "50.2655".
```

3. Python and JavaScript allow you to freely access an object's fields from outside of its own methods. Ruby and Smalltalk encapsulate instance state. Only methods on the class can access the raw fields, and it is up to the class to decide which state is exposed. Most statically typed languages offer modifiers like **private** and **public** to control which parts of a class are externally accessible on a per-member basis.

   What are the trade-offs between these approaches and why might a language prefer one or the other?

## DESIGN NOTE: PROTOTYPES AND POWER

In this chapter, we introduced two new runtime entities, LoxClass and LoxInstance. The former is where behavior for objects lives, and the latter is for state. What if you could define methods right on a single object, inside LoxInstance? In that case, we wouldn't need LoxClass at all. LoxInstance would be a complete package for defining the behavior and state of an object.

We'd still want some way, without classes, to reuse behavior across multiple instances. We could let a LoxInstance *delegate* directly to another LoxInstance to reuse its fields and methods, sort of like inheritance.

Users would model their program as a constellation of objects, some of which delegate to each other to reflect commonality. Objects used as delegates represent "canonical" or "prototypical" objects that others refine. The result is a simpler runtime with only a single internal construct, LoxInstance.

That's where the name **prototypes** comes from for this paradigm. It was invented by David Ungar and Randall Smith in a language called Self. They came up with it by starting with Smalltalk and following the above mental exercise to see how much they could pare it down.

Prototypes were an academic curiosity for a long time, a fascinating one that generated interesting research but didn't make a dent in the larger world of programming. That is, until Brendan Eich crammed prototypes into JavaScript, which then promptly took over the world. Many (many) words have been written about prototypes in JavaScript. Whether that shows that prototypes are brilliant or confusing—or both!—is an open question.

I won't get into whether or not I think prototypes are a good idea for a language. I've made languages that are prototypal and class-based, and my opinions of both are complex. What I want to discuss is the role of *simplicity* in a language.

Prototypes are simpler than classes—less code for the language implementer to write, and fewer concepts for the user to learn and understand. Does that make them better? We language nerds have a tendency to fetishize minimalism. Personally, I think simplicity is only part of the equation. What we really want to give the user is *power*, which I define as:

```
power = breadth × ease ÷ complexity
```

None of these are precise numeric measures. I'm using math as analogy here, not actual quantification.

- **Breadth** is the range of different things the language lets you express. C has a lot of breadth—it's been used for everything from operating systems to user applications to games. Domain-specific languages like AppleScript and Matlab have less breadth.

- **Ease** is how little effort it takes to make the language do what you want. "Usability" might be another term, though it carries more baggage than I want to bring in. "Higher-level" languages tend to have more ease than "lower-level" ones. Most languages have a "grain" to them where some things feel easier to express than others.

- **Complexity** is how big the language (including its runtime, core libraries, tools, ecosystem, etc.) is. People talk about how many pages are in a language's spec, or how many keywords it has. It's how much the user has to load into their wetware

Including more than a handful by yours truly:
→ craftinginterpreters.com/prototypes

Prototype-based Finch:
→ craftinginterpreters.com/finch

Class-based Wren:
→ craftinginterpreters.com/wren

before they can be productive in the system. It is the antonym of simplicity.

Reducing complexity *does* increase power. The smaller the denominator, the larger the resulting value, so our intuition that simplicity is good is valid. However, when reducing complexity, we must take care not to sacrifice breadth or ease in the process, or the total power may go down. Java would be a strictly *simpler* language if it removed strings, but it probably wouldn't handle text manipulation tasks well, nor would it be as easy to get things done.

The art, then, is finding *accidental* complexity that can be omitted—language features and interactions that don't carry their weight by increasing the breadth or ease of using the language.

If users want to express their program in terms of categories of objects, then baking classes into the language increases the ease of doing that, hopefully by a large enough margin to pay for the added complexity. But if that isn't how users are using your language, then by all means leave classes out.

# Inheritance

13

*"Once we were blobs in the sea, and then fishes, and then lizards and rats and then monkeys, and hundreds of things in between. This hand was once a fin, this hand once had claws! In my human mouth I have the pointy teeth of a wolf and the chisel teeth of a rabbit and the grinding teeth of a cow! Our blood is as salty as the sea we used to live in! When we're frightened, the hair on our skin stands up, just like it did when we had fur. We are history! Everything we've ever been on the way to becoming us, we still are."*

— Terry Pratchett, *A Hat Full of Sky*

Can you believe it? We've reached the last chapter of Part II. We're almost done with our first Lox interpreter. The previous chapter was a big ball of intertwined object-orientation features. I couldn't separate those from each other, but I did manage to untangle one piece. In this chapter, we'll finish off Lox's class support by adding inheritance.

Inheritance appears in object-oriented languages all the way back to the first one, Simula. Early on, Kristen Nygaard and Ole-Johan Dahl noticed commonalities across classes in the simulation programs they wrote. Inheritance gave them a way to reuse the code for those similar parts.

You could say all those other languages *inherited* it from Simula. Hey-ooo! I'll, uh, see myself out.

# 13.1 Superclasses and Subclasses

"Super-" and "sub-" mean "above" and "below" in Latin, respectively. Picture an inheritance tree like a family tree with the root at the top—subclasses are below their superclasses on the diagram. More generally, "sub-" refers to things that refine or are contained by some more general concept. In zoology, a subclass is a finer categorization of a larger class of living things.

   In set theory, a subset is contained by a larger superset which has all of the elements of the subset and possibly more. Set theory and programming languages meet each other in type theory. There, you have "supertypes" and "subtypes".

   In statically typed object-oriented languages, a subclass is also often a subtype of its superclass. Say we have a Doughnut superclass and a BostonCream subclass. Every BostonCream is also an instance of Doughnut, but there may be doughnut objects that are not BostonCreams (like Crullers).

   Think of a type as the set of all values of that type. The set of all Doughnut instances contains the set of all BostonCream instances since every BostonCream is also a Doughnut. So BostonCream is a subclass, and a subtype, and its instances are a subset. It all lines up.

Given that the concept is "inheritance", you would hope they would pick a consistent metaphor and call them "parent" and "child" classes, but that would be too easy. Way back when, C. A. R. Hoare coined the term "subclass" to refer to a record type that refines another type. Simula borrowed that term to refer to a *class* that inherits from another. I don't think it was until Smalltalk came along that someone flipped the Latin prefix to get "superclass" to refer to the other side of the relationship. From C++, you also hear "base" and "derived" classes. I'll mostly stick with "superclass" and "subclass".

   Our first step towards supporting inheritance in Lox is a way to specify a superclass when declaring a class. There's a lot of variety in syntax for this. C++ and C# place a : after the subclass's name, followed by the superclass name. Java uses extends instead of the colon. Python puts the superclass(es) in parentheses after the class name. Simula puts the superclass's name *before* the class keyword.

   This late in the game, I'd rather not add a new reserved word or token to the lexer. We don't have extends or even :, so we'll follow Ruby and use a less-than sign (<).

```
class Doughnut {
  // General doughnut stuff...
}

class BostonCream < Doughnut {
  // Boston Cream-specific stuff...
}
```

To work this into the grammar, we add a new optional clause in our existing classDecl rule.

```
classDecl      → "class" IDENTIFIER ( "<" IDENTIFIER )?
                 "{" function* "}" ;
```

After the class name, you can have a < followed by the superclass's name. The superclass clause is optional because you don't *have* to have a superclass. Unlike some other object-oriented languages like Java, Lox has no root "Object" class that everything inherits from, so when you omit the superclass clause, the class has *no* superclass, not even an implicit one.

   We want to capture this new syntax in the class declaration's AST node.

**tool/GenerateAst.java**
*in* main()
*replace 1 line*

```
      "Block     : List<Stmt> statements",
      "Class     : Token name, Expr.Variable superclass," +
      "            " + " List<Stmt.Function> methods",
      "Expression : Expr expression",
```

You might be surprised that we store the superclass name as an Expr.Variable, not a Token. The grammar restricts the superclass clause to a single identifier, but at runtime, that identifier is evaluated as a variable access. Wrapping the name in an Expr.Variable early on in the parser gives us an object that the resolver can hang the resolution information off of.

   The new parser code follows the grammar directly.

```
  Token name = consume(IDENTIFIER, "Expect class name.");

  Expr.Variable superclass = null;
  if (match(LESS)) {
    consume(IDENTIFIER, "Expect superclass name.");
    superclass = new Expr.Variable(previous());
  }

  consume(LEFT_BRACE, "Expect '{' before class body.");
```

lox/Parser.java
*in* classDeclaration()

Once we've (possibly) parsed a superclass declaration, we store it in the AST.

```
  consume(RIGHT_BRACE, "Expect '}' after class body.");
  return new Stmt.Class(name, superclass, methods);
}
```

lox/Parser.java
*in* classDeclaration()
*replace 1 line*

If we didn't parse a superclass clause, the superclass expression will be `null`. We'll have to make sure the later passes check for that. The first of those is the resolver.

```
  define(stmt.name);
  if (stmt.superclass != null) {
    resolve(stmt.superclass);
  }

  beginScope();
```

lox/Resolver.java
*in* visitClassStmt()

The class declaration AST node has a new subexpression, so we traverse into and resolve that. Since classes are usually declared at the top level, the superclass name will most likely be a global variable, so this doesn't usually do anything useful. However, Lox allows class declarations even inside blocks, so it's possible the superclass name refers to a local variable. In that case, we need to make sure it's resolved.

Because even well-intentioned programmers sometimes write weird code, there's a silly edge case we need to worry about while we're in here. Take a look at this:

```
class Oops < Oops {}
```

There's no way this will do anything useful, and if we let the runtime try to run this, it will break the expectation the interpreter has about there not being cycles in the inheritance chain. The safest thing is to detect this case statically and report it as an error.

```
  define(stmt.name);
  if (stmt.superclass != null &&
      stmt.name.lexeme.equals(stmt.superclass.name.lexeme)) {
    Lox.error(stmt.superclass.name,
        "A class can't inherit from itself.");
  }

  if (stmt.superclass != null) {
```

lox/Resolver.java
*in* visitClassStmt()

Assuming the code resolves without error, the AST travels to the interpreter.

lox/Interpreter.java
*in* visitClassStmt()

```java
public Void visitClassStmt(Stmt.Class stmt) {
  Object superclass = null;
  if (stmt.superclass != null) {
    superclass = evaluate(stmt.superclass);
    if (!(superclass instanceof LoxClass)) {
      throw new RuntimeError(stmt.superclass.name,
          "Superclass must be a class.");
    }
  }

  environment.define(stmt.name.lexeme, null);
```

If the class has a superclass expression, we evaluate it. Since that could potentially evaluate to some other kind of object, we have to check at runtime that the thing we want to be the superclass is actually a class. Bad things would happen if we allowed code like:

```java
var NotAClass = "I am totally not a class";

class Subclass < NotAClass {} // ?!
```

Assuming that check passes, we continue on. Executing a class declaration turns the syntactic representation of a class—its AST node—into its runtime representation, a LoxClass object. We need to plumb the superclass through to that too. We pass the superclass to the constructor.

lox/Interpreter.java
*in* visitClassStmt()
*replace 1 line*

```java
      methods.put(method.name.lexeme, function);
    }

    LoxClass klass = new LoxClass(stmt.name.lexeme,
        (LoxClass)superclass, methods);

    environment.assign(stmt.name, klass);
```

The constructor stores it in a field.

lox/LoxClass.java
*constructor* LoxClass()
*replace 1 line*

```java
LoxClass(String name, LoxClass superclass,
        Map<String, LoxFunction> methods) {
  this.superclass = superclass;
  this.name = name;
```

Which we declare here:

lox/LoxClass.java
*in class* LoxClass

```java
final String name;
final LoxClass superclass;
private final Map<String, LoxFunction> methods;
```

With that, we can define classes that are subclasses of other classes. Now, what does having a superclass actually *do*?

## 13.2 Inheriting Methods

Inheriting from another class means that everything that's true of the superclass should be true, more or less, of the subclass. In statically typed languages, that carries a lot of implications. The sub*class* must also be a sub*type*, and the memory layout is controlled so that you can pass an instance of a subclass to a function expecting a superclass and it can still access the inherited fields correctly.

Lox is a dynamically typed language, so our requirements are much simpler. Basically, it means that if you can call some method on an instance of the superclass, you should be able to call that method when given an instance of the subclass. In other words, methods are inherited from the superclass.

This lines up with one of the goals of inheritance—to give users a way to reuse code across classes. Implementing this in our interpreter is astonishingly easy.

> A fancier name for this hand-wavey guideline is the *Liskov substitution principle*. Barbara Liskov introduced it in a keynote during the formative period of object-oriented programming.

> lox/LoxClass.java
> *in* findMethod()

```
      return methods.get(name);
  }

  if (superclass != null) {
    return superclass.findMethod(name);
  }

  return null;
```

That's literally all there is to it. When we are looking up a method on an instance, if we don't find it on the instance's class, we recurse up through the superclass chain and look there. Give it a try:

```
class Doughnut {
  cook() {
    print "Fry until golden brown.";
  }
}

class BostonCream < Doughnut {}
BostonCream().cook();
```

There we go, half of our inheritance features are complete with only three lines of Java code.

## 13.3 Calling Superclass Methods

In findMethod() we look for a method on the current class *before* walking up the superclass chain. If a method with the same name exists in both the subclass and the superclass, the subclass one takes precedence or **overrides** the superclass method. Sort of like how variables in inner scopes shadow outer ones.

That's great if the subclass wants to *replace* some superclass behavior completely. But, in practice, subclasses often want to *refine* the superclass's behavior. They want to do a little work specific to the subclass, but also execute the original superclass behavior too.

However, since the subclass has overridden the method, there's no way to refer to the original one. If the subclass method tries to call it by name, it will just recursively hit its own override. We need a way to say "Call this method, but look for it directly on my superclass and ignore my override". Java uses `super` for this, and we'll use that same syntax in Lox. Here is an example:

```
class Doughnut {
  cook() {
    print "Fry until golden brown.";
  }
}

class BostonCream < Doughnut {
  cook() {
    super.cook();
    print "Pipe full of custard and coat with chocolate.";
  }
}

BostonCream().cook();
```

If you run this, it should print:

```
Fry until golden brown.
Pipe full of custard and coat with chocolate.
```

We have a new expression form. The `super` keyword, followed by a dot and an identifier, looks for a method with that name. Unlike calls on `this`, the search starts at the superclass.

### 13.3.1 Syntax

With `this`, the keyword works sort of like a magic variable, and the expression is that one lone token. But with `super`, the subsequent `.` and property name are inseparable parts of the `super` expression. You can't have a bare `super` token all by itself.

```
print super; // Syntax error.
```

So the new clause we add to the `primary` rule in our grammar includes the property access as well.

```
primary        → "true" | "false" | "nil" | "this"
               | NUMBER | STRING | IDENTIFIER | "(" expression ")"
               | "super" "." IDENTIFIER ;
```

Typically, a `super` expression is used for a method call, but, as with regular methods, the argument list is *not* part of the expression. Instead, a super *call* is a super *access* followed by a function call. Like other method calls, you can get a handle to a superclass method and invoke it separately.

```
var method = super.cook;
method();
```

So the super expression itself contains only the token for the super keyword and the name of the method being looked up. The corresponding syntax tree node is thus:

```
    "Set     : Expr object, Token name, Expr value",
    "Super   : Token keyword, Token method",
    "This    : Token keyword",
```

tool/GenerateAst.java
*in* main()

Following the grammar, the new parsing code goes inside our existing primary() method.

```
    return new Expr.Literal(previous().literal);
  }

  if (match(SUPER)) {
    Token keyword = previous();
    consume(DOT, "Expect '.' after 'super'.");
    Token method = consume(IDENTIFIER,
        "Expect superclass method name.");
    return new Expr.Super(keyword, method);
  }

  if (match(THIS)) return new Expr.This(previous());
```

lox/Parser.java
*in* primary()

A leading super keyword tells us we've hit a super expression. After that we consume the expected . and method name.

## 13.3.2 Semantics

Earlier, I said a super expression starts the method lookup from "the superclass", but *which* superclass? The naïve answer is the superclass of this, the object the surrounding method was called on. That coincidentally produces the right behavior in a lot of cases, but that's not actually correct. Gaze upon:

```
class A {
  method() {
    print "A method";
  }
}

class B < A {
  method() {
    print "B method";
  }
  test() {
    super.method();
  }
}

class C < B {}
C().test();
```

Translate this program to Java, C#, or C++ and it will print "A method", which is what we want Lox to do too. When this program runs, inside the body of `test()`, `this` is an instance of C. The superclass of C is B, but that is *not* where the lookup should start. If it did, we would hit B's `method()`.

Instead, lookup should start on the superclass of *the class containing the* `super` *expression*. In this case, since `test()` is defined inside B, the `super` expression inside it should start the lookup on *B's* superclass—A.

The execution flow goes like this:

1. We call `test()` on an instance of C.

2. That enters the `test()` method inherited from B. That calls `super.method()`.

3. The superclass of B is A, so that chains to `method()` on A, and the program prints "A method".

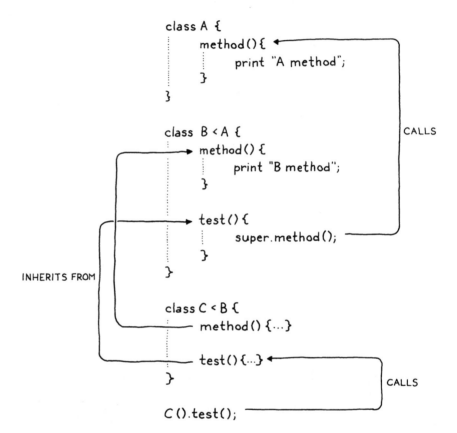

Thus, in order to evaluate a `super` expression, we need access to the superclass of the class definition surrounding the call. Alack and alas, at the point in the interpreter where we are executing a `super` expression, we don't have that easily available.

We *could* add a field to LoxFunction to store a reference to the LoxClass that owns that method. The interpreter would keep a reference to the currently executing LoxFunction so that we could look it up later when we hit a `super` expression. From there, we'd get the LoxClass of the method, then its superclass.

That's a lot of plumbing. In the last chapter, we had a similar problem when we needed to add support for `this`. In that case, we used our existing environment and closure mechanism to store a reference to the current object. Could we do something similar for storing the superclass? Well, I probably wouldn't be talking about it if the answer was no, so...yes.

Does anyone even like rhetorical questions?

One important difference is that we bound `this` when the method was *accessed*. The same method can be called on different instances and each needs its own `this`. With `super` expressions, the superclass is a fixed property of the *class declaration itself*. Every time you evaluate some `super` expression, the superclass is always the same.

That means we can create the environment for the superclass once, when the class definition is executed. Immediately before we define the methods, we make a new environment to bind the class's superclass to the name super.

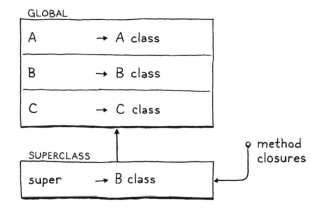

When we create the LoxFunction runtime representation for each method, that is the environment they will capture in their closure. Later, when a method is invoked and this is bound, the superclass environment becomes the parent for the method's environment, like so:

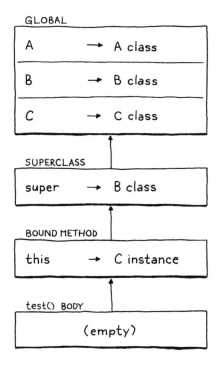

That's a lot of machinery, but we'll get through it a step at a time. Before we can get to creating the environment at runtime, we need to handle the corresponding scope chain in the resolver.

lox/Resolver.java
in visitClassStmt()

```
    resolve(stmt.superclass);
  }

  if (stmt.superclass != null) {
    beginScope();
    scopes.peek().put("super", true);
  }

  beginScope();
```

If the class declaration has a superclass, then we create a new scope surrounding all of its methods. In that scope, we define the name "super". Once we're done resolving the class's methods, we discard that scope.

lox/Resolver.java
in visitClassStmt()

```
  endScope();

  if (stmt.superclass != null) endScope();

  currentClass = enclosingClass;
```

It's a minor optimization, but we only create the superclass environment if the class actually *has* a superclass. There's no point creating it when there isn't a superclass since there'd be no superclass to store in it anyway.

With "super" defined in a scope chain, we are able to resolve the super expression itself.

lox/Resolver.java
add after visitSetExpr()

```
@Override
public Void visitSuperExpr(Expr.Super expr) {
  resolveLocal(expr, expr.keyword);
  return null;
}
```

We resolve the super token exactly as if it were a variable. The resolution stores the number of hops along the environment chain that the interpreter needs to walk to find the environment where the superclass is stored.

This code is mirrored in the interpreter. When we evaluate a subclass definition, we create a new environment.

lox/Interpreter.java
in visitClassStmt()

```
      throw new RuntimeError(stmt.superclass.name,
          "Superclass must be a class.");
    }
  }

  environment.define(stmt.name.lexeme, null);

  if (stmt.superclass != null) {
    environment = new Environment(environment);
    environment.define("super", superclass);
  }

  Map<String, LoxFunction> methods = new HashMap<>();
```

Inside that environment, we store a reference to the superclass—the actual LoxClass object for the superclass which we have now that we are in the runtime. Then we create the LoxFunctions for each method. Those will capture the current environment—the one where we just bound "super"—as their closure, holding on to the superclass like we need. Once that's done, we pop the environment.

```
LoxClass klass = new LoxClass(stmt.name.lexeme,
    (LoxClass)superclass, methods);

if (superclass != null) {
  environment = environment.enclosing;
}

environment.assign(stmt.name, klass);
```

lox/Interpreter.java
in visitClassStmt()

We're ready to interpret **super** expressions themselves. There are a few moving parts, so we'll build this method up in pieces.

```
@Override
public Object visitSuperExpr(Expr.Super expr) {
  int distance = locals.get(expr);
  LoxClass superclass = (LoxClass)environment.getAt(
      distance, "super");
}
```

lox/Interpreter.java
add after visitSetExpr()

First, the work we've been leading up to. We look up the surrounding class's superclass by looking up "super" in the proper environment.

When we access a method, we also need to bind **this** to the object the method is accessed from. In an expression like **doughnut.cook**, the object is whatever we get from evaluating **doughnut**. In a **super** expression like **super.cook**, the current object is implicitly the *same* current object that we're using. In other words, **this**. Even though we are looking up the *method* on the superclass, the *instance* is still **this**.

Unfortunately, inside the **super** expression, we don't have a convenient node for the resolver to hang the number of hops to **this** on. Fortunately, we do control the layout of the environment chains. The environment where "this" is bound is always right inside the environment where we store "super".

```
LoxClass superclass = (LoxClass)environment.getAt(
    distance, "super");

LoxInstance object = (LoxInstance)environment.getAt(
    distance - 1, "this");
}
```

lox/Interpreter.java
in visitSuperExpr()

Offsetting the distance by one looks up "this" in that inner environment. I admit this isn't the most elegant code, but it works.

Now we're ready to look up and bind the method, starting at the superclass.

Writing a book that includes every single line of code for a program means I can't hide the hacks by leaving them as an "exercise for the reader".

lox/Interpreter.java
*in* visitSuperExpr()

```
    LoxInstance object = (LoxInstance)environment.getAt(
        distance - 1, "this");

    LoxFunction method = superclass.findMethod(expr.method.lexeme);
    return method.bind(object);
  }
```

This is almost exactly like the code for looking up a method of a get expression, except that we call **findMethod()** on the superclass instead of on the class of the current object.

That's basically it. Except, of course, that we might *fail* to find the method. So we check for that too.

lox/Interpreter.java
*in* visitSuperExpr()

```
    LoxFunction method = superclass.findMethod(expr.method.lexeme);

    if (method == null) {
      throw new RuntimeError(expr.method,
          "Undefined property '" + expr.method.lexeme + "'.");
    }

    return method.bind(object);
  }
```

There you have it! Take that BostonCream example earlier and give it a try. Assuming you and I did everything right, it should fry it first, then stuff it with cream.

### 13.3.3  Invalid uses of super

As with previous language features, our implementation does the right thing when the user writes correct code, but we haven't bulletproofed the intepreter against bad code. In particular, consider:

```
class Eclair {
  cook() {
    super.cook();
    print "Pipe full of crème pâtissière.";
  }
}
```

This class has a **super** expression, but no superclass. At runtime, the code for evaluating **super** expressions assumes that "super" was successfully resolved and will be found in the environment. That's going to fail here because there is no surrounding environment for the superclass since there is no superclass. The JVM will throw an exception and bring our interpreter to its knees.

Heck, there are even simpler broken uses of super:

```
super.notEvenInAClass();
```

We could handle errors like these at runtime by checking to see if the lookup of "super" succeeded. But we can tell statically—just by looking at the source code—that Eclair has no superclass and thus no `super` expression will work inside it. Likewise, in the second example, we know that the `super` expression is not even inside a method body.

Even though Lox is dynamically typed, that doesn't mean we want to defer *everything* to runtime. If the user made a mistake, we'd like to help them find it sooner rather than later. So we'll report these errors statically, in the resolver.

First, we add a new case to the enum we use to keep track of what kind of class is surrounding the current code being visited.

```
  NONE,
  SUBCLASS
}
```

*lox/Resolver.java*
*in enum ClassType*
*add "," to previous line*

We'll use that to distinguish when we're inside a class that has a superclass versus one that doesn't. When we resolve a class declaration, we set that if the class is a subclass.

```
  if (stmt.superclass != null) {
    currentClass = ClassType.SUBCLASS;
    resolve(stmt.superclass);
```

*lox/Resolver.java*
*in visitClassStmt()*

Then, when we resolve a `super` expression, we check to see that we are currently inside a scope where that's allowed.

```
  public Void visitSuperExpr(Expr.Super expr) {
    if (currentClass == ClassType.NONE) {
      Lox.error(expr.keyword,
          "Can't use 'super' outside of a class.");
    } else if (currentClass != ClassType.SUBCLASS) {
      Lox.error(expr.keyword,
          "Can't use 'super' in a class with no superclass.");
    }

    resolveLocal(expr, expr.keyword);
```

*lox/Resolver.java*
*in visitSuperExpr()*

If not—oopsie!—the user made a mistake.

## 13.4  Conclusion

We made it! That final bit of error handling is the last chunk of code needed to complete our Java implementation of Lox. This is a real accomplishment and one you should be proud of. In the past dozen chapters and a thousand or so lines of code, we have learned and implemented... **tokens** and **lexing**, **abstract syntax trees**, **recursive descent parsing**, **prefix** and **infix expressions**, **runtime representation** of objects, interpreting code using the **Visitor pattern**, **lexical scope**, **environment chains** for storing variables, **control flow**, **functions** with **parameters**, **closures**, static **variable resolution** and **error detection**, **classes**, **constructors**, **fields**, **methods**, and finally, **inheritance**.

We did all of that from scratch, with no external dependencies or magic tools.

Just you and I, our respective text editors, a couple of collection classes in the Java standard library, and the JVM runtime.

This marks the end of Part II, but not the end of the book. Take a break. Maybe write a few fun Lox programs and run them in your interpreter. (You may want to add a few more native methods for things like reading user input.) When you're refreshed and ready, we'll embark on our next adventure.

## CHALLENGES

1. Lox supports only *single inheritance*—a class may have a single superclass and that's the only way to reuse methods across classes. Other languages have explored a variety of ways to more freely reuse and share capabilities across classes: mixins, traits, multiple inheritance, virtual inheritance, extension methods, etc.

   If you were to add some feature along these lines to Lox, which would you pick and why? If you're feeling courageous (and you should be at this point), go ahead and add it.

2. In Lox, as in most other object-oriented languages, when looking up a method, we start at the bottom of the class hierarchy and work our way up—a subclass's method is preferred over a superclass's. In order to get to the superclass method from within an overriding method, you use **super**.

   The language BETA takes the opposite approach. When you call a method, it starts at the *top* of the class hierarchy and works *down*. A superclass method wins over a subclass method. In order to get to the subclass method, the superclass method can call **inner**, which is sort of like the inverse of **super**. It chains to the next method down the hierarchy.

   The superclass method controls when and where the subclass is allowed to refine its behavior. If the superclass method doesn't call **inner** at all, then the subclass has no way of overriding or modifying the superclass's behavior.

   Take out Lox's current overriding and **super** behavior and replace it with BETA's semantics. In short:

   - When calling a method on a class, prefer the method *highest* on the class's inheritance chain.

   - Inside the body of a method, a call to **inner** looks for a method with the same name in the nearest subclass along the inheritance chain between the class containing the **inner** and the class of **this**. If there is no matching method, the **inner** call does nothing.

If you've never heard of BETA (likely), start here:
→ craftinginterpreters.com/beta

For example:

```
class Doughnut {
  cook() {
    print "Fry until golden brown.";
    inner();
    print "Place in a nice box.";
  }
}

class BostonCream < Doughnut {
  cook() {
    print "Pipe full of custard and coat with chocolate.";
  }
}

BostonCream().cook();
```

This should print:

```
Fry until golden brown.
Pipe full of custard and coat with chocolate.
Place in a nice box.
```

3. In the chapter where I introduced Lox, I challenged you to come up with a couple of features you think the language is missing. Now that you know how to build an interpreter, implement one of those features.

# A Bytecode Virtual Machine    PART

Our Java interpreter, jlox, taught us many of the fundamentals of programming languages, but we still have much to learn. First, if you run any interesting Lox programs in jlox, you'll discover it's achingly slow. The style of interpretation it uses—walking the AST directly—is good enough for *some* real-world uses, but leaves a lot to be desired for a general-purpose scripting language.

Also, we implicitly rely on runtime features of the JVM itself. We take for granted that things like `instanceof` in Java work *somehow*. And we never for a second worry about memory management because the JVM's garbage collector takes care of it for us.

When we were focused on high-level concepts, it was fine to gloss over those. But now that we know our way around an interpreter, it's time to dig down to those lower layers and build our own virtual machine from scratch using nothing more than the C standard library…

# Chunks of Bytecode

# 14

*"If you find that you're spending almost all your time on theory, start turning some attention to practical things; it will improve your theories. If you find that you're spending almost all your time on practice, start turning some attention to theoretical things; it will improve your practice."*

— Donald Knuth

We already have ourselves a complete implementation of Lox with jlox, so why isn't the book over yet? Part of this is because jlox relies on the JVM to do lots of things for us. If we want to understand how an interpreter works all the way down to the metal, we need to build those bits and pieces ourselves.

An even more fundamental reason that jlox isn't sufficient is that it's too damn slow. A tree-walk interpreter is fine for some kinds of high-level, declarative languages. But for a general-purpose, imperative language—even a "scripting" language like Lox—it won't fly.

Of course, our second interpreter relies on the C standard library for basics like memory allocation, and the C compiler frees us from details of the underlying machine code we're running it on. Heck, that machine code is probably implemented in terms of microcode on the chip. And the C runtime relies on the operating system to hand out pages of memory. But we have to stop *somewhere* if this book is going to fit on your bookshelf.

Take this little script:

```
fun fib(n) {
  if (n < 2) return n;
  return fib(n - 1) + fib(n - 2);
}

var before = clock();
print fib(40);
var after = clock();
print after - before;
```

This is a comically inefficient way to actually calculate Fibonacci numbers. Our goal is to see how fast the *interpreter* runs, not to see how fast of a program we can write. A slow program that does a lot of work—pointless or not—is a good test case for that.

On my laptop, that takes jlox about 72 seconds to execute. An equivalent C program finishes in half a second. Our dynamically typed scripting language is never going to be as fast as a statically typed language with manual memory management, but we don't need to settle for more than *two orders of magnitude slower*.

We could take jlox and run it in a profiler and start tuning and tweaking hotspots, but that will only get us so far. The execution model—walking the AST—is fundamentally the wrong design. We can't micro-optimize that to the performance we want any more than you can polish an AMC Gremlin into an SR-71 Blackbird.

We need to rethink the core model. This chapter introduces that model, bytecode, and begins our new interpreter, clox.

## 14.1  Bytecode?

In engineering, few choices are without trade-offs. To best understand why we're going with bytecode, let's stack it up against a couple of alternatives.

### 14.1.1  Why not walk the AST?

Our existing interpreter has a couple of things going for it:

- Well, first, we already wrote it. It's done. And the main reason it's done is because this style of interpreter is *really simple to implement*. The runtime representation of the code directly maps to the syntax. It's virtually effortless to get from the parser to the data structures we need at runtime.

- It's *portable*. Our current interpreter is written in Java and runs on any platform Java supports. We could write a new implementation in C using the same approach and compile and run our language on basically every platform under the sun.

Those are real advantages. But, on the other hand, it's *not memory-efficient*. Each piece of syntax becomes an AST node. A tiny Lox expression like 1 + 2 turns into a slew of objects with lots of pointers between them, something like:

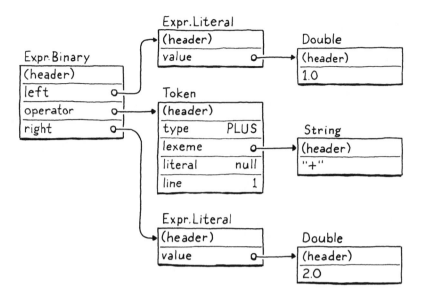

The "(header)" parts are the bookkeeping information the Java virtual machine uses to support memory management and store the object's type. Those take up space too!

Each of those pointers adds an extra 32 or 64 bits of overhead to the object. Worse, sprinkling our data across the heap in a loosely connected web of objects does bad things for *spatial locality*.

Modern CPUs process data way faster than they can pull it from RAM. To compensate for that, chips have multiple layers of caching. If a piece of memory it needs is already in the cache, it can be loaded more quickly. We're talking upwards of 100 *times* faster.

How does data get into that cache? The machine speculatively stuffs things in there for you. Its heuristic is pretty simple. Whenever the CPU reads a bit of data from RAM, it pulls in a whole little bundle of adjacent bytes and stuffs them in the cache.

If our program next requests some data close enough to be inside that cache line, our CPU runs like a well-oiled conveyor belt in a factory. We *really* want to take advantage of this. To use the cache effectively, the way we represent code in memory should be dense and ordered like it's read.

Now look up at that tree. Those sub-objects could be *anywhere*. Every step the tree-walker takes where it follows a reference to a child node may step outside the bounds of the cache and force the CPU to stall until a new lump of data can be slurped in from RAM. Just the *overhead* of those tree nodes with all of their pointer fields and object headers tends to push objects away from each other and out of the cache.

Our AST walker has other overhead too around interface dispatch and the Visitor pattern, but the locality issues alone are enough to justify a better code representation.

I wrote an entire chapter about this exact problem in my first book, *Game Programming Patterns*, if you want to really dig in:

→ craftinginterpreters.com/locality

Even if the objects happened to be allocated in sequential memory when the parser first produced them, after a couple of rounds of garbage collection—which may move objects around in memory—there's no telling where they'll be.

### 14.1.2 Why not compile to native code?

If you want to go *real* fast, you want to get all of those layers of indirection out of the way. Right down to the metal. Machine code. It even *sounds* fast. *Machine code.*

Yes, they actually wrote machine code by hand. On punched cards. Which, presumably, they punched *with their fists*.

Compiling directly to the native instruction set the chip supports is what the fastest languages do. Targeting native code has been the most efficient option since way back in the early days when engineers actually handwrote programs in machine code.

If you've never written any machine code, or its slightly more human-palatable cousin assembly code before, I'll give you the gentlest of introductions. Native code is a dense series of operations, encoded directly in binary. Each instruction is between one and a few bytes long, and is almost mind-numbingly low level. "Move a value from this address to this register." "Add the integers in these two registers." Stuff like that.

The CPU cranks through the instructions, decoding and executing each one in order. There is no tree structure like our AST, and control flow is handled by jumping from one point in the code directly to another. No indirection, no overhead, no unnecessary skipping around or chasing pointers.

Lightning fast, but that performance comes at a cost. First of all, compiling to native code ain't easy. Most chips in wide use today have sprawling Byzantine architectures with heaps of instructions that accreted over decades. They require sophisticated register allocation, pipelining, and instruction scheduling.

And, of course, you've thrown portability out. Spend a few years mastering some architecture and that still only gets you onto *one* of the several popular instruction sets out there. To get your language on all of them, you need to learn all of their instruction sets and write a separate back end for each one.

The situation isn't entirely dire. A well-architected compiler lets you share the front end and most of the middle layer optimization passes across the different architectures you support. It's mainly the code generation and some of the details around instruction selection that you'll need to write afresh each time.

The LLVM project gives you some of this out of the box. If your compiler outputs LLVM's own special intermediate language, LLVM in turn compiles that to native code for a plethora of architectures.

### 14.1.3  What is bytecode?

Fix those two points in your mind. On one end, a tree-walk interpreter is simple, portable, and slow. On the other, native code is complex and platform-specific but fast. Bytecode sits in the middle. It retains the portability of a tree-walker—we won't be getting our hands dirty with assembly code in this book. It sacrifices *some* simplicity to get a performance boost in return, though not as fast as going fully native.

Structurally, bytecode resembles machine code. It's a dense, linear sequence of binary instructions. That keeps overhead low and plays nice with the cache. However, it's a much simpler, higher-level instruction set than any real chip out there. (In many bytecode formats, each instruction is only a single byte long, hence "bytecode".)

Imagine you're writing a native compiler from some source language and you're given carte blanche to define the easiest possible architecture to target. Bytecode is kind of like that. It's an idealized fantasy instruction set that makes your life as the compiler writer easier.

One of the first bytecode formats was p-code, developed for Niklaus Wirth's Pascal language. You might think a PDP-11 running at 15MHz couldn't afford the overhead of emulating a virtual machine. But back then, computers were in their Cambrian explosion and new architectures appeared every day. Keeping up with the latest chips was worth more than squeezing the maximum performance from each one. That's why the "p" in p-code doesn't stand for "Pascal", but "portable".

The problem with a fantasy architecture, of course, is that it doesn't exist. We solve that by writing an *emulator*—a simulated chip written in software that interprets the bytecode one instruction at a time. A *virtual machine (VM)*, if you will.

That emulation layer adds overhead, which is a key reason bytecode is slower than native code. But in return, it gives us portability. Write our VM in a language like C that is already supported on all the machines we care about, and we can run our emulator on top of any hardware we like.

This is the path we'll take with our new interpreter, clox. We'll follow in the footsteps of the main implementations of Python, Ruby, Lua, OCaml, Erlang, and others.

In many ways, our VM's design will parallel the structure of our previous interpreter:

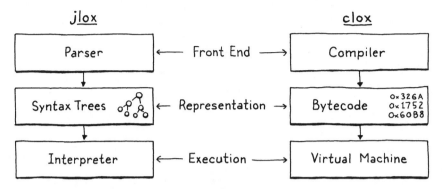

Of course, we won't implement the phases strictly in order. Like our previous interpreter, we'll bounce around, building up the implementation one language feature at a time. In this chapter, we'll get the skeleton of the application in place and create the data structures needed to store and represent a chunk of bytecode.

## 14.2  Getting Started

Where else to begin, but at `main()`? Fire up your trusty text editor and start typing.

Now is a good time to stretch, maybe crack your knuckles. A little montage music wouldn't hurt either.

**main.c**
*create new file*

```c
#include "common.h"

int main(int argc, const char* argv[]) {
  return 0;
}
```

From this tiny seed, we will grow our entire VM. Since C provides us with so little, we first need to spend some time amending the soil. Some of that goes into this header:

**common.h**
*create new file*

```c
#ifndef clox_common_h
#define clox_common_h

#include <stdbool.h>
#include <stddef.h>
#include <stdint.h>

#endif
```

There are a handful of types and constants we'll use throughout the interpreter, and this is a convenient place to put them. For now, it's the venerable NULL, `size_t`, the nice C99 Boolean `bool`, and explicit-sized integer types—`uint8_t` and friends.

## 14.3  Chunks of Instructions

Next, we need a module to define our code representation. I've been using "chunk" to refer to sequences of bytecode, so let's make that the official name for that module.

**chunk.h**
*create new file*

```
#ifndef clox_chunk_h
#define clox_chunk_h

#include "common.h"

#endif
```

In our bytecode format, each instruction has a one-byte **operation code** (universally shortened to **opcode**). That number controls what kind of instruction we're dealing with—add, subtract, look up variable, etc. We define those here:

**chunk.h**

```
#include "common.h"

typedef enum {
  OP_RETURN,
} OpCode;

#endif
```

For now, we start with a single instruction, OP_RETURN. When we have a full-featured VM, this instruction will mean "return from the current function". I admit this isn't exactly useful yet, but we have to start somewhere, and this is a particularly simple instruction, for reasons we'll get to later.

### 14.3.1  A dynamic array of instructions

Bytecode is a series of instructions. Eventually, we'll store some other data along with the instructions, so let's go ahead and create a struct to hold it all.

**chunk.h**
*add after enum OpCode*

```
} OpCode;

typedef struct {
  uint8_t* code;
} Chunk;

#endif
```

At the moment, this is simply a wrapper around an array of bytes. Since we don't know how big the array needs to be before we start compiling a chunk, it must be dynamic. Dynamic arrays are one of my favorite data structures. That sounds like claiming vanilla is my favorite ice cream flavor, but hear me out. Dynamic arrays provide:

Butter pecan is actually my favorite.

- Cache-friendly, dense storage

- Constant-time indexed element lookup

- Constant-time appending to the end of the array

Those features are exactly why we used dynamic arrays all the time in jlox under the guise of Java's ArrayList class. Now that we're in C, we get to roll our own. If you're rusty on dynamic arrays, the idea is pretty simple. In addition to the array itself, we keep two numbers: the number of elements in the array we have allocated ("capacity") and how many of those allocated entries are actually in use ("count").

```
typedef struct {
  int count;
  int capacity;
  uint8_t* code;
} Chunk;
```

chunk.h
*in struct* Chunk

When we add an element, if the count is less than the capacity, then there is already available space in the array. We store the new element right in there and bump the count.

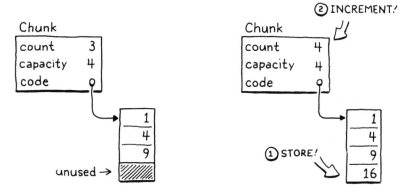

If we have no spare capacity, then the process is a little more involved.

1. Allocate a new array with more capacity.

2. Copy the existing elements from the old array to the new one.

3. Store the new **capacity**.

4. Delete the old array.

5. Update **code** to point to the new array.

6. Store the element in the new array now that there is room.

7. Update the **count**.

It looks like this:

Copying the existing elements when you grow the array makes it seem like appending an element is $O(n)$, not $O(1)$ like I said above. However, you need to do this copy step only on *some* of the appends. Most of the time, there is already extra capacity, so you don't need to copy.

To understand how this works, we need **amortized analysis**. That shows us that as long as we grow the array by a multiple of its current size, when we average out the cost of a *sequence* of appends, each append is $O(1)$.

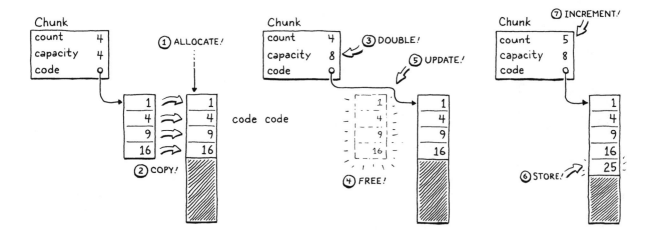

We have our struct ready, so let's implement the functions to work with it. C doesn't have constructors, so we declare a function to initialize a new chunk.

**chunk.h**
*add after struct* Chunk

```
} Chunk;

void initChunk(Chunk* chunk);

#endif
```

And implement it thusly:

**chunk.c**
*create new file*

```
#include <stdlib.h>

#include "chunk.h"

void initChunk(Chunk* chunk) {
  chunk->count = 0;
  chunk->capacity = 0;
  chunk->code = NULL;
}
```

The dynamic array starts off completely empty. We don't even allocate a raw array yet. To append a byte to the end of the chunk, we use a new function.

**chunk.h**
*add after* initChunk()

```
void initChunk(Chunk* chunk);
void writeChunk(Chunk* chunk, uint8_t byte);

#endif
```

This is where the interesting work happens.

**chunk.c**
*add after* initChunk()

```
void writeChunk(Chunk* chunk, uint8_t byte) {
  if (chunk->capacity < chunk->count + 1) {
    int oldCapacity = chunk->capacity;
    chunk->capacity = GROW_CAPACITY(oldCapacity);
    chunk->code = GROW_ARRAY(uint8_t, chunk->code,
        oldCapacity, chunk->capacity);
```

*continued on next page...*

```
  }

  chunk->code[chunk->count] = byte;
  chunk->count++;
}
```
…from previous page

The first thing we need to do is see if the current array already has capacity for the new byte. If it doesn't, then we first need to grow the array to make room. (We also hit this case on the very first write when the array is NULL and capacity is 0.)

To grow the array, first we figure out the new capacity and grow the array to that size. Both of those lower-level memory operations are defined in a new module.

```
#include "chunk.h"
#include "memory.h"

void initChunk(Chunk* chunk) {
```
chunk.c

This is enough to get us started.

```
#ifndef clox_memory_h
#define clox_memory_h

#include "common.h"

#define GROW_CAPACITY(capacity) \
    ((capacity) < 8 ? 8 : (capacity) * 2)

#endif
```
memory.h
*create new file*

This macro calculates a new capacity based on a given current capacity. In order to get the performance we want, the important part is that it *scales* based on the old size. We grow by a factor of two, which is pretty typical. 1.5× is another common choice.

We also handle when the current capacity is zero. In that case, we jump straight to eight elements instead of starting at one. That avoids a little extra memory churn when the array is very small, at the expense of wasting a few bytes on very small chunks.

Once we know the desired capacity, we create or grow the array to that size using GROW_ARRAY().

I picked the number eight somewhat arbitrarily for the book. Most dynamic array implementations have a minimum threshold like this. The right way to pick a value for this is to profile against real-world usage and see which constant makes the best performance trade-off between extra grows versus wasted space.

```
#define GROW_CAPACITY(capacity) \
    ((capacity) < 8 ? 8 : (capacity) * 2)

#define GROW_ARRAY(type, pointer, oldCount, newCount) \
    (type*)reallocate(pointer, sizeof(type) * (oldCount), \
        sizeof(type) * (newCount))

void* reallocate(void* pointer, size_t oldSize, size_t newSize);

#endif
```
memory.h

This macro pretties up a function call to `reallocate()` where the real work happens. The macro itself takes care of getting the size of the array's element type and casting the resulting `void*` back to a pointer of the right type.

This `reallocate()` function is the single function we'll use for all dynamic memory management in clox—allocating memory, freeing it, and changing the size of an existing allocation. Routing all of those operations through a single function will be important later when we add a garbage collector that needs to keep track of how much memory is in use.

The two size arguments passed to `reallocate()` control which operation to perform:

| oldSize  | newSize             | Operation                   |
| -------- | ------------------- | --------------------------- |
| 0        | Non-zero            | Allocate new block.         |
| Non-zero | 0                   | Free allocation.            |
| Non-zero | Smaller than `oldSize` | Shrink existing allocation. |
| Non-zero | Larger than `oldSize`  | Grow existing allocation.   |

That sounds like a lot of cases to handle, but here's the implementation:

memory.c
*create new file*

```c
#include <stdlib.h>

#include "memory.h"

void* reallocate(void* pointer, size_t oldSize, size_t newSize) {
  if (newSize == 0) {
    free(pointer);
    return NULL;
  }

  void* result = realloc(pointer, newSize);
  return result;
}
```

When `newSize` is zero, we handle the deallocation case ourselves by calling `free()`. Otherwise, we rely on the C standard library's `realloc()` function. That function conveniently supports the other three aspects of our policy. When `oldSize` is zero, `realloc()` is equivalent to calling `malloc()`.

The interesting cases are when both `oldSize` and `newSize` are not zero. Those tell `realloc()` to resize the previously allocated block. If the new size is smaller than the existing block of memory, it simply updates the size of the block and returns the same pointer you gave it. If the new size is larger, it attempts to grow the existing block of memory.

It can do that only if the memory after that block isn't already in use. If there isn't room to grow the block, `realloc()` instead allocates a *new* block of memory of the desired size, copies over the old bytes, frees the old block, and then returns a pointer to the new block. Remember, that's exactly the behavior we want for our dynamic array.

Since all we passed in was a bare pointer to the first byte of memory, what does it mean to "update" the block's size? Under the hood, the memory allocator maintains additional bookkeeping information for each block of heap-allocated memory, including its size.

Given a pointer to some previously allocated memory, it can find this bookkeeping information, which is necessary to be able to cleanly free it. It's this size metadata that `realloc()` updates.

Many implementations of `malloc()` store the allocated size in memory right *before* the returned address.

Because computers are finite lumps of matter and not the perfect mathematical abstractions computer science theory would have us believe, allocation can fail if there isn't enough memory and `realloc()` will return NULL. We should handle that.

```
void* result = realloc(pointer, newSize);
if (result == NULL) exit(1);
return result;
```

memory.c
*in* reallocate()

There's not really anything *useful* that our VM can do if it can't get the memory it needs, but we at least detect that and abort the process immediately instead of returning a NULL pointer and letting it go off the rails later.

OK, we can create new chunks and write instructions to them. Are we done? Nope! We're in C now, remember, we have to manage memory ourselves, like in Ye Olden Times, and that means *freeing* it too.

```
void initChunk(Chunk* chunk);
void freeChunk(Chunk* chunk);
void writeChunk(Chunk* chunk, uint8_t byte);
```

chunk.h
*add after* initChunk()

The implementation is:

```
void freeChunk(Chunk* chunk) {
  FREE_ARRAY(uint8_t, chunk->code, chunk->capacity);
  initChunk(chunk);
}
```

chunk.c
*add after* initChunk()

We deallocate all of the memory and then call `initChunk()` to zero out the fields leaving the chunk in a well-defined empty state. To free the memory, we add one more macro.

```
#define GROW_ARRAY(type, pointer, oldCount, newCount) \
    (type*)reallocate(pointer, sizeof(type) * (oldCount), \
        sizeof(type) * (newCount))

#define FREE_ARRAY(type, pointer, oldCount) \
    reallocate(pointer, sizeof(type) * (oldCount), 0)

void* reallocate(void* pointer, size_t oldSize, size_t newSize);
```

memory.h

Like `GROW_ARRAY()`, this is a wrapper around a call to `reallocate()`. This one frees the memory by passing in zero for the new size. I know, this is a lot of boring low-level stuff. Don't worry, we'll get a lot of use out of these in later chapters and will get to program at a higher level. Before we can do that, though, we gotta lay our own foundation.

## 14.4 Disassembling Chunks

Now we have a little module for creating chunks of bytecode. Let's try it out by hand-building a sample chunk.

main.c<br>in main()

```
int main(int argc, const char* argv[]) {
  Chunk chunk;
  initChunk(&chunk);
  writeChunk(&chunk, OP_RETURN);
  freeChunk(&chunk);
  return 0;
```

Don't forget the include.

main.c

```
#include "common.h"
#include "chunk.h"

int main(int argc, const char* argv[]) {
```

Run that and give it a try. Did it work? Uh…who knows? All we've done is push some bytes around in memory. We have no human-friendly way to see what's actually inside that chunk we made.

To fix this, we're going to create a **disassembler**. An **assembler** is an old-school program that takes a file containing human-readable mnemonic names for CPU instructions like "ADD" and "MULT" and translates them to their binary machine code equivalent. A *dis*assembler goes in the other direction—given a blob of machine code, it spits out a textual listing of the instructions.

We'll implement something similar. Given a chunk, it will print out all of the instructions in it. A Lox *user* won't use this, but we Lox *maintainers* will certainly benefit since it gives us a window into the interpreter's internal representation of code.

In main(), after we create the chunk, we pass it to the disassembler.

In jlox, our analogous tool was the AstPrinter class.

main.c<br>in main()

```
  initChunk(&chunk);
  writeChunk(&chunk, OP_RETURN);

  disassembleChunk(&chunk, "test chunk");
  freeChunk(&chunk);
```

I promise you we won't be creating this many new files in later chapters.

Again, we whip up yet another module.

main.c

```
#include "chunk.h"
#include "debug.h"

int main(int argc, const char* argv[]) {
```

Here's that header:

debug.h<br>create new file

```
#ifndef clox_debug_h
#define clox_debug_h

#include "chunk.h"

void disassembleChunk(Chunk* chunk, const char* name);
int disassembleInstruction(Chunk* chunk, int offset);

#endif
```

In main(), we call disassembleChunk() to disassemble all of the instructions in the entire chunk. That's implemented in terms of the other function, which just disassembles a single instruction. It shows up here in the header because we'll call it from the VM in later chapters.

Here's a start at the implementation file:

```c
#include <stdio.h>

#include "debug.h"

void disassembleChunk(Chunk* chunk, const char* name) {
  printf("== %s ==\n", name);
  for (int offset = 0; offset < chunk->count;) {
    offset = disassembleInstruction(chunk, offset);
  }
}
```

debug.c
*create new file*

To disassemble a chunk, we print a little header (so we can tell *which* chunk we're looking at) and then crank through the bytecode, disassembling each instruction. The way we iterate through the code is a little odd. Instead of incrementing offset in the loop, we let disassembleInstruction() do it for us. When we call that function, after disassembling the instruction at the given offset, it returns the offset of the *next* instruction. This is because, as we'll see later, instructions can have different sizes.

The core of the "debug" module is this function:

```c
int disassembleInstruction(Chunk* chunk, int offset) {
  printf("%04d ", offset);

  uint8_t instruction = chunk->code[offset];
  switch (instruction) {
    case OP_RETURN:
      return simpleInstruction("OP_RETURN", offset);
    default:
      printf("Unknown opcode %d\n", instruction);
      return offset + 1;
  }
}
```

debug.c
*add after* disassembleChunk()

First, it prints the byte offset of the given instruction—that tells us where in the chunk this instruction is. This will be a helpful signpost when we start doing control flow and jumping around in the bytecode.

Next, it reads a single byte from the bytecode at the given offset. That's our opcode. We switch on that. For each kind of instruction, we dispatch to a little utility function for displaying it. On the off chance that the given byte doesn't look like an instruction at all—a bug in our compiler—we print that too. For the one instruction we do have, OP_RETURN, the display function is:

We have only one instruction right now, but this switch will grow throughout the rest of the book.

```c
static int simpleInstruction(const char* name, int offset) {
  printf("%s\n", name);
  return offset + 1;
}
```

debug.c
*add after* disassembleChunk()

There isn't much to a return instruction, so all it does is print the name of the opcode, then return the next byte offset past this instruction. Other instructions will have more going on.

If we run our nascent interpreter now, it actually prints something:

```
== test chunk ==
0000 OP_RETURN
```

It worked! This is sort of the "Hello, world!" of our code representation. We can create a chunk, write an instruction to it, and then extract that instruction back out. Our encoding and decoding of the binary bytecode is working.

## 14.5  Constants

Now that we have a rudimentary chunk structure working, let's start making it more useful. We can store *code* in chunks, but what about *data*? Many values the interpreter works with are created at runtime as the result of operations.

```
1 + 2;
```

The value 3 appears nowhere in the code here. However, the literals 1 and 2 do. To compile that statement to bytecode, we need some sort of instruction that means "produce a constant" and those literal values need to get stored in the chunk somewhere. In jlox, the Expr.Literal AST node held the value. We need a different solution now that we don't have a syntax tree.

### 14.5.1  Representing values

We won't be *running* any code in this chapter, but since constants have a foot in both the static and dynamic worlds of our interpreter, they force us to start thinking at least a little bit about how our VM should represent values.

For now, we're going to start as simple as possible—we'll support only double-precision, floating-point numbers. This will obviously expand over time, so we'll set up a new module to give ourselves room to grow.

*value.h*
*create new file*

```
#ifndef clox_value_h
#define clox_value_h

#include "common.h"

typedef double Value;

#endif
```

This typedef abstracts how Lox values are concretely represented in C. That way, we can change that representation without needing to go back and fix existing code that passes around values.

Back to the question of where to store constants in a chunk. For small fixed-size values like integers, many instruction sets store the value directly in the code stream right after the opcode. These are called **immediate instructions** because the bits for the value are immediately after the opcode.

That doesn't work well for large or variable-sized constants like strings. In a native compiler to machine code, those bigger constants get stored in a separate "constant data" region in the binary executable. Then, the instruction to load a constant has an address or offset pointing to where the value is stored in that section.

Most virtual machines do something similar. For example, the Java Virtual Machine associates a **constant pool** with each compiled class. That sounds good enough for clox to me. Each chunk will carry with it a list of the values that appear as literals in the program. To keep things simpler, we'll put *all* constants in there, even simple integers.

In addition to needing two kinds of constant instructions—one for immediate values and one for constants in the constant table—immediates also force us to worry about alignment, padding, and endianness. Some architectures aren't happy if you try to say, stuff a 4-byte integer at an odd address.

### 14.5.2  Value arrays

The constant pool is an array of values. The instruction to load a constant looks up the value by index in that array. As with our bytecode array, the compiler doesn't know how big the array needs to be ahead of time. So, again, we need a dynamic one. Since C doesn't have generic data structures, we'll write another dynamic array data structure, this time for Value.

Defining a new struct and manipulation functions each time we need a dynamic array of a different type is a chore. We could cobble together some preprocessor macros to fake generics, but that's overkill for clox. We won't need many more of these.

```
typedef double Value;

typedef struct {
  int capacity;
  int count;
  Value* values;
} ValueArray;

#endif
```

value.h

As with the bytecode array in Chunk, this struct wraps a pointer to an array along with its allocated capacity and the number of elements in use. We also need the same three functions to work with value arrays.

```
} ValueArray;

void initValueArray(ValueArray* array);
void writeValueArray(ValueArray* array, Value value);
void freeValueArray(ValueArray* array);

#endif
```

value.h
*add after struct ValueArray*

The implementations will probably give you déjà vu. First, to create a new one:

```
#include <stdio.h>

#include "memory.h"
#include "value.h"
```

value.c
*create new file*

*continued on next page...*

*...from previous page*

```c
void initValueArray(ValueArray* array) {
  array->values = NULL;
  array->capacity = 0;
  array->count = 0;
}
```

*Fortunately, we don't need other operations like insertion and removal.*

Once we have an initialized array, we can start adding values to it.

**value.c**
*add after* initValueArray()

```c
void writeValueArray(ValueArray* array, Value value) {
  if (array->capacity < array->count + 1) {
    int oldCapacity = array->capacity;
    array->capacity = GROW_CAPACITY(oldCapacity);
    array->values = GROW_ARRAY(Value, array->values,
                               oldCapacity, array->capacity);
  }

  array->values[array->count] = value;
  array->count++;
}
```

The memory-management macros we wrote earlier do let us reuse some of the logic from the code array, so this isn't too bad. Finally, to release all memory used by the array:

**value.c**
*add after* writeValueArray()

```c
void freeValueArray(ValueArray* array) {
  FREE_ARRAY(Value, array->values, array->capacity);
  initValueArray(array);
}
```

Now that we have growable arrays of values, we can add one to Chunk to store the chunk's constants.

**chunk.h**
*in struct* Chunk

```c
  uint8_t* code;
  ValueArray constants;
} Chunk;
```

Don't forget the include.

**chunk.h**

```c
#include "common.h"
#include "value.h"

typedef enum {
```

Ah, C, and its Stone Age modularity story. Where were we? Right. When we initialize a new chunk, we initialize its constant list too.

**chunk.c**
*in* initChunk()

```c
  chunk->code = NULL;
  initValueArray(&chunk->constants);
}
```

Likewise, we free the constants when we free the chunk.

```
  FREE_ARRAY(uint8_t, chunk->code, chunk->capacity);
  freeValueArray(&chunk->constants);
  initChunk(chunk);
```

chunk.c
in freeChunk()

Next, we define a convenience method to add a new constant to the chunk. Our yet-to-be-written compiler could write to the constant array inside Chunk directly—it's not like C has private fields or anything—but it's a little nicer to add an explicit function.

```
void writeChunk(Chunk* chunk, uint8_t byte);
int addConstant(Chunk* chunk, Value value);

#endif
```

chunk.h
add after writeChunk()

Then we implement it.

```
int addConstant(Chunk* chunk, Value value) {
  writeValueArray(&chunk->constants, value);
  return chunk->constants.count - 1;
}
```

chunk.c
add after writeChunk()

After we add the constant, we return the index where the constant was appended so that we can locate that same constant later.

### 14.5.3  Constant instructions

We can *store* constants in chunks, but we also need to *execute* them. In a piece of code like:

```
print 1;
print 2;
```

The compiled chunk needs to not only contain the values 1 and 2, but know *when* to produce them so that they are printed in the right order. Thus, we need an instruction that produces a particular constant.

```
typedef enum {
  OP_CONSTANT,
  OP_RETURN,
```

chunk.h
in enum OpCode

When the VM executes a constant instruction, it "loads" the constant for use. This new instruction is a little more complex than OP_RETURN. In the above example, we load two different constants. A single bare opcode isn't enough to know *which* constant to load.

To handle cases like this, our bytecode—like most others—allows instructions to have **operands**. These are stored as binary data immediately after the opcode in the instruction stream and let us parameterize what the instruction does.

I'm being vague about what it means to "load" or "produce" a constant because we haven't learned how the virtual machine actually executes code at runtime yet. For that, you'll have to wait until you get to (or skip ahead to, I suppose) the next chapter.

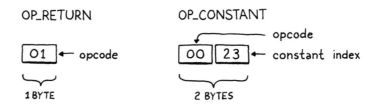

Bytecode instruction operands are *not* the same as the operands passed to an arithmetic operator. You'll see when we get to expressions that arithmetic operand values are tracked separately. Instruction operands are a lower-level notion that modify how the bytecode instruction itself behaves.

Each opcode determines how many operand bytes it has and what they mean. For example, a simple operation like "return" may have no operands, where an instruction for "load local variable" needs an operand to identify which variable to load. Each time we add a new opcode to clox, we specify what its operands look like—its **instruction format**.

In this case, OP_CONSTANT takes a single byte operand that specifies which constant to load from the chunk's constant array. Since we don't have a compiler yet, we "hand-compile" an instruction in our test chunk.

**main.c**
*in* main()

```
initChunk(&chunk);

int constant = addConstant(&chunk, 1.2);
writeChunk(&chunk, OP_CONSTANT);
writeChunk(&chunk, constant);

writeChunk(&chunk, OP_RETURN);
```

We add the constant value itself to the chunk's constant pool. That returns the index of the constant in the array. Then we write the constant instruction, starting with its opcode. After that, we write the one-byte constant index operand. Note that writeChunk() can write opcodes or operands. It's all raw bytes as far as that function is concerned.

If we try to run this now, the disassembler is going to yell at us because it doesn't know how to decode the new instruction. Let's fix that.

**debug.c**
*in* disassembleInstruction()

```
  switch (instruction) {
    case OP_CONSTANT:
      return constantInstruction("OP_CONSTANT", chunk, offset);
    case OP_RETURN:
```

This instruction has a different instruction format, so we write a new helper function to disassemble it.

**debug.c**
*add after* disassembleChunk()

```
static int constantInstruction(const char* name, Chunk* chunk,
                               int offset) {
  uint8_t constant = chunk->code[offset + 1];
  printf("%-16s %4d '", name, constant);
  printValue(chunk->constants.values[constant]);
  printf("'\n");
}
```

There's more going on here. As with OP_RETURN, we print out the name of the opcode. Then we pull out the constant index from the subsequent byte in the chunk. We print that index, but that isn't super useful to us human readers. So we also look up the actual constant value—since constants *are* known at compile time after all—and display the value itself too.

This requires some way to print a clox Value. That function will live in the "value" module, so we include that.

```
#include "debug.h"
#include "value.h"

void disassembleChunk(Chunk* chunk, const char* name) {
```
Over in that header, we declare:

```
void freeValueArray(ValueArray* array);
void printValue(Value value);

#endif
```

**value.h**
*add after* freeValueArray()

And here's an implementation:

```
void printValue(Value value) {
  printf("%g", value);
}
```

**value.c**
*add after* freeValueArray()

Magnificent, right? As you can imagine, this is going to get more complex once we add dynamic typing to Lox and have values of different types.

Back in constantInstruction(), the only remaining piece is the return value.

```
  printf("'\n");
  return offset + 2;
}
```

**debug.c**
*in* constantInstruction()

Remember that disassembleInstruction() also returns a number to tell the caller the offset of the beginning of the *next* instruction. Where OP_RETURN was only a single byte, OP_CONSTANT is two—one for the opcode and one for the operand.

## 14.6  Line Information

Chunks contain almost all of the information that the runtime needs from the user's source code. It's kind of crazy to think that we can reduce all of the different AST classes that we created in jlox down to an array of bytes and an array of constants. There's only one piece of data we're missing. We need it, even though the user hopes to never see it.

When a runtime error occurs, we show the user the line number of the offending source code. In jlox, those numbers live in tokens, which we in turn store in the AST nodes. We need a different solution for clox now that we've ditched syntax trees in favor of bytecode. Given any bytecode instruction, we need to be able to determine the line of the user's source program that it was compiled from.

There are a lot of clever ways we could encode this. I took the absolute sim-

This braindead encoding does do one thing right: it keeps the line information in a *separate* array instead of interleaving it in the bytecode itself. Since line information is only used when a runtime error occurs, we don't want it between the instructions, taking up precious space in the CPU cache and causing more cache misses as the interpreter skips past it to get to the opcodes and operands it cares about.

plest approach I could come up with, even though it's embarrassingly inefficient with memory. In the chunk, we store a separate array of integers that parallels the bytecode. Each number in the array is the line number for the corresponding byte in the bytecode. When a runtime error occurs, we look up the line number at the same index as the current instruction's offset in the code array.

To implement this, we add another array to Chunk.

chunk.h<br>in struct Chunk

```
uint8_t* code;
int* lines;
ValueArray constants;
```

Since it exactly parallels the bytecode array, we don't need a separate count or capacity. Every time we touch the code array, we make a corresponding change to the line number array, starting with initialization.

chunk.c<br>in initChunk()

```
chunk->code = NULL;
chunk->lines = NULL;
initValueArray(&chunk->constants);
```

And likewise deallocation:

chunk.c<br>in freeChunk()

```
FREE_ARRAY(uint8_t, chunk->code, chunk->capacity);
FREE_ARRAY(int, chunk->lines, chunk->capacity);
freeValueArray(&chunk->constants);
```

When we write a byte of code to the chunk, we need to know what source line it came from, so we add an extra parameter in the declaration of writeChunk().

chunk.h<br>function writeChunk()<br>replace 1 line

```
void freeChunk(Chunk* chunk);
void writeChunk(Chunk* chunk, uint8_t byte, int line);
int addConstant(Chunk* chunk, Value value);
```

And in the implementation:

chunk.c<br>function writeChunk()<br>replace 1 line

```
void writeChunk(Chunk* chunk, uint8_t byte, int line) {
  if (chunk->capacity < chunk->count + 1) {
```

When we allocate or grow the code array, we do the same for the line info too.

chunk.c<br>in writeChunk()

```
    chunk->code = GROW_ARRAY(uint8_t, chunk->code,
        oldCapacity, chunk->capacity);
    chunk->lines = GROW_ARRAY(int, chunk->lines,
        oldCapacity, chunk->capacity);
  }
```

Finally, we store the line number in the array.

chunk.c<br>in writeChunk()

```
  chunk->code[chunk->count] = byte;
  chunk->lines[chunk->count] = line;
  chunk->count++;
```

## 14.6.1 Disassembling line information

Alright, let's try this out with our little, uh, artisanal chunk. First, since we added a new parameter to `writeChunk()`, we need to fix those calls to pass in some—arbitrary at this point—line number.

```
int constant = addConstant(&chunk, 1.2);
writeChunk(&chunk, OP_CONSTANT, 123);
writeChunk(&chunk, constant, 123);

writeChunk(&chunk, OP_RETURN, 123);

disassembleChunk(&chunk, "test chunk");
```

main.c
in main()
replace 4 lines

Once we have a real front end, of course, the compiler will track the current line as it parses and pass that in.

Now that we have line information for every instruction, let's put it to good use. In our disassembler, it's helpful to show which source line each instruction was compiled from. That gives us a way to map back to the original code when we're trying to figure out what some blob of bytecode is supposed to do. After printing the offset of the instruction—the number of bytes from the beginning of the chunk—we show its source line.

```
int disassembleInstruction(Chunk* chunk, int offset) {
  printf("%04d ", offset);
  if (offset > 0 &&
      chunk->lines[offset] == chunk->lines[offset - 1]) {
    printf("   | ");
  } else {
    printf("%4d ", chunk->lines[offset]);
  }

  uint8_t instruction = chunk->code[offset];
```

debug.c
in disassembleInstruction()

Bytecode instructions tend to be pretty fine-grained. A single line of source code often compiles to a whole sequence of instructions. To make that more visually clear, we show a | for any instruction that comes from the same source line as the preceding one. The resulting output for our handwritten chunk looks like:

```
== test chunk ==
0000  123 OP_CONSTANT         0 '1.2'
0002    | OP_RETURN
```

We have a three-byte chunk. The first two bytes are a constant instruction that loads 1.2 from the chunk's constant pool. The first byte is the `OP_CONSTANT` opcode and the second is the index in the constant pool. The third byte (at offset 2) is a single-byte return instruction.

In the remaining chapters, we will flesh this out with lots more kinds of instructions. But the basic structure is here, and we have everything we need now to completely represent an executable piece of code at runtime in our virtual machine. Remember that whole family of AST classes we defined in jlox? In clox, we've reduced that down to three arrays: bytes of code, constant values, and line information for debugging.

This reduction is a key reason why our new interpreter will be faster than jlox. You can think of bytecode as a sort of compact serialization of the AST, highly optimized for how the interpreter will deserialize it in the order it needs as it executes. In the next chapter, we will see how the virtual machine does exactly that.

## CHALLENGES

1. Our encoding of line information is hilariously wasteful of memory. Given that a series of instructions often correspond to the same source line, a natural solution is something akin to run-length encoding of the line numbers.

   Devise an encoding that compresses the line information for a series of instructions on the same line. Change `writeChunk()` to write this compressed form, and implement a `getLine()` function that, given the index of an instruction, determines the line where the instruction occurs.

   *Hint: It's not necessary for `getLine()` to be particularly efficient. Since it is called only when a runtime error occurs, it is well off the critical path where performance matters.*

2. Because `OP_CONSTANT` uses only a single byte for its operand, a chunk may only contain up to 256 different constants. That's small enough that people writing real-world code will hit that limit. We could use two or more bytes to store the operand, but that makes *every* constant instruction take up more space. Most chunks won't need that many unique constants, so that wastes space and sacrifices some locality in the common case to support the rare case.

   To balance those two competing aims, many instruction sets feature multiple instructions that perform the same operation but with operands of different sizes. Leave our existing one-byte `OP_CONSTANT` instruction alone, and define a second `OP_CONSTANT_LONG` instruction. It stores the operand as a 24-bit number, which should be plenty.

   Implement this function:

   ```
   void writeConstant(Chunk* chunk, Value value, int line) {
     // Implement me...
   }
   ```

   It adds `value` to `chunk`'s constant array and then writes an appropriate instruction to load the constant. Also add support to the disassembler for `OP_CONSTANT_LONG` instructions.

   Defining two instructions seems to be the best of both worlds. What sacrifices, if any, does it force on us?

3. Our `reallocate()` function relies on the C standard library for dynamic memory allocation and freeing. `malloc()` and `free()` aren't magic. Find a couple of open source implementations of them and explain how they work. How do they keep track of which bytes are allocated and which are free? What is required to allocate a block of memory? Free it? How do they make that efficient? What do they do about fragmentation?

   *Hardcore mode:* Implement `reallocate()` without calling `realloc()`, `malloc()`, or `free()`. You are allowed to call `malloc()` *once*, at the beginning of the interpreter's execution, to allocate a single big block of memory, which your `reallocate()` function has access to. It parcels out blobs of memory from that single region, your own personal heap. It's your job to define how it does that.

## DESIGN NOTE: TEST YOUR LANGUAGE

We're almost halfway through the book and one thing we haven't talked about is *testing* your language implementation. That's not because testing isn't important. I can't possibly stress enough how vital it is to have a good, comprehensive test suite for your language.

You can find the test suite here:
↦ craftinginterpreters.com/tests

I wrote a test suite for Lox (which you are welcome to use on your own Lox implementation) before I wrote a single word of this book. Those tests found countless bugs in my implementations.

Tests are important in all software, but they're even more important for a programming language for at least a couple of reasons:

- **Users expect their programming languages to be rock solid.** We are so used to mature, stable compilers and interpreters that "It's your code, not the compiler" is an ingrained part of software culture. If there are bugs in your language implementation, users will go through the full five stages of grief before they can figure out what's going on, and you don't want to put them through all that.

- **A language implementation is a deeply interconnected piece of software.** Some codebases are broad and shallow. If the file loading code is broken in your text editor, it—hopefully!—won't cause failures in the text rendering on screen. Language implementations are narrower and deeper, especially the core of the interpreter that handles the language's actual semantics. That makes it easy for subtle bugs to creep in caused by weird interactions between various parts of the system. It takes good tests to flush those out.

- **The input to a language implementation is, by design, combinatorial.** There are an infinite number of possible programs a user could write, and your implementation needs to run them all correctly. You obviously can't test that exhaustively, but you need to work hard to cover as much of the input space as you can.

- **Language implementations are often complex, constantly changing, and full of optimizations.** That leads to gnarly code with lots of dark corners where bugs can hide.

All of that means you're gonna want a lot of tests. But *what* tests? Projects I've seen focus mostly on end-to-end "language tests". Each test is a program written in the language along with the output or errors it is expected to produce. Then you have a test runner that pushes the test program through your language implementation and validates that it does what it's supposed to. Writing your tests in the language itself has a few nice advantages:

- The tests aren't coupled to any particular API or internal architecture decisions of the implementation. This frees you to reorganize or rewrite parts of your interpreter or compiler without needing to update a slew of tests.

- You can use the same tests for multiple implementations of the language.

- Tests can often be terse and easy to read and maintain since they are simply scripts in your language.

It's not all rosy, though:

- End-to-end tests help you determine *if* there is a bug, but not *where* the bug is. It can be harder to figure out where the erroneous code in the implementation is because all the test tells you is that the right output didn't appear.

- It can be a chore to craft a valid program that tickles some obscure corner of the implementation. This is particularly true for highly optimized compilers where you may need to write convoluted code to ensure that you end up on just the right optimization path where a bug may be hiding.

- The overhead can be high to fire up the interpreter, parse, compile, and run each test script. With a big suite of tests—which you *do* want, remember—that can mean a lot of time spent waiting for the tests to finish running.

I could go on, but I don't want this to turn into a sermon. Also, I don't pretend to be an expert on *how* to test languages. I just want you to internalize how important it is *that* you test yours. Seriously. Test your language. You'll thank me for it.

# A Virtual Machine

15

*"Magicians protect their secrets not because the secrets are large and important, but because they are so small and trivial. The wonderful effects created on stage are often the result of a secret so absurd that the magician would be embarrassed to admit that that was how it was done."*

— Christopher Priest, *The Prestige*

We've spent a lot of time talking about how to represent a program as a sequence of bytecode instructions, but it feels like learning biology using only stuffed, dead animals. We know what instructions are in theory, but we've never seen them in action, so it's hard to really understand what they *do*. It would be hard to write a compiler that outputs bytecode when we don't have a good understanding of how that bytecode behaves.

So, before we go and build the front end of our new interpreter, we will begin with the back end—the virtual machine that executes instructions. It breathes life into the bytecode. Watching the instructions prance around gives us a clearer picture of how a compiler might translate the user's source code into a series of them.

## 15.1 An Instruction Execution Machine

The virtual machine is one part of our interpreter's internal architecture. You hand it a chunk of code—literally a Chunk—and it runs it. The code and data structures for the VM reside in a new module.

vm.h<br>create new file

```
#ifndef clox_vm_h
#define clox_vm_h

#include "chunk.h"

typedef struct {
  Chunk* chunk;
} VM;

void initVM();
void freeVM();

#endif
```

As usual, we start simple. The VM will gradually acquire a whole pile of state it needs to keep track of, so we define a struct now to stuff that all in. Currently, all we store is the chunk that it executes.

Like we do with most of the data structures we create, we also define functions to create and tear down a VM. Here's the implementation:

vm.c<br>create new file

```
#include "common.h"
#include "vm.h"

VM vm;

void initVM() {
}

void freeVM() {
}
```

The choice to have a static VM instance is a concession for the book, but not necessarily a sound engineering choice for a real language implementation. If you're building a VM that's designed to be embedded in other host applications, it gives the host more flexibility if you *do* explicitly take a VM pointer and pass it around.

That way, the host app can control when and where memory for the VM is allocated, run multiple VMs in parallel, etc.

What I'm doing here is a global variable, and everything bad you've heard about global variables is still true when programming in the large:

→ craftinginterpreters.com/singleton

But when keeping things small for a book…

OK, calling those functions "implementations" is a stretch. We don't have any interesting state to initialize or free yet, so the functions are empty. Trust me, we'll get there.

The slightly more interesting line here is that declaration of vm. This module is eventually going to have a slew of functions and it would be a chore to pass around a pointer to the VM to all of them. Instead, we declare a single global VM object. We need only one anyway, and this keeps the code in the book a little lighter on the page.

Before we start pumping fun code into our VM, let's go ahead and wire it up to the interpreter's main entrypoint.

main.c<br>in main()

```
int main(int argc, const char* argv[]) {
  initVM();

  Chunk chunk;
```

We spin up the VM when the interpreter first starts. Then when we're about to exit, we wind it down.

```
  disassembleChunk(&chunk, "test chunk");
  freeVM();
  freeChunk(&chunk);
```
*main.c*
*in* main()

One last ceremonial obligation:

```
#include "debug.h"
#include "vm.h"

int main(int argc, const char* argv[]) {
```
*main.c*

Now when you run clox, it starts up the VM before it creates that hand-authored chunk from the last chapter. The VM is ready and waiting, so let's teach it to do something.

## 15.1.1 Executing instructions

The VM springs into action when we command it to interpret a chunk of byte-code.

```
  disassembleChunk(&chunk, "test chunk");
  interpret(&chunk);
  freeVM();
```
*main.c*
*in* main()

This function is the main entrypoint into the VM. It's declared like so:

```
void freeVM();
InterpretResult interpret(Chunk* chunk);

#endif
```
*vm.h*
*add after* freeVM()

The VM runs the chunk and then responds with a value from this enum:

```
} VM;

typedef enum {
  INTERPRET_OK,
  INTERPRET_COMPILE_ERROR,
  INTERPRET_RUNTIME_ERROR
} InterpretResult;

void initVM();
void freeVM();
```
*vm.h*
*add after struct* VM

We aren't using the result yet, but when we have a compiler that reports static errors and a VM that detects runtime errors, the interpreter will use this to know how to set the exit code of the process.

We're inching towards some actual implementation.

vm.c
*add after* freeVM()

```
InterpretResult interpret(Chunk* chunk) {
  vm.chunk = chunk;
  vm.ip = vm.chunk->code;
  return run();
}
```

First, we store the chunk being executed in the VM. Then we call `run()`, an internal helper function that actually runs the bytecode instructions. Between those two parts is an intriguing line. What is this `ip` business?

As the VM works its way through the bytecode, it keeps track of where it is—the location of the instruction currently being executed. We don't use a local variable inside `run()` for this because eventually other functions will need to access it. Instead, we store it as a field in VM.

If we were trying to squeeze every ounce of speed out of our bytecode interpreter, we would store `ip` in a local variable. It gets modified so often during execution that we want the C compiler to keep it in a register.

vm.h
*in struct* VM

```
typedef struct {
  Chunk* chunk;
  uint8_t* ip;
} VM;
```

Its type is a byte pointer. We use an actual real C pointer pointing right into the middle of the bytecode array instead of something like an integer index because it's faster to dereference a pointer than look up an element in an array by index.

The name "IP" is traditional, and—unlike many traditional names in CS—actually makes sense: it's an **instruction pointer**. Almost every instruction set in the world, real and virtual, has a register or variable like this.

x86, x64, and the CLR call it "IP". 68k, PowerPC, ARM, p-code, and the JVM call it "PC", for **program counter**.

We initialize `ip` by pointing it at the first byte of code in the chunk. We haven't executed that instruction yet, so `ip` points to the instruction *about to be executed*. This will be true during the entire time the VM is running: the IP always points to the next instruction, not the one currently being handled.

The real fun happens in `run()`.

vm.c
*add after* freeVM()

```
static InterpretResult run() {
#define READ_BYTE() (*vm.ip++)

  for (;;) {
    uint8_t instruction;
    switch (instruction = READ_BYTE()) {
      case OP_RETURN: {
        return INTERPRET_OK;
      }
    }
  }

#undef READ_BYTE
}
```

Or, at least, it *will* be in a few chapters when it has enough content to be useful. Right now, it's not exactly a wonder of software wizardry.

This is the single most important function in all of clox, by far. When the interpreter executes a user's program, it will spend something like 90% of its time inside `run()`. It is the beating heart of the VM.

Despite that dramatic intro, it's conceptually pretty simple. We have an outer loop that goes and goes. Each turn through that loop, we read and execute a single bytecode instruction.

To process an instruction, we first figure out what kind of instruction we're dealing with. The READ_BYTE macro reads the byte currently pointed at by ip and then advances the instruction pointer. The first byte of any instruction is the opcode. Given a numeric opcode, we need to get to the right C code that implements that instruction's semantics. This process is called **decoding** or **dispatching** the instruction.

We do that process for every single instruction, every single time one is executed, so this is the most performance critical part of the entire virtual machine. Programming language lore is filled with clever techniques to do bytecode dispatch efficiently, going all the way back to the early days of computers.

Alas, the fastest solutions require either non-standard extensions to C, or handwritten assembly code. For clox, we'll keep it simple. Just like our disassembler, we have a single giant switch statement with a case for each opcode. The body of each case implements that opcode's behavior.

So far, we handle only a single instruction, OP_RETURN, and the only thing it does is exit the loop entirely. Eventually, that instruction will be used to return from the current Lox function, but we don't have functions yet, so we'll repurpose it temporarily to end the execution.

Let's go ahead and support our one other instruction.

> Note that ip advances as soon as we read the opcode, before we've actually started executing the instruction. So, again, ip points to the *next* byte of code to be used.

> If you want to learn some of these techniques, look up "direct threaded code", "jump table", and "computed goto".

```
  switch (instruction = READ_BYTE()) {
    case OP_CONSTANT: {
      Value constant = READ_CONSTANT();
      printValue(constant);
      printf("\n");
      break;
    }
    case OP_RETURN: {
```

> vm.c
> *in* run()

We don't have enough machinery in place yet to do anything useful with a constant. For now, we'll just print it out so we interpreter hackers can see what's going on inside our VM. That call to printf() necessitates an include.

```
#include <stdio.h>

#include "common.h"
```

> vm.c
> *add to top of file*

We also have a new macro to define.

```
#define READ_BYTE() (*vm.ip++)
#define READ_CONSTANT() (vm.chunk->constants.values[READ_BYTE()])

  for (;;) {
```

> vm.c
> *in* run()

READ_CONSTANT() reads the next byte from the bytecode, treats the resulting number as an index, and looks up the corresponding Value in the chunk's constant table. In later chapters, we'll add a few more instructions with operands that refer to constants, so we're setting up this helper macro now.

Like the previous READ_BYTE macro, READ_CONSTANT is only used inside run(). To make that scoping more explicit, the macro definitions themselves are confined to that function. We define them at the beginning and—because we care—undefine them at the end.

> Undefining these macros explicitly might seem needlessly fastidious, but C tends to punish sloppy users, and the C preprocessor doubly so.

```
vm.c          #undef READ_BYTE
in run()      #undef READ_CONSTANT
              }
```

## 15.1.2  Execution tracing

If you run clox now, it executes the chunk we hand-authored in the last chapter and spits out 1.2 to your terminal. We can see that it's working, but that's only because our implementation of OP_CONSTANT has temporary code to log the value. Once that instruction is doing what it's supposed to do and plumbing that constant along to other operations that want to consume it, the VM will become a black box. That makes our lives as VM implementers harder.

To help ourselves out, now is a good time to add some diagnostic logging to the VM like we did with chunks themselves. In fact, we'll even reuse the same code. We don't want this logging enabled all the time—it's just for us VM hackers, not Lox users—so first we create a flag to hide it behind.

```
common.h      #include <stdint.h>


              #define DEBUG_TRACE_EXECUTION


              #endif
```

When this flag is defined, the VM disassembles and prints each instruction right before executing it. Where our previous disassembler walked an entire chunk once, statically, this disassembles instructions dynamically, on the fly.

```
vm.c              for (;;) {
in run()      #ifdef DEBUG_TRACE_EXECUTION
                  disassembleInstruction(vm.chunk,
                                         (int)(vm.ip - vm.chunk->code));
              #endif

                  uint8_t instruction;
```

Since disassembleInstruction() takes an integer byte *offset* and we store the current instruction reference as a direct pointer, we first do a little pointer math to convert ip back to a relative offset from the beginning of the bytecode. Then we disassemble the instruction that begins at that byte.

As ever, we need to bring in the declaration of the function before we can call it.

```
vm.c          #include "common.h"
              #include "debug.h"
              #include "vm.h"
```

I know this code isn't super impressive so far—it's literally a switch statement wrapped in a for loop but, believe it or not, this is one of the two major components of our VM. With this, we can imperatively execute instructions. Its simplicity is a virtue—the less work it does, the faster it can do it. Contrast this

with all of the complexity and overhead we had in jlox with the Visitor pattern
for walking the AST.

## 15.2 A Value Stack Manipulator

In addition to imperative side effects, Lox has expressions that produce, modify,
and consume values. Thus, our compiled bytecode needs a way to shuttle values
around between the different instructions that need them. For example:

```
print 3 - 2;
```

We obviously need instructions for the constants 3 and 2, the `print` statement,
and the subtraction. But how does the subtraction instruction know that 3 is the
minuend and 2 is the subtrahend? How does the print instruction know to print
the result of that?

> Yes, I did have to look up "subtrahend"
> and "minuend" in a dictionary. But
> aren't they delightful words? "Minuend"
> sounds like a kind of Elizabethan dance
> and "subtrahend" might be some sort of
> underground Paleolithic monument.

To put a finer point on it, look at this thing right here:

```
fun echo(n) {
  print n;
  return n;
}
```

```
print echo(echo(1) + echo(2)) + echo(echo(4) + echo(5));
```

I wrapped each subexpression in a call to `echo()` that prints and returns its
argument. That side effect means we can see the exact order of operations.

Don't worry about the VM for a minute. Think about just the semantics of
Lox itself. The operands to an arithmetic operator obviously need to be evaluated
before we can perform the operation itself. (It's pretty hard to add a + b if you
don't know what a and b are.) Also, when we implemented expressions in jlox,
we decided that the left operand must be evaluated before the right.

Here is the syntax tree for the `print` statement:

> We could have left evaluation order
> unspecified and let each implementation
> decide. That leaves the door open for
> optimizing compilers to reorder arithmetic
> expressions for efficiency, even in cases
> where the operands have visible side
> effects. C and Scheme leave evaluation
> order unspecified. Java specifies left-to-
> right evaluation like we do for Lox.
>
> I think nailing down stuff like this
> is generally better for users. When
> expressions are not evaluated in the order
> users intuit—possibly in different orders
> across different implementations!—it can
> be a burning hellscape of pain to figure
> out what's going on.

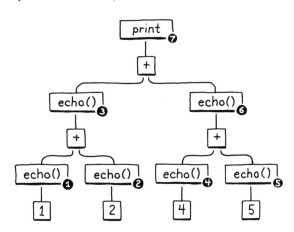

Given left-to-right evaluation, and the way the expressions are nested, any correct Lox implementation *must* print these numbers in this order:

```
 1  // from echo(1)
 2  // from echo(2)
 3  // from echo(1 + 2)
 4  // from echo(4)
 5  // from echo(5)
 9  // from echo(4 + 5)
12  // from print 3 + 9
```

Our old jlox interpreter accomplishes this by recursively traversing the AST. It does a postorder traversal. First it recurses down the left operand branch, then the right operand, then finally it evaluates the node itself.

After evaluating the left operand, jlox needs to store that result somewhere temporarily while it's busy traversing down through the right operand tree. We use a local variable in Java for that. Our recursive tree-walk interpreter creates a unique Java call frame for each node being evaluated, so we could have as many of these local variables as we needed.

In clox, our run() function is not recursive—the nested expression tree is flattened out into a linear series of instructions. We don't have the luxury of using C local variables, so how and where should we store these temporary values? You can probably guess already, but I want to really drill into this because it's an aspect of programming that we take for granted, but we rarely learn *why* computers are architected this way.

Hint: it's in the name of this section, and it's how Java and C manage recursive calls to functions.

Let's do a weird exercise. We'll walk through the execution of the above program a step at a time:

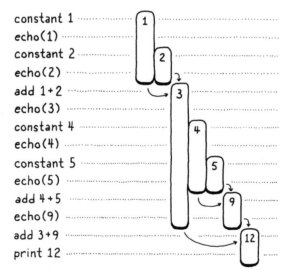

On the left are the steps of code. On the right are the values we're tracking. Each bar represents a number. It starts when the value is first produced—either a constant or the result of an addition. The length of the bar tracks when a previously produced value needs to be kept around, and it ends when that value finally gets consumed by an operation.

As you step through, you see values appear and then later get eaten. The longest-lived ones are the values produced from the left-hand side of an addition. Those stick around while we work through the right-hand operand expression.

In the above diagram, I gave each unique number its own visual column. Let's be a little more parsimonious. Once a number is consumed, we allow its column to be reused for another later value. In other words, we take all of those gaps in the previous illustration and fill them in, pushing in numbers from the right:

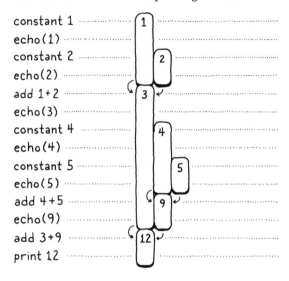

```
constant 1 ............... 1
echo(1) ...............
constant 2 ...............   2
echo(2) ...............
add 1+2 ...............  3
echo(3) ...............
constant 4 ...............   4
echo(4) ...............
constant 5 ...............    5
echo(5) ...............
add 4+5 ...............  9
echo(9) ...............
add 3+9 ...............  12
print 12 ...............
```

There's some interesting stuff going on here. When we shift everything over, each number still manages to stay in a single column for its entire life. Also, there are no gaps left. In other words, whenever a number appears earlier than another, then it will live at least as long as that second one. The first number to appear is the last to be consumed. Hmm... last-in, first-out... why, that's a stack!

In the second diagram, each time we introduce a number, we push it onto the stack from the right. When numbers are consumed, they are always popped off from rightmost to left.

Since the temporary values we need to track naturally have stack-like behavior, our VM will use a stack to manage them. When an instruction "produces" a value, it pushes it onto the stack. When it needs to consume one or more values, it gets them by popping them off the stack.

## 15.2.1 The VM's Stack

Maybe this doesn't seem like a revelation, but I *love* stack-based VMs. When you first see a magic trick, it feels like something actually magical. But then you learn how it works—usually some mechanical gimmick or misdirection—and the sense of wonder evaporates. There are a couple of ideas in computer science where even after I pulled them apart and learned all the ins and outs, some of the initial sparkle remained. Stack-based VMs are one of those.

As you'll see in this chapter, executing instructions in a stack-based VM is dead simple. In later chapters, you'll also discover that compiling a source language to a stack-based instruction set is a piece of cake. And yet, this architecture is fast enough to be used by production language implementations. It almost feels like cheating at the programming language game.

This is also a stack:

Heaps—the data structure, not the memory management thing—are another. And Vaughan Pratt's top-down operator precedence parsing scheme, which we'll learn about in due time.

To take a bit of the sheen off: stack-based interpreters aren't a silver bullet. They're often *adequate*, but modern implementations of the JVM, the CLR, and JavaScript all use sophisticated just-in-time compilation pipelines to generate *much* faster native code on the fly.

Alrighty, it's codin' time! Here's the stack:

**vm.h**
*in struct* **VM**

```
typedef struct {
  Chunk* chunk;
  uint8_t* ip;
  Value stack[STACK_MAX];
  Value* stackTop;
} VM;
```

We implement the stack semantics ourselves on top of a raw C array. The bottom of the stack—the first value pushed and the last to be popped—is at element zero in the array, and later pushed values follow it. If we push the letters of "crepe"— my favorite stackable breakfast item—onto the stack, in order, the resulting C array looks like this:

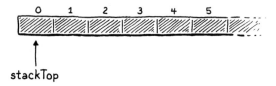

Since the stack grows and shrinks as values are pushed and popped, we need to track where the top of the stack is in the array. As with ip, we use a direct pointer instead of an integer index since it's faster to dereference the pointer than calculate the offset from the index each time we need it.

The pointer points at the array element just *past* the element containing the top value on the stack. That seems a little odd, but almost every implementation does this. It means we can indicate that the stack is empty by pointing at element zero in the array.

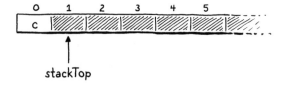

If we pointed to the top element, then for an empty stack we'd need to point at element -1. That's undefined in C. As we push values onto the stack...

What about when the stack is *full*, you ask, Clever Reader? The C standard is one step ahead of you. It *is* allowed and well-specified to have an array pointer that points just past the end of an array.

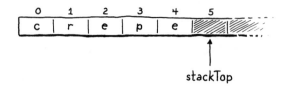

...stackTop always points just past the last item.

I remember it like this: stackTop points to where the next value to be pushed will go. The maximum number of values we can store on the stack (for now, at least) is:

```
#include "chunk.h"

#define STACK_MAX 256

typedef struct {
```
vm.h

Giving our VM a fixed stack size means it's possible for some sequence of instructions to push too many values and run out of stack space—the classic "stack overflow". We could grow the stack dynamically as needed, but for now we'll keep it simple. Since VM uses Value, we need to include its declaration.

```
#include "chunk.h"
#include "value.h"

#define STACK_MAX 256
```
vm.h

Now that VM has some interesting state, we get to initialize it.

```
void initVM() {
  resetStack();
}
```
vm.c
in initVM()

That uses this helper function:

```
static void resetStack() {
  vm.stackTop = vm.stack;
}
```
vm.c
add after variable vm

Since the stack array is declared directly inline in the VM struct, we don't need to allocate it. We don't even need to clear the unused cells in the array—we simply won't access them until after values have been stored in them. The only initialization we need is to set stackTop to point to the beginning of the array to indicate that the stack is empty.

The stack protocol supports two operations:

```
InterpretResult interpret(Chunk* chunk);
void push(Value value);
Value pop();

#endif
```
vm.h
add after interpret()

You can push a new value onto the top of the stack, and you can pop the most recently pushed value back off. Here's the first function:

```
void push(Value value) {
  *vm.stackTop = value;
  vm.stackTop++;
}
```
vm.c
add after freeVM()

If you're rusty on your C pointer syntax and operations, this is a good warm-up. The first line stores value in the array element at the top of the stack. Remember, stackTop points just *past* the last used element, at the next available one. This stores the value in that slot. Then we increment the pointer itself to point to the next unused slot in the array now that the previous slot is occupied.

Popping is the mirror image.

vm.c<br>add after push()

```c
Value pop() {
  vm.stackTop--;
  return *vm.stackTop;
}
```

First, we move the stack pointer *back* to get to the most recent used slot in the array. Then we look up the value at that index and return it. We don't need to explicitly "remove" it from the array—moving stackTop down is enough to mark that slot as no longer in use.

### 15.2.2 Stack tracing

We have a working stack, but it's hard to *see* that it's working. When we start implementing more complex instructions and compiling and running larger pieces of code, we'll end up with a lot of values crammed into that array. It would make our lives as VM hackers easier if we had some visibility into the stack.

To that end, whenever we're tracing execution, we'll also show the current contents of the stack before we interpret each instruction.

vm.c<br>in run()

```c
#ifdef DEBUG_TRACE_EXECUTION
    printf("          ");
    for (Value* slot = vm.stack; slot < vm.stackTop; slot++) {
      printf("[ ");
      printValue(*slot);
      printf(" ]");
    }
    printf("\n");
    disassembleInstruction(vm.chunk,
```

We loop, printing each value in the array, starting at the first (bottom of the stack) and ending when we reach the top. This lets us observe the effect of each instruction on the stack. The output is pretty verbose, but it's useful when we're surgically extracting a nasty bug from the bowels of the interpreter.

Stack in hand, let's revisit our two instructions. First up:

vm.c<br>in run()<br>replace 2 lines

```c
    case OP_CONSTANT: {
      Value constant = READ_CONSTANT();
      push(constant);
      break;
```

In the last chapter, I was hand-wavey about how the OP_CONSTANT instruction "loads" a constant. Now that we have a stack you know what it means to actually produce a value: it gets pushed onto the stack.

```
  case OP_RETURN: {
    printValue(pop());
    printf("\n");
    return INTERPRET_OK;
```

vm.c<br>in run()

Then we make **OP_RETURN** pop the stack and print the top value before exiting. When we add support for real functions to clox, we'll change this code. But, for now, it gives us a way to get the VM executing simple instruction sequences and displaying the result.

## 15.3  An Arithmetic Calculator

The heart and soul of our VM are in place now. The bytecode loop dispatches and executes instructions. The stack grows and shrinks as values flow through it. The two halves work, but it's hard to get a feel for how cleverly they interact with only the two rudimentary instructions we have so far. So let's teach our interpreter to do arithmetic.

We'll start with the simplest arithmetic operation, unary negation.

```
var a = 1.2;
print -a; // -1.2.
```

The prefix – operator takes one operand, the value to negate. It produces a single result. We aren't fussing with a parser yet, but we can add the bytecode instruction that the above syntax will compile to.

```
  OP_CONSTANT,
  OP_NEGATE,
  OP_RETURN,
```

chunk.h<br>in enum OpCode

We execute it like so:

```
    }
    case OP_NEGATE:   push(-pop()); break;
    case OP_RETURN: {
```

vm.c<br>in run()

The instruction needs a value to operate on, which it gets by popping from the stack. It negates that, then pushes the result back on for later instructions to use. Doesn't get much easier than that. We can disassemble it too.

```
  case OP_CONSTANT:
    return constantInstruction("OP_CONSTANT", chunk, offset);
  case OP_NEGATE:
    return simpleInstruction("OP_NEGATE", offset);
  case OP_RETURN:
```

debug.c<br>in disassembleInstruction()

And we can try it out in our test chunk.

main.c
in main()

```
writeChunk(&chunk, constant, 123);
writeChunk(&chunk, OP_NEGATE, 123);

writeChunk(&chunk, OP_RETURN, 123);
```

After loading the constant, but before returning, we execute the negate instruction. That replaces the constant on the stack with its negation. Then the return instruction prints that out:

```
-1.2
```

Magical!

### 15.3.1 Binary operators

OK, unary operators aren't *that* impressive. We still only ever have a single value on the stack. To really see some depth, we need binary operators. Lox has four binary arithmetic operators: addition, subtraction, multiplication, and division. We'll go ahead and implement them all at the same time.

Lox has some other binary operators—comparison and equality—but those don't produce numbers as a result, so we aren't ready for them yet.

chunk.h
in enum OpCode

```
  OP_CONSTANT,
  OP_ADD,
  OP_SUBTRACT,
  OP_MULTIPLY,
  OP_DIVIDE,
  OP_NEGATE,
```

Back in the bytecode loop, they are executed like this:

vm.c
in run()

```
      }
      case OP_ADD:      BINARY_OP(+); break;
      case OP_SUBTRACT: BINARY_OP(-); break;
      case OP_MULTIPLY: BINARY_OP(*); break;
      case OP_DIVIDE:   BINARY_OP(/); break;
      case OP_NEGATE:   push(-pop()); break;
```

The only difference between these four instructions is which underlying C operator they ultimately use to combine the two operands. Surrounding that core arithmetic expression is some boilerplate code to pull values off the stack and push the result. When we later add dynamic typing, that boilerplate will grow. To avoid repeating that code four times, I wrapped it up in a macro.

vm.c
in run()

```
#define READ_CONSTANT() (vm.chunk->constants.values[READ_BYTE()])
#define BINARY_OP(op) \
    do { \
      double b = pop(); \
      double a = pop(); \
      push(a op b); \
    } while (false)

  for (;;) {
```

I admit this is a fairly adventurous use of the C preprocessor. I hesitated to do this, but you'll be glad in later chapters when we need to add the type checking for each operand and stuff. It would be a chore to walk you through the same code four times.

If you aren't familiar with the trick already, that outer do while loop probably looks really weird. This macro needs to expand to a series of statements. To be careful macro authors, we want to ensure those statements all end up in the same scope when the macro is expanded. Imagine if you defined:

```
#define WAKE_UP() makeCoffee(); drinkCoffee();
```

And then used it like:

```
if (morning) WAKE_UP();
```

The intent is to execute both statements of the macro body only if morning is true. But it expands to:

```
if (morning) makeCoffee(); drinkCoffee();;
```

Oops. The if attaches only to the *first* statement. You might think you could fix this using a block.

```
#define WAKE_UP() { makeCoffee(); drinkCoffee(); }
```

That's better, but you still risk:

```
if (morning)
  WAKE_UP();
else
  sleepIn();
```

Now you get a compile error on the else because of that trailing ; after the macro's block. Using a do while loop in the macro looks funny, but it gives you a way to contain multiple statements inside a block that *also* permits a semicolon at the end.

Where were we? Right, so what the body of that macro does is straightforward. A binary operator takes two operands, so it pops twice. It performs the operation on those two values and then pushes the result.

Pay close attention to the *order* of the two pops. Note that we assign the first popped operand to b, not a. It looks backwards. When the operands themselves are calculated, the left is evaluated first, then the right. That means the left operand gets pushed before the right operand. So the right operand will be on top of the stack. Thus, the first value we pop is b.

For example, if we compile 3 - 1, the data flow between the instructions looks like so:

Did you even know you can pass an *operator* as an argument to a macro? Now you do. The preprocessor doesn't care that operators aren't first class in C. As far as it's concerned, it's all just text tokens.

I know, you can just *feel* the temptation to abuse this, can't you?

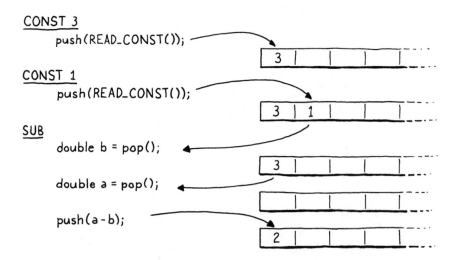

As we did with the other macros inside `run()`, we clean up after ourselves at the end of the function.

**vm.c**
*in* `run()`

```
#undef READ_CONSTANT
#undef BINARY_OP
}
```

Last is disassembler support.

**debug.c**
*in* `disassembleInstruction()`

```
  case OP_CONSTANT:
    return constantInstruction("OP_CONSTANT", chunk, offset);
  case OP_ADD:
    return simpleInstruction("OP_ADD", offset);
  case OP_SUBTRACT:
    return simpleInstruction("OP_SUBTRACT", offset);
  case OP_MULTIPLY:
    return simpleInstruction("OP_MULTIPLY", offset);
  case OP_DIVIDE:
    return simpleInstruction("OP_DIVIDE", offset);
  case OP_NEGATE:
```

The arithmetic instruction formats are simple, like OP_RETURN. Even though the arithmetic *operators* take operands—which are found on the stack—the arithmetic *bytecode instructions* do not.

Let's put some of our new instructions through their paces by evaluating a larger expression:

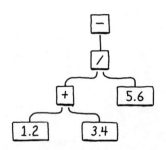

Building on our existing example chunk, here's the additional instructions we need to hand-compile that AST to bytecode.

main.c
in main()

```c
int constant = addConstant(&chunk, 1.2);
writeChunk(&chunk, OP_CONSTANT, 123);
writeChunk(&chunk, constant, 123);

constant = addConstant(&chunk, 3.4);
writeChunk(&chunk, OP_CONSTANT, 123);
writeChunk(&chunk, constant, 123);

writeChunk(&chunk, OP_ADD, 123);

constant = addConstant(&chunk, 5.6);
writeChunk(&chunk, OP_CONSTANT, 123);
writeChunk(&chunk, constant, 123);

writeChunk(&chunk, OP_DIVIDE, 123);
writeChunk(&chunk, OP_NEGATE, 123);

writeChunk(&chunk, OP_RETURN, 123);
```

The addition goes first. The instruction for the left constant, 1.2, is already there, so we add another for 3.4. Then we add those two using OP_ADD, leaving it on the stack. That covers the left side of the division. Next we push the 5.6, and divide the result of the addition by it. Finally, we negate the result of that.

Note how the output of the OP_ADD implicitly flows into being an operand of OP_DIVIDE without either instruction being directly coupled to each other. That's the magic of the stack. It lets us freely compose instructions without them needing any complexity or awareness of the data flow. The stack acts like a shared workspace that they all read from and write to.

In this tiny example chunk, the stack still only gets two values tall, but when we start compiling Lox source to bytecode, we'll have chunks that use much more of the stack. In the meantime, try playing around with this hand-authored chunk to calculate different nested arithmetic expressions and see how values flow through the instructions and stack.

You may as well get it out of your system now. This is the last chunk we'll build by hand. When we next revisit bytecode, we will be writing a compiler to generate it for us.

## CHALLENGES

1. What bytecode instruction sequences would you generate for the following expressions:

```
1 * 2 + 3
1 + 2 * 3
3 - 2 - 1
1 + 2 * 3 - 4 / -5
```

(Remember that Lox does not have a syntax for negative number literals, so the -5 is negating the number 5.)

2. If we really wanted a minimal instruction set, we could eliminate either **OP_NEGATE** or **OP_SUBTRACT**. Show the bytecode instruction sequence you would generate for:

```
4 - 3 * -2
```

First, without using **OP_NEGATE**. Then, without using **OP_SUBTRACT**.

Given the above, do you think it makes sense to have both instructions? Why or why not? Are there any other redundant instructions you would consider including?

3. Our VM's stack has a fixed size, and we don't check if pushing a value overflows it. This means the wrong series of instructions could cause our interpreter to crash or go into undefined behavior. Avoid that by dynamically growing the stack as needed.

What are the costs and benefits of doing so?

4. To interpret **OP_NEGATE**, we pop the operand, negate the value, and then push the result. That's a simple implementation, but it increments and decrements **stackTop** unnecessarily, since the stack ends up the same height in the end. It might be faster to simply negate the value in place on the stack and leave **stackTop** alone. Try that and see if you can measure a performance difference.

Are there other instructions where you can do a similar optimization?

## DESIGN NOTE: REGISTER-BASED BYTECODE

For the remainder of this book, we'll meticulously implement an interpreter around a stack-based bytecode instruction set. There's another family of bytecode architectures out there—*register-based*. Despite the name, these bytecode instructions aren't quite as difficult to work with as the registers in an actual chip like x64. With real hardware registers, you usually have only a handful for the entire program, so you spend a lot of effort trying to use them efficiently and shuttling stuff in and out of them.

In a register-based VM, you still have a stack. Temporary values still get pushed onto it and popped when no longer needed. The main difference is that instructions can read their inputs from anywhere in the stack and can store their outputs into specific stack slots.

Take this little Lox script:

```
var a = 1;
var b = 2;
var c = a + b;
```

In our stack-based VM, the last statement will get compiled to something like:

```
load <a>   // Read local variable a and push onto stack.
load <b>   // Read local variable b and push onto stack.
add        // Pop two values, add, push result.
store <c>  // Pop value and store in local variable c.
```

(Don't worry if you don't fully understand the load and store instructions yet. We'll go over them in much greater detail when we implement variables.) We have four separate instructions. That means four times through the bytecode interpret loop, four instructions to decode and dispatch. It's at least seven bytes of code—four for the opcodes and another three for the operands identifying which locals to load and store. Three pushes and three pops. A lot of work!

In a register-based instruction set, instructions can read from and store directly into local variables. The bytecode for the last statement above looks like:

```
add <a> <b> <c> // Read values from a and b, add, store in c.
```

The add instruction is bigger—it has three instruction operands that define where in the stack it reads its inputs from and writes the result to. But since local variables live on the stack, it can read directly from **a** and **b** and then store the result right into **c**.

There's only a single instruction to decode and dispatch, and the whole thing fits in four bytes. Decoding is more complex because of the additional operands, but it's still a net win. There's no pushing and popping or other stack manipulation.

The main implementation of Lua used to be stack-based. For Lua 5.0, the implementers switched to a register instruction set and noted a speed improvement. The amount of improvement, naturally, depends heavily on the details of the language semantics, specific instruction set, and compiler sophistication, but that should get your attention.

That raises the obvious question of why I'm going to spend the rest of the book doing a stack-based bytecode. Register VMs are neat, but they are quite a bit harder to write a compiler for. For what is likely to be your very first compiler, I wanted to stick with an instruction set that's easy to generate and easy to execute. Stack-based bytecode is marvelously simple.

Register-based bytecode is a little closer to the *register windows* supported by SPARC chips.

The Lua dev team—Roberto Ierusalimschy, Waldemar Celes, and Luiz Henrique de Figueiredo—wrote a *fantastic* paper on this, one of my all time favorite computer science papers, "The Implementation of Lua 5.0":

→ craftinginterpreters.com/lua5

It's also *much* better known in the literature and the community. Even though you may eventually move to something more advanced, it's a good common ground to share with the rest of your language hacker peers.

# Scanning on Demand

16

*"Literature is idiosyncratic arrangements in horizontal lines in only twenty-six phonetic symbols, ten Arabic numbers, and about eight punctuation marks."*

— Kurt Vonnegut, *Like Shaking Hands With God: A Conversation about Writing*

Our second interpreter, clox, has three phases—scanner, compiler, and virtual machine. A data structure joins each pair of phases. Tokens flow from scanner to compiler, and chunks of bytecode from compiler to VM. We began our implementation near the end with chunks and the VM. Now, we're going to hop back to the beginning and build a scanner that makes tokens. In the next chapter, we'll tie the two ends together with our bytecode compiler.

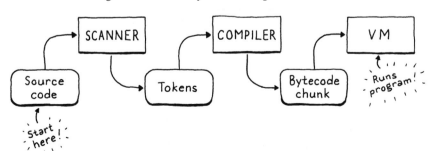

I'll admit, this is not the most exciting chapter in the book. With two implementations of the same language, there's bound to be some redundancy. I did sneak in a few interesting differences compared to jlox's scanner. Read on to see what they are.

## 16.1  Spinning Up the Interpreter

Now that we're building the front end, we can get clox running like a real interpreter. No more hand-authored chunks of bytecode. It's time for a REPL and script loading. Tear out most of the code in main() and replace it with:

main.c
in main()
replace 26 lines

```c
int main(int argc, const char* argv[]) {
  initVM();

  if (argc == 1) {
    repl();
  } else if (argc == 2) {
    runFile(argv[1]);
  } else {
    fprintf(stderr, "Usage: clox [path]\n");
    exit(64);
  }

  freeVM();
  return 0;
}
```

The code tests for one and two arguments, not zero and one, because the first argument in argv is always the name of the executable being run.

If you pass no arguments to the executable, you are dropped into the REPL. A single command line argument is understood to be the path to a script to run.

We'll need a few system headers, so let's get them all out of the way.

main.c
add to top of file

```c
#include <stdio.h>
#include <stdlib.h>
#include <string.h>

#include "common.h"
```

Next, we get the REPL up and REPL-ing.

main.c

```c
#include "vm.h"

static void repl() {
  char line[1024];
  for (;;) {
    printf("> ");

    if (!fgets(line, sizeof(line), stdin)) {
      printf("\n");
      break;
    }
```

continued on next page…

```
      interpret(line);
  }
}
```

… from previous page

A quality REPL handles input that spans multiple lines gracefully and doesn't have a hardcoded line length limit. This REPL here is a little more, ahem, austere, but it's fine for our purposes.

The real work happens in `interpret()`. We'll get to that soon, but first let's take care of loading scripts.

```
static void runFile(const char* path) {
  char* source = readFile(path);
  InterpretResult result = interpret(source);
  free(source);

  if (result == INTERPRET_COMPILE_ERROR) exit(65);
  if (result == INTERPRET_RUNTIME_ERROR) exit(70);
}
```

main.c
*add after* `repl()`

We read the file and execute the resulting string of Lox source code. Then, based on the result of that, we set the exit code appropriately because we're scrupulous tool builders and care about little details like that.

We also need to free the source code string because `readFile()` dynamically allocates it and passes ownership to its caller. That function looks like this:

```
static char* readFile(const char* path) {
  FILE* file = fopen(path, "rb");

  fseek(file, 0L, SEEK_END);
  size_t fileSize = ftell(file);
  rewind(file);

  char* buffer = (char*)malloc(fileSize + 1);
  size_t bytesRead = fread(buffer, sizeof(char), fileSize, file);
  buffer[bytesRead] = '\0';

  fclose(file);
  return buffer;
}
```

main.c
*add after* `repl()`

C asks us not just to manage memory explicitly, but *mentally*. We programmers have to remember the ownership rules and hand-implement them throughout the program. Java just does it for us. C++ gives us tools to encode the policy directly so that the compiler validates it for us.

I like C's simplicity, but we pay a real price for it—the language requires us to be more conscientious.

Like a lot of C code, it takes more effort than it seems like it should, especially for a language expressly designed for operating systems. The difficult part is that we want to allocate a big enough string to read the whole file, but we don't know how big the file is until we've read it.

The code here is the classic trick to solve that. We open the file, but before reading it, we seek to the very end using `fseek()`. Then we call `ftell()` which tells us how many bytes we are from the start of the file. Since we seeked (sought?) to the end, that's the size. We rewind back to the beginning, allocate a string of that size, and read the whole file in a single batch.

So we're done, right? Not quite. These function calls, like most calls in the C standard library, can fail. If this were Java, the failures would be thrown as

Well, that size *plus one*. Always gotta remember to make room for the null byte.

exceptions and automatically unwind the stack so we wouldn't *really* need to handle them. In C, if we don't check for them, they silently get ignored.

This isn't really a book on good C programming practice, but I hate to encourage bad style, so let's go ahead and handle the errors. It's good for us, like eating our vegetables or flossing.

Fortunately, we don't need to do anything particularly clever if a failure occurs. If we can't correctly read the user's script, all we can really do is tell the user and exit the interpreter gracefully. First of all, we might fail to open the file.

**main.c**
*in* readFile()

```c
FILE* file = fopen(path, "rb");
if (file == NULL) {
  fprintf(stderr, "Could not open file \"%s\".\n", path);
  exit(74);
}

fseek(file, 0L, SEEK_END);
```

This can happen if the file doesn't exist or the user doesn't have access to it. It's pretty common—people mistype paths all the time.

This failure is much rarer:

**main.c**
*in* readFile()

```c
char* buffer = (char*)malloc(fileSize + 1);
if (buffer == NULL) {
  fprintf(stderr, "Not enough memory to read \"%s\".\n", path);
  exit(74);
}

size_t bytesRead = fread(buffer, sizeof(char), fileSize, file);
```

If we can't even allocate enough memory to read the Lox script, the user's probably got bigger problems to worry about, but we should do our best to at least let them know.

Finally, the read itself may fail.

**main.c**
*in* readFile()

```c
size_t bytesRead = fread(buffer, sizeof(char), fileSize, file);
if (bytesRead < fileSize) {
  fprintf(stderr, "Could not read file \"%s\".\n", path);
  exit(74);
}

buffer[bytesRead] = '\0';
```

Even good old printf() can fail. Yup. How many times have you handled *that* error?

This is also unlikely. Actually, the calls to fseek(), ftell(), and rewind() could theoretically fail too, but let's not go too far off in the weeds, shall we?

### 16.1.1  Opening the compilation pipeline

We've got ourselves a string of Lox source code, so now we're ready to set up a pipeline to scan, compile, and execute it. It's driven by interpret(). Right now, that function runs our old hardcoded test chunk. Let's change it to something closer to its final incarnation.

```
void freeVM();
InterpretResult interpret(const char* source);
void push(Value value);
```
vm.h
*function* interpret()
*replace 1 line*

Where before we passed in a Chunk, now we pass in the string of source code.
Here's the new implementation:

```
InterpretResult interpret(const char* source) {
  compile(source);
  return INTERPRET_OK;
}
```
vm.c
*function* interpret()
*replace 4 lines*

We won't build the actual *compiler* yet in this chapter, but we can start laying out
its structure. It lives in a new module.

```
#include "common.h"
#include "compiler.h"
#include "debug.h"
```
vm.c

For now, the one function in it is declared like so:

```
#ifndef clox_compiler_h
#define clox_compiler_h

void compile(const char* source);

#endif
```
compiler.h
*create new file*

That signature will change, but it gets us going.
    The first phase of compilation is scanning—the thing we're doing in this
chapter—so right now all the compiler does is set that up.

```
#include <stdio.h>

#include "common.h"
#include "compiler.h"
#include "scanner.h"

void compile(const char* source) {
  initScanner(source);
}
```
compiler.c
*create new file*

This will also grow in later chapters, naturally.

## 16.1.2  The scanner scans

There are still a few more feet of scaffolding to stand up before we can start writing useful code. First, a new header:

**scanner.h**
*create new file*

```
#ifndef clox_scanner_h
#define clox_scanner_h

void initScanner(const char* source);

#endif
```

And its corresponding implementation:

**scanner.c**
*create new file*

```
#include <stdio.h>
#include <string.h>

#include "common.h"
#include "scanner.h"

typedef struct {
  const char* start;
  const char* current;
  int line;
} Scanner;

Scanner scanner;
```

As our scanner chews through the user's source code, it tracks how far it's gone. Like we did with the VM, we wrap that state in a struct and then create a single top-level module variable of that type so we don't have to pass it around all of the various functions.

There are surprisingly few fields. The `start` pointer marks the beginning of the current lexeme being scanned, and `current` points to the current character being looked at.

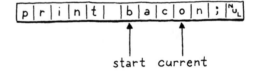

Here, we are in the middle of scanning the identifier **bacon**. The current character is o and the character we most recently consumed is c.

We have a `line` field to track what line the current lexeme is on for error reporting. That's it! We don't even keep a pointer to the beginning of the source code string. The scanner works its way through the code once and is done after that.

Since we have some state, we should initialize it.

**scanner.c**
*add after variable* scanner

```
void initScanner(const char* source) {
  scanner.start = source;
  scanner.current = source;
  scanner.line = 1;
}
```

We start at the very first character on the very first line, like a runner crouched at the starting line.

## 16.2  A Token at a Time

In jlox, when the starting gun went off, the scanner raced ahead and eagerly scanned the whole program, returning a list of tokens. This would be a challenge in clox. We'd need some sort of growable array or list to store the tokens in. We'd need to manage allocating and freeing the tokens, and the collection itself. That's a lot of code, and a lot of memory churn.

At any point in time, the compiler needs only one or two tokens—remember our grammar requires only a single token of lookahead—so we don't need to keep them *all* around at the same time. Instead, the simplest solution is to not scan a token until the compiler needs one. When the scanner provides one, it returns the token by value. It doesn't need to dynamically allocate anything—it can just pass tokens around on the C stack.

Unfortunately, we don't have a compiler yet that can ask the scanner for tokens, so the scanner will just sit there doing nothing. To kick it into action, we'll write some temporary code to drive it.

```
initScanner(source);
int line = -1;
for (;;) {
  Token token = scanToken();
  if (token.line != line) {
    printf("%4d ", token.line);
    line = token.line;
  } else {
    printf("   | ");
  }
  printf("%2d '%.*s'\n", token.type, token.length, token.start);

  if (token.type == TOKEN_EOF) break;
}
}
```

*compiler.c*
*in* compile()

That %.*s in the format string is a neat feature. Usually, you set the output precision—the number of characters to show—by placing a number inside the format string. Using * instead lets you pass the precision as an argument. So that printf() call prints the first token.length characters of the string at token.start. We need to limit the length like that because the lexeme points into the original source string and doesn't have a terminator at the end.

This loops indefinitely. Each turn through the loop, it scans one token and prints it. When it reaches a special "end of file" token or an error, it stops. For example, if we run the interpreter on this program:

```
print 1 + 2;
```

It prints out:

```
   1 31 'print'
   | 21 '1'
   |  7 '+'
   | 21 '2'
   |  8 ';'
   2 39 ''
```

The first column is the line number, the second is the numeric value of the token type, and then finally the lexeme. That last empty lexeme on line 2 is the EOF token.

The goal for the rest of the chapter is to make that blob of code work by imple-

Yeah, the raw index of the token type isn't exactly human readable, but it's all C gives us.

menting this key function:

scanner.h
*add after* initScanner()

```
void initScanner(const char* source);
Token scanToken();

#endif
```

Each call scans and returns the next token in the source code. A token looks like this:

scanner.h

```
#define clox_scanner_h

typedef struct {
  TokenType type;
  const char* start;
  int length;
  int line;
} Token;

void initScanner(const char* source);
```

It's pretty similar to jlox's Token class. We have an enum identifying what type of token it is—number, identifier, + operator, etc. The enum is virtually identical to the one in jlox, so let's just hammer out the whole thing.

scanner.h

```
#ifndef clox_scanner_h
#define clox_scanner_h

typedef enum {
  // Single-character tokens.
  TOKEN_LEFT_PAREN, TOKEN_RIGHT_PAREN,
  TOKEN_LEFT_BRACE, TOKEN_RIGHT_BRACE,
  TOKEN_COMMA, TOKEN_DOT, TOKEN_MINUS, TOKEN_PLUS,
  TOKEN_SEMICOLON, TOKEN_SLASH, TOKEN_STAR,
  // One or two character tokens.
  TOKEN_BANG, TOKEN_BANG_EQUAL,
  TOKEN_EQUAL, TOKEN_EQUAL_EQUAL,
  TOKEN_GREATER, TOKEN_GREATER_EQUAL,
  TOKEN_LESS, TOKEN_LESS_EQUAL,
  // Literals.
  TOKEN_IDENTIFIER, TOKEN_STRING, TOKEN_NUMBER,
  // Keywords.
  TOKEN_AND, TOKEN_CLASS, TOKEN_ELSE, TOKEN_FALSE,
  TOKEN_FOR, TOKEN_FUN, TOKEN_IF, TOKEN_NIL, TOKEN_OR,
  TOKEN_PRINT, TOKEN_RETURN, TOKEN_SUPER, TOKEN_THIS,
  TOKEN_TRUE, TOKEN_VAR, TOKEN_WHILE,

  TOKEN_ERROR, TOKEN_EOF
} TokenType;

typedef struct {
```

Aside from prefixing all the names with `TOKEN_` (since C tosses enum names in the top-level namespace) the only difference is that extra `TOKEN_ERROR` type. What's that about?

There are only a couple of errors that get detected during scanning: unterminated strings and unrecognized characters. In jlox, the scanner reports those itself. In clox, the scanner produces a synthetic "error" token for that error and passes it over to the compiler. This way, the compiler knows an error occurred and can kick off error recovery before reporting it.

The novel part in clox's Token type is how it represents the lexeme. In jlox, each Token stored the lexeme as its own separate little Java string. If we did that for clox, we'd have to figure out how to manage the memory for those strings. That's especially hard since we pass tokens by value—multiple tokens could point to the same lexeme string. Ownership gets weird.

Instead, we use the original source string as our character store. We represent a lexeme by a pointer to its first character and the number of characters it contains. This means we don't need to worry about managing memory for lexemes at all and we can freely copy tokens around. As long as the main source code string outlives all of the tokens, everything works fine.

> I don't mean to sound flippant. We really do need to think about and ensure that the source string, which is created far away over in the "main" module, has a long enough lifetime. That's why `runFile()` doesn't free the string until `interpret()` finishes executing the code and returns.

## 16.2.1  Scanning tokens

We're ready to scan some tokens. We'll work our way up to the complete implementation, starting with this:

```
Token scanToken() {
  scanner.start = scanner.current;

  if (isAtEnd()) return makeToken(TOKEN_EOF);

  return errorToken("Unexpected character.");
}
```

> scanner.c
> *add after* initScanner()

Since each call to this function scans a complete token, we know we are at the beginning of a new token when we enter the function. Thus, we set `scanner.start` to point to the current character so we remember where the lexeme we're about to scan starts.

Then we check to see if we've reached the end of the source code. If so, we return an EOF token and stop. This is a sentinel value that signals to the compiler to stop asking for more tokens.

If we aren't at the end, we do some…stuff…to scan the next token. But we haven't written that code yet. We'll get to that soon. If that code doesn't successfully scan and return a token, then we reach the end of the function. That must mean we're at a character that the scanner can't recognize, so we return an error token for that.

This function relies on a couple of helpers, most of which are familiar from jlox. First up:

```
static bool isAtEnd() {
  return *scanner.current == '\0';
}
```

> scanner.c
> *add after* initScanner()

We require the source string to be a good null-terminated C string. If the current character is the null byte, then we've reached the end.

To create a token, we have this constructor-like function:

scanner.c
*add after* isAtEnd()

```c
static Token makeToken(TokenType type) {
  Token token;
  token.type = type;
  token.start = scanner.start;
  token.length = (int)(scanner.current - scanner.start);
  token.line = scanner.line;
  return token;
}
```

It uses the scanner's `start` and `current` pointers to capture the token's lexeme. It sets a couple of other obvious fields then returns the token. It has a sister function for returning error tokens.

scanner.c
*add after* makeToken()

```c
static Token errorToken(const char* message) {
  Token token;
  token.type = TOKEN_ERROR;
  token.start = message;
  token.length = (int)strlen(message);
  token.line = scanner.line;
  return token;
}
```

This part of the chapter is pretty dry, so here's a picture of an axolotl.

The only difference is that the "lexeme" points to the error message string instead of pointing into the user's source code. Again, we need to ensure that the error message sticks around long enough for the compiler to read it. In practice, we only ever call this function with C string literals. Those are constant and eternal, so we're fine.

What we have now is basically a working scanner for a language with an empty lexical grammar. Since the grammar has no productions, every character is an error. That's not exactly a fun language to program in, so let's fill in the rules.

## 16.3  A Lexical Grammar for Lox

The simplest tokens are only a single character. We recognize those like so:

scanner.c
*in* scanToken()

```c
  if (isAtEnd()) return makeToken(TOKEN_EOF);

  char c = advance();

  switch (c) {
    case '(': return makeToken(TOKEN_LEFT_PAREN);
    case ')': return makeToken(TOKEN_RIGHT_PAREN);
    case '{': return makeToken(TOKEN_LEFT_BRACE);
    case '}': return makeToken(TOKEN_RIGHT_BRACE);
    case ';': return makeToken(TOKEN_SEMICOLON);
    case ',': return makeToken(TOKEN_COMMA);
```

*continued on next page...*

```
    case '.': return makeToken(TOKEN_DOT);
    case '-': return makeToken(TOKEN_MINUS);
    case '+': return makeToken(TOKEN_PLUS);
    case '/': return makeToken(TOKEN_SLASH);
    case '*': return makeToken(TOKEN_STAR);
  }

  return errorToken("Unexpected character.");
```

...from previous page

We read the next character from the source code, and then do a straightforward switch to see if it matches any of Lox's one-character lexemes. To read the next character, we use a new helper which consumes the current character and returns it.

```
static char advance() {
  scanner.current++;
  return scanner.current[-1];
}
```

scanner.c
add after isAtEnd()

Next up are the two-character punctuation tokens like != and >=. Each of these also has a corresponding single-character token. That means that when we see a character like !, we don't know if we're in a ! token or a != until we look at the next character too. We handle those like so:

```
    case '*': return makeToken(TOKEN_STAR);
    case '!':
      return makeToken(
          match('=') ? TOKEN_BANG_EQUAL : TOKEN_BANG);
    case '=':
      return makeToken(
          match('=') ? TOKEN_EQUAL_EQUAL : TOKEN_EQUAL);
    case '<':
      return makeToken(
          match('=') ? TOKEN_LESS_EQUAL : TOKEN_LESS);
    case '>':
      return makeToken(
          match('=') ? TOKEN_GREATER_EQUAL : TOKEN_GREATER);
  }
```

scanner.c
in scanToken()

After consuming the first character, we look for an =. If found, we consume it and return the corresponding two-character token. Otherwise, we leave the current character alone (so it can be part of the *next* token) and return the appropriate one-character token.

That logic for conditionally consuming the second character lives here:

```
static bool match(char expected) {
  if (isAtEnd()) return false;
  if (*scanner.current != expected) return false;
  scanner.current++;
  return true;
}
```

scanner.c
add after advance()

If the current character is the desired one, we advance and return `true`. Otherwise, we return `false` to indicate it wasn't matched.

Now our scanner supports all of the punctuation-like tokens. Before we get to the longer ones, let's take a little side trip to handle characters that aren't part of a token at all.

### 16.3.1 Whitespace

Our scanner needs to handle spaces, tabs, and newlines, but those characters don't become part of any token's lexeme. We could check for those inside the main character switch in `scanToken()` but it gets a little tricky to ensure that the function still correctly finds the next token *after* the whitespace when you call it. We'd have to wrap the whole body of the function in a loop or something.

Instead, before starting the token, we shunt off to a separate function.

scanner.c<br>in scanToken()

```
Token scanToken() {
  skipWhitespace();
  scanner.start = scanner.current;
```

This advances the scanner past any leading whitespace. After this call returns, we know the very next character is a meaningful one (or we're at the end of the source code).

scanner.c<br>add after errorToken()

```
static void skipWhitespace() {
  for (;;) {
    char c = peek();
    switch (c) {
      case ' ':
      case '\r':
      case '\t':
        advance();
        break;
      default:
        return;
    }
  }
}
```

It's sort of a separate mini-scanner. It loops, consuming every whitespace character it encounters. We need to be careful that it does *not* consume any *non-*whitespace characters. To support that, we use this:

scanner.c<br>add after advance()

```
static char peek() {
  return *scanner.current;
}
```

This simply returns the current character, but doesn't consume it. The previous code handles all the whitespace characters except for newlines.

```
      break;
  case '\n':
    scanner.line++;
    advance();
    break;
  default:
```
scanner.c
in skipWhitespace()

When we consume one of those, we also bump the current line number.

## 16.3.2 Comments

Comments aren't technically "whitespace", if you want to get all precise with your terminology, but as far as Lox is concerned, they may as well be, so we skip those too.

```
      break;
  case '/':
    if (peekNext() == '/') {
      // A comment goes until the end of the line.
      while (peek() != '\n' && !isAtEnd()) advance();
    } else {
      return;
    }
    break;
  default:
```
scanner.c
in skipWhitespace()

Comments start with // in Lox, so as with != and friends, we need a second character of lookahead. However, with !=, we still wanted to consume the ! even if the = wasn't found. Comments are different. If we don't find a second /, then skipWhitespace() needs to not consume the *first* slash either.

To handle that, we add:

```
static char peekNext() {
  if (isAtEnd()) return '\0';
  return scanner.current[1];
}
```
scanner.c
add after peek()

This is like peek() but for one character past the current one. If the current character and the next one are both /, we consume them and then any other characters until the next newline or the end of the source code.

We use peek() to check for the newline but not consume it. That way, the newline will be the current character on the next turn of the outer loop in skipWhitespace() and we'll recognize it and increment scanner.line.

## 16.3.3 Literal tokens

Number and string tokens are special because they have a runtime value associated with them. We'll start with strings because they are easy to recognize—they always begin with a double quote.

scanner.c
*in* scanToken()

```
                  match('=') ? TOKEN_GREATER_EQUAL : TOKEN_GREATER);
    case '"': return string();
  }
```

That calls a new function.

scanner.c
*add after* skipWhitespace()

```
static Token string() {
  while (peek() != '"' && !isAtEnd()) {
    if (peek() == '\n') scanner.line++;
    advance();
  }

  if (isAtEnd()) return errorToken("Unterminated string.");

  // The closing quote.
  advance();
  return makeToken(TOKEN_STRING);
}
```

Similar to jlox, we consume characters until we reach the closing quote. We also track newlines inside the string literal. (Lox supports multi-line strings.) And, as ever, we gracefully handle running out of source code before we find the end quote.

The main change here in clox is something that's *not* present. Again, it relates to memory management. In jlox, the Token class had a field of type Object to store the runtime value converted from the literal token's lexeme.

Implementing that in C would require a lot of work. We'd need some sort of union and type tag to tell whether the token contains a string or double value. If it's a string, we'd need to manage the memory for the string's character array somehow.

Doing the lexeme-to-value conversion in the compiler does introduce some redundancy. The work to scan a number literal is awfully similar to the work required to convert a sequence of digit characters to a number value. But there isn't *that* much redundancy, it isn't in anything performance critical, and it keeps our scanner simpler.

Instead of adding that complexity to the scanner, we defer converting the literal lexeme to a runtime value until later. In clox, tokens only store the lexeme—the character sequence exactly as it appears in the user's source code. Later in the compiler, we'll convert that lexeme to a runtime value right when we are ready to store it in the chunk's constant table.

Next up, numbers. Instead of adding a switch case for each of the ten digits that can start a number, we handle them here:

scanner.c
*in* scanToken()

```
  char c = advance();
  if (isDigit(c)) return number();

  switch (c) {
```

That uses this obvious utility function:

scanner.c
*add after* initScanner()

```
static bool isDigit(char c) {
  return c >= '0' && c <= '9';
}
```

We finish scanning the number using this:

```
static Token number() {
  while (isDigit(peek())) advance();

  // Look for a fractional part.
  if (peek() == '.' && isDigit(peekNext())) {
    // Consume the ".".
    advance();

    while (isDigit(peek())) advance();
  }

  return makeToken(TOKEN_NUMBER);
}
```

scanner.c
*add after* skipWhitespace()

It's virtually identical to jlox's version except, again, we don't convert the lexeme to a double yet.

## 16.4  Identifiers and Keywords

The last batch of tokens are identifiers, both user-defined and reserved. This section should be fun—the way we recognize keywords in clox is quite different from how we did it in jlox, and touches on some important data structures.

First, though, we have to scan the lexeme. Names start with a letter or underscore.

```
  char c = advance();

  if (isAlpha(c)) return identifier();
  if (isDigit(c)) return number();
```

scanner.c
*in* scanToken()

We recognize those using this:

```
static bool isAlpha(char c) {
  return (c >= 'a' && c <= 'z') ||
         (c >= 'A' && c <= 'Z') ||
          c == '_';
}
```

scanner.c
*add after* initScanner()

Once we've found an identifier, we scan the rest of it here:

```
static Token identifier() {
  while (isAlpha(peek()) || isDigit(peek())) advance();
  return makeToken(identifierType());
}
```

scanner.c
*add after* skipWhitespace()

After the first letter, we allow digits too, and we keep consuming alphanumerics until we run out of them. Then we produce a token with the proper type. Determining that "proper" type is the unique part of this chapter.

**scanner.c**
*add after* skipWhitespace()

```
static TokenType identifierType() {
  return TOKEN_IDENTIFIER;
}
```

Okay, I guess that's not very exciting yet. That's what it looks like if we have no reserved words at all. How should we go about recognizing keywords? In jlox, we stuffed them all in a Java Map and looked them up by name. We don't have any sort of hash table structure in clox, at least not yet.

Don't worry if this is unfamiliar to you. When we get to building our own hash table from scratch, we'll learn all about it in exquisite detail.

A hash table would be overkill anyway. To look up a string in a hash table, we need to walk the string to calculate its hash code, find the corresponding bucket in the hash table, and then do a character-by-character equality comparison on any string it happens to find there.

Let's say we've scanned the identifier "gorgonzola". How much work *should* we need to do to tell if that's a reserved word? Well, no Lox keyword starts with "g", so looking at the first character is enough to definitively answer no. That's a lot simpler than a hash table lookup.

What about "cardigan"? We do have a keyword in Lox that starts with "c": "class". But the second character in "cardigan", "a", rules that out. What about "forest"? Since "for" is a keyword, we have to go farther in the string before we can establish that we don't have a reserved word. But, in most cases, only a character or two is enough to tell we've got a user-defined name on our hands. We should be able to recognize that and fail fast.

Here's a visual representation of that branching character-inspection logic:

Read down each chain of nodes and you'll see Lox's keywords emerge.

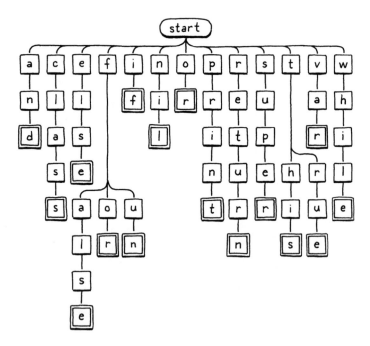

We start at the root node. If there is a child node whose letter matches the first character in the lexeme, we move to that node. Then repeat for the next letter in the lexeme and so on. If at any point the next letter in the lexeme doesn't match a child node, then the identifier must not be a keyword and we stop. If we reach a double-lined box, and we're at the last character of the lexeme, then we found a keyword.

## 16.4.1 Tries and state machines

This tree diagram is an example of a thing called a **trie**. A trie stores a set of strings. Most other data structures for storing strings contain the raw character arrays and then wrap them inside some larger construct that helps you search faster. A trie is different. Nowhere in the trie will you find a whole string.

Instead, each string the trie "contains" is represented as a *path* through the tree of character nodes, as in our traversal above. Nodes that match the last character in a string have a special marker—the double lined boxes in the illustration. That way, if your trie contains, say, "banquet" and "ban", you are able to tell that it does *not* contain "banque"—the "e" node won't have that marker, while the "n" and "t" nodes will.

Tries are a special case of an even more fundamental data structure: a **deterministic finite automaton** (**DFA**). You might also know these by other names: **finite-state machine**, or just **state machine**. State machines are rad. They end up useful in everything from game programming to implementing networking protocols.

In a DFA, you have a set of *states* with *transitions* between them, forming a graph. At any point in time, the machine is "in" exactly one state. It gets to other states by following transitions. When you use a DFA for lexical analysis, each transition is a character that gets matched from the string. Each state represents a set of allowed characters.

Our keyword tree is exactly a DFA that recognizes Lox keywords. But DFAs are more powerful than simple trees because they can be arbitrary *graphs*. Transitions can form cycles between states. That lets you recognize arbitrarily long strings. For example, here's a DFA that recognizes number literals:

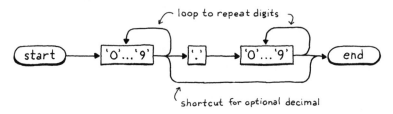

I've collapsed the nodes for the ten digits together to keep it more readable, but the basic process works the same—you work through the path, entering nodes whenever you consume a corresponding character in the lexeme. If we were so inclined, we could construct one big giant DFA that does *all* of the lexical analysis for Lox, a single state machine that recognizes and spits out all of the tokens we need.

However, crafting that mega-DFA by hand would be challenging. That's why Lex was created. You give it a simple textual description of your lexical grammar—a bunch of regular expressions—and it automatically generates a DFA for you and produces a pile of C code that implements it.

We won't go down that road. We already have a perfectly serviceable hand-rolled scanner. We just need a tiny trie for recognizing keywords. How should we map that to code?

The absolute simplest solution is to use a switch statement for each node with cases for each branch. We'll start with the root node and handle the easy keywords.

"Trie" is one of the most confusing names in CS. Edward Fredkin yanked it out of the middle of the word "retrieval", which means it should be pronounced like "tree". But, uh, there is already a pretty important data structure pronounced "tree" *which tries are a special case of*, so unless you never speak of these things out loud, no one can tell which one you're talking about. Thus, people these days often pronounce it like "try" to avoid the headache.

I wrote a chapter about state machines in my book on game programming:
→ craftinginterpreters.com/state

This style of diagram is called a **syntax diagram** or the more charming **railroad diagram**. The latter name is because it looks something like a switching yard for trains.

Back before Backus-Naur Form was a thing, this was one of the predominant ways of documenting a language's grammar. These days, we mostly use text, but there's something delightful about the official specification for a *textual language* relying on an *image*.

This is also how most regular expression engines in programming languages and text editors work under the hood. They take your regex string and convert it to a DFA, which they then use to match strings.

If you want to learn the algorithm to convert a regular expression into a DFA, the dragon book has you covered:
→ craftinginterpreters.com/dragon

Simple doesn't mean dumb. The same approach is essentially what V8 does, and that's currently one of the world's most sophisticated, fastest language implementations.

scanner.c
*in* identifierType()

```
static TokenType identifierType() {
  switch (scanner.start[0]) {
    case 'a': return checkKeyword(1, 2, "nd", TOKEN_AND);
    case 'c': return checkKeyword(1, 4, "lass", TOKEN_CLASS);
    case 'e': return checkKeyword(1, 3, "lse", TOKEN_ELSE);
    case 'i': return checkKeyword(1, 1, "f", TOKEN_IF);
    case 'n': return checkKeyword(1, 2, "il", TOKEN_NIL);
    case 'o': return checkKeyword(1, 1, "r", TOKEN_OR);
    case 'p': return checkKeyword(1, 4, "rint", TOKEN_PRINT);
    case 'r': return checkKeyword(1, 5, "eturn", TOKEN_RETURN);
    case 's': return checkKeyword(1, 4, "uper", TOKEN_SUPER);
    case 'v': return checkKeyword(1, 2, "ar", TOKEN_VAR);
    case 'w': return checkKeyword(1, 4, "hile", TOKEN_WHILE);
  }

  return TOKEN_IDENTIFIER;
```

These are the initial letters that correspond to a single keyword. If we see an "s", the only keyword the identifier could possibly be is super. It might not be, though, so we still need to check the rest of the letters too. In the tree diagram, this is basically that straight path hanging off the "s".

We won't roll a switch for each of those nodes. Instead, we have a utility function that tests the rest of a potential keyword's lexeme.

scanner.c
*add after* skipWhitespace()

```
static TokenType checkKeyword(int start, int length,
    const char* rest, TokenType type) {
  if (scanner.current - scanner.start == start + length &&
      memcmp(scanner.start + start, rest, length) == 0) {
    return type;
  }

  return TOKEN_IDENTIFIER;
}
```

We use this for all of the unbranching paths in the tree. Once we've found a prefix that could only be one possible reserved word, we need to verify two things. The lexeme must be exactly as long as the keyword. If the first letter is "s", the lexeme could still be "sup" or "superb". And the remaining characters must match exactly—"supar" isn't good enough.

If we do have the right number of characters, and they're the ones we want, then it's a keyword, and we return the associated token type. Otherwise, it must be a normal identifier.

We have a couple of keywords where the tree branches again after the first letter. If the lexeme starts with "f", it could be false, for, or fun. So we add another switch for the branches coming off the "f" node.

```
  case 'e': return checkKeyword(1, 3, "lse", TOKEN_ELSE);
  case 'f':
    if (scanner.current - scanner.start > 1) {
      switch (scanner.start[1]) {
        case 'a': return checkKeyword(2, 3, "lse", TOKEN_FALSE);
        case 'o': return checkKeyword(2, 1, "r", TOKEN_FOR);
        case 'u': return checkKeyword(2, 1, "n", TOKEN_FUN);
      }
    }
    break;
  case 'i': return checkKeyword(1, 1, "f", TOKEN_IF);
```

scanner.c
*in* identifierType()

Before we switch, we need to check that there even *is* a second letter. "f" by itself is a valid identifier too, after all. The other letter that branches is "t".

```
  case 's': return checkKeyword(1, 4, "uper", TOKEN_SUPER);
  case 't':
    if (scanner.current - scanner.start > 1) {
      switch (scanner.start[1]) {
        case 'h': return checkKeyword(2, 2, "is", TOKEN_THIS);
        case 'r': return checkKeyword(2, 2, "ue", TOKEN_TRUE);
      }
    }
    break;
  case 'v': return checkKeyword(1, 2, "ar", TOKEN_VAR);
```

scanner.c
*in* identifierType()

That's it. A couple of nested `switch` statements. Not only is this code short, but it's very, very fast. It does the minimum amount of work required to detect a keyword, and bails out as soon as it can tell the identifier will not be a reserved one.

And with that, our scanner is complete.

We sometimes fall into the trap of thinking that performance comes from complicated data structures, layers of caching, and other fancy optimizations. But, many times, all that's required is to do less work, and I often find that writing the simplest code I can is sufficient to accomplish that.

## CHALLENGES

1. Many newer languages support **string interpolation**. Inside a string literal, you have some sort of special delimiters—most commonly ${ at the beginning and } at the end. Between those delimiters, any expression can appear. When the string literal is executed, the inner expression is evaluated, converted to a string, and then merged with the surrounding string literal.

   For example, if Lox supported string interpolation, then this...

   ```
   var drink = "Tea";
   var steep = 4;
   var cool = 2;
   print "${drink} will be ready in ${steep + cool} minutes.";
   ```

   ...would print:

   ```
   Tea will be ready in 6 minutes.
   ```

   What token types would you define to implement a scanner for string interpolation? What sequence of tokens would you emit for the above string literal?
   What tokens would you emit for:

   ```
   "Nested ${"interpolation?! Are you ${"mad?!"}"}"
   ```

   Consider looking at other language implementations that support interpolation to see how they handle it.

2. Several languages use angle brackets for generics and also have a >> right shift operator. This led to a classic problem in early versions of C++:

   ```
   vector<vector<string>> nestedVectors;
   ```

   This would produce a compile error because the >> was lexed to a single right shift token, not two > tokens. Users were forced to avoid this by putting a space between the closing angle brackets.

   Later versions of C++ are smarter and can handle the above code. Java and C# never had the problem. How do those languages specify and implement this?

3. Many languages, especially later in their evolution, define "contextual keywords". These are identifiers that act like reserved words in some contexts but can be normal user-defined identifiers in others.

   For example, await is a keyword inside an async method in C#, but in other methods, you can use await as your own identifier.

   Name a few contextual keywords from other languages, and the context where they are meaningful. What are the pros and cons of having contextual keywords? How would you implement them in your language's front end if you needed to?

# Compiling Expressions

> *"In the middle of the journey of our life I found myself within a dark woods where the straight way was lost."*
>
> — Dante Alighieri, *Inferno*

This chapter is exciting for not one, not two, but *three* reasons. First, it provides the final segment of our VM's execution pipeline. Once in place, we can plumb the user's source code from scanning all the way through to executing it.

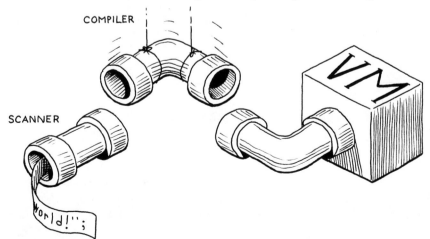

Bytecode was good enough for Niklaus Wirth, and no one questions his street cred.

Pratt parsers are a sort of oral tradition in industry. No compiler book I've read teaches them. Academia focuses on generated parsers, and Pratt's technique is for handwritten ones, so it gets overlooked.

But in production compilers, where hand-rolled parsers are common, you'd be surprised how many people know it. Ask where they learned it, and it's always, "Oh, I worked on this compiler years ago and my coworker said they took it from this old front end…"

Second, we get to write an actual, honest-to-God *compiler*. It parses source code and outputs a low-level series of binary instructions. Sure, it's bytecode and not some chip's native instruction set, but it's way closer to the metal than jlox was. We're about to be real language hackers.

Third and finally, I get to show you one of my absolute favorite algorithms: Vaughan Pratt's "top-down operator precedence parsing". It's the most elegant way I know to parse expressions. It gracefully handles prefix operators, postfix, infix, *mixfix*, any kind of *-fix* you got. It deals with precedence and associativity without breaking a sweat. I love it.

As usual, before we get to the fun stuff, we've got some preliminaries to work through. You have to eat your vegetables before you get dessert. First, let's ditch that temporary scaffolding we wrote for testing the scanner and replace it with something more useful.

vm.c
in interpret()
replace 2 lines

```
InterpretResult interpret(const char* source) {
  Chunk chunk;
  initChunk(&chunk);

  if (!compile(source, &chunk)) {
    freeChunk(&chunk);
    return INTERPRET_COMPILE_ERROR;
  }

  vm.chunk = &chunk;
  vm.ip = vm.chunk->code;

  InterpretResult result = run();

  freeChunk(&chunk);
  return result;
}
```

We create a new empty chunk and pass it over to the compiler. The compiler will take the user's program and fill up the chunk with bytecode. At least, that's what it will do if the program doesn't have any compile errors. If it does encounter an error, compile() returns false and we discard the unusable chunk.

Otherwise, we send the completed chunk over to the VM to be executed. When the VM finishes, we free the chunk and we're done. As you can see, the signature to compile() is different now.

compiler.h
replace 1 line

```
#define clox_compiler_h

#include "vm.h"

bool compile(const char* source, Chunk* chunk);

#endif
```

We pass in the chunk where the compiler will write the code, and then compile() returns whether or not compilation succeeded. We make the same change to the signature in the implementation.

```
#include "scanner.h"

bool compile(const char* source, Chunk* chunk) {
  initScanner(source);
```

compiler.c
function compile()
replace 1 line

That call to `initScanner()` is the only line that survives this chapter. Rip out the temporary code we wrote to test the scanner and replace it with these three lines:

```
  initScanner(source);
  advance();
  expression();
  consume(TOKEN_EOF, "Expect end of expression.");
}
```

compiler.c
in compile()
replace 13 lines

The call to `advance()` "primes the pump" on the scanner. We'll see what it does soon. Then we parse a single expression. We aren't going to do statements yet, so that's the only subset of the grammar we support. We'll revisit this when we add statements in a few chapters. After we compile the expression, we should be at the end of the source code, so we check for the sentinel EOF token.

We're going to spend the rest of the chapter making this function work, especially that little `expression()` call. Normally, we'd dive right into that function definition and work our way through the implementation from top to bottom.

This chapter is different. Pratt's parsing technique is remarkably simple once you have it all loaded in your head, but it's a little tricky to break into bite-sized pieces. It's recursive, of course, which is part of the problem. But it also relies on a big table of data. As we build up the algorithm, that table grows additional columns.

I don't want to revisit 40-something lines of code each time we extend the table. So we're going to work our way into the core of the parser from the outside and cover all of the surrounding bits before we get to the juicy center. This will require a little more patience and mental scratch space than most chapters, but it's the best I could do.

If this chapter isn't clicking with you and you'd like another take on the concepts, I wrote an article that teaches the same algorithm but using Java and an object-oriented style:

→ craftinginterpreters.com/pratt

## 17.1  Single-Pass Compilation

A compiler has roughly two jobs. It parses the user's source code to understand what it means. Then it takes that knowledge and outputs low-level instructions that produce the same semantics. Many languages split those two roles into two separate passes in the implementation. A parser produces an AST—just like jlox does—and then a code generator traverses the AST and outputs target code.

In clox, we're taking an old-school approach and merging these two passes into one. Back in the day, language hackers did this because computers literally didn't have enough memory to store an entire source file's AST. We're doing it because it keeps our compiler simpler, which is a real asset when programming in C.

Single-pass compilers like we're going to build don't work well for all languages. Since the compiler has only a peephole view into the user's program while generating code, the language must be designed such that you don't need much surrounding context to understand a piece of syntax. Fortunately, tiny,

In fact, most sophisticated optimizing compilers have a heck of a lot more than two passes. Determining not just *what* optimization passes to have, but how to order them to squeeze the most performance out of the compiler—since the optimizations often interact in complex ways—is somewhere between an "open area of research" and a "dark art".

Not that this should come as much of
a surprise. I did design the language
specifically for this book after all.

dynamically typed Lox is well-suited to that.

What this means in practical terms is that our "compiler" C module has functionality you'll recognize from jlox for parsing—consuming tokens, matching expected token types, etc. And it also has functions for code gen—emitting bytecode and adding constants to the destination chunk. (And it means I'll use "parsing" and "compiling" interchangeably throughout this and later chapters.)

We'll build the parsing and code generation halves first. Then we'll stitch them together with the code in the middle that uses Pratt's technique to parse Lox's particular grammar and output the right bytecode.

## 17.2  Parsing Tokens

First up, the front half of the compiler. This function's name should sound familiar.

compiler.c

```
#include "scanner.h"

static void advance() {
  parser.previous = parser.current;

  for (;;) {
    parser.current = scanToken();
    if (parser.current.type != TOKEN_ERROR) break;

    errorAtCurrent(parser.current.start);
  }
}
```

Just like in jlox, it steps forward through the token stream. It asks the scanner for the next token and stores it for later use. Before doing that, it takes the old **current** token and stashes that in a **previous** field. That will come in handy later so that we can get at the lexeme after we match a token.

The code to read the next token is wrapped in a loop. Remember, clox's scanner doesn't report lexical errors. Instead, it creates special *error tokens* and leaves it up to the parser to report them. We do that here.

We keep looping, reading tokens and reporting the errors, until we hit a non-error one or reach the end. That way, the rest of the parser sees only valid tokens. The current and previous token are stored in this struct:

compiler.c

```
#include "scanner.h"

typedef struct {
  Token current;
  Token previous;
} Parser;

Parser parser;

static void advance() {
```

Like we did in other modules, we have a single global variable of this struct type so we don't need to pass the state around from function to function in the compiler.

## 17.2.1  Handling syntax errors

If the scanner hands us an error token, we need to actually tell the user. That happens using this:

```
static void errorAtCurrent(const char* message) {
  errorAt(&parser.current, message);
}
```

*compiler.c*
*add after variable* parser

We pull the location out of the current token in order to tell the user where the error occurred and forward it to `errorAt()`. More often, we'll report an error at the location of the token we just consumed, so we give the shorter name to this other function:

```
static void error(const char* message) {
  errorAt(&parser.previous, message);
}
```

*compiler.c*
*add after variable* parser

The actual work happens here:

```
static void errorAt(Token* token, const char* message) {
  fprintf(stderr, "[line %d] Error", token->line);

  if (token->type == TOKEN_EOF) {
    fprintf(stderr, " at end");
  } else if (token->type == TOKEN_ERROR) {
    // Nothing.
  } else {
    fprintf(stderr, " at '%.*s'", token->length, token->start);
  }

  fprintf(stderr, ": %s\n", message);
  parser.hadError = true;
}
```

*compiler.c*
*add after variable* parser

First, we print where the error occurred. We try to show the lexeme if it's human-readable. Then we print the error message itself. After that, we set this `hadError` flag. That records whether any errors occurred during compilation. This field also lives in the parser struct.

```
  Token previous;
  bool hadError;
} Parser;
```

*compiler.c*
*in struct* Parser

Earlier I said that `compile()` should return `false` if an error occurred. Now we can make it do that.

CHAPTER 17: COMPILING EXPRESSIONS

*compiler.c*
*in* compile()

```
  consume(TOKEN_EOF, "Expect end of expression.");
  return !parser.hadError;
}
```

I've got another flag to introduce for error handling. We want to avoid error cascades. If the user has a mistake in their code and the parser gets confused about where it is in the grammar, we don't want it to spew out a whole pile of meaningless knock-on errors after the first one.

We fixed that in jlox using panic mode error recovery. In the Java interpreter, we threw an exception to unwind out of all of the parser code to a point where we could skip tokens and resynchronize. We don't have exceptions in C. Instead, we'll do a little smoke and mirrors. We add a flag to track whether we're currently in panic mode.

There is setjmp() and longjmp(), but I'd rather not go there. Those make it too easy to leak memory, forget to maintain invariants, or otherwise have a Very Bad Day.

*compiler.c*
*in struct* Parser

```
  bool hadError;
  bool panicMode;
} Parser;
```

When an error occurs, we set it.

*compiler.c*
*in* errorAt()

```
static void errorAt(Token* token, const char* message) {
  parser.panicMode = true;
  fprintf(stderr, "[line %d] Error", token->line);
```

After that, we go ahead and keep compiling as normal as if the error never occurred. The bytecode will never get executed, so it's harmless to keep on trucking. The trick is that while the panic mode flag is set, we simply suppress any other errors that get detected.

*compiler.c*
*in* errorAt()

```
static void errorAt(Token* token, const char* message) {
  if (parser.panicMode) return;
  parser.panicMode = true;
```

There's a good chance the parser will go off in the weeds, but the user won't know because the errors all get swallowed. Panic mode ends when the parser reaches a synchronization point. For Lox, we chose statement boundaries, so when we later add those to our compiler, we'll clear the flag there.

These new fields need to be initialized.

*compiler.c*
*in* compile()

```
  initScanner(source);

  parser.hadError = false;
  parser.panicMode = false;

  advance();
```

And to display the errors, we need a standard header.

*compiler.c*

```
#include <stdio.h>
#include <stdlib.h>

#include "common.h"
```

There's one last parsing function, another old friend from jlox.

```
static void consume(TokenType type, const char* message) {
  if (parser.current.type == type) {
    advance();
    return;
  }

  errorAtCurrent(message);
}
```

compiler.c  
*add after* advance()

It's similar to advance() in that it reads the next token. But it also validates that the token has an expected type. If not, it reports an error. This function is the foundation of most syntax errors in the compiler.

OK, that's enough on the front end for now.

## 17.3  Emitting Bytecode

After we parse and understand a piece of the user's program, the next step is to translate that to a series of bytecode instructions. It starts with the easiest possible step: appending a single byte to the chunk.

```
static void emitByte(uint8_t byte) {
  writeChunk(currentChunk(), byte, parser.previous.line);
}
```

compiler.c  
*add after* consume()

It's hard to believe great things will flow through such a simple function. It writes the given byte, which may be an opcode or an operand to an instruction. It sends in the previous token's line information so that runtime errors are associated with that line.

The chunk that we're writing gets passed into compile(), but it needs to make its way to emitByte(). To do that, we rely on this intermediary function:

```
Parser parser;
Chunk* compilingChunk;

static Chunk* currentChunk() {
  return compilingChunk;
}

static void errorAt(Token* token, const char* message) {
```

compiler.c  
*add after variable* parser

Right now, the chunk pointer is stored in a module-level variable like we store other global state. Later, when we start compiling user-defined functions, the notion of "current chunk" gets more complicated. To avoid having to go back and change a lot of code, I encapsulate that logic in the currentChunk() function.

We initialize this new module variable before we write any bytecode:

```
compiler.c      bool compile(const char* source, Chunk* chunk) {
in compile()      initScanner(source);
                  compilingChunk = chunk;

                  parser.hadError = false;
```

Then, at the very end, when we're done compiling the chunk, we wrap things up.

```
compiler.c        consume(TOKEN_EOF, "Expect end of expression.");
in compile()      endCompiler();
                  return !parser.hadError;
```

That calls this:

```
compiler.c      static void endCompiler() {
add after emitByte()    emitReturn();
                }
```

In this chapter, our VM deals only with expressions. When you run clox, it will parse, compile, and execute a single expression, then print the result. To print that value, we are temporarily using the OP_RETURN instruction. So we have the compiler add one of those to the end of the chunk.

```
compiler.c      static void emitReturn() {
add after emitByte()    emitByte(OP_RETURN);
                }
```

While we're here in the back end we may as well make our lives easier.

```
compiler.c      static void emitBytes(uint8_t byte1, uint8_t byte2) {
add after emitByte()    emitByte(byte1);
                    emitByte(byte2);
                }
```

Over time, we'll have enough cases where we need to write an opcode followed by a one-byte operand that it's worth defining this convenience function.

## 17.4 Parsing Prefix Expressions

We've assembled our parsing and code generation utility functions. The missing piece is the code in the middle that connects those together.

The only step in `compile()` that we have left to implement is this function:

```
static void expression() {
  // What goes here?
}
```

compiler.c
add after endCompiler()

We aren't ready to implement every kind of expression in Lox yet. Heck, we don't even have Booleans. For this chapter, we're only going to worry about four:

- Number literals: 123

- Parentheses for grouping: (123)

- Unary negation: -123

- The Four Horsemen of the Arithmetic: +, -, *, /

As we work through the functions to compile each of those kinds of expressions, we'll also assemble the requirements for the table-driven parser that calls them.

### 17.4.1 Parsers for tokens

For now, let's focus on the Lox expressions that are each only a single token. In this chapter, that's just number literals, but there will be more later. Here's how we can compile them:

We map each token type to a different kind of expression. We define a function for each expression that outputs the appropriate bytecode. Then we build an array of function pointers. The indexes in the array correspond to the `TokenType` enum values, and the function at each index is the code to compile an expression of that token type.

To compile number literals, we store a pointer to the following function at the `TOKEN_NUMBER` index in the array.

```
static void number() {
  double value = strtod(parser.previous.start, NULL);
  emitConstant(value);
}
```

compiler.c
add after endCompiler()

We assume the token for the number literal has already been consumed and is stored in `previous`. We take that lexeme and use the C standard library to convert it to a double value. Then we generate the code to load that value using this function:

```
static void emitConstant(Value value) {
  emitBytes(OP_CONSTANT, makeConstant(value));
}
```

compiler.c
add after emitReturn()

First, we add the value to the constant table, then we emit an `OP_CONSTANT` instruction that pushes it onto the stack at runtime. To insert an entry in the constant table, we rely on:

compiler.c
*add after* emitReturn()

```
static uint8_t makeConstant(Value value) {
  int constant = addConstant(currentChunk(), value);
  if (constant > UINT8_MAX) {
    error("Too many constants in one chunk.");
    return 0;
  }

  return (uint8_t)constant;
}
```

Most of the work happens in addConstant(), which we defined back in an earlier chapter. That adds the given value to the end of the chunk's constant table and returns its index. The new function's job is mostly to make sure we don't have too many constants. Since the OP_CONSTANT instruction uses a single byte for the index operand, we can store and load only up to 256 constants in a chunk.

That's basically all it takes. Provided there is some suitable code that consumes a TOKEN_NUMBER token, looks up number() in the function pointer array, and then calls it, we can now compile number literals to bytecode.

### 17.4.2  Parentheses for grouping

Our as-yet-imaginary array of parsing function pointers would be great if every expression was only a single token long. Alas, most are longer. However, many expressions *start* with a particular token. We call these *prefix* expressions. For example, when we're parsing an expression and the current token is (, we know we must be looking at a parenthesized grouping expression.

It turns out our function pointer array handles those too. The parsing function for an expression type can consume any additional tokens that it wants to, just like in a regular recursive descent parser. Here's how parentheses work:

compiler.c
*add after* endCompiler()

```
static void grouping() {
  expression();
  consume(TOKEN_RIGHT_PAREN, "Expect ')' after expression.");
}
```

Again, we assume the initial ( has already been consumed. We recursively call back into expression() to compile the expression between the parentheses, then parse the closing ) at the end.

As far as the back end is concerned, there's literally nothing to a grouping expression. Its sole function is syntactic—it lets you insert a lower-precedence expression where a higher precedence is expected. Thus, it has no runtime semantics on its own and therefore doesn't emit any bytecode. The inner call to expression() takes care of generating bytecode for the expression inside the parentheses.

### 17.4.3  Unary negation

Unary minus is also a prefix expression, so it works with our model too.

Yes, that limit is pretty low. If this were a full-sized language implementation, we'd want to add another instruction like OP_CONSTANT_16 that stores the index as a two-byte operand so we could handle more constants when needed.

The code to support that isn't particularly illuminating, so I omitted it from clox, but you'll want your VMs to scale to larger programs.

A Pratt parser isn't a recursive *descent* parser, but it's still recursive. That's to be expected since the grammar itself is recursive.

```
static void unary() {
  TokenType operatorType = parser.previous.type;

  // Compile the operand.
  expression();

  // Emit the operator instruction.
  switch (operatorType) {
    case TOKEN_MINUS: emitByte(OP_NEGATE); break;
    default: return; // Unreachable.
  }
}
```

compiler.c
*add after* number()

The leading – token has been consumed and is sitting in `parser.previous`. We grab the token type from that to note which unary operator we're dealing with. It's unnecessary right now, but this will make more sense when we use this same function to compile the `!` operator in the next chapter.

As in `grouping()`, we recursively call `expression()` to compile the operand. After that, we emit the bytecode to perform the negation. It might seem a little weird to write the negate instruction *after* its operand's bytecode since the – appears on the left, but think about it in terms of order of execution:

1. We evaluate the operand first which leaves its value on the stack.

2. Then we pop that value, negate it, and push the result.

So the `OP_NEGATE` instruction should be emitted last. This is part of the compiler's job—parsing the program in the order it appears in the source code and rearranging it into the order that execution happens.

There is one problem with this code, though. The `expression()` function it calls will parse any expression for the operand, regardless of precedence. Once we add binary operators and other syntax, that will do the wrong thing. Consider:

```
-a.b + c;
```

Here, the operand to – should be just the `a.b` expression, not the entire `a.b + c`. But if `unary()` calls `expression()`, the latter will happily chew through all of the remaining code including the `+`. It will erroneously treat the – as lower precedence than the `+`.

When parsing the operand to unary –, we need to compile only expressions at a certain precedence level or higher. In jlox's recursive descent parser we accomplished that by calling into the parsing method for the lowest-precedence expression we wanted to allow (in this case, `call()`). Each method for parsing a specific expression also parsed any expressions of higher precedence too, so that included the rest of the precedence table.

The parsing functions like `number()` and `unary()` here in clox are different. Each only parses exactly one type of expression. They don't cascade to include higher-precedence expression types too. We need a different solution, and it looks like this:

Emitting the `OP_NEGATE` instruction after the operands does mean that the current token when the bytecode is written is *not* the – token. That mostly doesn't matter, except that we use that token for the line number to associate with that instruction.

This means if you have a multi-line negation expression, like:

```
print -
  true;
```

Then the runtime error will be reported on the wrong line. Here, it would show the error on line 2, even though the – is on line 1. A more robust approach would be to store the token's line before compiling the operand and then pass that into `emitByte()`, but I wanted to keep things simple for the book.

compiler.c
add after unary()

```
static void parsePrecedence(Precedence precedence) {
  // What goes here?
}
```

This function—once we implement it—starts at the current token and parses any expression at the given precedence level or higher. We have some other setup to get through before we can write the body of this function, but you can probably guess that it will use that table of parsing function pointers I've been talking about. For now, don't worry too much about how it works. In order to take the "precedence" as a parameter, we define it numerically.

compiler.c
add after struct Parser

```
} Parser;

typedef enum {
  PREC_NONE,
  PREC_ASSIGNMENT,  // =
  PREC_OR,          // or
  PREC_AND,         // and
  PREC_EQUALITY,    // == !=
  PREC_COMPARISON,  // < > <= >=
  PREC_TERM,        // + -
  PREC_FACTOR,      // * /
  PREC_UNARY,       // ! -
  PREC_CALL,        // . ()
  PREC_PRIMARY
} Precedence;

Parser parser;
```

These are all of Lox's precedence levels in order from lowest to highest. Since C implicitly gives successively larger numbers for enums, this means that PREC_CALL is numerically larger than PREC_UNARY. For example, say the compiler is sitting on a chunk of code like:

```
-a.b + c
```

If we call parsePrecedence(PREC_ASSIGNMENT), then it will parse the entire expression because + has higher precedence than assignment. If instead we call parsePrecedence(PREC_UNARY), it will compile the -a.b and stop there. It doesn't keep going through the + because the addition has lower precedence than unary operators.

With this function in hand, it's a snap to fill in the missing body for expression().

compiler.c
in expression()
replace 1 line

```
static void expression() {
  parsePrecedence(PREC_ASSIGNMENT);
}
```

We simply parse the lowest precedence level, which subsumes all of the higher-precedence expressions too. Now, to compile the operand for a unary expression, we call this new function and limit it to the appropriate level:

```
  // Compile the operand.
  parsePrecedence(PREC_UNARY);

  // Emit the operator instruction.
```

compiler.c
*in* unary()
*replace 1 line*

We use the unary operator's own PREC_UNARY precedence to permit nested unary expressions like !!doubleNegative. Since unary operators have pretty high precedence, that correctly excludes things like binary operators. Speaking of which…

*Not that nesting unary expressions is particularly useful in Lox. But other languages let you do it, so we do too.*

## 17.5  Parsing Infix Expressions

Binary operators are different from the previous expressions because they are *infix*. With the other expressions, we know what we are parsing from the very first token. With infix expressions, we don't know we're in the middle of a binary operator until *after* we've parsed its left operand and then stumbled onto the operator token in the middle.

Here's an example:

```
1 + 2
```

Let's walk through trying to compile it with what we know so far:

1. We call expression(). That in turn calls parsePrecedence(PREC_ASSIGNMENT).

2. That function (once we implement it) sees the leading number token and recognizes it is parsing a number literal. It hands off control to number().

3. number() creates a constant, emits an OP_CONSTANT, and returns back to parsePrecedence().

Now what? The call to parsePrecedence() should consume the entire addition expression, so it needs to keep going somehow. Fortunately, the parser is right where we need it to be. Now that we've compiled the leading number expression, the next token is +. That's the exact token that parsePrecedence() needs to detect that we're in the middle of an infix expression and to realize that the expression we already compiled is actually an operand to that.

So this hypothetical array of function pointers doesn't just list functions to parse expressions that start with a given token. Instead, it's a *table* of function pointers. One column associates prefix parser functions with token types. The second column associates infix parser functions with token types.

The function we will use as the infix parser for TOKEN_PLUS, TOKEN_MINUS, TOKEN_STAR, and TOKEN_SLASH is this:

```
static void binary() {
  TokenType operatorType = parser.previous.type;
  ParseRule* rule = getRule(operatorType);
  parsePrecedence((Precedence)(rule->precedence + 1));
```

compiler.c
*add after* endCompiler()

*continued on next page…*

…from previous page

```
switch (operatorType) {
  case TOKEN_PLUS:          emitByte(OP_ADD); break;
  case TOKEN_MINUS:         emitByte(OP_SUBTRACT); break;
  case TOKEN_STAR:          emitByte(OP_MULTIPLY); break;
  case TOKEN_SLASH:         emitByte(OP_DIVIDE); break;
  default:
    return; // Unreachable.
  }
}
```

When a prefix parser function is called, the leading token has already been consumed. An infix parser function is even more *in medias res*—the entire left-hand operand expression has already been compiled and the subsequent infix operator consumed.

The fact that the left operand gets compiled first works out fine. It means at runtime, that code gets executed first. When it runs, the value it produces will end up on the stack. That's right where the infix operator is going to need it.

Then we come here to `binary()` to handle the rest of the arithmetic operators. This function compiles the right operand, much like how `unary()` compiles its own trailing operand. Finally, it emits the bytecode instruction that performs the binary operation.

When run, the VM will execute the left and right operand code, in that order, leaving their values on the stack. Then it executes the instruction for the operator. That pops the two values, computes the operation, and pushes the result.

The code that probably caught your eye here is that `getRule()` line. When we parse the right-hand operand, we again need to worry about precedence. Take an expression like:

```
2 * 3 + 4
```

When we parse the right operand of the * expression, we need to just capture 3, and not 3 + 4, because + is lower precedence than *. We could define a separate function for each binary operator. Each would call `parsePrecedence()` and pass in the correct precedence level for its operand.

But that's kind of tedious. Each binary operator's right-hand operand precedence is one level higher than its own. We can look that up dynamically with this `getRule()` thing we'll get to soon. Using that, we call `parsePrecedence()` with one level higher than this operator's level.

This way, we can use a single `binary()` function for all binary operators even though they have different precedences.

We use one *higher* level of precedence for the right operand because the binary operators are left-associative. Given a series of the *same* operator, like:

```
1 + 2 + 3 + 4
```

We want to parse it like:

```
((1 + 2) + 3) + 4
```

Thus, when parsing the right-hand operand to the first +, we want to consume the 2, but not the rest, so we use one level above +'s precedence. But if our operator was *right*-associative, this would be wrong. Given:

```
a = b = c = d
```

Since assignment is right-associative, we want to parse it as:

```
a = (b = (c = d))
```

To enable that, we would call `parsePrecedence()` with the *same* precedence as the current operator.

## 17.6  A Pratt Parser

We now have all of the pieces and parts of the compiler laid out. We have a function for each grammar production: `number()`, `grouping()`, `unary()`, and `binary()`. We still need to implement `parsePrecedence()`, and `getRule()`. We also know we need a table that, given a token type, lets us find

- the function to compile a prefix expression starting with a token of that type,

- the function to compile an infix expression whose left operand is followed by a token of that type, and

- the precedence of an infix expression that uses that token as an operator.

We don't need to track the precedence of the *prefix* expression starting with a given token because all prefix operators in Lox have the same precedence.

We wrap these three properties in a little struct which represents a single row in the parser table.

```
} Precedence;

typedef struct {
  ParseFn prefix;
  ParseFn infix;
  Precedence precedence;
} ParseRule;

Parser parser;
```

*compiler.c*
*add after enum* Precedence

That ParseFn type is a simple typedef for a function type that takes no arguments and returns nothing.

```
} Precedence;

typedef void (*ParseFn)();

typedef struct {
```

*compiler.c*
*add after enum* Precedence

C's syntax for function pointer types is so bad that I always hide it behind a typedef. I understand the intent behind the syntax—the whole "declaration reflects use" thing—but I think it was a failed syntactic experiment.

The table that drives our whole parser is an array of ParseRules. We've been talking about it forever, and finally you get to see it.

```
ParseRule rules[] = {
  [TOKEN_LEFT_PAREN]    = {grouping, NULL,   PREC_NONE},
  [TOKEN_RIGHT_PAREN]   = {NULL,     NULL,   PREC_NONE},
  [TOKEN_LEFT_BRACE]    = {NULL,     NULL,   PREC_NONE},
  [TOKEN_RIGHT_BRACE]   = {NULL,     NULL,   PREC_NONE},
  [TOKEN_COMMA]         = {NULL,     NULL,   PREC_NONE},
  [TOKEN_DOT]           = {NULL,     NULL,   PREC_NONE},
  [TOKEN_MINUS]         = {unary,    binary, PREC_TERM},
  [TOKEN_PLUS]          = {NULL,     binary, PREC_TERM},
  [TOKEN_SEMICOLON]     = {NULL,     NULL,   PREC_NONE},
  [TOKEN_SLASH]         = {NULL,     binary, PREC_FACTOR},
  [TOKEN_STAR]          = {NULL,     binary, PREC_FACTOR},
  [TOKEN_BANG]          = {NULL,     NULL,   PREC_NONE},
  [TOKEN_BANG_EQUAL]    = {NULL,     NULL,   PREC_NONE},
  [TOKEN_EQUAL]         = {NULL,     NULL,   PREC_NONE},
  [TOKEN_EQUAL_EQUAL]   = {NULL,     NULL,   PREC_NONE},
  [TOKEN_GREATER]       = {NULL,     NULL,   PREC_NONE},
  [TOKEN_GREATER_EQUAL] = {NULL,     NULL,   PREC_NONE},
  [TOKEN_LESS]          = {NULL,     NULL,   PREC_NONE},
  [TOKEN_LESS_EQUAL]    = {NULL,     NULL,   PREC_NONE},
  [TOKEN_IDENTIFIER]    = {NULL,     NULL,   PREC_NONE},
  [TOKEN_STRING]        = {NULL,     NULL,   PREC_NONE},
```

*compiler.c*
*add after* unary()

See what I mean about not wanting to revisit the table each time we needed a new column? It's a beast.

If you haven't seen the `[TOKEN_DOT]` = syntax in a C array literal, that is C99's designated initializer syntax. It's clearer than having to count array indexes by hand.

*continued on next page…*

*...from previous page*

```
  [TOKEN_NUMBER]        = {number,   NULL,   PREC_NONE},
  [TOKEN_AND]           = {NULL,     NULL,   PREC_NONE},
  [TOKEN_CLASS]         = {NULL,     NULL,   PREC_NONE},
  [TOKEN_ELSE]          = {NULL,     NULL,   PREC_NONE},
  [TOKEN_FALSE]         = {NULL,     NULL,   PREC_NONE},
  [TOKEN_FOR]           = {NULL,     NULL,   PREC_NONE},
  [TOKEN_FUN]           = {NULL,     NULL,   PREC_NONE},
  [TOKEN_IF]            = {NULL,     NULL,   PREC_NONE},
  [TOKEN_NIL]           = {NULL,     NULL,   PREC_NONE},
  [TOKEN_OR]            = {NULL,     NULL,   PREC_NONE},
  [TOKEN_PRINT]         = {NULL,     NULL,   PREC_NONE},
  [TOKEN_RETURN]        = {NULL,     NULL,   PREC_NONE},
  [TOKEN_SUPER]         = {NULL,     NULL,   PREC_NONE},
  [TOKEN_THIS]          = {NULL,     NULL,   PREC_NONE},
  [TOKEN_TRUE]          = {NULL,     NULL,   PREC_NONE},
  [TOKEN_VAR]           = {NULL,     NULL,   PREC_NONE},
  [TOKEN_WHILE]         = {NULL,     NULL,   PREC_NONE},
  [TOKEN_ERROR]         = {NULL,     NULL,   PREC_NONE},
  [TOKEN_EOF]           = {NULL,     NULL,   PREC_NONE},
};
```

You can see how `grouping` and `unary` are slotted into the prefix parser column for their respective token types. In the next column, `binary` is wired up to the four arithmetic infix operators. Those infix operators also have their precedences set in the last column.

Aside from those, the rest of the table is full of NULL and PREC_NONE. Most of those empty cells are because there is no expression associated with those tokens. You can't start an expression with, say, `else`, and `}` would make for a pretty confusing infix operator.

But, also, we haven't filled in the entire grammar yet. In later chapters, as we add new expression types, some of these slots will get functions in them. One of the things I like about this approach to parsing is that it makes it very easy to see which tokens are in use by the grammar and which are available.

Now that we have the table, we are finally ready to write the code that uses it. This is where our Pratt parser comes to life. The easiest function to define is `getRule()`.

*compiler.c*
*add after* `parsePrecedence()`

```
static ParseRule* getRule(TokenType type) {
  return &rules[type];
}
```

It simply returns the rule at the given index. It's called by `binary()` to look up the precedence of the current operator. This function exists solely to handle a declaration cycle in the C code. `binary()` is defined *before* the rules table so that the table can store a pointer to it. That means the body of `binary()` cannot access the table directly.

Instead, we wrap the lookup in a function. That lets us forward declare `getRule()` before the definition of `binary()`, and then *define* `getRule()` after the table. We'll need a couple of other forward declarations to handle the fact that our grammar is recursive, so let's get them all out of the way.

This is what happens when you write your VM in a language that was designed to be compiled on a PDP-11.

```
  emitReturn();
}


static void expression();
static ParseRule* getRule(TokenType type);
static void parsePrecedence(Precedence precedence);

static void binary() {
```

compiler.c
add after endCompiler()

If you're following along and implementing clox yourself, pay close attention to the little annotations that tell you where to put these code snippets. Don't worry, though, if you get it wrong, the C compiler will be happy to tell you.

## 17.6.1  Parsing with precedence

Now we're getting to the fun stuff. The maestro that orchestrates all of the parsing functions we've defined is **parsePrecedence()**. Let's start with parsing prefix expressions.

```
static void parsePrecedence(Precedence precedence) {
  advance();
  ParseFn prefixRule = getRule(parser.previous.type)->prefix;
  if (prefixRule == NULL) {
    error("Expect expression.");
    return;
  }

  prefixRule();
}
```

compiler.c
in parsePrecedence()
replace 1 line

We read the next token and look up the corresponding ParseRule. If there is no prefix parser, then the token must be a syntax error. We report that and return to the caller.

Otherwise, we call that prefix parse function and let it do its thing. That prefix parser compiles the rest of the prefix expression, consuming any other tokens it needs, and returns back here. Infix expressions are where it gets interesting since precedence comes into play. The implementation is remarkably simple.

```
  prefixRule();

  while (precedence <= getRule(parser.current.type)->precedence) {
    advance();
    ParseFn infixRule = getRule(parser.previous.type)->infix;
    infixRule();
  }
}
```

compiler.c
in parsePrecedence()

That's the whole thing. Really. Here's how the entire function works: At the beginning of **parsePrecedence()**, we look up a prefix parser for the current token. The first token is *always* going to belong to some kind of prefix expression, by definition. It may turn out to be nested as an operand inside one or more infix expressions, but as you read the code from left to right, the first token you hit always belongs to a prefix expression.

After parsing that, which may consume more tokens, the prefix expression is done. Now we look for an infix parser for the next token. If we find one, it means the prefix expression we already compiled might be an operand for it. But only if the call to `parsePrecedence()` has a `precedence` that is low enough to permit that infix operator.

If the next token is too low precedence, or isn't an infix operator at all, we're done. We've parsed as much expression as we can. Otherwise, we consume the operator and hand off control to the infix parser we found. It consumes whatever other tokens it needs (usually the right operand) and returns back to `parsePrecedence()`. Then we loop back around and see if the *next* token is also a valid infix operator that can take the entire preceding expression as its operand. We keep looping like that, crunching through infix operators and their operands until we hit a token that isn't an infix operator or is too low precedence and stop.

That's a lot of prose, but if you really want to mind meld with Vaughan Pratt and fully understand the algorithm, step through the parser in your debugger as it works through some expressions. Maybe a picture will help. There's only a handful of functions, but they are marvelously intertwined:

The ──▶ arrow connects a function to another function it directly calls. The ○─▶ arrow shows the table's pointers to the parsing functions.

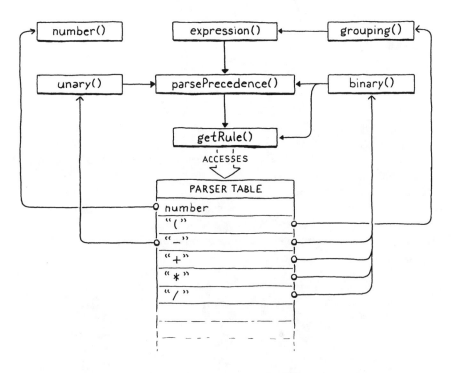

Later, we'll need to tweak the code in this chapter to handle assignment. But, otherwise, what we wrote covers all of our expression compiling needs for the rest of the book. We'll plug additional parsing functions into the table when we add new kinds of expressions, but `parsePrecedence()` is complete.

## 17.7  Dumping Chunks

While we're here in the core of our compiler, we should put in some instrumentation. To help debug the generated bytecode, we'll add support for dumping the chunk once the compiler finishes. We had some temporary logging earlier when we hand-authored the chunk. Now we'll put in some real code so that we can enable it whenever we want.

Since this isn't for end users, we hide it behind a flag.

```
#include <stdint.h>                                            common.h

#define DEBUG_PRINT_CODE
#define DEBUG_TRACE_EXECUTION
```

When that flag is defined, we use our existing "debug" module to print out the chunk's bytecode.

```
  emitReturn();                                                compiler.c
#ifdef DEBUG_PRINT_CODE                                     in endCompiler()
  if (!parser.hadError) {
    disassembleChunk(currentChunk(), "code");
  }
#endif
}
```

We do this only if the code was free of errors. After a syntax error, the compiler keeps on going but it's in kind of a weird state and might produce broken code. That's harmless because it won't get executed, but we'll just confuse ourselves if we try to read it.

Finally, to access disassembleChunk(), we need to include its header.

```
#include "scanner.h"                                          compiler.c

#ifdef DEBUG_PRINT_CODE
#include "debug.h"
#endif

typedef struct {
```

We made it! This was the last major section to install in our VM's compilation and execution pipeline. Our interpreter doesn't *look* like much, but inside it is scanning, parsing, compiling to bytecode, and executing.

Fire up the VM and type in an expression. If we did everything right, it should calculate and print the result. We now have a very over-engineered arithmetic calculator. We have a lot of language features to add in the coming chapters, but the foundation is in place.

## CHALLENGES

1. To really understand the parser, you need to see how execution threads through the interesting parsing functions—`parsePrecedence()` and the parser functions stored in the table. Take this (strange) expression:

   ```
   (-1 + 2) * 3 - -4
   ```

   Write a trace of how those functions are called. Show the order they are called, which calls which, and the arguments passed to them.

2. The ParseRule row for **TOKEN_MINUS** has both prefix and infix function pointers. That's because - is both a prefix operator (unary negation) and an infix one (subtraction).

   In the full Lox language, what other tokens can be used in both prefix and infix positions? What about in C or in another language of your choice?

3. You might be wondering about complex "mixfix" expressions that have more than two operands separated by tokens. C's conditional or "ternary" operator, ? :, is a widely known one.

   Add support for that operator to the compiler. You don't have to generate any bytecode, just show how you would hook it up to the parser and handle the operands.

## DESIGN NOTE: IT'S JUST PARSING

I'm going to make a claim here that will be unpopular with some compiler and language people. It's OK if you don't agree. Personally, I learn more from strongly stated opinions that I disagree with than I do from several pages of qualifiers and equivocation. My claim is that *parsing doesn't matter*.

Over the years, many programming language people, especially in academia, have gotten *really* into parsers and taken them very seriously. Initially, it was the compiler folks who got into compiler-compilers, LALR, and other stuff like that. The first half of the dragon book is a long love letter to the wonders of parser generators.

Later, the functional programming folks got into parser combinators, packrat parsers, and other sorts of things. Because, obviously, if you give a functional programmer a problem, the first thing they'll do is whip out a pocketful of higher-order functions.

Over in math and algorithm analysis land, there is a long legacy of research into proving time and memory usage for various parsing techniques, transforming parsing problems into other problems and back, and assigning complexity classes to different grammars.

At one level, this stuff is important. If you're implementing a language, you want some assurance that your parser won't go exponential and take 7,000 years to parse a weird edge case in the grammar. Parser theory gives you that bound. As an intellectual exercise, learning about parsing techniques is also fun and rewarding.

But if your goal is just to implement a language and get it in front of users, almost all of that stuff doesn't matter. It's really easy to get worked up by the enthusiasm of the people who *are* into it and think that your front end *needs* some whiz-bang generated combinator-parser-factory thing. I've seen people burn tons of time writing and rewriting their parser using whatever today's hot library or technique is.

That's time that doesn't add any value to your user's life. If you're just trying to get your parser done, pick one of the bog-standard techniques, use it, and move on. Recursive descent, Pratt parsing, and the popular parser generators like ANTLR or Bison are all fine.

Take the extra time you saved not rewriting your parsing code and spend it improving the compile error messages your compiler shows users. Good error handling and reporting is more valuable to users than almost anything else you can put time into in the front end.

All of us suffer from the vice of "when all you have is a hammer, everything looks like a nail", but perhaps none so visibly as compiler people. You wouldn't believe the breadth of software problems that miraculously seem to require a new little language in their solution as soon as you ask a compiler hacker for help.

Yacc and other compiler-compilers are the most delightfully recursive example. "Wow, writing compilers is a chore. I know, let's write a compiler to write our compiler for us."

For the record, I don't claim immunity to this affliction.

# Types of Values

# 18

*"When you are a Bear of Very Little Brain, and you Think of Things, you find sometimes that a Thing which seemed very Thing ish inside you is quite different when it gets out into the open and has other people looking at it."*

— A. A. Milne, *Winnie-the-Pooh*

The past few chapters were huge, packed full of complex techniques and pages of code. In this chapter, there's only one new concept to learn and a scattering of straightforward code. You've earned a respite.

Lox is dynamically typed. A single variable can hold a Boolean, number, or string at different points in time. At least, that's the idea. Right now, in clox, all values are numbers. By the end of the chapter, it will also support Booleans and nil. While those aren't super interesting, they force us to figure out how our value representation can dynamically handle different types.

> There is a third category next to statically typed and dynamically typed: **unityped**. In that paradigm, all variables have a single type, usually a machine register integer. Unityped languages aren't common today, but some Forths and BCPL, the language that inspired C, worked like this.
>
> As of this moment, clox is unityped.

## 18.1  Tagged Unions

The nice thing about working in C is that we can build our data structures from the raw bits up. The bad thing is that we *have* to do that. C doesn't give you much for free at compile time and even less at runtime. As far as C is concerned, the universe is an undifferentiated array of bytes. It's up to us to decide how many of those bytes to use and what they mean.

To choose a value representation, we need to answer two key questions:

1. **How do we represent the type of a value?** If you try to, say, multiply a number by `true`, we need to detect that error at runtime and report it. In order to do that, we need to be able to tell what a value's type is.

2. **How do we store the value itself?** We need to not only be able to tell that three is a number, but that it's different from the number four. I know, seems obvious, right? But we're operating at a level where it's good to spell these things out.

Since we're not just designing this language but building it ourselves, when answering these two questions we also have to keep in mind the implementer's eternal quest: to do it *efficiently*.

Language hackers over the years have come up with a variety of clever ways to pack the above information into as few bits as possible. For now, we'll start with the simplest, classic solution: a **tagged union**. A value contains two parts: a type "tag", and a payload for the actual value. To store the value's type, we define an enum for each kind of value the VM supports.

value.h

```
#include "common.h"

typedef enum {
  VAL_BOOL,
  VAL_NIL,
  VAL_NUMBER,
} ValueType;

typedef double Value;
```

The cases here cover each kind of value that has *built-in support in the VM*. When we get to adding classes to the language, each class the user defines doesn't need its own entry in this enum. As far as the VM is concerned, every instance of a class is the same type: "instance".

In other words, this is the VM's notion of "type", not the user's.

For now, we have only a couple of cases, but this will grow as we add strings, functions, and classes to clox. In addition to the type, we also need to store the data for the value—the `double` for a number, `true` or `false` for a Boolean. We could define a struct with fields for each possible type.

But this is a waste of memory. A value can't simultaneously be both a number and a Boolean. So at any point in time, only one of those fields will be used. C lets you optimize this by defining a union. A union looks like a struct except that all of its fields overlap in memory.

If you're familiar with a language in the ML family, structs and unions in C roughly mirror the difference between product and sum types, between tuples and algebraic data types.

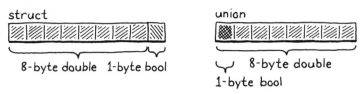

struct
8-byte double   1-byte bool

union
8-byte double
1-byte bool

Using a union to interpret bits as different types is the quintessence of C. It opens up clever optimizations and lets you slice and dice each byte of memory in ways that memory-safe languages disallow. But it is also wildly unsafe and will happily saw your fingers off if you don't watch out.

The size of a union is the size of its largest field. Since the fields all reuse the same bits, you have to be very careful when working with them. If you store data using one field and then access it using another, you will reinterpret what the underlying bits mean.

As the name "tagged union" implies, our new value representation combines these two parts into a single struct.

```
} ValueType;

typedef struct {
  ValueType type;
  union {
    bool boolean;
    double number;
  } as;
} Value;

typedef struct {
```

value.h
*add after enum ValueType*
*replace 1 line*

A smart language hacker gave me the idea to use "as" for the name of the union field because it reads nicely, almost like a cast, when you pull the various values out.

There's a field for the type tag, and then a second field containing the union of all of the underlying values. On a 64-bit machine with a typical C compiler, the layout looks like this:

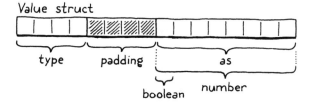

The four-byte type tag comes first, then the union. Most architectures prefer values be aligned to their size. Since the union field contains an eight-byte double, the compiler adds four bytes of padding after the type field to keep that double on the nearest eight-byte boundary. That means we're effectively spending eight bytes on the type tag, which only needs to represent a number between zero and three. We could stuff the enum in a smaller size, but all that would do is increase the padding.

So our Values are 16 bytes, which seems a little large. We'll improve it later. In the meantime, they're still small enough to store on the C stack and pass around by value. Lox's semantics allow that because the only types we support so far are **immutable**. If we pass a copy of a Value containing the number three to some function, we don't need to worry about the caller seeing modifications to the value. You can't "modify" three. It's three forever.

We could move the tag field *after* the union, but that doesn't help much either. Whenever we create an array of Values—which is where most of our memory usage for Values will be—the C compiler will insert that same padding *between* each Value to keep the doubles aligned.

## 18.2  Lox Values and C Values

That's our new value representation, but we aren't done. Right now, the rest of clox assumes Value is an alias for `double`. We have code that does a straight C cast from one to the other. That code is all broken now. So sad.

With our new representation, a Value can *contain* a double, but it's not *equivalent* to it. There is a conversion step to get from one to the other. We need to go through the code and insert those conversions to get clox working again.

We'll implement these conversions as a handful of macros, one for each type and operation. First, to promote a native C value to a clox Value:

```
} Value;

#define BOOL_VAL(value)     ((Value){VAL_BOOL, {.boolean = value}})
#define NIL_VAL             ((Value){VAL_NIL, {.number = 0}})
#define NUMBER_VAL(value)   ((Value){VAL_NUMBER, {.number = value}})

typedef struct {
```

Each one of these takes a C value of the appropriate type and produces a Value that has the correct type tag and contains the underlying value. This hoists statically typed values up into clox's dynamically typed universe. In order to *do* anything with a Value, though, we need to unpack it and get the C value back out.

```
} Value;

#define AS_BOOL(value)      ((value).as.boolean)
#define AS_NUMBER(value)    ((value).as.number)

#define BOOL_VAL(value)     ((Value){VAL_BOOL, {.boolean = value}})
```

There's no **AS_NIL** macro because there is only one **nil** value, so a Value with type **VAL_NIL** doesn't carry any extra data.

These macros go in the opposite direction. Given a Value of the right type, they unwrap it and return the corresponding raw C value. The "right type" part is important! These macros directly access the union fields. If we were to do something like:

```
Value value = BOOL_VAL(true);
double number = AS_NUMBER(value);
```

Then we may open a smoldering portal to the Shadow Realm. It's not safe to use any of the AS_ macros unless we know the Value contains the appropriate type. To that end, we define a last few macros to check a Value's type.

```
} Value;

#define IS_BOOL(value)      ((value).type == VAL_BOOL)
#define IS_NIL(value)       ((value).type == VAL_NIL)
#define IS_NUMBER(value)    ((value).type == VAL_NUMBER)

#define AS_BOOL(value)      ((value).as.boolean)
```

These macros return **true** if the Value has that type. Any time we call one of the AS_ macros, we need to guard it behind a call to one of these first. With these eight macros, we can now safely shuttle data between Lox's dynamic world and C's static one.

The _VAL macros lift a C value into the heavens. The AS_ macros bring it back down.

## 18.3 Dynamically Typed Numbers

We've got our value representation and the tools to convert to and from it. All that's left to get clox running again is to grind through the code and fix every place where data moves across that boundary. This is one of those sections of the book that isn't exactly mind-blowing, but I promised I'd show you every single line of code, so here we are.

The first values we create are the constants generated when we compile number literals. After we convert the lexeme to a C double, we simply wrap it in a Value before storing it in the constant table.

```
  double value = strtod(parser.previous.start, NULL);
  emitConstant(NUMBER_VAL(value));
}
```

compiler.c
in number()
replace 1 line

Over in the runtime, we have a function to print values.

```
void printValue(Value value) {
  printf("%g", AS_NUMBER(value));
}
```

value.c
in printValue()
replace 1 line

Right before we send the Value to `printf()`, we unwrap it and extract the double value. We'll revisit this function shortly to add the other types, but let's get our existing code working first.

## 18.3.1   Unary negation and runtime errors

The next simplest operation is unary negation. It pops a value off the stack, negates it, and pushes the result. Now that we have other types of values, we can't assume the operand is a number anymore. The user could just as well do:

```
print -false; // Uh...
```

We need to handle that gracefully, which means it's time for *runtime errors*. Before performing an operation that requires a certain type, we need to make sure the Value *is* that type.

For unary negation, the check looks like this:

```
      case OP_DIVIDE:   BINARY_OP(/); break;
      case OP_NEGATE:
        if (!IS_NUMBER(peek(0))) {
          runtimeError("Operand must be a number.");
          return INTERPRET_RUNTIME_ERROR;
        }
        push(NUMBER_VAL(-AS_NUMBER(pop())));
        break;
      case OP_RETURN: {
```

vm.c
in run()
replace 1 line

First, we check to see if the Value on top of the stack is a number. If it's not, we report the runtime error and stop the interpreter. Otherwise, we keep going. Only after this validation do we unwrap the operand, negate it, wrap the result and push it.

To access the Value, we use a new little function.

Lox's approach to error-handling is rather...*spare*. All errors are fatal and immediately halt the interpreter. There's no way for user code to recover from an error. If Lox were a real language, this is one of the first things I would remedy.

vm.c
add after pop()

```
static Value peek(int distance) {
  return vm.stackTop[-1 - distance];
}
```

It returns a Value from the stack but doesn't pop it. The distance argument is how far down from the top of the stack to look: zero is the top, one is one slot down, etc.

We report the runtime error using a new function that we'll get a lot of mileage out of over the remainder of the book.

Why not just pop the operand and then validate it? In later chapters, it will be important to leave operands on the stack to ensure the garbage collector can find them if a collection is triggered in the middle of the operation. I do the same thing here mostly out of habit.

vm.c
add after resetStack()

```
static void runtimeError(const char* format, ...) {
  va_list args;
  va_start(args, format);
  vfprintf(stderr, format, args);
  va_end(args);
  fputs("\n", stderr);

  size_t instruction = vm.ip - vm.chunk->code - 1;
  int line = vm.chunk->lines[instruction];
  fprintf(stderr, "[line %d] in script\n", line);
  resetStack();
}
```

You've certainly *called* variadic functions—ones that take a varying number of arguments—in C before: printf() is one. But you may not have *defined* your own. This book isn't a C tutorial, so I'll skim over it here, but basically the ... and va_list stuff let us pass an arbitrary number of arguments to runtimeError(). It forwards those on to vfprintf(), which is the flavor of printf() that takes an explicit va_list.

If you are looking for a C tutorial, I love *The C Programming Language*, usually called "K&R" in honor of its authors. It's not entirely up to date, but the quality of the writing more than makes up for it.

Callers can pass a format string to runtimeError() followed by a number of arguments, just like they can when calling printf() directly. runtimeError() then formats and prints those arguments. We won't take advantage of that in this chapter, but later chapters will produce formatted runtime error messages that contain other data.

After we show the hopefully helpful error message, we tell the user which line of their code was being executed when the error occurred. Since we left the tokens behind in the compiler, we look up the line in the debug information compiled into the chunk. If our compiler did its job right, that corresponds to the line of source code that the bytecode was compiled from.

Just showing the immediate line where the error occurred doesn't provide much context. Better would be a full stack trace. But we don't even have functions to call yet, so there is no call stack to trace.

We look into the chunk's debug line array using the current bytecode instruction index *minus one*. That's because the interpreter advances past each instruction before executing it. So, at the point that we call runtimeError(), the failed instruction is the previous one.

In order to use va_list and the macros for working with it, we need to bring in a standard header.

vm.c
add to top of file

```
#include <stdarg.h>
#include <stdio.h>
```

With this, our VM can not only do the right thing when we negate numbers (like it used to before we broke it), but it also gracefully handles erroneous attempts to negate other types (which we don't have yet, but still).

### 18.3.2 Binary arithmetic operators

We have our runtime error machinery in place now, so fixing the binary operators is easier even though they're more complex. We support four binary operators today: +, -, *, and /. The only difference between them is which underlying C operator they use. To minimize redundant code between the four operators, we wrapped up the commonality in a big preprocessor macro that takes the operator token as a parameter.

That macro seemed like overkill a few chapters ago, but we get the benefit from it today. It lets us add the necessary type checking and conversions in one place.

```
#define READ_CONSTANT() (vm.chunk->constants.values[READ_BYTE()])
#define BINARY_OP(valueType, op) \
    do { \
      if (!IS_NUMBER(peek(0)) || !IS_NUMBER(peek(1))) { \
        runtimeError("Operands must be numbers."); \
        return INTERPRET_RUNTIME_ERROR; \
      } \
      double b = AS_NUMBER(pop()); \
      double a = AS_NUMBER(pop()); \
      push(valueType(a op b)); \
    } while (false)

  for (;;) {
```

vm.c
in run()
replace 6 lines

Yeah, I realize that's a monster of a macro. It's not what I'd normally consider good C practice, but let's roll with it. The changes are similar to what we did for unary negate. First, we check that the two operands are both numbers. If either isn't, we report a runtime error and yank the ejection seat lever.

If the operands are fine, we pop them both and unwrap them. Then we apply the given operator, wrap the result, and push it back on the stack. Note that we don't wrap the result by directly using NUMBER_VAL(). Instead, the wrapper to use is passed in as a macro parameter. For our existing arithmetic operators, the result is a number, so we pass in the NUMBER_VAL macro.

> Did you know you can pass macros as parameters to macros? Now you do!

```
    }
    case OP_ADD:      BINARY_OP(NUMBER_VAL, +); break;
    case OP_SUBTRACT: BINARY_OP(NUMBER_VAL, -); break;
    case OP_MULTIPLY: BINARY_OP(NUMBER_VAL, *); break;
    case OP_DIVIDE:   BINARY_OP(NUMBER_VAL, /); break;
    case OP_NEGATE:
```

vm.c
in run()
replace 4 lines

Soon, I'll show you why we made the wrapping macro an argument.

## 18.4 Two New Types

All of our existing clox code is back in working order. Finally, it's time to add some new types. We've got a running numeric calculator that now does a number of pointless paranoid runtime type checks. We can represent other types

I'm not kidding about dedicated operations for certain constant values being faster. A bytecode VM spends much of its execution time reading and decoding instructions. The fewer, simpler instructions you need for a given piece of behavior, the faster it goes. Short instructions dedicated to common operations are a classic optimization.

The Java bytecode instruction set has dedicated instructions for loading 0.0, 1.0, 2.0, and the integer values from -1 through 5. (This ends up being a vestigial optimization given that most mature JVMs now JIT-compile the bytecode to machine code before execution anyway.)

internally, but there's no way for a user's program to ever create a Value of one of those types. Not until now, that is. We'll start by adding compiler support for the three new literals: `true`, `false`, and `nil`. They're all pretty simple, so we'll do all three in a single batch.

With number literals, we had to deal with the fact that there are billions of possible numeric values. We attended to that by storing the literal's value in the chunk's constant table and emitting a bytecode instruction that simply loaded that constant. We could do the same thing for the new types. We'd store, say, `true`, in the constant table, and use an `OP_CONSTANT` to read it out.

But given that there are literally (heh) only three possible values we need to worry about with these new types, it's gratuitous—and slow!—to waste a two-byte instruction and a constant table entry on them. Instead, we'll define three dedicated instructions to push each of these literals on the stack.

chunk.h<br>in enum OpCode

```
  OP_CONSTANT,
  OP_NIL,
  OP_TRUE,
  OP_FALSE,
  OP_ADD,
```

Our scanner already treats `true`, `false`, and `nil` as keywords, so we can skip right to the parser. With our table-based Pratt parser, we just need to slot parser functions into the rows associated with those keyword token types. We'll use the same function in all three slots. Here:

compiler.c<br>replace 1 line

```
  [TOKEN_ELSE]          = {NULL,     NULL,   PREC_NONE},
  [TOKEN_FALSE]         = {literal,  NULL,   PREC_NONE},
  [TOKEN_FOR]           = {NULL,     NULL,   PREC_NONE},
```

Here:

compiler.c<br>replace 1 line

```
  [TOKEN_THIS]          = {NULL,     NULL,   PREC_NONE},
  [TOKEN_TRUE]          = {literal,  NULL,   PREC_NONE},
  [TOKEN_VAR]           = {NULL,     NULL,   PREC_NONE},
```

And here:

compiler.c<br>replace 1 line

```
  [TOKEN_IF]            = {NULL,     NULL,   PREC_NONE},
  [TOKEN_NIL]           = {literal,  NULL,   PREC_NONE},
  [TOKEN_OR]            = {NULL,     NULL,   PREC_NONE},
```

When the parser encounters `false`, `nil`, or `true`, in prefix position, it calls this new parser function:

compiler.c<br>add after binary()

```
static void literal() {
  switch (parser.previous.type) {
    case TOKEN_FALSE: emitByte(OP_FALSE); break;
    case TOKEN_NIL: emitByte(OP_NIL); break;
    case TOKEN_TRUE: emitByte(OP_TRUE); break;
    default: return; // Unreachable.
  }
}
```

We could have used separate parser functions for each literal and saved ourselves a switch but that felt needlessly verbose to me. I think it's mostly a matter of taste.

Since `parsePrecedence()` has already consumed the keyword token, all we need to do is output the proper instruction. We figure that out based on the type of token we parsed. Our front end can now compile Boolean and nil literals to bytecode. Moving down the execution pipeline, we reach the interpreter.

```
case OP_CONSTANT: {
  Value constant = READ_CONSTANT();
  push(constant);
  break;
}
case OP_NIL: push(NIL_VAL); break;
case OP_TRUE: push(BOOL_VAL(true)); break;
case OP_FALSE: push(BOOL_VAL(false)); break;
case OP_ADD:      BINARY_OP(NUMBER_VAL, +); break;
```

vm.c
in run()

This is pretty self-explanatory. Each instruction summons the appropriate value and pushes it onto the stack. We shouldn't forget our disassembler either.

```
case OP_CONSTANT:
  return constantInstruction("OP_CONSTANT", chunk, offset);
case OP_NIL:
  return simpleInstruction("OP_NIL", offset);
case OP_TRUE:
  return simpleInstruction("OP_TRUE", offset);
case OP_FALSE:
  return simpleInstruction("OP_FALSE", offset);
case OP_ADD:
```

debug.c
in disassembleInstruction()

With this in place, we can run this Earth-shattering program:

```
true
```

Except that when the interpreter tries to print the result, it blows up. We need to extend `printValue()` to handle the new types too:

```
void printValue(Value value) {
  switch (value.type) {
    case VAL_BOOL:
      printf(AS_BOOL(value) ? "true" : "false");
      break;
    case VAL_NIL: printf("nil"); break;
    case VAL_NUMBER: printf("%g", AS_NUMBER(value)); break;
  }
}
```

value.c
in printValue()
replace 1 line

There we go! Now we have some new types. They just aren't very useful yet. Aside from the literals, you can't really *do* anything with them. It will be a while before `nil` comes into play, but we can start putting Booleans to work in the logical operators.

### 18.4.1 Logical not and falsiness

The simplest logical operator is our old exclamatory friend unary not.

```
print !true; // "false"
```

This new operation gets a new instruction.

chunk.h
*in enum* OpCode

```
  OP_DIVIDE,
  OP_NOT,
  OP_NEGATE,
```

We can reuse the unary() parser function we wrote for unary negation to compile a not expression. We just need to slot it into the parsing table.

compiler.c
*replace 1 line*

```
  [TOKEN_STAR]          = {NULL,     binary, PREC_FACTOR},
  [TOKEN_BANG]          = {unary,    NULL,   PREC_NONE},
  [TOKEN_BANG_EQUAL]    = {NULL,     NULL,   PREC_NONE},
```

Because I knew we were going to do this, the unary() function already has a switch on the token type to figure out which bytecode instruction to output. We merely add another case.

compiler.c
*in* unary()

```
  switch (operatorType) {
    case TOKEN_BANG: emitByte(OP_NOT); break;
    case TOKEN_MINUS: emitByte(OP_NEGATE); break;
    default: return; // Unreachable.
  }
```

That's it for the front end. Let's head over to the VM and conjure this instruction into life.

vm.c
*in* run()

```
    case OP_DIVIDE:   BINARY_OP(NUMBER_VAL, /); break;
    case OP_NOT:
      push(BOOL_VAL(isFalsey(pop())));
      break;
    case OP_NEGATE:
```

Like our previous unary operator, it pops the one operand, performs the operation, and pushes the result. And, as we did there, we have to worry about dynamic typing. Taking the logical not of true is easy, but there's nothing preventing an unruly programmer from writing something like this:

```
print !nil;
```

Now I can't help but try to figure out what it would mean to negate other types of values. nil is probably its own negation, sort of like a weird pseudo-zero. Negating a string could, uh, reverse it?

For unary minus, we made it an error to negate anything that isn't a number. But Lox, like most scripting languages, is more permissive when it comes to ! and other contexts where a Boolean is expected. The rule for how other types are handled is called "falsiness", and we implement it here:

```
static bool isFalsey(Value value) {
  return IS_NIL(value) || (IS_BOOL(value) && !AS_BOOL(value));
}
```

vm.c
add after peek()

Lox follows Ruby in that `nil` and `false` are falsey and every other value behaves like `true`. We've got a new instruction we can generate, so we also need to be able to *ungenerate* it in the disassembler.

```
    case OP_DIVIDE:
      return simpleInstruction("OP_DIVIDE", offset);
    case OP_NOT:
      return simpleInstruction("OP_NOT", offset);
    case OP_NEGATE:
```

debug.c
in disassembleInstruction()

## 18.4.2   Equality and comparison operators

That wasn't too bad. Let's keep the momentum going and knock out the equality and comparison operators too: ==, !=, <, >, <=, and >=. That covers all of the operators that return Boolean results except the logical operators and and or. Since those need to short-circuit (basically do a little control flow) we aren't ready for them yet.

Here are the new instructions for those operators:

```
  OP_FALSE,
  OP_EQUAL,
  OP_GREATER,
  OP_LESS,
  OP_ADD,
```

chunk.h
in enum OpCode

Wait, only three? What about !=, <=, and >=? We could create instructions for those too. Honestly, the VM would execute faster if we did, so we *should* do that if the goal is performance.

But my main goal is to teach you about bytecode compilers. I want you to start internalizing the idea that the bytecode instructions don't need to closely follow the user's source code. The VM has total freedom to use whatever instruction set and code sequences it wants as long as they have the right user-visible behavior.

The expression a != b has the same semantics as !(a == b), so the compiler is free to compile the former as if it were the latter. Instead of a dedicated OP_NOT_EQUAL instruction, it can output an OP_EQUAL followed by an OP_NOT. Likewise, a <= b is the same as !(a > b) and a >= b is !(a < b). Thus, we only need three new instructions.

Over in the parser, though, we do have six new operators to slot into the parse table. We use the same `binary()` parser function from before. Here's the row for !=:

*Is a <= b always the same as !(a > b)? According to IEEE 754, all comparison operators return false when an operand is NaN. That means NaN <= 1 is false and NaN > 1 is also false. But our desugaring assumes the latter is always the negation of the former.*

*For the book, we won't get hung up on this, but these kinds of details will matter in your real language implementations.*

compiler.c
replace 1 line

```
  [TOKEN_BANG]          = {unary,    NULL,   PREC_NONE},
  [TOKEN_BANG_EQUAL]    = {NULL,     binary, PREC_EQUALITY},
  [TOKEN_EQUAL]         = {NULL,     NULL,   PREC_NONE},
```

The remaining five operators are a little farther down in the table.

compiler.c
*replace 5 lines*

```
[TOKEN_EQUAL]         = {NULL,    NULL,   PREC_NONE},
[TOKEN_EQUAL_EQUAL]   = {NULL,    binary, PREC_EQUALITY},
[TOKEN_GREATER]       = {NULL,    binary, PREC_COMPARISON},
[TOKEN_GREATER_EQUAL] = {NULL,    binary, PREC_COMPARISON},
[TOKEN_LESS]          = {NULL,    binary, PREC_COMPARISON},
[TOKEN_LESS_EQUAL]    = {NULL,    binary, PREC_COMPARISON},
[TOKEN_IDENTIFIER]    = {NULL,    NULL,   PREC_NONE},
```

Inside `binary()` we already have a switch to generate the right bytecode for each token type. We add cases for the six new operators.

compiler.c
*in* binary()

```
switch (operatorType) {
  case TOKEN_BANG_EQUAL:    emitBytes(OP_EQUAL, OP_NOT); break;
  case TOKEN_EQUAL_EQUAL:   emitByte(OP_EQUAL); break;
  case TOKEN_GREATER:       emitByte(OP_GREATER); break;
  case TOKEN_GREATER_EQUAL: emitBytes(OP_LESS, OP_NOT); break;
  case TOKEN_LESS:          emitByte(OP_LESS); break;
  case TOKEN_LESS_EQUAL:    emitBytes(OP_GREATER, OP_NOT); break;
  case TOKEN_PLUS:          emitByte(OP_ADD); break;
```

The ==, <, and > operators output a single instruction. The others output a pair of instructions, one to evaluate the inverse operation, and then an OP_NOT to flip the result. Six operators for the price of three instructions!

That means over in the VM, our job is simpler. Equality is the most general operation.

vm.c
*in* run()

```
    case OP_FALSE: push(BOOL_VAL(false)); break;
    case OP_EQUAL: {
      Value b = pop();
      Value a = pop();
      push(BOOL_VAL(valuesEqual(a, b)));
      break;
    }
    case OP_ADD:      BINARY_OP(NUMBER_VAL, +); break;
```

You can evaluate == on any pair of objects, even objects of different types. There's enough complexity that it makes sense to shunt that logic over to a separate function. That function always returns a C bool, so we can safely wrap the result in a BOOL_VAL. The function relates to Values, so it lives over in the "value" module.

value.h
*add after struct* ValueArray

```
} ValueArray;

bool valuesEqual(Value a, Value b);
void initValueArray(ValueArray* array);
```

And here's the implementation:

```c
bool valuesEqual(Value a, Value b) {
  if (a.type != b.type) return false;
  switch (a.type) {
    case VAL_BOOL:   return AS_BOOL(a) == AS_BOOL(b);
    case VAL_NIL:    return true;
    case VAL_NUMBER: return AS_NUMBER(a) == AS_NUMBER(b);
    default:         return false; // Unreachable.
  }
}
```

value.c<br>add after printValue()

First, we check the types. If the Values have different types, they are definitely not equal. Otherwise, we unwrap the two Values and compare them directly.

For each value type, we have a separate case that handles comparing the value itself. Given how similar the cases are, you might wonder why we can't simply memcmp() the two Value structs and be done with it. The problem is that because of padding and different-sized union fields, a Value contains unused bits. C gives no guarantee about what is in those, so it's possible that two equal Values actually differ in memory that isn't used.

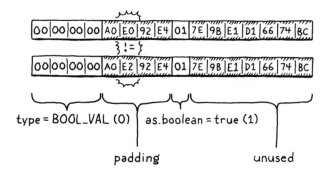

(You wouldn't believe how much pain I went through before learning this fact.)

Anyway, as we add more types to clox, this function will grow new cases. For now, these three are sufficient. The other comparison operators are easier since they work only on numbers.

```c
        push(BOOL_VAL(valuesEqual(a, b)));
        break;
      }
    case OP_GREATER:  BINARY_OP(BOOL_VAL, >); break;
    case OP_LESS:     BINARY_OP(BOOL_VAL, <); break;
    case OP_ADD:      BINARY_OP(NUMBER_VAL, +); break;
```

vm.c<br>in run()

We already extended the BINARY_OP macro to handle operators that return non-numeric types. Now we get to use that. We pass in BOOL_VAL since the result value type is Boolean. Otherwise, it's no different from plus or minus.

As always, the coda to today's aria is disassembling the new instructions.

```c
    case OP_FALSE:
      return simpleInstruction("OP_FALSE", offset);
    case OP_EQUAL:
      return simpleInstruction("OP_EQUAL", offset);
```

debug.c<br>in disassembleInstruction()

continued on next page…

Some languages have "implicit conversions" where values of different types may be considered equal if one can be converted to the other's type. For example, the number 0 is equivalent to the string "0" in JavaScript. This looseness was a large enough source of pain that JS added a separate "strict equality" operator, ===.

PHP considers the strings "1" and "01" to be equivalent because both can be converted to equivalent numbers, though the ultimate reason is because PHP was designed by a Lovecraftian eldritch god to destroy the mind.

Most dynamically typed languages that have separate integer and floating-point number types consider values of different number types equal if the numeric values are the same (so, say, 1.0 is equal to 1), though even that seemingly innocuous convenience can bite the unwary.

*…from previous page*

```
case OP_GREATER:
  return simpleInstruction("OP_GREATER", offset);
case OP_LESS:
  return simpleInstruction("OP_LESS", offset);
case OP_ADD:
```

With that, our numeric calculator has become something closer to a general expression evaluator. Fire up clox and type in:

```
!(5 - 4 > 3 * 2 == !nil)
```

OK, I'll admit that's maybe not the most *useful* expression, but we're making progress. We have one missing built-in type with its own literal form: strings. Those are much more complex because strings can vary in size. That tiny difference turns out to have implications so large that we give strings their very own chapter.

## CHALLENGES

1. We could reduce our binary operators even further than we did here. Which other instructions can you eliminate, and how would the compiler cope with their absence?

2. Conversely, we can improve the speed of our bytecode VM by adding more specific instructions that correspond to higher-level operations. What instructions would you define to speed up the kind of user code we added support for in this chapter?

# Strings

*"'Ah? A small aversion to menial labor?' The doctor cocked an eyebrow.
'Understandable, but misplaced. One should treasure those hum-
drum tasks that keep the body occupied but leave the mind and heart
unfettered.'"*

— Tad Williams, *The Dragonbone Chair*

Our little VM can represent three types of values right now: numbers, Booleans, and nil. Those types have two important things in common: they're immutable and they're small. Numbers are the largest, and they still fit into two 64-bit words. That's a small enough price that we can afford to pay it for all values, even Booleans and nils which don't need that much space.

Strings, unfortunately, are not so petite. There's no maximum length for a string. Even if we were to artificially cap it at some contrived limit like 255 characters, that's still too much memory to spend on every single value.

We need a way to support values whose sizes vary, sometimes greatly. This is exactly what dynamic allocation on the heap is designed for. We can allocate as many bytes as we need. We get back a pointer that we'll use to keep track of the value as it flows through the VM.

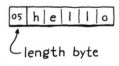

UCSD Pascal, one of the first implemen-tations of Pascal, had this exact limit. Instead of using a terminating null byte to indicate the end of the string like C, Pascal strings started with a length value. Since UCSD used only a single byte to store the length, strings couldn't be any longer than 255 characters.

## 19.1 Values and Objects

Using the heap for larger, variable-sized values and the stack for smaller, atomic ones leads to a two-level representation. Every Lox value that you can store in a variable or return from an expression will be a Value. For small, fixed-size types like numbers, the payload is stored directly inside the Value struct itself.

If the object is larger, its data lives on the heap. Then the Value's payload is a *pointer* to that blob of memory. We'll eventually have a handful of heap-allocated types in clox: strings, instances, functions, you get the idea. Each type has its own unique data, but there is also state they all share that our future garbage collector will use to manage their memory.

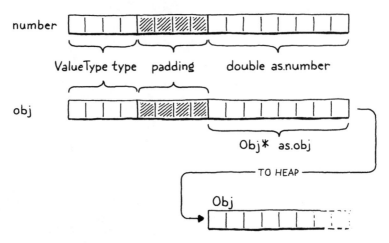

"Obj" is short for "object", natch.

We'll call this common representation "Obj". Each Lox value whose state lives on the heap is an Obj. We can thus use a single new ValueType case to refer to all heap-allocated types.

**value.h**
*in enum ValueType*

```
  VAL_NUMBER,
  VAL_OBJ
} ValueType;
```

When a Value's type is VAL_OBJ, the payload is a pointer to the heap memory, so we add another case to the union for that.

**value.h**
*in struct Value*

```
    double number;
  Obj* obj;
} as;
```

As we did with the other value types, we crank out a couple of helpful macros for working with Obj values.

**value.h**
*add after struct Value*

```
#define IS_NUMBER(value)   ((value).type == VAL_NUMBER)
#define IS_OBJ(value)      ((value).type == VAL_OBJ)

#define AS_BOOL(value)     ((value).as.boolean)
```

This evaluates to true if the given Value is an Obj. If so, we can use this:

```
#define IS_OBJ(value)        ((value).type == VAL_OBJ)
```
value.h

```
#define AS_OBJ(value)        ((value).as.obj)
#define AS_BOOL(value)       ((value).as.boolean)
```

It extracts the Obj pointer from the value. We can also go the other way.

```
#define NUMBER_VAL(value) ((Value){VAL_NUMBER, {.number = value}})
#define OBJ_VAL(object)   ((Value){VAL_OBJ, {.obj = (Obj*)object}})

typedef struct {
```
value.h

This takes a bare Obj pointer and wraps it in a full Value.

## 19.2  Struct Inheritance

Every heap-allocated value is an Obj, but Objs are not all the same. For strings, we need the array of characters. When we get to instances, they will need their data fields. A function object will need its chunk of bytecode. How do we handle different payloads and sizes? We can't use another union like we did for Value since the sizes are all over the place.

No, I don't know how to pronounce "objs" either. Feels like there should be a vowel in there somewhere.

Instead, we'll use another technique. It's been around for ages, to the point that the C specification carves out specific support for it, but I don't know that it has a canonical name. It's an example of *type punning*, but that term is too broad. In the absence of any better ideas, I'll call it **struct inheritance**, because it relies on structs and roughly follows how single-inheritance of state works in object-oriented languages.

Like a tagged union, each Obj starts with a tag field that identifies what kind of object it is—string, instance, etc. Following that are the payload fields. Instead of a union with cases for each type, each type is its own separate struct. The tricky part is how to treat these structs uniformly since C has no concept of inheritance or polymorphism. I'll explain that soon, but first lets get the preliminary stuff out of the way.

The name "Obj" itself refers to a struct that contains the state shared across all object types. It's sort of the "base class" for objects. Because of cyclic dependencies between values and objects, we forward-declare it in the "value" module.

```
#include "common.h"

typedef struct Obj Obj;

typedef enum {
```
value.h

And the actual definition is in a new module.

```
#ifndef clox_object_h
#define clox_object_h

#include "common.h"
#include "value.h"
```
object.h<br>create new file

continued on next page…

...from previous page

```
struct Obj {
  ObjType type;
};

#endif
```

Right now, it contains only the type tag. Shortly, we'll add some other bookkeeping information for memory management. The type enum is this:

object.h

```
#include "value.h"

typedef enum {
  OBJ_STRING,
} ObjType;

struct Obj {
```

Obviously, that will be more useful in later chapters after we add more heap-allocated types. Since we'll be accessing these tag types frequently, it's worth making a little macro that extracts the object type tag from a given Value.

object.h

```
#include "value.h"

#define OBJ_TYPE(value)        (AS_OBJ(value)->type)

typedef enum {
```

That's our foundation.

Now, let's build strings on top of it. The payload for strings is defined in a separate struct. Again, we need to forward-declare it.

value.h

```
typedef struct Obj Obj;
typedef struct ObjString ObjString;

typedef enum {
```

The definition lives alongside Obj.

object.h
add after struct Obj

```
};

struct ObjString {
  Obj obj;
  int length;
  char* chars;
};

#endif
```

A string object contains an array of characters. Those are stored in a separate, heap-allocated array so that we set aside only as much room as needed for each string. We also store the number of bytes in the array. This isn't strictly necessary but lets us tell how much memory is allocated for the string without walking the character array to find the null terminator.

Because ObjString is an Obj, it also needs the state all Objs share. It accomplishes that by having its first field be an Obj. C specifies that struct fields are arranged in memory in the order that they are declared. Also, when you nest structs, the inner struct's fields are expanded right in place. So the memory for Obj and for ObjString looks like this:

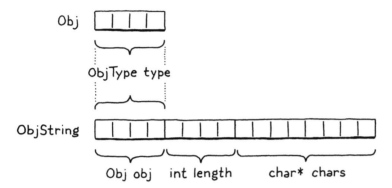

Note how the first bytes of ObjString exactly line up with Obj. This is not a coincidence—C mandates it. This is designed to enable a clever pattern: You can take a pointer to a struct and safely convert it to a pointer to its first field and back.

Given an `ObjString*`, you can safely cast it to `Obj*` and then access the `type` field from it. Every ObjString "is" an Obj in the OOP sense of "is". When we later add other object types, each struct will have an Obj as its first field. Any code that wants to work with all objects can treat them as base `Obj*` and ignore any other fields that may happen to follow.

You can go in the other direction too. Given an `Obj*`, you can "downcast" it to an `ObjString*`. Of course, you need to ensure that the `Obj*` pointer you have does point to the `obj` field of an actual ObjString. Otherwise, you are unsafely reinterpreting random bits of memory. To detect that such a cast is safe, we add another macro.

> The key part of the spec is:
>
> *§ 6.7.2.1 13 – Within a structure object, the non-bit-field members and the units in which bit-fields reside have addresses that increase in the order in which they are declared. A pointer to a structure object, suitably converted, points to its initial member (or if that member is a bit-field, then to the unit in which it resides), and vice versa. There may be unnamed padding within a structure object, but not at its beginning.*

```
#define OBJ_TYPE(value)        (AS_OBJ(value)->type)

#define IS_STRING(value)       isObjType(value, OBJ_STRING)

typedef enum {
```
**object.h**

It takes a Value, not a raw `Obj*` because most code in the VM works with Values. It relies on this inline function:

```
};

static inline bool isObjType(Value value, ObjType type) {
  return IS_OBJ(value) && AS_OBJ(value)->type == type;
}

#endif
```
**object.h**
*add after struct ObjString*

Pop quiz: Why not just put the body of this function right in the macro? What's different about this one compared to the others? Right, it's because the body uses `value` twice. A macro is expanded by inserting the argument *expression* every place the parameter name appears in the body. If a macro uses a parameter more than once, that expression gets evaluated multiple times.

That's bad if the expression has side effects. If we put the body of `isObjType()` into the macro definition and then you did, say,

```
IS_STRING(POP())
```

then it would pop two values off the stack! Using a function fixes that.

As long as we ensure that we set the type tag correctly whenever we create an Obj of some type, this macro will tell us when it's safe to cast a value to a specific object type. We can do that using these:

object.h

```
#define IS_STRING(value)        isObjType(value, OBJ_STRING)

#define AS_STRING(value)        ((ObjString*)AS_OBJ(value))
#define AS_CSTRING(value)       (((ObjString*)AS_OBJ(value))->chars)

typedef enum {
```

These two macros take a Value that is expected to contain a pointer to a valid ObjString on the heap. The first one returns the `ObjString*` pointer. The second one steps through that to return the character array itself, since that's often what we'll end up needing.

## 19.3  Strings

OK, our VM can now represent string values. It's time to add strings to the language itself. As usual, we begin in the front end. The lexer already tokenizes string literals, so it's the parser's turn.

compiler.c<br>*replace 1 line*

```
    [TOKEN_IDENTIFIER]    = {NULL,     NULL,   PREC_NONE},
    [TOKEN_STRING]        = {string,   NULL,   PREC_NONE},
    [TOKEN_NUMBER]        = {number,   NULL,   PREC_NONE},
```

When the parser hits a string token, it calls this parse function:

compiler.c<br>*add after* number()

```
static void string() {
  emitConstant(OBJ_VAL(copyString(parser.previous.start + 1,
                                  parser.previous.length - 2)));
}
```

If Lox supported string escape sequences like \n, we'd translate those here. Since it doesn't, we can take the characters as they are.

This takes the string's characters directly from the lexeme. The + 1 and − 2 parts trim the leading and trailing quotation marks. It then creates a string object, wraps it in a Value, and stuffs it into the constant table.

To create the string, we use `copyString()`, which is declared in `object.h`.

```
};

ObjString* copyString(const char* chars, int length);

static inline bool isObjType(Value value, ObjType type) {
```

object.h
*add after struct ObjString*

The compiler module needs to include that.

```
#define clox_compiler_h

#include "object.h"
#include "vm.h"
```

compiler.h

Our "object" module gets an implementation file where we define the new function.

```
#include <stdio.h>
#include <string.h>

#include "memory.h"
#include "object.h"
#include "value.h"
#include "vm.h"

ObjString* copyString(const char* chars, int length) {
  char* heapChars = ALLOCATE(char, length + 1);
  memcpy(heapChars, chars, length);
  heapChars[length] = '\0';
  return allocateString(heapChars, length);
}
```

object.c
*create new file*

We need to terminate the string ourselves because the lexeme points at a range of characters inside the monolithic source string and isn't terminated.

Since ObjString stores the length explicitly, we *could* leave the character array unterminated, but slapping a terminator on the end costs us only a byte and lets us pass the character array to C standard library functions that expect a terminated string.

First, we allocate a new array on the heap, just big enough for the string's characters and the trailing terminator, using this low-level macro that allocates an array with a given element type and count:

```
#include "common.h"

#define ALLOCATE(type, count) \
    (type*)reallocate(NULL, 0, sizeof(type) * (count))

#define GROW_CAPACITY(capacity) \
```

memory.h

Once we have the array, we copy over the characters from the lexeme and terminate it.

You might wonder why the ObjString can't just point back to the original characters in the source string. Some ObjStrings will be created dynamically at runtime as a result of string operations like concatenation. Those strings obviously need to dynamically allocate memory for the characters, which means the string needs to *free* that memory when it's no longer needed.

If we had an ObjString for a string literal, and tried to free its character array that pointed into the original source code string, bad things would happen. So, for literals, we preemptively copy the characters over to the heap. This way, every ObjString reliably owns its character array and can free it.

The real work of creating a string object happens in this function:

object.c

```
#include "vm.h"

static ObjString* allocateString(char* chars, int length) {
  ObjString* string = ALLOCATE_OBJ(ObjString, OBJ_STRING);
  string->length = length;
  string->chars = chars;
  return string;
}
```

It creates a new ObjString on the heap and then initializes its fields. It's sort of like a constructor in an OOP language. As such, it first calls the "base class" constructor to initialize the Obj state, using a new macro.

object.c

```
#include "vm.h"

#define ALLOCATE_OBJ(type, objectType) \
    (type*)allocateObject(sizeof(type), objectType)

static ObjString* allocateString(char* chars, int length) {
```

I admit this chapter has a sea of helper functions and macros to wade through. I try to keep the code nicely factored, but that leads to a scattering of tiny functions. They will pay off when we reuse them later.

Like the previous macro, this exists mainly to avoid the need to redundantly cast a void* back to the desired type. The actual functionality is here:

object.c

```
#define ALLOCATE_OBJ(type, objectType) \
    (type*)allocateObject(sizeof(type), objectType)

static Obj* allocateObject(size_t size, ObjType type) {
  Obj* object = (Obj*)reallocate(NULL, 0, size);
  object->type = type;
  return object;
}

static ObjString* allocateString(char* chars, int length) {
```

It allocates an object of the given size on the heap. Note that the size is *not* just the size of Obj itself. The caller passes in the number of bytes so that there is room for the extra payload fields needed by the specific object type being created.

Then it initializes the Obj state—right now, that's just the type tag. This function returns to allocateString(), which finishes initializing the ObjString fields. *Voilà*, we can compile and execute string literals.

Don't get "voilà" confused with "viola". One means "there it is" and the other is a string instrument, the middle child between a violin and a cello. Yes, I did spend two hours drawing a viola just to mention that.

## 19.4  Operations on Strings

Our fancy strings are there, but they don't do much of anything yet. A good first step is to make the existing print code not barf on the new value type.

```
    case VAL_NUMBER: printf("%g", AS_NUMBER(value)); break;
    case VAL_OBJ: printObject(value); break;
  }
```

value.c
in printValue()

If the value is a heap-allocated object, it defers to a helper function over in the "object" module.

```
ObjString* copyString(const char* chars, int length);
void printObject(Value value);

static inline bool isObjType(Value value, ObjType type) {
```

object.h
add after copyString()

The implementation looks like this:

```
void printObject(Value value) {
  switch (OBJ_TYPE(value)) {
    case OBJ_STRING:
      printf("%s", AS_CSTRING(value));
      break;
  }
}
```

object.c
add after copyString()

We have only a single object type now, but this function will sprout additional switch cases in later chapters. For string objects, it simply prints the character array as a C string.

I told you terminating the string would come in handy.

The equality operators also need to gracefully handle strings. Consider:

```
"string" == "string"
```

These are two separate string literals. The compiler will make two separate calls to copyString(), create two distinct ObjString objects and store them as two constants in the chunk. They are different objects in the heap. But our users (and thus we) expect strings to have value equality. The above expression should evaluate to true. That requires a little special support.

```
    case VAL_NUMBER: return AS_NUMBER(a) == AS_NUMBER(b);
    case VAL_OBJ: {
      ObjString* aString = AS_STRING(a);
      ObjString* bString = AS_STRING(b);
      return aString->length == bString->length &&
          memcmp(aString->chars, bString->chars,
              aString->length) == 0;
    }
    default:         return false; // Unreachable.
```

value.c
in valuesEqual()

If the two values are both strings, then they are equal if their character arrays contain the same characters, regardless of whether they are two separate objects or the exact same one. This does mean that string equality is slower than equality on other types since it has to walk the whole string. We'll revise that later, but this gives us the right semantics for now.

Finally, in order to use memcmp() and the new stuff in the "object" module, we need a couple of includes. Here:

```
value.c    #include <stdio.h>
           #include <string.h>

           #include "memory.h"
```

And here:

```
value.c    #include <string.h>

           #include "object.h"
           #include "memory.h"
```

## 19.4.1 Concatenation

Full-grown languages provide lots of operations for working with strings—access to individual characters, the string's length, changing case, splitting, joining, searching, etc. When you implement your language, you'll likely want all that. But for this book, we keep things *very* minimal.

The only interesting operation we support on strings is +. If you use that operator on two string objects, it produces a new string that's a concatenation of the two operands. Since Lox is dynamically typed, we can't tell which behavior is needed at compile time because we don't know the types of the operands until runtime. Thus, the OP_ADD instruction dynamically inspects the operands and chooses the right operation.

```
vm.c        case OP_LESS:      BINARY_OP(BOOL_VAL, <); break;
in run()    case OP_ADD: {
replace 1 line  if (IS_STRING(peek(0)) && IS_STRING(peek(1))) {
              concatenate();
            } else if (IS_NUMBER(peek(0)) && IS_NUMBER(peek(1))) {
              double b = AS_NUMBER(pop());
              double a = AS_NUMBER(pop());
              push(NUMBER_VAL(a + b));
            } else {
              runtimeError(
                  "Operands must be two numbers or two strings.");
              return INTERPRET_RUNTIME_ERROR;
            }
            break;
          }
            case OP_SUBTRACT: BINARY_OP(NUMBER_VAL, -); break;
```

This is more conservative than most languages. In other languages, if one operand is a string, the other can be any type and it will be implicitly converted to a string before concatenating the two.

I think that's a fine feature, but would require writing tedious "convert to string" code for each type, so I left it out of Lox.

If both operands are strings, it concatenates. If they're both numbers, it adds them. Any other combination of operand types is a runtime error.

To concatenate strings, we define a new function.

```
vm.c                    static void concatenate() {
add after isFalsey()      ObjString* b = AS_STRING(pop());
                          ObjString* a = AS_STRING(pop());
```

*continued on next page…*

```
    int length = a->length + b->length;                              ...from previous page
    char* chars = ALLOCATE(char, length + 1);
    memcpy(chars, a->chars, a->length);
    memcpy(chars + a->length, b->chars, b->length);
    chars[length] = '\0';

    ObjString* result = takeString(chars, length);
    push(OBJ_VAL(result));
}
```

It's pretty verbose, as C code that works with strings tends to be. First, we calculate the length of the result string based on the lengths of the operands. We allocate a character array for the result and then copy the two halves in. As always, we carefully ensure the string is terminated.

In order to call **memcpy()**, the VM needs an include.

```
#include <stdio.h>                                                    vm.c
#include <string.h>

#include "common.h"
```

Finally, we produce an ObjString to contain those characters. This time we use a new function, **takeString()**.

```
};                                                                   object.h
                                                                     add after struct ObjString
ObjString* takeString(char* chars, int length);
ObjString* copyString(const char* chars, int length);
```

The implementation looks like this:

```
ObjString* takeString(char* chars, int length) {                     object.c
  return allocateString(chars, length);                              add after allocateString()
}
```

The previous **copyString()** function assumes it *cannot* take ownership of the characters you pass in. Instead, it conservatively creates a copy of the characters on the heap that the ObjString can own. That's the right thing for string literals where the passed-in characters are in the middle of the source string.

But, for concatenation, we've already dynamically allocated a character array on the heap. Making another copy of that would be redundant (and would mean **concatenate()** has to remember to free its copy). Instead, this function claims ownership of the string you give it.

As usual, stitching this functionality together requires a couple of includes.

```
#include "debug.h"                                                   vm.c
#include "object.h"
#include "memory.h"
#include "vm.h"
```

## 19.5  Freeing Objects

Behold this innocuous-seeming expression:

```
"st" + "ri" + "ng"
```

When the compiler chews through this, it allocates an ObjString for each of those three string literals and stores them in the chunk's constant table and generates this bytecode:

Here's the stack after each instruction:

```
OP_CONSTANT O
  ┌──────┐
  │ "st" │
  └──────┘
OP_CONSTANT 1
  ┌──────┬──────┐
  │ "st" │ "ri" │
  └──────┴──────┘
OP_ADD
  ┌───────┐
  │ "stri"│
  └───────┘
OP_CONSTANT 2
  ┌───────┬──────┐
  │ "stri"│ "ng" │
  └───────┴──────┘
OP_ADD
  ┌─────────┐
  │"string" │
  └─────────┘
```

```
0000      OP_CONSTANT           0 "st"
0002      OP_CONSTANT           1 "ri"
0004      OP_ADD
0005      OP_CONSTANT           2 "ng"
0007      OP_ADD
0008      OP_RETURN
```

The first two instructions push "st" and "ri" onto the stack. Then the OP_ADD pops those and concatenates them. That dynamically allocates a new "stri" string on the heap. The VM pushes that and then pushes the "ng" constant. The last OP_ADD pops "stri" and "ng", concatenates them, and pushes the result: "string". Great, that's what we expect.

But, wait. What happened to that "stri" string? We dynamically allocated it, then the VM discarded it after concatenating it with "ng". We popped it from the stack and no longer have a reference to it, but we never freed its memory. We've got ourselves a classic memory leak.

Of course, it's perfectly fine for the *Lox program* to forget about intermediate strings and not worry about freeing them. Lox automatically manages memory on the user's behalf. The responsibility to manage memory doesn't *disappear*. Instead, it falls on our shoulders as VM implementers.

The full solution is a garbage collector that reclaims unused memory while the program is running. We've got some other stuff to get in place before we're ready to tackle that project. Until then, we are living on borrowed time. The longer we wait to add the collector, the harder it is to do.

Today, we should at least do the bare minimum: avoid *leaking* memory by making sure the VM can still find every allocated object even if the Lox program itself no longer references them. There are many sophisticated techniques that advanced memory managers use to allocate and track memory for objects. We're going to take the simplest practical approach.

We'll create a linked list that stores every Obj. The VM can traverse that list to find every single object that has been allocated on the heap, whether or not the user's program or the VM's stack still has a reference to it.

We could define a separate linked list node struct but then we'd have to allocate those too. Instead, we'll use an **intrusive list**—the Obj struct itself will be the linked list node. Each Obj gets a pointer to the next Obj in the chain.

I've seen a number of people implement large swathes of their language before trying to start on the GC. For the kind of toy programs you typically run while a language is being developed, you actually don't run out of memory before reaching the end of the program, so this gets you surprisingly far.

But that underestimates how *hard* it is to add a garbage collector later. The collector *must* ensure it can find every bit of memory that *is* still being used so that it doesn't collect live data. There are hundreds of places a language implementation can squirrel away a reference to some object. If you don't find all of them, you get nightmarish bugs.

I've seen language implementations die because it was too hard to get the GC in later. If your language needs GC, get it working as soon as you can. It's a crosscutting concern that touches the entire codebase.

*object.h*
*in struct* Obj

```
struct Obj {
  ObjType type;
  struct Obj* next;
};
```

The VM stores a pointer to the head of the list.

```
  Value* stackTop;
  Obj* objects;
} VM;
```
vm.h
*in struct* VM

When we first initialize the VM, there are no allocated objects.

```
  resetStack();
  vm.objects = NULL;
}
```
vm.c
*in* initVM()

Every time we allocate an Obj, we insert it in the list.

```
  object->type = type;

  object->next = vm.objects;
  vm.objects = object;
  return object;
```
object.c
*in* allocateObject()

Since this is a singly linked list, the easiest place to insert it is as the head. That way, we don't need to also store a pointer to the tail and keep it updated.

The "object" module is directly using the global vm variable from the "vm" module, so we need to expose that externally.

```
} InterpretResult;

extern VM vm;

void initVM();
```
vm.h
*add after enum* InterpretResult

Eventually, the garbage collector will free memory while the VM is still running. But, even then, there will usually be unused objects still lingering in memory when the user's program completes. The VM should free those too.

There's no sophisticated logic for that. Once the program is done, we can free *every* object. We can and should implement that now.

```
void freeVM() {
  freeObjects();
}
```
vm.c
*in* freeVM()

That empty function we defined way back when finally does something! It calls this:

```
void* reallocate(void* pointer, size_t oldSize, size_t newSize);
void freeObjects();

#endif
```
memory.h
*add after* reallocate()

Here's how we free the objects:

**memory.c**
*add after* `reallocate()`

```c
void freeObjects() {
  Obj* object = vm.objects;
  while (object != NULL) {
    Obj* next = object->next;
    freeObject(object);
    object = next;
  }
}
```

This is a CS 101 textbook implementation of walking a linked list and freeing its nodes. For each node, we call:

**memory.c**
*add after* `reallocate()`

```c
static void freeObject(Obj* object) {
  switch (object->type) {
    case OBJ_STRING: {
      ObjString* string = (ObjString*)object;
      FREE_ARRAY(char, string->chars, string->length + 1);
      FREE(ObjString, object);
      break;
    }
  }
}
```

We aren't only freeing the Obj itself. Since some object types also allocate other memory that they own, we also need a little type-specific code to handle each object type's special needs. Here, that means we free the character array and then free the ObjString. Those both use one last memory management macro.

```c
    (type*)reallocate(NULL, 0, sizeof(type) * (count))
```

**memory.h**

```c
#define FREE(type, pointer) reallocate(pointer, sizeof(type), 0)

#define GROW_CAPACITY(capacity) \
```

Going through `reallocate()` instead of calling `free()` directly seems pointless. But later, having everything go through `reallocate()` will make it easier to keep track of how much memory is in use.

It's a tiny wrapper around `reallocate()` that "resizes" an allocation down to zero bytes.

As usual, we need an include to wire everything together.

**memory.h**

```c
#include "common.h"
#include "object.h"

#define ALLOCATE(type, count) \
```

Then in the implementation file:

**memory.c**

```c
#include "memory.h"
#include "vm.h"

void* reallocate(void* pointer, size_t oldSize, size_t newSize) {
```

With this, our VM no longer leaks memory. Like a good C program, it cleans up its mess before exiting. But it doesn't free any objects while the VM is running.

Later, when it's possible to write longer-running Lox programs, the VM will eat more and more memory as it goes, not relinquishing a single byte until the entire program is done.

We won't address that until we've added a real garbage collector, but this is a big step. We now have the infrastructure to support a variety of different kinds of dynamically allocated objects. And we've used that to add strings to clox, one of the most used types in most programming languages. Strings in turn enable us to build another fundamental data type, especially in dynamic languages: the venerable hash table. But that's for the next chapter…

## CHALLENGES

1. Each string requires two separate dynamic allocations—one for the ObjString and a second for the character array. Accessing the characters from a value requires two pointer indirections, which can be bad for performance. A more efficient solution relies on a technique called **flexible array members**. Use that to store the ObjString and its character array in a single contiguous allocation.

2. When we create the ObjString for each string literal, we copy the characters onto the heap. That way, when the string is later freed, we know it is safe to free the characters too.

   This is a simpler approach but wastes some memory, which might be a problem on very constrained devices. Instead, we could keep track of which ObjStrings own their character array and which are "constant strings" that just point back to the original source string or some other non-freeable location. Add support for this.

3. If Lox was your language, what would you have it do when a user tries to use + with one string operand and the other some other type? Justify your choice. What do other languages do?

## DESIGN NOTE: STRING ENCODING

In this book, I try not to shy away from the gnarly problems you'll run into in a real language implementation. We might not always use the most *sophisticated* solution—it's an intro book after all—but I don't think it's honest to pretend the problem doesn't exist at all. However, I did skirt around one really nasty conundrum: deciding how to represent strings.

There are two facets to a string encoding:

- **What is a single "character" in a string?** How many different values are there and what do they represent? The first widely adopted standard answer to this was ASCII. It gave you 127 different character values and specified what they were. It was great…if you only ever cared about English. While it has weird, mostly forgotten characters like "record separator" and "synchronous idle", it doesn't have a single umlaut, acute, or grave. It can't represent "jalapeño", "naïve", "Gruyère", or "Mötley Crüe".

  Next came Unicode. Initially, it supported 16,384 different characters (**code points**), which fit nicely in 16 bits with a couple of bits to spare. Later that grew and grew, and now there are well over 100,000 different code points including such vital instruments of human communication as 💩 (Unicode Character 'PILE OF POO', U+1F4A9).

  Even that long list of code points is not enough to represent each possible visible glyph a language might support. To handle that, Unicode also has **combining characters** that modify a preceding code point. For example, "a" followed by the combining character "¨" gives you "ä". (To make things more confusing Unicode *also* has a single code point that looks like "ä".)

  If a user accesses the fourth "character" in "naïve", do they expect to get back "v" or "¨"? The former means they are thinking of each code point and its combining character as a single unit—what Unicode calls an **extended grapheme cluster**—the latter means they are thinking in individual code points. Which do your users expect?

- **How is a single unit represented in memory?** Most systems using ASCII gave a single byte to each character and left the high bit unused. Unicode has a handful of common encodings. UTF-16 packs most code points into 16 bits. That was great when every code point fit in that size. When that overflowed, they added *surrogate pairs* that use multiple 16-bit code units to represent a single code point. UTF-32 is the next evolution of UTF-16—it gives a full 32 bits to each and every code point.

  UTF-8 is more complex than either of those. It uses a variable number of bytes to encode a code point. Lower-valued code points fit in fewer bytes. Since each character may occupy a different number of bytes, you can't directly index into the string to find a specific code point. If you want, say, the 10th code point, you don't know how many bytes into the string that is without walking and decoding all of the preceding ones.

Choosing a character representation and encoding involves fundamental trade-offs. Like many things in engineering, there's no perfect solution:

- ASCII is memory efficient and fast, but it kicks non-Latin languages to the side.

- UTF-32 is fast and supports the whole Unicode range, but wastes a lot of memory given that most code points do tend to be in the lower range of values, where a full

*It goes without saying that a language that does not let one discuss Gruyère or Mötley Crüe is a language not worth using.*

*An example of how difficult this problem is comes from Python. The achingly long transition from Python 2 to 3 is painful mostly because of its changes around string encoding.*

32 bits aren't needed.

- UTF-8 is memory efficient and supports the whole Unicode range, but its variable-length encoding makes it slow to access arbitrary code points.

- UTF-16 is worse than all of them—an ugly consequence of Unicode outgrowing its earlier 16-bit range. It's less memory efficient than UTF-8 but is still a variable-length encoding thanks to surrogate pairs. Avoid it if you can. Alas, if your language needs to run on or interoperate with the browser, the JVM, or the CLR, you might be stuck with it, since those all use UTF-16 for their strings and you don't want to have to convert every time you pass a string to the underlying system.

One option is to take the maximal approach and do the "rightest" thing. Support all the Unicode code points. Internally, select an encoding for each string based on its contents—use ASCII if every code point fits in a byte, UTF-16 if there are no surrogate pairs, etc. Provide APIs to let users iterate over both code points and extended grapheme clusters.

This covers all your bases but is really complex. It's a lot to implement, debug, and optimize. When serializing strings or interoperating with other systems, you have to deal with all of the encodings. Users need to understand the two indexing APIs and know which to use when. This is the approach that newer, big languages tend to take—like Raku and Swift.

A simpler compromise is to always encode using UTF-8 and only expose an API that works with code points. For users that want to work with grapheme clusters, let them use a third-party library for that. This is less Latin-centric than ASCII but not much more complex. You lose fast direct indexing by code point, but you can usually live without that or afford to make it $O(n)$ instead of $O(1)$.

If I were designing a big workhorse language for people writing large applications, I'd probably go with the maximal approach. For my little embedded scripting language Wren, I went with UTF-8 and code points.

# Hash Tables

20

*"Hash, x. There is no definition for this word—nobody knows what hash is."*

— Ambrose Bierce, *The Unabridged Devil's Dictionary*

Before we can add variables to our burgeoning virtual machine, we need some way to look up a value given a variable's name. Later, when we add classes, we'll also need a way to store fields on instances. The perfect data structure for these problems and others is a hash table.

You probably already know what a hash table is, even if you don't know it by that name. If you're a Java programmer, you call them "HashMaps". C# and Python users call them "dictionaries". In C++, it's an "unordered map". "Objects" in JavaScript and "tables" in Lua are hash tables under the hood, which is what gives them their flexibility.

A hash table, whatever your language calls it, associates a set of **keys** with a set of **values**. Each key/value pair is an **entry** in the table. Given a key, you can look up its corresponding value. You can add new key/value pairs and remove entries by key. If you add a new value for an existing key, it replaces the previous entry.

Hash tables appear in so many languages because they are incredibly power-ful. Much of this power comes from one metric: given a key, a hash table returns the corresponding value in constant time, *regardless of how many keys are in the hash table*.

That's pretty remarkable when you think about it. Imagine you've got a big stack of business cards and I ask you to find a certain person. The bigger the pile is, the longer it will take. Even if the pile is nicely sorted and you've got the manual dexterity to do a binary search by hand, you're still talking *O(log n)*. But with a hash table, it takes the same time to find that business card when the stack has ten cards as when it has a million.

More specifically, the *average-case* lookup time is constant. Worst-case performance can be, well, worse. In practice, it's easy to avoid degenerate behavior and stay on the happy path.

Stuff all those cards in a Rolodex—does anyone even remember those things anymore?—with dividers for each letter, and you improve your speed dramatically. As we'll see, that's not too far from the trick a hash table uses.

## 20.1  An Array of Buckets

A complete, fast hash table has a couple of moving parts. I'll introduce them one at a time by working through a couple of toy problems and their solutions. Eventually, we'll build up to a data structure that can associate any set of names with their values.

For now, imagine if Lox was a *lot* more restricted in variable names. What if a variable's name could only be a single lowercase letter. How could we very efficiently represent a set of variable names and their values?

This limitation isn't *too* far-fetched. The initial versions of BASIC out of Dartmouth allowed variable names to be only a single letter followed by one optional digit.

With only 26 possible variables (27 if you consider underscore a "letter", I guess), the answer is easy. Declare a fixed-size array with 26 elements. We'll follow tradition and call each element a **bucket**. Each represents a variable with a starting at index zero. If there's a value in the array at some letter's index, then that key is present with that value. Otherwise, the bucket is empty and that key/value pair isn't in the data structure.

Memory usage is great—just a single, reasonably sized array. There's some waste from the empty buckets, but it's not huge. There's no overhead for node pointers, padding, or other stuff you'd get with something like a linked list or tree.

Performance is even better. Given a variable name—its character—you can subtract the ASCII value of a and use the result to index directly into the array. Then you can either look up the existing value or store a new value directly into that slot. It doesn't get much faster than that.

This is sort of our Platonic ideal data structure. Lightning fast, dead simple, and compact in memory. As we add support for more complex keys, we'll have to make some concessions, but this is what we're aiming for. Even once you add in hash functions, dynamic resizing, and collision resolution, this is still the core of every hash table out there—a contiguous array of buckets that you index directly into.

### 20.1.1  Load factor and wrapped keys

Again, this restriction isn't so crazy. Early linkers for C treated only the first six characters of external identifiers as meaningful. Everything after that was ignored. If you've ever wondered why the C standard library is so enamored of abbreviation—looking at you, `strncmp()`—it turns out it wasn't entirely because of the small screens (or teletypes!) of the day.

Confining Lox to single-letter variables would make our job as implementers easier, but it's probably no fun programming in a language that gives you only 26 storage locations. What if we loosened it a little and allowed variables up to eight characters long?

That's small enough that we can pack all eight characters into a 64-bit integer and easily turn the string into a number. We can then use it as an array index. Or, at least, we could if we could somehow allocate a 295,148 *petabyte* array. Memory's gotten cheaper over time, but not quite *that* cheap. Even if we could make an array that big, it would be heinously wasteful. Almost every bucket would be empty unless users started writing way bigger Lox programs than we've anticipated.

Even though our variable keys cover the full 64-bit numeric range, we clearly don't need an array that large. Instead, we allocate an array with more than enough capacity for the entries we need, but not unreasonably large. We map the full 64-bit keys down to that smaller range by taking the value modulo the size of the array. Doing that essentially folds the larger numeric range onto itself until it fits the smaller range of array elements.

For example, say we want to store "bagel". We allocate an array with eight elements, plenty enough to store it and more later. We treat the key string as a 64-bit integer. On a little-endian machine like Intel, packing those characters into a 64-bit word puts the first letter, "b" (ASCII value 98), in the least-significant byte. We take that integer modulo the array size (8) to fit it in the bounds and get a bucket index, 2. Then we store the value there as usual.

Using the array size as a modulus lets us map the key's numeric range down to fit an array of any size. We can thus control the number of buckets independently of the key range. That solves our waste problem, but introduces a new one. Any two variables whose key number has the same remainder when divided by the array size will end up in the same bucket. Keys can **collide**. For example, if we try to add "jam", it also ends up in bucket 2.

I'm using powers of two for the array sizes here, but they don't need to be. Some styles of hash tables work best with powers of two, including the one we'll build in this book. Others prefer prime number array sizes or have other rules.

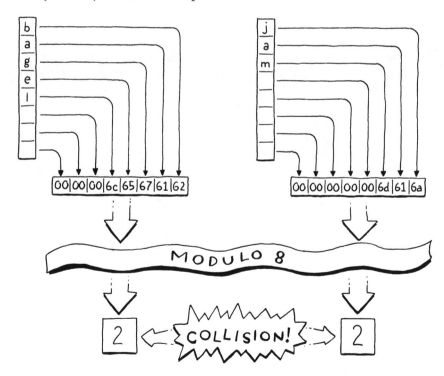

We have some control over this by tuning the array size. The bigger the array, the fewer the indexes that get mapped to the same bucket and the fewer the collisions that are likely to occur. Hash table implementers track this collision likelihood by measuring the table's **load factor**. It's defined as the number of entries divided by the number of buckets. So a hash table with five entries and an array of 16 elements has a load factor of 0.3125. The higher the load factor, the greater the chance of collisions.

One way we mitigate collisions is by resizing the array. Just like the dynamic arrays we implemented earlier, we reallocate and grow the hash table's array as it fills up. Unlike a regular dynamic array, though, we won't wait until the array is *full*. Instead, we pick a desired load factor and grow the array when it goes over that.

## 20.2  Collision Resolution

Even with a very low load factor, collisions can still occur. The *birthday paradox* tells us that as the number of entries in the hash table increases, the chance of collision increases very quickly. We can pick a large array size to reduce that, but it's a losing game. Say we wanted to store a hundred items in a hash table. To keep the chance of collision below a still-pretty-high 10%, we need an array with at least 47,015 elements. To get the chance below 1% requires an array with 492,555 elements, over 4,000 empty buckets for each one in use.

A low load factor can make collisions rarer, but the *pigeonhole principle* tells us we can never eliminate them entirely. If you've got five pet pigeons and four holes to put them in, at least one hole is going to end up with more than one pigeon. With 18,446,744,073,709,551,616 different variable names, any reasonably sized array can potentially end up with multiple keys in the same bucket.

Thus we still have to handle collisions gracefully when they occur. Users don't like it when their programming language can look up variables correctly only *most* of the time.

### 20.2.1  Separate chaining

Techniques for resolving collisions fall into two broad categories. The first is **separate chaining**. Instead of each bucket containing a single entry, we let it contain a collection of them. In the classic implementation, each bucket points to a linked list of entries. To look up an entry, you find its bucket and then walk the list until you find an entry with the matching key.

Put these two funny-named mathematical rules together and you get this observation: Take a birdhouse containing 365 pigeonholes, and use each pigeon's birthday to assign it to a pigeonhole. You'll need only about 26 randomly chosen pigeons before you get a greater than 50% chance of two pigeons in the same box.

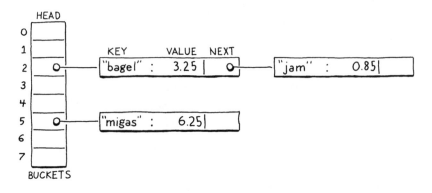

In catastrophically bad cases where every entry collides in the same bucket, the data structure degrades into a single unsorted linked list with $O(n)$ lookup. In practice, it's easy to avoid that by controlling the load factor and how entries get scattered across buckets. In typical separate-chained hash tables, it's rare for a bucket to have more than one or two entries.

Separate chaining is conceptually simple—it's literally an array of linked lists. Most operations are straightforward to implement, even deletion which, as we'll see, can be a pain. But it's not a great fit for modern CPUs. It has a lot of overhead from pointers and tends to scatter little linked list nodes around in memory which isn't great for cache usage.

There are a few tricks to optimize this. Many implementations store the first entry right in the bucket so that in the common case where there's only one, no extra pointer indirection is needed. You can also make each linked list node store a few entries to reduce the pointer overhead.

## 20.2.2 Open addressing

The other technique is called **open addressing** or (confusingly) **closed hashing**. With this technique, all entries live directly in the bucket array, with one entry per bucket. If two entries collide in the same bucket, we find a different empty bucket to use instead.

It's called "open" addressing because the entry may end up at an address (bucket) outside of its preferred one. It's called "closed" hashing because all of the entries stay inside the array of buckets.

Storing all entries in a single, big, contiguous array is great for keeping the memory representation simple and fast. But it makes all of the operations on the hash table more complex. When inserting an entry, its bucket may be full, sending us to look at another bucket. That bucket itself may be occupied and so on. This process of finding an available bucket is called **probing**, and the order that you examine buckets is a **probe sequence**.

There are a number of algorithms for determining which buckets to probe and how to decide which entry goes in which bucket. There's been a ton of research here because even slight tweaks can have a large performance impact. And, on a data structure as heavily used as hash tables, that performance impact touches a very large number of real-world programs across a range of hardware capabilities.

If you'd like to learn more (and you should, because some of these are really cool), look into "double hashing", "cuckoo hashing", "Robin Hood hashing", and anything those lead you to.

As usual in this book, we'll pick the simplest one that gets the job done efficiently. That's good old **linear probing**. When looking for an entry, we look in the first bucket its key maps to. If it's not in there, we look in the very next element in the array, and so on. If we reach the end, we wrap back around to the beginning.

The good thing about linear probing is that it's cache friendly. Since you walk the array directly in memory order, it keeps the CPU's cache lines full and happy. The bad thing is that it's prone to **clustering**. If you have a lot of entries with numerically similar key values, you can end up with a lot of colliding, overflowing buckets right next to each other.

Compared to separate chaining, open addressing can be harder to wrap your head around. I think of open addressing as similar to separate chaining except that the "list" of nodes is threaded through the bucket array itself. Instead of storing the links between them in pointers, the connections are calculated implicitly by the order that you look through the buckets.

The tricky part is that more than one of these implicit lists may be interleaved together. Let's walk through an example that covers all the interesting cases. We'll ignore values for now and just worry about a set of keys. We start with an empty array of 8 buckets.

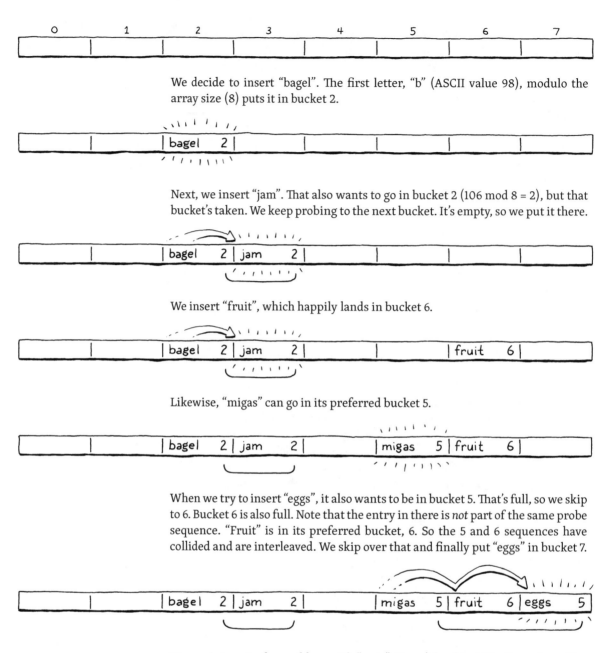

We decide to insert "bagel". The first letter, "b" (ASCII value 98), modulo the array size (8) puts it in bucket 2.

Next, we insert "jam". That also wants to go in bucket 2 (106 mod 8 = 2), but that bucket's taken. We keep probing to the next bucket. It's empty, so we put it there.

We insert "fruit", which happily lands in bucket 6.

Likewise, "migas" can go in its preferred bucket 5.

When we try to insert "eggs", it also wants to be in bucket 5. That's full, so we skip to 6. Bucket 6 is also full. Note that the entry in there is *not* part of the same probe sequence. "Fruit" is in its preferred bucket, 6. So the 5 and 6 sequences have collided and are interleaved. We skip over that and finally put "eggs" in bucket 7.

We run into a similar problem with "nuts". It can't land in 6 like it wants to. Nor can it go into 7. So we keep going. But we've reached the end of the array, so we wrap back around to 0 and put it there.

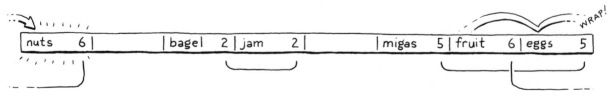

In practice, the interleaving turns out to not be much of a problem. Even in separate chaining, we need to walk the list to check each entry's key because multiple keys can reduce to the same bucket. With open addressing, we need to do that same check, and that also covers the case where you are stepping over entries that "belong" to a different original bucket.

## 20.3  Hash Functions

We can now build ourselves a reasonably efficient table for storing variable names up to eight characters long, but that limitation is still annoying. In order to relax the last constraint, we need a way to take a string of any length and convert it to a fixed-size integer.

Finally, we get to the "hash" part of "hash table". A **hash function** takes some larger blob of data and "hashes" it to produce a fixed-size integer **hash code** whose value depends on all of the bits of the original data. A good hash function has three main goals:

- **It must be *deterministic*.** The same input must always hash to the same number. If the same variable ends up in different buckets at different points in time, it's gonna get really hard to find it.

- **It must be *uniform*.** Given a typical set of inputs, it should produce a wide and evenly distributed range of output numbers, with as few clumps or patterns as possible. We want it to scatter values across the whole numeric range to minimize collisions and clustering.

- **It must be *fast*.** Every operation on the hash table requires us to hash the key first. If hashing is slow, it can potentially cancel out the speed of the underlying array storage.

There is a veritable pile of hash functions out there. Some are old and optimized for architectures no one uses anymore. Some are designed to be fast, others cryptographically secure. Some take advantage of vector instructions and cache sizes for specific chips, others aim to maximize portability.

There are people out there for whom designing and evaluating hash functions is, like, their *jam*. I admire them, but I'm not mathematically astute enough to *be* one. So for clox, I picked a simple, well-worn hash function called FNV-1a that's served me fine over the years. Consider trying out different ones in your code and see if they make a difference.

OK, that's a quick run through of buckets, load factors, open addressing, collision resolution, and hash functions. That's an awful lot of text and not a lot of real code. Don't worry if it still seems vague. Once we're done coding it up, it will all click into place.

Hash functions are also used for cryptography. In that domain, "good" has a *much* more stringent definition to avoid exposing details about the data being hashed. We, thankfully, don't need to worry about those concerns for this book.

One of the original names for a hash table was "scatter table" because it takes the entries and scatters them throughout the array. The word "hash" came from the idea that a hash function takes the input data, chops it up, and tosses it all together into a pile to come up with a single number from all of those bits.

Who knows, maybe hash functions could turn out to be your thing too?

## 20.4  Building a Hash Table

The great thing about hash tables compared to other classic techniques like balanced search trees is that the actual data structure is so simple. Ours goes into a new module.

**table.h**
*create new file*

```
#ifndef clox_table_h
#define clox_table_h

#include "common.h"
#include "value.h"

typedef struct {
  int count;
  int capacity;
  Entry* entries;
} Table;

#endif
```

A hash table is an array of entries. As in our dynamic array earlier, we keep track of both the allocated size of the array (`capacity`) and the number of key/value pairs currently stored in it (`count`). The ratio of count to capacity is exactly the load factor of the hash table.

Each entry is one of these:

**table.h**

```
#include "value.h"

typedef struct {
  ObjString* key;
  Value value;
} Entry;

typedef struct {
```

In clox, we only need to support keys that are strings. Handling other types of keys doesn't add much complexity. As long as you can compare two objects for equality and reduce them to sequences of bits, it's easy to use them as hash keys.

It's a simple key/value pair. Since the key is always a string, we store the ObjString pointer directly instead of wrapping it in a Value. It's a little faster and smaller this way.

To create a new, empty hash table, we declare a constructor-like function.

**table.h**
*add after struct Table*

```
} Table;

void initTable(Table* table);

#endif
```

We need a new implementation file to define that. While we're at it, let's get all of the pesky includes out of the way.

**table.c**
*create new file*

```
#include <stdlib.h>
#include <string.h>

#include "memory.h"
#include "object.h"
#include "table.h"
#include "value.h"
```

*continued on next page…*

```
void initTable(Table* table) {
  table->count = 0;
  table->capacity = 0;
  table->entries = NULL;
}
```

…from previous page

As in our dynamic value array type, a hash table initially starts with zero capacity and a NULL array. We don't allocate anything until needed. Assuming we do eventually allocate something, we need to be able to free it too.

```
void initTable(Table* table);
void freeTable(Table* table);

#endif
```

table.h
*add after* initTable()

And its glorious implementation:

```
void freeTable(Table* table) {
  FREE_ARRAY(Entry, table->entries, table->capacity);
  initTable(table);
}
```

table.c
*add after* initTable()

Again, it looks just like a dynamic array. In fact, you can think of a hash table as basically a dynamic array with a really strange policy for inserting items. We don't need to check for NULL here since FREE_ARRAY() already handles that gracefully.

## 20.4.1  Hashing strings

Before we can start putting entries in the table, we need to, well, hash them. To ensure that the entries get distributed uniformly throughout the array, we want a good hash function that looks at all of the bits of the key string. If it looked at, say, only the first few characters, then a series of strings that all shared the same prefix would end up colliding in the same bucket.

On the other hand, walking the entire string to calculate the hash is kind of slow. We'd lose some of the performance benefit of the hash table if we had to walk the string every time we looked for a key in the table. So we'll do the obvious thing: cache it.

Over in the "object" module in ObjString, we add:

```
  char* chars;
  uint32_t hash;
};
```

object.h
*in struct* ObjString

Each ObjString stores the hash code for its string. Since strings are immutable in Lox, we can calculate the hash code once up front and be certain that it will never get invalidated. Caching it eagerly makes a kind of sense: allocating the string and copying its characters over is already an $O(n)$ operation, so it's a good time to also do the $O(n)$ calculation of the string's hash.

Whenever we call the internal function to allocate a string, we pass in its hash code.

**object.c**
*function* allocateString()
*replace 1 line*

```c
static ObjString* allocateString(char* chars, int length,
                                 uint32_t hash) {
  ObjString* string = ALLOCATE_OBJ(ObjString, OBJ_STRING);
```

That function simply stores the hash in the struct.

**object.c**
*in* allocateString()

```c
  string->chars = chars;
  string->hash = hash;
  return string;
}
```

The fun happens over at the callers. `allocateString()` is called from two places: the function that copies a string and the one that takes ownership of an existing dynamically allocated string. We'll start with the first.

**object.c**
*in* copyString()

```c
ObjString* copyString(const char* chars, int length) {
  uint32_t hash = hashString(chars, length);
  char* heapChars = ALLOCATE(char, length + 1);
```

No magic here. We calculate the hash code and then pass it along.

**object.c**
*in* copyString()
*replace 1 line*

```c
  memcpy(heapChars, chars, length);
  heapChars[length] = '\0';
  return allocateString(heapChars, length, hash);
}
```

The other string function is similar.

**object.c**
*in* takeString()
*replace 1 line*

```c
ObjString* takeString(char* chars, int length) {
  uint32_t hash = hashString(chars, length);
  return allocateString(chars, length, hash);
}
```

The interesting code is over here:

**object.c**
*add after* allocateString()

```c
static uint32_t hashString(const char* key, int length) {
  uint32_t hash = 2166136261u;
  for (int i = 0; i < length; i++) {
    hash ^= (uint8_t)key[i];
    hash *= 16777619;
  }
  return hash;
}
```

This is the actual bona fide "hash function" in clox. The algorithm is called "FNV-1a", and is the shortest decent hash function I know. Brevity is certainly a virtue in a book that aims to show you every line of code.

The basic idea is pretty simple, and many hash functions follow the same pattern. You start with some initial hash value, usually a constant with certain carefully chosen mathematical properties. Then you walk the data to be hashed. For each byte (or sometimes word), you mix the bits into the hash value somehow, and then scramble the resulting bits around some.

What it means to "mix" and "scramble" can get pretty sophisticated. Ultimately, though, the basic goal is *uniformity*—we want the resulting hash values to be as widely scattered around the numeric range as possible to avoid collisions and clustering.

## 20.4.2  Inserting entries

Now that string objects know their hash code, we can start putting them into hash tables.

```
void freeTable(Table* table);
bool tableSet(Table* table, ObjString* key, Value value);

#endif
```

table.h
*add after* freeTable()

This function adds the given key/value pair to the given hash table. If an entry for that key is already present, the new value overwrites the old value. The function returns true if a new entry was added. Here's the implementation:

```
bool tableSet(Table* table, ObjString* key, Value value) {
  Entry* entry = findEntry(table->entries, table->capacity, key);
  bool isNewKey = entry->key == NULL;
  if (isNewKey) table->count++;

  entry->key = key;
  entry->value = value;
  return isNewKey;
}
```

table.c
*add after* freeTable()

Most of the interesting logic is in findEntry() which we'll get to soon. That function's job is to take a key and figure out which bucket in the array it should go in. It returns a pointer to that bucket—the address of the Entry in the array.

Once we have a bucket, inserting is straightforward. We update the hash table's size, taking care to not increase the count if we overwrote the value for an already-present key. Then we copy the key and value into the corresponding fields in the Entry.

We're missing a little something here, though. We haven't actually allocated the Entry array yet. Oops! Before we can insert anything, we need to make sure we have an array, and that it's big enough.

```
bool tableSet(Table* table, ObjString* key, Value value) {
  if (table->count + 1 > table->capacity * TABLE_MAX_LOAD) {
    int capacity = GROW_CAPACITY(table->capacity);
    adjustCapacity(table, capacity);
  }

  Entry* entry = findEntry(table->entries, table->capacity, key);
```

table.c
*in* tableSet()

This is similar to the code we wrote a while back for growing a dynamic array. If we don't have enough capacity to insert an item, we reallocate and grow the array. The GROW_CAPACITY() macro takes an existing capacity and grows it by a multiple to ensure that we get amortized constant performance over a series of inserts.

The interesting difference here is that `TABLE_MAX_LOAD` constant.

table.c

```
#include "value.h"

#define TABLE_MAX_LOAD 0.75

void initTable(Table* table) {
```

Ideal max load factor varies based on the hash function, collision-handling strategy, and typical keysets you'll see. Since a toy language like Lox doesn't have "real world" data sets, it's hard to optimize this, and I picked 75% somewhat arbitrarily. When you build your own hash tables, benchmark and tune this.

This is how we manage the table's load factor. We don't grow when the capacity is completely full. Instead, we grow the array before then, when the array becomes at least 75% full.

We'll get to the implementation of `adjustCapacity()` soon. First, let's look at that `findEntry()` function you've been wondering about.

table.c
*add after* freeTable()

```
static Entry* findEntry(Entry* entries, int capacity,
                        ObjString* key) {
  uint32_t index = key->hash % capacity;
  for (;;) {
    Entry* entry = &entries[index];
    if (entry->key == key || entry->key == NULL) {
      return entry;
    }

    index = (index + 1) % capacity;
  }
}
```

This function is the real core of the hash table. It's responsible for taking a key and an array of buckets, and figuring out which bucket the entry belongs in. This function is also where linear probing and collision handling come into play. We'll use `findEntry()` both to look up existing entries in the hash table and to decide where to insert new ones.

For all that, there isn't much to it. First, we use modulo to map the key's hash code to an index within the array's bounds. That gives us a bucket index where, ideally, we'll be able to find or place the entry.

There are a few cases to check for:

- If the key for the Entry at that array index is `NULL`, then the bucket is empty. If we're using `findEntry()` to look up something in the hash table, this means it isn't there. If we're using it to insert, it means we've found a place to add the new entry.

It looks like we're using == to see if two strings are equal. That doesn't work, does it? There could be two copies of the same string at different places in memory. Fear not, astute reader. We'll solve this further on. And, strangely enough, it's a hash table that provides the tool we need.

- If the key in the bucket is equal to the key we're looking for, then that key is already present in the table. If we're doing a lookup, that's good—we've found the key we seek. If we're doing an insert, this means we'll be replacing the value for that key instead of adding a new entry.

- Otherwise, the bucket has an entry in it, but with a different key. This is a collision. In that case, we start probing. That's what that `for` loop does. We start at the bucket where the entry would ideally go. If that bucket is empty or has the same key, we're done. Otherwise, we advance to the next element—this is the *linear* part of "linear probing"—and check there. If we go past the end of the array, that second modulo operator wraps us back around to the beginning.

We exit the loop when we find either an empty bucket or a bucket with the same key as the one we're looking for. You might be wondering about an infinite loop. What if we collide with *every* bucket? Fortunately, that can't happen thanks to our load factor. Because we grow the array as soon as it gets close to being full, we know there will always be empty buckets.

We return directly from within the loop, yielding a pointer to the found Entry so the caller can either insert something into it or read from it. Way back in `tableSet()`, the function that first kicked this off, we store the new entry in that returned bucket and we're done.

## 20.4.3 Allocating and resizing

Before we can put entries in the hash table, we do need a place to actually store them. We need to allocate an array of buckets. That happens in this function:

```
static void adjustCapacity(Table* table, int capacity) {
  Entry* entries = ALLOCATE(Entry, capacity);
  for (int i = 0; i < capacity; i++) {
    entries[i].key = NULL;
    entries[i].value = NIL_VAL;
  }

  table->entries = entries;
  table->capacity = capacity;
}
```

table.c
*add after* findEntry()

We create a bucket array with `capacity` entries. After we allocate the array, we initialize every element to be an empty bucket and then store the array (and its capacity) in the hash table's main struct. This code is fine for when we insert the very first entry into the table, and we require the first allocation of the array. But what about when we already have one and we need to grow it?

Back when we were doing a dynamic array, we could just use `realloc()` and let the C standard library copy everything over. That doesn't work for a hash table. Remember that to choose the bucket for each entry, we take its hash key *modulo the array size*. That means that when the array size changes, entries may end up in different buckets.

Those new buckets may have new collisions that we need to deal with. So the simplest way to get every entry where it belongs is to rebuild the table from scratch by re-inserting every entry into the new empty array.

```
    entries[i].value = NIL_VAL;
  }

  for (int i = 0; i < table->capacity; i++) {
    Entry* entry = &table->entries[i];
    if (entry->key == NULL) continue;
```

table.c
*in* adjustCapacity()

*continued on next page...*

*...from previous page*

```
  Entry* dest = findEntry(entries, capacity, entry->key);
  dest->key = entry->key;
  dest->value = entry->value;
}

table->entries = entries;
```

We walk through the old array front to back. Any time we find a non-empty bucket, we insert that entry into the new array. We use findEntry(), passing in the *new* array instead of the one currently stored in the Table. (This is why findEntry() takes a pointer directly to an Entry array and not the whole Table struct. That way, we can pass the new array and capacity before we've stored those in the struct.)

After that's done, we can release the memory for the old array.

**table.c**
*in* adjustCapacity()

```
    dest->value = entry->value;
  }

  FREE_ARRAY(Entry, table->entries, table->capacity);
  table->entries = entries;
```

With that, we have a hash table that we can stuff as many entries into as we like. It handles overwriting existing keys and growing itself as needed to maintain the desired load capacity.

While we're at it, let's also define a helper function for copying all of the entries of one hash table into another.

**table.h**
*add after* tableSet()

```
bool tableSet(Table* table, ObjString* key, Value value);
void tableAddAll(Table* from, Table* to);

#endif
```

We won't need this until much later when we support method inheritance, but we may as well implement it now while we've got all the hash table stuff fresh in our minds.

**table.c**
*add after* tableSet()

```
void tableAddAll(Table* from, Table* to) {
  for (int i = 0; i < from->capacity; i++) {
    Entry* entry = &from->entries[i];
    if (entry->key != NULL) {
      tableSet(to, entry->key, entry->value);
    }
  }
}
```

There's not much to say about this. It walks the bucket array of the source hash table. Whenever it finds a non-empty bucket, it adds the entry to the destination hash table using the tableSet() function we recently defined.

## 20.4.4 Retrieving values

Now that our hash table contains some stuff, let's start pulling things back out. Given a key, we can look up the corresponding value, if there is one, with this function:

```
void freeTable(Table* table);
bool tableGet(Table* table, ObjString* key, Value* value);
bool tableSet(Table* table, ObjString* key, Value value);
```

**table.h**
*add after* freeTable()

You pass in a table and a key. If it finds an entry with that key, it returns `true`, otherwise it returns `false`. If the entry exists, the `value` output parameter points to the resulting value.

Since `findEntry()` already does the hard work, the implementation isn't bad.

```
bool tableGet(Table* table, ObjString* key, Value* value) {
  if (table->count == 0) return false;

  Entry* entry = findEntry(table->entries, table->capacity, key);
  if (entry->key == NULL) return false;

  *value = entry->value;
  return true;
}
```

**table.c**
*add after* findEntry()

If the table is completely empty, we definitely won't find the entry, so we check for that first. This isn't just an optimization—it also ensures that we don't try to access the bucket array when the array is NULL. Otherwise, we let `findEntry()` work its magic. That returns a pointer to a bucket. If the bucket is empty, which we detect by seeing if the key is NULL, then we didn't find an Entry with our key. If `findEntry()` does return a non-empty Entry, then that's our match. We take the Entry's value and copy it to the output parameter so the caller can get it. Piece of cake.

## 20.4.5 Deleting entries

There is one more fundamental operation a full-featured hash table needs to support: removing an entry. This seems pretty obvious, if you can add things, you should be able to *un*-add them, right? But you'd be surprised how many tutorials on hash tables omit this.

I could have taken that route too. In fact, we use deletion in clox only in a tiny edge case in the VM. But if you want to actually understand how to completely implement a hash table, this feels important. I can sympathize with their desire to overlook it. As we'll see, deleting from a hash table that uses open addressing is tricky.

At least the declaration is simple.

With separate chaining, deleting is as easy as removing a node from a linked list.

```
bool tableSet(Table* table, ObjString* key, Value value);
bool tableDelete(Table* table, ObjString* key);
void tableAddAll(Table* from, Table* to);
```

**table.h**
*add after* tableSet()

The obvious approach is to mirror insertion. Use `findEntry()` to look up the entry's bucket. Then clear out the bucket. Done!

In cases where there are no collisions, that works fine. But if a collision has occurred, then the bucket where the entry lives may be part of one or more implicit probe sequences. For example, here's a hash table containing three keys all with the same preferred bucket, 2:

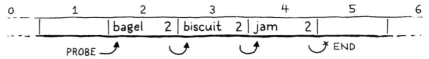

Remember that when we're walking a probe sequence to find an entry, we know we've reached the end of a sequence and that the entry isn't present when we hit an empty bucket. It's like the probe sequence is a list of entries and an empty entry terminates that list.

If we delete "biscuit" by simply clearing the Entry, then we break that probe sequence in the middle, leaving the trailing entries orphaned and unreachable. Sort of like removing a node from a linked list without relinking the pointer from the previous node to the next one.

If we later try to look for "jam", we'd start at "bagel", stop at the next empty Entry, and never find it.

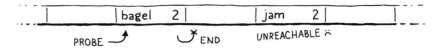

To solve this, most implementations use a trick called **tombstones**. Instead of clearing the entry on deletion, we replace it with a special sentinel entry called a "tombstone". When we are following a probe sequence during a lookup, and we hit a tombstone, we *don't* treat it like an empty slot and stop iterating. Instead, we keep going so that deleting an entry doesn't break any implicit collision chains and we can still find entries after it.

The code looks like this:

*table.c*
*add after* `tableSet()`

```c
bool tableDelete(Table* table, ObjString* key) {
  if (table->count == 0) return false;

  // Find the entry.
  Entry* entry = findEntry(table->entries, table->capacity, key);
  if (entry->key == NULL) return false;

  // Place a tombstone in the entry.
  entry->key = NULL;
  entry->value = BOOL_VAL(true);
  return true;
}
```

First, we find the bucket containing the entry we want to delete. (If we don't find it, there's nothing to delete, so we bail out.) We replace the entry with a tombstone. In clox, we use a NULL key and a true value to represent that, but any representation that can't be confused with an empty bucket or a valid entry works.

That's all we need to do to delete an entry. Simple and fast. But all of the other operations need to correctly handle tombstones too. A tombstone is a sort of "half" entry. It has some of the characteristics of a present entry, and some of the characteristics of an empty one.

When we are following a probe sequence during a lookup, and we hit a tombstone, we note it and keep going.

```
for (;;) {
  Entry* entry = &entries[index];
  if (entry->key == NULL) {
    if (IS_NIL(entry->value)) {
      // Empty entry.
      return tombstone != NULL ? tombstone : entry;
    } else {
      // We found a tombstone.
      if (tombstone == NULL) tombstone = entry;
    }
  } else if (entry->key == key) {
    // We found the key.
    return entry;
  }

  index = (index + 1) % capacity;
```

table.c
in findEntry()
replace 3 lines

The first time we pass a tombstone, we store it in this local variable:

```
  uint32_t index = key->hash % capacity;
  Entry* tombstone = NULL;

  for (;;) {
```

table.c
in findEntry()

If we reach a truly empty entry, then the key isn't present. In that case, if we have passed a tombstone, we return its bucket instead of the later empty one. If we're calling findEntry() in order to insert a node, that lets us treat the tombstone bucket as empty and reuse it for the new entry.

Reusing tombstone slots automatically like this helps reduce the number of tombstones wasting space in the bucket array. In typical use cases where there is a mixture of insertions and deletions, the number of tombstones grows for a while and then tends to stabilize.

Even so, there's no guarantee that a large number of deletes won't cause the array to be full of tombstones. In the very worst case, we could end up with *no* empty buckets. That would be bad because, remember, the only thing preventing an infinite loop in findEntry() is the assumption that we'll eventually hit an empty bucket.

So we need to be thoughtful about how tombstones interact with the table's load factor and resizing. The key question is, when calculating the load factor, should we treat tombstones like full buckets or empty ones?

### 20.4.6  Counting tombstones

If we treat tombstones like full buckets, then we may end up with a bigger array than we probably need because it artificially inflates the load factor. There are tombstones we could reuse, but they aren't treated as unused so we end up growing the array prematurely.

But if we treat tombstones like empty buckets and *don't* include them in the load factor, then we run the risk of ending up with *no* actual empty buckets to terminate a lookup. An infinite loop is a much worse problem than a few extra array slots, so for load factor, we consider tombstones to be full buckets.

That's why we don't reduce the count when deleting an entry in the previous code. The count is no longer the number of entries in the hash table, it's the number of entries plus tombstones. That implies that we increment the count during insertion only if the new entry goes into an entirely empty bucket.

table.c<br>in tableSet()<br>replace 1 line

```
bool isNewKey = entry->key == NULL;
if (isNewKey && IS_NIL(entry->value)) table->count++;

entry->key = key;
```

If we are replacing a tombstone with a new entry, the bucket has already been accounted for and the count doesn't change.

When we resize the array, we allocate a new array and re-insert all of the existing entries into it. During that process, we *don't* copy the tombstones over. They don't add any value since we're rebuilding the probe sequences anyway, and would just slow down lookups. That means we need to recalculate the count since it may change during a resize. So we clear it out:

table.c<br>in adjustCapacity()

```
  }

  table->count = 0;
  for (int i = 0; i < table->capacity; i++) {
```

Then each time we find a non-tombstone entry, we increment it.

table.c<br>in adjustCapacity()

```
    dest->value = entry->value;
    table->count++;
  }
```

This means that when we grow the capacity, we may end up with *fewer* entries in the resulting larger array because all of the tombstones get discarded. That's a little wasteful, but not a huge practical problem.

I find it interesting that much of the work to support deleting entries is in findEntry() and adjustCapacity(). The actual delete logic is quite simple and fast. In practice, deletions tend to be rare, so you'd expect a hash table to do as much work as it can in the delete function and leave the other functions alone to keep them faster. With our tombstone approach, deletes are fast, but lookups get penalized.

I did a little benchmarking to test this out in a few different deletion scenarios. I was surprised to discover that tombstones did end up being faster overall compared to doing all the work during deletion to reinsert the affected entries.

But if you think about it, it's not that the tombstone approach pushes the work of fully deleting an entry to other operations, it's more that it makes deleting *lazy*. At first, it does the minimal work to turn the entry into a tombstone. That can cause a penalty when later lookups have to skip over it. But it also allows that tombstone bucket to be reused by a later insert too. That reuse is a very efficient way to avoid the cost of rearranging all of the following affected entries. You basically recycle a node in the chain of probed entries. It's a neat trick.

## 20.5  String Interning

We've got ourselves a hash table that mostly works, though it has a critical flaw in its center. Also, we aren't using it for anything yet. It's time to address both of those and, in the process, learn a classic technique used by interpreters.

The reason the hash table doesn't totally work is that when `findEntry()` checks to see if an existing key matches the one it's looking for, it uses `==` to compare two strings for equality. That only returns true if the two keys are the exact same string in memory. Two separate strings with the same characters should be considered equal, but aren't.

Remember, back when we added strings in the last chapter, we added explicit support to compare the strings character-by-character in order to get true value equality. We could do that in `findEntry()`, but that's slow.

Instead, we'll use a technique called **string interning**. The core problem is that it's possible to have different strings in memory with the same characters. Those need to behave like equivalent values even though they are distinct objects. They're essentially duplicates, and we have to compare all of their bytes to detect that.

String interning is a process of deduplication. We create a collection of "interned" strings. Any string in that collection is guaranteed to be textually distinct from all others. When you intern a string, you look for a matching string in the collection. If found, you use that original one. Otherwise, the string you have is unique, so you add it to the collection.

In this way, you know that each sequence of characters is represented by only one string in memory. This makes value equality trivial. If two strings point to the same address in memory, they are obviously the same string and must be equal. And, because we know strings are unique, if two strings point to different addresses, they must be distinct strings.

Thus, pointer equality exactly matches value equality. Which in turn means that our existing `==` in `findEntry()` does the right thing. Or, at least, it will once we intern all the strings. In order to reliably deduplicate all strings, the VM needs to be able to find every string that's created. We do that by giving it a hash table to store them all.

In practice, we would first compare the hash codes of the two strings. That quickly detects almost all different strings—it wouldn't be a very good hash function if it didn't. But when the two hashes are the same, we still have to compare characters to make sure we didn't have a hash collision on different strings.

I'm guessing "intern" is short for "internal". I think the idea is that the language's runtime keeps its own "internal" collection of these strings, whereas other strings could be user created and floating around in memory. When you intern a string, you ask the runtime to add the string to that internal collection and return a pointer to it.

Languages vary in how much string interning they do and how it's exposed to the user. Lua interns *all* strings, which is what clox will do too. Lisp, Scheme, Smalltalk, Ruby and others have a separate string-like type called "symbol" that is implicitly interned. (This is why they say symbols are "faster" in Ruby.) Java interns constant strings by default, and provides an API to let you explicitly intern any string you give it.

```
  Value* stackTop;
  Table strings;
  Obj* objects;
```

**vm.h**
*in struct VM*

As usual, we need an include.

```
#include "chunk.h"
#include "table.h"
#include "value.h"
```

**vm.h**

When we spin up a new VM, the string table is empty.

vm.c<br>in initVM()

```
vm.objects = NULL;
  initTable(&vm.strings);
}
```

And when we shut down the VM, we clean up any resources used by the table.

vm.c<br>in freeVM()

```
void freeVM() {
  freeTable(&vm.strings);
  freeObjects();
```

Some languages have a separate type or an explicit step to intern a string. For clox, we'll automatically intern every one. That means whenever we create a new unique string, we add it to the table.

object.c<br>in allocateString()

```
string->hash = hash;
  tableSet(&vm.strings, string, NIL_VAL);
  return string;
```

We're using the table more like a hash *set* than a hash *table*. The keys are the strings and those are all we care about, so we just use nil for the values.

This gets a string into the table assuming that it's unique, but we need to actually check for duplication before we get here. We do that in the two higher-level functions that call allocateString(). Here's one:

object.c<br>in copyString()

```
uint32_t hash = hashString(chars, length);
  ObjString* interned = tableFindString(&vm.strings, chars, length,
                                         hash);
  if (interned != NULL) return interned;

  char* heapChars = ALLOCATE(char, length + 1);
```

When copying a string into a new LoxString, we look it up in the string table first. If we find it, instead of "copying", we just return a reference to that string. Otherwise, we fall through, allocate a new string, and store it in the string table.

Taking ownership of a string is a little different.

object.c<br>in takeString()

```
uint32_t hash = hashString(chars, length);
  ObjString* interned = tableFindString(&vm.strings, chars, length,
                                         hash);
  if (interned != NULL) {
    FREE_ARRAY(char, chars, length + 1);
    return interned;
  }

  return allocateString(chars, length, hash);
```

Again, we look up the string in the string table first. If we find it, before we return it, we free the memory for the string that was passed in. Since ownership is being passed to this function and we no longer need the duplicate string, it's up to us to free it.

Before we get to the new function we need to write, there's one more include.

```
#include "object.h"
#include "table.h"
#include "value.h"
```
object.c

To look for a string in the table, we can't use the normal `tableGet()` function because that calls `findEntry()`, which has the exact problem with duplicate strings that we're trying to fix right now. Instead, we use this new function:

```
void tableAddAll(Table* from, Table* to);
ObjString* tableFindString(Table* table, const char* chars,
                           int length, uint32_t hash);

#endif
```
table.h
*add after* tableAddAll()

The implementation looks like so:

```
ObjString* tableFindString(Table* table, const char* chars,
                           int length, uint32_t hash) {
  if (table->count == 0) return NULL;

  uint32_t index = hash % table->capacity;
  for (;;) {
    Entry* entry = &table->entries[index];
    if (entry->key == NULL) {
      // Stop if we find an empty non-tombstone entry.
      if (IS_NIL(entry->value)) return NULL;
    } else if (entry->key->length == length &&
        entry->key->hash == hash &&
        memcmp(entry->key->chars, chars, length) == 0) {
      // We found it.
      return entry->key;
    }

    index = (index + 1) % table->capacity;
  }
}
```
table.c
*add after* tableAddAll()

It appears we have copy-pasted `findEntry()`. There is a lot of redundancy, but also a couple of key differences. First, we pass in the raw character array of the key we're looking for instead of an ObjString. At the point that we call this, we haven't created an ObjString yet.

Second, when checking to see if we found the key, we look at the actual strings. We first see if they have matching lengths and hashes. Those are quick to check and if they aren't equal, the strings definitely aren't the same.

If there is a hash collision, we do an actual character-by-character string comparison. This is the one place in the VM where we actually test strings for textual equality. We do it here to deduplicate strings and then the rest of the VM can take for granted that any two strings at different addresses in memory must have different contents.

In fact, now that we've interned all the strings, we can take advantage of it in the bytecode interpreter. When a user does == on two objects that happen to be strings, we don't need to test the characters any more.

**value.c**
*in* valuesEqual()
*replace 7 lines*

```
  case VAL_NUMBER: return AS_NUMBER(a) == AS_NUMBER(b);
  case VAL_OBJ:    return AS_OBJ(a) == AS_OBJ(b);
  default:         return false; // Unreachable.
```

We've added a little overhead when creating strings to intern them. But in return, at runtime, the equality operator on strings is much faster. With that, we have a full-featured hash table ready for us to use for tracking variables, instances, or any other key-value pairs that might show up.

We also sped up testing strings for equality. This is nice for when the user does == on strings. But it's even more critical in a dynamically typed language like Lox where method calls and instance fields are looked up by name at runtime. If testing a string for equality is slow, then that means looking up a method by name is slow. And if *that's* slow in your object-oriented language, then *everything* is slow.

> Well, at least that wasn't the *only* reason they were created. Whether that was the *main* reason is up for debate.

## CHALLENGES

1. In clox, we happen to only need keys that are strings, so the hash table we built is hardcoded for that key type. If we exposed hash tables to Lox users as a first-class collection, it would be useful to support different kinds of keys.

   Add support for keys of the other primitive types: numbers, Booleans, and nil. Later, clox will support user-defined classes. If we want to support keys that are instances of those classes, what kind of complexity does that add?

2. Hash tables have a lot of knobs you can tweak that affect their performance. You decide whether to use separate chaining or open addressing. Depending on which fork in that road you take, you can tune how many entries are stored in each node, or the probing strategy you use. You control the hash function, load factor, and growth rate.

   All of this variety wasn't created just to give CS doctoral candidates something to publish theses on: each has its uses in the many varied domains and hardware scenarios where hashing comes into play. Look up a few hash table implementations in different open source systems, research the choices they made, and try to figure out why they did things that way.

3. Benchmarking a hash table is notoriously difficult. A hash table implementation may perform well with some keysets and poorly with others. It may work well at small sizes but degrade as it grows, or vice versa. It may choke when deletions are common, but fly when they aren't. Creating benchmarks that accurately represent how your users will use the hash table is a challenge.

   Write a handful of different benchmark programs to validate our hash table implementation. How does the performance vary between them? Why did you choose the specific test cases you chose?

# Global Variables

21

*"If only there could be an invention that bottled up a memory, like scent. And it never faded, and it never got stale. And then, when one wanted it, the bottle could be uncorked, and it would be like living the moment all over again."*

— Daphne du Maurier, *Rebecca*

The previous chapter was a long exploration of one big, deep, fundamental computer science data structure. Heavy on theory and concept. There may have been some discussion of big-O notation and algorithms. This chapter has fewer intellectual pretensions. There are no large ideas to learn. Instead, it's a handful of straightforward engineering tasks. Once we've completed them, our virtual machine will support variables.

Actually, it will support only *global* variables. Locals are coming in the next chapter. In jlox, we managed to cram them both into a single chapter because we used the same implementation technique for all variables. We built a chain of environments, one for each scope, all the way up to the top. That was a simple, clean way to learn how to manage state.

But it's also *slow*. Allocating a hash table each time you enter a block or call a function is not the road to a fast VM. Given how much code uses variables, if variables go slow, everything goes slow. For clox, we'll improve that by using a more efficient strategy for local variables, but globals aren't as easily optimized.

This is a common meta-strategy in sophisticated language implementations. Often, the same language feature will have multiple implementation techniques, each tuned for different use patterns. For example, JavaScript VMs often have a faster representation for objects that are used more like instances of classes compared to other objects whose set of properties is more freely modified. C and C++ compilers usually have a variety of ways to compile `switch` statements based on the number of cases and how densely packed the case values are.

A quick refresher on Lox semantics: Global variables in Lox are "late bound", or resolved dynamically. This means you can compile a chunk of code that refers to a global variable before it's defined. As long as the code doesn't *execute* before the definition happens, everything is fine. In practice, that means you can refer to later variables inside the body of functions.

```
fun showVariable() {
  print global;
}

var global = "after";
showVariable();
```

Code like this might seem odd, but it's handy for defining mutually recursive functions. It also plays nicer with the REPL. You can write a little function in one line, then define the variable it uses in the next.

Local variables work differently. Since a local variable's declaration *always* occurs before it is used, the VM can resolve them at compile time, even in a simple single-pass compiler. That will let us use a smarter representation for locals. But that's for the next chapter. Right now, let's just worry about globals.

## 21.1  Statements

Variables come into being using variable declarations, which means now is also the time to add support for statements to our compiler. If you recall, Lox splits statements into two categories. "Declarations" are those statements that bind a new name to a value. The other kinds of statements—control flow, print, etc.— are just called "statements". We disallow declarations directly inside control flow statements, like this:

```
if (monday) var croissant = "yes"; // Error.
```

Allowing it would raise confusing questions around the scope of the variable. So, like other languages, we prohibit it syntactically by having a separate grammar rule for the subset of statements that *are* allowed inside a control flow body.

```
statement        → exprStmt
                 | forStmt
                 | ifStmt
                 | printStmt
                 | returnStmt
                 | whileStmt
                 | block ;
```

Then we use a separate rule for the top level of a script and inside a block.

```
declaration      → classDecl
                 | funDecl
                 | varDecl
                 | statement ;
```

The `declaration` rule contains the statements that declare names, and also includes `statement` so that all statement types are allowed. Since `block` itself is in `statement`, you can put declarations inside a control flow construct by nesting them inside a block.

In this chapter, we'll cover only a couple of statements and one declaration.

```
statement       → exprStmt
                | printStmt ;

declaration     → varDecl
                | statement ;
```

Blocks work sort of like parentheses do for expressions. A block lets you put the "lower-precedence" declaration statements in places where only a "higher-precedence" non-declaring statement is allowed.

Up to now, our VM considered a "program" to be a single expression since that's all we could parse and compile. In a full Lox implementation, a program is a sequence of declarations. We're ready to support that now.

```
  advance();

  while (!match(TOKEN_EOF)) {
    declaration();
  }

  endCompiler();
```

compiler.c
*in* compile()
*replace 2 lines*

We keep compiling declarations until we hit the end of the source file. We compile a single declaration using this:

```
static void declaration() {
  statement();
}
```

compiler.c
*add after* expression()

We'll get to variable declarations later in the chapter, so for now, we simply forward to `statement()`.

```
static void statement() {
  if (match(TOKEN_PRINT)) {
    printStatement();
  }
}
```

compiler.c
*add after* declaration()

Blocks can contain declarations, and control flow statements can contain other statements. That means these two functions will eventually be recursive. We may as well write out the forward declarations now.

```
static void expression();
static void statement();
static void declaration();
static ParseRule* getRule(TokenType type);
```

compiler.c
*add after* expression()

### 21.1.1 Print statements

We have two statement types to support in this chapter. Let's start with `print` statements, which begin, naturally enough, with a `print` token. We detect that using this helper function:

compiler.c<br>add after consume()

```c
static bool match(TokenType type) {
  if (!check(type)) return false;
  advance();
  return true;
}
```

You may recognize it from jlox. If the current token has the given type, we consume the token and return `true`. Otherwise we leave the token alone and return `false`. This helper function is implemented in terms of this other helper:

It's helpers all the way down!

compiler.c<br>add after consume()

```c
static bool check(TokenType type) {
  return parser.current.type == type;
}
```

The `check()` function returns `true` if the current token has the given type. It seems a little silly to wrap this in a function, but we'll use it more later, and I think short verb-named functions like this make the parser easier to read.

This sounds trivial, but handwritten parsers for non-toy languages get pretty big. When you have thousands of lines of code, a utility function that turns two lines into one and makes the result a little more readable easily earns its keep.

If we did match the `print` token, then we compile the rest of the statement here:

compiler.c<br>add after expression()

```c
static void printStatement() {
  expression();
  consume(TOKEN_SEMICOLON, "Expect ';' after value.");
  emitByte(OP_PRINT);
}
```

A `print` statement evaluates an expression and prints the result, so we first parse and compile that expression. The grammar expects a semicolon after that, so we consume it. Finally, we emit a new instruction to print the result.

chunk.h<br>in enum OpCode

```c
  OP_NEGATE,
  OP_PRINT,
  OP_RETURN,
```

At runtime, we execute this instruction like so:

vm.c<br>in run()

```c
        break;
      case OP_PRINT: {
        printValue(pop());
        printf("\n");
        break;
      }
      case OP_RETURN: {
```

When the interpreter reaches this instruction, it has already executed the code for the expression, leaving the result value on top of the stack. Now we simply pop and print it.

Note that we don't push anything else after that. This is a key difference between expressions and statements in the VM. Every bytecode instruction has a **stack effect** that describes how the instruction modifies the stack. For example, OP_ADD pops two values and pushes one, leaving the stack one element smaller than before.

You can sum the stack effects of a series of instructions to get their total effect. When you add the stack effects of the series of instructions compiled from any complete expression, it will total one. Each expression leaves one result value on the stack.

The bytecode for an entire statement has a total stack effect of zero. Since a statement produces no values, it ultimately leaves the stack unchanged, though it of course uses the stack while it's doing its thing. This is important because when we get to control flow and looping, a program might execute a long series of statements. If each statement grew or shrank the stack, it might eventually overflow or underflow.

While we're in the interpreter loop, we should delete a bit of code.

> The stack is one element shorter after an OP_ADD, so its effect is -1:

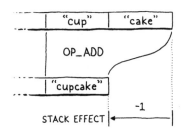

```
    case OP_RETURN: {
      // Exit interpreter.
      return INTERPRET_OK;
```

> **vm.c**
> *in* run()
> *replace 2 lines*

When the VM only compiled and evaluated a single expression, we had some temporary code in OP_RETURN to output the value. Now that we have statements and `print`, we don't need that anymore. We're one step closer to the complete implementation of clox.

As usual, a new instruction needs support in the disassembler.

> We're only one step closer, though. We will revisit **OP_RETURN** again when we add functions. Right now, it exits the entire interpreter loop.

```
      return simpleInstruction("OP_NEGATE", offset);
    case OP_PRINT:
      return simpleInstruction("OP_PRINT", offset);
    case OP_RETURN:
```

> **debug.c**
> *in* disassembleInstruction()

That's our `print` statement. If you want, give it a whirl:

```
print 1 + 2;
print 3 * 4;
```

Exciting! OK, maybe not thrilling, but we can build scripts that contain as many statements as we want now, which feels like progress.

## 21.1.2  Expression statements

Wait until you see the next statement. If we *don't* see a `print` keyword, then we must be looking at an expression statement.

```
    printStatement();
  } else {
    expressionStatement();
  }
```

> **compiler.c**
> *in* statement()

It's parsed like so:

compiler.c
*add after* expression()

```
static void expressionStatement() {
  expression();
  consume(TOKEN_SEMICOLON, "Expect ';' after expression.");
  emitByte(OP_POP);
}
```

An "expression statement" is simply an expression followed by a semicolon. They're how you write an expression in a context where a statement is expected. Usually, it's so that you can call a function or evaluate an assignment for its side effect, like this:

```
brunch = "quiche";
eat(brunch);
```

Semantically, an expression statement evaluates the expression and discards the result. The compiler directly encodes that behavior. It compiles the expression, and then emits an OP_POP instruction.

chunk.h
*in enum* OpCode

```
  OP_FALSE,
  OP_POP,
  OP_EQUAL,
```

As the name implies, that instruction pops the top value off the stack and forgets it.

vm.c
*in* run()

```
    case OP_FALSE: push(BOOL_VAL(false)); break;
    case OP_POP: pop(); break;
    case OP_EQUAL: {
```

We can disassemble it too.

debug.c
*in* disassembleInstruction()

```
    return simpleInstruction("OP_FALSE", offset);
  case OP_POP:
    return simpleInstruction("OP_POP", offset);
  case OP_EQUAL:
```

Expression statements aren't very useful yet since we can't create any expressions that have side effects, but they'll be essential when we add functions later. The majority of statements in real-world code in languages like C are expression statements.

By my count, 80 of the 149 statements, in the version of "compiler.c" that we have at the end of this chapter are expression statements.

### 21.1.3  Error synchronization

While we're getting this initial work done in the compiler, we can tie off a loose end we left several chapters back. Like jlox, clox uses panic mode error recovery to minimize the number of cascaded compile errors that it reports. The compiler exits panic mode when it reaches a synchronization point. For Lox, we chose statement boundaries as that point. Now that we have statements, we can implement synchronization.

```
  statement();

  if (parser.panicMode) synchronize();
}
```

compiler.c
in declaration()

If we hit a compile error while parsing the previous statement, we enter panic mode. When that happens, after the statement we start synchronizing.

```
static void synchronize() {
  parser.panicMode = false;

  while (parser.current.type != TOKEN_EOF) {
    if (parser.previous.type == TOKEN_SEMICOLON) return;
    switch (parser.current.type) {
      case TOKEN_CLASS:
      case TOKEN_FUN:
      case TOKEN_VAR:
      case TOKEN_FOR:
      case TOKEN_IF:
      case TOKEN_WHILE:
      case TOKEN_PRINT:
      case TOKEN_RETURN:
        return;

      default:
        ; // Do nothing.
    }

    advance();
  }
}
```

compiler.c
add after printStatement()

We skip tokens indiscriminately until we reach something that looks like a statement boundary. We recognize the boundary by looking for a preceding token that can end a statement, like a semicolon. Or we'll look for a subsequent token that begins a statement, usually one of the control flow or declaration keywords.

## 21.2  Variable Declarations

Merely being able to *print* doesn't win your language any prizes at the programming language fair, so let's move on to something a little more ambitious and get variables going. There are three operations we need to support:

- Declaring a new variable using a `var` statement.

- Accessing the value of a variable using an identifier expression.

- Storing a new value in an existing variable using an assignment expression.

We can't do either of the last two until we have some variables, so we start with

I can't help but imagine a "language fair" like some country 4H thing. Rows of straw-lined stalls full of baby languages *mooing* and *baaing* at each other.

declarations.

compiler.c
*in* declaration()
*replace 1 line*

```
static void declaration() {
  if (match(TOKEN_VAR)) {
    varDeclaration();
  } else {
    statement();
  }

  if (parser.panicMode) synchronize();
```

The placeholder parsing function we sketched out for the declaration grammar rule has an actual production now. If we match a var token, we jump here:

compiler.c
*add after* expression()

```
static void varDeclaration() {
  uint8_t global = parseVariable("Expect variable name.");

  if (match(TOKEN_EQUAL)) {
    expression();
  } else {
    emitByte(OP_NIL);
  }
  consume(TOKEN_SEMICOLON,
          "Expect ';' after variable declaration.");

  defineVariable(global);
}
```

Essentially, the compiler desugars a variable declaration like:

var a;

into:

var a = nil;

The code it generates for both is identical.

The keyword is followed by the variable name. That's compiled by parseVariable(), which we'll get to in a second. Then we look for an = followed by an initializer expression. If the user doesn't initialize the variable, the compiler implicitly initializes it to nil by emitting an OP_NIL instruction. Either way, we expect the statement to be terminated with a semicolon.

There are two new functions here for working with variables and identifiers. Here is the first:

compiler.c
*add after* parsePrecedence()

```
static void parsePrecedence(Precedence precedence);

static uint8_t parseVariable(const char* errorMessage) {
  consume(TOKEN_IDENTIFIER, errorMessage);
  return identifierConstant(&parser.previous);
}
```

It requires the next token to be an identifier, which it consumes and sends here:

compiler.c
*add after* parsePrecedence()

```
static void parsePrecedence(Precedence precedence);

static uint8_t identifierConstant(Token* name) {
  return makeConstant(OBJ_VAL(copyString(name->start,
                                         name->length)));
}
```

This function takes the given token and adds its lexeme to the chunk's constant table as a string. It then returns the index of that constant in the constant table.

Global variables are looked up *by name* at runtime. That means the VM—the bytecode interpreter loop—needs access to the name. A whole string is too big to stuff into the bytecode stream as an operand. Instead, we store the string in the constant table and the instruction then refers to the name by its index in the table.

This function returns that index all the way to `varDeclaration()` which later hands it over to here:

```
static void defineVariable(uint8_t global) {
  emitBytes(OP_DEFINE_GLOBAL, global);
}
```

compiler.c
*add after* parseVariable()

This outputs the bytecode instruction that defines the new variable and stores its initial value. The index of the variable's name in the constant table is the instruction's operand. As usual in a stack-based VM, we emit this instruction last. At runtime, we execute the code for the variable's initializer first. That leaves the value on the stack. Then this instruction takes that value and stores it away for later.

Over in the runtime, we begin with this new instruction:

I know some of these functions seem pretty pointless right now. But we'll get more mileage out of them as we add more language features for working with names. Function and class declarations both declare new variables, and variable and assignment expressions access them.

```
  OP_POP,
  OP_DEFINE_GLOBAL,
  OP_EQUAL,
```

chunk.h
*in enum* OpCode

Thanks to our handy-dandy hash table, the implementation isn't too hard.

```
    case OP_POP: pop(); break;
    case OP_DEFINE_GLOBAL: {
      ObjString* name = READ_STRING();
      tableSet(&vm.globals, name, peek(0));
      pop();
      break;
    }
    case OP_EQUAL: {
```

vm.c
*in* run()

We get the name of the variable from the constant table. Then we take the value from the top of the stack and store it in a hash table with that name as the key.

This code doesn't check to see if the key is already in the table. Lox is pretty lax with global variables and lets you redefine them without error. That's useful in a REPL session, so the VM supports that by simply overwriting the value if the key happens to already be in the hash table.

There's another little helper macro:

Note that we don't *pop* the value until *after* we add it to the hash table. That ensures the VM can still find the value if a garbage collection is triggered right in the middle of adding it to the hash table. That's a distinct possibility since the hash table requires dynamic allocation when it resizes.

```
#define READ_CONSTANT() (vm.chunk->constants.values[READ_BYTE()])
#define READ_STRING() AS_STRING(READ_CONSTANT())
#define BINARY_OP(valueType, op) \
```

vm.c
*in* run()

It reads a one-byte operand from the bytecode chunk. It treats that as an index into the chunk's constant table and returns the string at that index. It doesn't check that the value *is* a string—it just indiscriminately casts it. That's safe because the compiler never emits an instruction that refers to a non-string constant.

Because we care about lexical hygiene, we also undefine this macro at the end of the interpret function.

vm.c<br/>in <code>run()</code>

```
#undef READ_CONSTANT
#undef READ_STRING
#undef BINARY_OP
```

I keep saying "the hash table", but we don't actually have one yet. We need a place to store these globals. Since we want them to persist as long as clox is running, we store them right in the VM.

vm.h<br/>in struct VM

```
  Value* stackTop;
  Table globals;
  Table strings;
```

As we did with the string table, we need to initialize the hash table to a valid state when the VM boots up.

vm.c<br/>in <code>initVM()</code>

```
  vm.objects = NULL;

  initTable(&vm.globals);
  initTable(&vm.strings);
```

And we tear it down when we exit.

vm.c<br/>in <code>freeVM()</code>

```
void freeVM() {
  freeTable(&vm.globals);
  freeTable(&vm.strings);
```

As usual, we want to be able to disassemble the new instruction too.

debug.c<br/>in <code>disassembleInstruction()</code>

```
      return simpleInstruction("OP_POP", offset);
    case OP_DEFINE_GLOBAL:
      return constantInstruction("OP_DEFINE_GLOBAL", chunk,
                                 offset);
    case OP_EQUAL:
```

And with that, we can define global variables. Not that users can *tell* that they've done so, because they can't actually *use* them. So let's fix that next.

## 21.3  Reading Variables

As in every programming language ever, we access a variable's value using its name. We hook up identifier tokens to the expression parser here:

compiler.c<br/>replace 1 line

```
  [TOKEN_LESS_EQUAL]    = {NULL,     binary, PREC_COMPARISON},
  [TOKEN_IDENTIFIER]    = {variable, NULL,   PREC_NONE},
  [TOKEN_STRING]        = {string,   NULL,   PREC_NONE},
```

That calls this new parser function:

```
static void variable() {
  namedVariable(parser.previous);
}
```

compiler.c
add after string()

Like with declarations, there are a couple of tiny helper functions that seem pointless now but will become more useful in later chapters. I promise.

```
static void namedVariable(Token name) {
  uint8_t arg = identifierConstant(&name);
  emitBytes(OP_GET_GLOBAL, arg);
}
```

compiler.c
add after string()

This calls the same `identifierConstant()` function from before to take the given identifier token and add its lexeme to the chunk's constant table as a string. All that remains is to emit an instruction that loads the global variable with that name. Here's the instruction:

```
  OP_POP,
  OP_GET_GLOBAL,
  OP_DEFINE_GLOBAL,
```

chunk.h
in enum OpCode

Over in the interpreter, the implementation mirrors `OP_DEFINE_GLOBAL`.

```
      case OP_POP: pop(); break;
      case OP_GET_GLOBAL: {
        ObjString* name = READ_STRING();
        Value value;
        if (!tableGet(&vm.globals, name, &value)) {
          runtimeError("Undefined variable '%s'.", name->chars);
          return INTERPRET_RUNTIME_ERROR;
        }
        push(value);
        break;
      }
      case OP_DEFINE_GLOBAL: {
```

vm.c
in run()

We pull the constant table index from the instruction's operand and get the variable name. Then we use that as a key to look up the variable's value in the globals hash table.

If the key isn't present in the hash table, it means that global variable has never been defined. That's a runtime error in Lox, so we report it and exit the interpreter loop if that happens. Otherwise, we take the value and push it onto the stack.

```
      return simpleInstruction("OP_POP", offset);
    case OP_GET_GLOBAL:
      return constantInstruction("OP_GET_GLOBAL", chunk, offset);
    case OP_DEFINE_GLOBAL:
```

debug.c
in disassembleInstruction()

A little bit of disassembling, and we're done. Our interpreter is now able to run code like this:

```
var beverage = "cafe au lait";
var breakfast = "beignets with " + beverage;
print breakfast;
```

There's only one operation left.

## 21.4 Assignment

If you recall, assignment was pretty easy in jlox.

Throughout this book, I've tried to keep you on a fairly safe and easy path. I don't avoid hard *problems*, but I try to not make the *solutions* more complex than they need to be. Alas, other design choices in our bytecode compiler make assignment annoying to implement.

Our bytecode VM uses a single-pass compiler. It parses and generates bytecode on the fly without any intermediate AST. As soon as it recognizes a piece of syntax, it emits code for it. Assignment doesn't naturally fit that. Consider:

```
menu.brunch(sunday).beverage = "mimosa";
```

In this code, the parser doesn't realize `menu.brunch(sunday).beverage` is the target of an assignment and not a normal expression until it reaches =, many tokens after the first `menu`. By then, the compiler has already emitted bytecode for the whole thing.

The problem is not as dire as it might seem, though. Look at how the parser sees that example:

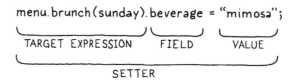

Even though the `.beverage` part must not be compiled as a get expression, everything to the left of the `.` is an expression, with the normal expression semantics. The `menu.brunch(sunday)` part can be compiled and executed as usual.

Fortunately for us, the only semantic differences on the left side of an assignment appear at the very right-most end of the tokens, immediately preceding the =. Even though the receiver of a setter may be an arbitrarily long expression, the part whose behavior differs from a get expression is only the trailing identifier, which is right before the =. We don't need much lookahead to realize `beverage` should be compiled as a set expression and not a getter.

Variables are even easier since they are just a single bare identifier before an =. The idea then is that right *before* compiling an expression that can also be used as an assignment target, we look for a subsequent = token. If we see one, we compile it as an assignment or setter instead of a variable access or getter.

We don't have setters to worry about yet, so all we need to handle are variables.

```
  uint8_t arg = identifierConstant(&name);

  if (match(TOKEN_EQUAL)) {
    expression();
    emitBytes(OP_SET_GLOBAL, arg);
  } else {
    emitBytes(OP_GET_GLOBAL, arg);
  }
}
```

**compiler.c**
*in* namedVariable()
*replace 1 line*

In the parse function for identifier expressions, we look for an equals sign after the identifier. If we find one, instead of emitting code for a variable access, we compile the assigned value and then emit an assignment instruction.

That's the last instruction we need to add in this chapter.

```
  OP_DEFINE_GLOBAL,
  OP_SET_GLOBAL,
  OP_EQUAL,
```

**chunk.h**
*in enum* OpCode

As you'd expect, its runtime behavior is similar to defining a new variable.

```
      }
      case OP_SET_GLOBAL: {
        ObjString* name = READ_STRING();
        if (tableSet(&vm.globals, name, peek(0))) {
          tableDelete(&vm.globals, name);
          runtimeError("Undefined variable '%s'.", name->chars);
          return INTERPRET_RUNTIME_ERROR;
        }
        break;
      }
      case OP_EQUAL: {
```

**vm.c**
*in* run()

The call to **tableSet()** stores the value in the global variable table even if the variable wasn't previously defined. That fact is visible in a REPL session, since it keeps running even after the runtime error is reported. So we also take care to delete that zombie value from the table.

The main difference is what happens when the key doesn't already exist in the globals hash table. If the variable hasn't been defined yet, it's a runtime error to try to assign to it. Lox doesn't do implicit variable declaration.

The other difference is that setting a variable doesn't pop the value off the stack. Remember, assignment is an expression, so it needs to leave that value there in case the assignment is nested inside some larger expression.

Add a dash of disassembly:

```
      return constantInstruction("OP_DEFINE_GLOBAL", chunk,
                                 offset);
    case OP_SET_GLOBAL:
      return constantInstruction("OP_SET_GLOBAL", chunk, offset);
    case OP_EQUAL:
```

**debug.c**
*in* disassembleInstruction()

So we're done, right? Well...not quite. We've made a mistake! Take a gander at:

```
a * b = c + d;
```

According to Lox's grammar, = has the lowest precedence, so this should be parsed roughly like:

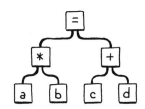

Wouldn't it be wild if a * b *was* a valid assignment target, though? You could imagine some algebra-like language that tried to divide the assigned value up in some reasonable way and distribute it to a and b…that's probably a terrible idea.

Obviously, a * b isn't a valid assignment target, so this should be a syntax error. But here's what our parser does:

1. First, `parsePrecedence()` parses a using the `variable()` prefix parser.

2. After that, it enters the infix parsing loop.

3. It reaches the * and calls `binary()`.

4. That recursively calls `parsePrecedence()` to parse the right operand.

5. That calls `variable()` again for parsing b.

6. Inside that call to `variable()`, it looks for a trailing =. It sees one and thus parses the rest of the line as an assignment.

In other words, the parser sees the above code like:

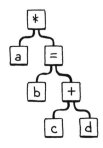

We've messed up the precedence handling because `variable()` doesn't take into account the precedence of the surrounding expression that contains the variable. If the variable happens to be the right-hand side of an infix operator, or the operand of a unary operator, then that containing expression is too high precedence to permit the =.

To fix this, `variable()` should look for and consume the = only if it's in the context of a low-precedence expression. The code that knows the current precedence is, logically enough, `parsePrecedence()`. The `variable()` function doesn't need to know the actual level. It just cares that the precedence is low enough to allow assignment, so we pass that fact in as a Boolean.

```
  }

  bool canAssign = precedence <= PREC_ASSIGNMENT;
  prefixRule(canAssign);

  while (precedence <= getRule(parser.current.type)->precedence) {
```

Since assignment is the lowest-precedence expression, the only time we allow an assignment is when parsing an assignment expression or top-level expression like in an expression statement. That flag makes its way to the parser function here:

```
static void variable(bool canAssign) {
  namedVariable(parser.previous, canAssign);
}
```

compiler.c
*function* variable()
*replace 3 lines*

Which passes it through a new parameter:

```
static void namedVariable(Token name, bool canAssign) {
  uint8_t arg = identifierConstant(&name);
```

compiler.c
*function* namedVariable()
*replace 1 line*

And then finally uses it here:

```
  uint8_t arg = identifierConstant(&name);

  if (canAssign && match(TOKEN_EQUAL)) {
    expression();
```

compiler.c
*in* namedVariable()
*replace 1 line*

That's a lot of plumbing to get literally one bit of data to the right place in the compiler, but arrived it has. If the variable is nested inside some expression with higher precedence, `canAssign` will be `false` and this will ignore the = even if there is one there. Then `namedVariable()` returns, and execution eventually makes its way back to `parsePrecedence()`.

Then what? What does the compiler do with our broken example from before? Right now, `variable()` won't consume the =, so that will be the current token. The compiler returns back to `parsePrecedence()` from the `variable()` prefix parser and then tries to enter the infix parsing loop. There is no parsing function associated with =, so it skips that loop.

Then `parsePrecedence()` silently returns back to the caller. That also isn't right. If the = doesn't get consumed as part of the expression, nothing else is going to consume it. It's an error and we should report it.

```
    infixRule();
  }

  if (canAssign && match(TOKEN_EQUAL)) {
    error("Invalid assignment target.");
  }
}
```

compiler.c
*in* parsePrecedence()

With that, the previous bad program correctly gets an error at compile time. OK, *now* are we done? Still not quite. See, we're passing an argument to one of the parse functions. But those functions are stored in a table of function pointers, so all of the parse functions need to have the same type. Even though most parse functions don't support being used as an assignment target—setters are the only other one—our friendly C compiler requires them *all* to accept the parameter.

So we're going to finish off this chapter with some grunt work. First, let's go ahead and pass the flag to the infix parse functions.

If Lox had arrays and subscript operators like `array[index]` then an infix `[` would also allow assignment to support `array[index] = value`.

compiler.c
*in* parsePrecedence()
*replace 1 line*

```
    ParseFn infixRule = getRule(parser.previous.type)->infix;
    infixRule(canAssign);
  }
```

We'll need that for setters eventually. Then we'll fix the typedef for the function type.

compiler.c
*add after enum* Precedence
*replace 1 line*

```
} Precedence;

typedef void (*ParseFn)(bool canAssign);

typedef struct {
```

And some completely tedious code to accept this parameter in all of our existing parse functions. Here:

compiler.c
*function* binary()
*replace 1 line*

```
static void binary(bool canAssign) {
  TokenType operatorType = parser.previous.type;
```

And here:

compiler.c
*function* literal()
*replace 1 line*

```
static void literal(bool canAssign) {
  switch (parser.previous.type) {
```

And here:

compiler.c
*function* grouping()
*replace 1 line*

```
static void grouping(bool canAssign) {
  expression();
```

And here:

compiler.c
*function* number()
*replace 1 line*

```
static void number(bool canAssign) {
  double value = strtod(parser.previous.start, NULL);
```

And here too:

compiler.c
*function* string()
*replace 1 line*

```
static void string(bool canAssign) {
  emitConstant(OBJ_VAL(copyString(parser.previous.start + 1,
```

And, finally:

compiler.c
*function* unary()
*replace 1 line*

```
static void unary(bool canAssign) {
  TokenType operatorType = parser.previous.type;
```

Phew! We're back to a C program we can compile. Fire it up and you can run this:

```
var breakfast = "beignets";
var beverage = "cafe au lait";
breakfast = "beignets with " + beverage;
print breakfast;
```

It's starting to look like real code for an actual language!

## CHALLENGES

1. The compiler adds a global variable's name to the constant table as a string every time an identifier is encountered. It creates a new constant each time, even if that variable name is already in a previous slot in the constant table. That's wasteful in cases where the same variable is referenced multiple times by the same function. That, in turn, increases the odds of filling up the constant table and running out of slots since we allow only 256 constants in a single chunk.

   Optimize this. How does your optimization affect the performance of the compiler compared to the runtime? Is this the right trade-off?

2. Looking up a global variable by name in a hash table each time it is used is pretty slow, even with a good hash table. Can you come up with a more efficient way to store and access global variables without changing the semantics?

3. When running in the REPL, a user might write a function that references an unknown global variable. Then, in the next line, they declare the variable. Lox should handle this gracefully by not reporting an "unknown variable" compile error when the function is first defined.

   But when a user runs a Lox *script*, the compiler has access to the full text of the entire program before any code is run. Consider this program:

```
fun useVar() {
  print oops;
}

var ooops = "too many o's!";
```

   Here, we can tell statically that **oops** will not be defined because there is *no* declaration of that global anywhere in the program. Note that **useVar()** is never called either, so even though the variable isn't defined, no runtime error will occur because it's never used either.

   We could report mistakes like this as compile errors, at least when running from a script. Do you think we should? Justify your answer. What do other scripting languages you know do?

# Local Variables

22

*"And as imagination bodies forth*
*The forms of things unknown, the poet's pen*
*Turns them to shapes and gives to airy nothing*
*A local habitation and a name."*

— William Shakespeare, *A Midsummer Night's Dream*

The last chapter introduced variables to clox, but only of the global variety. In this chapter, we'll add blocks, block scope, and local variables. In jlox, we managed to pack all of that and globals into one chapter. For clox, that's two chapters worth of work partially because, frankly, everything takes more effort in C.

There's probably some dumb "think globally, act locally" joke here, but I'm struggling to find it.

But an even more important reason is that our approach to local variables will be quite different from how we implemented globals. Global variables are late bound in Lox. "Late" in this context means "resolved after compile time". That's good for keeping the compiler simple, but not great for performance. Local variables are one of the most-used parts of a language. If locals are slow, *everything* is slow. So we want a strategy for local variables that's as efficient as possible.

Fortunately, lexical scoping is here to help us. As the name implies, lexical scope means we can resolve a local variable just by looking at the text of the program—locals are *not* late bound. Any processing work we do in the compiler is work we *don't* have to do at runtime, so our implementation of local variables will lean heavily on the compiler.

Function parameters are also heavily used. They work like local variables too, so we'll use the same implementation technique for them.

## 22.1  Representing Local Variables

The nice thing about hacking on a programming language in modern times is there's a long lineage of other languages to learn from. So how do C and Java manage their local variables? Why, on the stack, of course! They typically use the native stack mechanisms supported by the chip and OS. That's a little too low level for us, but inside the virtual world of clox, we have our own stack we can use.

Right now, we only use it for holding on to **temporaries**—short-lived blobs of data that we need to remember while computing an expression. As long as we don't get in the way of those, we can stuff our local variables onto the stack too. This is great for performance. Allocating space for a new local requires only incrementing the `stackTop` pointer, and freeing is likewise a decrement. Accessing a variable from a known stack slot is an indexed array lookup.

We do need to be careful, though. The VM expects the stack to behave like, well, a stack. We have to be OK with allocating new locals only on the top of the stack, and we have to accept that we can discard a local only when nothing is above it on the stack. Also, we need to make sure temporaries don't interfere.

Conveniently, the design of Lox is in harmony with these constraints. New locals are always created by declaration statements. Statements don't nest inside expressions, so there are never any temporaries on the stack when a statement begins executing. Blocks are strictly nested. When a block ends, it always takes the innermost, most recently declared locals with it. Since those are also the locals that came into scope last, they should be on top of the stack where we need them.

Step through this example program and watch how the local variables come in and go out of scope:

This alignment obviously isn't coincidental. I designed Lox to be amenable to single-pass compilation to stack-based bytecode. But I didn't have to tweak the language too much to fit in those restrictions. Most of its design should feel pretty natural.

This is in large part because the history of languages is deeply tied to single-pass compilation and—to a lesser degree—stack-based architectures. Lox's block scoping follows a tradition stretching back to BCPL. As programmers, our intuition of what's "normal" in a language is informed even today by the hardware limitations of yesteryear.

See how they fit a stack perfectly? It seems that the stack will work for storing locals at runtime. But we can go further than that. Not only do we know *that* they will be on the stack, but we can even pin down precisely *where* they will be on the stack. Since the compiler knows exactly which local variables are in scope at any point in time, it can effectively simulate the stack during compilation and note where in the stack each variable lives.

We'll take advantage of this by using these stack offsets as operands for the bytecode instructions that read and store local variables. This makes working with locals deliciously fast—as simple as indexing into an array.

There's a lot of state we need to track in the compiler to make this whole thing go, so let's get started there. In jlox, we used a linked chain of "environment" HashMaps to track which local variables were currently in scope. That's sort of the classic, schoolbook way of representing lexical scope. For clox, as usual, we're going a little closer to the metal. All of the state lives in a new struct.

```
} ParseRule;

typedef struct {
  Local locals[UINT8_COUNT];
  int localCount;
  int scopeDepth;
} Compiler;

Parser parser;
```

compiler.c
add after struct ParseRule

We have a simple, flat array of all locals that are in scope during each point in the compilation process. They are ordered in the array in the order that their declarations appear in the code. Since the instruction operand we'll use to encode a local is a single byte, our VM has a hard limit on the number of locals that can be in scope at once. That means we can also give the locals array a fixed size.

```
#define DEBUG_TRACE_EXECUTION

#define UINT8_COUNT (UINT8_MAX + 1)

#endif
```

common.h

Back in the Compiler struct, the localCount field tracks how many locals are in scope—how many of those array slots are in use. We also track the "scope depth". This is the number of blocks surrounding the current bit of code we're compiling.

Our Java interpreter used a chain of maps to keep each block's variables separate from other blocks'. This time, we'll simply number variables with the level of nesting where they appear. Zero is the global scope, one is the first top-level block, two is inside that, you get the idea. We use this to track which block each local belongs to so that we know which locals to discard when a block ends.

Each local in the array is one of these:

```
} ParseRule;

typedef struct {
  Token name;
  int depth;
} Local;

typedef struct {
```

compiler.c
add after struct ParseRule

In this chapter, locals start at the bottom of the VM's stack array and are indexed from there. When we add functions, that scheme gets a little more complex. Each function needs its own region of the stack for its parameters and local variables. But, as we'll see, that doesn't add as much complexity as you might expect.

We're writing a single-pass compiler, so it's not like we have *too* many other options for how to order them in the array.

We store the name of the variable. When we're resolving an identifier, we compare the identifier's lexeme with each local's name to find a match. It's pretty hard to resolve a variable if you don't know its name. The `depth` field records the scope depth of the block where the local variable was declared. That's all the state we need for now.

This is a very different representation from what we had in jlox, but it still lets us answer all of the same questions our compiler needs to ask of the lexical environment. The next step is figuring out how the compiler *gets* at this state. If we were principled engineers, we'd give each function in the front end a parameter that accepts a pointer to a Compiler. We'd create a Compiler at the beginning and carefully thread it through each function call…but that would mean a lot of boring changes to the code we already wrote, so here's a global variable instead:

In particular, if we ever want to use our compiler in a multi-threaded application, possibly with multiple compilers running in parallel, then using a global variable is a *bad* idea.

**compiler.c**
*add after variable* parser

```
Parser parser;
Compiler* current = NULL;
Chunk* compilingChunk;
```

Here's a little function to initialize the compiler:

**compiler.c**
*add after* emitConstant()

```
static void initCompiler(Compiler* compiler) {
  compiler->localCount = 0;
  compiler->scopeDepth = 0;
  current = compiler;
}
```

When we first start up the VM, we call it to get everything into a clean state.

**compiler.c**
*in* compile()

```
  initScanner(source);
  Compiler compiler;
  initCompiler(&compiler);
  compilingChunk = chunk;
```

Our compiler has the data it needs, but not the operations on that data. There's no way to create and destroy scopes, or add and resolve variables. We'll add those as we need them. First, let's start building some language features.

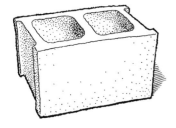

When you think about it, "block" is a weird name. Used metaphorically, "block" usually means a small indivisible unit, but for some reason, the ALGOL 60 committee decided to use it to refer to a *compound* structure—a series of statements. It could be worse, I suppose. Algol 58 called **begin** and **end** "statement parentheses".

## 22.2  Block Statements

Before we can have any local variables, we need some local scopes. These come from two things: function bodies and blocks. Functions are a big chunk of work that we'll tackle in a later chapter, so for now we're only going to do blocks. As usual, we start with the syntax. The new grammar we'll introduce is:

```
statement       → exprStmt
                | printStmt
                | block ;

block           → "{" declaration* "}" ;
```

Blocks are a kind of statement, so the rule for them goes in the `statement` production. The corresponding code to compile one looks like this:

```
  if (match(TOKEN_PRINT)) {
    printStatement();
  } else if (match(TOKEN_LEFT_BRACE)) {
    beginScope();
    block();
    endScope();
  } else {
```

compiler.c
in statement()

After parsing the initial curly brace, we use this helper function to compile the rest of the block:

This function will come in handy later for compiling function bodies.

```
static void block() {
  while (!check(TOKEN_RIGHT_BRACE) && !check(TOKEN_EOF)) {
    declaration();
  }

  consume(TOKEN_RIGHT_BRACE, "Expect '}' after block.");
}
```

compiler.c
add after expression()

It keeps parsing declarations and statements until it hits the closing brace. As we do with any loop in the parser, we also check for the end of the token stream. This way, if there's a malformed program with a missing closing curly, the compiler doesn't get stuck in a loop.

Executing a block simply means executing the statements it contains, one after the other, so there isn't much to compiling them. The semantically interesting thing blocks do is create scopes. Before we compile the body of a block, we call this function to enter a new local scope:

```
static void beginScope() {
  current->scopeDepth++;
}
```

compiler.c
add after endCompiler()

In order to "create" a scope, all we do is increment the current depth. This is certainly much faster than jlox, which allocated an entire new HashMap for each one. Given beginScope(), you can probably guess what endScope() does.

```
static void endScope() {
  current->scopeDepth--;
}
```

compiler.c
add after beginScope()

That's it for blocks and scopes—more or less—so we're ready to stuff some variables into them.

## 22.3  Declaring Local Variables

Usually we start with parsing here, but our compiler already supports parsing and compiling variable declarations. We've got var statements, identifier expressions and assignment in there now. It's just that the compiler assumes all variables are global. So we don't need any new parsing support, we just need to hook up the new scoping semantics to the existing code.

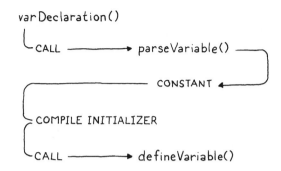

Variable declaration parsing begins in `varDeclaration()` and relies on a couple of other functions. First, `parseVariable()` consumes the identifier token for the variable name, adds its lexeme to the chunk's constant table as a string, and then returns the constant table index where it was added. Then, after `varDeclaration()` compiles the initializer, it calls `defineVariable()` to emit the bytecode for storing the variable's value in the global variable hash table.

Both of those helpers need a few changes to support local variables. In `parseVariable()`, we add:

compiler.c<br>in parseVariable()

```
  consume(TOKEN_IDENTIFIER, errorMessage);

  declareVariable();
  if (current->scopeDepth > 0) return 0;

  return identifierConstant(&parser.previous);
```

First, we "declare" the variable. I'll get to what that means in a second. After that, we exit the function if we're in a local scope. At runtime, locals aren't looked up by name. There's no need to stuff the variable's name into the constant table, so if the declaration is inside a local scope, we return a dummy table index instead.

Over in `defineVariable()`, we need to emit the code to store a local variable if we're in a local scope. It looks like this:

compiler.c<br>in defineVariable()

```
static void defineVariable(uint8_t global) {
  if (current->scopeDepth > 0) {
    return;
  }

  emitBytes(OP_DEFINE_GLOBAL, global);
```

Wait, what? Yup. That's it. There is no code to create a local variable at runtime. Think about what state the VM is in. It has already executed the code for the variable's initializer (or the implicit `nil` if the user omitted an initializer), and that value is sitting right on top of the stack as the only remaining temporary. We also know that new locals are allocated at the top of the stack...right where that value already is. Thus, there's nothing to do. The temporary simply *becomes* the local variable. It doesn't get much more efficient than that.

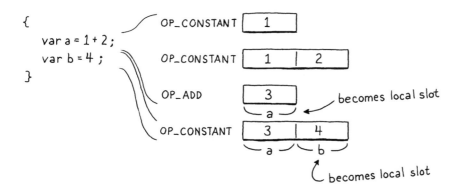

The code on the left compiles to the sequence of instructions on the right.

OK, so what's "declaring" about? Here's what that does:

```c
static void declareVariable() {
  if (current->scopeDepth == 0) return;

  Token* name = &parser.previous;
  addLocal(*name);
}
```

compiler.c
add after identifierConstant()

This is the point where the compiler records the existence of the variable. We only do this for locals, so if we're in the top-level global scope, we just bail out. Because global variables are late bound, the compiler doesn't keep track of which declarations for them it has seen.

But for local variables, the compiler does need to remember that the variable exists. That's what declaring it does—it adds it to the compiler's list of variables in the current scope. We implement that using another new function.

```c
static void addLocal(Token name) {
  Local* local = &current->locals[current->localCount++];
  local->name = name;
  local->depth = current->scopeDepth;
}
```

compiler.c
add after identifierConstant()

Worried about the lifetime of the string for the variable's name? The Local directly stores a copy of the Token struct for the identifier. Tokens store a pointer to the first character of their lexeme and the lexeme's length. That pointer points into the original source string for the script or REPL entry being compiled.

As long as that string stays around during the entire compilation process—which it must since, you know, we're compiling it—then all of the tokens pointing into it are fine.

This initializes the next available Local in the compiler's array of variables. It stores the variable's name and the depth of the scope that owns the variable.

Our implementation is fine for a correct Lox program, but what about invalid code? Let's aim to be robust. The first error to handle is not really the user's fault, but more a limitation of the VM. The instructions to work with local variables refer to them by slot index. That index is stored in a single-byte operand, which means the VM only supports up to 256 local variables in scope at one time.

If we try to go over that, not only could we not refer to them at runtime, but the compiler would overwrite its own locals array, too. Let's prevent that.

```c
static void addLocal(Token name) {
  if (current->localCount == UINT8_COUNT) {
    error("Too many local variables in function.");
    return;
  }

  Local* local = &current->locals[current->localCount++];
```

compiler.c
in addLocal()

The next case is trickier. Consider:

```
{
  var a = "first";
  var a = "second";
}
```

At the top level, Lox allows redeclaring a variable with the same name as a previous declaration because that's useful for the REPL. But inside a local scope, that's a pretty weird thing to do. It's likely to be a mistake, and many languages, including our own Lox, enshrine that assumption by making this an error.

Note that the above program is different from this one:

Interestingly, the Rust programming language *does* allow this, and idiomatic code relies on it.

```
{
  var a = "outer";
  {
    var a = "inner";
  }
}
```

It's OK to have two variables with the same name in *different* scopes, even when the scopes overlap such that both are visible at the same time. That's shadowing, and Lox does allow that. It's only an error to have two variables with the same name in the *same* local scope. We detect that error like so:

**compiler.c**
*in* declareVariable()

Don't worry about that odd depth != -1 part yet. We'll get to what that's about later.

```
Token* name = &parser.previous;
  for (int i = current->localCount - 1; i >= 0; i--) {
    Local* local = &current->locals[i];
    if (local->depth != -1 && local->depth < current->scopeDepth) {
      break;
    }

    if (identifiersEqual(name, &local->name)) {
      error("Already a variable with this name in this scope.");
    }
  }

  addLocal(*name);
}
```

Local variables are appended to the array when they're declared, which means the current scope is always at the end of the array. When we declare a new variable, we start at the end and work backward, looking for an existing variable with the same name. If we find one in the current scope, we report the error. Otherwise, if we reach the beginning of the array or a variable owned by another scope, then we know we've checked all of the existing variables in the scope.

To see if two identifiers are the same, we use this:

**compiler.c**
*add after* identifierConstant()

```
static bool identifiersEqual(Token* a, Token* b) {
  if (a->length != b->length) return false;
  return memcmp(a->start, b->start, a->length) == 0;
}
```

Since we know the lengths of both lexemes, we check that first. That will fail quickly for many non-equal strings. If the lengths are the same, we check the characters using memcmp(). To get to memcmp(), we need an include.

It would be a nice little optimization if we could check their hashes, but tokens aren't full LoxStrings, so we haven't calculated their hashes yet.

compiler.c

```
#include <stdlib.h>
#include <string.h>

#include "common.h"
```

With this, we're able to bring variables into being. But, like ghosts, they linger on beyond the scope where they are declared. When a block ends, we need to put them to rest.

compiler.c
in endScope()

```
  current->scopeDepth--;

  while (current->localCount > 0 &&
         current->locals[current->localCount - 1].depth >
            current->scopeDepth) {
    emitByte(OP_POP);
    current->localCount--;
  }
}
```

When we pop a scope, we walk backward through the local array looking for any variables declared at the scope depth we just left. We discard them by simply decrementing the length of the array.

There is a runtime component to this too. Local variables occupy slots on the stack. When a local variable goes out of scope, that slot is no longer needed and should be freed. So, for each variable that we discard, we also emit an OP_POP instruction to pop it from the stack.

When multiple local variables go out of scope at once, you get a series of OP_POP instructions that get interpreted one at a time. A simple optimization you could add to your Lox implementation is a specialized OP_POPN instruction that takes an operand for the number of slots to pop and pops them all at once.

## 22.4  Using Locals

We can now compile and execute local variable declarations. At runtime, their values are sitting where they should be on the stack. Let's start using them. We'll do both variable access and assignment at the same time since they touch the same functions in the compiler.

We already have code for getting and setting global variables, and—like good little software engineers—we want to reuse as much of that existing code as we can. Something like this:

compiler.c
in namedVariable()
*replace 1 line*

```
static void namedVariable(Token name, bool canAssign) {
  uint8_t getOp, setOp;
  int arg = resolveLocal(current, &name);
  if (arg != -1) {
    getOp = OP_GET_LOCAL;
    setOp = OP_SET_LOCAL;
  } else {
    arg = identifierConstant(&name);
    getOp = OP_GET_GLOBAL;
```

*continued on next page...*

*…from previous page*

```
    setOp = OP_SET_GLOBAL;
  }

  if (canAssign && match(TOKEN_EQUAL)) {
```

Instead of hardcoding the bytecode instructions emitted for variable access and assignment, we use a couple of C variables. First, we try to find a local variable with the given name. If we find one, we use the instructions for working with locals. Otherwise, we assume it's a global variable and use the existing bytecode instructions for globals.

A little further down, we use those variables to emit the right instructions. For assignment:

*compiler.c*
*in namedVariable()*
*replace 1 line*

```
  if (canAssign && match(TOKEN_EQUAL)) {
    expression();
    emitBytes(setOp, (uint8_t)arg);
  } else {
```

And for access:

*compiler.c*
*in namedVariable()*
*replace 1 line*

```
    emitBytes(setOp, (uint8_t)arg);
  } else {
    emitBytes(getOp, (uint8_t)arg);
  }
```

The real heart of this chapter, the part where we resolve a local variable, is here:

*compiler.c*
*add after identifiersEqual()*

```
static int resolveLocal(Compiler* compiler, Token* name) {
  for (int i = compiler->localCount - 1; i >= 0; i--) {
    Local* local = &compiler->locals[i];
    if (identifiersEqual(name, &local->name)) {
      return i;
    }
  }

  return -1;
}
```

For all that, it's straightforward. We walk the list of locals that are currently in scope. If one has the same name as the identifier token, the identifier must refer to that variable. We've found it! We walk the array backward so that we find the *last* declared variable with the identifier. That ensures that inner local variables correctly shadow locals with the same name in surrounding scopes.

At runtime, we load and store locals using the stack slot index, so that's what the compiler needs to calculate after it resolves the variable. Whenever a variable is declared, we append it to the locals array in Compiler. That means the first local variable is at index zero, the next one is at index one, and so on. In other words, the locals array in the compiler has the *exact* same layout as the VM's stack will have at runtime. The variable's index in the locals array is the same as its stack slot. How convenient!

If we make it through the whole array without finding a variable with the given name, it must not be a local. In that case, we return −1 to signal that it wasn't found and should be assumed to be a global variable instead.

## 22.4.1 Interpreting local variables

Our compiler is emitting two new instructions, so let's get them working. First is loading a local variable:

```
  OP_POP,
  OP_GET_LOCAL,
  OP_GET_GLOBAL,
```

chunk.h
in enum OpCode

And its implementation:

```
    case OP_POP: pop(); break;
    case OP_GET_LOCAL: {
      uint8_t slot = READ_BYTE();
      push(vm.stack[slot]);
      break;
    }
    case OP_GET_GLOBAL: {
```

vm.c
in run()

It seems redundant to push the local's value onto the stack since it's already on the stack lower down somewhere. The problem is that the other bytecode instructions only look for data at the *top* of the stack. This is the core aspect that makes our bytecode instruction set *stack*-based. Register-based bytecode instruction sets avoid this stack juggling at the cost of having larger instructions with more operands.

It takes a single-byte operand for the stack slot where the local lives. It loads the value from that index and then pushes it on top of the stack where later instructions can find it.

Next is assignment:

```
  OP_GET_LOCAL,
  OP_SET_LOCAL,
  OP_GET_GLOBAL,
```

chunk.h
in enum OpCode

You can probably predict the implementation.

```
    }
    case OP_SET_LOCAL: {
      uint8_t slot = READ_BYTE();
      vm.stack[slot] = peek(0);
      break;
    }
    case OP_GET_GLOBAL: {
```

vm.c
in run()

It takes the assigned value from the top of the stack and stores it in the stack slot corresponding to the local variable. Note that it doesn't pop the value from the stack. Remember, assignment is an expression, and every expression produces a value. The value of an assignment expression is the assigned value itself, so the VM just leaves the value on the stack.

Our disassembler is incomplete without support for these two new instructions.

debug.c
in disassembleInstruction()

```
      return simpleInstruction("OP_POP", offset);
    case OP_GET_LOCAL:
      return byteInstruction("OP_GET_LOCAL", chunk, offset);
    case OP_SET_LOCAL:
      return byteInstruction("OP_SET_LOCAL", chunk, offset);
    case OP_GET_GLOBAL:
```

The compiler compiles local variables to direct slot access. The local variable's name never leaves the compiler to make it into the chunk at all. That's great for performance, but not so great for introspection. When we disassemble these instructions, we can't show the variable's name like we could with globals. Instead, we just show the slot number.

debug.c
add after simpleInstruction()

```
static int byteInstruction(const char* name, Chunk* chunk,
                           int offset) {
  uint8_t slot = chunk->code[offset + 1];
  printf("%-16s %4d\n", name, slot);
  return offset + 2;
}
```

Erasing local variable names in the compiler is a real issue if we ever want to implement a debugger for our VM. When users step through code, they expect to see the values of local variables organized by their names. To support that, we'd need to output some additional information that tracks the name of each local variable at each stack slot.

No, not even Scheme.

### 22.4.2 Another scope edge case

We already sunk some time into handling a couple of weird edge cases around scopes. We made sure shadowing works correctly. We report an error if two variables in the same local scope have the same name. For reasons that aren't entirely clear to me, variable scoping seems to have a lot of these wrinkles. I've never seen a language where it feels completely elegant.

We've got one more edge case to deal with before we end this chapter. Recall this strange beastie we first met in jlox's implementation of variable resolution:

```
{
  var a = "outer";
  {
    var a = a;
  }
}
```

We slayed it then by splitting a variable's declaration into two phases, and we'll do that again here:

As soon as the variable declaration begins—in other words, before its initializer—the name is declared in the current scope. The variable exists, but in a special "uninitialized" state. Then we compile the initializer. If at any point in that expression we resolve an identifier that points back to this variable, we'll see that it is not initialized yet and report an error. After we finish compiling the initializer, we mark the variable as initialized and ready for use.

To implement this, when we declare a local, we need to indicate the "unini-tialized" state somehow. We could add a new field to Local, but let's be a little more parsimonious with memory. Instead, we'll set the variable's scope depth to a special sentinel value, -1.

```
  local->name = name;
  local->depth = -1;
}
```
compiler.c
in addLocal()
replace 1 line

Later, once the variable's initializer has been compiled, we mark it initialized.

```
  if (current->scopeDepth > 0) {
    markInitialized();
    return;
  }
```
compiler.c
in defineVariable()

That is implemented like so:

```
static void markInitialized() {
  current->locals[current->localCount - 1].depth =
      current->scopeDepth;
}
```
compiler.c
add after parseVariable()

So this is *really* what "declaring" and "defining" a variable means in the compiler. "Declaring" is when the variable is added to the scope, and "defining" is when it becomes available for use.

When we resolve a reference to a local variable, we check the scope depth to see if it's fully defined.

```
    if (identifiersEqual(name, &local->name)) {
      if (local->depth == -1) {
        error("Can't read local variable in its own initializer.");
      }
      return i;
```
compiler.c
in resolveLocal()

If the variable has the sentinel depth, it must be a reference to a variable in its own initializer, and we report that as an error.

That's it for this chapter! We added blocks, local variables, and real, honest-to-God lexical scoping. Given that we introduced an entirely different runtime representation for variables, we didn't have to write a lot of code. The implementation ended up being pretty clean and efficient.

You'll notice that almost all of the code we wrote is in the compiler. Over in the runtime, it's just two little instructions. You'll see this as a continuing trend in clox compared to jlox. One of the biggest hammers in the optimizer's toolbox is pulling work forward into the compiler so that you don't have to do it at runtime. In this chapter, that meant resolving exactly which stack slot every local variable occupies. That way, at runtime, no lookup or resolution needs to happen.

You can look at static types as an extreme example of this trend. A statically typed language takes all of the type analysis and type error handling and sorts it all out during compilation. Then the runtime doesn't have to waste any time checking that values have the proper type for their operation. In fact, in some statically typed languages like C, you don't even *know* the type at runtime. The compiler completely erases any representation of a value's type leaving just the bare bits.

## CHALLENGES

1. Our simple local array makes it easy to calculate the stack slot of each local variable. But it means that when the compiler resolves a reference to a variable, we have to do a linear scan through the array.

   Come up with something more efficient. Do you think the additional complexity is worth it?

2. How do other languages handle code like this:

   ```
   var a = a;
   ```

   What would you do if it was your language? Why?

3. Many languages make a distinction between variables that can be reassigned and those that can't. In Java, the `final` modifier prevents you from assigning to a variable. In JavaScript, a variable declared with `let` can be assigned, but one declared using `const` can't. Swift treats `let` as single-assignment and uses `var` for assignable variables. Scala and Kotlin use `val` and `var`.

   Pick a keyword for a single-assignment variable form to add to Lox. Justify your choice, then implement it. An attempt to assign to a variable declared using your new keyword should cause a compile error.

4. Extend clox to allow more than 256 local variables to be in scope at a time.

# Jumping Back and Forth

*"The order that our mind imagines is like a net, or like a ladder, built to attain something. But afterward you must throw the ladder away, because you discover that, even if it was useful, it was meaningless."*

— Umberto Eco, *The Name of the Rose*

It's taken a while to get here, but we're finally ready to add control flow to our virtual machine. In the tree-walk interpreter we built for jlox, we implemented Lox's control flow in terms of Java's. To execute a Lox `if` statement, we used a Java `if` statement to run the chosen branch. That works, but isn't entirely satisfying. By what magic does the *JVM itself* or a native CPU implement `if` statements? Now that we have our own bytecode VM to hack on, we can answer that.

When we talk about "control flow", what are we referring to? By "flow" we mean the way execution moves through the text of the program. Almost like there is a little robot inside the computer wandering through our code, executing bits and pieces here and there. Flow is the path that robot takes, and by *controlling* the robot, we drive which pieces of code it executes.

In jlox, the robot's locus of attention—the *current* bit of code—was implicit based on which AST nodes were stored in various Java variables and what Java code we were in the middle of running. In clox, it is much more explicit. The VM's `ip` field stores the address of the current bytecode instruction. The value of that field is exactly "where we are" in the program.

Execution proceeds normally by incrementing the `ip`. But we can mutate that variable however we want to. In order to implement control flow, all that's necessary is to change the `ip` in more interesting ways. The simplest control flow construct is an `if` statement with no `else` clause:

```
if (condition) print("condition was truthy");
```

The VM evaluates the bytecode for the condition expression. If the result is truthy, then it continues along and executes the `print` statement in the body. The interesting case is when the condition is falsey. When that happens, execution skips over the then branch and proceeds to the next statement.

To skip over a chunk of code, we simply set the `ip` field to the address of the bytecode instruction following that code. To *conditionally* skip over some code, we need an instruction that looks at the value on top of the stack. If it's falsey, it adds a given offset to the `ip` to jump over a range of instructions. Otherwise, it does nothing and lets execution proceed to the next instruction as usual.

When we compile to bytecode, the explicit nested block structure of the code evaporates, leaving only a flat series of instructions behind. Lox is a structured programming language, but clox bytecode isn't. The right—or wrong, depending on how you look at it—set of bytecode instructions could jump into the middle of a block, or from one scope into another.

The VM will happily execute that, even if the result leaves the stack in an unknown, inconsistent state. So even though the bytecode is unstructured, we'll take care to ensure that our compiler only generates clean code that maintains the same structure and nesting that Lox itself does.

This is exactly how real CPUs behave. Even though we might program them using higher-level languages that mandate structured control flow, the compiler lowers that down to raw jumps. At the bottom, it turns out goto is the only real control flow.

Anyway, I didn't mean to get all philosophical. The important bit is that if we have that one conditional jump instruction, that's enough to implement Lox's `if` statement, as long as it doesn't have an `else` clause. So let's go ahead and get started with that.

## 23.1  If Statements

This many chapters in, you know the drill. Any new feature starts in the front end and works its way through the pipeline. An `if` statement is, well, a statement, so that's where we hook it into the parser.

compiler.c<br>*in* statement()

```
  if (match(TOKEN_PRINT)) {
    printStatement();
  } else if (match(TOKEN_IF)) {
    ifStatement();
  } else if (match(TOKEN_LEFT_BRACE)) {
```

When we see an `if` keyword, we hand off compilation to this function:

```
static void ifStatement() {
  consume(TOKEN_LEFT_PAREN, "Expect '(' after 'if'.");
  expression();
  consume(TOKEN_RIGHT_PAREN, "Expect ')' after condition.");

  int thenJump = emitJump(OP_JUMP_IF_FALSE);
  statement();

  patchJump(thenJump);
}
```

compiler.c
*add after* expressionStatement()

Have you ever noticed that the ( after the if keyword doesn't actually do anything useful? The language would be just as unambiguous and easy to parse without it, like:

```
if condition)
  print("looks weird");
```

The closing ) is useful because it separates the condition expression from the body. Some languages use a **then** keyword instead. But the opening ( doesn't do anything. It's just there because unmatched parentheses look bad to us humans.

First we compile the condition expression, bracketed by parentheses. At runtime, that will leave the condition value on top of the stack. We'll use that to determine whether to execute the then branch or skip it.

Then we emit a new OP_JUMP_IF_FALSE instruction. It has an operand for how much to offset the ip—how many bytes of code to skip. If the condition is falsey, it adjusts the ip by that amount. Something like this:

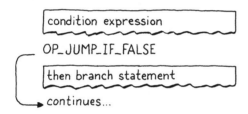

The boxes with the torn edges here represent the blob of bytecode generated by compiling some sub-clause of a control flow construct. So the "condition expression" box is all of the instructions emitted when we compiled that expression.

But we have a problem. When we're writing the OP_JUMP_IF_FALSE instruction's operand, how do we know how far to jump? We haven't compiled the then branch yet, so we don't know how much bytecode it contains.

To fix that, we use a classic trick called **backpatching**. We emit the jump instruction first with a placeholder offset operand. We keep track of where that half-finished instruction is. Next, we compile the then body. Once that's done, we know how far to jump. So we go back and replace that placeholder offset with the real one now that we can calculate it. Sort of like sewing a patch onto the existing fabric of the compiled code.

We encode this trick into two helper functions.

compiler.c
*add after* emitBytes()

```
static int emitJump(uint8_t instruction) {
  emitByte(instruction);
  emitByte(0xff);
  emitByte(0xff);
  return currentChunk()->count - 2;
}
```

The first emits a bytecode instruction and writes a placeholder operand for the jump offset. We pass in the opcode as an argument because later we'll have two different instructions that use this helper. We use two bytes for the jump offset operand. A 16-bit offset lets us jump over up to 65,535 bytes of code, which should be plenty for our needs.

> Some instruction sets have separate "long" jump instructions that take larger operands for when you need to jump a greater distance.

The function returns the offset of the emitted instruction in the chunk. After compiling the then branch, we take that offset and pass it to this:

compiler.c
*add after* emitConstant()

```
static void patchJump(int offset) {
  // -2 to adjust for the bytecode for the jump offset itself.
  int jump = currentChunk()->count - offset - 2;

  if (jump > UINT16_MAX) {
    error("Too much code to jump over.");
  }

  currentChunk()->code[offset] = (jump >> 8) & 0xff;
  currentChunk()->code[offset + 1] = jump & 0xff;
}
```

This goes back into the bytecode and replaces the operand at the given location with the calculated jump offset. We call patchJump() right before we emit the next instruction that we want the jump to land on, so it uses the current bytecode count to determine how far to jump. In the case of an if statement, that means right after we compile the then branch and before we compile the next statement.

That's all we need at compile time. Let's define the new instruction.

chunk.h
*in enum* OpCode

```
  OP_PRINT,
  OP_JUMP_IF_FALSE,
  OP_RETURN,
```

Over in the VM, we get it working like so:

vm.c
*in* run()

```
        break;
      }
      case OP_JUMP_IF_FALSE: {
        uint16_t offset = READ_SHORT();
        if (isFalsey(peek(0))) vm.ip += offset;
        break;
      }
      case OP_RETURN: {
```

This is the first instruction we've added that takes a 16-bit operand. To read that from the chunk, we use a new macro.

```
#define READ_CONSTANT() (vm.chunk->constants.values[READ_BYTE()])
#define READ_SHORT() \
    (vm.ip += 2, (uint16_t)((vm.ip[-2] << 8) | vm.ip[-1]))
#define READ_STRING() AS_STRING(READ_CONSTANT())
```

vm.c
in run()

It yanks the next two bytes from the chunk and builds a 16-bit unsigned integer out of them. As usual, we clean up our macro when we're done with it.

```
#undef READ_BYTE
#undef READ_SHORT
#undef READ_CONSTANT
```

vm.c
in run()

After reading the offset, we check the condition value on top of the stack. If it's falsey, we apply this jump offset to the ip. Otherwise, we leave the ip alone and execution will automatically proceed to the next instruction following the jump instruction.

In the case where the condition is falsey, we don't need to do any other work. We've offset the ip, so when the outer instruction dispatch loop turns again, it will pick up execution at that new instruction, past all of the code in the then branch.

Note that the jump instruction doesn't pop the condition value off the stack. So we aren't totally done here, since this leaves an extra value floating around on the stack. We'll clean that up soon. Ignoring that for the moment, we do have a working if statement in Lox now, with only one little instruction required to support it at runtime in the VM.

## 23.1.1 Else clauses

An if statement without support for else clauses is like Morticia Addams without Gomez. So, after we compile the then branch, we look for an else keyword. If we find one, we compile the else branch.

```
    patchJump(thenJump);

    if (match(TOKEN_ELSE)) statement();
}
```

compiler.c
in ifStatement()

When the condition is falsey, we'll jump over the then branch. If there's an else branch, the ip will land right at the beginning of its code. But that's not enough, though. Here's the flow that leads to:

I said we wouldn't use C's if statement to implement Lox's control flow, but we do use one here to determine whether or not to offset the instruction pointer. But we aren't really using C for *control flow*. If we wanted to, we could do the same thing purely arithmetically. Let's assume we have a function falsey() that takes a Lox Value and returns 1 if it's falsey or 0 otherwise. Then we could implement the jump instruction like:

```
case OP_JUMP_IF_FALSE: {
  uint16_t offset =
    READ_SHORT();
  vm.ip += falsey()
    * offset;
  break;
}
```

The falsey() function might use control flow to handle the different value types, but that's an implementation detail of that function and doesn't affect how our VM does its own control flow.

condition expression

OP_JUMP_IF_FALSE

then branch statement

else branch statement

FALLS THROUGH!

continues...

If the condition is truthy, we execute the then branch like we want. But after that, execution rolls right on through into the else branch. Oops! When the condition is true, after we run the then branch, we need to jump over the else branch. That way, in either case, we only execute a single branch, like this:

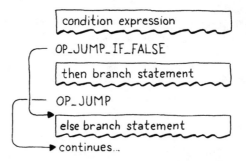

To implement that, we need another jump from the end of the then branch.

compiler.c<br>in ifStatement()

```
    statement();

    int elseJump = emitJump(OP_JUMP);

    patchJump(thenJump);
```

We patch that offset after the end of the else body.

compiler.c<br>in ifStatement()

```
    if (match(TOKEN_ELSE)) statement();
    patchJump(elseJump);
}
```

After executing the then branch, this jumps to the next statement after the else branch. Unlike the other jump, this jump is unconditional. We always take it, so we need another instruction that expresses that.

chunk.h<br>in enum OpCode

```
    OP_PRINT,
    OP_JUMP,
    OP_JUMP_IF_FALSE,
```

We interpret it like so:

vm.c<br>in run()

```
        break;
      }
      case OP_JUMP: {
        uint16_t offset = READ_SHORT();
        vm.ip += offset;
        break;
      }
      case OP_JUMP_IF_FALSE: {
```

Nothing too surprising here—the only difference is that it doesn't check a condition and always applies the offset.

We have then and else branches working now, so we're close. The last bit is to clean up that condition value we left on the stack. Remember, each statement is required to have zero stack effect—after the statement is finished executing, the stack should be as tall as it was before.

We could have the `OP_JUMP_IF_FALSE` instruction pop the condition itself, but soon we'll use that same instruction for the logical operators where we don't want the condition popped. Instead, we'll have the compiler emit a couple of explicit `OP_POP` instructions when compiling an `if` statement. We need to take care that every execution path through the generated code pops the condition.

When the condition is truthy, we pop it right before the code inside the then branch.

```
int thenJump = emitJump(OP_JUMP_IF_FALSE);
emitByte(OP_POP);
statement();
```

compiler.c
*in* ifStatement()

Otherwise, we pop it at the beginning of the else branch.

```
patchJump(thenJump);
emitByte(OP_POP);

if (match(TOKEN_ELSE)) statement();
```

compiler.c
*in* ifStatement()

This little instruction here also means that every `if` statement has an implicit else branch even if the user didn't write an `else` clause. In the case where they left it off, all the branch does is discard the condition value.

The full correct flow looks like this:

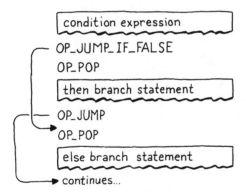

If you trace through, you can see that it always executes a single branch and ensures the condition is popped first. All that remains is a little disassembler support.

```
    return simpleInstruction("OP_PRINT", offset);
  case OP_JUMP:
    return jumpInstruction("OP_JUMP", 1, chunk, offset);
  case OP_JUMP_IF_FALSE:
    return jumpInstruction("OP_JUMP_IF_FALSE", 1, chunk, offset);
  case OP_RETURN:
```

debug.c
*in* disassembleInstruction()

These two instructions have a new format with a 16-bit operand, so we add a new utility function to disassemble them.

debug.c
add after byteInstruction()

```
static int jumpInstruction(const char* name, int sign,
                           Chunk* chunk, int offset) {
  uint16_t jump = (uint16_t)(chunk->code[offset + 1] << 8);
  jump |= chunk->code[offset + 2];
  printf("%-16s %4d -> %d\n", name, offset,
         offset + 3 + sign * jump);
  return offset + 3;
}
```

There we go, that's one complete control flow construct. If this were an '80s movie, the montage music would kick in and the rest of the control flow syntax would take care of itself. Alas, the '80s are long over, so we'll have to grind it out ourselves.

My enduring love of Depeche Mode notwithstanding.

## 23.2  Logical Operators

You probably remember this from jlox, but the logical operators and and or aren't just another pair of binary operators like + and −. Because they short-circuit and may not evaluate their right operand depending on the value of the left one, they work more like control flow expressions.

They're basically a little variation on an if statement with an else clause. The easiest way to explain them is to just show you the compiler code and the control flow it produces in the resulting bytecode. Starting with and, we hook it into the expression parsing table here:

compiler.c
replace 1 line

```
  [TOKEN_NUMBER]      = {number,    NULL,    PREC_NONE},
  [TOKEN_AND]         = {NULL,      and_,    PREC_AND},
  [TOKEN_CLASS]       = {NULL,      NULL,    PREC_NONE},
```

That hands off to a new parser function.

compiler.c
add after defineVariable()

```
static void and_(bool canAssign) {
  int endJump = emitJump(OP_JUMP_IF_FALSE);

  emitByte(OP_POP);
  parsePrecedence(PREC_AND);

  patchJump(endJump);
}
```

At the point this is called, the left-hand side expression has already been compiled. That means at runtime, its value will be on top of the stack. If that value is falsey, then we know the entire and must be false, so we skip the right operand and leave the left-hand side value as the result of the entire expression. Otherwise, we discard the left-hand value and evaluate the right operand which becomes the result of the whole and expression.

Those four lines of code right there produce exactly that. The flow looks like this:

Now you can see why `OP_JUMP_IF_FALSE` leaves the value on top of the stack. When the left-hand side of the and is falsey, that value sticks around to become the result of the entire expression.

### 23.2.1   Logical or operator

The or operator is a little more complex. First we add it to the parse table.

```
  [TOKEN_NIL]            = {literal,  NULL,   PREC_NONE},
  [TOKEN_OR]             = {NULL,     or_,    PREC_OR},
  [TOKEN_PRINT]          = {NULL,     NULL,   PREC_NONE},
```

*compiler.c*
*replace 1 line*

When that parser consumes an infix or token, it calls this:

```
static void or_(bool canAssign) {
  int elseJump = emitJump(OP_JUMP_IF_FALSE);
  int endJump = emitJump(OP_JUMP);

  patchJump(elseJump);
  emitByte(OP_POP);

  parsePrecedence(PREC_OR);
  patchJump(endJump);
}
```

*compiler.c*
*add after* number()

In an or expression, if the left-hand side is *truthy*, then we skip over the right operand. Thus we need to jump when a value is truthy. We could add a separate instruction, but just to show how our compiler is free to map the language's semantics to whatever instruction sequence it wants, I implemented it in terms of the jump instructions we already have.

When the left-hand side is falsey, it does a tiny jump over the next statement. That statement is an unconditional jump over the code for the right operand. This little dance effectively does a jump when the value is truthy. The flow looks like this:

We've got plenty of space left in our opcode range, so we could have separate instructions for conditional jumps that implicitly pop and those that don't, I suppose. But I'm trying to keep things minimal for the book. In your bytecode VM, it's worth exploring adding more specialized instructions and seeing how they affect performance.

If I'm honest with you, this isn't the best way to do this. There are more instructions to dispatch and more overhead. There's no good reason why or should be slower than and. But it is kind of fun to see that it's possible to implement both operators without adding any new instructions. Forgive me my indulgences.

OK, those are the three *branching* constructs in Lox. By that, I mean, these are the control flow features that only jump *forward* over code. Other languages often have some kind of multi-way branching statement like switch and maybe a conditional expression like ?:, but Lox keeps it simple.

## 23.3  While Statements

That takes us to the *looping* statements, which jump *backward* so that code can be executed more than once. Lox only has two loop constructs, while and for. A while loop is (much) simpler, so we start the party there.

compiler.c
*in* statement()

```
    ifStatement();
  } else if (match(TOKEN_WHILE)) {
    whileStatement();
  } else if (match(TOKEN_LEFT_BRACE)) {
```

When we reach a while token, we call:

compiler.c
*add after* printStatement()

```
static void whileStatement() {
  consume(TOKEN_LEFT_PAREN, "Expect '(' after 'while'.");
  expression();
  consume(TOKEN_RIGHT_PAREN, "Expect ')' after condition.");

  int exitJump = emitJump(OP_JUMP_IF_FALSE);
  emitByte(OP_POP);
  statement();

  patchJump(exitJump);
  emitByte(OP_POP);
}
```

Most of this mirrors if statements—we compile the condition expression, surrounded by mandatory parentheses. That's followed by a jump instruction that skips over the subsequent body statement if the condition is falsey.

We patch the jump after compiling the body and take care to pop the condition value from the stack on either path. The only difference from an if statement is the loop. That looks like this:

Really starting to second-guess my decision to use the same jump instructions for the logical operators.

compiler.c
*in* whileStatement()

```
  statement();
  emitLoop(loopStart);

  patchJump(exitJump);
```

After the body, we call this function to emit a "loop" instruction. That instruction needs to know how far back to jump. When jumping forward, we had to emit the instruction in two stages since we didn't know how far we were going to jump until after we emitted the jump instruction. We don't have that problem now. We've already compiled the point in code that we want to jump back to—it's right before the condition expression.

All we need to do is capture that location as we compile it.

```
static void whileStatement() {
  int loopStart = currentChunk()->count;
  consume(TOKEN_LEFT_PAREN, "Expect '(' after 'while'.");
```

compiler.c
in whileStatement()

After executing the body of a while loop, we jump all the way back to before the condition. That way, we re-evaluate the condition expression on each iteration. We store the chunk's current instruction count in loopStart to record the offset in the bytecode right before the condition expression we're about to compile. Then we pass that into this helper function:

```
static void emitLoop(int loopStart) {
  emitByte(OP_LOOP);

  int offset = currentChunk()->count - loopStart + 2;
  if (offset > UINT16_MAX) error("Loop body too large.");

  emitByte((offset >> 8) & 0xff);
  emitByte(offset & 0xff);
}
```

compiler.c
add after emitBytes()

It's a bit like emitJump() and patchJump() combined. It emits a new loop instruction, which unconditionally jumps *backwards* by a given offset. Like the jump instructions, after that we have a 16-bit operand. We calculate the offset from the instruction we're currently at to the loopStart point that we want to jump back to. The + 2 is to take into account the size of the OP_LOOP instruction's own operands which we also need to jump over.

From the VM's perspective, there really is no semantic difference between OP_LOOP and OP_JUMP. Both just add an offset to the ip. We could have used a single instruction for both and given it a signed offset operand. But I figured it was a little easier to sidestep the annoying bit twiddling required to manually pack a signed 16-bit integer into two bytes, and we've got the opcode space available, so why not use it?

The new instruction is here:

```
  OP_JUMP_IF_FALSE,
  OP_LOOP,
  OP_RETURN,
```

chunk.h
in enum OpCode

And in the VM, we implement it thusly:

```
    }
    case OP_LOOP: {
      uint16_t offset = READ_SHORT();
      vm.ip -= offset;
      break;
    }
    case OP_RETURN: {
```

vm.c
in run()

The only difference from `OP_JUMP` is a subtraction instead of an addition. Disassembly is similar too.

debug.c
*in* disassembleInstruction()

```
    return jumpInstruction("OP_JUMP_IF_FALSE", 1, chunk, offset);
  case OP_LOOP:
    return jumpInstruction("OP_LOOP", -1, chunk, offset);
  case OP_RETURN:
```

That's our `while` statement. It contains two jumps—a conditional forward one to escape the loop when the condition is not met, and an unconditional loop backward after we have executed the body. The flow looks like this:

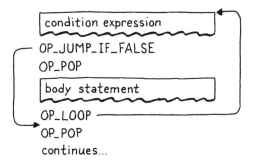

## 23.4  For Statements

The other looping statement in Lox is the venerable `for` loop, inherited from C. It's got a lot more going on with it compared to a `while` loop. It has three clauses, all of which are optional:

If you want a refresher, chapter "Control Flow", section 9.5 goes through the semantics in more detail.

- The initializer can be a variable declaration or an expression. It runs once at the beginning of the statement.

- The condition clause is an expression. Like in a `while` loop, we exit the loop when it evaluates to something falsey.

- The increment expression runs once at the end of each loop iteration.

In jlox, the parser desugared a `for` loop to a synthesized AST for a `while` loop with some extra stuff before it and at the end of the body. We'll do something similar, though we won't go through anything like an AST. Instead, our bytecode compiler will use the jump and loop instructions we already have.

We'll work our way through the implementation a piece at a time, starting with the `for` keyword.

compiler.c
*in* statement()

```
    printStatement();
  } else if (match(TOKEN_FOR)) {
    forStatement();
  } else if (match(TOKEN_IF)) {
```

It calls a helper function. If we only supported `for` loops with empty clauses like `for (;;)`, then we could implement it like this:

```
static void forStatement() {
  consume(TOKEN_LEFT_PAREN, "Expect '(' after 'for'.");
  consume(TOKEN_SEMICOLON, "Expect ';'.");

  int loopStart = currentChunk()->count;
  consume(TOKEN_SEMICOLON, "Expect ';'.");
  consume(TOKEN_RIGHT_PAREN, "Expect ')' after for clauses.");

  statement();
  emitLoop(loopStart);
}
```

compiler.c
*add after* expressionStatement()

There's a bunch of mandatory punctuation at the top. Then we compile the body. Like we did for `while` loops, we record the bytecode offset at the top of the body and emit a loop to jump back to that point after it. We've got a working implementation of infinite loops now.

Alas, without **return** statements, there isn't any way to terminate it short of a runtime error.

### 23.4.1  Initializer clause

Now we'll add the first clause, the initializer. It executes only once, before the body, so compiling is straightforward.

```
  consume(TOKEN_LEFT_PAREN, "Expect '(' after 'for'.");
  if (match(TOKEN_SEMICOLON)) {
    // No initializer.
  } else if (match(TOKEN_VAR)) {
    varDeclaration();
  } else {
    expressionStatement();
  }

  int loopStart = currentChunk()->count;
```

compiler.c
*in* forStatement()
*replace 1 line*

The syntax is a little complex since we allow either a variable declaration or an expression. We use the presence of the `var` keyword to tell which we have. For the expression case, we call `expressionStatement()` instead of `expression()`. That looks for a semicolon, which we need here too, and also emits an `OP_POP` instruction to discard the value. We don't want the initializer to leave anything on the stack.

If a `for` statement declares a variable, that variable should be scoped to the loop body. We ensure that by wrapping the whole statement in a scope.

```
static void forStatement() {
  beginScope();
  consume(TOKEN_LEFT_PAREN, "Expect '(' after 'for'.");
```

compiler.c
*in* forStatement()

Then we close it at the end.

```
  emitLoop(loopStart);
  endScope();
}
```

compiler.c
*in* forStatement()

### 23.4.2  Condition clause

Next, is the condition expression that can be used to exit the loop.

compiler.c
in forStatement()
replace 1 line

```
int loopStart = currentChunk()->count;
int exitJump = -1;
if (!match(TOKEN_SEMICOLON)) {
  expression();
  consume(TOKEN_SEMICOLON, "Expect ';' after loop condition.");

  // Jump out of the loop if the condition is false.
  exitJump = emitJump(OP_JUMP_IF_FALSE);
  emitByte(OP_POP); // Condition.
}

consume(TOKEN_RIGHT_PAREN, "Expect ')' after for clauses.");
```

Since the clause is optional, we need to see if it's actually present. If the clause is omitted, the next token must be a semicolon, so we look for that to tell. If there isn't a semicolon, there must be a condition expression.

In that case, we compile it. Then, just like with while, we emit a conditional jump that exits the loop if the condition is falsey. Since the jump leaves the value on the stack, we pop it before executing the body. That ensures we discard the value when the condition is true.

After the loop body, we need to patch that jump.

compiler.c
in forStatement()

```
emitLoop(loopStart);

if (exitJump != -1) {
  patchJump(exitJump);
  emitByte(OP_POP); // Condition.
}

endScope();
```

We do this only when there is a condition clause. If there isn't, there's no jump to patch and no condition value on the stack to pop.

### 23.4.3  Increment clause

I've saved the best for last, the increment clause. It's pretty convoluted. It appears textually before the body, but executes *after* it. If we parsed to an AST and generated code in a separate pass, we could simply traverse into and compile the for statement AST's body field before its increment clause.

Unfortunately, we can't compile the increment clause later, since our compiler only makes a single pass over the code. Instead, we'll *jump over* the increment, run the body, jump *back* up to the increment, run it, and then go to the next iteration.

I know, a little weird, but hey, it beats manually managing ASTs in memory in C, right? Here's the code:

compiler.c
*in* forStatement()
*replace 1 line*

```
  }

  if (!match(TOKEN_RIGHT_PAREN)) {
    int bodyJump = emitJump(OP_JUMP);
    int incrementStart = currentChunk()->count;
    expression();
    emitByte(OP_POP);
    consume(TOKEN_RIGHT_PAREN, "Expect ')' after for clauses.");

    emitLoop(loopStart);
    loopStart = incrementStart;
    patchJump(bodyJump);
  }

  statement();
```

Again, it's optional. Since this is the last clause, when omitted, the next token will be the closing parenthesis. When an increment is present, we need to compile it now, but it shouldn't execute yet. So, first, we emit an unconditional jump that hops over the increment clause's code to the body of the loop.

Next, we compile the increment expression itself. This is usually an assignment. Whatever it is, we only execute it for its side effect, so we also emit a pop to discard its value.

The last part is a little tricky. First, we emit a loop instruction. This is the main loop that takes us back to the top of the for loop—right before the condition expression if there is one. That loop happens right after the increment, since the increment executes at the end of each loop iteration.

Then we change loopStart to point to the offset where the increment expression begins. Later, when we emit the loop instruction after the body statement, this will cause it to jump up to the *increment* expression instead of the top of the loop like it does when there is no increment. This is how we weave the increment in to run after the body.

It's convoluted, but it all works out. A complete loop with all the clauses compiles to a flow like this:

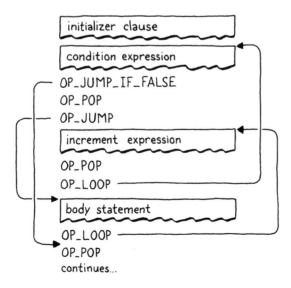

I couldn't resist the pun. I regret nothing.

As with implementing `for` loops in jlox, we didn't need to touch the runtime. It all gets compiled down to primitive control flow operations the VM already supports. In this chapter, we've taken a big leap forward—clox is now Turing-complete. We've also covered quite a bit of new syntax: three statements and two expression forms. Even so, it only took three new simple instructions. That's a pretty good effort-to-reward ratio for the architecture of our VM.

## CHALLENGES

1.  In addition to `if` statements, most C-family languages have a multi-way `switch` statement. Add one to clox. The grammar is:

    ```
    switchStmt     → "switch" "(" expression ")"
                     "{" switchCase* defaultCase? "}" ;
    switchCase     → "case" expression ":" statement* ;
    defaultCase    → "default" ":" statement* ;
    ```

    To execute a `switch` statement, first evaluate the parenthesized switch value expression. Then walk the cases. For each case, evaluate its value expression. If the case value is equal to the switch value, execute the statements under the case and then exit the `switch` statement. Otherwise, try the next case. If no case matches and there is a `default` clause, execute its statements.

    To keep things simpler, we're omitting fallthrough and `break` statements. Each case automatically jumps to the end of the switch statement after its statements are done.

2.  In jlox, we had a challenge to add support for `break` statements. This time, let's do `continue`:

    ```
    continueStmt    → "continue" ";" ;
    ```

    A `continue` statement jumps directly to the top of the nearest enclosing loop, skipping the rest of the loop body. Inside a `for` loop, a `continue` jumps to the increment clause, if there is one. It's a compile-time error to have a `continue` statement not enclosed in a loop.

    Make sure to think about scope. What should happen to local variables declared inside the body of the loop or in blocks nested inside the loop when a `continue` is executed?

3.  Control flow constructs have been mostly unchanged since ALGOL 68. Language evolution since then has focused on making code more declarative and high level, so imperative control flow hasn't gotten much attention.

    For fun, try to invent a useful novel control flow feature for Lox. It can be a refinement of an existing form or something entirely new. In practice, it's hard to come up with something useful enough at this low expressiveness level to outweigh the cost of forcing a user to learn an unfamiliar notation and behavior, but it's a good chance to practice your design skills.

## DESIGN NOTE: CONSIDERING GOTO HARMFUL

Discovering that all of our beautiful structured control flow in Lox is actually compiled to raw unstructured jumps is like the moment in Scooby Doo when the monster rips the mask off their face. It was goto all along! Except in this case, the monster is *under* the mask. We all know goto is evil. But…why?

It is true that you can write outrageously unmaintainable code using goto. But I don't think most programmers around today have seen that first hand. It's been a long time since that style was common. These days, it's a boogie man we invoke in scary stories around the campfire.

The reason we rarely confront that monster in person is because Edsger Dijkstra slayed it with his famous letter "Go To Statement Considered Harmful", published in *Communications of the ACM* (March, 1968). Debate around structured programming had been fierce for some time with adherents on both sides, but I think Dijkstra deserves the most credit for effectively ending it. Most new languages today have no unstructured jump statements.

A one-and-a-half page letter that almost single-handedly destroyed a language feature must be pretty impressive stuff. If you haven't read it, I encourage you to do so. It's a seminal piece of computer science lore, one of our tribe's ancestral songs. Also, it's a nice, short bit of practice for reading academic CS writing, which is a useful skill to develop.

I've read it through a number of times, along with a few critiques, responses, and commentaries. I ended up with mixed feelings, at best. At a very high level, I'm with him. His general argument is something like this:

1. As programmers, we write programs—static text—but what we care about is the actual running program—its dynamic behavior.

2. We're better at reasoning about static things than dynamic things. (He doesn't provide any evidence to support this claim, but I accept it.)

3. Thus, the more we can make the dynamic execution of the program reflect its textual structure, the better.

This is a good start. Drawing our attention to the separation between the code we write and the code as it runs inside the machine is an interesting insight. Then he tries to define a "correspondence" between program text and execution. For someone who spent literally his entire career advocating greater rigor in programming, his definition is pretty hand-wavey. He says:

> Let us now consider how we can characterize the progress of a process. (You may think about this question in a very concrete manner: suppose that a process, considered as a time succession of actions, is stopped after an arbitrary action, what data do we have to fix in order that we can redo the process until the very same point?)

Imagine it like this. You have two computers with the same program running on the exact same inputs—so totally deterministic. You pause one of them at an arbitrary point in its execution. What data would you need to send to the other computer to be able to stop it exactly as far along as the first one was?

If your program allows only simple statements like assignment, it's easy. You just need to know the point after the last statement you executed. Basically a breakpoint, the **ip** in our VM, or the line number in an error message. Adding branching control

That is, if you can get past Dijkstra's insufferable faux-modest self-aggrandizing writing style:

> More recently I discovered why the use of the go to statement has such disastrous effects. …At that time I did not attach too much importance to this discovery; I now submit my considerations for publication because in very recent discussions in which the subject turned up, I have been urged to do so.

Ah, yet another one of my many discoveries. I couldn't even be bothered to write it up until the clamoring masses begged me to.

flow like `if` and `switch` doesn't add any more to this. Even if the marker points inside a branch, we can still tell where we are.

Once you add function calls, you need something more. You could have paused the first computer in the middle of a function, but that function may be called from multiple places. To pause the second machine at exactly the same point in *the entire program's* execution, you need to pause it on the *right* call to that function.

So you need to know not just the current statement, but, for function calls that haven't returned yet, you need to know the locations of the callsites. In other words, a call stack, though I don't think that term existed when Dijkstra wrote this. Groovy.

He notes that loops make things harder. If you pause in the middle of a loop body, you don't know how many iterations have run. So he says you also need to keep an iteration count. And, since loops can nest, you need a stack of those (presumably interleaved with the call stack pointers since you can be in loops in outer calls too).

This is where it gets weird. So we're really building to something now, and you expect him to explain how goto breaks all of this. Instead, he just says:

> The unbridled use of the go to statement has an immediate consequence that it becomes terribly hard to find a meaningful set of coordinates in which to describe the process progress.

He doesn't prove that this is hard, or say why. He just says it. He does say that one approach is unsatisfactory:

> With the go to statement one can, of course, still describe the progress uniquely by a counter counting the number of actions performed since program start (viz. a kind of normalized clock). The difficulty is that such a coordinate, although unique, is utterly unhelpful.

But…that's effectively what loop counters do, and he was fine with those. It's not like every loop is a simple "for every integer from 0 to 10" incrementing count. Many are `while` loops with complex conditionals.

Taking an example close to home, consider the core bytecode execution loop at the heart of clox. Dijkstra argues that that loop is tractable because we can simply count how many times the loop has run to reason about its progress. But that loop runs once for each executed instruction in some user's compiled Lox program. Does knowing that it executed 6,201 bytecode instructions really tell us VM maintainers *anything* edifying about the state of the interpreter?

In fact, this particular example points to a deeper truth. Böhm and Jacopini's *structured program theorem* proved that *any* control flow using goto can be transformed into one using just sequencing, loops, and branches. Our bytecode interpreter loop is a living example of that proof: it implements the unstructured control flow of the clox bytecode instruction set without using any gotos itself.

That seems to offer a counter-argument to Dijkstra's claim: you *can* define a correspondence for a program using gotos by transforming it to one that doesn't and then use the correspondence from that program, which—according to him—is acceptable because it uses only branches and loops.

But, honestly, my argument here is also weak. I think both of us are basically doing pretend math and using fake logic to make what should be an empirical, human-centered argument. Dijkstra is right that some code using goto is really bad. Much of that could and should be turned into clearer code by using structured control flow.

By eliminating goto completely from languages, you're definitely prevented from writing bad code using gotos. It may be that forcing users to use structured control flow and making it an uphill battle to write goto-like code using those constructs is a net win for all of our productivity.

But I do wonder sometimes if we threw out the baby with the bathwater. In the absence of goto, we often resort to more complex structured patterns. The "switch inside a loop" is a classic one. Another is using a guard variable to exit out of a series of nested loops:

```
// See if the matrix contains a zero.
bool found = false;
for (int x = 0; x < xSize; x++) {
  for (int y = 0; y < ySize; y++) {
    for (int z = 0; z < zSize; z++) {
      if (matrix[x][y][z] == 0) {
        printf("found");
        found = true;
        break;
      }
    }
    if (found) break;
  }
  if (found) break;
}
```

You could do this without **break** statements—themselves a limited goto-ish construct—by inserting ! **found** && at the beginning of the condition clause of each loop.

Is that really better than:

```
for (int x = 0; x < xSize; x++) {
  for (int y = 0; y < ySize; y++) {
    for (int z = 0; z < zSize; z++) {
      if (matrix[x][y][z] == 0) {
        printf("found");
        goto done;
      }
    }
  }
}
done:
```

I guess what I really don't like is that we're making language design and engineering decisions today based on fear. Few people today have any subtle understanding of the problems and benefits of goto. Instead, we just think it's "considered harmful". Personally, I've never found dogma a good starting place for quality creative work.

# Calls and Functions

24

*"Any problem in computer science can be solved with another level of indirection. Except for the problem of too many layers of indirection."*

— David Wheeler

This chapter is a beast. I try to break features into bite-sized pieces, but sometimes you gotta swallow the whole meal. Our next task is functions. We could start with only function declarations, but that's not very useful when you can't call them. We could do calls, but there's nothing to call. And all of the runtime support needed in the VM to support both of those isn't very rewarding if it isn't hooked up to anything you can see. So we're going to do it all. It's a lot, but we'll feel good when we're done.

Eating—consumption—is a weird metaphor for a creative act. But most of the biological processes that produce "output" are a little less, ahem, decorous.

## 24.1 Function Objects

The most interesting structural change in the VM is around the stack. We already *have* a stack for local variables and temporaries, so we're partway there. But we have no notion of a *call* stack. Before we can make much progress, we'll have to fix that. But first, let's write some code. I always feel better once I start moving. We can't do much without having some kind of representation for functions, so we'll start there. From the VM's perspective, what is a function?

A function has a body that can be executed, so that means some bytecode. We could compile the entire program and all of its function declarations into one big monolithic Chunk. Each function would have a pointer to the first instruction of its code inside the Chunk.

This is roughly how compilation to native code works where you end up with one solid blob of machine code. But for our bytecode VM, we can do something a little higher level. I think a cleaner model is to give each function its own Chunk. We'll want some other metadata too, so let's go ahead and stuff it all in a struct now.

object.h<br>add after struct Obj

```
  struct Obj* next;
};

typedef struct {
  Obj obj;
  int arity;
  Chunk chunk;
  ObjString* name;
} ObjFunction;

struct ObjString {
```

Functions are first class in Lox, so they need to be actual Lox objects. Thus ObjFunction has the same Obj header that all object types share. The `arity` field stores the number of parameters the function expects. Then, in addition to the chunk, we store the function's name. That will be handy for reporting readable runtime errors.

Humans don't seem to find numeric bytecode offsets particularly illuminating in crash dumps.

This is the first time the "object" module has needed to reference Chunk, so we get an include.

object.h

```
#include "common.h"
#include "chunk.h"
#include "value.h"
```

Like we did with strings, we define some accessories to make Lox functions easier to work with in C. Sort of a poor man's object orientation. First, we'll declare a C function to create a new Lox function.

object.h<br>add after struct ObjString

```
  uint32_t hash;
};

ObjFunction* newFunction();
ObjString* takeString(char* chars, int length);
```

The implementation is over here:

```
ObjFunction* newFunction() {
  ObjFunction* function = ALLOCATE_OBJ(ObjFunction, OBJ_FUNCTION);
  function->arity = 0;
  function->name = NULL;
  initChunk(&function->chunk);
  return function;
}
```

object.c
*add after* allocateObject()

We use our friend `ALLOCATE_OBJ()` to allocate memory and initialize the object's header so that the VM knows what type of object it is. Instead of passing in arguments to initialize the function like we did with ObjString, we set the function up in a sort of blank state—zero arity, no name, and no code. That will get filled in later after the function is created.

Since we have a new kind of object, we need a new object type in the enum.

```
typedef enum {
  OBJ_FUNCTION,
  OBJ_STRING,
} ObjType;
```

object.h
*in enum* ObjType

When we're done with a function object, we must return the bits it borrowed back to the operating system.

```
  switch (object->type) {
    case OBJ_FUNCTION: {
      ObjFunction* function = (ObjFunction*)object;
      freeChunk(&function->chunk);
      FREE(ObjFunction, object);
      break;
    }
    case OBJ_STRING: {
```

memory.c
*in* freeObject()

This switch case is responsible for freeing the ObjFunction itself as well as any other memory it owns. Functions own their chunk, so we call Chunk's destructor-like function.

Lox lets you print any object, and functions are first-class objects, so we need to handle them too.

We don't need to explicitly free the function's name because it's an ObjString. That means we can let the garbage collector manage its lifetime for us. Or, at least, we'll be able to once we implement a garbage collector.

```
  switch (OBJ_TYPE(value)) {
    case OBJ_FUNCTION:
      printFunction(AS_FUNCTION(value));
      break;
    case OBJ_STRING:
```

object.c
*in* printObject()

This calls out to:

```
static void printFunction(ObjFunction* function) {
  printf("<fn %s>", function->name->chars);
}
```

object.c
*add after* copyString()

Since a function knows its name, it may as well say it.

Finally, we have a couple of macros for converting values to functions. First, make sure your value actually *is* a function.

object.h

```
#define OBJ_TYPE(value)          (AS_OBJ(value)->type)

#define IS_FUNCTION(value)       isObjType(value, OBJ_FUNCTION)
#define IS_STRING(value)         isObjType(value, OBJ_STRING)
```

Assuming that evaluates to true, you can then safely cast the Value to an ObjFunction pointer using this:

object.h

```
#define IS_STRING(value)         isObjType(value, OBJ_STRING)

#define AS_FUNCTION(value)       ((ObjFunction*)AS_OBJ(value))
#define AS_STRING(value)         ((ObjString*)AS_OBJ(value))
```

With that, our object model knows how to represent functions. I'm feeling warmed up now. You ready for something a little harder?

## 24.2  Compiling to Function Objects

Right now, our compiler assumes it is always compiling to one single chunk. With each function's code living in separate chunks, that gets more complex. When the compiler reaches a function declaration, it needs to emit code into the function's chunk when compiling its body. At the end of the function body, the compiler needs to return to the previous chunk it was working with.

That's fine for code inside function bodies, but what about code that isn't? The "top level" of a Lox program is also imperative code and we need a chunk to compile that into. We can simplify the compiler and VM by placing that top-level code inside an automatically defined function too. That way, the compiler is always within some kind of function body, and the VM always runs code by invoking a function. It's as if the entire program is wrapped inside an implicit `main()` function.

One semantic corner where that analogy breaks down is global variables. They have special scoping rules different from local variables, so in that way, the top level of a script isn't like a function body.

Before we get to user-defined functions, then, let's do the reorganization to support that implicit top-level function. It starts with the Compiler struct. Instead of pointing directly to a Chunk that the compiler writes to, it instead has a reference to the function object being built.

compiler.c
*in struct* Compiler

```
typedef struct {
  ObjFunction* function;
  FunctionType type;

  Local locals[UINT8_COUNT];
```

We also have a little FunctionType enum. This lets the compiler tell when it's compiling top-level code versus the body of a function. Most of the compiler doesn't care about this—that's why it's a useful abstraction—but in one or two places the distinction is meaningful. We'll get to one later.

```
typedef enum {
  TYPE_FUNCTION,
  TYPE_SCRIPT
} FunctionType;
```

compiler.c
*add after struct* Local

Every place in the compiler that was writing to the Chunk now needs to go through that `function` pointer. Fortunately, many chapters ago, we encapsulated access to the chunk in the `currentChunk()` function. We only need to fix that and the rest of the compiler is happy.

It's almost like I had a crystal ball that could see into the future and knew we'd need to change the code later. But, really, it's because I wrote all the code for the book before any of the text.

```
Compiler* current = NULL;

static Chunk* currentChunk() {
  return &current->function->chunk;
}

static void errorAt(Token* token, const char* message) {
```

compiler.c
*add after variable* current
*replace 5 lines*

The current chunk is always the chunk owned by the function we're in the middle of compiling. Next, we need to actually create that function. Previously, the VM passed a Chunk to the compiler which filled it with code. Instead, the compiler will create and return a function that contains the compiled top-level code—which is all we support right now—of the user's program.

### 24.2.1  Creating functions at compile time

We start threading this through in `compile()`, which is the main entry point into the compiler.

```
  Compiler compiler;
  initCompiler(&compiler, TYPE_SCRIPT);

  parser.hadError = false;
```

compiler.c
*in* compile()
*replace 2 lines*

There are a bunch of changes in how the compiler is initialized. First, we initialize the new Compiler fields.

```
static void initCompiler(Compiler* compiler, FunctionType type) {
  compiler->function = NULL;
  compiler->type = type;
  compiler->localCount = 0;
```

compiler.c
*function* initCompiler()
*replace 1 line*

Then we allocate a new function object to compile into.

```
  compiler->scopeDepth = 0;
  compiler->function = newFunction();
  current = compiler;
```

I know, it looks dumb to null the `function` field only to immediately assign it a value a few lines later. More garbage collection-related paranoia.

compiler.c
*in* initCompiler()

Creating an ObjFunction in the compiler might seem a little strange. A function object is the *runtime* representation of a function, but here we are creating it at compile time. The way to think of it is that a function is similar to a string or number literal. It forms a bridge between the compile time and runtime worlds. When we get to function *declarations*, those really *are* literals—they are a notation that produces values of a built-in type. So the compiler creates function objects during compilation. Then, at runtime, they are simply invoked.

Here is another strange piece of code:

```
  current = compiler;

  Local* local = &current->locals[current->localCount++];
  local->depth = 0;
  local->name.start = "";
  local->name.length = 0;
}
```

We can create functions at compile time because they contain only data available at compile time. The function's code, name, and arity are all fixed. When we add closures in the next chapter, which capture variables at runtime, the story gets more complex.

Remember that the compiler's `locals` array keeps track of which stack slots are associated with which local variables or temporaries. From now on, the compiler implicitly claims stack slot zero for the VM's own internal use. We give it an empty name so that the user can't write an identifier that refers to it. I'll explain what this is about when it becomes useful.

That's the initialization side. We also need a couple of changes on the other end when we finish compiling some code.

```
static ObjFunction* endCompiler() {
  emitReturn();
```

Previously, when `interpret()` called into the compiler, it passed in a Chunk to be written to. Now that the compiler creates the function object itself, we return that function. We grab it from the current compiler here:

```
  emitReturn();
  ObjFunction* function = current->function;

#ifdef DEBUG_PRINT_CODE
```

And then return it to `compile()` like so:

```
#endif

  return function;
}
```

Now is a good time to make another tweak in this function. Earlier, we added some diagnostic code to have the VM dump the disassembled bytecode so we could debug the compiler. We should fix that to keep working now that the generated chunk is wrapped in a function.

```
#ifdef DEBUG_PRINT_CODE
  if (!parser.hadError) {
    disassembleChunk(currentChunk(), function->name != NULL
        ? function->name->chars : "<script>");
  }
#endif
```

Notice the check in here to see if the function's name is NULL? User-defined functions have names, but the implicit function we create for the top-level code does not, and we need to handle that gracefully even in our own diagnostic code. Speaking of which:

```
static void printFunction(ObjFunction* function) {
  if (function->name == NULL) {
    printf("<script>");
    return;
  }
  printf("<fn %s>", function->name->chars);
```

object.c
*in* printFunction()

There's no way for a *user* to get a reference to the top-level function and try to print it, but our DEBUG_TRACE_EXECUTION diagnostic code that prints the entire stack can and does.

It is no fun if the diagnostic code we use to find bugs itself causes the VM to segfault!

Bumping up a level to compile(), we adjust its signature.

```
#include "vm.h"

ObjFunction* compile(const char* source);

#endif
```

compiler.h
*function* compile()
*replace 1 line*

Instead of taking a chunk, now it returns a function. Over in the implementation:

```
ObjFunction* compile(const char* source) {
  initScanner(source);
```

compiler.c
*function* compile()
*replace 1 line*

Finally we get to some actual code. We change the very end of the function to this:

```
  while (!match(TOKEN_EOF)) {
    declaration();
  }

  ObjFunction* function = endCompiler();
  return parser.hadError ? NULL : function;
}
```

compiler.c
*in* compile()
*replace 2 lines*

We get the function object from the compiler. If there were no compile errors, we return it. Otherwise, we signal an error by returning NULL. This way, the VM doesn't try to execute a function that may contain invalid bytecode.

Eventually, we will update interpret() to handle the new declaration of compile(), but first we have some other changes to make.

## 24.3  Call Frames

It's time for a big conceptual leap. Before we can implement function declarations and calls, we need to get the VM ready to handle them. There are two main problems we need to worry about:

### 24.3.1  Allocating local variables

The compiler allocates stack slots for local variables. How should that work when the set of local variables in a program is distributed across multiple functions?

It's basically what you'd get if you declared every local variable in a C program using static.

One option would be to keep them totally separate. Each function would get its own dedicated set of slots in the VM stack that it would own forever, even when the function isn't being called. Each local variable in the entire program would have a bit of memory in the VM that it keeps to itself.

Believe it or not, early programming language implementations worked this way. The first Fortran compilers statically allocated memory for each variable. The obvious problem is that it's really inefficient. Most functions are not in the middle of being called at any point in time, so sitting on unused memory for them is wasteful.

Fortran avoided this problem by disallowing recursion entirely. Recursion was considered an advanced, esoteric feature at the time.

The more fundamental problem, though, is recursion. With recursion, you can be "in" multiple calls to the same function at the same time. Each needs its own memory for its local variables. In jlox, we solved this by dynamically allocating memory for an environment each time a function was called or a block entered. In clox, we don't want that kind of performance cost on every function call.

Instead, our solution lies somewhere between Fortran's static allocation and jlox's dynamic approach. The value stack in the VM works on the observation that local variables and temporaries behave in a last-in first-out fashion. Fortunately for us, that's still true even when you add function calls into the mix. Here's an example:

```
fun first() {
  var a = 1;
  second();
  var b = 2;
}

fun second() {
  var c = 3;
  var d = 4;
}

first();
```

Step through the program and look at which variables are in memory at each point in time:

As execution flows through the two calls, every local variable obeys the principle that any variable declared after it will be discarded before the first variable needs to be. This is true even across calls. We know we'll be done with c and d before we are done with a. It seems we should be able to allocate local variables on the VM's value stack.

Ideally, we still determine *where* on the stack each variable will go at compile time. That keeps the bytecode instructions for working with variables simple and fast. In the above example, we could imagine doing so in a straightforward way, but that doesn't always work out. Consider:

I say "imagine" because the compiler can't actually figure this out. Because functions are first class in Lox, we can't determine which functions call which others at compile time.

```
fun first() {
  var a = 1;
  second();
  var b = 2;
  second();
}

fun second() {
  var c = 3;
  var d = 4;
}

first();
```

In the first call to second(), c and d would go into slots 1 and 2. But in the second call, we need to have made room for b, so c and d need to be in slots 2 and 3. Thus the compiler can't pin down an exact slot for each local variable across function calls. But *within* a given function, the *relative* locations of each local variable are fixed. Variable d is always in the slot right after c. This is the key insight.

When a function is called, we don't know where the top of the stack will be because it can be called from different contexts. But, wherever that top happens to be, we do know where all of the function's local variables will be relative to that starting point. So, like many problems, we solve our allocation problem with a level of indirection.

At the beginning of each function call, the VM records the location of the first slot where that function's own locals begin. The instructions for working with local variables access them by a slot index relative to that, instead of relative to the bottom of the stack like they do today. At compile time, we calculate those relative slots. At runtime, we convert that relative slot to an absolute stack index by adding the function call's starting slot.

It's as if the function gets a "window" or "frame" within the larger stack where it can store its locals. The position of the **call frame** is determined at runtime, but within and relative to that region, we know where to find things.

The historical name for this recorded location where the function's locals start is a **frame pointer** because it points to the beginning of the function's call frame. Sometimes you hear **base pointer**, because it points to the base stack slot on top of which all of the function's variables live.

That's the first piece of data we need to track. Every time we call a function, the VM determines the first stack slot where that function's variables begin.

### 24.3.2  Return addresses

Right now, the VM works its way through the instruction stream by incrementing the `ip` field. The only interesting behavior is around control flow instructions which offset the `ip` by larger amounts. *Calling* a function is pretty straightforward—simply set `ip` to point to the first instruction in that function's chunk. But what about when the function is done?

The VM needs to return back to the chunk where the function was called from and resume execution at the instruction immediately after the call. Thus, for each function call, we need to track where we jump back to when the call completes. This is called a **return address** because it's the address of the instruction that the VM returns to after the call.

Again, thanks to recursion, there may be multiple return addresses for a single function, so this is a property of each *invocation* and not the function itself.

### 24.3.3  The call stack

So for each live function invocation—each call that hasn't returned yet—we need to track where on the stack that function's locals begin, and where the caller should resume. We'll put this, along with some other stuff, in a new struct.

vm.h

```
#define STACK_MAX 256

typedef struct {
  ObjFunction* function;
  uint8_t* ip;
  Value* slots;
} CallFrame;

typedef struct {
```

A CallFrame represents a single ongoing function call. The `slots` field points into the VM's value stack at the first slot that this function can use. I gave it a plural name because—thanks to C's weird "pointers are sort of arrays" thing—we'll treat it like an array.

The implementation of return addresses is a little different from what I described above. Instead of storing the return address in the callee's frame, the caller stores its own `ip`. When we return from a function, the VM will jump to the `ip` of the caller's CallFrame and resume from there.

I also stuffed a pointer to the function being called in here. We'll use that to

The authors of early Fortran compilers had a clever trick for implementing return addresses. Since they *didn't* support recursion, any given function needed only a single return address at any point in time. So when a function was called at runtime, the program would *modify its own code* to change a jump instruction at the end of the function to jump back to its caller. Sometimes the line between genius and madness is hair thin.

look up constants and for a few other things.

Each time a function is called, we create one of these structs. We could dynamically allocate them on the heap, but that's slow. Function calls are a core operation, so they need to be as fast as possible. Fortunately, we can make the same observation we made for variables: function calls have stack semantics. If `first()` calls `second()`, the call to `second()` will complete before `first()` does.

So over in the VM, we create an array of these CallFrame structs up front and treat it as a stack, like we do with the value array.

```
typedef struct {
  CallFrame frames[FRAMES_MAX];
  int frameCount;

  Value stack[STACK_MAX];
```

vm.h
in struct **VM**
replace 2 lines

This array replaces the `chunk` and `ip` fields we used to have directly in the VM. Now each CallFrame has its own `ip` and its own pointer to the ObjFunction that it's executing. From there, we can get to the function's chunk.

The new `frameCount` field in the VM stores the current height of the CallFrame stack—the number of ongoing function calls. To keep clox simple, the array's capacity is fixed. This means, as in many language implementations, there is a maximum call depth we can handle. For clox, it's defined here:

```
#include "value.h"

#define FRAMES_MAX 64
#define STACK_MAX (FRAMES_MAX * UINT8_COUNT)

typedef struct {
```

vm.h
replace 1 line

It is still possible to overflow the stack if enough function calls use enough temporaries in addition to locals. A robust implementation would guard against this, but I'm trying to keep things simple.

We also redefine the value stack's size in terms of that to make sure we have plenty of stack slots even in very deep call trees. When the VM starts up, the CallFrame stack is empty.

```
  vm.stackTop = vm.stack;
  vm.frameCount = 0;
}
```

vm.c
in resetStack()

The "vm.h" header needs access to ObjFunction, so we add an include.

```
#define clox_vm_h

#include "object.h"
#include "table.h"
```

vm.h
replace 1 line

Now we're ready to move over to the VM's implementation file. We've got some grunt work ahead of us. We've moved `ip` out of the VM struct and into CallFrame. We need to fix every line of code in the VM that touches `ip` to handle that. Also, the instructions that access local variables by stack slot need to be updated to do so relative to the current CallFrame's `slots` field.

We'll start at the top and plow through it.

Many Lisp implementations dynamically allocate stack frames because it simplifies implementing continuations. If your language supports continuations, then function calls do *not* always have stack semantics.

vm.c
in run()
replace 4 lines

```
static InterpretResult run() {
  CallFrame* frame = &vm.frames[vm.frameCount - 1];

#define READ_BYTE() (*frame->ip++)

#define READ_SHORT() \
    (frame->ip += 2, \
    (uint16_t)((frame->ip[-2] << 8) | frame->ip[-1]))

#define READ_CONSTANT() \
    (frame->function->chunk.constants.values[READ_BYTE()])

#define READ_STRING() AS_STRING(READ_CONSTANT())
```

We could access the current frame by going through the CallFrame array every time, but that's verbose. More importantly, storing the frame in a local variable encourages the C compiler to keep that pointer in a register. That speeds up access to the frame's ip. There's no *guarantee* that the compiler will do this, but there's a good chance it will.

First, we store the current topmost CallFrame in a local variable inside the main bytecode execution function. Then we replace the bytecode access macros with versions that access ip through that variable.

Now onto each instruction that needs a little tender loving care.

vm.c
in run()
replace 1 line

```
    case OP_GET_LOCAL: {
      uint8_t slot = READ_BYTE();
      push(frame->slots[slot]);
      break;
```

Previously, OP_GET_LOCAL read the given local slot directly from the VM's stack array, which meant it indexed the slot starting from the bottom of the stack. Now, it accesses the current frame's slots array, which means it accesses the given numbered slot relative to the beginning of that frame.

Setting a local variable works the same way.

vm.c
in run()
replace 1 line

```
    case OP_SET_LOCAL: {
      uint8_t slot = READ_BYTE();
      frame->slots[slot] = peek(0);
      break;
```

The jump instructions used to modify the VM's ip field. Now, they do the same for the current frame's ip.

vm.c
in run()
replace 1 line

```
    case OP_JUMP: {
      uint16_t offset = READ_SHORT();
      frame->ip += offset;
      break;
```

Same with the conditional jump:

vm.c
in run()
replace 1 line

```
    case OP_JUMP_IF_FALSE: {
      uint16_t offset = READ_SHORT();
      if (isFalsey(peek(0))) frame->ip += offset;
      break;
```

And our backward-jumping loop instruction:

```
    case OP_LOOP: {
      uint16_t offset = READ_SHORT();
      frame->ip -= offset;
      break;
```
vm.c
in run()
replace 1 line

We have some diagnostic code that prints each instruction as it executes to help us debug our VM. That needs to work with the new structure too.

```
    printf("\n");
    disassembleInstruction(&frame->function->chunk,
        (int)(frame->ip - frame->function->chunk.code));
#endif
```
vm.c
in run()
replace 2 lines

Instead of passing in the VM's chunk and ip fields, now we read from the current CallFrame.

You know, that wasn't too bad, actually. Most instructions just use the macros so didn't need to be touched. Next, we jump up a level to the code that calls run().

```
InterpretResult interpret(const char* source) {
  ObjFunction* function = compile(source);
  if (function == NULL) return INTERPRET_COMPILE_ERROR;

  push(OBJ_VAL(function));
  CallFrame* frame = &vm.frames[vm.frameCount++];
  frame->function = function;
  frame->ip = function->chunk.code;
  frame->slots = vm.stack;

  InterpretResult result = run();
```
vm.c
in interpret()
replace 10 lines

We finally get to wire up our earlier compiler changes to the back-end changes we just made. First, we pass the source code to the compiler. It returns us a new ObjFunction containing the compiled top-level code. If we get NULL back, it means there was some compile-time error which the compiler has already reported. In that case, we bail out since we can't run anything.

Otherwise, we store the function on the stack and prepare an initial CallFrame to execute its code. Now you can see why the compiler sets aside stack slot zero—that stores the function being called. In the new CallFrame, we point to the function, initialize its ip to point to the beginning of the function's bytecode, and set up its stack window to start at the very bottom of the VM's value stack.

This gets the interpreter ready to start executing code. After finishing, the VM used to free the hardcoded chunk. Now that the ObjFunction owns that code, we don't need to do that anymore, so the end of interpret() is simply this:

```
  frame->slots = vm.stack;

  return run();
}
```
vm.c
in interpret()
replace 4 lines

The last piece of code referring to the old VM fields is runtimeError(). We'll revisit that later in the chapter, but for now let's change it to this:

**vm.c**
*in* runtimeError()
*replace 2 lines*

```
  fputs("\n", stderr);

  CallFrame* frame = &vm.frames[vm.frameCount - 1];
  size_t instruction = frame->ip - frame->function->chunk.code - 1;
  int line = frame->function->chunk.lines[instruction];
  fprintf(stderr, "[line %d] in script\n", line);
```

Instead of reading the chunk and `ip` directly from the VM, it pulls those from the topmost CallFrame on the stack. That should get the function working again and behaving as it did before.

Assuming we did all of that correctly, we got clox back to a runnable state. Fire it up and it does...exactly what it did before. We haven't added any new features yet, so this is kind of a let down. But all of the infrastructure is there and ready for us now. Let's take advantage of it.

## 24.4  Function Declarations

Yes, I am going to make a joke about the
**fun** keyword every time it comes up.

Before we can do call expressions, we need something to call, so we'll do function declarations first. The fun starts with a keyword.

**compiler.c**
*in* declaration()
*replace 1 line*

```
static void declaration() {
  if (match(TOKEN_FUN)) {
    funDeclaration();
  } else if (match(TOKEN_VAR)) {
    varDeclaration();
```

That passes control to here:

**compiler.c**
*add after* block()

```
static void funDeclaration() {
  uint8_t global = parseVariable("Expect function name.");
  markInitialized();
  function(TYPE_FUNCTION);
  defineVariable(global);
}
```

Functions are first-class values, and a function declaration simply creates and stores one in a newly declared variable. So we parse the name just like any other variable declaration. A function declaration at the top level will bind the function to a global variable. Inside a block or other function, a function declaration creates a local variable.

In an earlier chapter, I explained how variables get defined in two stages. This ensures you can't access a variable's value inside the variable's own initializer. That would be bad because the variable doesn't *have* a value yet.

Functions don't suffer from this problem. It's safe for a function to refer to its own name inside its body. You can't *call* the function and execute the body until after it's fully defined, so you'll never see the variable in an uninitialized state. Practically speaking, it's useful to allow this in order to support recursive local functions.

To make that work, we mark the function declaration's variable "initialized" as soon as we compile the name, before we compile the body. That way the name can be referenced inside the body without generating an error.

We do need one check, though.

```
static void markInitialized() {
  if (current->scopeDepth == 0) return;
  current->locals[current->localCount - 1].depth =
```

compiler.c
*in* markInitialized()

Before, we called `markInitialized()` only when we already knew we were in a local scope. Now, a top-level function declaration will also call this function. When that happens, there is no local variable to mark initialized—the function is bound to a global variable.

Next, we compile the function itself—its parameter list and block body. For that, we use a separate helper function. That helper generates code that leaves the resulting function object on top of the stack. After that, we call `defineVariable()` to store that function back into the variable we declared for it.

I split out the code to compile the parameters and body because we'll reuse it later for parsing method declarations inside classes. Let's build it incrementally, starting with this:

```
static void function(FunctionType type) {
  Compiler compiler;
  initCompiler(&compiler, type);
  beginScope();

  consume(TOKEN_LEFT_PAREN, "Expect '(' after function name.");
  consume(TOKEN_RIGHT_PAREN, "Expect ')' after parameters.");
  consume(TOKEN_LEFT_BRACE, "Expect '{' before function body.");
  block();

  ObjFunction* function = endCompiler();
  emitBytes(OP_CONSTANT, makeConstant(OBJ_VAL(function)));
}
```

compiler.c
*add after* block()

This `beginScope()` doesn't have a corresponding `endScope()` call. Because we end Compiler completely when we reach the end of the function body, there's no need to close the lingering outermost scope.

For now, we won't worry about parameters. We parse an empty pair of parentheses followed by the body. The body starts with a left curly brace, which we parse here. Then we call our existing `block()` function, which knows how to compile the rest of a block including the closing brace.

### 24.4.1 A stack of compilers

The interesting parts are the compiler stuff at the top and bottom. The Compiler struct stores data like which slots are owned by which local variables, how many blocks of nesting we're currently in, etc. All of that is specific to a single function. But now the front end needs to handle compiling multiple functions nested within each other.

The trick for managing that is to create a separate Compiler for each function being compiled. When we start compiling a function declaration, we create a new Compiler on the C stack and initialize it. `initCompiler()` sets that Compiler to be the current one. Then, as we compile the body, all of the functions that emit bytecode write to the chunk owned by the new Compiler's function.

Remember that the compiler treats top-level code as the body of an implicit function, so as soon as we add *any* function declarations, we're in a world of nested functions.

After we reach the end of the function's block body, we call `endCompiler()`. That yields the newly compiled function object, which we store as a constant in the *surrounding* function's constant table. But, wait, how do we get back to the surrounding function? We lost it when `initCompiler()` overwrote the current compiler pointer.

We fix that by treating the series of nested Compiler structs as a stack. Unlike the Value and CallFrame stacks in the VM, we won't use an array. Instead, we use a linked list. Each Compiler points back to the Compiler for the function that encloses it, all the way back to the root Compiler for the top-level code.

compiler.c
*add after enum* FunctionType
*replace 1 line*

```
} FunctionType;

typedef struct Compiler {
  struct Compiler* enclosing;
  ObjFunction* function;
```

Inside the Compiler struct, we can't reference the Compiler *typedef* since that declaration hasn't finished yet. Instead, we give a name to the struct itself and use that for the field's type. C is weird.

When initializing a new Compiler, we capture the about-to-no-longer-be-current one in that pointer.

compiler.c
*in* initCompiler()

```
static void initCompiler(Compiler* compiler, FunctionType type) {
  compiler->enclosing = current;
  compiler->function = NULL;
```

Then when a Compiler finishes, it pops itself off the stack by restoring the previous compiler to be the new current one.

compiler.c
*in* endCompiler()

```
#endif

  current = current->enclosing;
  return function;
```

Using the native stack for Compiler structs does mean our compiler has a practical limit on how deeply nested function declarations can be. Go too far and you could overflow the C stack. If we want the compiler to be more robust against pathological or even malicious code—a real concern for tools like JavaScript VMs—it would be good to have our compiler artificially limit the amount of function nesting it permits.

Note that we don't even need to dynamically allocate the Compiler structs. Each is stored as a local variable in the C stack—either in `compile()` or `function()`. The linked list of Compilers threads through the C stack. The reason we can get an unbounded number of them is because our compiler uses recursive descent, so `function()` ends up calling itself recursively when you have nested function declarations.

### 24.4.2  Function parameters

Functions aren't very useful if you can't pass arguments to them, so let's do parameters next.

compiler.c
*in* function()

```
  consume(TOKEN_LEFT_PAREN, "Expect '(' after function name.");
  if (!check(TOKEN_RIGHT_PAREN)) {
    do {
      current->function->arity++;
      if (current->function->arity > 255) {
```

*continued on next page…*

```
        errorAtCurrent("Can't have more than 255 parameters.");
      }
      uint8_t constant = parseVariable("Expect parameter name.");
      defineVariable(constant);
    } while (match(TOKEN_COMMA));
  }
  consume(TOKEN_RIGHT_PAREN, "Expect ')' after parameters.");
```

*...from previous page*

Semantically, a parameter is simply a local variable declared in the outermost lexical scope of the function body. We get to use the existing compiler support for declaring named local variables to parse and compile parameters. Unlike local variables, which have initializers, there's no code here to initialize the parameter's value. We'll see how they are initialized later when we do argument passing in function calls.

While we're at it, we note the function's arity by counting how many parameters we parse. The other piece of metadata we store with a function is its name. When compiling a function declaration, we call `initCompiler()` right after we parse the function's name. That means we can grab the name right then from the previous token.

```
  current = compiler;
  if (type != TYPE_SCRIPT) {
    current->function->name = copyString(parser.previous.start,
                                         parser.previous.length);
  }

  Local* local = &current->locals[current->localCount++];
```

compiler.c
*in* `initCompiler()`

Note that we're careful to create a copy of the name string. Remember, the lexeme points directly into the original source code string. That string may get freed once the code is finished compiling. The function object we create in the compiler outlives the compiler and persists until runtime. So it needs its own heap-allocated name string that it can keep around.

Rad. Now we can compile function declarations, like this:

```
fun areWeHavingItYet() {
  print "Yes we are!";
}

print areWeHavingItYet;
```

We just can't do anything useful with them.

We can print them! I guess that's not very useful, though.

## 24.5 Function Calls

By the end of this section, we'll start to see some interesting behavior. The next step is calling functions. We don't usually think of it this way, but a function call expression is kind of an infix ( operator. You have a high-precedence expression on the left for the thing being called—usually just a single identifier. Then the ( in the middle, followed by the argument expressions separated by commas, and a final ) to wrap it up at the end.

That odd grammatical perspective explains how to hook the syntax into our parsing table.

compiler.c
*add after* unary()
*replace 1 line*

```
ParseRule rules[] = {
  [TOKEN_LEFT_PAREN]     = {grouping, call,   PREC_CALL},
  [TOKEN_RIGHT_PAREN]    = {NULL,     NULL,   PREC_NONE},
```

When the parser encounters a left parenthesis following an expression, it dispatches to a new parser function.

compiler.c
*add after* binary()

```
static void call(bool canAssign) {
  uint8_t argCount = argumentList();
  emitBytes(OP_CALL, argCount);
}
```

We've already consumed the ( token, so next we compile the arguments using a separate argumentList() helper. That function returns the number of arguments it compiled. Each argument expression generates code that leaves its value on the stack in preparation for the call. After that, we emit a new OP_CALL instruction to invoke the function, using the argument count as an operand.

We compile the arguments using this friend:

compiler.c
*add after* defineVariable()

```
static uint8_t argumentList() {
  uint8_t argCount = 0;
  if (!check(TOKEN_RIGHT_PAREN)) {
    do {
      expression();
      argCount++;
    } while (match(TOKEN_COMMA));
  }
  consume(TOKEN_RIGHT_PAREN, "Expect ')' after arguments.");
  return argCount;
}
```

That code should look familiar from jlox. We chew through arguments as long as we find commas after each expression. Once we run out, we consume the final closing parenthesis and we're done.

Well, almost. Back in jlox, we added a compile-time check that you don't pass more than 255 arguments to a call. At the time, I said that was because clox would need a similar limit. Now you can see why—since we stuff the argument count into the bytecode as a single-byte operand, we can only go up to 255. We need to verify that in this compiler too.

compiler.c
*in* argumentList()

```
    expression();
    if (argCount == 255) {
      error("Can't have more than 255 arguments.");
    }
    argCount++;
```

That's the front end. Let's skip over to the back end, with a quick stop in the middle to declare the new instruction.

```
OP_LOOP,
OP_CALL,
OP_RETURN,
```

chunk.h
*in enum* OpCode

## 24.5.1 Binding arguments to parameters

Before we get to the implementation, we should think about what the stack looks like at the point of a call and what we need to do from there. When we reach the call instruction, we have already executed the expression for the function being called, followed by its arguments. Say our program looks like this:

```
fun sum(a, b, c) {
  return a + b + c;
}

print 4 + sum(5, 6, 7);
```

If we pause the VM right on the OP_CALL instruction for that call to sum(), the stack looks like this:

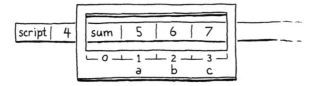

Picture this from the perspective of sum() itself. When the compiler compiled sum(), it automatically allocated slot zero. Then, after that, it allocated local slots for the parameters a, b, and c, in order. To perform a call to sum(), we need a CallFrame initialized with the function being called and a region of stack slots that it can use. Then we need to collect the arguments passed to the function and get them into the corresponding slots for the parameters.

When the VM starts executing the body of sum(), we want its stack window to look like this:

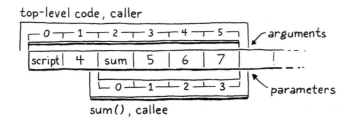

Do you notice how the argument slots that the caller sets up and the parameter slots the callee needs are both in exactly the right order? How convenient! This is no coincidence. When I talked about each CallFrame having its own window into the stack, I never said those windows must be *disjoint*. There's nothing preventing us from overlapping them, like this:

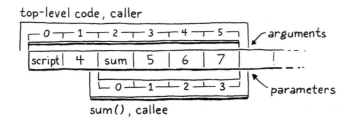

The top of the caller's stack contains the function being called followed by the

Different bytecode VMs and real CPU architectures have different *calling conventions*, which is the specific mechanism they use to pass arguments, store the return address, etc. The mechanism I use here is based on Lua's clean, fast virtual machine.

arguments in order. We know the caller doesn't have any other slots above those in use because any temporaries needed when evaluating argument expressions have been discarded by now. The bottom of the callee's stack overlaps so that the parameter slots exactly line up with where the argument values already live.

This means that we don't need to do *any* work to "bind an argument to a parameter". There's no copying values between slots or across environments. The arguments are already exactly where they need to be. It's hard to beat that for performance.

Time to implement the call instruction.

**vm.c**
*in* run()

```
    }
    case OP_CALL: {
      int argCount = READ_BYTE();
      if (!callValue(peek(argCount), argCount)) {
        return INTERPRET_RUNTIME_ERROR;
      }
      break;
    }
    case OP_RETURN: {
```

We need to know the function being called and the number of arguments passed to it. We get the latter from the instruction's operand. That also tells us where to find the function on the stack by counting past the argument slots from the top of the stack. We hand that data off to a separate `callValue()` function. If that returns `false`, it means the call caused some sort of runtime error. When that happens, we abort the interpreter.

If `callValue()` is successful, there will be a new frame on the CallFrame stack for the called function. The `run()` function has its own cached pointer to the current frame, so we need to update that.

**vm.c**
*in* run()

```
        return INTERPRET_RUNTIME_ERROR;
      }
      frame = &vm.frames[vm.frameCount - 1];
      break;
```

Since the bytecode dispatch loop reads from that `frame` variable, when the VM goes to execute the next instruction, it will read the `ip` from the newly called function's CallFrame and jump to its code. The work for executing that call begins here:

**vm.c**
*add after* peek()

Using a `switch` statement to check a single type is overkill now, but will make sense when we add cases to handle other callable types.

```
static bool callValue(Value callee, int argCount) {
  if (IS_OBJ(callee)) {
    switch (OBJ_TYPE(callee)) {
      case OBJ_FUNCTION:
        return call(AS_FUNCTION(callee), argCount);
      default:
        break; // Non-callable object type.
    }
  }
  runtimeError("Can only call functions and classes.");
  return false;
}
```

There's more going on here than just initializing a new CallFrame. Because Lox is dynamically typed, there's nothing to prevent a user from writing bad code like:

```
var notAFunction = 123;
notAFunction();
```

If that happens, the runtime needs to safely report an error and halt. So the first thing we do is check the type of the value that we're trying to call. If it's not a function, we error out. Otherwise, the actual call happens here:

```
static bool call(ObjFunction* function, int argCount) {
  CallFrame* frame = &vm.frames[vm.frameCount++];
  frame->function = function;
  frame->ip = function->chunk.code;
  frame->slots = vm.stackTop - argCount - 1;
  return true;
}
```

vm.c
*add after* peek()

This simply initializes the next CallFrame on the stack. It stores a pointer to the function being called and points the frame's ip to the beginning of the function's bytecode. Finally, it sets up the slots pointer to give the frame its window into the stack. The arithmetic there ensures that the arguments already on the stack line up with the function's parameters:

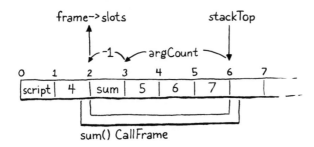

The funny little − 1 is to account for stack slot zero which the compiler set aside for when we add methods later. The parameters start at slot one so we make the window start one slot earlier to align them with the arguments.

Before we move on, let's add the new instruction to our disassembler.

```
    return jumpInstruction("OP_LOOP", -1, chunk, offset);
  case OP_CALL:
    return byteInstruction("OP_CALL", chunk, offset);
  case OP_RETURN:
```

debug.c
*in* disassembleInstruction()

And one more quick side trip. Now that we have a handy function for initiating a CallFrame, we may as well use it to set up the first frame for executing the top-level code.

```
  push(OBJ_VAL(function));
  call(function, 0);

  return run();
```

vm.c
*in* interpret()
*replace 4 lines*

OK, now back to calls...

### 24.5.2  Runtime error checking

The overlapping stack windows work based on the assumption that a call passes exactly one argument for each of the function's parameters. But, again, because Lox ain't statically typed, a foolish user could pass too many or too few arguments. In Lox, we've defined that to be a runtime error, which we report like so:

vm.c<br>in call()

```
static bool call(ObjFunction* function, int argCount) {
  if (argCount != function->arity) {
    runtimeError("Expected %d arguments but got %d.",
        function->arity, argCount);
    return false;
  }

  CallFrame* frame = &vm.frames[vm.frameCount++];
```

Pretty straightforward. This is why we store the arity of each function inside the ObjFunction for it.

There's another error we need to report that's less to do with the user's foolishness than our own. Because the CallFrame array has a fixed size, we need to ensure a deep call chain doesn't overflow it.

vm.c<br>in call()

```
  }

  if (vm.frameCount == FRAMES_MAX) {
    runtimeError("Stack overflow.");
    return false;
  }

  CallFrame* frame = &vm.frames[vm.frameCount++];
```

In practice, if a program gets anywhere close to this limit, there's most likely a bug in some runaway recursive code.

### 24.5.3  Printing stack traces

While we're on the subject of runtime errors, let's spend a little time making them more useful. Stopping on a runtime error is important to prevent the VM from crashing and burning in some ill-defined way. But simply aborting doesn't help the user fix their code that *caused* that error.

The classic tool to aid debugging runtime failures is a **stack trace**—a print out of each function that was still executing when the program died, and where the execution was at the point that it died. Now that we have a call stack and we've conveniently stored each function's name, we can show that entire stack when a runtime error disrupts the harmony of the user's existence. It looks like this:

```
  fputs("\n", stderr);

  for (int i = vm.frameCount - 1; i >= 0; i--) {
    CallFrame* frame = &vm.frames[i];
    ObjFunction* function = frame->function;
    size_t instruction = frame->ip - function->chunk.code - 1;
    fprintf(stderr, "[line %d] in ",
            function->chunk.lines[instruction]);
    if (function->name == NULL) {
      fprintf(stderr, "script\n");
    } else {
      fprintf(stderr, "%s()\n", function->name->chars);
    }
  }

  resetStack();
}
```

vm.c
*in* runtimeError()
*replace 4 lines*

The – 1 is because the IP is already sitting on the next instruction to be executed but we want the stack trace to point to the previous failed instruction.

After printing the error message itself, we walk the call stack from top (the most recently called function) to bottom (the top-level code). For each frame, we find the line number that corresponds to the current ip inside that frame's function. Then we print that line number along with the function name.

For example, if you run this broken program:

```
fun a() { b(); }
fun b() { c(); }
fun c() {
  c("too", "many");
}

a();
```

It prints out:

```
Expected 0 arguments but got 2.
[line 4] in c()
[line 2] in b()
[line 1] in a()
[line 7] in script
```

That doesn't look too bad, does it?

There is some disagreement on which order stack frames should be shown in a trace. Most put the innermost function as the first line and work their way towards the bottom of the stack. Python prints them out in the opposite order. So reading from top to bottom tells you how your program got to where it is, and the last line is where the error actually occurred.

There's a logic to that style. It ensures you can always see the innermost function even if the stack trace is too long to fit on one screen. On the other hand, the "inverted pyramid" from journalism tells us we should put the most important information *first* in a block of text. In a stack trace, that's the function where the error actually occurred. Most other language implementations do that.

## 24.5.4 Returning from functions

We're getting close. We can call functions, and the VM will execute them. But we can't *return* from them yet. We've had an OP_RETURN instruction for quite some time, but it's always had some kind of temporary code hanging out in it just to get us out of the bytecode loop. The time has arrived for a real implementation.

**vm.c**
*in* run()
*replace 2 lines*

```
case OP_RETURN: {
  Value result = pop();
  vm.frameCount--;
  if (vm.frameCount == 0) {
    pop();
    return INTERPRET_OK;
  }

  vm.stackTop = frame->slots;
  push(result);
  frame = &vm.frames[vm.frameCount - 1];
  break;
}
```

When a function returns a value, that value will be on top of the stack. We're about to discard the called function's entire stack window, so we pop that return value off and hang on to it. Then we discard the CallFrame for the returning function. If that was the very last CallFrame, it means we've finished executing the top-level code. The entire program is done, so we pop the main script function from the stack and then exit the interpreter.

Otherwise, we discard all of the slots the callee was using for its parameters and local variables. That includes the same slots the caller used to pass the arguments. Now that the call is done, the caller doesn't need them anymore. This means the top of the stack ends up right at the beginning of the returning function's stack window.

We push the return value back onto the stack at that new, lower location. Then we update the run() function's cached pointer to the current frame. Just like when we began a call, on the next iteration of the bytecode dispatch loop, the VM will read ip from that frame, and execution will jump back to the caller, right where it left off, immediately after the OP_CALL instruction.

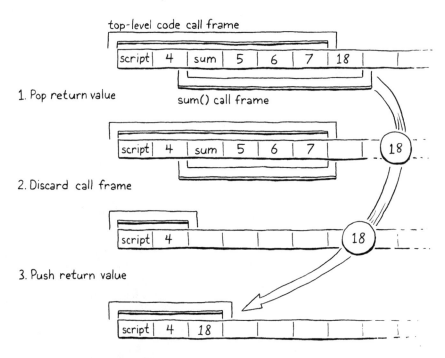

Note that we assume here that the function *did* actually return a value, but a function can implicitly return by reaching the end of its body:

```
fun noReturn() {
  print "Do stuff";
  // No return here.
}

print noReturn(); // ???
```

We need to handle that correctly too. The language is specified to implicitly return `nil` in that case. To make that happen, we add this:

```
static void emitReturn() {
  emitByte(OP_NIL);
  emitByte(OP_RETURN);
}
```

*compiler.c*
*in* emitReturn()

The compiler calls `emitReturn()` to write the `OP_RETURN` instruction at the end of a function body. Now, before that, it emits an instruction to push `nil` onto the stack. And with that, we have working function calls! They can even take parameters! It almost looks like we know what we're doing here.

## 24.6  Return Statements

If you want a function that returns something other than the implicit `nil`, you need a `return` statement. Let's get that working.

```
    ifStatement();
  } else if (match(TOKEN_RETURN)) {
    returnStatement();
  } else if (match(TOKEN_WHILE)) {
```

*compiler.c*
*in* statement()

When the compiler sees a `return` keyword, it goes here:

```
static void returnStatement() {
  if (match(TOKEN_SEMICOLON)) {
    emitReturn();
  } else {
    expression();
    consume(TOKEN_SEMICOLON, "Expect ';' after return value.");
    emitByte(OP_RETURN);
  }
}
```

*compiler.c*
*add after* printStatement()

The return value expression is optional, so the parser looks for a semicolon token to tell if a value was provided. If there is no return value, the statement implicitly returns `nil`. We implement that by calling `emitReturn()`, which emits an `OP_NIL` instruction. Otherwise, we compile the return value expression and return it with an `OP_RETURN` instruction.

This is the same `OP_RETURN` instruction we've already implemented—we don't need any new runtime code. This is quite a difference from jlox. There, we had to use exceptions to unwind the stack when a `return` statement was executed. That was because you could return from deep inside some nested blocks. Since jlox recursively walks the AST, that meant there were a bunch of Java method calls we needed to escape out of.

Our bytecode compiler flattens that all out. We do recursive descent during parsing, but at runtime, the VM's bytecode dispatch loop is completely flat. There is no recursion going on at the C level at all. So returning, even from within some nested blocks, is as straightforward as returning from the end of the function's body.

We're not totally done, though. The new `return` statement gives us a new compile error to worry about. Returns are useful for returning from functions but the top level of a Lox program is imperative code too. You shouldn't be able to return from there.

```
return "What?!";
```

Allowing `return` at the top level isn't the worst idea in the world. It would give you a natural way to terminate a script early. You could maybe even use a returned number to indicate the process's exit code.

We've specified that it's a compile error to have a `return` statement outside of any function, which we implement like so:

compiler.c
in returnStatement()

```
static void returnStatement() {
  if (current->type == TYPE_SCRIPT) {
    error("Can't return from top-level code.");
  }

  if (match(TOKEN_SEMICOLON)) {
```

This is one of the reasons we added that FunctionType enum to the compiler.

## 24.7  Native Functions

Our VM is getting more powerful. We've got functions, calls, parameters, returns. You can define lots of different functions that can call each other in interesting ways. But, ultimately, they can't really *do* anything. The only user-visible thing a Lox program can do, regardless of its complexity, is print. To add more capabilities, we need to expose them to the user.

A programming language implementation reaches out and touches the material world through **native functions**. If you want to be able to write programs that check the time, read user input, or access the file system, we need to add native functions—callable from Lox but implemented in C—that expose those capabilities.

At the language level, Lox is fairly complete—it's got closures, classes, inheritance, and other fun stuff. One reason it feels like a toy language is because it has almost no native capabilities. We could turn it into a real language by adding a long list of them.

However, grinding through a pile of OS operations isn't actually very educational. Once you've seen how to bind one piece of C code to Lox, you get the idea. But you do need to see *one*, and even a single native function requires us to build out all the machinery for interfacing Lox with C. So we'll go through that and do all the hard work. Then, when that's done, we'll add one tiny native function just to prove that it works.

The reason we need new machinery is because, from the implementation's perspective, native functions are different from Lox functions. When they are called, they don't push a CallFrame, because there's no bytecode code for that frame to point to. They have no bytecode chunk. Instead, they somehow reference a piece of native C code.

We handle this in clox by defining native functions as an entirely different object type.

```
} ObjFunction;

typedef Value (*NativeFn)(int argCount, Value* args);

typedef struct {
  Obj obj;
  NativeFn function;
} ObjNative;

struct ObjString {
```

object.h
*add after struct* ObjFunction

The representation is simpler than ObjFunction—merely an Obj header and a pointer to the C function that implements the native behavior. The native function takes the argument count and a pointer to the first argument on the stack. It accesses the arguments through that pointer. Once it's done, it returns the result value.

As always, a new object type carries some accoutrements with it. To create an ObjNative, we declare a constructor-like function.

```
ObjFunction* newFunction();
ObjNative* newNative(NativeFn function);
ObjString* takeString(char* chars, int length);
```

object.h
*add after* newFunction()

We implement that like so:

```
ObjNative* newNative(NativeFn function) {
  ObjNative* native = ALLOCATE_OBJ(ObjNative, OBJ_NATIVE);
  native->function = function;
  return native;
}
```

object.c
*add after* newFunction()

The constructor takes a C function pointer to wrap in an ObjNative. It sets up the object header and stores the function. For the header, we need a new object type.

```
typedef enum {
  OBJ_FUNCTION,
  OBJ_NATIVE,
  OBJ_STRING,
} ObjType;
```

object.h
*in enum* ObjType

The VM also needs to know how to deallocate a native function object.

```
        }
      case OBJ_NATIVE:
        FREE(ObjNative, object);
        break;
      case OBJ_STRING: {
```

There isn't much here since ObjNative doesn't own any extra memory. The other capability all Lox objects support is being printed.

```
        break;
      case OBJ_NATIVE:
        printf("<native fn>");
        break;
      case OBJ_STRING:
```

In order to support dynamic typing, we have a macro to see if a value is a native function.

```
#define IS_FUNCTION(value)      isObjType(value, OBJ_FUNCTION)
#define IS_NATIVE(value)        isObjType(value, OBJ_NATIVE)
#define IS_STRING(value)        isObjType(value, OBJ_STRING)
```

Assuming that returns true, this macro extracts the C function pointer from a Value representing a native function:

```
#define AS_FUNCTION(value)      ((ObjFunction*)AS_OBJ(value))
#define AS_NATIVE(value) \
    (((ObjNative*)AS_OBJ(value))->function)
#define AS_STRING(value)        ((ObjString*)AS_OBJ(value))
```

All of this baggage lets the VM treat native functions like any other object. You can store them in variables, pass them around, throw them birthday parties, etc. Of course, the operation we actually care about is *calling* them—using one as the left-hand operand in a call expression.

Over in `callValue()` we add another type case.

```
      case OBJ_FUNCTION:
        return call(AS_FUNCTION(callee), argCount);
      case OBJ_NATIVE: {
        NativeFn native = AS_NATIVE(callee);
        Value result = native(argCount, vm.stackTop - argCount);
        vm.stackTop -= argCount + 1;
        push(result);
        return true;
      }
      default:
```

If the object being called is a native function, we invoke the C function right then and there. There's no need to muck with CallFrames or anything. We just hand off to C, get the result, and stuff it back in the stack. This makes native functions as fast as we can get.

With this, users should be able to call native functions, but there aren't any to call. Without something like a foreign function interface, users can't define their own native functions. That's our job as VM implementers. We'll start with a helper to define a new native function exposed to Lox programs.

```
static void defineNative(const char* name, NativeFn function) {
  push(OBJ_VAL(copyString(name, (int)strlen(name))));
  push(OBJ_VAL(newNative(function)));
  tableSet(&vm.globals, AS_STRING(vm.stack[0]), vm.stack[1]);
  pop();
  pop();
}
```
*vm.c*
*add after* runtimeError()

It takes a pointer to a C function and the name it will be known as in Lox. We wrap the function in an ObjNative and then store that in a global variable with the given name.

You're probably wondering why we push and pop the name and function on the stack. That looks weird, right? This is the kind of stuff you have to worry about when garbage collection gets involved. Both copyString() and newNative() dynamically allocate memory. That means once we have a GC, they can potentially trigger a collection. If that happens, we need to ensure the collector knows we're not done with the name and ObjFunction so that it doesn't free them out from under us. Storing them on the value stack accomplishes that.

It feels silly, but after all of that work, we're going to add only one little native function.

Don't worry if you didn't follow all that. It will make a lot more sense once we get around to implementing the GC.

```
static Value clockNative(int argCount, Value* args) {
  return NUMBER_VAL((double)clock() / CLOCKS_PER_SEC);
}
```
*vm.c*
*add after variable* vm

This returns the elapsed time since the program started running, in seconds. It's handy for benchmarking Lox programs. In Lox, we'll name it clock().

```
  initTable(&vm.strings);

  defineNative("clock", clockNative);
}
```
*vm.c*
*in* initVM()

To get to the C standard library clock() function, the "vm" module needs an include.

```
#include <string.h>
#include <time.h>

#include "common.h"
```
*vm.c*

That was a lot of material to work through, but we did it! Type this in and try it out:

```
fun fib(n) {
  if (n < 2) return n;
  return fib(n - 2) + fib(n - 1);
}

var start = clock();
print fib(35);
print clock() - start;
```

It's a little slower than a comparable Ruby program run in Ruby 2.4.3p205, and about 3x faster than one run in Python 3.7.3. And we still have a lot of simple optimizations we can do in our VM.

We can write a really inefficient recursive Fibonacci function. Even better, we can measure just *how* inefficient it is. This is, of course, not the smartest way to calculate a Fibonacci number. But it is a good way to stress test a language implementation's support for function calls. On my machine, running this in clox is about five times faster than in jlox. That's quite an improvement.

## CHALLENGES

1. Reading and writing the **ip** field is one of the most frequent operations inside the bytecode loop. Right now, we access it through a pointer to the current CallFrame. That requires a pointer indirection which may force the CPU to by-pass the cache and hit main memory. That can be a real performance sink.

   Ideally, we'd keep the **ip** in a native CPU register. C doesn't let us *require* that without dropping into inline assembly, but we can structure the code to encourage the compiler to make that optimization. If we store the **ip** directly in a C local variable and mark it **register**, there's a good chance the C compiler will accede to our polite request.

   This does mean we need to be careful to load and store the local **ip** back into the correct CallFrame when starting and ending function calls. Implement this optimization. Write a couple of benchmarks and see how it affects the performance. Do you think the extra code complexity is worth it?

2. Native function calls are fast in part because we don't validate that the call passes as many arguments as the function expects. We really should, or an incorrect call to a native function without enough arguments could cause the function to read uninitialized memory. Add arity checking.

3. Right now, there's no way for a native function to signal a runtime error. In a real implementation, this is something we'd need to support because native functions live in the statically typed world of C but are called from dynamically typed Lox land. If a user, say, tries to pass a string to **sqrt()**, that native function needs to report a runtime error.

   Extend the native function system to support that. How does this capability affect the performance of native calls?

4. Add some more native functions to do things you find useful. Write some programs using those. What did you add? How do they affect the feel of the language and how practical it is?

# Closures

> *"As the man said, for every complex problem there's a simple solution, and it's wrong."*
>
> — Umberto Eco, *Foucault's Pendulum*

Thanks to our diligent labor in the last chapter, we have a virtual machine with working functions. What it lacks is closures. Aside from global variables, which are their own breed of animal, a function has no way to reference a variable declared outside of its own body.

```
var x = "global";
fun outer() {
  var x = "outer";
  fun inner() {
    print x;
  }
  inner();
}
outer();
```

Run this example now and it prints "global". It's supposed to print "outer". To fix this, we need to include the entire lexical scope of all surrounding functions when resolving a variable.

This problem is harder in clox than it was in jlox because our bytecode VM stores locals on a stack. We used a stack because I claimed locals have stack semantics—variables are discarded in the reverse order that they are created. But with closures, that's only *mostly* true.

```
fun makeClosure() {
  var local = "local";
  fun closure() {
    print local;
  }
  return closure;
}

var closure = makeClosure();
closure();
```

Oh no, it's escaping!

The function `makeClosure()` declares a variable, `local`. It also creates an inner function, `closure()` that captures that variable. Then `makeClosure()` returns a reference to that function. Since the closure escapes while holding on to the local variable, `local` must outlive the function call where it was created.

There is a reason that C and Java use the stack for their local variables, after all.

We could solve this problem by dynamically allocating memory for all local variables. That's what jlox does by putting everything in those Environment objects that float around in Java's heap. But we don't want to. Using a stack is *really* fast. Most local variables are *not* captured by closures and do have stack semantics. It would suck to make all of those slower for the benefit of the rare local that is captured.

This means a more complex approach than we used in our Java interpreter. Because some locals have very different lifetimes, we will have two implementation strategies. For locals that aren't used in closures, we'll keep them just as they are on the stack. When a local is captured by a closure, we'll adopt another solution that lifts them onto the heap where they can live as long as needed.

Closures have been around since the early Lisp days when bytes of memory and CPU cycles were more precious than emeralds. Over the intervening decades, hackers devised all manner of ways to compile closures to optimized runtime representations. Some are more efficient but require a more complex compilation process than we could easily retrofit into clox.

Search for "closure conversion" or "lambda lifting" to start exploring.

The technique I explain here comes from the design of the Lua VM. It is fast, parsimonious with memory, and implemented with relatively little code. Even more impressive, it fits naturally into the single-pass compilers clox and Lua both use. It is somewhat intricate, though. It might take a while before all the pieces click together in your mind. We'll build them one step at a time, and I'll try to introduce the concepts in stages.

## 25.1  Closure Objects

In other words, a function declaration in Lox *is* a kind of literal—a piece of syntax that defines a constant value of a built-in type.

Our VM represents functions at runtime using ObjFunction. These objects are created by the front end during compilation. At runtime, all the VM does is load the function object from a constant table and bind it to a name. There is no operation to "create" a function at runtime. Much like string and number literals, they are constants instantiated purely at compile time.

That made sense because all of the data that composes a function is known at compile time: the chunk of bytecode compiled from the function's body, and the constants used in the body. Once we introduce closures, though, that representation is no longer sufficient. Take a gander at:

```
fun makeClosure(value) {
  fun closure() {
    print value;
  }
  return closure;
}

var doughnut = makeClosure("doughnut");
var bagel = makeClosure("bagel");
doughnut();
bagel();
```

The `makeClosure()` function defines and returns a function. We call it twice and get two closures back. They are created by the same nested function declaration, `closure`, but close over different values. When we call the two closures, each prints a different string. That implies we need some runtime representation for a closure that captures the local variables surrounding the function as they exist when the function declaration is *executed*, not just when it is compiled.

We'll work our way up to capturing variables, but a good first step is defining that object representation. Our existing ObjFunction type represents the "raw" compile-time state of a function declaration, since all closures created from a single declaration share the same code and constants. At runtime, when we execute a function declaration, we wrap the ObjFunction in a new ObjClosure structure. The latter has a reference to the underlying bare function along with runtime state for the variables the function closes over.

> The Lua implementation refers to the raw function object containing the bytecode as a "prototype", which is a great word to describe this, except that word also gets overloaded to refer to prototypal inheritance.

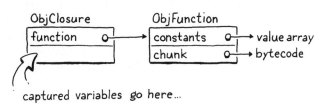

captured variables go here...

We'll wrap every function in an ObjClosure, even if the function doesn't actually close over and capture any surrounding local variables. This is a little wasteful, but it simplifies the VM because we can always assume that the function we're calling is an ObjClosure. That new struct starts out like this:

```
typedef struct {
  Obj obj;
  ObjFunction* function;
} ObjClosure;
```

> object.h
> *add after struct* ObjString

Right now, it simply points to an ObjFunction and adds the necessary object header stuff. Grinding through the usual ceremony for adding a new object type to clox, we declare a C function to create a new closure.

**object.h**
*add after struct ObjClosure*

```
} ObjClosure;

ObjClosure* newClosure(ObjFunction* function);
ObjFunction* newFunction();
```

Then we implement it here:

**object.c**
*add after* allocateObject()

```
ObjClosure* newClosure(ObjFunction* function) {
  ObjClosure* closure = ALLOCATE_OBJ(ObjClosure, OBJ_CLOSURE);
  closure->function = function;
  return closure;
}
```

It takes a pointer to the ObjFunction it wraps. It also initializes the type field to a new type.

**object.h**
*in enum* ObjType

```
typedef enum {
  OBJ_CLOSURE,
  OBJ_FUNCTION,
```

And when we're done with a closure, we release its memory.

**memory.c**
*in* freeObject()

```
  switch (object->type) {
    case OBJ_CLOSURE: {
      FREE(ObjClosure, object);
      break;
    }
    case OBJ_FUNCTION: {
```

Perhaps I should have defined a macro to make it easier to generate these macros. Maybe that would be a little too meta.

We free only the ObjClosure itself, not the ObjFunction. That's because the closure doesn't *own* the function. There may be multiple closures that all reference the same function, and none of them claims any special privilege over it. We can't free the ObjFunction until *all* objects referencing it are gone—including even the surrounding function whose constant table contains it. Tracking that sounds tricky, and it is! That's why we'll write a garbage collector soon to manage it for us.

We also have the usual macros for checking a value's type.

**object.h**

```
#define OBJ_TYPE(value)         (AS_OBJ(value)->type)

#define IS_CLOSURE(value)       isObjType(value, OBJ_CLOSURE)
#define IS_FUNCTION(value)      isObjType(value, OBJ_FUNCTION)
```

And to cast a value:

**object.h**

```
#define IS_STRING(value)        isObjType(value, OBJ_STRING)

#define AS_CLOSURE(value)       ((ObjClosure*)AS_OBJ(value))
#define AS_FUNCTION(value)      ((ObjFunction*)AS_OBJ(value))
```

Closures are first-class objects, so you can print them.

```
switch (OBJ_TYPE(value)) {
  case OBJ_CLOSURE:
    printFunction(AS_CLOSURE(value)->function);
    break;
  case OBJ_FUNCTION:
```

object.c
in printObject()

They display exactly as ObjFunction does. From the user's perspective, the difference between ObjFunction and ObjClosure is purely a hidden implementation detail. With that out of the way, we have a working but empty representation for closures.

## 25.1.1  Compiling to closure objects

We have closure objects, but our VM never creates them. The next step is getting the compiler to emit instructions to tell the runtime when to create a new ObjClosure to wrap a given ObjFunction. This happens right at the end of a function declaration.

```
  ObjFunction* function = endCompiler();
  emitBytes(OP_CLOSURE, makeConstant(OBJ_VAL(function)));
}
```

compiler.c
in function()
replace 1 line

Before, the final bytecode for a function declaration was a single OP_CONSTANT instruction to load the compiled function from the surrounding function's constant table and push it onto the stack. Now we have a new instruction.

```
  OP_CALL,
  OP_CLOSURE,
  OP_RETURN,
```

chunk.h
in enum OpCode

Like OP_CONSTANT, it takes a single operand that represents a constant table index for the function. But when we get over to the runtime implementation, we do something more interesting.

First, let's be diligent VM hackers and slot in disassembler support for the instruction.

```
  case OP_CALL:
    return byteInstruction("OP_CALL", chunk, offset);
  case OP_CLOSURE: {
    offset++;
    uint8_t constant = chunk->code[offset++];
    printf("%-16s %4d ", "OP_CLOSURE", constant);
    printValue(chunk->constants.values[constant]);
    printf("\n");
    return offset;
  }
  case OP_RETURN:
```

debug.c
in disassembleInstruction()

There's more going on here than we usually have in the disassembler. By the end of the chapter, you'll discover that OP_CLOSURE is quite an unusual instruction. It's straightforward right now—just a single byte operand—but we'll be adding to it. This code here anticipates that future.

## 25.1.2  Interpreting function declarations

Most of the work we need to do is in the runtime. We have to handle the new instruction, naturally. But we also need to touch every piece of code in the VM that works with ObjFunction and change it to use ObjClosure instead—function calls, call frames, etc. We'll start with the instruction, though.

**vm.c**
*in* run()

```
      }
    case OP_CLOSURE: {
      ObjFunction* function = AS_FUNCTION(READ_CONSTANT());
      ObjClosure* closure = newClosure(function);
      push(OBJ_VAL(closure));
      break;
    }
    case OP_RETURN: {
```

Like the OP_CONSTANT instruction we used before, first we load the compiled function from the constant table. The difference now is that we wrap that function in a new ObjClosure and push the result onto the stack.

Once you have a closure, you'll eventually want to call it.

**vm.c**
*in* callValue()
*replace 2 lines*

```
  switch (OBJ_TYPE(callee)) {
    case OBJ_CLOSURE:
      return call(AS_CLOSURE(callee), argCount);
    case OBJ_NATIVE: {
```

We remove the code for calling objects whose type is OBJ_FUNCTION. Since we wrap all functions in ObjClosures, the runtime will never try to invoke a bare ObjFunction anymore. Those objects live only in constant tables and get immediately wrapped in closures before anything else sees them.

We don't want any naked functions wandering around the VM! What would the neighbors say?

We replace the old code with very similar code for calling a closure instead. The only difference is the type of object we pass to call(). The real changes are over in that function. First, we update its signature.

**vm.c**
*function* call()
*replace 1 line*

```
static bool call(ObjClosure* closure, int argCount) {
  if (argCount != function->arity) {
```

Then, in the body, we need to fix everything that referenced the function to handle the fact that we've introduced a layer of indirection. We start with the arity checking:

**vm.c**
*in* call()
*replace 3 lines*

```
static bool call(ObjClosure* closure, int argCount) {
  if (argCount != closure->function->arity) {
    runtimeError("Expected %d arguments but got %d.",
        closure->function->arity, argCount);
    return false;
```

The only change is that we unwrap the closure to get to the underlying function. The next thing call() does is create a new CallFrame. We change that code to store the closure in the CallFrame and get the bytecode pointer from the closure's function.

```
CallFrame* frame = &vm.frames[vm.frameCount++];
frame->closure = closure;
frame->ip = closure->function->chunk.code;
frame->slots = vm.stackTop - argCount - 1;
```

vm.c
in call()
replace 2 lines

This necessitates changing the declaration of CallFrame too.

```
typedef struct {
  ObjClosure* closure;
  uint8_t* ip;
```

vm.h
in struct CallFrame
replace 1 line

That change triggers a few other cascading changes. Every place in the VM that accessed CallFrame's function needs to use a closure instead. First, the macro for reading a constant from the current function's constant table:

```
    (uint16_t)((frame->ip[-2] << 8) | frame->ip[-1]))

#define READ_CONSTANT() \
    (frame->closure->function->chunk.constants.values[READ_BYTE()])

#define READ_STRING() AS_STRING(READ_CONSTANT())
```

vm.c
in run()
replace 2 lines

When DEBUG_TRACE_EXECUTION is enabled, it needs to get to the chunk from the closure.

```
    printf("\n");
    disassembleInstruction(&frame->closure->function->chunk,
        (int)(frame->ip - frame->closure->function->chunk.code));
#endif
```

vm.c
in run()
replace 2 lines

Likewise when reporting a runtime error:

```
    CallFrame* frame = &vm.frames[i];
    ObjFunction* function = frame->closure->function;
    size_t instruction = frame->ip - function->chunk.code - 1;
```

vm.c
in runtimeError()
replace 1 line

Almost there. The last piece is the blob of code that sets up the very first CallFrame to begin executing the top-level code for a Lox script.

```
push(OBJ_VAL(function));
ObjClosure* closure = newClosure(function);
pop();
push(OBJ_VAL(closure));
call(closure, 0);

return run();
```

vm.c
in interpret()
replace 1 line

The compiler still returns a raw ObjFunction when compiling a script. That's fine, but it means we need to wrap it in an ObjClosure here, before the VM can

The previous code looks a little silly because we still push the original ObjFunction onto the stack. Then we pop it after creating the closure, only to then push the closure. Why put the ObjFunction on there at all? As usual, when you see weird stack stuff going on, it's to keep the forthcoming garbage collector aware of some heap-allocated objects.

execute it.

We are back to a working interpreter. The *user* can't tell any difference, but the compiler now generates code telling the VM to create a closure for each function declaration. Every time the VM executes a function declaration, it wraps the ObjFunction in a new ObjClosure. The rest of the VM now handles those ObjClosures floating around. That's the boring stuff out of the way. Now we're ready to make these closures actually *do* something.

## 25.2  Upvalues

Our existing instructions for reading and writing local variables are limited to a single function's stack window. Locals from a surrounding function are outside of the inner function's window. We're going to need some new instructions.

The easiest approach might be an instruction that takes a relative stack slot offset that can reach *before* the current function's window. That would work if closed-over variables were always on the stack. But as we saw earlier, these variables sometimes outlive the function where they are declared. That means they won't always be on the stack.

The next easiest approach, then, would be to take any local variable that gets closed over and have it always live on the heap. When the local variable declaration in the surrounding function is executed, the VM would allocate memory for it dynamically. That way it could live as long as needed.

This would be a fine approach if clox didn't have a single-pass compiler. But that restriction we chose in our implementation makes things harder. Take a look at this example:

```
fun outer() {
  var x = 1;      // (1)
  x = 2;          // (2)

  fun inner() { // (3)
    print x;
  }

  inner();
}
```

Here, the compiler compiles the declaration of x at (1) and emits code for the assignment at (2). It does that before reaching the declaration of inner() at (3) and discovering that x is in fact closed over. We don't have an easy way to go back and fix that already-emitted code to treat x specially. Instead, we want a solution that allows a closed-over variable to live on the stack exactly like a normal local variable *until the point that it is closed over*.

Fortunately, thanks to the Lua dev team, we have a solution. We use a level of indirection that they call an **upvalue**. An upvalue refers to a local variable in an enclosing function. Every closure maintains an array of upvalues, one for each surrounding local variable that the closure uses.

The upvalue points back into the stack to where the variable it captured lives. When the closure needs to access a closed-over variable, it goes through the corresponding upvalue to reach it. When a function declaration is first executed and we create a closure for it, the VM creates the array of upvalues and wires them up to "capture" the surrounding local variables that the closure needs.

For example, if we throw this program at clox,

```
{
  var a = 3;

  fun f() {
    print a;
  }
}
```

the compiler and runtime will conspire together to build up a set of objects in memory like this:

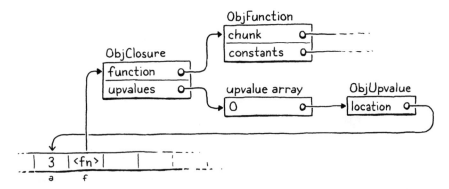

That might look overwhelming, but fear not. We'll work our way through it. The important part is that upvalues serve as the layer of indirection needed to continue to find a captured local variable even after it moves off the stack. But before we get to all that, let's focus on compiling captured variables.

## 25.2.1 Compiling upvalues

As usual, we want to do as much work as possible during compilation to keep execution simple and fast. Since local variables are lexically scoped in Lox, we have enough knowledge at compile time to resolve which surrounding local variables a function accesses and where those locals are declared. That, in turn, means we know *how many* upvalues a closure needs, *which* variables they capture, and *which stack slots* contain those variables in the declaring function's stack window.

Currently, when the compiler resolves an identifier, it walks the block scopes for the current function from innermost to outermost. If we don't find the variable in that function, we assume the variable must be a global. We don't consider the local scopes of enclosing functions—they get skipped right over. The first change, then, is inserting a resolution step for those outer local scopes.

compiler.c
*in* namedVariable()

```
  if (arg != -1) {
    getOp = OP_GET_LOCAL;
    setOp = OP_SET_LOCAL;
  } else if ((arg = resolveUpvalue(current, &name)) != -1) {
    getOp = OP_GET_UPVALUE;
    setOp = OP_SET_UPVALUE;
  } else {
```

This new `resolveUpvalue()` function looks for a local variable declared in any of the surrounding functions. If it finds one, it returns an "upvalue index" for that variable. (We'll get into what that means later.) Otherwise, it returns -1 to indicate the variable wasn't found. If it was found, we use these two new instructions for reading or writing to the variable through its upvalue:

chunk.h
*in enum* OpCode

```
  OP_SET_GLOBAL,
  OP_GET_UPVALUE,
  OP_SET_UPVALUE,
  OP_EQUAL,
```

We're implementing this sort of top-down, so I'll show you how these work at runtime soon. The part to focus on now is how the compiler actually resolves the identifier.

compiler.c
*add after* resolveLocal()

```
static int resolveUpvalue(Compiler* compiler, Token* name) {
  if (compiler->enclosing == NULL) return -1;

  int local = resolveLocal(compiler->enclosing, name);
  if (local != -1) {
    return addUpvalue(compiler, (uint8_t)local, true);
  }

  return -1;
}
```

We call this after failing to resolve a local variable in the current function's scope, so we know the variable isn't in the current compiler. Recall that Compiler stores a pointer to the Compiler for the enclosing function, and these pointers form a linked chain that goes all the way to the root Compiler for the top-level code. Thus, if the enclosing Compiler is NULL, we know we've reached the outermost function without finding a local variable. The variable must be global, so we return -1.

It might end up being an entirely undefined variable and not even global. But in Lox, we don't detect that error until runtime, so from the compiler's perspective, it's "hopefully global".

Otherwise, we try to resolve the identifier as a *local* variable in the *enclosing* compiler. In other words, we look for it right outside the current function. For example:

```
fun outer() {
  var x = 1;
  fun inner() {
    print x; // (1)
  }
  inner();
}
```

When compiling the identifier expression at (1), `resolveUpvalue()` looks for a local variable x declared in `outer()`. If found—like it is in this example—then we've successfully resolved the variable. We create an upvalue so that the inner function can access the variable through that. The upvalue is created here:

```c
static int addUpvalue(Compiler* compiler, uint8_t index,
                      bool isLocal) {
  int upvalueCount = compiler->function->upvalueCount;
  compiler->upvalues[upvalueCount].isLocal = isLocal;
  compiler->upvalues[upvalueCount].index = index;
  return compiler->function->upvalueCount++;
}
```

compiler.c
*add after* resolveLocal()

The compiler keeps an array of upvalue structures to track the closed-over identifiers that it has resolved in the body of each function. Remember how the compiler's Local array mirrors the stack slot indexes where locals live at runtime? This new upvalue array works the same way. The indexes in the compiler's array match the indexes where upvalues will live in the ObjClosure at runtime.

This function adds a new upvalue to that array. It also keeps track of the number of upvalues the function uses. It stores that count directly in the ObjFunction itself because we'll also need that number for use at runtime.

The `index` field tracks the closed-over local variable's slot index. That way the compiler knows *which* variable in the enclosing function needs to be captured. We'll circle back to what that `isLocal` field is for before too long. Finally, `addUpvalue()` returns the index of the created upvalue in the function's upvalue list. That index becomes the operand to the `OP_GET_UPVALUE` and `OP_SET_UPVALUE` instructions.

That's the basic idea for resolving upvalues, but the function isn't fully baked. A closure may reference the same variable in a surrounding function multiple times. In that case, we don't want to waste time and memory creating a separate upvalue for each identifier expression. To fix that, before we add a new upvalue, we first check to see if the function already has an upvalue that closes over that variable.

Like constants and function arity, the upvalue count is another one of those little pieces of data that form the bridge between the compiler and runtime.

```c
  int upvalueCount = compiler->function->upvalueCount;

  for (int i = 0; i < upvalueCount; i++) {
    Upvalue* upvalue = &compiler->upvalues[i];
    if (upvalue->index == index && upvalue->isLocal == isLocal) {
      return i;
    }
  }

  compiler->upvalues[upvalueCount].isLocal = isLocal;
```

compiler.c
*in* addUpvalue()

If we find an upvalue in the array whose slot index matches the one we're adding, we just return that *upvalue* index and reuse it. Otherwise, we fall through and add the new upvalue.

These two functions access and modify a bunch of new state, so let's define that. First, we add the upvalue count to ObjFunction.

**object.h**
*in struct* ObjFunction

```
  int arity;
  int upvalueCount;
  Chunk chunk;
```

We're conscientious C programmers, so we zero-initialize that when an ObjFunction is first allocated.

**object.c**
*in* newFunction()

```
  function->arity = 0;
  function->upvalueCount = 0;
  function->name = NULL;
```

In the compiler, we add a field for the upvalue array.

**compiler.c**
*in struct* Compiler

```
  int localCount;
  Upvalue upvalues[UINT8_COUNT];
  int scopeDepth;
```

For simplicity, I gave it a fixed size. The OP_GET_UPVALUE and OP_SET_UPVALUE instructions encode an upvalue index using a single byte operand, so there's a restriction on how many upvalues a function can have—how many unique variables it can close over. Given that, we can afford a static array that large. We also need to make sure the compiler doesn't overflow that limit.

**compiler.c**
*in* addUpvalue()

```
    if (upvalue->index == index && upvalue->isLocal == isLocal) {
      return i;
    }
  }

  if (upvalueCount == UINT8_COUNT) {
    error("Too many closure variables in function.");
    return 0;
  }

  compiler->upvalues[upvalueCount].isLocal = isLocal;
```

Finally, the Upvalue struct type itself.

**compiler.c**
*add after struct* Local

```
typedef struct {
  uint8_t index;
  bool isLocal;
} Upvalue;
```

The index field stores which local slot the upvalue is capturing. The isLocal field deserves its own section, which we'll get to next.

## 25.2.2  Flattening upvalues

In the example I showed before, the closure is accessing a variable declared in the immediately enclosing function. Lox also supports accessing local variables declared in *any* enclosing scope, as in:

```
fun outer() {
  var x = 1;

  fun middle() {
    fun inner() {
      print x;
    }
  }
}
```

Here, we're accessing x in `inner()`. That variable is defined not in `middle()`, but all the way out in `outer()`. We need to handle cases like this too. You *might* think that this isn't much harder since the variable will simply be somewhere farther down on the stack. But consider this devious example:

```
fun outer() {
  var x = "value";

  fun middle() {
    fun inner() {
      print x;
    }

    print "create inner closure";
    return inner;
  }

  print "return from outer";
  return middle;
}

var mid = outer();
var in = mid();
in();
```

When you run this, it should print:

```
return from outer
create inner closure
value
```

I know, it's convoluted. The important part is that `outer()`—where x is declared—returns and pops all of its variables off the stack before the *declaration* of `inner()` executes. So, at the point in time that we create the closure for `inner()`, x is already off the stack.

Here, I traced out the execution flow for you:

If you work on programming languages long enough, you will develop a finely honed skill at creating bizarre programs like this that are technically valid but likely to trip up an implementation written by someone with a less perverse imagination than you.

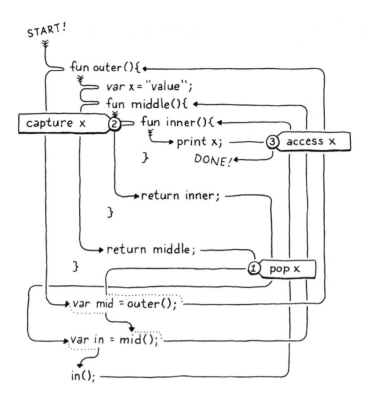

See how x is popped **①** before it is captured **②** and then later accessed **③**? We really have two problems:

1. We need to resolve local variables that are declared in surrounding functions beyond the immediately enclosing one.

2. We need to be able to capture variables that have already left the stack.

Fortunately, we're in the middle of adding upvalues to the VM, and upvalues are explicitly designed for tracking variables that have escaped the stack. So, in a clever bit of self-reference, we can use upvalues to allow upvalues to capture variables declared outside of the immediately surrounding function.

The solution is to allow a closure to capture either a local variable or *an existing upvalue* in the immediately enclosing function. If a deeply nested function references a local variable declared several hops away, we'll thread it through all of the intermediate functions by having each function capture an upvalue for the next function to grab.

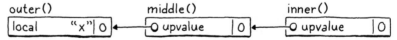

In the above example, middle() captures the local variable x in the immediately enclosing function outer() and stores it in its own upvalue. It does this even though middle() itself doesn't reference x. Then, when the declaration of inner() executes, its closure grabs the *upvalue* from the ObjClosure for middle() that captured x. A function captures—either a local or upvalue—*only* from the immediately surrounding function, which is guaranteed to still be around at the point that the inner function declaration executes.

In order to implement this, `resolveUpvalue()` becomes recursive.

```
if (local != -1) {
  return addUpvalue(compiler, (uint8_t)local, true);
}

int upvalue = resolveUpvalue(compiler->enclosing, name);
if (upvalue != -1) {
  return addUpvalue(compiler, (uint8_t)upvalue, false);
}

return -1;
```

compiler.c
in resolveUpvalue()

It's only another three lines of code, but I found this function really challenging to get right the first time. This in spite of the fact that I wasn't inventing anything new, just porting the concept over from Lua. Most recursive functions either do all their work before the recursive call (a **pre-order traversal**, or "on the way down"), or they do all the work after the recursive call (a **post-order traversal**, or "on the way back up"). This function does both. The recursive call is right in the middle.

We'll walk through it slowly. First, we look for a matching local variable in the enclosing function. If we find one, we capture that local and return. That's the base case.

Otherwise, we look for a local variable beyond the immediately enclosing function. We do that by recursively calling `resolveUpvalue()` on the *enclosing* compiler, not the current one. This series of `resolveUpvalue()` calls works its way along the chain of nested compilers until it hits one of the base cases—either it finds an actual local variable to capture or it runs out of compilers.

When a local variable is found, the most deeply nested call to `resolveUpvalue()` captures it and returns the upvalue index. That returns to the next call for the inner function declaration. That call captures the *upvalue* from the surrounding function, and so on. As each nested call to `resolveUpvalue()` returns, we drill back down into the innermost function declaration where the identifier we are resolving appears. At each step along the way, we add an upvalue to the intervening function and pass the resulting upvalue index down to the next call.

It might help to walk through the original example when resolving x:

The other base case, of course, is if there is no enclosing function. In that case, the variable can't be resolved lexically and is treated as global.

Each recursive call to `resolveUpvalue()` walks *out* one level of function nesting. So an inner *recursive call* refers to an *outer* nested declaration. The innermost recursive call to `resolveUpvalue()` that finds the local variable will be for the *outermost* function, just inside the enclosing function where that variable is actually declared.

Note that the new call to `addUpvalue()` passes `false` for the `isLocal` parameter. Now you see that that flag controls whether the closure captures a local variable or an upvalue from the surrounding function.

By the time the compiler reaches the end of a function declaration, every variable reference has been resolved as either a local, an upvalue, or a global. Each upvalue may in turn capture a local variable from the surrounding function, or an upvalue in the case of transitive closures. We finally have enough data to emit bytecode which creates a closure at runtime that captures all of the correct variables.

**compiler.c**
*in* function()

```
emitBytes(OP_CLOSURE, makeConstant(OBJ_VAL(function)));

  for (int i = 0; i < function->upvalueCount; i++) {
    emitByte(compiler.upvalues[i].isLocal ? 1 : 0);
    emitByte(compiler.upvalues[i].index);
  }
}
```

The `OP_CLOSURE` instruction is unique in that it has a variably sized encoding. For each upvalue the closure captures, there are two single-byte operands. Each pair of operands specifies what that upvalue captures. If the first byte is one, it captures a local variable in the enclosing function. If zero, it captures one of the function's upvalues. The next byte is the local slot or upvalue index to capture.

This odd encoding means we need some bespoke support in the disassembly code for `OP_CLOSURE`.

**debug.c**
*in* disassembleInstruction()

```
  printf("\n");

    ObjFunction* function = AS_FUNCTION(
        chunk->constants.values[constant]);
    for (int j = 0; j < function->upvalueCount; j++) {
      int isLocal = chunk->code[offset++];
      int index = chunk->code[offset++];
      printf("%04d      |                    %s %d\n",
             offset - 2, isLocal ? "local" : "upvalue", index);
    }

  return offset;
```

For example, take this script:

```
fun outer() {
  var a = 1;
  var b = 2;
  fun middle() {
    var c = 3;
    var d = 4;
    fun inner() {
      print a + c + b + d;
    }
  }
}
```

If we disassemble the instruction that creates the closure for `inner()`, it prints this:

```
0004    9 OP_CLOSURE          2 <fn inner>
0006    |                       upvalue 0
0008    |                       local 1
0010    |                       upvalue 1
0012    |                       local 2
```

We have two other, simpler instructions to add disassembler support for.

```
    case OP_SET_GLOBAL:
      return constantInstruction("OP_SET_GLOBAL", chunk, offset);
    case OP_GET_UPVALUE:
      return byteInstruction("OP_GET_UPVALUE", chunk, offset);
    case OP_SET_UPVALUE:
      return byteInstruction("OP_SET_UPVALUE", chunk, offset);
    case OP_EQUAL:
```

debug.c<br>*in* disassembleInstruction()

These both have a single-byte operand, so there's nothing exciting going on. We do need to add an include so the debug module can get to `AS_FUNCTION()`.

```
#include "debug.h"
#include "object.h"
#include "value.h"
```

debug.c

With that, our compiler is where we want it. For each function declaration, it outputs an `OP_CLOSURE` instruction followed by a series of operand byte pairs for each upvalue it needs to capture at runtime. It's time to hop over to that side of the VM and get things running.

## 25.3  Upvalue Objects

Each `OP_CLOSURE` instruction is now followed by the series of bytes that specify the upvalues the ObjClosure should own. Before we process those operands, we need a runtime representation for upvalues.

```
typedef struct ObjUpvalue {
  Obj obj;
  Value* location;
} ObjUpvalue;
```

object.h<br>*add after struct* ObjString

We know upvalues must manage closed-over variables that no longer live on the stack, which implies some amount of dynamic allocation. The easiest way to do that in our VM is by building on the object system we already have. That way, when we implement a garbage collector in the next chapter, the GC can manage memory for upvalues too.

Thus, our runtime upvalue structure is an ObjUpvalue with the typical Obj header field. Following that is a `location` field that points to the closed-over variable. Note that this is a *pointer* to a Value, not a Value itself. It's a reference to a *variable*, not a *value*. This is important because it means that when we assign to the variable the upvalue captures, we're assigning to the actual variable, not a copy. For example:

```
fun outer() {
  var x = "before";
  fun inner() {
    x = "assigned";
  }
  inner();
  print x;
}
outer();
```

This program should print "assigned" even though the closure assigns to x and the surrounding function accesses it.

Because upvalues are objects, we've got all the usual object machinery, starting with a constructor-like function:

**object.h**
*add after* copyString()

```
ObjString* copyString(const char* chars, int length);
ObjUpvalue* newUpvalue(Value* slot);
void printObject(Value value);
```

It takes the address of the slot where the closed-over variable lives. Here is the implementation:

**object.c**
*add after* copyString()

```
ObjUpvalue* newUpvalue(Value* slot) {
  ObjUpvalue* upvalue = ALLOCATE_OBJ(ObjUpvalue, OBJ_UPVALUE);
  upvalue->location = slot;
  return upvalue;
}
```

We simply initialize the object and store the pointer. That requires a new object type.

**object.h**
*in enum* ObjType

```
  OBJ_STRING,
  OBJ_UPVALUE
} ObjType;
```

And on the back side, a destructor-like function:

**memory.c**
*in* freeObject()

```
      FREE(ObjString, object);
      break;
    }
    case OBJ_UPVALUE:
      FREE(ObjUpvalue, object);
      break;
  }
```

Multiple closures can close over the same variable, so ObjUpvalue does not own the variable it references. Thus, the only thing to free is the ObjUpvalue itself.

And, finally, to print:

```
  case OBJ_STRING:
    printf("%s", AS_CSTRING(value));
    break;
  case OBJ_UPVALUE:
    printf("upvalue");
    break;
}
```

object.c
in printObject()

Printing isn't useful to end users. Upvalues are objects only so that we can take advantage of the VM's memory management. They aren't first-class values that a Lox user can directly access in a program. So this code will never actually execute...but it keeps the compiler from yelling at us about an unhandled switch case, so here we are.

### 25.3.1  Upvalues in closures

When I first introduced upvalues, I said each closure has an array of them. We've finally worked our way back to implementing that.

```
  ObjFunction* function;
  ObjUpvalue** upvalues;
  int upvalueCount;
} ObjClosure;
```

object.h
in struct ObjClosure

Storing the upvalue count in the closure is redundant because the ObjFunction that the ObjClosure references also keeps that count. As usual, this weird code is to appease the GC. The collector may need to know an ObjClosure's upvalue array size after the closure's corresponding ObjFunction has already been freed.

Different closures may have different numbers of upvalues, so we need a dynamic array. The upvalues themselves are dynamically allocated too, so we end up with a double pointer—a pointer to a dynamically allocated array of pointers to upvalues. We also store the number of elements in the array.

When we create an ObjClosure, we allocate an upvalue array of the proper size, which we determined at compile time and stored in the ObjFunction.

```
ObjClosure* newClosure(ObjFunction* function) {
  ObjUpvalue** upvalues = ALLOCATE(ObjUpvalue*,
                                   function->upvalueCount);
  for (int i = 0; i < function->upvalueCount; i++) {
    upvalues[i] = NULL;
  }

  ObjClosure* closure = ALLOCATE_OBJ(ObjClosure, OBJ_CLOSURE);
```

object.c
in newClosure()

Before creating the closure object itself, we allocate the array of upvalues and initialize them all to NULL. This weird ceremony around memory is a careful dance to please the (forthcoming) garbage collection deities. It ensures the memory manager never sees uninitialized memory.

Then we store the array in the new closure, as well as copy the count over from the ObjFunction.

```
  closure->function = function;
  closure->upvalues = upvalues;
  closure->upvalueCount = function->upvalueCount;
  return closure;
```

object.c
in newClosure()

When we free an ObjClosure, we also free the upvalue array.

**memory.c**
*in* freeObject()

```
case OBJ_CLOSURE: {
  ObjClosure* closure = (ObjClosure*)object;
  FREE_ARRAY(ObjUpvalue*, closure->upvalues,
             closure->upvalueCount);
  FREE(ObjClosure, object);
```

ObjClosure does not own the ObjUpvalue objects themselves, but it does own *the array* containing pointers to those upvalues.

We fill the upvalue array over in the interpreter when it creates a closure. This is where we walk through all of the operands after OP_CLOSURE to see what kind of upvalue each slot captures.

**vm.c**
*in* run()

```
      push(OBJ_VAL(closure));
      for (int i = 0; i < closure->upvalueCount; i++) {
        uint8_t isLocal = READ_BYTE();
        uint8_t index = READ_BYTE();
        if (isLocal) {
          closure->upvalues[i] =
              captureUpvalue(frame->slots + index);
        } else {
          closure->upvalues[i] = frame->closure->upvalues[index];
        }
      }
      break;
```

This code is the magic moment when a closure comes to life. We iterate over each upvalue the closure expects. For each one, we read a pair of operand bytes. If the upvalue closes over a local variable in the enclosing function, we let captureUpvalue() do the work.

Otherwise, we capture an upvalue from the surrounding function. An OP_CLOSURE instruction is emitted at the end of a function declaration. At the moment that we are executing that declaration, the *current* function is the surrounding one. That means the current function's closure is stored in the CallFrame at the top of the callstack. So, to grab an upvalue from the enclosing function, we can read it right from the `frame` local variable, which caches a reference to that CallFrame.

Closing over a local variable is more interesting. Most of the work happens in a separate function, but first we calculate the argument to pass to it. We need to grab a pointer to the captured local's slot in the surrounding function's stack window. That window begins at `frame->slots`, which points to slot zero. Adding `index` offsets that to the local slot we want to capture. We pass that pointer here:

**vm.c**
*add after* callValue()

```
static ObjUpvalue* captureUpvalue(Value* local) {
  ObjUpvalue* createdUpvalue = newUpvalue(local);
  return createdUpvalue;
}
```

This seems a little silly. All it does is create a new ObjUpvalue that captures the given stack slot and returns it. Did we need a separate function for this? Well, no, not *yet*. But you know we are going to end up sticking more code in here.

First, let's wrap up what we're working on. Back in the interpreter code for handling OP_CLOSURE, we eventually finish iterating through the upvalue array and initialize each one. When that completes, we have a new closure with an array full of upvalues pointing to variables.

With that in hand, we can implement the instructions that work with those upvalues.

```
      }
    case OP_GET_UPVALUE: {
      uint8_t slot = READ_BYTE();
      push(*frame->closure->upvalues[slot]->location);
      break;
    }
    case OP_EQUAL: {
```
vm.c<br>*in* run()

The operand is the index into the current function's upvalue array. So we simply look up the corresponding upvalue and dereference its location pointer to read the value in that slot. Setting a variable is similar.

```
      }
    case OP_SET_UPVALUE: {
      uint8_t slot = READ_BYTE();
      *frame->closure->upvalues[slot]->location = peek(0);
      break;
    }
    case OP_EQUAL: {
```
vm.c<br>*in* run()

We take the value on top of the stack and store it into the slot pointed to by the chosen upvalue. Just as with the instructions for local variables, it's important that these instructions are fast. User programs are constantly reading and writing variables, so if that's slow, everything is slow. And, as usual, the way we make them fast is by keeping them simple. These two new instructions are pretty good: no control flow, no complex arithmetic, just a couple of pointer indirections and a push().

> The set instruction doesn't *pop* the value from the stack because, remember, assignment is an expression in Lox. So the result of the assignment—the assigned value—needs to remain on the stack for the surrounding expression.

This is a milestone. As long as all of the variables remain on the stack, we have working closures. Try this:

```
fun outer() {
  var x = "outside";
  fun inner() {
    print x;
  }
  inner();
}
outer();
```

Run this, and it correctly prints "outside".

## 25.4  Closed Upvalues

Of course, a key feature of closures is that they hold on to the variable as long as needed, even after the function that declares the variable has returned. Here's another example that *should* work:

```
fun outer() {
  var x = "outside";
  fun inner() {
    print x;
  }

  return inner;
}

var closure = outer();
closure();
```

But if you run it right now...who knows what it does? At runtime, it will end up reading from a stack slot that no longer contains the closed-over variable. Like I've mentioned a few times, the crux of the issue is that variables in closures don't have stack semantics. That means we've got to hoist them off the stack when the function where they were declared returns. This final section of the chapter does that.

### 25.4.1  Values and variables

If Lox didn't allow assignment, it *would* be an academic question.

Before we get to writing code, I want to dig into an important semantic point. Does a closure close over a *value* or a *variable*? This isn't purely an academic question. I'm not just splitting hairs. Consider:

The fact that I'm using a couple of global variables isn't significant. I needed some way to return two values from a function, and without any kind of collection type in Lox, my options were limited.

```
var globalSet;
var globalGet;

fun main() {
  var a = "initial";

  fun set() { a = "updated"; }
  fun get() { print a; }

  globalSet = set;
  globalGet = get;
}

main();
globalSet();
globalGet();
```

The outer `main()` function creates two closures and stores them in global variables so that they outlive the execution of `main()` itself. Both of those closures capture the same variable. The first closure assigns a new value to it and the second closure reads the variable.

What does the call to `globalGet()` print? If closures capture *values* then each closure gets its own copy of a with the value that a had at the point in time that the closure's function declaration executed. The call to `globalSet()` will modify `set()`'s copy of a, but `get()`'s copy will be unaffected. Thus, the call to `globalGet()` will print "initial".

If closures close over variables, then `get()` and `set()` will both capture—reference—the *same mutable variable*. When `set()` changes a, it changes the same a that `get()` reads from. There is only one a. That, in turn, implies the call to `globalGet()` will print "updated".

Which is it? The answer for Lox and most other languages I know with closures is the latter. Closures capture variables. You can think of them as capturing *the place the value lives*. This is important to keep in mind as we deal with closed-over variables that are no longer on the stack. When a variable moves to the heap, we need to ensure that all closures capturing that variable retain a reference to its *one* new location. That way, when the variable is mutated, all closures see the change.

## 25.4.2  Closing upvalues

We know that local variables always start out on the stack. This is faster, and lets our single-pass compiler emit code before it discovers the variable has been captured. We also know that closed-over variables need to move to the heap if the closure outlives the function where the captured variable is declared.

Following Lua, we'll use **open upvalue** to refer to an upvalue that points to a local variable still on the stack. When a variable moves to the heap, we are *closing* the upvalue and the result is, naturally, a **closed upvalue**. The two questions we need to answer are:

1. Where on the heap does the closed-over variable go?

2. When do we close the upvalue?

The answer to the first question is easy. We already have a convenient object on the heap that represents a reference to a variable—ObjUpvalue itself. The closed-over variable will move into a new field right inside the ObjUpvalue struct. That way we don't need to do any additional heap allocation to close an upvalue.

The second question is straightforward too. As long as the variable is on the stack, there may be code that refers to it there, and that code must work correctly. So the logical time to hoist the variable to the heap is as late as possible. If we move the local variable right when it goes out of scope, we are certain that no code after that point will try to access it from the stack. After the variable is out of scope, the compiler will have reported an error if any code tried to use it.

The compiler already emits an `OP_POP` instruction when a local variable goes out of scope. If a variable is captured by a closure, we will instead emit a different instruction to hoist that variable out of the stack and into its corresponding upvalue. To do that, the compiler needs to know which locals are closed over.

The compiler already maintains an array of Upvalue structs for each local variable in the function to track exactly that state. That array is good for answering "Which variables does this closure use?" But it's poorly suited for answering, "Does *any* function capture this local variable?" In particular, once the Compiler

By "after" here, I mean in the lexical or textual sense—code past the } for the block containing the declaration of the closed-over variable.

The compiler doesn't pop parameters and locals declared immediately inside the body of a function. We'll handle those too, in the runtime.

for some closure has finished, the Compiler for the enclosing function whose variable has been captured no longer has access to any of the upvalue state.

In other words, the compiler maintains pointers from upvalues to the locals they capture, but not in the other direction. So we first need to add some extra tracking inside the existing Local struct so that we can tell if a given local is captured by a closure.

compiler.c<br>in struct Local

```
  int depth;
  bool isCaptured;
} Local;
```

This field is `true` if the local is captured by any later nested function declaration. Initially, all locals are not captured.

compiler.c<br>in addLocal()

```
  local->depth = -1;
  local->isCaptured = false;
}
```

Later in the book, it *will* become possible for a user to capture this variable. Just building some anticipation here.

Likewise, the special "slot zero local" that the compiler implicitly declares is not captured.

compiler.c<br>in initCompiler()

```
  local->depth = 0;
  local->isCaptured = false;
  local->name.start = "";
```

When resolving an identifier, if we end up creating an upvalue for a local variable, we mark it as captured.

compiler.c<br>in resolveUpvalue()

```
  if (local != -1) {
    compiler->enclosing->locals[local].isCaptured = true;
    return addUpvalue(compiler, (uint8_t)local, true);
```

Now, at the end of a block scope when the compiler emits code to free the stack slots for the locals, we can tell which ones need to get hoisted onto the heap. We'll use a new instruction for that.

compiler.c<br>in endScope()<br>replace 1 line

```
  while (current->localCount > 0 &&
         current->locals[current->localCount - 1].depth >
            current->scopeDepth) {
    if (current->locals[current->localCount - 1].isCaptured) {
      emitByte(OP_CLOSE_UPVALUE);
    } else {
      emitByte(OP_POP);
    }
    current->localCount--;
  }
```

The instruction requires no operand. We know that the variable will always be right on top of the stack at the point that this instruction executes. We declare the instruction.

```
  OP_CLOSURE,
  OP_CLOSE_UPVALUE,
  OP_RETURN,
```

chunk.h
in enum OpCode

And add trivial disassembler support for it:

```
  }
  case OP_CLOSE_UPVALUE:
    return simpleInstruction("OP_CLOSE_UPVALUE", offset);
  case OP_RETURN:
```

debug.c
in disassembleInstruction()

Excellent. Now the generated bytecode tells the runtime exactly when each captured local variable must move to the heap. Better, it does so only for the locals that *are* used by a closure and need this special treatment. This aligns with our general performance goal that we want users to pay only for functionality that they use. Variables that aren't used by closures live and die entirely on the stack just as they did before.

### 25.4.3  Tracking open upvalues

Let's move over to the runtime side. Before we can interpret OP_CLOSE_UPVALUE instructions, we have an issue to resolve. Earlier, when I talked about whether closures capture variables or values, I said it was important that if multiple closures access the same variable that they end up with a reference to the exact same storage location in memory. That way if one closure writes to the variable, the other closure sees the change.

Right now, if two closures capture the same local variable, the VM creates a separate Upvalue for each one. The necessary sharing is missing. When we move the variable off the stack, if we move it into only one of the upvalues, the other upvalue will have an orphaned value.

To fix that, whenever the VM needs an upvalue that captures a particular local variable slot, we will first search for an existing upvalue pointing to that slot. If found, we reuse that. The challenge is that all of the previously created upvalues are squirreled away inside the upvalue arrays of the various closures. Those closures could be anywhere in the VM's memory.

The first step is to give the VM its own list of all open upvalues that point to variables still on the stack. Searching a list each time the VM needs an upvalue sounds like it might be slow, but in practice, it's not bad. The number of variables on the stack that actually get closed over tends to be small. And function declarations that create closures are rarely on performance critical execution paths in the user's program.

Even better, we can order the list of open upvalues by the stack slot index they point to. The common case is that a slot has *not* already been captured—sharing variables between closures is uncommon—and closures tend to capture locals near the top of the stack. If we store the open upvalue array in stack slot order, as soon as we step past the slot where the local we're capturing lives, we know it won't be found. When that local is near the top of the stack, we can exit the loop pretty early.

Maintaining a sorted list requires inserting elements in the middle efficiently. That suggests using a linked list instead of a dynamic array. Since we defined the ObjUpvalue struct ourselves, the easiest implementation is an intrusive list

The VM *does* share upvalues if one closure captures an *upvalue* from a surrounding function. The nested case works correctly. But if two *sibling* closures capture the same local variable, they each create a separate ObjUpvalue.

Closures are frequently *invoked* inside hot loops. Think about the closures passed to typical higher-order functions on collections like map() and filter(). That should be fast. But the function declaration that *creates* the closure happens only once and is usually outside of the loop.

that puts the next pointer right inside the ObjUpvalue struct itself.

**object.h**
*in struct ObjUpvalue*

```
  Value* location;
  struct ObjUpvalue* next;
} ObjUpvalue;
```

When we allocate an upvalue, it is not attached to any list yet so the link is NULL.

**object.c**
*in newUpvalue()*

```
  upvalue->location = slot;
  upvalue->next = NULL;
  return upvalue;
```

The VM owns the list, so the head pointer goes right inside the main VM struct.

**vm.h**
*in struct VM*

```
  Table strings;
  ObjUpvalue* openUpvalues;
  Obj* objects;
```

The list starts out empty.

**vm.c**
*in resetStack()*

```
  vm.frameCount = 0;
  vm.openUpvalues = NULL;
}
```

Starting with the first upvalue pointed to by the VM, each open upvalue points to the next open upvalue that references a local variable farther down the stack. This script, for example,

```
{
  var a = 1;
  fun f() { print a; }
  var b = 2;
  fun g() { print b; }
  var c = 3;
  fun h() { print c; }
}
```

should produce a series of linked upvalues like so:

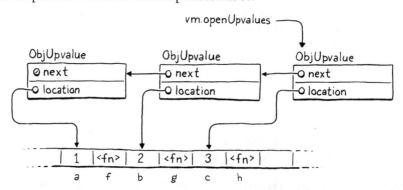

Whenever we close over a local variable, before creating a new upvalue, we look for an existing one in the list.

```
static ObjUpvalue* captureUpvalue(Value* local) {
  ObjUpvalue* prevUpvalue = NULL;
  ObjUpvalue* upvalue = vm.openUpvalues;
  while (upvalue != NULL && upvalue->location > local) {
    prevUpvalue = upvalue;
    upvalue = upvalue->next;
  }

  if (upvalue != NULL && upvalue->location == local) {
    return upvalue;
  }

  ObjUpvalue* createdUpvalue = newUpvalue(local);
```

vm.c
in captureUpvalue()

We start at the head of the list, which is the upvalue closest to the top of the stack. We walk through the list, using a little pointer comparison to iterate past every upvalue pointing to slots above the one we're looking for. While we do that, we keep track of the preceding upvalue on the list. We'll need to update that node's next pointer if we end up inserting a node after it.

It's a singly linked list. It's not like we have any other choice than to start at the head and go forward from there.

There are three reasons we can exit the loop:

1. **The local slot we stopped at is the slot we're looking for.** We found an existing upvalue capturing the variable, so we reuse that upvalue.

2. **We ran out of upvalues to search.** When upvalue is NULL, it means every open upvalue in the list points to locals above the slot we're looking for, or (more likely) the upvalue list is empty. Either way, we didn't find an upvalue for our slot.

3. **We found an upvalue whose local slot is *below* the one we're looking for.** Since the list is sorted, that means we've gone past the slot we are closing over, and thus there must not be an existing upvalue for it.

In the first case, we're done and we've returned. Otherwise, we create a new upvalue for our local slot and insert it into the list at the right location.

```
  ObjUpvalue* createdUpvalue = newUpvalue(local);
  createdUpvalue->next = upvalue;

  if (prevUpvalue == NULL) {
    vm.openUpvalues = createdUpvalue;
  } else {
    prevUpvalue->next = createdUpvalue;
  }

  return createdUpvalue;
```

vm.c
in captureUpvalue()

The current incarnation of this function already creates the upvalue, so we only need to add code to insert the upvalue into the list. We exited the list traversal by either going past the end of the list, or by stopping on the first upvalue whose stack slot is below the one we're looking for. In either case, that means we need to insert the new upvalue *before* the object pointed at by upvalue (which may be

NULL if we hit the end of the list).

As you may have learned in Data Structures 101, to insert a node into a linked list, you set the `next` pointer of the previous node to point to your new one. We have been conveniently keeping track of that preceding node as we walked the list. We also need to handle the special case where we are inserting a new upvalue at the head of the list, in which case the "next" pointer is the VM's head pointer.

With this updated function, the VM now ensures that there is only ever a single ObjUpvalue for any given local slot. If two closures capture the same variable, they will get the same upvalue. We're ready to move those upvalues off the stack now.

There is a shorter implementation that handles updating either the head pointer or the previous upvalue's `next` pointer uniformly by using a pointer to a pointer, but that kind of code confuses almost everyone who hasn't reached some Zen master level of pointer expertise. I went with the basic `if` statement approach.

### 25.4.4  Closing upvalues at runtime

The compiler helpfully emits an `OP_CLOSE_UPVALUE` instruction to tell the VM exactly when a local variable should be hoisted onto the heap. Executing that instruction is the interpreter's responsibility.

vm.c
*in* run()

```
      }

    case OP_CLOSE_UPVALUE:
      closeUpvalues(vm.stackTop - 1);
      pop();
      break;
    case OP_RETURN: {
```

When we reach the instruction, the variable we are hoisting is right on top of the stack. We call a helper function, passing the address of that stack slot. That function is responsible for closing the upvalue and moving the local from the stack to the heap. After that, the VM is free to discard the stack slot, which it does by calling `pop()`.

The fun stuff happens here:

vm.c
*add after* captureUpvalue()

```
static void closeUpvalues(Value* last) {
  while (vm.openUpvalues != NULL &&
         vm.openUpvalues->location >= last) {
    ObjUpvalue* upvalue = vm.openUpvalues;
    upvalue->closed = *upvalue->location;
    upvalue->location = &upvalue->closed;
    vm.openUpvalues = upvalue->next;
  }
}
```

This function takes a pointer to a stack slot. It closes every open upvalue it can find that points to that slot or any slot above it on the stack. Right now, we pass a pointer only to the top slot on the stack, so the "or above it" part doesn't come into play, but it will soon.

To do this, we walk the VM's list of open upvalues, again from top to bottom. If an upvalue's location points into the range of slots we're closing, we close the upvalue. Otherwise, once we reach an upvalue outside of the range, we know the rest will be too, so we stop iterating.

The way an upvalue gets closed is pretty cool. First, we copy the variable's value into the `closed` field in the ObjUpvalue. That's where closed-over variables live on the heap. The `OP_GET_UPVALUE` and `OP_SET_UPVALUE` instructions need to look for the variable there after it's been moved. We could add some conditional logic in the interpreter code for those instructions to check some flag for whether the upvalue is open or closed.

But there is already a level of indirection in play—those instructions dereference the `location` pointer to get to the variable's value. When the variable moves from the stack to the `closed` field, we simply update that `location` to the address of the ObjUpvalue's *own* `closed` field.

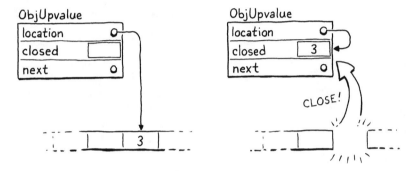

We don't need to change how `OP_GET_UPVALUE` and `OP_SET_UPVALUE` are interpreted at all. That keeps them simple, which in turn keeps them fast. We do need to add the new field to ObjUpvalue, though.

```
Value* location;
Value closed;
struct ObjUpvalue* next;
```
> object.h
> *in struct* ObjUpvalue

And we should zero it out when we create an ObjUpvalue so there's no uninitialized memory floating around.

```
ObjUpvalue* upvalue = ALLOCATE_OBJ(ObjUpvalue, OBJ_UPVALUE);
upvalue->closed = NIL_VAL;
upvalue->location = slot;
```
> object.c
> *in* newUpvalue()

Whenever the compiler reaches the end of a block, it discards all local variables in that block and emits an `OP_CLOSE_UPVALUE` for each local variable that was closed over. The compiler does *not* emit any instructions at the end of the outermost block scope that defines a function body. That scope contains the function's parameters and any locals declared immediately inside the function. Those need to get closed too.

This is the reason `closeUpvalues()` accepts a pointer to a stack slot. When a function returns, we call that same helper and pass in the first stack slot owned by the function.

```
Value result = pop();
closeUpvalues(frame->slots);
vm.frameCount--;
```
> vm.c
> *in* run()

I'm not praising myself here. This is all the Lua dev team's innovation.

There's nothing *preventing* us from closing the outermost function scope in the compiler and emitting `OP_POP` and `OP_CLOSE_UPVALUE` instructions. Doing so is just unnecessary because the runtime discards all of the stack slots used by the function implicitly when it pops the call frame.

By passing the first slot in the function's stack window, we close every remaining open upvalue owned by the returning function. And with that, we now have a fully functioning closure implementation. Closed-over variables live as long as they are needed by the functions that capture them.

This was a lot of work! In jlox, closures fell out naturally from our environment representation. In clox, we had to add a lot of code—new bytecode instructions, more data structures in the compiler, and new runtime objects. The VM very much treats variables in closures as different from other variables.

There is a rationale for that. In terms of implementation complexity, jlox gave us closures "for free". But in terms of *performance*, jlox's closures are anything but. By allocating *all* environments on the heap, jlox pays a significant performance price for *all* local variables, even the majority which are never captured by closures.

With clox, we have a more complex system, but that allows us to tailor the implementation to fit the two use patterns we observe for local variables. For most variables which do have stack semantics, we allocate them entirely on the stack which is simple and fast. Then, for the few local variables where that doesn't work, we have a second slower path we can opt in to as needed.

Fortunately, users don't perceive the complexity. From their perspective, local variables in Lox are simple and uniform. The *language itself* is as simple as jlox's implementation. But under the hood, clox is watching what the user does and optimizing for their specific uses. As your language implementations grow in sophistication, you'll find yourself doing this more. A large fraction of "optimization" is about adding special case code that detects certain uses and provides a custom-built, faster path for code that fits that pattern.

We have lexical scoping fully working in clox now, which is a major milestone. And, now that we have functions and variables with complex lifetimes, we also have a *lot* of objects floating around in clox's heap, with a web of pointers stringing them together. The next step is figuring out how to manage that memory so that we can free some of those objects when they're no longer needed.

## CHALLENGES

1. Wrapping every ObjFunction in an ObjClosure introduces a level of indirection that has a performance cost. That cost isn't necessary for functions that do not close over any variables, but it does let the runtime treat all calls uniformly.

   Change clox to only wrap functions in ObjClosures that need upvalues. How does the code complexity and performance compare to always wrapping functions? Take care to benchmark programs that do and do not use closures. How should you weight the importance of each benchmark? If one gets slower and one faster, how do you decide what trade-off to make to choose an implementation strategy?

2. Read the design note below. I'll wait. Now, how do you think Lox *should* behave? Change the implementation to create a new variable for each loop iteration.

3. A famous koan teaches us that "objects are a poor man's closure" (and vice versa). Our VM doesn't support objects yet, but now that we have closures we can approximate them. Using closures, write a Lox program that models two-dimensional vector "objects". It should:

   Meditate on:
   → craftinginterpreters.com/koan

   - Define a "constructor" function to create a new vector with the given *x* and *y* coordinates.

   - Provide "methods" to access the *x* and *y* coordinates of values returned from that constructor.

   - Define an addition "method" that adds two vectors and produces a third.

## DESIGN NOTE: CLOSING OVER THE LOOP VARIABLE

Closures capture variables. When two closures capture the same variable, they share a reference to the same underlying storage location. This fact is visible when new values are assigned to the variable. Obviously, if two closures capture *different* variables, there is no sharing.

```
var globalOne;
var globalTwo;

fun main() {
  {
    var a = "one";
    fun one() { print a; }

    globalOne = one;
  }

  {
    var a = "two";
    fun two() { print a; }

    globalTwo = two;
  }
}

main();
globalOne();
globalTwo();
```

This prints "one" then "two". In this example, it's pretty clear that the two a variables are different. But it's not always so obvious. Consider:

```
var globalOne;
var globalTwo;

fun main() {
  for (var a = 1; a <= 2; a = a + 1) {
    fun closure() { print a; }

    if (globalOne == nil) {
      globalOne = closure;
    } else {
      globalTwo = closure;
    }
  }
}

main();
globalOne();
globalTwo();
```

The code is convoluted because Lox has no collection types. The important part is that the `main()` function does two iterations of a `for` loop. Each time through the loop, it creates a closure that captures the loop variable. It stores the first closure in `globalOne` and the second in `globalTwo`.

There are definitely two different closures. Do they close over two different variables? Is there only one **a** for the entire duration of the loop, or does each iteration get its own distinct **a** variable?

The script here is strange and contrived, but this does show up in real code in languages that aren't as minimal as clox. Here's a JavaScript example:

```
var closures = [];
for (var i = 1; i <= 2; i++) {
  closures.push(function () { console.log(i); });
}

closures[0]();
closures[1]();
```

Does this print "1" then "2", or does it print "3" twice? You may be surprised to hear that it prints "3" twice. In this JavaScript program, there is only a single `i` variable whose lifetime includes all iterations of the loop, including the final exit.

If you're familiar with JavaScript, you probably know that variables declared using `var` are implicitly *hoisted* to the surrounding function or top-level scope. It's as if you really wrote this:

```
var closures = [];
var i;
for (i = 1; i <= 2; i++) {
  closures.push(function () { console.log(i); });
}

closures[0]();
closures[1]();
```

At that point, it's clearer that there is only a single `i`. Now consider if you change the program to use the newer `let` keyword:

```
var closures = [];
for (let i = 1; i <= 2; i++) {
  closures.push(function () { console.log(i); });
}

closures[0]();
closures[1]();
```

Does this new program behave the same? Nope. In this case, it prints "1" then "2". Each closure gets its own `i`. That's sort of strange when you think about it. The increment clause is `i++`. That looks very much like it is assigning to and mutating an existing variable, not creating a new one.

Let's try some other languages. Here's Python:

You're wondering how *three* enters the picture? After the second iteration, `i++` is executed, which increments `i` to three. That's what causes `i  <=  2` to evaluate to false and end the loop. If `i` never reached three, the loop would run forever.

```
closures = []
for i in range(1, 3):
  closures.append(lambda: print(i))

closures[0]()
closures[1]()
```

Python doesn't really have block scope. Variables are implicitly declared and are au-tomatically scoped to the surrounding function. Kind of like hoisting in JS, now that I think about it. So both closures capture the same variable. Unlike C, though, we don't exit the loop by incrementing *i past* the last value, so this prints "2" twice.

What about Ruby? Ruby has two typical ways to iterate numerically. Here's the classic imperative style:

```
closures = []
for i in 1..2 do
  closures << lambda { puts i }
end

closures[0].call
closures[1].call
```

This, like Python, prints "2" twice. But the more idiomatic Ruby style is using a high-er-order **each()** method on range objects:

```
closures = []
(1..2).each do |i|
  closures << lambda { puts i }
end

closures[0].call
closures[1].call
```

If you're not familiar with Ruby, the do |i| ... end part is basically a closure that gets created and passed to the **each()** method. The |i| is the parameter signature for the closure. The **each()** method invokes that closure twice, passing in 1 for **i** the first time and 2 the second time.

In this case, the "loop variable" is really a function parameter. And, since each iter-ation of the loop is a separate invocation of the function, those are definitely separate variables for each call. So this prints "1" then "2".

If a language has a higher-level iterator-based looping structure like **foreach** in C#, Java's "enhanced for", **for-of** in JavaScript, **for-in** in Dart, etc., then I think it's natural to the reader to have each iteration create a new variable. The code *looks* like a new variable because the loop header looks like a variable declaration. And there's no increment expression that looks like it's mutating that variable to advance to the next step.

If you dig around StackOverflow and other places, you find evidence that this is what users expect, because they are very surprised when they *don't* get it. In partic-ular, C# originally did *not* create a new loop variable for each iteration of a **foreach** loop. This was such a frequent source of user confusion that they took the very rare step of shipping a breaking change to the language. In C# 5, each iteration creates a fresh variable.

Old C-style `for` loops are harder. The increment clause really does look like muta-tion. That implies there is a single variable that's getting updated each step. But it's almost never *useful* for each iteration to share a loop variable. The only time you can even detect this is when closures capture it. And it's rarely helpful to have a closure that references a variable whose value is whatever value caused you to exit the loop.

The pragmatically useful answer is probably to do what JavaScript does with `let` in `for` loops. Make it look like mutation but actually create a new variable each time, because that's what users want. It is kind of weird when you think about it, though.

# Garbage Collection

26

> *"I wanna, I wanna,*
> *I wanna, I wanna,*
> *I wanna be trash."*

— The Whip, "Trash"

We say Lox is a "high-level" language because it frees programmers from worrying about details irrelevant to the problem they're solving. The user becomes an executive, giving the machine abstract goals and letting the lowly computer figure out how to get there.

Dynamic memory allocation is a perfect candidate for automation. It's necessary for a working program, tedious to do by hand, and yet still error-prone. The inevitable mistakes can be catastrophic, leading to crashes, memory corruption, or security violations. It's the kind of risky-yet-boring work that machines excel at over humans.

This is why Lox is a **managed language**, which means that the language implementation manages memory allocation and freeing on the user's behalf. When a user performs an operation that requires some dynamic memory, the VM automatically allocates it. The programmer never worries about deallocating anything. The machine ensures any memory the program is using sticks around as long as needed.

Recycling would really be a better metaphor for this. The GC doesn't *throw away* the memory, it reclaims it to be reused for new data. But managed languages are older than Earth Day, so the inventors went with the analogy they knew.

I'm using "conservative" in the general sense. There is such a thing as a "conservative garbage collector" which means something more specific. All garbage collectors are "conservative" in that they keep memory alive if it *could* be accessed, instead of having a Magic 8-Ball that lets them more precisely know what data *will* be accessed.

A **conservative GC** is a special kind of collector that considers any piece of memory to be a pointer if the value in there looks like it could be an address. This is in contrast to a **precise GC**—which is what we'll implement—that knows exactly which words in memory are pointers and which store other kinds of values like numbers or strings.

Lox provides the illusion that the computer has an infinite amount of memory. Users can allocate and allocate and allocate and never once think about where all these bytes are coming from. Of course, computers do not yet *have* infinite memory. So the way managed languages maintain this illusion is by going behind the programmer's back and reclaiming memory that the program no longer needs. The component that does this is called a **garbage collector**.

## 26.1 Reachability

This raises a surprisingly difficult question: how does a VM tell what memory is *not* needed? Memory is only needed if it is read in the future, but short of having a time machine, how can an implementation tell what code the program *will* execute and which data it *will* use? Spoiler alert: VMs cannot travel into the future. Instead, the language makes a conservative approximation: it considers a piece of memory to still be in use if it *could possibly* be read in the future.

That sounds *too* conservative. Couldn't *any* bit of memory potentially be read? Actually, no, at least not in a memory-safe language like Lox. Here's an example:

```
var a = "first value";
a = "updated";
// GC here.
print a;
```

Say we run the GC after the assignment has completed on the second line. The string "first value" is still sitting in memory, but there is no way for the user's program to ever get to it. Once a got reassigned, the program lost any reference to that string. We can safely free it. A value is **reachable** if there is some way for a user program to reference it. Otherwise, like the string "first value" here, it is **unreachable**.

Many values can be directly accessed by the VM. Take a look at:

```
var global = "string";
{
  var local = "another";
  print global + local;
}
```

Pause the program right after the two strings have been concatenated but before the `print` statement has executed. The VM can reach `"string"` by looking through the global variable table and finding the entry for `global`. It can find `"another"` by walking the value stack and hitting the slot for the local variable `local`. It can even find the concatenated string `"stringanother"` since that temporary value is also sitting on the VM's stack at the point when we paused our program.

All of these values are called **roots**. A root is any object that the VM can reach directly without going through a reference in some other object. Most roots are global variables or on the stack, but as we'll see, there are a couple of other places the VM stores references to objects that it can find.

Other values can be found by going through a reference inside another value. Fields on instances of classes are the most obvious case, but we don't have those

We'll get there soon, though!

yet. Even without those, our VM still has indirect references. Consider:

```
fun makeClosure() {
  var a = "data";

  fun f() { print a; }
  return f;
}

{
  var closure = makeClosure();
  // GC here.
  closure();
}
```

Say we pause the program on the marked line and run the garbage collector. When the collector is done and the program resumes, it will call the closure, which will in turn print `"data"`. So the collector needs to *not* free that string. But here's what the stack looks like when we pause the program:

closure

The `"data"` string is nowhere on it. It has already been hoisted off the stack and moved into the closed upvalue that the closure uses. The closure itself is on the stack. But to get to the string, we need to trace through the closure and its upvalue array. Since it *is* possible for the user's program to do that, all of these indirectly accessible objects are also considered reachable.

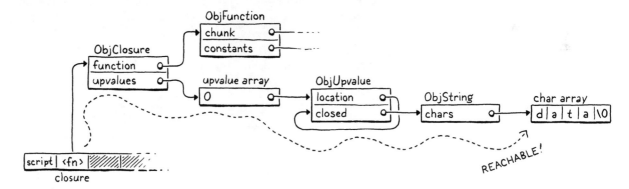

This gives us an inductive definition of reachability:

- All roots are reachable.

- Any object referred to from a reachable object is itself reachable.

These are the values that are still "live" and need to stay in memory. Any value that *doesn't* meet this definition is fair game for the collector to reap. That recursive pair of rules hints at a recursive algorithm we can use to free up unneeded memory:

1. Starting with the roots, traverse through object references to find the full set of reachable objects.

2. Free all objects *not* in that set.

If you want to explore other GC algorithms, *The Garbage Collection Handbook* (Jones, et al.) is the canonical reference. For a large book on such a deep, narrow topic, it is quite enjoyable to read. Or perhaps I have a strange idea of fun.

Many different garbage collection algorithms are in use today, but they all roughly follow that same structure. Some may interleave the steps or mix them, but the two fundamental operations are there. They mostly differ in *how* they perform each step.

## 26.2  Mark-Sweep Garbage Collection

The first managed language was Lisp, the second "high-level" language to be invented, right after Fortran. John McCarthy considered using manual memory management or reference counting, but eventually settled on (and coined) garbage collection—once the program was out of memory, it would go back and find unused storage it could reclaim.

In John McCarthy's "History of Lisp", he notes: "Once we decided on garbage collection, its actual implementation could be postponed, because only toy examples were being done." Our choice to procrastinate adding the GC to clox follows in the footsteps of giants.

He designed the very first, simplest garbage collection algorithm, called **mark-and-sweep** or just **mark-sweep**. Its description fits in three short paragraphs in the initial paper on Lisp. Despite its age and simplicity, the same fundamental algorithm underlies many modern memory managers. Some corners of CS seem to be timeless.

As the name implies, mark-sweep works in two phases:

A **tracing garbage collector** is any algorithm that traces through the graph of object references. This is in contrast with reference counting, which has a different strategy for tracking the reachable objects.

- **Marking:** We start with the roots and traverse or *trace* through all of the objects those roots refer to. This is a classic graph traversal of all of the reachable objects. Each time we visit an object, we *mark* it in some way. (Implementations differ in how they record the mark.)

- **Sweeping:** Once the mark phase completes, every reachable object in the heap has been marked. That means any unmarked object is unreachable and ripe for reclamation. We go through the unmarked objects and free each one.

It looks something like this:

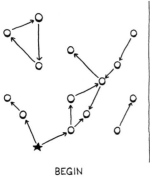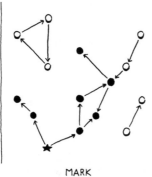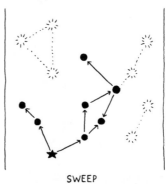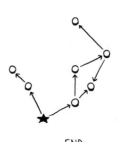

BEGIN                MARK                SWEEP                END

That's what we're gonna implement. Whenever we decide it's time to reclaim some bytes, we'll trace everything and mark all the reachable objects, free what didn't get marked, and then resume the user's program.

## 26.2.1  Collecting garbage

This entire chapter is about implementing this one function:

```
void* reallocate(void* pointer, size_t oldSize, size_t newSize);
void collectGarbage();
void freeObjects();
```

We'll work our way up to a full implementation starting with this empty shell:

```
void collectGarbage() {
}
```

The first question you might ask is, When does this function get called? It turns out that's a subtle question that we'll spend some time on later in the chapter. For now we'll sidestep the issue and build ourselves a handy diagnostic tool in the process.

```
#define DEBUG_TRACE_EXECUTION

#define DEBUG_STRESS_GC

#define UINT8_COUNT (UINT8_MAX + 1)
```

We'll add an optional "stress test" mode for the garbage collector. When this flag is defined, the GC runs as often as it possibly can. This is, obviously, horrendous for performance. But it's great for flushing out memory management bugs that occur only when a GC is triggered at just the right moment. If *every* moment triggers a GC, you're likely to find those bugs.

```
void* reallocate(void* pointer, size_t oldSize, size_t newSize) {
  if (newSize > oldSize) {
#ifdef DEBUG_STRESS_GC
    collectGarbage();
#endif
  }

  if (newSize == 0) {
```

Whenever we call `reallocate()` to acquire more memory, we force a collection to run. The if check is because `reallocate()` is also called to free or shrink an allocation. We don't want to trigger a GC for that—in particular because the GC itself will call `reallocate()` to free memory.

Collecting right before allocation is the classic way to wire a GC into a VM. You're already calling into the memory manager, so it's an easy place to hook in the code. Also, allocation is the only time when you really *need* some freed up memory so that you can reuse it. If you *don't* use allocation to trigger a GC, you have to make sure every possible place in code where you can loop and allocate memory also has a way to trigger the collector. Otherwise, the VM can get into a starved state where it needs more memory but never collects any.

Of course, we'll end up adding a bunch of helper functions too.

**memory.h**
*add after* `reallocate()`

**memory.c**
*add after* `freeObject()`

**common.h**

**memory.c**
*in* `reallocate()`

More sophisticated collectors might run on a separate thread or be interleaved periodically during program execution—often at function call boundaries or when a backward jump occurs.

### 26.2.2  Debug logging

While we're on the subject of diagnostics, let's put some more in. A real challenge I've found with garbage collectors is that they are opaque. We've been running lots of Lox programs just fine without any GC *at all* so far. Once we add one, how do we tell if it's doing anything useful? Can we tell only if we write programs that plow through acres of memory? How do we debug that?

An easy way to shine a light into the GC's inner workings is with some logging.

common.h

```
#define DEBUG_STRESS_GC
#define DEBUG_LOG_GC

#define UINT8_COUNT (UINT8_MAX + 1)
```

When this is enabled, clox prints information to the console when it does something with dynamic memory.

We need a couple of includes.

memory.c

```
#include "vm.h"

#ifdef DEBUG_LOG_GC
#include <stdio.h>
#include "debug.h"
#endif

void* reallocate(void* pointer, size_t oldSize, size_t newSize) {
```

We don't have a collector yet, but we can start putting in some of the logging now. We'll want to know when a collection run starts.

memory.c<br>in collectGarbage()

```
void collectGarbage() {
#ifdef DEBUG_LOG_GC
  printf("-- gc begin\n");
#endif
}
```

Eventually we will log some other operations during the collection, so we'll also want to know when the show's over.

memory.c<br>in collectGarbage()

```
  printf("-- gc begin\n");
#endif

#ifdef DEBUG_LOG_GC
  printf("-- gc end\n");
#endif
}
```

We don't have any code for the collector yet, but we do have functions for allocating and freeing, so we can instrument those now.

```
  vm.objects = object;

#ifdef DEBUG_LOG_GC
  printf("%p allocate %zu for %d\n", (void*)object, size, type);
#endif

  return object;
```

object.c
in allocateObject()

And at the end of an object's lifespan:

```
static void freeObject(Obj* object) {
#ifdef DEBUG_LOG_GC
  printf("%p free type %d\n", (void*)object, object->type);
#endif

  switch (object->type) {
```

memory.c
in freeObject()

With these two flags, we should be able to see that we're making progress as we work through the rest of the chapter.

## 26.3  Marking the Roots

Objects are scattered across the heap like stars in the inky night sky. A reference from one object to another forms a connection, and these constellations are the graph that the mark phase traverses. Marking begins at the roots.

```
#ifdef DEBUG_LOG_GC
  printf("-- gc begin\n");
#endif

  markRoots();

#ifdef DEBUG_LOG_GC
```

memory.c
in collectGarbage()

Most roots are local variables or temporaries sitting right in the VM's stack, so we start by walking that.

```
static void markRoots() {
  for (Value* slot = vm.stack; slot < vm.stackTop; slot++) {
    markValue(*slot);
  }
}
```

memory.c
add after freeObject()

To mark a Lox value, we use this new function:

```
void* reallocate(void* pointer, size_t oldSize, size_t newSize);
void markValue(Value value);
void collectGarbage();
```

memory.h
add after reallocate()

Its implementation is here:

**memory.c**
*add after* reallocate()

```
void markValue(Value value) {
  if (IS_OBJ(value)) markObject(AS_OBJ(value));
}
```

Some Lox values—numbers, Booleans, and nil—are stored directly inline in Value and require no heap allocation. The garbage collector doesn't need to worry about them at all, so the first thing we do is ensure that the value is an actual heap object. If so, the real work happens in this function:

**memory.h**
*add after* reallocate()

```
void* reallocate(void* pointer, size_t oldSize, size_t newSize);
void markObject(Obj* object);
void markValue(Value value);
```

Which is defined here:

**memory.c**
*add after* reallocate()

```
void markObject(Obj* object) {
  if (object == NULL) return;
  object->isMarked = true;
}
```

The NULL check is unnecessary when called from markValue(). A Lox Value that is some kind of Obj type will always have a valid pointer. But later we will call this function directly from other code, and in some of those places, the object being pointed to is optional.

Assuming we do have a valid object, we mark it by setting a flag. That new field lives in the Obj header struct all objects share.

**object.h**
*in struct* Obj

```
  ObjType type;
  bool isMarked;
  struct Obj* next;
```

Every new object begins life unmarked because we haven't yet determined if it is reachable or not.

**object.c**
*in* allocateObject()

```
  object->type = type;
  object->isMarked = false;

  object->next = vm.objects;
```

Before we go any farther, let's add some logging to markObject().

**memory.c**
*in* markObject()

```
void markObject(Obj* object) {
  if (object == NULL) return;
#ifdef DEBUG_LOG_GC
  printf("%p mark ", (void*)object);
  printValue(OBJ_VAL(object));
  printf("\n");
#endif

  object->isMarked = true;
```

This way we can see what the mark phase is doing. Marking the stack takes care of local variables and temporaries. The other main source of roots are the global variables.

```
    markValue(*slot);
  }


  markTable(&vm.globals);
}
```

memory.c
in markRoots()

Those live in a hash table owned by the VM, so we'll declare another helper function for marking all of the objects in a table.

```
ObjString* tableFindString(Table* table, const char* chars,
                           int length, uint32_t hash);
void markTable(Table* table);

#endif
```

table.h
add after tableFindString()

We implement that in the "table" module here:

```
void markTable(Table* table) {
  for (int i = 0; i < table->capacity; i++) {
    Entry* entry = &table->entries[i];
    markObject((Obj*)entry->key);
    markValue(entry->value);
  }
}
```

table.c
add after tableFindString()

Pretty straightforward. We walk the entry array. For each one, we mark its value. We also mark the key strings for each entry since the GC manages those strings too.

## 26.3.1 Less obvious roots

Those cover the roots that we typically think of—the values that are obviously reachable because they're stored in variables the user's program can see. But the VM has a few of its own hidey-holes where it squirrels away references to values that it directly accesses.

Most function call state lives in the value stack, but the VM maintains a separate stack of CallFrames. Each CallFrame contains a pointer to the closure being called. The VM uses those pointers to access constants and upvalues, so those closures need to be kept around too.

```
  }

  for (int i = 0; i < vm.frameCount; i++) {
    markObject((Obj*)vm.frames[i].closure);
  }

  markTable(&vm.globals);
```

memory.c
in markRoots()

Speaking of upvalues, the open upvalue list is another set of values that the VM can directly reach.

**memory.c**
*in* markRoots()

```
  for (int i = 0; i < vm.frameCount; i++) {
    markObject((Obj*)vm.frames[i].closure);
  }

  for (ObjUpvalue* upvalue = vm.openUpvalues;
       upvalue != NULL;
       upvalue = upvalue->next) {
    markObject((Obj*)upvalue);
  }

  markTable(&vm.globals);
```

Remember also that a collection can begin during *any* allocation. Those allocations don't just happen while the user's program is running. The compiler itself periodically grabs memory from the heap for literals and the constant table. If the GC runs while we're in the middle of compiling, then any values the compiler directly accesses need to be treated as roots too.

To keep the compiler module cleanly separated from the rest of the VM, we'll do that in a separate function.

**memory.c**
*in* markRoots()

```
  markTable(&vm.globals);
  markCompilerRoots();
}
```

It's declared here:

**compiler.h**
*add after* compile()

```
ObjFunction* compile(const char* source);
void markCompilerRoots();

#endif
```

Which means the "memory" module needs an include.

**memory.c**

```
#include <stdlib.h>

#include "compiler.h"
#include "memory.h"
```

And the definition is over in the "compiler" module.

**compiler.c**
*add after* compile()

```
void markCompilerRoots() {
  Compiler* compiler = current;
  while (compiler != NULL) {
    markObject((Obj*)compiler->function);
    compiler = compiler->enclosing;
  }
}
```

Fortunately, the compiler doesn't have too many values that it hangs on to. The only object it uses is the ObjFunction it is compiling into. Since function declarations can nest, the compiler has a linked list of those and we walk the whole list.

Since the "compiler" module is calling `markObject()`, it also needs an include.

```
#include "compiler.h"
#include "memory.h"
#include "scanner.h"
```

compiler.c

Those are all the roots. After running this, every object that the VM—runtime and compiler—can get to *without* going through some other object has its mark bit set.

## 26.4  Tracing Object References

The next step in the marking process is tracing through the graph of references between objects to find the indirectly reachable values. We don't have instances with fields yet, so there aren't many objects that contain references, but we do have some. In particular, ObjClosure has the list of ObjUpvalues it closes over as well as a reference to the raw ObjFunction that it wraps. ObjFunction, in turn, has a constant table containing references to all of the literals created in the function's body. This is enough to build a fairly complex web of objects for our collector to crawl through.

Now it's time to implement that traversal. We can go breadth-first, depth-first, or in some other order. Since we just need to find the *set* of all reachable objects, the order we visit them mostly doesn't matter.

### 26.4.1  The tricolor abstraction

As the collector wanders through the graph of objects, we need to make sure it doesn't lose track of where it is or get stuck going in circles. This is particularly a concern for advanced implementations like incremental GCs that interleave marking with running pieces of the user's program. The collector needs to be able to pause and then pick up where it left off later.

To help us soft-brained humans reason about this complex process, VM hackers came up with a metaphor called the **tricolor abstraction**. Each object has a conceptual "color" that tracks what state the object is in, and what work is left to do.

- ○ At the beginning of a garbage collection, every object is white. This color means we have not reached or processed the object at all.

- ⊘ During marking, when we first reach an object, we darken it gray. This color means we know the object itself is reachable and should not be collected. But we have not yet traced *through* it to see what *other* objects it references. In graph algorithm terms, this is the *worklist*—the set of objects we know about but haven't processed yet.

I slotted this chapter into the book right here specifically *because* we now have closures which give us interesting objects for the garbage collector to process.

I say "mostly" because some garbage collectors move objects in the order that they are visited, so traversal order determines which objects end up adjacent in memory. That impacts performance because the CPU uses locality to determine which memory to preload into the caches.

Even when traversal order does matter, it's not clear which order is *best*. It's very difficult to determine which order objects will be used in the future, so it's hard for the GC to know which order will help performance.

Advanced garbage collection algorithms often add other colors to the abstraction. I've seen multiple shades of gray, and even purple in some designs. My puce-chartreuse-fuchsia-malachite collector paper was, alas, not accepted for publication.

- ● When we take a gray object and mark all of the objects it references, we then turn the gray object black. This color means the mark phase is done processing that object.

In terms of that abstraction, the marking process now looks like this:

1. Start off with all objects white.

2. Find all the roots and mark them gray.

3. Repeat as long as there are still gray objects:

   1. Pick a gray object. Turn any white objects that the object mentions to gray.

   2. Mark the original gray object black.

I find it helps to visualize this. You have a web of objects with references between them. Initially, they are all little white dots. Off to the side are some incoming edges from the VM that point to the roots. Those roots turn gray. Then each gray object's siblings turn gray while the object itself turns black. The full effect is a gray wavefront that passes through the graph, leaving a field of reachable black objects behind it. Unreachable objects are not touched by the wavefront and stay white.

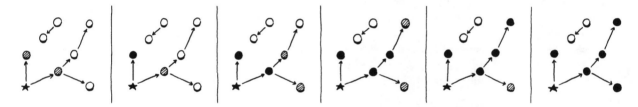

Note that at every step of this process no black node ever points to a white node. This property is called the **tricolor invariant**. The traversal process maintains this invariant to ensure that no reachable object is ever collected.

At the end, you're left with a sea of reached, black objects sprinkled with islands of white objects that can be swept up and freed. Once the unreachable objects are freed, the remaining objects—all black—are reset to white for the next garbage collection cycle.

## 26.4.2  A worklist for gray objects

In our implementation we have already marked the roots. They're all gray. The next step is to start picking them and traversing their references. But we don't have any easy way to find them. We set a field on the object, but that's it. We don't want to have to traverse the entire object list looking for objects with that field set.

Instead, we'll create a separate worklist to keep track of all of the gray objects. When an object turns gray, in addition to setting the mark field we'll also add it to the worklist.

**memory.c**
*in* markObject()

*continued on next page...*

```
object->isMarked = true;

if (vm.grayCapacity < vm.grayCount + 1) {
  vm.grayCapacity = GROW_CAPACITY(vm.grayCapacity);
```

```
    vm.grayStack = (Obj**)realloc(vm.grayStack,
                                  sizeof(Obj*) * vm.grayCapacity);
  }

  vm.grayStack[vm.grayCount++] = object;
}
```

…from previous page

We could use any kind of data structure that lets us put items in and take them out easily. I picked a stack because that's the simplest to implement with a dynamic array in C. It works mostly like other dynamic arrays we've built in Lox, *except*, note that it calls the *system* `realloc()` function and not our own `reallocate()` wrapper. The memory for the gray stack itself is *not* managed by the garbage collector. We don't want growing the gray stack during a GC to cause the GC to recursively start a new GC. That could tear a hole in the space-time continuum.

We'll manage its memory ourselves, explicitly. The VM owns the gray stack.

```
  Obj* objects;
  int grayCount;
  int grayCapacity;
  Obj** grayStack;
} VM;
```

**vm.h**
*in struct* VM

It starts out empty.

```
  vm.objects = NULL;

  vm.grayCount = 0;
  vm.grayCapacity = 0;
  vm.grayStack = NULL;

  initTable(&vm.globals);
```

**vm.c**
*in* initVM()

And we need to free it when the VM shuts down.

```
    object = next;
  }

  free(vm.grayStack);
}
```

**memory.c**
*in* freeObjects()

We take full responsibility for this array. That includes allocation failure. If we can't create or grow the gray stack, then we can't finish the garbage collection. This is bad news for the VM, but fortunately rare since the gray stack tends to be pretty small. It would be nice to do something more graceful, but to keep the code in this book simple, we just abort.

To be more robust, we can allocate a "rainy day fund" block of memory when we start the VM. If the gray stack allocation fails, we free the rainy day block and try again. That may give us enough wiggle room on the heap to create the gray stack, finish the GC, and free up more memory.

```
    vm.grayStack = (Obj**)realloc(vm.grayStack,
                                  sizeof(Obj*) * vm.grayCapacity);

    if (vm.grayStack == NULL) exit(1);
  }
```

**memory.c**
*in* markObject()

### 26.4.3  Processing gray objects

OK, now when we're done marking the roots, we have both set a bunch of fields and filled our work list with objects to chew through. It's time for the next phase.

memory.c
*in* collectGarbage()

```
  markRoots();
  traceReferences();

#ifdef DEBUG_LOG_GC
```

Here's the implementation:

memory.c
*add after* markRoots()

```
static void traceReferences() {
  while (vm.grayCount > 0) {
    Obj* object = vm.grayStack[--vm.grayCount];
    blackenObject(object);
  }
}
```

It's as close to that textual algorithm as you can get. Until the stack empties, we keep pulling out gray objects, traversing their references, and then marking them black. Traversing an object's references may turn up new white objects that get marked gray and added to the stack. So this function swings back and forth between turning white objects gray and gray objects black, gradually advancing the entire wavefront forward.

Here's where we traverse a single object's references:

memory.c
*add after* markValue()

```
static void blackenObject(Obj* object) {
  switch (object->type) {
    case OBJ_NATIVE:
    case OBJ_STRING:
      break;
  }
}
```

An easy optimization we could do in markObject() is to skip adding strings and native functions to the gray stack at all since we know they don't need to be processed. Instead, they could darken from white straight to black.

You may rightly wonder why we have the isMarked field at all. All in good time, friend.

Each object kind has different fields that might reference other objects, so we need a specific blob of code for each type. We start with the easy ones—strings and native function objects contain no outgoing references so there is nothing to traverse.

Note that we don't set any state in the traversed object itself. There is no direct encoding of "black" in the object's state. A black object is any object whose isMarked field is set and that is no longer in the gray stack.

Now let's start adding in the other object types. The simplest is upvalues.

memory.c
*in* blackenObject()

```
static void blackenObject(Obj* object) {
  switch (object->type) {
    case OBJ_UPVALUE:
      markValue(((ObjUpvalue*)object)->closed);
      break;
    case OBJ_NATIVE:
```

When an upvalue is closed, it contains a reference to the closed-over value. Since the value is no longer on the stack, we need to make sure we trace the reference to it from the upvalue.

Next are functions.

```
switch (object->type) {
    case OBJ_FUNCTION: {
      ObjFunction* function = (ObjFunction*)object;
      markObject((Obj*)function->name);
      markArray(&function->chunk.constants);
      break;
    }
    case OBJ_UPVALUE:
```

memory.c
in blackenObject()

Each function has a reference to an ObjString containing the function's name. More importantly, the function has a constant table packed full of references to other objects. We trace all of those using this helper:

```
static void markArray(ValueArray* array) {
  for (int i = 0; i < array->count; i++) {
    markValue(array->values[i]);
  }
}
```

memory.c
add after markValue()

The last object type we have now—we'll add more in later chapters—is closures.

```
switch (object->type) {
    case OBJ_CLOSURE: {
      ObjClosure* closure = (ObjClosure*)object;
      markObject((Obj*)closure->function);
      for (int i = 0; i < closure->upvalueCount; i++) {
        markObject((Obj*)closure->upvalues[i]);
      }
      break;
    }
    case OBJ_FUNCTION: {
```

memory.c
in blackenObject()

Each closure has a reference to the bare function it wraps, as well as an array of pointers to the upvalues it captures. We trace all of those.

That's the basic mechanism for processing a gray object, but there are two loose ends to tie up. First, some logging.

```
static void blackenObject(Obj* object) {
#ifdef DEBUG_LOG_GC
  printf("%p blacken ", (void*)object);
  printValue(OBJ_VAL(object));
  printf("\n");
#endif

  switch (object->type) {
```

memory.c
in blackenObject()

This way, we can watch the tracing percolate through the object graph. Speaking of which, note that I said *graph*. References between objects are directed, but that doesn't mean they're *acyclic!* It's entirely possible to have cycles of objects. When that happens, we need to ensure our collector doesn't get stuck in an infinite loop as it continually re-adds the same series of objects to the gray stack.

The fix is easy.

memory.c
*in* markObject()

```
  if (object == NULL) return;
  if (object->isMarked) return;

#ifdef DEBUG_LOG_GC
```

If the object is already marked, we don't mark it again and thus don't add it to the gray stack. This ensures that an already-gray object is not redundantly added and that a black object is not inadvertently turned back to gray. In other words, it keeps the wavefront moving forward through only the white objects.

## 26.5  Sweeping Unused Objects

When the loop in traceReferences() exits, we have processed all the objects we could get our hands on. The gray stack is empty, and every object in the heap is either black or white. The black objects are reachable, and we want to hang on to them. Anything still white never got touched by the trace and is thus garbage. All that's left is to reclaim them.

memory.c
*in* collectGarbage()

```
  traceReferences();
  sweep();

#ifdef DEBUG_LOG_GC
```

All of the logic lives in one function.

memory.c
*add after* traceReferences()

```
static void sweep() {
  Obj* previous = NULL;
  Obj* object = vm.objects;
  while (object != NULL) {
    if (object->isMarked) {
      previous = object;
      object = object->next;
    } else {
      Obj* unreached = object;
      object = object->next;
      if (previous != NULL) {
        previous->next = object;
      } else {
        vm.objects = object;
      }

      freeObject(unreached);
    }
  }
}
```

I know that's kind of a lot of code and pointer shenanigans, but there isn't much to it once you work through it. The outer `while` loop walks the linked list of every object in the heap, checking their mark bits. If an object is marked (black), we leave it alone and continue past it. If it is unmarked (white), we unlink it from the list and free it using the `freeObject()` function we already wrote.

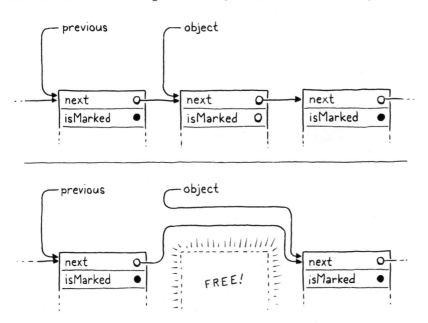

Most of the other code in here deals with the fact that removing a node from a singly linked list is cumbersome. We have to continuously remember the previous node so we can unlink its next pointer, and we have to handle the edge case where we are freeing the first node. But, otherwise, it's pretty simple—delete every node in a linked list that doesn't have a bit set in it.

There's one little addition:

```
    if (object->isMarked) {
      object->isMarked = false;
      previous = object;
```

memory.c
*in* sweep()

After `sweep()` completes, the only remaining objects are the live black ones with their mark bits set. That's correct, but when the *next* collection cycle starts, we need every object to be white. So whenever we reach a black object, we go ahead and clear the bit now in anticipation of the next run.

### 26.5.1   Weak references and the string pool

We are almost done collecting. There is one remaining corner of the VM that has some unusual requirements around memory. Recall that when we added strings to clox we made the VM intern them all. That means the VM has a hash table containing a pointer to every single string in the heap. The VM uses this to de-duplicate strings.

During the mark phase, we deliberately did *not* treat the VM's string table as a source of roots. If we had, no string would *ever* be collected. The string table

This can be a real problem. Java does not intern *all* strings, but it does intern string *literals*. It also provides an API to add strings to the string table. For many years, the capacity of that table was fixed, and strings added to it could never be removed. If users weren't careful about their use of `String.intern()`, they could run out of memory and crash.

Ruby had a similar problem for years where symbols—interned string-like values—were not garbage collected. Both eventually enabled the GC to collect these strings.

would grow and grow and never yield a single byte of memory back to the operating system. That would be bad.

At the same time, if we *do* let the GC free strings, then the VM's string table will be left with dangling pointers to freed memory. That would be even worse.

The string table is special and we need special support for it. In particular, it needs a special kind of reference. The table should be able to refer to a string, but that link should not be considered a root when determining reachability. That implies that the referenced object can be freed. When that happens, the dangling reference must be fixed too, sort of like a magic, self-clearing pointer. This particular set of semantics comes up frequently enough that it has a name: a **weak reference**.

We have already implicitly implemented half of the string table's unique behavior by virtue of the fact that we *don't* traverse it during marking. That means it doesn't force strings to be reachable. The remaining piece is clearing out any dangling pointers for strings that are freed.

To remove references to unreachable strings, we need to know which strings *are* unreachable. We don't know that until after the mark phase has completed. But we can't wait until after the sweep phase is done because by then the objects—and their mark bits—are no longer around to check. So the right time is exactly between the marking and sweeping phases.

**memory.c**
*in* `collectGarbage()`

```
  traceReferences();
  tableRemoveWhite(&vm.strings);
  sweep();
```

The logic for removing the about-to-be-deleted strings exists in a new function in the "table" module.

**table.h**
*add after* `tableFindString()`

```
ObjString* tableFindString(Table* table, const char* chars,
                           int length, uint32_t hash);

void tableRemoveWhite(Table* table);
void markTable(Table* table);
```

The implementation is here:

**table.c**
*add after* `tableFindString()`

```
void tableRemoveWhite(Table* table) {
  for (int i = 0; i < table->capacity; i++) {
    Entry* entry = &table->entries[i];
    if (entry->key != NULL && !entry->key->obj.isMarked) {
      tableDelete(table, entry->key);
    }
  }
}
```

We walk every entry in the table. The string intern table uses only the key of each entry—it's basically a hash *set* not a hash *map*. If the key string object's mark bit is not set, then it is a white object that is moments from being swept away. We delete it from the hash table first and thus ensure we won't see any dangling pointers.

# 26.6  When to Collect

We have a fully functioning mark-sweep garbage collector now. When the stress testing flag is enabled, it gets called all the time, and with the logging enabled too, we can watch it do its thing and see that it is indeed reclaiming memory. But, when the stress testing flag is off, it never runs at all. It's time to decide when the collector should be invoked during normal program execution.

As far as I can tell, this question is poorly answered by the literature. When garbage collectors were first invented, computers had a tiny, fixed amount of memory. Many of the early GC papers assumed that you set aside a few thousand words of memory—in other words, most of it—and invoked the collector whenever you ran out. Simple.

Modern machines have gigs of physical RAM, hidden behind the operating system's even larger virtual memory abstraction, which is shared among a slew of other programs all fighting for their chunk of memory. The operating system will let your program request as much as it wants and then page in and out from the disc when physical memory gets full. You never really "run out" of memory, you just get slower and slower.

## 26.6.1  Latency and throughput

It no longer makes sense to wait until you "have to", to run the GC, so we need a more subtle timing strategy. To reason about this more precisely, it's time to introduce two fundamental numbers used when measuring a memory manager's performance: *throughput* and *latency*.

Every managed language pays a performance price compared to explicit, user-authored deallocation. The time spent actually freeing memory is the same, but the GC spends cycles figuring out *which* memory to free. That is time *not* spent running the user's code and doing useful work. In our implementation, that's the entirety of the mark phase. The goal of a sophisticated garbage collector is to minimize that overhead.

There are two key metrics we can use to understand that cost better:

- **Throughput** is the total fraction of time spent running user code versus doing garbage collection work. Say you run a clox program for ten seconds and it spends a second of that inside `collectGarbage()`. That means the throughput is 90%—it spent 90% of the time running the program and 10% on GC overhead.

  Throughput is the most fundamental measure because it tracks the total cost of collection overhead. All else being equal, you want to maximize throughput. Up until this chapter, clox had no GC at all and thus 100% throughput. That's pretty hard to beat. Of course, it came at the slight expense of potentially running out of memory and crashing if the user's program ran long enough. You can look at the goal of a GC as fixing that "glitch" while sacrificing as little throughput as possible.

- **Latency** is the longest *continuous* chunk of time where the user's program is completely paused while garbage collection happens. It's a measure of how "chunky" the collector is. Latency is an entirely different metric than throughput.

  Consider two runs of a clox program that both take ten seconds. In the first

Well, not *exactly* 100%. It did still put the allocated objects into a linked list, so there was some tiny overhead for setting those pointers.

run, the GC kicks in once and spends a solid second in `collectGarbage()` in one massive collection. In the second run, the GC gets invoked five times, each for a fifth of a second. The *total* amount of time spent collecting is still a second, so the throughput is 90% in both cases. But in the second run, the latency is only 1/5th of a second, five times less than in the first.

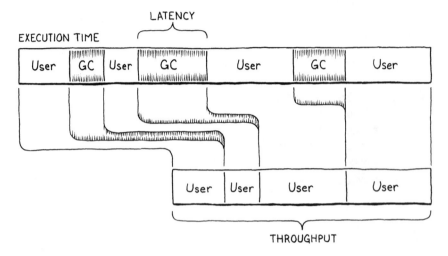

The bar represents the execution of a program, divided into time spent running user code and time spent in the GC. The size of the largest single slice of time running the GC is the latency. The size of all of the user code slices added up is the throughput.

If each person represents a thread, then an obvious optimization is to have separate threads running garbage collection, giving you a **concurrent garbage collector**. In other words, hire some dishwashers to clean while others bake. This is how very sophisticated GCs work because it does let the bakers—the worker threads—keep running user code with little interruption.

However, coordination is required. You don't want a dishwasher grabbing a bowl out of a baker's hands! This coordination adds overhead and a lot of complexity. Concurrent collectors are fast, but challenging to implement correctly.

Clearly the baking analogy is going to my head.

In contrast, an **incremental garbage collector** can do a little collection, then run some user code, then collect a little more, and so on.

If you like analogies, imagine your program is a bakery selling fresh-baked bread to customers. Throughput is the total number of warm, crusty baguettes you can serve to customers in a single day. Latency is how long the unluckiest customer has to wait in line before they get served.

Running the garbage collector is like shutting down the bakery temporarily to go through all of the dishes, sort out the dirty from the clean, and then wash the used ones. In our analogy, we don't have dedicated dishwashers, so while this is going on, no baking is happening. The baker is washing up.

Selling fewer loaves of bread a day is bad, and making any particular customer sit and wait while you clean all the dishes is too. The goal is to maximize throughput and minimize latency, but there is no free lunch, even inside a bakery. Garbage collectors make different trade-offs between how much throughput they sacrifice and latency they tolerate.

Being able to make these trade-offs is useful because different user programs have different needs. An overnight batch job that is generating a report from a terabyte of data just needs to get as much work done as fast as possible. Throughput is queen. Meanwhile, an app running on a user's smartphone needs to always respond immediately to user input so that dragging on the screen feels buttery smooth. The app can't freeze for a few seconds while the GC mucks around in the heap.

As a garbage collector author, you control some of the trade-off between throughput and latency by your choice of collection algorithm. But even within a single algorithm, we have a lot of control over *how frequently* the collector runs.

Our collector is a **stop-the-world GC** which means the user's program is paused until the entire garbage collection process has completed. If we wait a long time before we run the collector, then a large number of dead objects will accumulate. That leads to a very long pause while the collector runs, and thus high latency. So, clearly, we want to run the collector really frequently.

But every time the collector runs, it spends some time visiting live objects. That doesn't really *do* anything useful (aside from ensuring that they don't incorrectly get deleted). Time visiting live objects is time not freeing memory and also time not running user code. If you run the GC *really* frequently, then the user's program doesn't have enough time to even generate new garbage for the VM to collect. The VM will spend all of its time obsessively revisiting the same set of live objects over and over, and throughput will suffer. So, clearly, we want to run the collector really *in*frequently.

In fact, we want something in the middle, and the frequency of when the collector runs is one of our main knobs for tuning the trade-off between latency and throughput.

## 26.6.2  Self-adjusting heap

We want our GC to run frequently enough to minimize latency but infrequently enough to maintain decent throughput. But how do we find the balance between these when we have no idea how much memory the user's program needs and how often it allocates? We could pawn the problem onto the user and force them to pick by exposing GC tuning parameters. Many VMs do this. But if we, the GC authors, don't know how to tune it well, odds are good most users won't either. They deserve a reasonable default behavior.

I'll be honest with you, this is not my area of expertise. I've talked to a number of professional GC hackers—this is something you can build an entire career on—and read a lot of the literature, and all of the answers I got were...vague. The strategy I ended up picking is common, pretty simple, and (I hope!) good enough for most uses.

The idea is that the collector frequency automatically adjusts based on the live size of the heap. We track the total number of bytes of managed memory that the VM has allocated. When it goes above some threshold, we trigger a GC. After that, we note how many bytes of memory remain—how many were *not* freed. Then we adjust the threshold to some value larger than that.

The result is that as the amount of live memory increases, we collect less frequently in order to avoid sacrificing throughput by re-traversing the growing pile of live objects. As the amount of live memory goes down, we collect more frequently so that we don't lose too much latency by waiting too long.

The implementation requires two new bookkeeping fields in the VM.

```
ObjUpvalue* openUpvalues;

size_t bytesAllocated;
size_t nextGC;
Obj* objects;
```

**vm.h**
*in struct* **VM**

The first is a running total of the number of bytes of managed memory the VM has allocated. The second is the threshold that triggers the next collection. We initialize them when the VM starts up.

```
vm.objects = NULL;
vm.bytesAllocated = 0;
vm.nextGC = 1024 * 1024;

vm.grayCount = 0;
```

**vm.c**
*in* initVM()

A challenge with learning garbage collectors is that it's *very* hard to discover the best practices in an isolated lab environment. You don't see how a collector actually performs unless you run it on the kind of large, messy real-world programs it is actually intended for. It's like tuning a rally car—you need to take it out on the course.

The starting threshold here is arbitrary. It's similar to the initial capacity we picked for our various dynamic arrays. The goal is to not trigger the first few GCs *too* quickly but also to not wait too long. If we had some real-world Lox programs, we could profile those to tune this. But since all we have are toy programs, I just picked a number.

Every time we allocate or free some memory, we adjust the counter by that delta.

**memory.c**
*in* reallocate()

```
void* reallocate(void* pointer, size_t oldSize, size_t newSize) {
  vm.bytesAllocated += newSize - oldSize;
  if (newSize > oldSize) {
```

When the total crosses the limit, we run the collector.

**memory.c**
*in* reallocate()

```
    collectGarbage();
#endif

    if (vm.bytesAllocated > vm.nextGC) {
      collectGarbage();
    }
  }
```

Now, finally, our garbage collector actually does something when the user runs a program without our hidden diagnostic flag enabled. The sweep phase frees objects by calling `reallocate()`, which lowers the value of `bytesAllocated`, so after the collection completes, we know how many live bytes remain. We adjust the threshold of the next GC based on that.

**memory.c**
*in* collectGarbage()

```
  sweep();

  vm.nextGC = vm.bytesAllocated * GC_HEAP_GROW_FACTOR;

#ifdef DEBUG_LOG_GC
```

The threshold is a multiple of the heap size. This way, as the amount of memory the program uses grows, the threshold moves farther out to limit the total time spent re-traversing the larger live set. Like other numbers in this chapter, the scaling factor is basically arbitrary.

**memory.c**

```
#endif

#define GC_HEAP_GROW_FACTOR 2

void* reallocate(void* pointer, size_t oldSize, size_t newSize) {
```

You'd want to tune this in your implementation once you had some real programs to benchmark it on. Right now, we can at least log some of the statistics that we have. We capture the heap size before the collection.

**memory.c**
*in* collectGarbage()

```
  printf("-- gc begin\n");
  size_t before = vm.bytesAllocated;
#endif
```

And then print the results at the end.

```
printf("-- gc end\n");
printf("   collected %zu bytes (from %zu to %zu) next at %zu\n",
       before - vm.bytesAllocated, before, vm.bytesAllocated,
       vm.nextGC);
#endif
```

memory.c
*in* collectGarbage()

This way we can see how much the garbage collector accomplished while it ran.

## 26.7 Garbage Collection Bugs

In theory, we are all done now. We have a GC. It kicks in periodically, collects what it can, and leaves the rest. If this were a typical textbook, we would wipe the dust from our hands and bask in the soft glow of the flawless marble edifice we have created.

But I aim to teach you not just the theory of programming languages but the sometimes painful reality. I am going to roll over a rotten log and show you the nasty bugs that live under it, and garbage collector bugs really are some of the grossest invertebrates out there.

The collector's job is to free dead objects and preserve live ones. Mistakes are easy to make in both directions. If the VM fails to free objects that aren't needed, it slowly leaks memory. If it frees an object that is in use, the user's program can access invalid memory. These failures often don't immediately cause a crash, which makes it hard for us to trace backward in time to find the bug.

This is made harder by the fact that we don't know when the collector will run. Any call that eventually allocates some memory is a place in the VM where a collection could happen. It's like musical chairs. At any point, the GC might stop the music. Every single heap-allocated object that we want to keep needs to find a chair quickly—get marked as a root or stored as a reference in some other object—before the sweep phase comes to kick it out of the game.

How is it possible for the VM to use an object later—one that the GC itself doesn't see? How can the VM find it? The most common answer is through a pointer stored in some local variable on the C stack. The GC walks the *VM's* value and CallFrame stacks, but the C stack is hidden to it.

In previous chapters, we wrote seemingly pointless code that pushed an object onto the VM's value stack, did a little work, and then popped it right back off. Most times, I said this was for the GC's benefit. Now you see why. The code between pushing and popping potentially allocates memory and thus can trigger a GC. We had to make sure the object was on the value stack so that the collector's mark phase would find it and keep it alive.

I wrote the entire clox implementation before splitting it into chapters and writing the prose, so I had plenty of time to find all of these corners and flush out most of these bugs. The stress testing code we put in at the beginning of this chapter and a pretty good test suite were very helpful.

But I fixed only *most* of them. I left a couple in because I want to give you a hint of what it's like to encounter these bugs in the wild. If you enable the stress test flag and run some toy Lox programs, you can probably stumble onto a few. Give it a try and *see if you can fix any yourself.*

Our GC can't find addresses in the C stack, but many can. Conservative garbage collectors look all through memory, including the native stack. The most well-known of this variety is the **Boehm-Demers-Weiser garbage collector**, usually just called the "Boehm collector". (The shortest path to fame in CS is a last name that's alphabetically early so that it shows up first in sorted lists of names.)

Many precise GCs walk the C stack too. Even those have to be careful about pointers to live objects that exist only in *CPU registers*.

### 26.7.1  Adding to the constant table

You are very likely to hit the first bug. The constant table each chunk owns is a dynamic array. When the compiler adds a new constant to the current function's table, that array may need to grow. The constant itself may also be some heap-allocated object like a string or a nested function.

The new object being added to the constant table is passed to addConstant(). At that moment, the object can be found only in the parameter to that function on the C stack. That function appends the object to the constant table. If the table doesn't have enough capacity and needs to grow, it calls reallocate(). That in turn triggers a GC, which fails to mark the new constant object and thus sweeps it right before we have a chance to add it to the table. Crash.

The fix, as you've seen in other places, is to push the constant onto the stack temporarily.

**chunk.c**
*in* addConstant()

```
int addConstant(Chunk* chunk, Value value) {
  push(value);
  writeValueArray(&chunk->constants, value);
```

Once the constant table contains the object, we pop it off the stack.

**chunk.c**
*in* addConstant()

```
  writeValueArray(&chunk->constants, value);
  pop();
  return chunk->constants.count - 1;
```

When the GC is marking roots, it walks the chain of compilers and marks each of their functions, so the new constant is reachable now. We do need an include to call into the VM from the "chunk" module.

**chunk.c**

```
#include "memory.h"
#include "vm.h"

void initChunk(Chunk* chunk) {
```

### 26.7.2  Interning strings

Here's another similar one. All strings are interned in clox, so whenever we create a new string, we also add it to the intern table. You can see where this is going. Since the string is brand new, it isn't reachable anywhere. And resizing the string pool can trigger a collection. Again, we go ahead and stash the string on the stack first.

**object.c**
*in* allocateString()

```
  string->chars = chars;
  string->hash = hash;

  push(OBJ_VAL(string));
  tableSet(&vm.strings, string, NIL_VAL);
```

And then pop it back off once it's safely nestled in the table.

```
    tableSet(&vm.strings, string, NIL_VAL);
    pop();

    return string;
}
```

object.c
in allocateString()

This ensures the string is safe while the table is being resized. Once it survives that, `allocateString()` will return it to some caller which can then take responsibility for ensuring the string is still reachable before the next heap allocation occurs.

### 26.7.3  Concatenating strings

One last example: Over in the interpreter, the `OP_ADD` instruction can be used to concatenate two strings. As it does with numbers, it pops the two operands from the stack, computes the result, and pushes that new value back onto the stack. For numbers that's perfectly safe.

But concatenating two strings requires allocating a new character array on the heap, which can in turn trigger a GC. Since we've already popped the operand strings by that point, they can potentially be missed by the mark phase and get swept away. Instead of popping them off the stack eagerly, we peek them.

```
static void concatenate() {
  ObjString* b = AS_STRING(peek(0));
  ObjString* a = AS_STRING(peek(1));

  int length = a->length + b->length;
```

vm.c
in concatenate()
replace 2 lines

That way, they are still hanging out on the stack when we create the result string. Once that's done, we can safely pop them off and replace them with the result.

```
  ObjString* result = takeString(chars, length);
  pop();
  pop();
  push(OBJ_VAL(result));
```

vm.c
in concatenate()

Those were all pretty easy, especially because I *showed* you where the fix was. In practice, *finding* them is the hard part. All you see is an object that *should* be there but isn't. It's not like other bugs where you're looking for the code that *causes* some problem. You're looking for the *absence* of code which fails to *prevent* a problem, and that's a much harder search.

But, for now at least, you can rest easy. As far as I know, we've found all of the collection bugs in clox, and now we have a working, robust, self-tuning, mark-sweep garbage collector.

## CHALLENGES

1. The Obj header struct at the top of each object now has three fields: `type`, `isMarked`, and `next`. How much memory do those take up (on your machine)? Can you come up with something more compact? Is there a runtime cost to doing so?

2. When the sweep phase traverses a live object, it clears the `isMarked` field to prepare it for the next collection cycle. Can you come up with a more efficient approach?

3. Mark-sweep is only one of a variety of garbage collection algorithms out there. Explore those by replacing or augmenting the current collector with another one. Good candidates to consider are reference counting, Cheney's algorithm, or the Lisp 2 mark-compact algorithm.

## DESIGN NOTE: GENERATIONAL COLLECTORS

A collector loses throughput if it spends a long time re-visiting objects that are still alive. But it can increase latency if it avoids collecting and accumulates a large pile of garbage to wade through. If only there were some way to tell which objects were likely to be long-lived and which weren't. Then the GC could avoid revisiting the long-lived ones as often and clean up the ephemeral ones more frequently.

It turns out there kind of is. Many years ago, GC researchers gathered metrics on the lifetime of objects in real-world running programs. They tracked every object when it was allocated, and eventually when it was no longer needed, and then graphed out how long objects tended to live.

They discovered something they called the **generational hypothesis**, or the much less tactful term **infant mortality**. Their observation was that most objects are very short-lived but once they survive beyond a certain age, they tend to stick around quite a long time. The longer an object *has* lived, the longer it likely will *continue* to live. This observation is powerful because it gave them a handle on how to partition objects into groups that benefit from frequent collections and those that don't.

They designed a technique called **generational garbage collection**. It works like this: Every time a new object is allocated, it goes into a special, relatively small region of the heap called the "nursery". Since objects tend to die young, the garbage collector is invoked frequently over the objects just in this region.

Each time the GC runs over the nursery is called a "generation". Any objects that are no longer needed get freed. Those that survive are now considered one generation older, and the GC tracks this for each object. If an object survives a certain number of generations—often just a single collection—it gets *tenured*. At this point, it is copied out of the nursery into a much larger heap region for long-lived objects. The garbage collector runs over that region too, but much less frequently since odds are good that most of those objects will still be alive.

Generational collectors are a beautiful marriage of empirical data—the observation that object lifetimes are *not* evenly distributed—and clever algorithm design that takes advantage of that fact. They're also conceptually quite simple. You can think of one as just two separately tuned GCs and a pretty simple policy for moving objects from one to the other.

Nurseries are also usually managed using a copying collector which is faster at allocating and freeing objects than a mark-sweep collector.

# Classes and Instances

27

> *"Caring too much for objects can destroy you. Only—if you care for a thing enough, it takes on a life of its own, doesn't it? And isn't the whole point of things—beautiful things—that they connect you to some larger beauty?"*

> — Donna Tartt, *The Goldfinch*

The last area left to implement in clox is object-oriented programming. OOP is a bundle of intertwined features: classes, instances, fields, methods, initializers, and inheritance. Using relatively high-level Java, we packed all that into two chapters. Now that we're coding in C, which feels like building a model of the Eiffel tower out of toothpicks, we'll devote three chapters to covering the same territory. This makes for a leisurely stroll through the implementation. After strenuous chapters like closures and the garbage collector, you have earned a rest. In fact, the book should be easy from here on out.

In this chapter, we cover the first three features: classes, instances, and fields. This is the stateful side of object orientation. Then in the next two chapters, we will hang behavior and code reuse off of those objects.

People who have strong opinions about object-oriented programming—read "everyone"—tend to assume OOP means some very specific list of language features, but really there's a whole space to explore, and each language has its own ingredients and recipes.

Self has objects but no classes. CLOS has methods but doesn't attach them to specific classes. C++ initially had no runtime polymorphism—no virtual methods. Python has multiple inheritance, but Java does not. Ruby attaches methods to classes, but you can also define methods on a single object.

## 27.1 Class Objects

In a class-based object-oriented language, everything begins with classes. They define what sorts of objects exist in the program and are the factories used to produce new instances. Going bottom-up, we'll start with their runtime representation and then hook that into the language.

By this point, we're well-acquainted with the process of adding a new object type to the VM. We start with a struct.

**object.h**
*add after struct* ObjClosure

```
} ObjClosure;

typedef struct {
  Obj obj;
  ObjString* name;
} ObjClass;

ObjClosure* newClosure(ObjFunction* function);
```

After the Obj header, we store the class's name. This isn't strictly needed for the user's program, but it lets us show the name at runtime for things like stack traces.

The new type needs a corresponding case in the ObjType enum.

**object.h**
*in enum* ObjType

```
typedef enum {
  OBJ_CLASS,
  OBJ_CLOSURE,
```

And that type gets a corresponding pair of macros. First, for testing an object's type:

**object.h**

```
#define OBJ_TYPE(value)        (AS_OBJ(value)->type)

#define IS_CLASS(value)        isObjType(value, OBJ_CLASS)
#define IS_CLOSURE(value)      isObjType(value, OBJ_CLOSURE)
```

And then for casting a Value to an ObjClass pointer:

**object.h**

```
#define IS_STRING(value)       isObjType(value, OBJ_STRING)

#define AS_CLASS(value)        ((ObjClass*)AS_OBJ(value))
#define AS_CLOSURE(value)      ((ObjClosure*)AS_OBJ(value))
```

The VM creates new class objects using this function:

**object.h**
*add after struct* ObjClass

```
} ObjClass;

ObjClass* newClass(ObjString* name);
ObjClosure* newClosure(ObjFunction* function);
```

The implementation lives over here:

```
ObjClass* newClass(ObjString* name) {
  ObjClass* klass = ALLOCATE_OBJ(ObjClass, OBJ_CLASS);
  klass->name = name;
  return klass;
}
```

object.c
*add after* allocateObject()

I named the variable "klass" not just to give the VM a zany preschool "Kidz Korner" feel. It makes it easier to get clox compiling as C++ where "class" is a reserved word.

Pretty much all boilerplate. It takes in the class's name as a string and stores it. Every time the user declares a new class, the VM will create a new one of these ObjClass structs to represent it.

When the VM no longer needs a class, it frees it like so:

```
  switch (object->type) {
    case OBJ_CLASS: {
      FREE(ObjClass, object);
      break;
    }
    case OBJ_CLOSURE: {
```

memory.c
*in* freeObject()

The braces here are pointless now, but will be useful in the next chapter when we add some more code to the switch case.

We have a memory manager now, so we also need to support tracing through class objects.

```
  switch (object->type) {
    case OBJ_CLASS: {
      ObjClass* klass = (ObjClass*)object;
      markObject((Obj*)klass->name);
      break;
    }
    case OBJ_CLOSURE: {
```

memory.c
*in* blackenObject()

When the GC reaches a class object, it marks the class's name to keep that string alive too.

The last operation the VM can perform on a class is printing it.

```
  switch (OBJ_TYPE(value)) {
    case OBJ_CLASS:
      printf("%s", AS_CLASS(value)->name->chars);
      break;
    case OBJ_CLOSURE:
```

object.c
*in* printObject()

A class simply says its own name.

## 27.2  Class Declarations

Runtime representation in hand, we are ready to move into the parser.

```
static void declaration() {
  if (match(TOKEN_CLASS)) {
    classDeclaration();
  } else if (match(TOKEN_FUN)) {
    funDeclaration();
```

compiler.c
*in* declaration()
*replace 1 line*

Class declarations are statements, and the parser recognizes one by the leading class keyword. The rest of the compilation happens over here:

```c
static void classDeclaration() {
  consume(TOKEN_IDENTIFIER, "Expect class name.");
  uint8_t nameConstant = identifierConstant(&parser.previous);
  declareVariable();

  emitBytes(OP_CLASS, nameConstant);
  defineVariable(nameConstant);

  consume(TOKEN_LEFT_BRACE, "Expect '{' before class body.");
  consume(TOKEN_RIGHT_BRACE, "Expect '}' after class body.");
}
```

Immediately after the class keyword is the class's name. We take that identifier and add it to the surrounding function's constant table as a string. As you just saw, printing a class shows its name, so the compiler needs to stuff the name string somewhere that the runtime can find. The constant table is the way to do that.

The class's name is also used to bind the class object to a variable of the same name. So we declare a variable with that identifier right after consuming its token.

Next, we emit a new instruction to actually create the class object at runtime. That instruction takes the constant table index of the class's name as an operand.

After that, but before compiling the body of the class, we define the variable for the class's name. *Declaring* the variable adds it to the scope, but recall from a previous chapter that we can't *use* the variable until it's *defined*. For classes, we define the variable before the body. That way, users can refer to the containing class inside the bodies of its own methods. That's useful for things like factory methods that produce new instances of the class.

Finally, we compile the body. We don't have methods yet, so right now it's simply an empty pair of braces. Lox doesn't require fields to be declared in the class, so we're done with the body—and the parser—for now.

The compiler is emitting a new instruction, so let's define that.

We could have made class declarations be *expressions* instead of statements—they are essentially a literal that produces a value after all. Then users would have to explicitly bind the class to a variable themselves like:

```
var Pie = class {}
```

Sort of like lambda functions but for classes. But since we generally want classes to be named anyway, it makes sense to treat them as declarations.

```c
  OP_RETURN,
  OP_CLASS,
} OpCode;
```

And add it to the disassembler:

```c
    case OP_RETURN:
      return simpleInstruction("OP_RETURN", offset);
    case OP_CLASS:
      return constantInstruction("OP_CLASS", chunk, offset);
    default:
```

For such a large-seeming feature, the interpreter support is minimal.

```
      break;
    }
    case OP_CLASS:
      push(OBJ_VAL(newClass(READ_STRING())));
      break;
  }
```

vm.c
in run()

We load the string for the class's name from the constant table and pass that to `newClass()`. That creates a new class object with the given name. We push that onto the stack and we're good. If the class is bound to a global variable, then the compiler's call to `defineVariable()` will emit code to store that object from the stack into the global variable table. Otherwise, it's right where it needs to be on the stack for a new local variable.

There you have it, our VM supports classes now. You can run this:

```
class Brioche {}
print Brioche;
```

Unfortunately, printing is about *all* you can do with classes, so next is making them more useful.

"Local" classes—classes declared inside the body of a function or block, are an unusual concept. Many languages don't allow them at all. But since Lox is a dynamically typed scripting language, it treats the top level of a program and the bodies of functions and blocks uniformly. Classes are just another kind of declaration, and since you can declare variables and functions inside blocks, you can declare classes in there too.

## 27.3 Instances of Classes

Classes serve two main purposes in a language:

- **They are how you create new instances.** Sometimes this involves a `new` keyword, other times it's a method call on the class object, but you usually mention the class by name *somehow* to get a new instance.

- **They contain methods.** These define how all instances of the class behave.

We won't get to methods until the next chapter, so for now we will only worry about the first part. Before classes can create instances, we need a representation for them.

```
} ObjClass;

typedef struct {
  Obj obj;
  ObjClass* klass;
  Table fields;
} ObjInstance;

ObjClass* newClass(ObjString* name);
```

object.h
add after struct ObjClass

Adding fields to an object at runtime is a big practical difference between most dynamic and static languages. The latter usually require fields to be explicitly declared so the compiler knows what fields each instance has. It uses that to determine the memory needed for each instance and the offsets where each field can be found.

In Lox and other dynamic languages, accessing a field is usually a hash table lookup. Constant time, but still pretty heavyweight. In a language like C++, accessing a field is as fast as offsetting a pointer by an integer constant.

Instances know their class—each instance has a pointer to the class that it is an instance of. We won't use this much in this chapter, but it will become critical when we add methods.

More important to this chapter is how instances store their state. Lox lets users freely add fields to an instance at runtime. This means we need a storage mechanism that can grow. We could use a dynamic array, but we also want to look up fields by name as quickly as possible. There's a data structure that's just perfect for quickly accessing a set of values by name and—even more conveniently—we've already implemented it. Each instance stores its fields using a hash table.

We only need to add an include, and we've got it.

object.h

```
#include "chunk.h"
#include "table.h"
#include "value.h"
```

This new struct gets a new object type.

object.h<br>in enum ObjType

```
  OBJ_FUNCTION,
  OBJ_INSTANCE,
  OBJ_NATIVE,
```

I want to slow down a bit here because the Lox *language's* notion of "type" and the VM *implementation's* notion of "type" brush against each other in ways that can be confusing. Inside the C code that makes clox, there are a number of different types of Obj—ObjString, ObjClosure, etc. Each has its own internal representation and semantics.

In the Lox *language*, users can define their own classes—say Cake and Pie— and then create instances of those classes. From the user's perspective, an instance of Cake is a different type of object than an instance of Pie. But, from the VM's perspective, every class the user defines is simply another value of type ObjClass. Likewise, each instance in the user's program, no matter what class it is an instance of, is an ObjInstance. That one VM object type covers instances of all classes. The two worlds map to each other something like this:

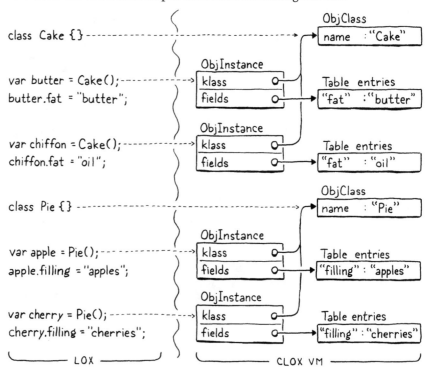

Got it? OK, back to the implementation. We also get our usual macros.

```
#define IS_FUNCTION(value)    isObjType(value, OBJ_FUNCTION)
#define IS_INSTANCE(value)    isObjType(value, OBJ_INSTANCE)
#define IS_NATIVE(value)      isObjType(value, OBJ_NATIVE)
```

object.h

And:

```
#define AS_FUNCTION(value)    ((ObjFunction*)AS_OBJ(value))
#define AS_INSTANCE(value)    ((ObjInstance*)AS_OBJ(value))
#define AS_NATIVE(value) \
```

object.h

Since fields are added after the instance is created, the "constructor" function only needs to know the class.

```
ObjFunction* newFunction();
ObjInstance* newInstance(ObjClass* klass);
ObjNative* newNative(NativeFn function);
```

object.h
*add after* newFunction()

We implement that function here:

```
ObjInstance* newInstance(ObjClass* klass) {
  ObjInstance* instance = ALLOCATE_OBJ(ObjInstance, OBJ_INSTANCE);
  instance->klass = klass;
  initTable(&instance->fields);
  return instance;
}
```

object.c
*add after* newFunction()

We store a reference to the instance's class. Then we initialize the field table to an empty hash table. A new baby object is born!

At the sadder end of the instance's lifespan, it gets freed.

```
      FREE(ObjFunction, object);
      break;
    }
    case OBJ_INSTANCE: {
      ObjInstance* instance = (ObjInstance*)object;
      freeTable(&instance->fields);
      FREE(ObjInstance, object);
      break;
    }
    case OBJ_NATIVE:
```

memory.c
*in* freeObject()

The instance owns its field table so when freeing the instance, we also free the table. We don't explicitly free the entries *in* the table, because there may be other references to those objects. The garbage collector will take care of those for us. Here we free only the entry array of the table itself.

Speaking of the garbage collector, it needs support for tracing through instances.

memory.c
*in* blackenObject()

```
    markArray(&function->chunk.constants);
    break;
  }
  case OBJ_INSTANCE: {
    ObjInstance* instance = (ObjInstance*)object;
    markObject((Obj*)instance->klass);
    markTable(&instance->fields);
    break;
  }
  case OBJ_UPVALUE:
```

If the instance is alive, we need to keep its class around. Also, we need to keep every object referenced by the instance's fields. Most live objects that are not roots are reachable because some instance refers to the object in a field. Fortunately, we already have a nice markTable() function to make tracing them easy.

Less critical but still important is printing.

object.c
*in* printObject()

```
    break;
  case OBJ_INSTANCE:
    printf("%s instance",
            AS_INSTANCE(value)->klass->name->chars);
    break;
  case OBJ_NATIVE:
```

Most object-oriented languages let a class define some sort of toString() method that lets the class specify how its instances are converted to a string and printed. If Lox was less of a toy language, I would want to support that too.

An instance prints its name followed by "instance". (The "instance" part is mainly so that classes and instances don't print the same.)

The real fun happens over in the interpreter. Lox has no special new keyword. The way to create an instance of a class is to invoke the class itself as if it were a function. The runtime already supports function calls, and it checks the type of object being called to make sure the user doesn't try to invoke a number or other invalid type.

We extend that runtime checking with a new case.

vm.c
*in* callValue()

```
    switch (OBJ_TYPE(callee)) {
      case OBJ_CLASS: {
        ObjClass* klass = AS_CLASS(callee);
        vm.stackTop[-argCount - 1] = OBJ_VAL(newInstance(klass));
        return true;
      }
      case OBJ_CLOSURE:
```

If the value being called—the object that results when evaluating the expression to the left of the opening parenthesis—is a class, then we treat it as a constructor call. We create a new instance of the called class and store the result on the stack.

We ignore any arguments passed to the call for now. We'll revisit this code in the next chapter when we add support for initializers.

We're one step farther. Now we can define classes and create instances of them.

```
class Brioche {}
print Brioche();
```

Note the parentheses after Brioche on the second line now. This prints "Brioche instance".

## 27.4  Get and Set Expressions

Our object representation for instances can already store state, so all that re-mains is exposing that functionality to the user. Fields are accessed and modified using get and set expressions. Not one to break with tradition, Lox uses the clas-sic "dot" syntax:

```
eclair.filling = "pastry creme";
print eclair.filling;
```

The period—full stop for my English friends—works sort of like an infix oper-ator. There is an expression to the left that is evaluated first and produces an instance. After that is the `.` followed by a field name. Since there is a preceding operand, we hook this into the parse table as an infix expression.

> I say "sort of" because the right-hand side after the `.` is not an expression, but a single identifier whose semantics are handled by the get or set expression itself. It's really closer to a postfix expression.

```
    [TOKEN_COMMA]         = {NULL,     NULL,    PREC_NONE},
    [TOKEN_DOT]           = {NULL,     dot,     PREC_CALL},
    [TOKEN_MINUS]         = {unary,    binary,  PREC_TERM},
```

> compiler.c
> *replace 1 line*

As in other languages, the `.` operator binds tightly, with precedence as high as the parentheses in a function call. After the parser consumes the dot token, it dispatches to a new parse function.

```
static void dot(bool canAssign) {
  consume(TOKEN_IDENTIFIER, "Expect property name after '.'.");
  uint8_t name = identifierConstant(&parser.previous);

  if (canAssign && match(TOKEN_EQUAL)) {
    expression();
    emitBytes(OP_SET_PROPERTY, name);
  } else {
    emitBytes(OP_GET_PROPERTY, name);
  }
}
```

> compiler.c
> *add after* call()

The parser expects to find a property name immediately after the dot. We load that token's lexeme into the constant table as a string so that the name is avail-able at runtime.

We have two new expression forms—getters and setters—that this one function handles. If we see an equals sign after the field name, it must be a set expression that is assigning to a field. But we don't *always* allow an equals sign after the field to be compiled. Consider:

> The compiler uses "property" instead of "field" here because, remember, Lox also lets you use dot syntax to access a meth-od without calling it. "Property" is the general term we use to refer to any named entity you can access on an instance. Fields are the subset of properties that are backed by the instance's state.

```
a + b.c = 3
```

This is syntactically invalid according to Lox's grammar, which means our Lox implementation is obligated to detect and report the error. If `dot()` silently parsed the `= 3` part, we would incorrectly interpret the code as if the user had written:

```
a + (b.c = 3)
```

The problem is that the = side of a set expression has much lower precedence than the . part. The parser may call dot() in a context that is too high precedence to permit a setter to appear. To avoid incorrectly allowing that, we parse and compile the equals part only when canAssign is true. If an equals token appears when canAssign is false, dot() leaves it alone and returns. In that case, the compiler will eventually unwind up to parsePrecedence(), which stops at the unexpected = still sitting as the next token and reports an error.

If we find an = in a context where it *is* allowed, then we compile the expression that follows. After that, we emit a new OP_SET_PROPERTY instruction. That takes a single operand for the index of the property name in the constant table. If we didn't compile a set expression, we assume it's a getter and emit an OP_GET_PROPERTY instruction, which also takes an operand for the property name.

Now is a good time to define these two new instructions.

You can't *set* a non-field property, so I suppose that instruction could have been OP_SET_FIELD, but I thought it looked nicer to be consistent with the get instruction.

*chunk.h*
*in enum* OpCode

```
OP_SET_UPVALUE,
OP_GET_PROPERTY,
OP_SET_PROPERTY,
OP_EQUAL,
```

And add support for disassembling them:

*debug.c*
*in* disassembleInstruction()

```
    return byteInstruction("OP_SET_UPVALUE", chunk, offset);
  case OP_GET_PROPERTY:
    return constantInstruction("OP_GET_PROPERTY", chunk, offset);
  case OP_SET_PROPERTY:
    return constantInstruction("OP_SET_PROPERTY", chunk, offset);
  case OP_EQUAL:
```

### 27.4.1 Interpreting getter and setter expressions

Sliding over to the runtime, we'll start with get expressions since those are a little simpler.

*vm.c*
*in* run()

```
    }
    case OP_GET_PROPERTY: {
      ObjInstance* instance = AS_INSTANCE(peek(0));
      ObjString* name = READ_STRING();

      Value value;
      if (tableGet(&instance->fields, name, &value)) {
        pop(); // Instance.
        push(value);
        break;
      }
    }
    case OP_EQUAL: {
```

When the interpreter reaches this instruction, the expression to the left of the dot has already been executed and the resulting instance is on top of the stack. We read the field name from the constant pool and look it up in the instance's field table. If the hash table contains an entry with that name, we pop the instance and push the entry's value as the result.

Of course, the field might not exist. In Lox, we've defined that to be a runtime error. So we add a check for that and abort if it happens.

```
    push(value);
    break;
  }

    runtimeError("Undefined property '%s'.", name->chars);
    return INTERPRET_RUNTIME_ERROR;
  }
  case OP_EQUAL: {
```

vm.c
in run()

There is another failure mode to handle which you've probably noticed. The above code assumes the expression to the left of the dot did evaluate to an ObjInstance. But there's nothing preventing a user from writing this:

```
var obj = "not an instance";
print obj.field;
```

The user's program is wrong, but the VM still has to handle it with some grace. Right now, it will misinterpret the bits of the ObjString as an ObjInstance and, I don't know, catch on fire or something definitely not graceful.

In Lox, only instances are allowed to have fields. You can't stuff a field onto a string or number. So we need to check that the value is an instance before accessing any fields on it.

Lox *could* support adding fields to values of other types. It's our language and we can do what we want. But it's likely a bad idea. It significantly complicates the implementation in ways that hurt performance—for example, string interning gets a lot harder.

Also, it raises gnarly semantic questions around the equality and identity of values. If I attach a field to the number 3, does the result of $1 + 2$ have that field as well? If so, how does the implementation track that? If not, are those two resulting "threes" still considered equal?

```
  case OP_GET_PROPERTY: {
    if (!IS_INSTANCE(peek(0))) {
      runtimeError("Only instances have properties.");
      return INTERPRET_RUNTIME_ERROR;
    }

    ObjInstance* instance = AS_INSTANCE(peek(0));
```

vm.c
in run()

If the value on the stack isn't an instance, we report a runtime error and safely exit.

Of course, get expressions are not very useful when no instances have any fields. For that we need setters.

```
    return INTERPRET_RUNTIME_ERROR;
  }
  case OP_SET_PROPERTY: {
    ObjInstance* instance = AS_INSTANCE(peek(1));
    tableSet(&instance->fields, READ_STRING(), peek(0));
    Value value = pop();
    pop();
    push(value);
    break;
  }
  case OP_EQUAL: {
```

vm.c
in run()

This is a little more complex than OP_GET_PROPERTY. When this executes, the top of the stack has the instance whose field is being set and above that, the value to be stored. Like before, we read the instruction's operand and find the field name string. Using that, we store the value on top of the stack into the instance's field table.

After that is a little stack juggling. We pop the stored value off, then pop the instance, and finally push the value back on. In other words, we remove the *second* element from the stack while leaving the top alone. A setter is itself an expression whose result is the assigned value, so we need to leave that value on the stack. Here's what I mean:

The stack operations go like this:

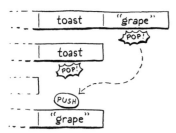

```
class Toast {}
var toast = Toast();
print toast.jam = "grape"; // Prints "grape".
```

Unlike when reading a field, we don't need to worry about the hash table not containing the field. A setter implicitly creates the field if needed. We do need to handle the user incorrectly trying to store a field on a value that isn't an instance.

*vm.c*
*in* run()

```
    case OP_SET_PROPERTY: {
      if (!IS_INSTANCE(peek(1))) {
        runtimeError("Only instances have fields.");
        return INTERPRET_RUNTIME_ERROR;
      }

      ObjInstance* instance = AS_INSTANCE(peek(1));
```

Exactly like with get expressions, we check the value's type and report a runtime error if it's invalid. And, with that, the stateful side of Lox's support for object-oriented programming is in place. Give it a try:

```
class Pair {}

var pair = Pair();
pair.first = 1;
pair.second = 2;
print pair.first + pair.second; // 3.
```

This doesn't really feel very *object*-oriented. It's more like a strange, dynamically typed variant of C where objects are loose struct-like bags of data. Sort of a dynamic procedural language. But this is a big step in expressiveness. Our Lox implementation now lets users freely aggregate data into bigger units. In the next chapter, we will breathe life into those inert blobs.

## CHALLENGES

1. Trying to access a non-existent field on an object immediately aborts the entire VM. The user has no way to recover from this runtime error, nor is there any way to see if a field exists *before* trying to access it. It's up to the user to ensure on their own that only valid fields are read.

   How do other dynamically typed languages handle missing fields? What do you think Lox should do? Implement your solution.

2. Fields are accessed at runtime by their *string* name. But that name must always appear directly in the source code as an *identifier token*. A user program cannot imperatively build a string value and then use that as the name of a field. Do you think they should be able to? Devise a language feature that enables that and implement it.

3. Conversely, Lox offers no way to *remove* a field from an instance. You can set a field's value to `nil`, but the entry in the hash table is still there. How do other languages handle this? Choose and implement a strategy for Lox.

4. Because fields are accessed by name at runtime, working with instance state is slow. It's technically a constant-time operation—thanks, hash tables—but the constant factors are relatively large. This is a major component of why dynamic languages are slower than statically typed ones.

   How do sophisticated implementations of dynamically typed languages cope with and optimize this?

# Methods and Initializers

28

*"When you are on the dancefloor, there is nothing to do but dance."*

— Umberto Eco, *The Mysterious Flame of Queen Loana*

It is time for our virtual machine to bring its nascent objects to life with behavior. That means methods and method calls. And, since they are a special kind of method, initializers too.

All of this is familiar territory from our previous jlox interpreter. What's new in this second trip is an important optimization we'll implement to make method calls over seven times faster than our baseline performance. But before we get to that fun, we gotta get the basic stuff working.

## 28.1 Method Declarations

We can't optimize method calls before we have method calls, and we can't call methods without having methods to call, so we'll start with declarations.

### 28.1.1 Representing methods

We usually start in the compiler, but let's knock the object model out first this time. The runtime representation for methods in clox is similar to that of jlox. Each class stores a hash table of methods. Keys are method names, and each value is an ObjClosure for the body of the method.

*object.h*
*in struct ObjClass*

```
typedef struct {
  Obj obj;
  ObjString* name;
  Table methods;
} ObjClass;
```

A brand new class begins with an empty method table.

*object.c*
*in newClass()*

```
  klass->name = name;
  initTable(&klass->methods);
  return klass;
```

The ObjClass struct owns the memory for this table, so when the memory manager deallocates a class, the table should be freed too.

*memory.c*
*in freeObject()*

```
    case OBJ_CLASS: {
      ObjClass* klass = (ObjClass*)object;
      freeTable(&klass->methods);
      FREE(ObjClass, object);
```

Speaking of memory managers, the GC needs to trace through classes into the method table. If a class is still reachable (likely through some instance), then all of its methods certainly need to stick around too.

*memory.c*
*in blackenObject()*

```
      markObject((Obj*)klass->name);
      markTable(&klass->methods);
      break;
```

We use the existing `markTable()` function, which traces through the key string and value in each table entry.

Storing a class's methods is pretty familiar coming from jlox. The different part is how that table gets populated. Our previous interpreter had access to the entire AST node for the class declaration and all of the methods it contained. At runtime, the interpreter simply walked that list of declarations.

Now every piece of information the compiler wants to shunt over to the runtime has to squeeze through the interface of a flat series of bytecode instructions. How do we take a class declaration, which can contain an arbitrarily large set of methods, and represent it as bytecode? Let's hop over to the compiler and find out.

## 28.1.2  Compiling method declarations

The last chapter left us with a compiler that parses classes but allows only an empty body. Now we insert a little code to compile a series of method declarations between the braces.

```
consume(TOKEN_LEFT_BRACE, "Expect '{' before class body.");
while (!check(TOKEN_RIGHT_BRACE) && !check(TOKEN_EOF)) {
  method();
}
consume(TOKEN_RIGHT_BRACE, "Expect '}' after class body.");
```

compiler.c
*in* classDeclaration()

Lox doesn't have field declarations, so anything before the closing brace at the end of the class body must be a method. We stop compiling methods when we hit that final curly or if we reach the end of the file. The latter check ensures our compiler doesn't get stuck in an infinite loop if the user accidentally forgets the closing brace.

The tricky part with compiling a class declaration is that a class may declare any number of methods. Somehow the runtime needs to look up and bind all of them. That would be a lot to pack into a single OP_CLASS instruction. Instead, the bytecode we generate for a class declaration will split the process into a *series* of instructions. The compiler already emits an OP_CLASS instruction that creates a new empty ObjClass object. Then it emits instructions to store the class in a variable with its name.

Now, for each method declaration, we emit a new OP_METHOD instruction that adds a single method to that class. When all of the OP_METHOD instructions have executed, we're left with a fully formed class. While the user sees a class declaration as a single atomic operation, the VM implements it as a series of mutations.

To define a new method, the VM needs three things:

1. The name of the method.

2. The closure for the method body.

3. The class to bind the method to.

We'll incrementally write the compiler code to see how those all get through to the runtime, starting here:

```
static void method() {
  consume(TOKEN_IDENTIFIER, "Expect method name.");
  uint8_t constant = identifierConstant(&parser.previous);
  emitBytes(OP_METHOD, constant);
}
```

compiler.c
*add after* function()

Like OP_GET_PROPERTY and other instructions that need names at runtime, the compiler adds the method name token's lexeme to the constant table, getting back a table index. Then we emit an OP_METHOD instruction with that index as the operand. That's the name. Next is the method body:

We did something similar for closures. The OP_CLOSURE instruction needs to know the type and index for each captured upvalue. We encoded that using a series of pseudo-instructions following the main OP_CLOSURE instruction— basically a variable number of operands. The VM processes all of those extra bytes immediately when interpreting the OP_CLOSURE instruction.

Here our approach is a little different because from the VM's perspective, each instruction to define a method is a separate stand-alone operation. Either approach would work. A variable-sized pseudo-instruction is possibly marginally faster, but class declarations are rarely in hot loops, so it doesn't matter much.

compiler.c
*in* method()

```
uint8_t constant = identifierConstant(&parser.previous);

FunctionType type = TYPE_FUNCTION;
function(type);
emitBytes(OP_METHOD, constant);
```

We use the same `function()` helper that we wrote for compiling function declarations. That utility function compiles the subsequent parameter list and function body. Then it emits the code to create an ObjClosure and leave it on top of the stack. At runtime, the VM will find the closure there.

Last is the class to bind the method to. Where can the VM find that? Unfortunately, by the time we reach the `OP_METHOD` instruction, we don't know where it is. It could be on the stack, if the user declared the class in a local scope. But a top-level class declaration ends up with the ObjClass in the global variable table.

Fear not. The compiler does know the *name* of the class. We can capture it right after we consume its token.

If Lox supported declaring classes only at the top level, the VM could assume that any class could be found by looking it up directly from the global variable table. Alas, because we support local classes, we need to handle that case too.

compiler.c
*in* classDeclaration()

```
consume(TOKEN_IDENTIFIER, "Expect class name.");
Token className = parser.previous;
uint8_t nameConstant = identifierConstant(&parser.previous);
```

And we know that no other declaration with that name could possibly shadow the class. So we do the easy fix. Before we start binding methods, we emit whatever code is necessary to load the class back on top of the stack.

compiler.c
*in* classDeclaration()

```
defineVariable(nameConstant);

namedVariable(className, false);
consume(TOKEN_LEFT_BRACE, "Expect '{' before class body.");
```

The preceding call to
`defineVariable()` pops
the class, so it seems silly to call
`namedVariable()` to load it right
back onto the stack. Why not simply
leave it on the stack in the first place?
We could, but in the next chapter we will
insert code between these two calls to
support inheritance. At that point, it will
be simpler if the class isn't sitting around
on the stack.

Right before compiling the class body, we call `namedVariable()`. That helper function generates code to load a variable with the given name onto the stack. Then we compile the methods.

This means that when we execute each `OP_METHOD` instruction, the stack has the method's closure on top with the class right under it. Once we've reached the end of the methods, we no longer need the class and tell the VM to pop it off the stack.

compiler.c
*in* classDeclaration()

```
consume(TOKEN_RIGHT_BRACE, "Expect '}' after class body.");
emitByte(OP_POP);
}
```

Putting all of that together, here is an example class declaration to throw at the compiler:

```
class Brunch {
  bacon() {}
  eggs() {}
}
```

Given that, here is what the compiler generates and how those instructions affect the stack at runtime:

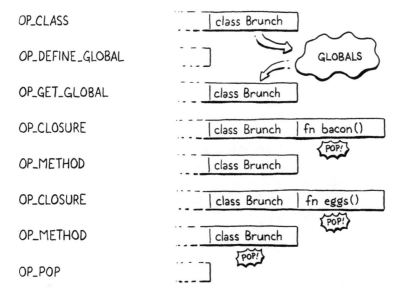

All that remains for us is to implement the runtime for that new `OP_METHOD` instruction.

### 28.1.3  Executing method declarations

First we define the opcode.

```
  OP_CLASS,
  OP_METHOD
} OpCode;
```
*chunk.h*
*in enum OpCode*

We disassemble it like other instructions that have string constant operands.

```
  case OP_CLASS:
    return constantInstruction("OP_CLASS", chunk, offset);
  case OP_METHOD:
    return constantInstruction("OP_METHOD", chunk, offset);
  default:
```
*debug.c*
*in* `disassembleInstruction()`

And over in the interpreter, we add a new case too.

```
      break;
    case OP_METHOD:
      defineMethod(READ_STRING());
      break;
  }
```
*vm.c*
*in* `run()`

There, we read the method name from the constant table and pass it here:

```
static void defineMethod(ObjString* name) {
  Value method = peek(0);
  ObjClass* klass = AS_CLASS(peek(1));
  tableSet(&klass->methods, name, method);
  pop();
}
```

The method closure is on top of the stack, above the class it will be bound to. We read those two stack slots and store the closure in the class's method table. Then we pop the closure since we're done with it.

Note that we don't do any runtime type checking on the closure or class object. That `AS_CLASS()` call is safe because the compiler itself generated the code that causes the class to be in that stack slot. The VM trusts its own compiler.

After the series of `OP_METHOD` instructions is done and the `OP_POP` has popped the class, we will have a class with a nicely populated method table, ready to start doing things. The next step is pulling those methods back out and using them.

The VM trusts that the instructions it executes are valid because the *only* way to get code to the bytecode interpreter is by going through clox's own compiler. Many bytecode VMs, like the JVM and CPython, support executing bytecode that has been compiled separately. That leads to a different security story. Maliciously crafted bytecode could crash the VM or worse.

To prevent that, the JVM does a bytecode verification pass before it executes any loaded code. CPython says it's up to the user to ensure any bytecode they run is safe.

## 28.2  Method References

Most of the time, methods are accessed and immediately called, leading to this familiar syntax:

```
instance.method(argument);
```

But remember, in Lox and some other languages, those two steps are distinct and can be separated.

```
var closure = instance.method;
closure(argument);
```

Since users *can* separate the operations, we have to implement them separately. The first step is using our existing dotted property syntax to access a method defined on the instance's class. That should return some kind of object that the user can then call like a function.

The obvious approach is to look up the method in the class's method table and return the ObjClosure associated with that name. But we also need to remember that when you access a method, `this` gets bound to the instance the method was accessed from. Here's the example from when we added methods to jlox:

```
class Person {
  sayName() {
    print this.name;
  }
}

var jane = Person();
jane.name = "Jane";
var method = jane.sayName;
method(); // ?
```

This should print "Jane", so the object returned by `.sayName` somehow needs to remember the instance it was accessed from when it later gets called. In jlox, we implemented that "memory" using the interpreter's existing heap-allocated Environment class, which handled all variable storage.

Our bytecode VM has a more complex architecture for storing state. Local variables and temporaries are on the stack, globals are in a hash table, and variables in closures use upvalues. That necessitates a somewhat more complex solution for tracking a method's receiver in clox, and a new runtime type.

### 28.2.1   Bound methods

When the user executes a method access, we'll find the closure for that method and wrap it in a new "bound method" object that tracks the instance that the method was accessed from. This bound object can be called later like a function. When invoked, the VM will do some shenanigans to wire up `this` to point to the receiver inside the method's body.

Here's the new object type:

I took the name "bound method" from CPython. Python behaves similar to Lox here, and I used its implementation for inspiration.

```
} ObjInstance;

typedef struct {
  Obj obj;
  Value receiver;
  ObjClosure* method;
} ObjBoundMethod;

ObjClass* newClass(ObjString* name);
```

object.h
*add after struct* ObjInstance

It wraps the receiver and the method closure together. The receiver's type is Value even though methods can be called only on ObjInstances. Since the VM doesn't care what kind of receiver it has anyway, using Value means we don't have to keep converting the pointer back to a Value when it gets passed to more general functions.

The new struct implies the usual boilerplate you're used to by now. A new case in the object type enum:

```
typedef enum {
  OBJ_BOUND_METHOD,
  OBJ_CLASS,
```

object.h
*in enum* ObjType

A macro to check a value's type:

```
#define OBJ_TYPE(value)        (AS_OBJ(value)->type)

#define IS_BOUND_METHOD(value) isObjType(value, OBJ_BOUND_METHOD)
#define IS_CLASS(value)        isObjType(value, OBJ_CLASS)
```

object.h

Another macro to cast the value to an ObjBoundMethod pointer:

**object.h**

```
#define IS_STRING(value)         isObjType(value, OBJ_STRING)

#define AS_BOUND_METHOD(value) ((ObjBoundMethod*)AS_OBJ(value))
#define AS_CLASS(value)          ((ObjClass*)AS_OBJ(value))
```

A function to create a new ObjBoundMethod:

**object.h**
*add after struct* ObjBoundMethod

```
} ObjBoundMethod;

ObjBoundMethod* newBoundMethod(Value receiver,
                               ObjClosure* method);
ObjClass* newClass(ObjString* name);
```

And an implementation of that function here:

**object.c**
*add after* allocateObject()

```
ObjBoundMethod* newBoundMethod(Value receiver,
                               ObjClosure* method) {
  ObjBoundMethod* bound = ALLOCATE_OBJ(ObjBoundMethod,
                                       OBJ_BOUND_METHOD);
  bound->receiver = receiver;
  bound->method = method;
  return bound;
}
```

The constructor-like function simply stores the given closure and receiver. When the bound method is no longer needed, we free it.

**memory.c**
*in* freeObject()

```
  switch (object->type) {
    case OBJ_BOUND_METHOD:
      FREE(ObjBoundMethod, object);
      break;
    case OBJ_CLASS: {
```

The bound method has a couple of references, but it doesn't *own* them, so it frees nothing but itself. However, those references do get traced by the garbage collector.

**memory.c**
*in* blackenObject()

```
  switch (object->type) {
    case OBJ_BOUND_METHOD: {
      ObjBoundMethod* bound = (ObjBoundMethod*)object;
      markValue(bound->receiver);
      markObject((Obj*)bound->method);
      break;
    }
    case OBJ_CLASS: {
```

Tracing the method closure isn't really necessary. The receiver is an ObjInstance, which has a pointer to its ObjClass, which has a table for all of the methods. But it feels dubious to me in some vague way to have ObjBoundMethod rely on that.

This ensures that a handle to a method keeps the receiver around in memory so that this can still find the object when you invoke the handle later. We also trace the method closure.

The last operation all objects support is printing.

```
switch (OBJ_TYPE(value)) {
  case OBJ_BOUND_METHOD:
    printFunction(AS_BOUND_METHOD(value)->method->function);
    break;
  case OBJ_CLASS:
```

object.c
*in* printObject()

A bound method prints exactly the same way as a function. From the user's perspective, a bound method *is* a function. It's an object they can call. We don't expose that the VM implements bound methods using a different object type.

Put on your party hat because we just reached a little milestone. ObjBoundMethod is the very last runtime type to add to clox. You've written your last IS_ and AS_ macros. We're only a few chapters from the end of the book, and we're getting close to a complete VM.

## 28.2.2 Accessing methods

Let's get our new object type doing something. Methods are accessed using the same "dot" property syntax we implemented in the last chapter. The compiler already parses the right expressions and emits OP_GET_PROPERTY instructions for them. The only changes we need to make are in the runtime.

When a property access instruction executes, the instance is on top of the stack. The instruction's job is to find a field or method with the given name and replace the top of the stack with the accessed property.

The interpreter already handles fields, so we simply extend the OP_GET_PROPERTY case with another section.

```
      pop(); // Instance.
      push(value);
      break;
    }

  if (!bindMethod(instance->klass, name)) {
    return INTERPRET_RUNTIME_ERROR;
  }
  break;
  }
```

vm.c
*in* run()
*replace 2 lines*

We insert this after the code to look up a field on the receiver instance. Fields take priority over and shadow methods, so we look for a field first. If the instance does not have a field with the given property name, then the name may refer to a method.

We take the instance's class and pass it to a new bindMethod() helper. If that function finds a method, it places the method on the stack and returns true. Otherwise it returns false to indicate a method with that name couldn't be found. Since the name also wasn't a field, that means we have a runtime error, which aborts the interpreter.

Here is the good stuff:

vm.c
*add after* callValue()

```
static bool bindMethod(ObjClass* klass, ObjString* name) {
  Value method;
  if (!tableGet(&klass->methods, name, &method)) {
    runtimeError("Undefined property '%s'.", name->chars);
    return false;
  }

  ObjBoundMethod* bound = newBoundMethod(peek(0),
                                         AS_CLOSURE(method));
  pop();
  push(OBJ_VAL(bound));
  return true;
}
```

First we look for a method with the given name in the class's method table. If we don't find one, we report a runtime error and bail out. Otherwise, we take the method and wrap it in a new ObjBoundMethod. We grab the receiver from its home on top of the stack. Finally, we pop the instance and replace the top of the stack with the bound method.

For example:

```
class Brunch {
  eggs() {}
}

var brunch = Brunch();
var eggs = brunch.eggs;
```

Here is what happens when the VM executes the bindMethod() call for the brunch.eggs expression:

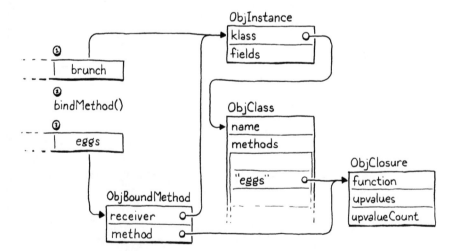

That's a lot of machinery under the hood, but from the user's perspective, they simply get a function that they can call.

### 28.2.3  Calling methods

Users can declare methods on classes, access them on instances, and get bound methods onto the stack. They just can't *do* anything useful with those bound method objects. The operation we're missing is calling them. Calls are implemented in `callValue()`, so we add a case there for the new object type.

A bound method *is* a first-class value, so they can store it in variables, pass it to functions, and otherwise do "value"-y stuff with it.

**vm.c**
*in* `callValue()`

```
  switch (OBJ_TYPE(callee)) {
    case OBJ_BOUND_METHOD: {
      ObjBoundMethod* bound = AS_BOUND_METHOD(callee);
      return call(bound->method, argCount);
    }
    case OBJ_CLASS: {
```

We pull the raw closure back out of the ObjBoundMethod and use the existing `call()` helper to begin an invocation of that closure by pushing a CallFrame for it onto the call stack. That's all it takes to be able to run this Lox program:

```
class Scone {
  topping(first, second) {
    print "scone with " + first + " and " + second;
  }
}

var scone = Scone();
scone.topping("berries", "cream");
```

That's three big steps. We can declare, access, and invoke methods. But something is missing. We went to all that trouble to wrap the method closure in an object that binds the receiver, but when we invoke the method, we don't use that receiver at all.

## 28.3  This

The reason bound methods need to keep hold of the receiver is so that it can be accessed inside the body of the method. Lox exposes a method's receiver through `this` expressions. It's time for some new syntax. The lexer already treats `this` as a special token type, so the first step is wiring that token up in the parse table.

**compiler.c**
*replace 1 line*

```
  [TOKEN_SUPER]         = {NULL,     NULL,   PREC_NONE},
  [TOKEN_THIS]          = {this_,    NULL,   PREC_NONE},
  [TOKEN_TRUE]          = {literal,  NULL,   PREC_NONE},
```

When the parser encounters a `this` in prefix position, it dispatches to a new parser function.

**compiler.c**
*add after* `variable()`

```
static void this_(bool canAssign) {
  variable(false);
}
```

The underscore at the end of the name of the parser function is because this is a reserved word in C++ and we support compiling clox as C++.

We'll apply the same implementation technique for this in clox that we used in jlox. We treat this as a lexically scoped local variable whose value gets magically initialized. Compiling it like a local variable means we get a lot of behavior for free. In particular, closures inside a method that reference this will do the right thing and capture the receiver in an upvalue.

When the parser function is called, the this token has just been consumed and is stored as the previous token. We call our existing variable() function which compiles identifier expressions as variable accesses. It takes a single Boolean parameter for whether the compiler should look for a following = operator and parse a setter. You can't assign to this, so we pass false to disallow that.

The variable() function doesn't care that this has its own token type and isn't an identifier. It is happy to treat the lexeme "this" as if it were a variable name and then look it up using the existing scope resolution machinery. Right now, that lookup will fail because we never declared a variable whose name is "this". It's time to think about where the receiver should live in memory.

At least until they get captured by closures, clox stores every local variable on the VM's stack. The compiler keeps track of which slots in the function's stack window are owned by which local variables. If you recall, the compiler sets aside stack slot zero by declaring a local variable whose name is an empty string.

For function calls, that slot ends up holding the function being called. Since the slot has no name, the function body never accesses it. You can guess where this is going. For *method* calls, we can repurpose that slot to store the receiver. Slot zero will store the instance that this is bound to. In order to compile this expressions, the compiler simply needs to give the correct name to that local variable.

compiler.c
in initCompiler()
replace 2 lines

```
  local->isCaptured = false;
  if (type != TYPE_FUNCTION) {
    local->name.start = "this";
    local->name.length = 4;
  } else {
    local->name.start = "";
    local->name.length = 0;
  }
}
```

We want to do this only for methods. Function declarations don't have a this. And, in fact, they *must not* declare a variable named "this", so that if you write a this expression inside a function declaration which is itself inside a method, the this correctly resolves to the outer method's receiver.

```
class Nested {
  method() {
    fun function() {
      print this;
    }
    function();
  }
}

Nested().method();
```

This program should print "Nested instance". To decide what name to give to local slot zero, the compiler needs to know whether it's compiling a function or method declaration, so we add a new case to our FunctionType enum to distinguish methods.

```
  TYPE_FUNCTION,
  TYPE_METHOD,
  TYPE_SCRIPT
```

compiler.c
*in enum* FunctionType

When we compile a method, we use that type.

```
  uint8_t constant = identifierConstant(&parser.previous);

  FunctionType type = TYPE_METHOD;
  function(type);
```

compiler.c
*in* method()
*replace 1 line*

Now we can correctly compile references to the special "this" variable, and the compiler will emit the right OP_GET_LOCAL instructions to access it. Closures can even capture this and store the receiver in upvalues. Pretty cool.

Except that at runtime, the receiver isn't actually *in* slot zero. The interpreter isn't holding up its end of the bargain yet. Here is the fix:

```
    case OBJ_BOUND_METHOD: {
      ObjBoundMethod* bound = AS_BOUND_METHOD(callee);
      vm.stackTop[-argCount - 1] = bound->receiver;
      return call(bound->method, argCount);
    }
```

vm.c
*in* callValue()

When a method is called, the top of the stack contains all of the arguments, and then just under those is the closure of the called method. That's where slot zero in the new CallFrame will be. This line of code inserts the receiver into that slot. For example, given a method call like this:

```
scone.topping("berries", "cream");
```

We calculate the slot to store the receiver like so:

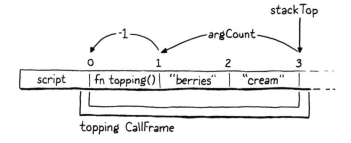

The -argCount skips past the arguments and the - 1 adjusts for the fact that stackTop points just *past* the last used stack slot.

### 28.3.1 Misusing this

Our VM now supports users *correctly* using `this`, but we also need to make sure it properly handles users *misusing* `this`. Lox says it is a compile error for a `this` expression to appear outside of the body of a method. These two wrong uses should be caught by the compiler:

```
print this; // At top level.
```

```
fun notMethod() {
  print this; // In a function.
}
```

So how does the compiler know if it's inside a method? The obvious answer is to look at the FunctionType of the current Compiler. We did just add an enum case there to treat methods specially. However, that wouldn't correctly handle code like the earlier example where you are inside a function which is, itself, nested inside a method.

We could try to resolve "this" and then report an error if it wasn't found in any of the surrounding lexical scopes. That would work, but would require us to shuffle around a bunch of code, since right now the code for resolving a variable implicitly considers it a global access if no declaration is found.

In the next chapter, we will need information about the nearest enclosing class. If we had that, we could use it here to determine if we are inside a method. So we may as well make our future selves' lives a little easier and put that machinery in place now.

**compiler.c**
*add after variable* current

```
Compiler* current = NULL;
ClassCompiler* currentClass = NULL;

static Chunk* currentChunk() {
```

This module variable points to a struct representing the current, innermost class being compiled. The new type looks like this:

**compiler.c**
*add after struct* Compiler

```
} Compiler;

typedef struct ClassCompiler {
  struct ClassCompiler* enclosing;
} ClassCompiler;

Parser parser;
```

Right now we store only a pointer to the ClassCompiler for the enclosing class, if any. Nesting a class declaration inside a method in some other class is an uncommon thing to do, but Lox supports it. Just like the Compiler struct, this means ClassCompiler forms a linked list from the current innermost class being compiled out through all of the enclosing classes.

If we aren't inside any class declaration at all, the module variable `currentClass` is NULL. When the compiler begins compiling a class, it pushes a new ClassCompiler onto that implicit linked stack.

```
    defineVariable(nameConstant);

    ClassCompiler classCompiler;
    classCompiler.enclosing = currentClass;
    currentClass = &classCompiler;

    namedVariable(className, false);
```

compiler.c
in classDeclaration()

The memory for the ClassCompiler struct lives right on the C stack, a handy capability we get by writing our compiler using recursive descent. At the end of the class body, we pop that compiler off the stack and restore the enclosing one.

```
    emitByte(OP_POP);

    currentClass = currentClass->enclosing;
}
```

compiler.c
in classDeclaration()

When an outermost class body ends, `enclosing` will be NULL, so this resets `currentClass` to NULL. Thus, to see if we are inside a class—and therefore inside a method—we simply check that module variable.

```
static void this_(bool canAssign) {
  if (currentClass == NULL) {
    error("Can't use 'this' outside of a class.");
    return;
  }

  variable(false);
```

compiler.c
in this_()

With that, `this` outside of a class is correctly forbidden. Now our methods really feel like *methods* in the object-oriented sense. Accessing the receiver lets them affect the instance you called the method on. We're getting there!

## 28.4  Instance Initializers

The reason object-oriented languages tie state and behavior together—one of the core tenets of the paradigm—is to ensure that objects are always in a valid, meaningful state. When the only way to touch an object's state is through its methods, the methods can make sure nothing goes awry. But that presumes the object is *already* in a proper state. What about when it's first created?

Object-oriented languages ensure that brand new objects are properly set up through constructors, which both produce a new instance and initialize its state. In Lox, the runtime allocates new raw instances, and a class may declare an initializer to set up any fields. Initializers work mostly like normal methods, with a few tweaks:

1. The runtime automatically invokes the initializer method whenever an instance of a class is created.

2. The caller that constructs an instance always gets the instance back after the

Of course, Lox does let outside code directly access and modify an instance's fields without going through its methods. This is unlike Ruby and Smalltalk, which completely encapsulate state inside objects. Our toy scripting language, alas, isn't so principled.

It's as if the initializer is implicitly wrapped in a bundle of code like this:

```
fun create(klass) {
  var obj = newInstance(
      klass);
  obj.init();
  return obj;
}
```

Note how the value returned by `init()` is discarded.

initializer finishes, regardless of what the initializer function itself returns. The initializer method doesn't need to explicitly return `this`.

3. In fact, an initializer is *prohibited* from returning any value at all since the value would never be seen anyway.

Now that we support methods, to add initializers, we merely need to implement those three special rules. We'll go in order.

### 28.4.1 Invoking initializers

First, automatically calling `init()` on new instances:

**vm.c**
*in* callValue()

```
vm.stackTop[-argCount - 1] = OBJ_VAL(newInstance(klass));
Value initializer;
if (tableGet(&klass->methods, vm.initString,
             &initializer)) {
  return call(AS_CLOSURE(initializer), argCount);
}
return true;
```

After the runtime allocates the new instance, we look for an `init()` method on the class. If we find one, we initiate a call to it. This pushes a new CallFrame for the initializer's closure. Say we run this program:

```
class Brunch {
  init(food, drink) {}
}

Brunch("eggs", "coffee");
```

When the VM executes the call to `Brunch()`, it goes like this:

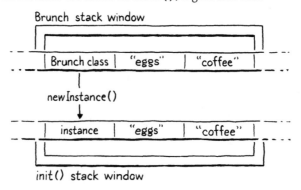

Any arguments passed to the class when we called it are still sitting on the stack above the instance. The new CallFrame for the `init()` method shares that stack window, so those arguments implicitly get forwarded to the initializer.

Lox doesn't require a class to define an initializer. If omitted, the runtime simply returns the new uninitialized instance. However, if there is no `init()` method, then it doesn't make any sense to pass arguments to the class when creating the instance. We make that an error.

```
          return call(AS_CLOSURE(initializer), argCount);
        } else if (argCount != 0) {
          runtimeError("Expected 0 arguments but got %d.",
                       argCount);
          return false;
        }
```
vm.c
in callValue()

When the class *does* provide an initializer, we also need to ensure that the number of arguments passed matches the initializer's arity. Fortunately, the call() helper does that for us already.

To call the initializer, the runtime looks up the init() method by name. We want that to be fast since it happens every time an instance is constructed. That means it would be good to take advantage of the string interning we've already implemented. To do that, the VM creates an ObjString for "init" and reuses it. The string lives right in the VM struct.

```
  Table strings;
  ObjString* initString;
  ObjUpvalue* openUpvalues;
```
vm.h
in struct VM

We create and intern the string when the VM boots up.

```
  initTable(&vm.strings);

  vm.initString = copyString("init", 4);

  defineNative("clock", clockNative);
```
vm.c
in initVM()

We want it to stick around, so the GC considers it a root.

```
  markCompilerRoots();
  markObject((Obj*)vm.initString);
}
```
memory.c
in markRoots()

Look carefully. See any bug waiting to happen? No? It's a subtle one. The garbage collector now reads vm.initString. That field is initialized from the result of calling copyString(). But copying a string allocates memory, which can trigger a GC. If the collector ran at just the wrong time, it would read vm.initString before it had been initialized. So, first we zero the field out.

```
  initTable(&vm.strings);

  vm.initString = NULL;
  vm.initString = copyString("init", 4);
```
vm.c
in initVM()

We clear the pointer when the VM shuts down since the next line will free it.

```
  freeTable(&vm.strings);
  vm.initString = NULL;
  freeObjects();
```
vm.c
in freeVM()

OK, that lets us call initializers.

### 28.4.2  Initializer return values

The next step is ensuring that constructing an instance of a class with an initializer always returns the new instance, and not `nil` or whatever the body of the initializer returns. Right now, if a class defines an initializer, then when an instance is constructed, the VM pushes a call to that initializer onto the CallFrame stack. Then it just keeps on trucking.

The user's invocation on the class to create the instance will complete whenever that initializer method returns, and will leave on the stack whatever value the initializer puts there. That means that unless the user takes care to put `return this;` at the end of the initializer, no instance will come out. Not very helpful.

To fix this, whenever the front end compiles an initializer method, it will emit different bytecode at the end of the body to return `this` from the method instead of the usual implicit `nil` most functions return. In order to do *that*, the compiler needs to actually know when it is compiling an initializer. We detect that by checking to see if the name of the method we're compiling is "init".

*compiler.c*
*in* method()

```
FunctionType type = TYPE_METHOD;
if (parser.previous.length == 4 &&
    memcmp(parser.previous.start, "init", 4) == 0) {
  type = TYPE_INITIALIZER;
}

function(type);
```

We define a new function type to distinguish initializers from other methods.

*compiler.c*
*in enum* FunctionType

```
TYPE_FUNCTION,
TYPE_INITIALIZER,
TYPE_METHOD,
```

Whenever the compiler emits the implicit return at the end of a body, we check the type to decide whether to insert the initializer-specific behavior.

*compiler.c*
*in* emitReturn()
*replace 1 line*

```
static void emitReturn() {
  if (current->type == TYPE_INITIALIZER) {
    emitBytes(OP_GET_LOCAL, 0);
  } else {
    emitByte(OP_NIL);
  }

  emitByte(OP_RETURN);
```

In an initializer, instead of pushing `nil` onto the stack before returning, we load slot zero, which contains the instance. This `emitReturn()` function is also called when compiling a `return` statement without a value, so this also correctly handles cases where the user does an early return inside the initializer.

### 28.4.3  Incorrect returns in initializers

The last step, the last item in our list of special features of initializers, is making it an error to try to return anything *else* from an initializer. Now that the compiler tracks the method type, this is straightforward.

```
  if (match(TOKEN_SEMICOLON)) {
    emitReturn();
  } else {
    if (current->type == TYPE_INITIALIZER) {
      error("Can't return a value from an initializer.");
    }

    expression();
```

compiler.c
in returnStatement()

We report an error if a `return` statement in an initializer has a value. We still go ahead and compile the value afterwards so that the compiler doesn't get confused by the trailing expression and report a bunch of cascaded errors.

Aside from inheritance, which we'll get to soon, we now have a fairly full-featured class system working in clox.

```
class CoffeeMaker {
  init(coffee) {
    this.coffee = coffee;
  }

  brew() {
    print "Enjoy your cup of " + this.coffee;

    // No reusing the grounds!
    this.coffee = nil;
  }
}

var maker = CoffeeMaker("coffee and chicory");
maker.brew();
```

Pretty fancy for a C program that would fit on an old floppy disk.

I acknowledge that "floppy disk" may no longer be a useful size reference for current generations of programmers. Maybe I should have said "a few tweets" or something.

## 28.5  Optimized Invocations

Our VM correctly implements the language's semantics for method calls and initializers. We could stop here. But the main reason we are building an entire second implementation of Lox from scratch is to execute faster than our old Java interpreter. Right now, method calls even in clox are slow.

Lox's semantics define a method invocation as two operations—accessing the method and then calling the result. Our VM must support those as separate operations because the user *can* separate them. You can access a method without calling it and then invoke the bound method later. Nothing we've implemented so far is unnecessary.

But *always* executing those as separate operations has a significant cost. Every single time a Lox program accesses and invokes a method, the runtime heap allocates a new ObjBoundMethod, initializes its fields, then pulls them right back out. Later, the GC has to spend time freeing all of those ephemeral bound methods.

Most of the time, a Lox program accesses a method and then immediately calls it. The bound method is created by one bytecode instruction and then consumed by the very next one. In fact, it's so immediate that the compiler can even textually *see* that it's happening—a dotted property access followed by an opening parenthesis is most likely a method call.

Since we can recognize this pair of operations at compile time, we have the opportunity to emit a new, special instruction that performs an optimized method call.

We start in the function that compiles dotted property expressions.

compiler.c<br>in dot()

```
  if (canAssign && match(TOKEN_EQUAL)) {
    expression();
    emitBytes(OP_SET_PROPERTY, name);
  } else if (match(TOKEN_LEFT_PAREN)) {
    uint8_t argCount = argumentList();
    emitBytes(OP_INVOKE, name);
    emitByte(argCount);
  } else {
```

If you spend enough time watching your bytecode VM run, you'll notice it often executes the same series of bytecode instructions one after the other. A classic optimization is to define a new single instruction called a **superinstruction** that fuses those into a single instruction with the same behavior as the entire sequence.

One of the largest performance drains in a bytecode interpreter is decoding and dispatching each instruction. Fusing instructions eliminates some of that.

The challenge is determining *which* instruction sequences are common enough to benefit from this optimization. Every new superinstruction claims an opcode for its own use and there are only so many of those to go around. Add too many, and you'll need a larger encoding for opcodes, which then increases code size and makes decoding *all* instructions slower.

After the compiler has parsed the property name, we look for a left parenthesis. If we match one, we switch to a new code path. There, we compile the argument list exactly like we do when compiling a call expression. Then we emit a single new OP_INVOKE instruction. It takes two operands:

1. The index of the property name in the constant table.

2. The number of arguments passed to the method.

In other words, this single instruction combines the operands of the OP_GET_PROPERTY and OP_CALL instructions it replaces, in that order. It really is a fusion of those two instructions. Let's define it.

chunk.h<br>in enum OpCode

```
  OP_CALL,
  OP_INVOKE,
  OP_CLOSURE,
```

And add it to the disassembler:

debug.c<br>in disassembleInstruction()

```
    case OP_CALL:
      return byteInstruction("OP_CALL", chunk, offset);
    case OP_INVOKE:
      return invokeInstruction("OP_INVOKE", chunk, offset);
    case OP_CLOSURE: {
```

This is a new, special instruction format, so it needs a little custom disassembly logic.

```
static int invokeInstruction(const char* name, Chunk* chunk,
                             int offset) {
  uint8_t constant = chunk->code[offset + 1];
  uint8_t argCount = chunk->code[offset + 2];
  printf("%-16s (%d args) %4d '", name, argCount, constant);
  printValue(chunk->constants.values[constant]);
  printf("'\n");
  return offset + 3;
}
```

debug.c
*add after* constantInstruction()

We read the two operands and then print out both the method name and the argument count. Over in the interpreter's bytecode dispatch loop is where the real action begins.

```
      }
      case OP_INVOKE: {
        ObjString* method = READ_STRING();
        int argCount = READ_BYTE();
        if (!invoke(method, argCount)) {
          return INTERPRET_RUNTIME_ERROR;
        }
        frame = &vm.frames[vm.frameCount - 1];
        break;
      }
      case OP_CLOSURE: {
```

vm.c
*in* run()

Most of the work happens in invoke(), which we'll get to. Here, we look up the method name from the first operand and then read the argument count operand. Then we hand off to invoke() to do the heavy lifting. That function returns true if the invocation succeeds. As usual, a false return means a runtime error occurred. We check for that here and abort the interpreter if disaster has struck.

Finally, assuming the invocation succeeded, then there is a new CallFrame on the stack, so we refresh our cached copy of the current frame in frame.

The interesting work happens here:

```
static bool invoke(ObjString* name, int argCount) {
  Value receiver = peek(argCount);
  ObjInstance* instance = AS_INSTANCE(receiver);
  return invokeFromClass(instance->klass, name, argCount);
}
```

vm.c
*add after* callValue()

First we grab the receiver off the stack. The arguments passed to the method are above it on the stack, so we peek that many slots down. Then it's a simple matter to cast the object to an instance and invoke the method on it.

That does assume the object *is* an instance. As with OP_GET_PROPERTY instructions, we also need to handle the case where a user incorrectly tries to call a method on a value of the wrong type.

vm.c
*in* invoke()

```
Value receiver = peek(argCount);

if (!IS_INSTANCE(receiver)) {
  runtimeError("Only instances have methods.");
  return false;
}

ObjInstance* instance = AS_INSTANCE(receiver);
```

As you can guess by now, we split this code into a separate function because we're going to reuse it later—in this case for **super** calls.

vm.c
*add after* callValue()

That's a runtime error, so we report that and bail out. Otherwise, we get the instance's class and jump over to this other new utility function:

```
static bool invokeFromClass(ObjClass* klass, ObjString* name,
                            int argCount) {
  Value method;
  if (!tableGet(&klass->methods, name, &method)) {
    runtimeError("Undefined property '%s'.", name->chars);
    return false;
  }
  return call(AS_CLOSURE(method), argCount);
}
```

This function combines the logic of how the VM implements `OP_GET_PROPERTY` and `OP_CALL` instructions, in that order. First we look up the method by name in the class's method table. If we don't find one, we report that runtime error and exit.

This is a key reason *why* we use stack slot zero to store the receiver—it's how the caller already organizes the stack for a method call. An efficient calling convention is an important part of a bytecode VM's performance story.

Otherwise, we take the method's closure and push a call to it onto the CallFrame stack. We don't need to heap allocate and initialize an ObjBoundMethod. In fact, we don't even need to juggle anything on the stack. The receiver and method arguments are already right where they need to be.

If you fire up the VM and run a little program that calls methods now, you should see the exact same behavior as before. But, if we did our job right, the *performance* should be much improved. I wrote a little microbenchmark that does a batch of 10,000 method calls. Then it tests how many of these batches it can execute in 10 seconds. On my computer, without the new `OP_INVOKE` instruction, it got through 1,089 batches. With this new optimization, it finished 8,324 batches in the same time. That's *7.6 times faster*, which is a huge improvement when it comes to programming language optimization.

We shouldn't pat ourselves on the back *too* firmly. This performance improvement is relative to our own unoptimized method call implementation which was quite slow. Doing a heap allocation for every single method call isn't going to win any races.

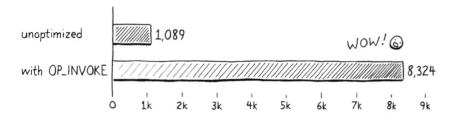

### 28.5.1 Invoking fields

The fundamental creed of optimization is: "Thou shalt not break correctness." Users like it when a language implementation gives them an answer faster, but only if it's the *right* answer. Alas, our implementation of faster method invocations fails to uphold that principle:

```
class Oops {
  init() {
    fun f() {
      print "not a method";
    }

    this.field = f;
  }
}

var oops = Oops();
oops.field();
```

The last line looks like a method call. The compiler thinks that it is and dutifully emits an `OP_INVOKE` instruction for it. However, it's not. What is actually happening is a *field* access that returns a function which then gets called. Right now, instead of executing that correctly, our VM reports a runtime error when it can't find a method named "field".

Earlier, when we implemented `OP_GET_PROPERTY`, we handled both field and method accesses. To squash this new bug, we need to do the same thing for `OP_INVOKE`.

```
    ObjInstance* instance = AS_INSTANCE(receiver);

    Value value;
    if (tableGet(&instance->fields, name, &value)) {
      vm.stackTop[-argCount - 1] = value;
      return callValue(value, argCount);
    }

    return invokeFromClass(instance->klass, name, argCount);
```

*vm.c*
*in* `invoke()`

Pretty simple fix. Before looking up a method on the instance's class, we look for a field with the same name. If we find a field, then we store it on the stack in place of the receiver, *under* the argument list. This is how `OP_GET_PROPERTY` behaves since the latter instruction executes before a subsequent parenthesized list of arguments has been evaluated.

Then we try to call that field's value like the callable that it hopefully is. The `callValue()` helper will check the value's type and call it as appropriate or report a runtime error if the field's value isn't a callable type like a closure.

That's all it takes to make our optimization fully safe. We do sacrifice a little performance, unfortunately. But that's the price you have to pay sometimes. You occasionally get frustrated by optimizations you *could* do if only the language wouldn't allow some annoying corner case. But, as language implementers, we have to play the game we're given.

The code we wrote here follows a typical pattern in optimization:

1. Recognize a common operation or sequence of operations that is performance critical. In this case, it is a method access followed by a call.

There are cases where users may be satisfied when a program sometimes returns the wrong answer in return for running significantly faster or with a better bound on the performance. These are the field of **Monte Carlo algorithms**. For some use cases, this is a good trade-off.

The important part, though, is that the user is *choosing* to apply one of these algorithms. We language implementers can't unilaterally decide to sacrifice their program's correctness.

As language *designers*, our role is very different. If we do control the language itself, we may sometimes choose to restrict or change the language in ways that enable optimizations. Users want expressive languages, but they also want fast implementations. Sometimes it is good language design to sacrifice a little power if you can give them perf in return.

2. Add an optimized implementation of that pattern. That's our OP_INVOKE instruction.

3. Guard the optimized code with some conditional logic that validates that the pattern actually applies. If it does, stay on the fast path. Otherwise, fall back to a slower but more robust unoptimized behavior. Here, that means checking that we are actually calling a method and not accessing a field.

As your language work moves from getting the implementation working *at all* to getting it to work *faster*, you will find yourself spending more and more time looking for patterns like this and adding guarded optimizations for them. Full-time VM engineers spend much of their careers in this loop.

But we can stop here for now. With this, clox now supports most of the features of an object-oriented programming language, and with respectable performance.

## CHALLENGES

1. The hash table lookup to find a class's `init()` method is constant time, but still fairly slow. Implement something faster. Write a benchmark and measure the performance difference.

2. In a dynamically typed language like Lox, a single callsite may invoke a variety of methods on a number of classes throughout a program's execution. Even so, in practice, most of the time a callsite ends up calling the exact same method on the exact same class for the duration of the run. Most calls are actually not polymorphic even if the language says they can be.

   How do advanced language implementations optimize based on that observation?

3. When interpreting an `OP_INVOKE` instruction, the VM has to do two hash table lookups. First, it looks for a field that could shadow a method, and only if that fails does it look for a method. The former check is rarely useful—most fields do not contain functions. But it is *necessary* because the language says fields and methods are accessed using the same syntax, and fields shadow methods.

   That is a language *choice* that affects the performance of our implementation. Was it the right choice? If Lox were your language, what would you do?

## DESIGN NOTE: NOVELTY BUDGET

I still remember the first time I wrote a tiny BASIC program on a TRS-80 and made a computer do something it hadn't done before. It felt like a superpower. The first time I cobbled together just enough of a parser and interpreter to let me write a tiny program in *my own language* that made a computer do a thing was like some sort of higher-order meta-superpower. It was and remains a wonderful feeling.

I realized I could design a language that looked and behaved however I chose. It was like I'd been going to a private school that required uniforms my whole life and then one day transferred to a public school where I could wear whatever I wanted. I don't need to use curly braces for blocks? I can use something other than an equals sign for assignment? I can do objects without classes? Multiple inheritance *and* multimethods? A dynamic language that overloads statically, by arity?

Naturally, I took that freedom and ran with it. I made the weirdest, most arbitrary language design decisions. Apostrophes for generics. No commas between arguments. Overload resolution that can fail at runtime. I did things differently just for difference's sake.

This is a very fun experience that I highly recommend. We need more weird, avant-garde programming languages. I want to see more art languages. I still make oddball toy languages for fun sometimes.

*However*, if your goal is success where "success" is defined as a large number of users, then your priorities must be different. In that case, your primary goal is to have your language loaded into the brains of as many people as possible. That's *really hard*. It takes a lot of human effort to move a language's syntax and semantics from a computer into trillions of neurons.

Programmers are naturally conservative with their time and cautious about what languages are worth uploading into their wetware. They don't want to waste their time on a language that ends up not being useful to them. As a language designer, your goal is thus to give them as much language power as you can with as little required learning as possible.

One natural approach is *simplicity*. The fewer concepts and features your language has, the less total volume of stuff there is to learn. This is one of the reasons minimal scripting languages often find success even though they aren't as powerful as the big industrial languages—they are easier to get started with, and once they are in someone's brain, the user wants to keep using them.

The problem with simplicity is that simply cutting features often sacrifices power and expressiveness. There is an art to finding features that punch above their weight, but often minimal languages simply do less.

There is another path that avoids much of that problem. The trick is to realize that a user doesn't have to load your entire language into their head, *just the part they don't already have in there*. As I mentioned in an earlier design note, learning is about transferring the *delta* between what they already know and what they need to know.

Many potential users of your language already know some other programming language. Any features your language shares with that language are essentially "free" when it comes to learning. It's already in their head, they just have to recognize that your language does the same thing.

In other words, *familiarity* is another key tool to lower the adoption cost of your language. Of course, if you fully maximize that attribute, the end result is a language that is completely identical to some existing one. That's not a recipe for success, because at that point there's no incentive for users to switch to your language at all.

So you do need to provide some compelling differences. Some things your language can do that other languages can't, or at least can't do as well. I believe this is one of the

In particular, this is a big advantage of dynamically typed languages. A static language requires you to learn *two* languages—the runtime semantics and the static type system—before you can get to the point where you are making the computer do stuff. Dynamic languages require you to learn only the former.

Eventually, programs get big enough that the value of static analysis pays for the effort to learn that second static language, but the value proposition isn't as obvious at the outset.

Klabnik writes about the strangeness budget here:

→ craftinginterpreters.com/budget

A related concept in psychology is **idiosyncrasy credit**, the idea that other people in society grant you a finite amount of deviations from social norms. You earn credit by fitting in and doing in-group things, which you can then spend on oddball activities that might otherwise raise eyebrows. In other words, demonstrating that you are "one of the good ones" gives you license to raise your freak flag, but only so far.

fundamental balancing acts of language design: similarity to other languages lowers learning cost, while divergence raises the compelling advantages.

I think of this balancing act in terms of a **novelty budget**, or as Steve Klabnik calls it, a "strangeness budget". Users have a low threshold for the total amount of new stuff they are willing to accept to learn a new language. Exceed that, and they won't show up.

Anytime you add something new to your language that other languages don't have, or anytime your language does something other languages do in a different way, you spend some of that budget. That's OK—you *need* to spend it to make your language compelling. But your goal is to spend it *wisely*. For each feature or difference, ask yourself how much compelling power it adds to your language and then evaluate critically whether it pays its way. Is the change so valuable that it is worth blowing some of your novelty budget?

In practice, I find this means that you end up being pretty conservative with syntax and more adventurous with semantics. As fun as it is to put on a new change of clothes, swapping out curly braces with some other block delimiter is very unlikely to add much real power to the language, but it does spend some novelty. It's hard for syntax differences to carry their weight.

On the other hand, new semantics can significantly increase the power of the language. Multimethods, mixins, traits, reflection, dependent types, runtime metaprogramming, etc. can radically level up what a user can do with the language.

Alas, being conservative like this is not as fun as just changing everything. But it's up to you to decide whether you want to chase mainstream success or not in the first place. We don't all need to be radio-friendly pop bands. If you want your language to be like free jazz or drone metal and are happy with the proportionally smaller (but likely more devoted) audience size, go for it.

# Superclasses

29

*"You can choose your friends but you sho' can't choose your family, an'
they're still kin to you no matter whether you acknowledge 'em or not,
and it makes you look right silly when you don't."*

— Harper Lee, *To Kill a Mockingbird*

This is the very last chapter where we add new functionality to our VM. We've packed almost the entire Lox language in there already. All that remains is inheriting methods and calling superclass methods. We have another chapter after this one, but it introduces no new behavior. It only makes existing stuff faster. Make it to the end of this one, and you'll have a complete Lox implementation.

Some of the material in this chapter will remind you of jlox. The way we resolve super calls is pretty much the same, though viewed through clox's more complex mechanism for storing state on the stack. But we have an entirely different, much faster, way of handling inherited method calls this time around.

That "only" should not imply that making stuff faster isn't important! After all, the whole purpose of our entire second virtual machine is better performance over jlox. You could argue that *all* of the past fifteen chapters are "optimization".

## 29.1  Inheriting Methods

We'll kick things off with method inheritance since it's the simpler piece. To refresh your memory, Lox inheritance syntax looks like this:

```
class Doughnut {
  cook() { print "Dunk in the fryer."; }
}

class Cruller < Doughnut {
  finish() { print "Glaze with icing."; }
}
```

Here, the Cruller class inherits from Doughnut and thus, instances of Cruller inherit the `cook()` method. I don't know why I'm belaboring this. You know how inheritance works. Let's start compiling the new syntax.

compiler.c
*in* classDeclaration()

```
currentClass = &classCompiler;

if (match(TOKEN_LESS)) {
  consume(TOKEN_IDENTIFIER, "Expect superclass name.");
  variable(false);
  namedVariable(className, false);
  emitByte(OP_INHERIT);
}

namedVariable(className, false);
```

After we compile the class name, if the next token is a `<`, then we found a superclass clause. We consume the superclass's identifier token, then call `variable()`. That function takes the previously consumed token, treats it as a variable reference, and emits code to load the variable's value. In other words, it looks up the superclass by name and pushes it onto the stack.

After that, we call `namedVariable()` to load the subclass doing the inheriting onto the stack, followed by an `OP_INHERIT` instruction. That instruction wires up the superclass to the new subclass. In the last chapter, we defined an `OP_METHOD` instruction to mutate an existing class object by adding a method to its method table. This is similar—the `OP_INHERIT` instruction takes an existing class and applies the effect of inheritance to it.

In the previous example, when the compiler works through this bit of syntax:

```
class Cruller < Doughnut {
```

The result is this bytecode:

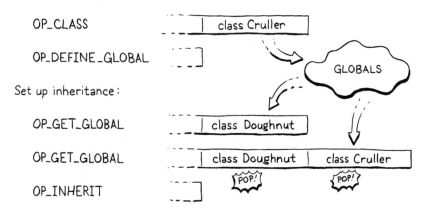

Before we implement the new `OP_INHERIT` instruction, we have an edge case to detect.

```
variable(false);

if (identifiersEqual(&className, &parser.previous)) {
  error("A class can't inherit from itself.");
}

namedVariable(className, false);
```

compiler.c
in classDeclaration()

A class cannot be its own superclass. Unless you have access to a deranged nuclear physicist and a very heavily modified DeLorean, you cannot inherit from yourself.

*Interestingly, with the way we implement method inheritance, I don't think allowing cycles would actually cause any problems in clox. It wouldn't do anything* useful, *but I don't think it would cause a crash or infinite loop.*

## 29.1.1 Executing inheritance

Now onto the new instruction.

```
OP_CLASS,
OP_INHERIT,
OP_METHOD
```

chunk.h
in enum OpCode

There are no operands to worry about. The two values we need—superclass and subclass—are both found on the stack. That means disassembling is easy.

```
    return constantInstruction("OP_CLASS", chunk, offset);
  case OP_INHERIT:
    return simpleInstruction("OP_INHERIT", offset);
  case OP_METHOD:
```

debug.c
in disassembleInstruction()

The interpreter is where the action happens.

```
    break;
  case OP_INHERIT: {
    Value superclass = peek(1);
    ObjClass* subclass = AS_CLASS(peek(0));
    tableAddAll(&AS_CLASS(superclass)->methods,
                &subclass->methods);
    pop(); // Subclass.
    break;
  }
  case OP_METHOD:
```

vm.c
in run()

From the top of the stack down, we have the subclass then the superclass. We grab both of those and then do the inherit-y bit. This is where clox takes a different path than jlox. In our first interpreter, each subclass stored a reference to its superclass. On method access, if we didn't find the method in the subclass's method table, we recursed through the inheritance chain looking at each ancestor's method table until we found it.

For example, calling **cook()** on a Cruller instance sends jlox on this journey:

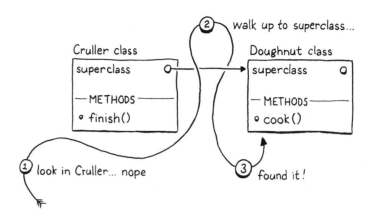

That's a lot of work to perform during method *invocation* time. It's slow, and worse, the farther an inherited method is up the ancestor chain, the slower it gets. Not a great performance story.

The new approach is much faster. When the subclass is declared, we copy all of the inherited class's methods down into the subclass's own method table. Later, when *calling* a method, any method inherited from a superclass will be found right in the subclass's own method table. There is no extra runtime work needed for inheritance at all. By the time the class is declared, the work is done. This means inherited method calls are exactly as fast as normal method calls—a single hash table lookup.

<aside>
Well, two hash table lookups, I guess. Because first we have to make sure a field on the instance doesn't shadow the method.
</aside>

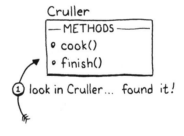

I've sometimes heard this technique called "copy-down inheritance". It's simple and fast, but, like most optimizations, you get to use it only under certain constraints. It works in Lox because Lox classes are *closed*. Once a class declaration is finished executing, the set of methods for that class can never change.

In languages like Ruby, Python, and JavaScript, it's possible to crack open an existing class and jam some new methods into it or even remove them. That would break our optimization because if those modifications happened to a superclass *after* the subclass declaration executed, the subclass would not pick up those changes. That breaks a user's expectation that inheritance always reflects the current state of the superclass.

<aside>
As you can imagine, changing the set of methods a class defines imperatively at runtime can make it hard to reason about a program. It is a very powerful tool, but also a dangerous tool.

Those who find this tool maybe a little *too* dangerous gave it the unbecoming name "monkey patching", or the even less decorous "duck punching".
</aside>

Fortunately for us (but not for users who like the feature, I guess), Lox doesn't let you patch monkeys or punch ducks, so we can safely apply this optimization.

What about method overrides? Won't copying the superclass's methods into the subclass's method table clash with the subclass's own methods? Fortunately, no. We emit the OP_INHERIT after the OP_CLASS instruction that creates the subclass but before any method declarations and OP_METHOD instructions have been compiled. At the point that we copy the superclass's methods down, the subclass's method table is empty. Any methods the subclass overrides will overwrite those inherited entries in the table.

## 29.1.2  Invalid superclasses

Our implementation is simple and fast, which is just the way I like my VM code. But it's not robust. Nothing prevents a user from inheriting from an object that isn't a class at all:

```
var NotClass = "So not a class";
class OhNo < NotClass {}
```

Obviously, no self-respecting programmer would write that, but we have to guard against potential Lox users who have no self respect. A simple runtime check fixes that.

```
    Value superclass = peek(1);
    if (!IS_CLASS(superclass)) {
      runtimeError("Superclass must be a class.");
      return INTERPRET_RUNTIME_ERROR;
    }

    ObjClass* subclass = AS_CLASS(peek(0));
```

vm.c
in run()

If the value we loaded from the identifier in the superclass clause isn't an ObjClass, we report a runtime error to let the user know what we think of them and their code.

## 29.2  Storing Superclasses

Did you notice that when we added method inheritance, we didn't actually add any reference from a subclass to its superclass? After we copy the inherited methods over, we forget the superclass entirely. We don't need to keep a handle on the superclass, so we don't.

That won't be sufficient to support super calls. Since a subclass may override the superclass method, we need to be able to get our hands on superclass method tables. Before we get to that mechanism, I want to refresh your memory on how super calls are statically resolved.

Back in the halcyon days of jlox, I showed you this tricky example to explain the way super calls are dispatched:

"May" might not be a strong enough word. Presumably the method *has* been overridden. Otherwise, why are you bothering to use **super** instead of just calling it directly?

```
class A {
  method() { print "A method"; }
}

class B < A {
  method() { print "B method"; }

  test() { super.method(); }
}

class C < B {}
C().test();
```

Inside the body of the `test()` method, `this` is an instance of C. If super calls were resolved relative to the superclass of the *receiver*, then we would look in C's superclass, B. But super calls are resolved relative to the superclass of the *surrounding class where the super call occurs*. In this case, we are in B's `test()` method, so the superclass is A, and the program should print "A method".

This means that super calls are not resolved dynamically based on the runtime instance. The superclass used to look up the method is a static—practically lexical—property of where the call occurs. When we added inheritance to jlox, we took advantage of that static aspect by storing the superclass in the same Environment structure we used for all lexical scopes. Almost as if the interpreter saw the above program like this:

```
class A {
  method() { print "A method"; }
}

var Bs_super = A;
class B < A {
  method() { print "B method"; }

  test() { runtimeSuperCall(Bs_super, "method"); }
}

var Cs_super = B;
class C < B {}

C().test();
```

Each subclass has a hidden variable storing a reference to its superclass. Whenever we need to perform a super call, we access the superclass from that variable and tell the runtime to start looking for methods there.

We'll take the same path with clox. The difference is that instead of jlox's heap-allocated Environment class, we have the bytecode VM's value stack and upvalue system. The machinery is a little different, but the overall effect is the same.

### 29.2.1  A superclass local variable

Our compiler already emits code to load the superclass onto the stack. Instead of leaving that slot as a temporary, we create a new scope and make it a local variable.

compiler.c<br>in classDeclaration()

```
  }

  beginScope();
  addLocal(syntheticToken("super"));
  defineVariable(0);

  namedVariable(className, false);
  emitByte(OP_INHERIT);
```

Creating a new lexical scope ensures that if we declare two classes in the same scope, each has a different local slot to store its superclass. Since we always name this variable "super", if we didn't make a scope for each subclass, the variables would collide.

We name the variable "super" for the same reason we use "this" as the name of the hidden local variable that `this` expressions resolve to: "super" is a reserved word, which guarantees the compiler's hidden variable won't collide with a user-defined one.

The difference is that when compiling `this` expressions, we conveniently have a token sitting around whose lexeme is "this". We aren't so lucky here. Instead, we add a little helper function to create a synthetic token for the given constant string.

I say "constant string" because tokens don't do any memory management of their lexeme. If we tried to use a heap-allocated string for this, we'd end up leaking memory because it never gets freed. But the memory for C string literals lives in the executable's constant data section and never needs to be freed, so we're fine.

```
static Token syntheticToken(const char* text) {
  Token token;
  token.start = text;
  token.length = (int)strlen(text);
  return token;
}
```

compiler.c
*add after* variable()

Since we opened a local scope for the superclass variable, we need to close it.

```
    emitByte(OP_POP);

  if (classCompiler.hasSuperclass) {
    endScope();
  }

  currentClass = currentClass->enclosing;
```

compiler.c
*in* classDeclaration()

We pop the scope and discard the "super" variable after compiling the class body and its methods. That way, the variable is accessible in all of the methods of the subclass. It's a somewhat pointless optimization, but we create the scope only if there *is* a superclass clause. Thus we need to close the scope only if there is one.

To track that, we could declare a little local variable in classDeclaration(). But soon, other functions in the compiler will need to know whether the surrounding class is a subclass or not. So we may as well give our future selves a hand and store this fact as a field in the ClassCompiler now.

```
typedef struct ClassCompiler {
  struct ClassCompiler* enclosing;
  bool hasSuperclass;
} ClassCompiler;
```

compiler.c
*in struct* ClassCompiler

When we first initialize a ClassCompiler, we assume it is not a subclass.

```
  ClassCompiler classCompiler;
  classCompiler.hasSuperclass = false;
  classCompiler.enclosing = currentClass;
```

compiler.c
*in* classDeclaration()

Then, if we see a superclass clause, we know we are compiling a subclass.

compiler.c
in classDeclaration()

```
  emitByte(OP_INHERIT);
  classCompiler.hasSuperclass = true;
}
```

This machinery gives us a mechanism at runtime to access the superclass object of the surrounding subclass from within any of the subclass's methods—simply emit code to load the variable named "super". That variable is a local outside of the method body, but our existing upvalue support enables the VM to capture that local inside the body of the method or even in functions nested inside that method.

## 29.3  Super Calls

This is it, friend. The very last entry you'll add to the parsing table.

With that runtime support in place, we are ready to implement super calls. As usual, we go front to back, starting with the new syntax. A super call begins, naturally enough, with the super keyword.

compiler.c
replace 1 line

```
  [TOKEN_RETURN]    = {NULL,     NULL,    PREC_NONE},
  [TOKEN_SUPER]     = {super_,   NULL,    PREC_NONE},
  [TOKEN_THIS]      = {this_,    NULL,    PREC_NONE},
```

When the expression parser lands on a super token, control jumps to a new parsing function which starts off like so:

compiler.c
add after syntheticToken()

```
static void super_(bool canAssign) {
  consume(TOKEN_DOT, "Expect '.' after 'super'.");
  consume(TOKEN_IDENTIFIER, "Expect superclass method name.");
  uint8_t name = identifierConstant(&parser.previous);
}
```

Hypothetical question: If a bare super token *was* an expression, what kind of object would it evaluate to?

This is pretty different from how we compiled this expressions. Unlike this, a super token is not a standalone expression. Instead, the dot and method name following it are inseparable parts of the syntax. However, the parenthesized argument list is separate. As with normal method access, Lox supports getting a reference to a superclass method as a closure without invoking it:

```
class A {
  method() { print "A"; }
}

class B < A {
  method() {
    var closure = super.method;
    closure(); // Prints "A".
  }
}
```

In other words, Lox doesn't really have super *call* expressions, it has super *access* expressions, which you can choose to immediately invoke if you want. So when the compiler hits a super token, we consume the subsequent . token and then look for a method name. Methods are looked up dynamically, so we use `identifierConstant()` to take the lexeme of the method name token and store it in the constant table just like we do for property access expressions.

Here is what the compiler does after consuming those tokens:

```
  uint8_t name = identifierConstant(&parser.previous);

  namedVariable(syntheticToken("this"), false);
  namedVariable(syntheticToken("super"), false);
  emitBytes(OP_GET_SUPER, name);
}
```

compiler.c
in super_()

In order to access a *superclass method* on *the current instance*, the runtime needs both the receiver *and* the superclass of the surrounding method's class. The first `namedVariable()` call generates code to look up the current receiver stored in the hidden variable "this" and push it onto the stack. The second `namedVariable()` call emits code to look up the superclass from its "super" variable and push that on top.

Finally, we emit a new `OP_GET_SUPER` instruction with an operand for the constant table index of the method name. That's a lot to hold in your head. To make it tangible, consider this example program:

```
class Doughnut {
  cook() {
    print "Dunk in the fryer.";
    this.finish("sprinkles");
  }

  finish(ingredient) { print "Finish with " + ingredient; }
}

class Cruller < Doughnut {
  finish(ingredient) {
    // No sprinkles, always icing.
    super.finish("icing");
  }
}
```

The bytecode emitted for the `super.finish("icing")` expression looks and works like this:

The first three instructions give the runtime access to the three pieces of information it needs to perform the super access:

1. The first instruction loads **the instance** onto the stack.

2. The second instruction loads **the superclass where the method is resolved.**

3. Then the new OP_GET_SUPER instuction encodes **the name of the method to access** as an operand.

The remaining instructions are the normal bytecode for evaluating an argument list and calling a function.

We're almost ready to implement the new OP_GET_SUPER instruction in the interpreter. But before we do, the compiler has some errors it is responsible for reporting.

compiler.c<br>in super_()

```c
static void super_(bool canAssign) {
  if (currentClass == NULL) {
    error("Can't use 'super' outside of a class.");
  } else if (!currentClass->hasSuperclass) {
    error("Can't use 'super' in a class with no superclass.");
  }

  consume(TOKEN_DOT, "Expect '.' after 'super'.");
```

A super call is meaningful only inside the body of a method (or in a function nested inside a method), and only inside the method of a class that has a superclass. We detect both of these cases using the value of currentClass. If that's NULL or points to a class with no superclass, we report those errors.

### 29.3.1 Executing super accesses

Assuming the user didn't put a super expression where it's not allowed, their code passes from the compiler over to the runtime. We've got ourselves a new instruction.

chunk.h<br>in enum OpCode

```c
  OP_SET_PROPERTY,
  OP_GET_SUPER,
  OP_EQUAL,
```

We disassemble it like other opcodes that take a constant table index operand.

debug.c<br>in disassembleInstruction()

```c
    return constantInstruction("OP_SET_PROPERTY", chunk, offset);
  case OP_GET_SUPER:
    return constantInstruction("OP_GET_SUPER", chunk, offset);
  case OP_EQUAL:
```

You might anticipate something harder, but interpreting the new instruction is similar to executing a normal property access.

```
    }
  case OP_GET_SUPER: {
    ObjString* name = READ_STRING();
    ObjClass* superclass = AS_CLASS(pop());

    if (!bindMethod(superclass, name)) {
      return INTERPRET_RUNTIME_ERROR;
    }
    break;
  }
  case OP_EQUAL: {
```

vm.c
in run()

As with properties, we read the method name from the constant table. Then we pass that to bindMethod() which looks up the method in the given class's method table and creates an ObjBoundMethod to bundle the resulting closure to the current instance.

The key difference is *which* class we pass to bindMethod(). With a normal property access, we use the ObjInstances's own class, which gives us the dynamic dispatch we want. For a super call, we don't use the instance's class. Instead, we use the statically resolved superclass of the containing class, which the compiler has conveniently ensured is sitting on top of the stack waiting for us.

We pop that superclass and pass it to bindMethod(), which correctly skips over any overriding methods in any of the subclasses between that superclass and the instance's own class. It also correctly includes any methods inherited by the superclass from any of *its* superclasses.

The rest of the behavior is the same. Popping the superclass leaves the instance at the top of the stack. When bindMethod() succeeds, it pops the instance and pushes the new bound method. Otherwise, it reports a runtime error and returns false. In that case, we abort the interpreter.

Another difference compared to OP_GET_PROPERTY is that we don't try to look for a shadowing field first. Fields are not inherited, so **super** expressions always resolve to methods.

If Lox were a prototype-based language that used *delegation* instead of *inheritance*, then instead of one *class* inheriting from another *class*, instances would inherit from ("delegate to") other instances. In that case, fields *could* be inherited, and we would need to check for them here.

## 29.3.2  Faster super calls

We have superclass method accesses working now. And since the returned object is an ObjBoundMethod that you can then invoke, we've got super *calls* working too. Just like last chapter, we've reached a point where our VM has the complete, correct semantics.

But, also like last chapter, it's pretty slow. Again, we're heap allocating an ObjBoundMethod for each super call even though most of the time the very next instruction is an OP_CALL that immediately unpacks that bound method, invokes it, and then discards it. In fact, this is even more likely to be true for super calls than for regular method calls. At least with method calls there is a chance that the user is actually invoking a function stored in a field. With super calls, you're *always* looking up a method. The only question is whether you invoke it immediately or not.

The compiler can certainly answer that question for itself if it sees a left parenthesis after the superclass method name, so we'll go ahead and perform the same optimization we did for method calls. Take out the two lines of code that load the superclass and emit OP_GET_SUPER, and replace them with this:

compiler.c
*in* super_()
*replace 2 lines*

```
  namedVariable(syntheticToken("this"), false);
  if (match(TOKEN_LEFT_PAREN)) {
    uint8_t argCount = argumentList();
    namedVariable(syntheticToken("super"), false);
    emitBytes(OP_SUPER_INVOKE, name);
    emitByte(argCount);
  } else {
    namedVariable(syntheticToken("super"), false);
    emitBytes(OP_GET_SUPER, name);
  }
}
```

Now before we emit anything, we look for a parenthesized argument list. If we find one, we compile that. Then we load the superclass. After that, we emit a new OP_SUPER_INVOKE instruction. This superinstruction combines the behavior of OP_GET_SUPER and OP_CALL, so it takes two operands: the constant table index of the method name to look up and the number of arguments to pass to it.

This is a particularly *super* superinstruction, if you get what I'm saying. I...I'm sorry for this terrible joke.

Otherwise, if we don't find a (, we continue to compile the expression as a super access like we did before and emit an OP_GET_SUPER.

Drifting down the compilation pipeline, our first stop is a new instruction.

chunk.h
*in enum* OpCode

```
  OP_INVOKE,
  OP_SUPER_INVOKE,
  OP_CLOSURE,
```

And just past that, its disassembler support.

debug.c
*in* disassembleInstruction()

```
      return invokeInstruction("OP_INVOKE", chunk, offset);
    case OP_SUPER_INVOKE:
      return invokeInstruction("OP_SUPER_INVOKE", chunk, offset);
    case OP_CLOSURE: {
```

A super invocation instruction has the same set of operands as OP_INVOKE, so we reuse the same helper to disassemble it. Finally, the pipeline dumps us into the interpreter.

vm.c
*in* run()

```
        break;
      }
      case OP_SUPER_INVOKE: {
        ObjString* method = READ_STRING();
        int argCount = READ_BYTE();
        ObjClass* superclass = AS_CLASS(pop());
        if (!invokeFromClass(superclass, method, argCount)) {
          return INTERPRET_RUNTIME_ERROR;
        }
        frame = &vm.frames[vm.frameCount - 1];
        break;
      }
      case OP_CLOSURE: {
```

This handful of code is basically our implementation of OP_INVOKE mixed together with a dash of OP_GET_SUPER. There are some differences in how the stack is organized, though. With an unoptimized super call, the superclass is popped and replaced by the ObjBoundMethod for the resolved function *before* the arguments to the call are executed. This ensures that by the time the OP_CALL is executed, the bound method is *under* the argument list, where the runtime expects it to be for a closure call.

With our optimized instructions, things are shuffled a bit:

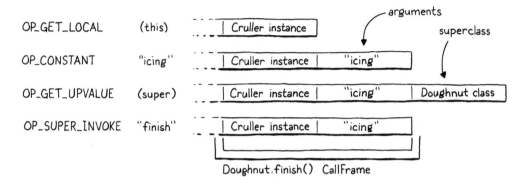

Now resolving the superclass method is part of the *invocation*, so the arguments need to already be on the stack at the point that we look up the method. This means the superclass object is on top of the arguments.

Aside from that, the behavior is roughly the same as an OP_GET_SUPER followed by an OP_CALL. First, we pull out the method name and argument count operands. Then we pop the superclass off the top of the stack so that we can look up the method in its method table. This conveniently leaves the stack set up just right for a method call.

We pass the superclass, method name, and argument count to our existing invokeFromClass() function. That function looks up the given method on the given class and attempts to create a call to it with the given arity. If a method could not be found, it returns false, and we bail out of the interpreter. Otherwise, invokeFromClass() pushes a new CallFrame onto the call stack for the method's closure. That invalidates the interpreter's cached CallFrame pointer, so we refresh frame.

## 29.4  A Complete Virtual Machine

Take a look back at what we've created. By my count, we wrote around 2,500 lines of fairly clean, straightforward C. That little program contains a complete implementation of the—quite high-level!—Lox language, with a whole precedence table full of expression types and a suite of control flow statements. We implemented variables, functions, closures, classes, fields, methods, and inheritance.

Even more impressive, our implementation is portable to any platform with a C compiler, and is fast enough for real-world production use. We have a single-pass bytecode compiler, a tight virtual machine interpreter for our internal instruction set, compact object representations, a stack for storing variables without heap allocation, and a precise garbage collector.

If you go out and start poking around in the implementations of Lua, Python, or Ruby, you will be surprised by how much of it now looks familiar to you. You have seriously leveled up your knowledge of how programming languages work, which in turn gives you a deeper understanding of programming itself. It's like you used to be a race car driver, and now you can pop the hood and repair the engine too.

You can stop here if you like. The two implementations of Lox you have are complete and full featured. You built the car and can drive it wherever you want now. But if you are looking to have more fun tuning and tweaking for even greater performance out on the track, there is one more chapter. We don't add any new capabilities, but we roll in a couple of classic optimizations to squeeze even more perf out. If that sounds fun, keep reading…

## CHALLENGES

1. A tenet of object-oriented programming is that a class should ensure new objects are in a valid state. In Lox, that means defining an initializer that populates the instance's fields. Inheritance complicates invariants because the instance must be in a valid state according to all of the classes in the object's inheritance chain.

   The easy part is remembering to call `super.init()` in each subclass's `init()` method. The harder part is fields. There is nothing preventing two classes in the inheritance chain from accidentally claiming the same field name. When this happens, they will step on each other's fields and possibly leave you with an instance in a broken state.

   If Lox was your language, how would you address this, if at all? If you would change the language, implement your change.

2. Our copy-down inheritance optimization is valid only because Lox does not permit you to modify a class's methods after its declaration. This means we don't have to worry about the copied methods in the subclass getting out of sync with later changes to the superclass.

   Other languages, like Ruby, *do* allow classes to be modified after the fact. How do implementations of languages like that support class modification while keeping method resolution efficient?

3. In the jlox chapter on inheritance, we had a challenge to implement the BETA language's approach to method overriding. Solve the challenge again, but this time in clox. Here's the description of the previous challenge:

   In Lox, as in most other object-oriented languages, when looking up a method, we start at the bottom of the class hierarchy and work our way up—a subclass's method is preferred over a superclass's. In order to get to the superclass method from within an overriding method, you use `super`.

   The language BETA takes the opposite approach. When you call a method, it starts at the *top* of the class hierarchy and works *down*. A superclass method wins over a subclass method. In order to get to the subclass method, the superclass method can call `inner`, which is sort of like the inverse of `super`. It chains to the next method down the hierarchy.

The superclass method controls when and where the subclass is allowed to refine its behavior. If the superclass method doesn't call `inner` at all, then the subclass has no way of overriding or modifying the superclass's behavior.

Take out Lox's current overriding and `super` behavior, and replace it with BETA's semantics. In short:

- When calling a method on a class, the method *highest* on the class's inheritance chain takes precedence.

- Inside the body of a method, a call to `inner` looks for a method with the same name in the nearest subclass along the inheritance chain between the class containing the `inner` and the class of `this`. If there is no matching method, the `inner` call does nothing.

  For example:

```
class Doughnut {
  cook() {
    print "Fry until golden brown.";
    inner();
    print "Place in a nice box.";
  }
}

class BostonCream < Doughnut {
  cook() {
    print "Pipe full of custard and coat with chocolate.";
  }
}

BostonCream().cook();
```

This should print:

```
Fry until golden brown.
Pipe full of custard and coat with chocolate.
Place in a nice box.
```

Since clox is about not just implementing Lox, but doing so with good performance, this time around try to solve the challenge with an eye towards efficiency.

# Optimization

*"The evening's the best part of the day. You've done your day's work. Now you can put your feet up and enjoy it."*

— Kazuo Ishiguro, *The Remains of the Day*

If I still lived in New Orleans, I'd call this chapter a *lagniappe*, a little something extra given for free to a customer. You've got a whole book and a complete virtual machine already, but I want you to have some more fun hacking on clox. This time, we're going for pure performance. We'll apply two very different optimizations to our virtual machine. In the process, you'll get a feel for measuring and improving the performance of a language implementation—or any program, really.

# 30.1  Measuring Performance

**Optimization** means taking a working application and improving its performance. An optimized program does the same thing, it just takes less resources to do so. The resource we usually think of when optimizing is runtime speed, but it can also be important to reduce memory usage, startup time, persistent storage size, or network bandwidth. All physical resources have some cost—even if the cost is mostly in wasted human time—so optimization work often pays off.

There was a time in the early days of computing that a skilled programmer could hold the entire hardware architecture and compiler pipeline in their head and understand a program's performance just by thinking real hard. Those days are long gone, separated from the present by microcode, cache lines, branch prediction, deep compiler pipelines, and mammoth instruction sets. We like to pretend C is a "low-level" language, but the stack of technology between

```
printf("Hello, world!");
```

and a greeting appearing on screen is now perilously tall.

Optimization today is an empirical science. Our program is a border collie sprinting through the hardware's obstacle course. If we want her to reach the end faster, we can't just sit and ruminate on canine physiology until enlightenment strikes. Instead, we need to *observe* her performance, see where she stumbles, and then find faster paths for her to take.

Much like agility training is particular to one dog and one obstacle course, we can't assume that our virtual machine optimizations will make *all* Lox programs run faster on *all* hardware. Different Lox programs stress different areas of the VM, and different architectures have their own strengths and weaknesses.

## 30.1.1  Benchmarks

When we add new functionality, we validate correctness by writing tests—Lox programs that use a feature and validate the VM's behavior. Tests pin down semantics and ensure we don't break existing features when we add new ones. We have similar needs when it comes to performance:

1.  How do we validate that an optimization *does* improve performance, and by how much?

2.  How do we ensure that other unrelated changes don't *regress* performance?

The Lox programs we write to accomplish those goals are **benchmarks**. These are carefully crafted programs that stress some part of the language implementation. They measure not *what* the program does, but how *long* it takes to do it.

By measuring the performance of a benchmark before and after a change, you can see what your change does. When you land an optimization, all of the tests should behave exactly the same as they did before, but hopefully the benchmarks run faster.

Once you have an entire *suite* of benchmarks, you can measure not just *that* an optimization changes performance, but on which *kinds* of code. Often you'll find that some benchmarks get faster while others get slower. Then you have to make hard decisions about what kinds of code your language implementation

Most benchmarks measure running time. But, of course, you'll eventually find yourself needing to write benchmarks that measure memory allocation, how much time is spent in the garbage collector, startup time, etc.

optimizes for.

The suite of benchmarks you choose to write is a key part of that decision. In the same way that your tests encode your choices around what correct behavior looks like, your benchmarks are the embodiment of your priorities when it comes to performance. They will guide which optimizations you implement, so choose your benchmarks carefully, and don't forget to periodically reflect on whether they are helping you reach your larger goals.

Benchmarking is a subtle art. Like tests, you need to balance not overfitting to your implementation while ensuring that the benchmark does actually tickle the code paths that you care about. When you measure performance, you need to compensate for variance caused by CPU throttling, caching, and other weird hardware and operating system quirks. I won't give you a whole sermon here, but treat benchmarking as its own skill that improves with practice.

### 30.1.2 Profiling

OK, so you've got a few benchmarks now. You want to make them go faster. Now what? First of all, let's assume you've done all the obvious, easy work. You are using the right algorithms and data structures—or, at least, you aren't using ones that are aggressively wrong. I don't consider using a hash table instead of a linear search through a huge unsorted array "optimization" so much as "good software engineering".

Since the hardware is too complex to reason about our program's performance from first principles, we have to go out into the field. That means *profiling*. A **profiler**, if you've never used one, is a tool that runs your program and tracks hardware resource use as the code executes. Simple ones show you how much time was spent in each function in your program. Sophisticated ones log data cache misses, instruction cache misses, branch mispredictions, memory allocations, and all sorts of other metrics.

There are many profilers out there for various operating systems and languages. On whatever platform you program, it's worth getting familiar with a decent profiler. You don't need to be a master. I have learned things within minutes of throwing a program at a profiler that would have taken me *days* to discover on my own through trial and error. Profilers are wonderful, magical tools.

## 30.2 Faster Hash Table Probing

Enough pontificating, let's get some performance charts going up and to the right. The first optimization we'll do, it turns out, is about the *tiniest* possible change we could make to our VM.

When I first got the bytecode virtual machine that clox is descended from working, I did what any self-respecting VM hacker would do. I cobbled together a couple of benchmarks, fired up a profiler, and ran those scripts through my interpreter. In a dynamically typed language like Lox, a large fraction of user code is field accesses and method calls, so one of my benchmarks looked something like this:

In the early proliferation of JavaScript VMs, the first widely used benchmark suite was SunSpider from WebKit. During the browser wars, marketing folks used SunSpider results to claim their browser was fastest. That highly incentivized VM hackers to optimize to those benchmarks.

Unfortunately, SunSpider programs often didn't match real-world JavaScript. They were mostly microbenchmarks—tiny toy programs that completed quickly. Those benchmarks penalize complex just-in-time compilers that start off slower but get *much* faster once the JIT has had enough time to optimize and re-compile hot code paths. This put VM hackers in the unfortunate position of having to choose between making the SunSpider numbers get better, or actually optimizing the kinds of programs real users ran.

Google's V8 team responded by sharing their Octane benchmark suite, which was closer to real-world code at the time. Years later, as JavaScript use patterns continued to evolve, even Octane outlived its usefulness. Expect that your benchmarks will evolve as your language's ecosystem does.

Remember, the ultimate goal is to make *user programs* faster, and benchmarks are only a proxy for that.

"Your program" here means the Lox VM itself running some *other* Lox program. We are trying to optimize clox, not the user's Lox script. Of course, the choice of which Lox program to load into our VM will highly affect which parts of clox get stressed, which is why benchmarks are so important.

A profiler *won't* show us how much time is spent in each *Lox* function in the script being run. We'd have to write our own "Lox profiler" to do that, which is slightly out of scope for this book.

```
class Zoo {
  init() {
    this.aardvark = 1;
    this.baboon   = 1;
    this.cat      = 1;
    this.donkey   = 1;
    this.elephant = 1;
    this.fox      = 1;
  }
  ant()    { return this.aardvark; }
  banana() { return this.baboon; }
  tuna()   { return this.cat; }
  hay()    { return this.donkey; }
  grass()  { return this.elephant; }
  mouse()  { return this.fox; }
}

var zoo = Zoo();
var sum = 0;
var start = clock();
while (sum < 100000000) {
  sum = sum + zoo.ant()
            + zoo.banana()
            + zoo.tuna()
            + zoo.hay()
            + zoo.grass()
            + zoo.mouse();
}

print clock() - start;
print sum;
```

Another thing this benchmark is careful to do is *use* the result of the code it executes. By calculating a rolling sum and printing the result, we ensure the VM *must* execute all that Lox code. This is an important habit. Unlike our simple Lox VM, many compilers do aggressive dead code elimination and are smart enough to discard a computation whose result is never used.

Many a programming language hacker has been impressed by the blazing performance of a VM on some benchmark, only to realize that it's because the compiler optimized the entire benchmark program away to nothing.

If you really want to benchmark hash table performance, you should use many tables of different sizes. The six keys we add to each table here aren't even enough to get over our hash table's eight-element minimum threshold. But I didn't want to throw an enormous benchmark script at you. Feel free to add more critters and treats if you like.

If you've never seen a benchmark before, this might seem ludicrous. *What* is going on here? The program itself doesn't intend to do anything useful. What it does do is call a bunch of methods and access a bunch of fields since those are the parts of the language we're interested in. Fields and methods live in hash tables, so it takes care to populate at least a *few* interesting keys in those tables. That is all wrapped in a big loop to ensure our profiler has enough execution time to dig in and see where the cycles are going.

Before I tell you what my profiler showed me, spend a minute taking a few guesses. Where in clox's codebase do you think the VM spent most of its time? Is there any code we've written in previous chapters that you suspect is particularly slow?

Here's what I found: Naturally, the function with the greatest inclusive time is run(). (**Inclusive time** means the total time spent in some function and all other functions it calls—the total time between when you enter the function and when it returns.) Since run() is the main bytecode execution loop, it drives everything.

Inside run(), there are small chunks of time sprinkled in various cases in the bytecode switch for common instructions like OP_POP, OP_RETURN, and OP_ADD. The big heavy instructions are OP_GET_GLOBAL with 17% of the execution time, OP_GET_PROPERTY at 12%, and OP_INVOKE which takes a whopping

42% of the total running time.

So we've got three hotspots to optimize? Actually, no. Because it turns out those three instructions spend almost all of their time inside calls to the same function: `tableGet()`. That function claims a whole 72% of the execution time (again, inclusive). Now, in a dynamically typed language, we expect to spend a fair bit of time looking stuff up in hash tables—it's sort of the price of dynamism. But, still, *wow*.

### 30.2.1  Slow key wrapping

If you take a look at `tableGet()`, you'll see it's mostly a wrapper around a call to `findEntry()` where the actual hash table lookup happens. To refresh your memory, here it is in full:

```
static Entry* findEntry(Entry* entries, int capacity,
                        ObjString* key) {
  uint32_t index = key->hash % capacity;
  Entry* tombstone = NULL;

  for (;;) {
    Entry* entry = &entries[index];
    if (entry->key == NULL) {
      if (IS_NIL(entry->value)) {
        // Empty entry.
        return tombstone != NULL ? tombstone : entry;
      } else {
        // We found a tombstone.
        if (tombstone == NULL) tombstone = entry;
      }
    } else if (entry->key == key) {
      // We found the key.
      return entry;
    }

    index = (index + 1) % capacity;
  }
}
```

When running that previous benchmark—on my machine, at least—the VM spends 70% of the total execution time on *one line* in this function. Any guesses as to which one? No? It's this:

```
  uint32_t index = key->hash % capacity;
```

That pointer dereference isn't the problem. It's the little %. It turns out the modulo operator is *really* slow. Much slower than other arithmetic operators. Can we do something better?

In the general case, it's really hard to re-implement a fundamental arithmetic operator in user code in a way that's faster than what the CPU itself can do. After all, our C code ultimately compiles down to the CPU's own arithmetic operations. If there were tricks we could use to go faster, the chip would be using them.

Pipelining makes it hard to talk about the performance of an individual CPU instruction, but to give you a feel for things, division and modulo are about 30-50 *times* slower than addition and subtraction on x86.

However, we can take advantage of the fact that we know more about our problem than the CPU does. We use modulo here to take a key string's hash code and wrap it to fit within the bounds of the table's entry array. That array starts out at eight elements and grows by a factor of two each time. We know—and the CPU and C compiler do not—that our table's size is always a power of two.

Because we're clever bit twiddlers, we know a faster way to calculate the remainder of a number modulo a power of two: **bit masking**. Let's say we want to calculate 229 modulo 64. The answer is 37, which is not particularly apparent in decimal, but is clearer when you view those numbers in binary:

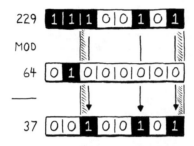 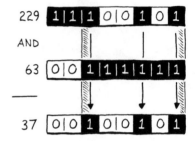

On the left side of the illustration, notice how the result (37) is simply the dividend (229) with the highest two bits shaved off? Those two highest bits are the bits at or to the left of the divisor's single 1 bit.

On the right side, we get the same result by taking 229 and bitwise AND-ing it with 63, which is one less than our original power of two divisor. Subtracting one from a power of two gives you a series of 1 bits. That is exactly the mask we need in order to strip out those two leftmost bits.

In other words, you can calculate a number modulo any power of two by simply AND-ing it with that power of two minus one. I'm not enough of a mathematician to *prove* to you that this works, but if you think it through, it should make sense. We can replace that slow modulo operator with a very fast decrement and bitwise AND. We simply change the offending line of code to this:

**table.c**
*in* `findEntry()`
*replace 1 line*

```
static Entry* findEntry(Entry* entries, int capacity,
                        ObjString* key) {
  uint32_t index = key->hash & (capacity - 1);
  Entry* tombstone = NULL;
```

CPUs love bitwise operators, so it's hard to improve on that.

Our linear probing search may need to wrap around the end of the array, so there is another modulo in `findEntry()` to update.

**table.c**
*in* `findEntry()`
*replace 1 line*

```
    // We found the key.
    return entry;
  }

  index = (index + 1) & (capacity - 1);
}
```

This line didn't show up in the profiler since most searches don't wrap.

The `findEntry()` function has a sister function, `tableFindString()` that does a hash table lookup for interning strings. We may as well apply the same optimizations there too. This function is called only when interning strings, which

Another potential improvement is to eliminate the decrement by storing the bit mask directly instead of the capacity. In my tests, that didn't make a difference. Instruction pipelining makes some operations essentially free if the CPU is bottlenecked elsewhere.

wasn't heavily stressed by our benchmark. But a Lox program that created lots
of strings might noticeably benefit from this change.

```
if (table->count == 0) return NULL;

uint32_t index = hash & (table->capacity - 1);
for (;;) {
  Entry* entry = &table->entries[index];
```

table.c
*in* tableFindString()
*replace 1 line*

And also when the linear probing wraps around.

```
    return entry->key;
  }

  index = (index + 1) & (table->capacity - 1);
}
```

table.c
*in* tableFindString()
*replace 1 line*

Let's see if our fixes were worth it. I tweaked that zoological benchmark to count
how many batches of 10,000 calls it can run in ten seconds. More batches equals
faster performance. On my machine using the unoptimized code, the benchmark gets through 3,192 batches. After this optimization, that jumps to 6,249.

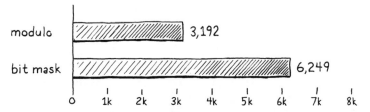

That's almost exactly twice as much work in the same amount of time. We made
the VM twice as fast (usual caveat: on this benchmark). That is a massive win
when it comes to optimization. Usually you feel good if you can claw a few per-
centage points here or there. Since methods, fields, and global variables are so
prevalent in Lox programs, this tiny optimization improves performance across
the board. Almost every Lox program benefits.

Now, the point of this section is *not* that the modulo operator is profoundly
evil and you should stamp it out of every program you ever write. Nor is it that
micro-optimization is a vital engineering skill. It's rare that a performance problem has such a narrow, effective solution. We got lucky.

The point is that we didn't *know* that the modulo operator was a performance
drain until our profiler told us so. If we had wandered around our VM's codebase
blindly guessing at hotspots, we likely wouldn't have noticed it. What I want you
to take away from this is how important it is to have a profiler in your toolbox.

To reinforce that point, let's go ahead and run the original benchmark in
our now-optimized VM and see what the profiler shows us. On my machine,
`tableGet()` is still a fairly large chunk of execution time. That's to be expected
for a dynamically typed language. But it has dropped from 72% of the total execution time down to 35%. That's much more in line with what we'd like to see
and shows that our optimization didn't just make the program faster, but made
it faster *in the way we expected*. Profilers are as useful for verifying solutions as
they are for discovering problems.

Our original benchmark fixed the amount
of *work* and then measured the *time*.
Changing the script to count how many
batches of calls it can do in ten seconds
fixes the time and measures the work.
For performance comparisons, I like the
latter measure because the reported
number represents *speed*. You can directly
compare the numbers before and after an
optimization. When measuring execution
time, you have to do a little arithmetic
to get to a good relative measure of
performance.

## 30.3  NaN Boxing

This next optimization has a very different feel. Thankfully, despite the odd name, it does not involve punching your grandmother. It's different, but not, like, *that* different. With our previous optimization, the profiler told us where the problem was, and we merely had to use some ingenuity to come up with a solution.

This optimization is more subtle, and its performance effects more scattered across the virtual machine. The profiler won't help us come up with this. Instead, it was invented by someone thinking deeply about the lowest levels of machine architecture.

I'm not sure who first came up with this trick. The earliest source I can find is David Gudeman's 1993 paper "Representing Type Information in Dynamically Typed Languages". Everyone else cites that. But Gudeman himself says the paper isn't novel work, but instead "gathers together a body of folklore".

Maybe the inventor has been lost to the mists of time, or maybe it's been reinvented a number of times. Anyone who ruminates on IEEE 754 long enough probably starts thinking about trying to stuff something useful into all those unused NaN bits.

Like the heading says, this optimization is called **NaN boxing** or sometimes **NaN tagging**. Personally I like the latter name because "boxing" tends to imply some kind of heap-allocated representation, but the former seems to be the more widely used term. This technique changes how we represent values in the VM.

On a 64-bit machine, our Value type takes up 16 bytes. The struct has two fields, a type tag and a union for the payload. The largest fields in the union are an Obj pointer and a double, which are both 8 bytes. To keep the union field aligned to an 8-byte boundary, the compiler adds padding after the tag too:

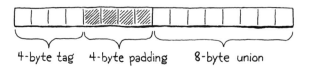

That's pretty big. If we could cut that down, then the VM could pack more values into the same amount of memory. Most computers have plenty of RAM these days, so the direct memory savings aren't a huge deal. But a smaller representation means more Values fit in a cache line. That means fewer cache misses, which affects *speed*.

If Values need to be aligned to their largest payload size, and a Lox number or Obj pointer needs a full 8 bytes, how can we get any smaller? In a dynamically typed language like Lox, each value needs to carry not just its payload, but enough additional information to determine the value's type at runtime. If a Lox number is already using the full 8 bytes, where could we squirrel away a couple of extra bits to tell the runtime "this is a number"?

This is one of the perennial problems for dynamic language hackers. It particularly bugs them because statically typed languages don't generally have this problem. The type of each value is known at compile time, so no extra memory is needed at runtime to track it. When your C compiler compiles a 32-bit int, the resulting variable gets *exactly* 32 bits of storage.

Dynamic language folks hate losing ground to the static camp, so they've come up with a number of very clever ways to pack type information and a payload into a small number of bits. NaN boxing is one of those. It's a particularly good fit for languages like JavaScript and Lua, where all numbers are double-precision floating point. Lox is in that same boat.

### 30.3.1  What is (and is not) a number?

Before we start optimizing, we need to really understand how our friend the CPU represents floating-point numbers. Almost all machines today use the same scheme, encoded in the venerable scroll IEEE 754, known to mortals as the "IEEE Standard for Floating-Point Arithmetic".

In the eyes of your computer, a 64-bit, double-precision, IEEE floating-point number looks like this:

That's a lot of hyphens for one sentence.

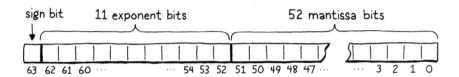

- Starting from the right, the first 52 bits are the **fraction**, **mantissa**, or **significand** bits. They represent the significant digits of the number, as a binary integer.

- Next to that are 11 **exponent** bits. These tell you how far the mantissa is shifted away from the decimal (well, binary) point.

- The highest bit is the **sign bit**, which indicates whether the number is positive or negative.

Since the sign bit is always present, even if the number is zero, that implies that "positive zero" and "negative zero" have different bit representations, and indeed, IEEE 754 does distinguish those.

I know that's a little vague, but this chapter isn't a deep dive on floating point representation. If you want to know how the exponent and mantissa play together, there are already better explanations out there than I could write.

The important part for our purposes is that the spec carves out a special case exponent. When all of the exponent bits are set, then instead of just representing a really big number, the value has a different meaning. These values are "Not a Number" (hence, **NaN**) values. They represent concepts like infinity or the result of division by zero.

*Any* double whose exponent bits are all set is a NaN, regardless of the mantissa bits. That means there's lots and lots of *different* NaN bit patterns. IEEE 754 divides those into two categories. Values where the highest mantissa bit is 0 are called **signalling NaNs**, and the others are **quiet NaNs**. Signalling NaNs are intended to be the result of erroneous computations, like division by zero. A chip may detect when one of these values is produced and abort a program completely. They may self-destruct if you try to read one.

I don't know if any CPUs actually *do* trap signalling NaNs and abort. The spec just says they *could*.

Quiet NaNs are supposed to be safer to use. They don't represent useful numeric values, but they should at least not set your hand on fire if you touch them.

Every double with all of its exponent bits set and its highest mantissa bit set is a quiet NaN. That leaves 52 bits unaccounted for. We'll avoid one of those so that we don't step on Intel's "QNaN Floating-Point Indefinite" value, leaving us 51 bits. Those remaining bits can be anything. We're talking 2,251,799,813,685,248 unique quiet NaN bit patterns.

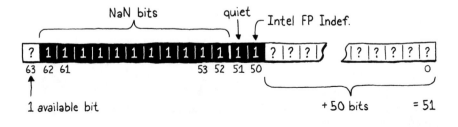

This means a 64-bit double has enough room to store all of the various different numeric floating-point values and *also* has room for another 51 bits of data that we can use however we want. That's plenty of room to set aside a couple of bit patterns to represent Lox's `nil`, `true`, and `false` values. But what about Obj pointers? Don't pointers need a full 64 bits too?

Fortunately, we have another trick up our other sleeve. Yes, technically pointers on a 64-bit architecture are 64 bits. But, no architecture I know of actually uses that entire address space. Instead, most widely used chips today only ever use the low 48 bits. The remaining 16 bits are either unspecified or always zero.

If we've got 51 bits, we can stuff a 48-bit pointer in there with three bits to spare. Those three bits are just enough to store tiny type tags to distinguish between `nil`, Booleans, and Obj pointers.

That's NaN boxing. Within a single 64-bit double, you can store all of the different floating-point numeric values, a pointer, or any of a couple of other special sentinel values. Half the memory usage of our current Value struct, while retaining all of the fidelity.

What's particularly nice about this representation is that there is no need to *convert* a numeric double value into a "boxed" form. Lox numbers *are* just normal, 64-bit doubles. We still need to *check* their type before we use them, since Lox is dynamically typed, but we don't need to do any bit shifting or pointer indirection to go from "value" to "number".

For the other value types, there is a conversion step, of course. But, fortunately, our VM hides all of the mechanism to go from values to raw types behind a handful of macros. Rewrite those to implement NaN boxing, and the rest of the VM should just work.

> 48 bits is enough to address 262,144 gigabytes of memory. Modern operating systems also give each process its own address space, so that should be plenty.

## 30.3.2  Conditional support

I know the details of this new representation aren't clear in your head yet. Don't worry, they will crystallize as we work through the implementation. Before we get to that, we're going to put some compile-time scaffolding in place.

For our previous optimization, we rewrote the previous slow code and called it done. This one is a little different. NaN boxing relies on some very low-level details of how a chip represents floating-point numbers and pointers. It *probably* works on most CPUs you're likely to encounter, but you can never be totally sure.

It would suck if our VM completely lost support for an architecture just because of its value representation. To avoid that, we'll maintain support for *both* the old tagged union implementation of Value and the new NaN-boxed form. We select which representation we want at compile time using this flag:

common.h

```
#include <stdint.h>

#define NAN_BOXING
#define DEBUG_PRINT_CODE
```

If that's defined, the VM uses the new form. Otherwise, it reverts to the old style. The few pieces of code that care about the details of the value representation—mainly the handful of macros for wrapping and unwrapping Values—vary based on whether this flag is set. The rest of the VM can continue along its merry way.

Most of the work happens in the "value" module where we add a section for the new type.

```
typedef struct ObjString ObjString;

#ifdef NAN_BOXING

typedef uint64_t Value;

#else

typedef enum {
```

value.h

When NaN boxing is enabled, the actual type of a Value is a flat, unsigned 64-bit integer. We could use double instead, which would make the macros for dealing with Lox numbers a little simpler. But all of the other macros need to do bitwise operations and uint64_t is a much friendlier type for that. Outside of this module, the rest of the VM doesn't really care one way or the other.

Before we start re-implementing those macros, we close the #else branch of the #ifdef at the end of the definitions for the old representation.

```
#define OBJ_VAL(object)   ((Value){VAL_OBJ, {.obj = (Obj*)object}})

#endif

typedef struct {
```

value.h

Our remaining task is simply to fill in that first #ifdef section with new implementations of all the stuff already in the #else side. We'll work through it one value type at a time, from easiest to hardest.

### 30.3.3  Numbers

We'll start with numbers since they're easiest. To "convert" a C double to a NaN-boxed clox Value, we don't need to touch a single bit—the representation is exactly the same. But we do need to convince our C compiler of that fact, which we made harder by defining Value to be uint64_t.

We need to get the compiler to take a set of bits that it thinks are a double and use those same bits as a uint64_t, or vice versa. This is called **type punning**. C and C++ programmers have been doing this since the days of bell bottoms and 8-tracks, but the language specifications have hesitated to say which of the many ways to do this is officially sanctioned.

I know one way to convert a double to Value and back that I believe is supported by both the C and C++ specs. Unfortunately, it doesn't fit in a single expression, so the conversion macros have to call out to helper functions. Here's the first macro:

```
typedef uint64_t Value;

#define NUMBER_VAL(num)  numToValue(num)

#else
```

value.h

That macro passes the double here:

Spec authors don't like type punning because it makes optimization harder. A key optimization technique is reordering instructions to fill the CPU's execution pipelines. A compiler can reorder code only when doing so doesn't have a user-visible effect, obviously.

Pointers make that harder. If two pointers point to the same value, then a write through one and a read through the other cannot be reordered. But what about two pointers of *different* types? If those could point to the same object, then basically *any* two pointers could be aliases to the same value. That drastically limits the amount of code the compiler is free to rearrange.

To avoid that, compilers want to assume **strict aliasing**—pointers of incompatible types cannot point to the same value. Type punning, by nature, breaks that assumption.

<table>
<tr><td>value.h</td><td>

```
#define NUMBER_VAL(num) numToValue(num)

static inline Value numToValue(double num) {
  Value value;
  memcpy(&value, &num, sizeof(double));
  return value;
}

#else
```

</td></tr>
</table>

I know, weird, right? The way to treat a series of bytes as having a different type without changing their value at all is memcpy()? This looks horrendously slow: Create a local variable. Pass its address to the operating system through a syscall to copy a few bytes. Then return the result, which is the exact same bytes as the input. Thankfully, because this *is* the supported idiom for type punning, most compilers recognize the pattern and optimize away the memcpy() entirely.

"Unwrapping" a Lox number is the mirror image.

<table>
<tr><td>value.h</td><td>

```
typedef uint64_t Value;

#define AS_NUMBER(value)     valueToNum(value)

#define NUMBER_VAL(num) numToValue(num)
```

</td></tr>
</table>

That macro calls this function:

<table>
<tr><td>value.h</td><td>

```
#define NUMBER_VAL(num) numToValue(num)

static inline double valueToNum(Value value) {
  double num;
  memcpy(&num, &value, sizeof(Value));
  return num;
}

static inline Value numToValue(double num) {
```

</td></tr>
</table>

It works exactly the same except we swap the types. Again, the compiler will eliminate all of it. Even though those calls to memcpy() will disappear, we still need to show the compiler *which* memcpy() we're calling so we also need an include.

If you find yourself with a compiler that does not optimize the **memcpy()** away, try this instead:

```
double valueToNum(
    Value value) {
  union {
    uint64_t bits;
    double num;
  } data;
  data.bits = value;
  return data.num;
}
```

<table>
<tr><td>value.h</td><td>

```
#define clox_value_h

#include <string.h>

#include "common.h"
```

</td></tr>
</table>

That was a lot of code to ultimately do nothing but silence the C type checker. Doing a runtime type *test* on a Lox number is a little more interesting. If all we have are exactly the bits for a double, how do we tell that it *is* a double? It's time to get bit twiddling.

```
typedef uint64_t Value;

#define IS_NUMBER(value)     (((value) & QNAN) != QNAN)

#define AS_NUMBER(value)     valueToNum(value)
```
value.h

We know that every Value that is *not* a number will use a special quiet NaN representation. And we presume we have correctly avoided any of the meaningful NaN representations that may actually be produced by doing arithmetic on numbers.

If the double has all of its NaN bits set, and the quiet NaN bit set, and one more for good measure, we can be pretty certain it is one of the bit patterns we ourselves have set aside for other types. To check that, we mask out all of the bits except for our set of quiet NaN bits. If *all* of those bits are set, it must be a NaN-boxed value of some other Lox type. Otherwise, it is actually a number.

The set of quiet NaN bits are declared like this:

Pretty certain, but not strictly guaranteed. As far as I know, there is nothing preventing a CPU from producing a NaN value as the result of some operation whose bit representation collides with ones we have claimed. But in my tests across a number of architectures, I haven't seen it happen.

```
#ifdef NAN_BOXING

#define QNAN      ((uint64_t)0x7ffc000000000000)

typedef uint64_t Value;
```
value.h

It would be nice if C supported binary literals. But if you do the conversion, you'll see that value is the same as this:
This is exactly all of the exponent bits, plus the quiet NaN bit, plus one extra to dodge that Intel value.

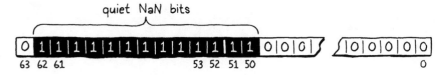

### 30.3.4 Nil, true, and false

The next type to handle is nil. That's pretty simple since there's only one nil value and thus we need only a single bit pattern to represent it. There are two other singleton values, the two Booleans, true and false. This calls for three total unique bit patterns.

Two bits give us four different combinations, which is plenty. We claim the two lowest bits of our unused mantissa space as a "type tag" to determine which of these three singleton values we're looking at. The three type tags are defined like so:

```
#define QNAN      ((uint64_t)0x7ffc000000000000)

#define TAG_NIL   1 // 01.
#define TAG_FALSE 2 // 10.
#define TAG_TRUE  3 // 11.

typedef uint64_t Value;
```
value.h

Our representation of nil is thus all of the bits required to define our quiet NaN representation along with the nil type tag bits:

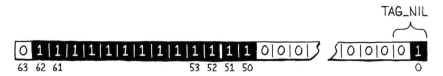

In code, we check the bits like so:

value.h

```
#define AS_NUMBER(value)     valueToNum(value)

#define NIL_VAL            ((Value)(uint64_t)(QNAN | TAG_NIL))
#define NUMBER_VAL(num) numToValue(num)
```

We simply bitwise OR the quiet NaN bits and the type tag, and then do a little cast dance to teach the C compiler what we want those bits to mean.

Since nil has only a single bit representation, we can use equality on uint64_t to see if a Value is nil.

value.h

```
typedef uint64_t Value;

#define IS_NIL(value)          ((value) == NIL_VAL)
#define IS_NUMBER(value)     (((value) & QNAN) != QNAN)
```

You can guess how we define the true and false values.

value.h

```
#define AS_NUMBER(value)     valueToNum(value)

#define FALSE_VAL          ((Value)(uint64_t)(QNAN | TAG_FALSE))
#define TRUE_VAL           ((Value)(uint64_t)(QNAN | TAG_TRUE))
#define NIL_VAL            ((Value)(uint64_t)(QNAN | TAG_NIL))
```

The bits look like this:

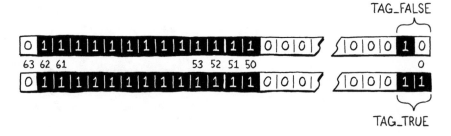

To convert a C bool into a Lox Boolean, we rely on these two singleton values and the good old conditional operator.

value.h

```
#define AS_NUMBER(value)     valueToNum(value)

#define BOOL_VAL(b)        ((b) ? TRUE_VAL : FALSE_VAL)
#define FALSE_VAL          ((Value)(uint64_t)(QNAN | TAG_FALSE))
```

There's probably a cleverer bitwise way to do this, but my hunch is that the compiler can figure one out faster than I can. Going the other direction is simpler.

```
#define IS_NUMBER(value)    (((value) & QNAN) != QNAN)

#define AS_BOOL(value)      ((value) == TRUE_VAL)
#define AS_NUMBER(value)    valueToNum(value)
```
value.h

Since we know there are exactly two Boolean bit representations in Lox—unlike in C where any non-zero value can be considered "true"—if it ain't `true`, it must be `false`. This macro does assume you call it only on a Value that you know is a Lox Boolean. To check that, there's one more macro.

```
typedef uint64_t Value;

#define IS_BOOL(value)      (((value) | 1) == TRUE_VAL)
#define IS_NIL(value)       ((value) == NIL_VAL)
```
value.h

That looks a little strange. A more obvious macro would look like this:

```
#define IS_BOOL(v) ((v) == TRUE_VAL || (v) == FALSE_VAL)
```

Unfortunately, that's not safe. The expansion mentions v twice, which means if that expression has any side effects, they will be executed twice. We could have the macro call out to a separate function, but, ugh, what a chore.

Instead, we bitwise OR a 1 onto the value to merge the only two valid Boolean bit patterns. That leaves three potential states the value can be in:

1. It was FALSE_VAL and has now been converted to TRUE_VAL.

2. It was TRUE_VAL and the | 1 did nothing and it's still TRUE_VAL.

3. It's some other, non-Boolean value.

At that point, we can simply compare the result to TRUE_VAL to see if we're in the first two states or the third.

## 30.3.5 Objects

The last value type is the hardest. Unlike the singleton values, there are billions of different pointer values we need to box inside a NaN. This means we need both some kind of tag to indicate that these particular NaNs *are* Obj pointers, and room for the addresses themselves.

The tag bits we used for the singleton values are in the region where I decided to store the pointer itself, so we can't easily use a different bit there to indicate that the value is an object reference. However, there is another bit we aren't using. Since all our NaN values are not numbers—it's right there in the name—the sign bit isn't used for anything. We'll go ahead and use that as the type tag for objects. If one of our quiet NaNs has its sign bit set, then it's an Obj pointer. Otherwise, it must be one of the previous singleton values.

We actually *could* use the lowest bits to store the type tag even when the value is an Obj pointer. That's because Obj pointers are always aligned to an 8-byte boundary since Obj contains a 64-bit field. That, in turn, implies that the three lowest bits of an Obj pointer will always be zero. We could store whatever we wanted in there and just mask it off before dereferencing the pointer.

This is another value representation optimization called **pointer tagging**.

If the sign bit is set, then the remaining low bits store the pointer to the Obj:

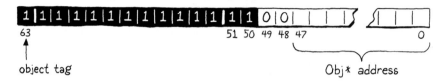

To convert a raw Obj pointer to a Value, we take the pointer and set all of the quiet NaN bits and the sign bit.

value.h

```
#define NUMBER_VAL(num)  numToValue(num)
#define OBJ_VAL(obj) \
    (Value)(SIGN_BIT | QNAN | (uint64_t)(uintptr_t)(obj))

static inline double valueToNum(Value value) {
```

The pointer itself is a full 64 bits, and in principle, it could thus overlap with some of those quiet NaN and sign bits. But in practice, at least on the architectures I've tested, everything above the 48th bit in a pointer is always zero. There's a lot of casting going on here, which I've found is necessary to satisfy some of the pickiest C compilers, but the end result is just jamming some bits together.

We define the sign bit like so:

value.h

```
#ifdef NAN_BOXING

#define SIGN_BIT ((uint64_t)0x8000000000000000)
#define QNAN     ((uint64_t)0x7ffc000000000000)
```

To get the Obj pointer back out, we simply mask off all of those extra bits.

value.h

```
#define AS_NUMBER(value)    valueToNum(value)
#define AS_OBJ(value) \
    ((Obj*)(uintptr_t)((value) & ~(SIGN_BIT | QNAN)))

#define BOOL_VAL(b)    ((b) ? TRUE_VAL : FALSE_VAL)
```

The tilde (~), if you haven't done enough bit manipulation to encounter it before, is bitwise NOT. It toggles all ones and zeroes in its operand. By masking the value with the bitwise negation of the quiet NaN and sign bits, we *clear* those bits and let the pointer bits remain.

One last macro:

value.h

```
#define IS_NUMBER(value)    (((value) & QNAN) != QNAN)
#define IS_OBJ(value) \
    (((value) & (QNAN | SIGN_BIT)) == (QNAN | SIGN_BIT))

#define AS_BOOL(value)    ((value) == TRUE_VAL)
```

A Value storing an Obj pointer has its sign bit set, but so does any negative number. To tell if a Value is an Obj pointer, we need to check that both the sign bit and

I try to follow the letter of the law when it comes to the code in this book, so this paragraph is dubious. There comes a point when optimizing where you push the boundary of not just what the *spec says* you can do, but what a real compiler and chip let you get away with.

There are risks when stepping outside of the spec, but there are rewards in that lawless territory too. It's up to you to decide if the gains are worth it.

all of the quiet NaN bits are set. This is similar to how we detect the type of the singleton values, except this time we use the sign bit as the tag.

### 30.3.6 Value functions

The rest of the VM usually goes through the macros when working with Values, so we are almost done. However, there are a couple of functions in the "value" module that peek inside the otherwise black box of Value and work with its encoding directly. We need to fix those too.

The first is `printValue()`. It has separate code for each value type. We no longer have an explicit type enum we can switch on, so instead we use a series of type tests to handle each kind of value.

```c
void printValue(Value value) {
#ifdef NAN_BOXING
  if (IS_BOOL(value)) {
    printf(AS_BOOL(value) ? "true" : "false");
  } else if (IS_NIL(value)) {
    printf("nil");
  } else if (IS_NUMBER(value)) {
    printf("%g", AS_NUMBER(value));
  } else if (IS_OBJ(value)) {
    printObject(value);
  }
#else
  switch (value.type) {
```

value.c<br>in printValue()

This is technically a tiny bit slower than a switch, but compared to the overhead of actually writing to a stream, it's negligible.

We still support the original tagged union representation, so we keep the old code and enclose it in the `#else` conditional section.

```c
  }
#endif
}
```

value.c<br>in printValue()

The other operation is testing two values for equality.

```c
bool valuesEqual(Value a, Value b) {
#ifdef NAN_BOXING
  return a == b;
#else
  if (a.type != b.type) return false;
```

value.c<br>in valuesEqual()

It doesn't get much simpler than that! If the two bit representations are identical, the values are equal. That does the right thing for the singleton values since each has a unique bit representation and they are only equal to themselves. It also does the right thing for Obj pointers, since objects use identity for equality—two Obj references are equal only if they point to the exact same object.

It's *mostly* correct for numbers too. Most floating-point numbers with different bit representations are distinct numeric values. Alas, IEEE 754 contains a pothole to trip us up. For reasons that aren't entirely clear to me, the spec mandates that NaN values are *not* equal to *themselves*. This isn't a problem for the special quiet NaNs that we are using for our own purposes. But it's possible to produce a "real" arithmetic NaN in Lox, and if we want to correctly implement IEEE 754 numbers, then the resulting value is not supposed to be equal to itself. More concretely:

```
var nan = 0/0;
print nan == nan;
```

IEEE 754 says this program is supposed to print "false". It does the right thing with our old tagged union representation because the VAL_NUMBER case applies == to two values that the C compiler knows are doubles. Thus the compiler generates the right CPU instruction to perform an IEEE floating-point equality.

Our new representation breaks that by defining Value to be a uint64_t. If we want to be *fully* compliant with IEEE 754, we need to handle this case.

value.c<br>*in* valuesEqual()

```
#ifdef NAN_BOXING
  if (IS_NUMBER(a) && IS_NUMBER(b)) {
    return AS_NUMBER(a) == AS_NUMBER(b);
  }
  return a == b;
```

I know, it's weird. And there is a performance cost to doing this type test every time we check two Lox values for equality. If we are willing to sacrifice a little compatibility—who *really* cares if NaN is not equal to itself?—we could leave this off. I'll leave it up to you to decide how pedantic you want to be.

In fact, jlox gets NaN equality wrong. Java does the right thing when you compare primitive doubles using ==, but not if you box those to Double or Object and compare them using **equals()**, which is how jlox implements equality.

Finally, we close the conditional compilation section around the old implementation.

value.c<br>*in* valuesEqual()

```
  }
#endif
}
```

And that's it. This optimization is complete, as is our clox virtual machine. That was the last line of new code in the book.

### 30.3.7  Evaluating performance

The code is done, but we still need to figure out if we actually made anything better with these changes. Evaluating an optimization like this is very different from the previous one. There, we had a clear hotspot visible in the profiler. We fixed that part of the code and could instantly see the hotspot get faster.

The effects of changing the value representation are more diffused. The macros are expanded in place wherever they are used, so the performance changes are spread across the codebase in a way that's hard for many profilers to track well, especially in an optimized build.

When doing profiling work, you almost always want to profile an optimized "release" build of your program since that reflects the performance story your end users experience. Compiler optimizations, like inlining, can dramatically affect which parts of the code are performance hotspots. Hand-optimizing a debug build risks sending you off "fixing" problems that the optimizing compiler will already solve for you.

Make sure you don't accidentally benchmark and optimize your debug build. I seem to make that mistake at least once a year.

We also can't easily *reason* about the effects of our change. We've made values smaller, which reduces cache misses all across the VM. But the actual real-world performance effect of that change is highly dependent on the memory use of the Lox program being run. A tiny Lox microbenchmark may not have enough values scattered around in memory for the effect to be noticeable, and even things like the addresses handed out to us by the C memory allocator can impact the results.

If we did our job right, basically everything gets a little faster, especially on larger, more complex Lox programs. But it is possible that the extra bitwise operations we do when NaN-boxing values nullify the gains from the better memory use. Doing performance work like this is unnerving because you can't easily *prove* that you've made the VM better. You can't point to a single surgically targeted microbenchmark and say, "There, see?"

Instead, what we really need is a *suite* of larger benchmarks. Ideally, they would be distilled from real-world applications—not that such a thing exists for a toy language like Lox. Then we can measure the aggregate performance changes across all of those. I did my best to cobble together a handful of larger Lox programs. On my machine, the new value representation seems to make everything roughly 10% faster across the board.

That's not a huge improvement, especially compared to the profound effect of making hash table lookups faster. I added this optimization in large part because it's a good example of a certain *kind* of performance work you may experience, and honestly, because I think it's technically really cool. It might not be the first thing I would reach for if I were seriously trying to make clox faster. There is probably other, lower-hanging fruit.

But, if you find yourself working on a program where all of the easy wins have been taken, then at some point you may want to think about tuning your value representation. I hope this chapter has shined a light on some of the options you have in that area.

## 30.4  Where to Next

We'll stop here with the Lox language and our two interpreters. We could tinker on it forever, adding new language features and clever speed improvements. But, for this book, I think we've reached a natural place to call our work complete. I won't rehash everything we've learned in the past many pages. You were there with me and you remember. Instead, I'd like to take a minute to talk about where you might go from here. What is the next step in your programming language journey?

Most of you probably won't spend a significant part of your career working in compilers or interpreters. It's a pretty small slice of the computer science academia pie, and an even smaller segment of software engineering in industry. That's OK. Even if you never work on a compiler again in your life, you will certainly *use* one, and I hope this book has equipped you with a better understanding of how the programming languages you use are designed and implemented.

You have also learned a handful of important, fundamental data structures and gotten some practice doing low-level profiling and optimization work. That kind of expertise is helpful no matter what domain you program in.

I also hope I gave you a new way of looking at and solving problems. Even if you never work on a language again, you may be surprised to discover how many programming problems can be seen as language-*like*. Maybe that report generator you need to write can be modeled as a series of stack-based "instructions" that the generator "executes". That user interface you need to render looks an awful lot like traversing an AST.

This goes for other domains too. I don't think there's a single topic I've learned in programming—or even outside of programming—that I haven't ended up finding useful in other areas. One of my favorite aspects of software engineering is how much it rewards those with eclectic interests.

If you do want to go further down the programming language rabbit hole, here are some suggestions for which branches in the tunnel to explore:

I like Cooper and Torczon's *Engineering a Compiler* for this. Appel's *Modern Compiler Implementation* books are also well regarded.

- Our simple, single-pass bytecode compiler pushed us towards mostly runtime optimization. In a mature language implementation, compile-time optimization is generally more important, and the field of compiler optimizations is incredibly rich. Grab a classic compilers book, and rebuild the front end of clox or jlox to be a sophisticated compilation pipeline with some interesting intermediate representations and optimization passes.

  Dynamic typing will place some restrictions on how far you can go, but there is still a lot you can do. Or maybe you want to take a big leap and add static types and a type checker to Lox. That will certainly give your front end a lot more to chew on.

- In this book, I aim to be correct, but not particularly rigorous. My goal is mostly to give you an *intuition* and a feel for doing language work. If you like more precision, then the whole world of programming language academia is waiting for you. Languages and compilers have been studied formally since before we even had computers, so there is no shortage of books and papers on parser theory, type systems, semantics, and formal logic. Going down this path will also teach you how to read CS papers, which is a valuable skill in its own right.

- Or, if you just really enjoy hacking on and making languages, you can take Lox and turn it into your own plaything. Change the syntax to something that delights your eye. Add missing features or remove ones you don't like. Jam new optimizations in there.

  Eventually you may get to a point where you have something you think others could use as well. That gets you into the very distinct world of programming language *popularity*. Expect to spend a ton of time writing documentation, example programs, tools, and useful libraries. The field is crowded with languages vying for users. To thrive in that space you'll have to put on your marketing hat and *sell*. Not everyone enjoys that kind of public-facing work, but if you do, it can be incredibly gratifying to see people use your language to express themselves.

Or maybe this book has satisfied your craving and you'll stop here. Whichever way you go, or don't go, there is one lesson I hope to lodge in your heart. Like I was, you may have initially been intimidated by programming languages. But in these chapters, you've seen that even really challenging material can be tackled by us mortals if we get our hands dirty and take it a step at a time. If you can handle compilers and interpreters, you can do anything you put your mind to.

## CHALLENGES

Assigning homework on the last day of school seems cruel but if you really want something to do during your summer vacation:

1. Fire up your profiler, run a couple of benchmarks, and look for other hotspots in the VM. Do you see anything in the runtime that you can improve?

2. Many strings in real-world user programs are small, often only a character or two. This is less of a concern in clox because we intern strings, but most VMs don't. For those that don't, heap allocating a tiny character array for each of those little strings and then representing the value as a pointer to that array is wasteful. Often, the pointer is larger than the string's characters. A classic trick is to have a separate value representation for small strings that stores the characters inline in the value.

   Starting from clox's original tagged union representation, implement that optimization. Write a couple of relevant benchmarks and see if it helps.

3. Reflect back on your experience with this book. What parts of it worked well for you? What didn't? Was it easier for you to learn bottom-up or top-down? Did the illustrations help or distract? Did the analogies clarify or confuse?

   The more you understand your personal learning style, the more effectively you can upload knowledge into your head. You can specifically target material that teaches you the way you learn best.

# Appendix I

Here is a complete grammar for Lox. The chapters that introduce each part of the language include the grammar rules there, but this collects them all into one place.

## A1.1 Syntax Grammar

The syntactic grammar is used to parse the linear sequence of tokens into the nested syntax tree structure. It starts with the first rule that matches an entire Lox program (or a single REPL entry).

```
program        → declaration* EOF ;
```

### A1.1.1 Declarations

A program is a series of declarations, which are the statements that bind new identifiers or any of the other statement types.

```
declaration    → classDecl | funDecl | varDecl | statement ;

classDecl      → "class" IDENTIFIER ( "<" IDENTIFIER )?
                 "{" function* "}" ;
funDecl        → "fun" function ;
varDecl        → "var" IDENTIFIER ( "=" expression )? ";" ;
```

## A1.1.2 Statements

The remaining statement rules produce side effects, but do not introduce bindings.

```
statement        → exprStmt
                 | forStmt
                 | ifStmt
                 | printStmt
                 | returnStmt
                 | whileStmt
                 | block ;


exprStmt         → expression ";" ;
forStmt          → "for" "(" ( varDecl | exprStmt | ";" )
                            expression? ";"
                            expression? ")" statement ;
ifStmt           → "if" "(" expression ")" statement
                   ( "else" statement )? ;
printStmt        → "print" expression ";" ;
returnStmt       → "return" expression? ";" ;
whileStmt        → "while" "(" expression ")" statement ;
block            → "{" declaration* "}" ;
```

Note that block is a statement rule, but is also used as a nonterminal in a couple of other rules for things like function bodies.

## A1.1.3 Expressions

Expressions produce values. Lox has a number of unary and binary operators with different levels of precedence. Some grammars for languages do not directly encode the precedence relationships and specify that elsewhere. Here, we use a separate rule for each precedence level to make it explicit.

```
expression       → assignment ;

assignment       → ( call "." )? IDENTIFIER "=" assignment
                 | logic_or ;

logic_or         → logic_and ( "or" logic_and )* ;
logic_and        → equality ( "and" equality )* ;
equality         → comparison ( ( "!=" | "==" ) comparison )* ;
comparison       → term ( ( ">" | ">=" | "<" | "<=" ) term )* ;
term             → factor ( ( "-" | "+" ) factor )* ;
factor           → unary ( ( "/" | "*" ) unary )* ;

unary            → ( "!" | "-" ) unary | call ;
call             → primary ( "(" arguments? ")" | "." IDENTIFIER )* ;
primary          → "true" | "false" | "nil" | "this"
                 | NUMBER | STRING | IDENTIFIER | "(" expression ")"
                 | "super" "." IDENTIFIER ;
```

### A1.1.4  Utility rules

In order to keep the above rules a little cleaner, some of the grammar is split out
into a few reused helper rules.

```
function     → IDENTIFIER "(" parameters? ")" block ;
parameters   → IDENTIFIER ( "," IDENTIFIER )* ;
arguments    → expression ( "," expression )* ;
```

## A1.2  Lexical Grammar

The lexical grammar is used by the scanner to group characters into tokens.
Where the syntax is context free, the lexical grammar is regular—note that
there are no recursive rules.

```
NUMBER       → DIGIT+ ( "." DIGIT+ )? ;
STRING       → "\"" <any char except "\"">* "\"" ;
IDENTIFIER   → ALPHA ( ALPHA | DIGIT )* ;
ALPHA        → "a" ... "z" | "A" ... "Z" | "_" ;
DIGIT        → "0" ... "9" ;
```

# Appendix II

For your edification, here is the code produced by the little script we built to automate generating the syntax tree classes for jlox.

## A2.1 Expressions

Expressions are the first syntax tree nodes we see, introduced in Chapter 5, "Representing Code". The main Expr class defines the visitor interface used to dispatch against the specific expression types, and contains the other expression subclasses as nested classes.

```java
package com.craftinginterpreters.lox;

import java.util.List;

abstract class Expr {
  interface Visitor<R> {
    R visitAssignExpr(Assign expr);
    R visitBinaryExpr(Binary expr);
    R visitCallExpr(Call expr);
    R visitGetExpr(Get expr);
    R visitGroupingExpr(Grouping expr);
    R visitLiteralExpr(Literal expr);
    R visitLogicalExpr(Logical expr);
    R visitSetExpr(Set expr);
    R visitSuperExpr(Super expr);
```

**lox/Expr.java**
*create new file*

*continued on next page…*

...from previous page

```
    R visitThisExpr(This expr);
    R visitUnaryExpr(Unary expr);
    R visitVariableExpr(Variable expr);
  }

  // Nested Expr classes here...

  abstract <R> R accept(Visitor<R> visitor);
}
```

### A2.1.1  Assign expression

Variable assignment is introduced in Chapter 8, "Statements and State".

*lox/Expr.java*
*nest inside class* Expr

```
static class Assign extends Expr {
  Assign(Token name, Expr value) {
    this.name = name;
    this.value = value;
  }

  @Override
  <R> R accept(Visitor<R> visitor) {
    return visitor.visitAssignExpr(this);
  }

  final Token name;
  final Expr value;
}
```

### A2.1.2  Binary expression

Binary operators are introduced in Chapter 5, "Representing Code".

*lox/Expr.java*
*nest inside class* Expr

```
static class Binary extends Expr {
  Binary(Expr left, Token operator, Expr right) {
    this.left = left;
    this.operator = operator;
    this.right = right;
  }

  @Override
  <R> R accept(Visitor<R> visitor) {
    return visitor.visitBinaryExpr(this);
  }

  final Expr left;
  final Token operator;
  final Expr right;
}
```

### A2.1.3 Call expression

Function call expressions are introduced in Chapter 10, "Functions".

```java
static class Call extends Expr {
  Call(Expr callee, Token paren, List<Expr> arguments) {
    this.callee = callee;
    this.paren = paren;
    this.arguments = arguments;
  }

  @Override
  <R> R accept(Visitor<R> visitor) {
    return visitor.visitCallExpr(this);
  }

  final Expr callee;
  final Token paren;
  final List<Expr> arguments;
}
```

*lox/Expr.java*
*nest inside class Expr*

### A2.1.4 Get expression

Property access "get" expressions are introduced in Chapter 12, "Classes".

```java
static class Get extends Expr {
  Get(Expr object, Token name) {
    this.object = object;
    this.name = name;
  }

  @Override
  <R> R accept(Visitor<R> visitor) {
    return visitor.visitGetExpr(this);
  }

  final Expr object;
  final Token name;
}
```

*lox/Expr.java*
*nest inside class Expr*

### A2.1.5 Grouping expression

Using parentheses to group expressions is introduced in Chapter 5, "Representing Code".

```java
static class Grouping extends Expr {
  Grouping(Expr expression) {
    this.expression = expression;
  }
```

*lox/Expr.java*
*nest inside class Expr*

*continued on next page…*

*…from previous page*

```
  @Override
  <R> R accept(Visitor<R> visitor) {
    return visitor.visitGroupingExpr(this);
  }

  final Expr expression;
}
```

### A2.1.6  Literal expression

Literal value expressions are introduced in Chapter 5, "Representing Code".

*lox/Expr.java*
*nest inside class* Expr

```
static class Literal extends Expr {
  Literal(Object value) {
    this.value = value;
  }

  @Override
  <R> R accept(Visitor<R> visitor) {
    return visitor.visitLiteralExpr(this);
  }

  final Object value;
}
```

### A2.1.7  Logical expression

The logical and and or operators are introduced in Chapter 9, "Control Flow".

*lox/Expr.java*
*nest inside class* Expr

```
static class Logical extends Expr {
  Logical(Expr left, Token operator, Expr right) {
    this.left = left;
    this.operator = operator;
    this.right = right;
  }

  @Override
  <R> R accept(Visitor<R> visitor) {
    return visitor.visitLogicalExpr(this);
  }

  final Expr left;
  final Token operator;
  final Expr right;
}
```

### A2.1.8  Set expression

Property assignment "set" expressions are introduced in Chapter 12, "Classes".

```
static class Set extends Expr {
  Set(Expr object, Token name, Expr value) {
    this.object = object;
    this.name = name;
    this.value = value;
  }

  @Override
  <R> R accept(Visitor<R> visitor) {
    return visitor.visitSetExpr(this);
  }

  final Expr object;
  final Token name;
  final Expr value;
}
```

lox/Expr.java
*nest inside class* Expr

## A2.1.9  Super expression

The super expression is introduced in Chapter 13, "Inheritance".

```
static class Super extends Expr {
  Super(Token keyword, Token method) {
    this.keyword = keyword;
    this.method = method;
  }

  @Override
  <R> R accept(Visitor<R> visitor) {
    return visitor.visitSuperExpr(this);
  }

  final Token keyword;
  final Token method;
}
```

lox/Expr.java
*nest inside class* Expr

## A2.1.10  This expression

The this expression is introduced in Chapter 12, "Classes".

```
static class This extends Expr {
  This(Token keyword) {
    this.keyword = keyword;
  }

  @Override
  <R> R accept(Visitor<R> visitor) {
    return visitor.visitThisExpr(this);
  }
}
```

lox/Expr.java
*nest inside class* Expr

*continued on next page...*

*…from previous page*

```
    final Token keyword;
  }
```

### A2.1.11 Unary expression

Unary operators are introduced in Chapter 5, "Representing Code".

lox/Expr.java
*nest inside class* Expr

```
static class Unary extends Expr {
  Unary(Token operator, Expr right) {
    this.operator = operator;
    this.right = right;
  }

  @Override
  <R> R accept(Visitor<R> visitor) {
    return visitor.visitUnaryExpr(this);
  }

  final Token operator;
  final Expr right;
}
```

### A2.1.12 Variable expression

Variable access expressions are introduced in Chapter 8, "Statements and State".

lox/Expr.java
*nest inside class* Expr

```
static class Variable extends Expr {
  Variable(Token name) {
    this.name = name;
  }

  @Override
  <R> R accept(Visitor<R> visitor) {
    return visitor.visitVariableExpr(this);
  }

  final Token name;
}
```

## A2.2 Statements

Statements form a second hierarchy of syntax tree nodes independent of expressions. We add the first couple of them in Chapter 8, "Statements and State".

lox/Stmt.java
*create new file*

```
package com.craftinginterpreters.lox;

import java.util.List;
```

*continued on next page…*

```
abstract class Stmt {
  interface Visitor<R> {
    R visitBlockStmt(Block stmt);
    R visitClassStmt(Class stmt);
    R visitExpressionStmt(Expression stmt);
    R visitFunctionStmt(Function stmt);
    R visitIfStmt(If stmt);
    R visitPrintStmt(Print stmt);
    R visitReturnStmt(Return stmt);
    R visitVarStmt(Var stmt);
    R visitWhileStmt(While stmt);
  }

  // Nested Stmt classes here...

  abstract <R> R accept(Visitor<R> visitor);
}
```

*...from previous page*

## A2.2.1  Block statement

The curly-braced block statement that defines a local scope is introduced in Chapter 8, "Statements and State".

```
static class Block extends Stmt {
  Block(List<Stmt> statements) {
    this.statements = statements;
  }

  @Override
  <R> R accept(Visitor<R> visitor) {
    return visitor.visitBlockStmt(this);
  }

  final List<Stmt> statements;
}
```

lox/Stmt.java
*nest inside class* Stmt

## A2.2.2  Class statement

Class declarations are introduced in, unsurprisingly, Chapter 12, "Classes".

```
static class Class extends Stmt {
  Class(Token name,
        Expr.Variable superclass,
        List<Stmt.Function> methods) {
    this.name = name;
    this.superclass = superclass;
    this.methods = methods;
  }
```

lox/Stmt.java
*nest inside class* Stmt

*continued on next page...*

...from previous page

```
  @Override
  <R> R accept(Visitor<R> visitor) {
    return visitor.visitClassStmt(this);
  }

  final Token name;
  final Expr.Variable superclass;
  final List<Stmt.Function> methods;
}
```

### A2.2.3  Expression statement

The expression statement is introduced in Chapter 8, "Statements and State".

lox/Stmt.java
*nest inside class* Stmt

```
static class Expression extends Stmt {
  Expression(Expr expression) {
    this.expression = expression;
  }

  @Override
  <R> R accept(Visitor<R> visitor) {
    return visitor.visitExpressionStmt(this);
  }

  final Expr expression;
}
```

### A2.2.4  Function statement

Function declarations are introduced in, you guessed it, Chapter 10, "Functions".

lox/Stmt.java
*nest inside class* Stmt

```
static class Function extends Stmt {
  Function(Token name, List<Token> params, List<Stmt> body) {
    this.name = name;
    this.params = params;
    this.body = body;
  }

  @Override
  <R> R accept(Visitor<R> visitor) {
    return visitor.visitFunctionStmt(this);
  }

  final Token name;
  final List<Token> params;
  final List<Stmt> body;
}
```

## A2.2.5  If statement

The if statement is introduced in Chapter 9, "Control Flow".

```
static class If extends Stmt {
  If(Expr condition, Stmt thenBranch, Stmt elseBranch) {
    this.condition = condition;
    this.thenBranch = thenBranch;
    this.elseBranch = elseBranch;
  }

  @Override
  <R> R accept(Visitor<R> visitor) {
    return visitor.visitIfStmt(this);
  }

  final Expr condition;
  final Stmt thenBranch;
  final Stmt elseBranch;
}
```

*lox/Stmt.java*
*nest inside class Stmt*

## A2.2.6  Print statement

The print statement is introduced in Chapter 8, "Statements and State".

```
static class Print extends Stmt {
  Print(Expr expression) {
    this.expression = expression;
  }

  @Override
  <R> R accept(Visitor<R> visitor) {
    return visitor.visitPrintStmt(this);
  }

  final Expr expression;
}
```

*lox/Stmt.java*
*nest inside class Stmt*

## A2.2.7  Return statement

You need a function to return from, so return statements are introduced in Chapter 10, "Functions".

```
static class Return extends Stmt {
  Return(Token keyword, Expr value) {
    this.keyword = keyword;
    this.value = value;
  }
```

*lox/Stmt.java*
*nest inside class Stmt*

*continued on next page...*

*...from previous page*

```
  @Override
  <R> R accept(Visitor<R> visitor) {
    return visitor.visitReturnStmt(this);
  }

  final Token keyword;
  final Expr value;
}
```

## A2.2.8 Variable statement

Variable declarations are introduced in Chapter 8, "Statements and State".

lox/Stmt.java
*nest inside class* Stmt

```
static class Var extends Stmt {
  Var(Token name, Expr initializer) {
    this.name = name;
    this.initializer = initializer;
  }

  @Override
  <R> R accept(Visitor<R> visitor) {
    return visitor.visitVarStmt(this);
  }

  final Token name;
  final Expr initializer;
}
```

## A2.2.9 While statement

The while statement is introduced in Chapter 9, "Control Flow".

lox/Stmt.java
*nest inside class* Stmt

```
static class While extends Stmt {
  While(Expr condition, Stmt body) {
    this.condition = condition;
    this.body = body;
  }

  @Override
  <R> R accept(Visitor<R> visitor) {
    return visitor.visitWhileStmt(this);
  }

  final Expr condition;
  final Stmt body;
}
```

# Index

14432260R00354